RACE AND RELATIONS 97/98

Seventh Edition

Editor

John A. Kromkowski

Catholic University of America

John A. Kromkowski is president of The National Center for Urban Ethnic Affairs in Washington, D.C., a nonprofit research and educational institute that has sponsored and published many books and articles on ethnic relations, urban affairs, and economic revitalization. He is Assistant Dean of the College of Arts and Sciences at the Catholic University of America, and he coordinates international seminars and internship programs in the United States, England, Ireland, and Belgium. He has served on national advisory boards for the Campaign for Human development, the U.S. Department of Education Ethnic Heritage Studies Program, the White House Fellows Program, the National Neighborhood Coalition, and the American Revolution Bicentennial Administration. Dr. Kromkowski has edited a series sponsored by the Council for Research in Values and Philosophy titled *Cultural Heritage and Contemporary Change*. These volumes include scholarly findings and reflections on urbanization, cultural affairs, personhood, community, and political economy.

A Library of Information from the Public Press

Dushkin/McGraw·Hill

Sluice Dock, Guilford, Connecticut 06437

***Visit us on the Internet*—http://www.dushkin.com**

The Annual Editions Series

ANNUAL EDITIONS is a series of over 65 volumes designed to provide the reader with convenient, low-cost access to a wide range of current, carefully selected articles from some of the most important magazines, newspapers, and journals published today. ANNUAL EDITIONS are updated on an annual basis through a continuous monitoring of over 300 periodical sources. All ANNUAL EDITIONS have a number of features that are designed to make them particularly useful, including topic guides, annotated tables of contents, unit overviews, and indexes. For the teacher using ANNUAL EDITIONS in the classroom, an Instructor's Resource Guide with test questions is available for each volume.

VOLUMES AVAILABLE

Abnormal Psychology
Adolescent Psychology
Africa
Aging
American Foreign Policy
American Government
American History, Pre-Civil War
American History, Post-Civil War
American Public Policy
Anthropology
Archaeology
Biopsychology
Business Ethics
Child Growth and Development
China
Comparative Politics
Computers in Education
Computers in Society
Criminal Justice
Criminology
Developing World
Deviant Behavior
Drugs, Society, and Behavior
Dying, Death, and Bereavement
Early Childhood Education
Economics
Educating Exceptional Children
Education
Educational Psychology
Environment
Geography
Global Issues
Health
Human Development
Human Resources
Human Sexuality
India and South Asia
International Business
Japan and the Pacific Rim
Latin America
Life Management
Macroeconomics
Management
Marketing
Marriage and Family
Mass Media
Microeconomics
Middle East and the Islamic World
Multicultural Education
Nutrition
Personal Growth and Behavior
Physical Anthropology
Psychology
Public Administration
Race and Ethnic Relations
Russia, the Eurasian Republics, and Central/Eastern Europe
Social Problems
Social Psychology
Sociology
State and Local Government
Urban Society
Western Civilization, Pre-Reformation
Western Civilization, Post-Reformation
Western Europe
World History, Pre-Modern
World History, Modern
World Politics

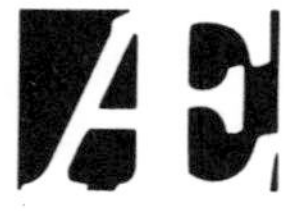

Cataloging in Publication Data
Main entry under title: Annual editions: Race and ethnic relations. 1997/98.
1. Race relations—Periodicals. 2. United States—Race relations—Periodicals. 3. Culture conflict—United States—Periodicals. I. Kromkowski, John A., *comp.* II. Title: Race and ethnic relations.
ISBN 0–697–37351-7 305.8′073′05

Seventh Edition

(Cover: The Million Man March on the Mall, Washington, DC, October 16, 1995. Photo by Porter Gifford/Gamma Liaison)

Printed in the United States of America

Printed on Recycled Paper

Editors/Advisory Board

Members of the Advisory Board are instrumental in the final selection of articles for each edition of ANNUAL EDITIONS. Their review of articles for content, level, currentness, and appropriateness provides critical direction to the editor and staff. We think that you will find their careful consideration well reflected in this volume.

Staff

Ian A. Nielsen, Publisher

EDITORIAL STAFF

Roberta Monaco, Developmental Editor
Dorothy Fink, Associate Developmental Editor
Addie Raucci, Administrative Editor
Cheryl Greenleaf, Permissions Editor
Deanna Herrschaft, Permissions Assistant
Diane Barker, Proofreader
Lisa Holmes-Doebrick, Program Coordinator

PRODUCTION STAFF

Brenda S. Filley, Production Manager
Charles Vitelli, Designer
Shawn Callahan, Graphics
Lara M. Johnson, Graphics
Laura Levine, Graphics
Mike Campbell, Graphics
Joseph Offredi, Graphics
Juliana Arbo, Typesetting Supervisor
Jane Jaegersen, Typesetter
Marie Lazauskas, Word Processor
Kathleen D'Amico, Word Processor
Larry Killian, Copier Coordinator

To the Reader

In publishing ANNUAL EDITIONS we recognize the enormous role played by the magazines, newspapers, and journals of the *public press* in providing current, first-rate educational information in a broad spectrum of interest areas. Many of these articles are appropriate for students, researchers, and professionals seeking accurate, current material to help bridge the gap between principles and theories and the real world. These articles, however, become more useful for study when those of lasting value are carefully *collected, organized, indexed,* and *reproduced* in a *low-cost format,* which provides easy and permanent access when the material is needed. That is the role played by ANNUAL EDITIONS. Under the direction of each volume's *academic editor,* who is an expert in the subject area, and with the guidance of an *Advisory Board,* each year we seek to provide in each ANNUAL EDITION a current, well-balanced, carefully selected collection of the best of the public press for your study and enjoyment. We think that you will find this volume useful, and we hope that you will take a moment to let us know what you think.

The information explosion and expansion of knowledge about the range of diversity among and within societies have increased awareness of ethnicity and race. During previous periods of history, society was discussed in terms of a universal sense of common humanity. Differences between societies and the arrangements of economic production were noted, but they were usually explained in terms of theories of progressive development or of class conflict that was leading toward a universal and homogenized humanity. Consciousness of the enduring pluralism expressed in ethnic, racial, and cultural diversity that constitutes the human condition has emerged throughout the world. It appears, however, that the dimensions of diversity are significantly, if not essentially, shaped by social, economic, cultural, and, most importantly, political and communitarian processes. Creativity, imagination, and religion influence ethnic and racial relations.

This collection of essays was designed to assist you in understanding ethnic and racial pluralism in the United States and several other countries. Unit 1, for example, illustrates how the most basic legal principles of a society—and especially the U.S. Supreme Court's historical interpretation of them—are especially significant for the delineation of ethnic groups, for the acceptance of cultural pluralism, and for the political and moral foundations from which contemporary challenges to the promise of American liberties may be addressed. Subsequent sections include illustrative articles of ethnic interaction with and within American society. The immigration of persons, the focus of unit 2, into a relatively young society such as America is of particular concern, because the fragility of social continuity is exposed by the recognition of changes in the ethnic composition of American society.

The contemporary experiences of indigenous groups, including Native Americans, are arranged in unit 3. Discussion of the experiences of the descendants of the earliest and the most recently arrived ethnic populations and the legal framework for participating in America is extended in unit 4 on Hispanic/Latino Americans and unit 5 on African Americans. Unit 6 explores various dimensions of the Asian American experience. The experiences of these ethnicities form a cluster of concerns addressed in the traditional literature that focused on marginality, minority, and alienation. New voices from within these traditions suggest bridges to the topics included in unit 7, titled "The Ethnic Legacy," which articulates neglected dimensions of ethnicity derived from the industrial and urban development of America, as well as a pluralistic vision of diversity and moral imagination. Unit 8, "The Ethnic Factor: International Challenges for the 1990s," extends prior concerns and addresses national and international implications of ethnic exclusivity and the imperatives of new approaches to group relations. Unit 9 focuses on understanding the origins of racialism and the religious and ethical origins that shape consciousness of group affinities and, especially, the emergence of scientific claims of racialism and religious exclusion in public affairs. This section ends with suggestions that our inability to bridge racial and ethnic gaps as well as our misunderstandings of the paradoxes of integration could impose heavy burdens on efforts to resolve differences. Our national and universal moral sensibilities compel us to search for new paradigms and new approaches that foster values of institutional and attitudinal inclusiveness. Yet, curiously, the arena most in flux includes personal identity manifested in ethnic and religious terms that pose primordial questions: Who am I? Who are we? How can we order our aspirations for liberty and justice so that all may participate in and benefit from a heightened level of ethnic interdependence? What large-scale communal projects can be initiated that will uplift the well-being of the human condition and enrich our experiences of the other—the alien—and our appreciation of the stunning variety of cultures? That our racial and ethnic differences need not be divisive is abundantly clear.

Readers may have input into the next edition of *Annual Editions: Race and Ethnic Relations* by completing and returning the postpaid article rating form in the back of the book.

John A. Kromkowski
Editor

Contents

UNIT 1

Race and Ethnicity in the American Legal Tradition

Eight articles in this section include Supreme Court decisions that established the legal definitions of race, citizenship, and the historic landmarks of equal protection and due process, as well as discussions of civil rights doctrine and implementation and the rise of new critical legal theories that challenge traditional remedies.

The concepts in bold italics are developed in the article. For further expansion please refer to the Topic Guide and the Index.

UNIT 2

Immigration and the American Experience

Six articles in this section review the historical record of immigration and current concerns regarding patterns of immigration and the legal, social, cultural, and economic issues that are related to immigrants in the American experience.

The concepts in bold italics are developed in the article. For further expansion please refer to the Topic Guide and the Index.

UNIT 3

Indigenous Ethnic Groups

Seven articles in this section review the issues and problems of indigenous peoples. They portray the new relationship that indigenous people are forging with concurrent governments and the processes that protect indigenous traditions within pluralistic societies.

UNIT 4

Hispanic/Latino Americans

Five articles in this section reveal the demographics of Hispanic/Latino Americans as well as the economic and political cultural dynamics of these diverse ethnicities.

UNIT 5

African Americans

Six articles in this section review historical experiences derived from slavery and segregation and then explore current contexts and persistent concerns of African Americans.

The concepts in bold italics are developed in the article. For further expansion please refer to the Topic Guide and the Index.

UNIT 6

Asian Americans

Four articles in this section explore dimensions of pluralism among Asian Americans and their issues related to the cultural, economic, and political dynamics of pluralism.

UNIT 7

The Ethnic Legacy

Five articles in this section examine neglected dimensions of ethnic communities, their intersection with each other, and the influence of interethnic protocols within American society.

UNIT 8

The Ethnic Factor: International Challenges for the 1990s

Five articles in this section look at the intersections of ethnicities and the impact of ethnic conflict and cooperation on international affairs and the prospect of peace.

UNIT 9

Understanding Cultural Pluralism

Six articles in this section examine the origins of misunderstandings regarding human variety, indicate the influence of race and ethnic opinions in selected contexts, and discuss the range of challenges that must be addressed to forge new approaches to understanding cultural pluralism.

The concepts in bold italics are developed in the article. For further expansion please refer to the Topic Guide and the Index.

Topic Guide

This topic guide suggests how the selections in this book relate to topics of traditional concern to students and professionals involved with the study of race and ethnic relations. It is useful for locating articles that relate to each other for reading and research. The guide is arranged alphabetically according to topic. Articles may, of course, treat topics that do not appear in the topic guide. In turn, entries in the topic guide do not necessarily constitute a comprehensive listing of all the contents of each selection.

TOPIC AREA	TREATED IN
Affirmative Action	5. Court Grows Critical 7. Proposition 209 8. Long Retreat Back to 'Separate-but-Equal' 28. 10 Most Dramatic Events 29. Color Blind 47. So You want to Be Color-Blind
Canada	15. UN Working Group 18. Canada Pressed on Indian Rights 43. No Canada?
Civil Rights	1. *Dred Scott v. Sandford* 2. Racial Restrictions in Law of Citizenship 3. *Brown v. Board of Education* 5. Court Grows Critical 7. Proposition 209 8. Long Retreat Back to 'Separate-but-Equal' 12. Solidarity Doesn't Mean Lost Identity 13. Citizenship Is Malleable Concept 15. UN Working Group 16. American Indians in the 1990s 28. 10 Most Dramatic Events 32. From Scottsboro to Simpson 38. Italian Americans 47. So You Want to Be Color-Blind 51. One Drop of Blood
Class	4. Is Racial Integration Essential? 9. Nation of Immigrants 11. Is Latest Wave Drain or Boon? 12. Solidarity Doesn't Mean Lost Identity 16. American Indians in the 1990s 23. Ballad of Freddy Gonzalez 25. Out of the Shadows 46. Military-Civilian Schism Widens
Courts	1. *Dred Scott v. Sandford* 2. Racial Restrictions in Law of Citizenship 3. *Brown v. Board of Education* 5. Court Grows Critical 6. New Tolerance in the South? 7. Proposition 209 8. Long Retreat Back to 'Separate-but-Equal' 20. Dispute over Indian Casinos 28. 10 Most Dramatic Events 38. Italian Americans 41. A Riddle
Demography	2. Racial Restrictions in Law of Citizenship 5. Court Grows Critical 9. Nation of Immigrants 10. American Ethnicities and Politics of Inclusions *and* Not Quite So Welcome Anymore 11. Is Latest Wave Drain or Boon? 16. American Indians in the 1990s 22. Specific Hispanics
Demography (continued)	33. Misperceived Minorities 34. Neighboring Faiths 36. Asian-Indian Americans 44. Germania Irredenta 49. Geometer of Race 51. One Drop of Blood
Discrimination	1. *Dred Scott v. Sandford* 2. Racial Restrictions in Law of Citizenship 3. *Brown v. Board of Education* 5. Court Grows Critical 6. New Tolerance in the South? 7. Proposition 209 8. Long Retreat Back to 'Separate-but-Equal' 9. Nation of Immigrants 10. Not Quite So Welcome Anymore 13. Citizenship Is Malleable Concept 15. UN Working Group 16. American Indians in the 1990s 21. Native-American Women in History 24. Baiting Immigrants 28. 10 Most Dramatic Events 29. Color Blind 30. Alternative Afrocentrisms: Three Paths 31. God and the Civil Rights Movement 32. From Scottsboro to Simpson 33. Misperceived Minorities 38. Italian Americans 41. A Riddle 42. Resurgence of Ethnic Nationalism 47. So You Want to Be Color-Blind 51. One Drop of Blood
Economy	9. Nation of Immigrants 10. Not Quite So Welcome Anymore 11. Is Latest Wave Drain or Boon? 16. American Indians in the 1990s 20. Dispute over Indian Casinos 25. Out of the Shadows 26. Magazines 33. Misperceived Minorities 35. Chinese Diaspora
Education	3. *Brown v. Board of Education* 4. "Is Racial Integration Essential?" 5. Court Grows Critical 8. Long Retreat Back to 'Separate-but-Equal' 12. Solidarity Doesn't Mean Lost Identity 17. Good, Bad, and Intolerable 21. Native-American Women in History 27. Understanding Afrocentrism 28. 10 Most Dramatic Events 29. Color Blind 30. Alternative Afrocentrisms: Three Paths 31. God and the Civil Rights Movement *and* Josephites Mark 125 Years 34. Neighboring Faiths 40. Polish Americans and the Holocaust

TOPIC AREA	TREATED IN	TOPIC AREA	TREATED IN
Education (continued)	42. Resurgence of Ethnic Nationalism 46. Military-Civilian Schism Widens 49. Geometer of Race 50. Minority Rights 52. Place of Faith in Public Life	**Prejudice**	2. Racial Restrictions in Law of Citizenship 3. *Brown v. Board of Education* 6. New Tolerance in the South? 9. Nation of Immigrants 10. Not Quite So Welcome Anymore 12. Solidarity Doesn't Mean Lost Identity 13. Citizenship Is Malleable Concept 15. UN Working Group 18. Canada Pressed on Indian Rights 23. Ballad of Freddy Gonzalez 24. Baiting Immigrants 25. Out of the Shadows 26. Magazines 28. 10 Most Dramatic Events 29. Color Blind 33. Misperceived Minorities 37. New Ethnicity 38. Italian Americans 40. Polish Americans and the Holocaust 41. A Riddle 44. Germania Irredenta 51. One Drop of Blood 52. Place of Faith in Public Life
Family	9. Nation of Immigrants 11. Is Latest Wave Drain or Boon? 19. Amity in Indian Adoptions 25. Out of the Shadows 26. Magazines 41. A Riddle 48. Goin' Gangsta, Choosin' Cholita 51. One Drop of Blood	**Refugees**	2. Racial Restrictions in Law of Citizenship 9. Nation of Immigrants 10. Not Quite So Welcome Anymore 13. Citizenship Is Malleable Concept 14. Held in War, Latins Seek Reparations 42. Resurgence of Ethnic Nationalism 44. Germania Irredenta 45. Size, Scope of Hutu Crisis 50. Minority Rights
Gender	6. New Tolerance in the South? 7. Proposition 209 21. Native-American Women in History 24. Baiting Immigrants 25. Out of the Shadows 26. Magazines 41. A Riddle 48. Goin' Gangsta, Choosin' Cholita	**Religion**	31. God and the Civil Rights Movement *and* Josephites Mark 125 Years 34. Neighboring Faiths 40. Polish Americans and the Holocaust 41. A Riddle 52. Place of Faith in Public Life
Germany	42. Resurgence of Ethnic Nationalism 44. Germania Irredenta	**Segregation**	1. *Dred Scott v. Sandford* 2. Racial Restrictions in Law of Citizenship 3. *Brown v. Board of Education* 5. Court Grows Critical 6. New Tolerance in the South? 8. Long Retreat Back to 'Separate-but-Equal' 14. Held in War, Latins Seek Reparations 28. 10 Most Dramatic Events 50. Minority Rights 51. One Drop of Blood
Identity	1. *Dred Scott v. Sandford* 2. Racial Restrictions in Law of Citizenship 9. Nation of Immigrants 10. American Ethnicities and Politics of Inclusion 12. Solidarity Doesn't Mean Lost Identity 14. Held in War, Latins Seek Reparations 16. American Indians in the 1990s 17. Good, Bad, and Intolerable 23. Ballad of Freddy Gonzalez 24. Baiting Immigrants 30. Alternative Afrocentrisms: Three Paths 31. God and the Civil Rights Movement 38. Italian Americans 39. Greek-Americans in Political Life 40. Polish Americans and the Holocaust 41. A Riddle 42. Resurgence of Ethnic Nationalism 43. No Canada? 44. Germania Irredenta 48. Goin' Gangsta, Choosin' Cholita 49. Geometer of Race 51. One Drop of Blood 52. Place of Faith in Public Life	**Violence**	14. Held in War, Latins Seek Reparations 20. Dispute Over Indian Casinos 23. Ballad of Freddy Gonzalez 28. 10 Most Dramatic Events 42. Resurgence of Ethnic Nationalism
Migration	7. Proposition 209 9. Nation of Immigrants 10. Not Quite So Welcome Anymore 13. Citizenship Is Malleable Concept 22. Specific Hispanics 33. Misperceived Minorities 34. Neighboring Faiths 35. Chinese Diaspora 36. Asian-Indian Americans 37. New Ethnicity 41. A Riddle 42. Resurgence of Ethnic Nationalism 44. Germania Irredenta 45. Size, Scope of Hutu Crisis 50. Minority Rights		

Race and Ethnicity in the American Legal Tradition

• **The Foundations (Articles 1 and 2)**
• **The Civil Rights Era (Article 3)**
• **Contemporary Challenges (Articles 4–8)**

The legal framework established by the original U.S. Constitution illustrates the way the American founders handled ethnic pluralism. In most respects, they ignored the cultural and linguistic variety within and between the 13 original states, adopting instead a legal system that guaranteed religious exercise free from government interference, due process of law, and the freedom of speech and of the press. The founders, however, conspicuously compromised their claims of unalienable rights and democratic republicanism with regard to the constitutional status of Africans in bondage and the indigenous Native Americans. Even after the Civil War and the inclusion of constitutional amendments that ended slavery and guaranteed equal protection under the law to all, exclusionary practices continued. Decisions by the U.S. Supreme Court helped to establish a legal system in which inequality and ethnic discrimination—both political and private—were legally permissible. Only recently has the Supreme Court attempted to redress the complex relationship between our constitutional system and the diverse society it governs.

Moreover, the history of American immigration legislation, from the Alien and Sedition Laws at the founding to the most recent statutes, reveals an ambiguous legacy. This legal framework continues to mirror the political forces that influence the definition of citizenship and the constitution of ethnic identity and ethnic groups in America.

The legacies of African slavery, racial segregation, and ethnic discrimination established by the Constitution and by subsequent Court doctrines are traced in the following abbreviated U.S. Supreme Court opinions.

In *Dred Scott v. Sandford* (1856), the Supreme Court addressed the constitutional status of an African held in bondage who had been moved to a state that prohibited slavery. U.S. Supreme Court Chief Justice Roger B. Taney attempted to resolve the increasingly divisive issue of slavery by declaring that the "Negro African race"—whether free or slave—was "not intended to be included under the word 'citizens' in the Constitution, and can therefore claim none of the rights and privileges that instrument provides for and secures to citizens of the United States." Contrary to Taney's intentions, however, *Dred Scott* further fractured the nation, ensuring that only the Civil War would resolve the slavery issue.

In *Plessy v. Ferguson* (1896), the Supreme Court upheld the constitutionality of "Jim Crow" laws that segregated public facilities on the basis of an individual's racial ancestry. The Court reasoned that this "separate but equal" segregation did not violate any rights guaranteed by the U.S. Constitution, nor did it stamp "the colored race with a badge of inferiority." Instead, the Court argued that if "this be so, it is not by reason of anything found in the act but solely because the colored race chooses to put that construction upon it." In contrast, Justice John M. Harlan's vigorous dissent from the Court's *Plessy* opinion contends that "our Constitution is color-blind, and neither knows nor tolerates classes among citizens." The history of the Court's attention to citizenship provides a view of a culturally embedded character of color consciousness and the strict textual dependence of the Justices that interpreted the Constitution. Another perspective, however, emerges from the congressional debate that occurred when a civil rights law ensuring equal protection and voting rights was passed shortly after the Civil War. That legislative history is cited extensively in *Shaare Tefila/Alkhasraji* (1987). This expansive view of protection for all ethnic groups cited in these decisions and the origin of these views in congressional intention voiced by elected legislators are indications of the Court's new directions. The Court's dependence on statutes rather than the exercise of constitutional judicial authority (and thus as a policymaker and initiator) appears to be waning. Moreover, the Court, under the influence of a color-blind doctrine, seems ready to challenge policies that significantly rely on race and ethnicity, thus changing the landscape as well as the discussion of race and ethnicity, inviting all of us to reexamine both the intentions and outcomes of all legislation in this field.

In *Brown v. Board of Education of Topeka* (1954), the Supreme Court began the ambitious project of dismantling state-supported racial segregation. In *Brown,* a unan-

UNIT 1

imous Court overturned *Plessy v. Ferguson,* arguing that "in the field of public education the doctrine of 'separate but equal' has no place," because "separate educational facilities are inherently unequal."

However, this era of civil rights consensus embodied in the landmark actions of the Supreme Court has been challenged by contemporary plaintiffs who have turned to the Court for clarification regarding specific cases related to the significance of race and ethnic criteria in public affairs. The lack of popular support for the administration and implementation of policies and the judicial leadership of those policies in California emerged in Proposition 209. This issue of popular concern was played out in the referendum that was supported by the electorate, but their decision will be played out in the Court as the country braces itself for another cycle of tension and acrimony between the will of the people in a particular state and the rule and supremacy of national law. The mediation between law and popular expression, the political nexus of state and federal legitimacy, will no doubt be challenged by these contentions.

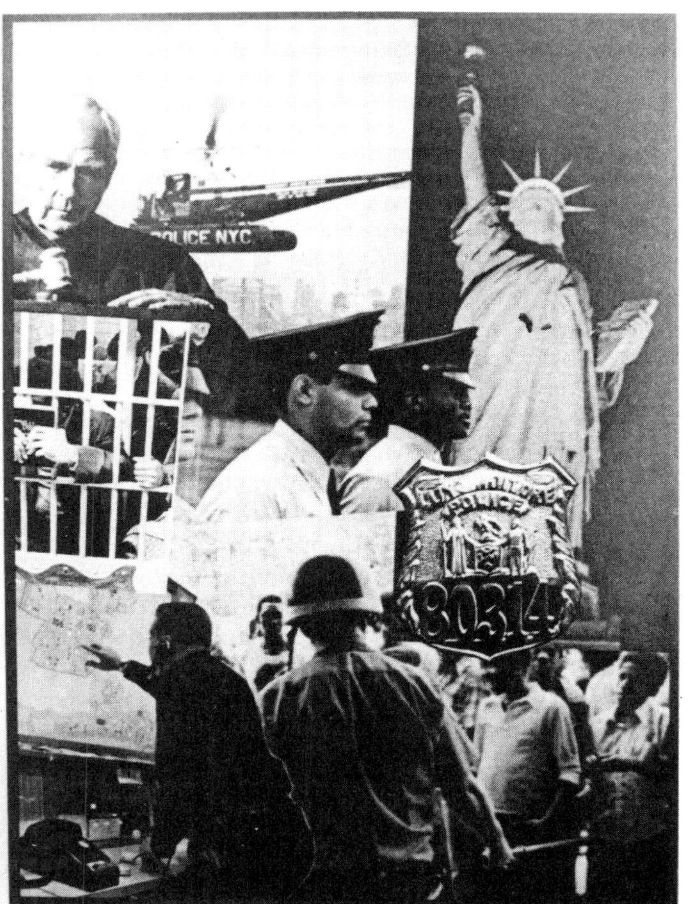

The impact of these reconsiderations and of the remedies that should be applied will undoubtedly reverberate in a variety of ways. The implementation of the voting rights remedies, by contriving clusters of black, Hispanic, and Asian populations rather than increasing the number of legislative districts, has exacerbated racial and ethnic competition for public participation. In the late 1960s, proposals that sought to depolarize race issues argued for a policy of benign neglect, meaning that although equal protection and opportunity were essential, economic and education policy should focus on the needs of persons and groups and regions, not on their race, and that these should be the driving criteria and the redistributive thrust of the nation's policy of remediation. What does this philosophy of public policy contribute to the current context?

Looking Ahead: Challenge Questions

Comment on the idea that the American political process has relied too extensively on the Supreme Court for doctrine and dogma regarding race and ethnicity.

The U.S. Congress is the lawmaking institution that authorized national policies of equal protection that are constitutionally guaranteed to all. What explains the disparity between the patently clear proclamation of equality and the painfully obvious practices of racial/ethnic discrimination?

DRED SCOTT V. SANDFORD

December Term 1856.

MR. CHIEF JUSTICE TANEY delivered the opinion of the court.

This case has been twice argued. After the argument at the last term, differences of opinion were found to exist among the members of the court; and as the questions in controversy are of the highest importance, and the court was at that time much pressed by the ordinary business of the term, it was deemed advisable to continue the case, and direct a re-argument on some of the points, in order that we might have an opportunity of giving to the whole subject a more deliberate consideration. It has accordingly been again argued by counsel, and considered by the court; and I now proceed to deliver its opinion.

There are two leading questions presented by the record:

1. Had the Circuit Court of the United States jurisdiction to hear and determine the case between these parties? And

2. If it had jurisdiction, is the judgment it has given erroneous or not?

The plaintiff in error, who was also the plaintiff in the court below, was, with his wife and children, held as slaves by the defendant, in the State of Missouri; and he brought this action in the Circuit Court of the United States for that district, to assert the title of himself and his family to freedom.

The declaration is in the form usually adopted in that State to try questions of this description, and contains the averment necessary to give the court jurisdiction; that he and the defendant are citizens of different States; that is, that he is a citizen of Missouri, and the defendant a citizen of New York.

The defendant pleaded in abatement to the jurisdiction of the court, that the plaintiff was not a citizen of the State of Missouri, as alleged in his declaration, being a negro of African descent, whose ancestors were of pure African blood, and who were brought into this country and sold as slaves.

To this plea the plaintiff demurred, and the defendant joined in demurrer. The court overruled the plea, and gave judgment that the defendant should answer over. And he thereupon put in sundry pleas in bar, upon which issues were joined; and at the trial the verdict and judgment were in his favor. Whereupon the plaintiff brought this writ of error.

Before we speak of the pleas in bar, it will be proper to dispose of the questions which have arisen on the plea in abatement.

That plea denies the right of the plaintiff to sue in a court of the United States, for the reasons therein stated.

If the question raised by it is legally before us, and the court should be of opinion that the facts stated in it disqualify the plaintiff from becoming a citizen, in the sense in which that word is used in the Constitution of the United States, then the judgment of the Circuit Court is erroneous, and must be reversed.

It is suggested, however, that this plea is not before us; and that as the judgment in the court below on this plea was in favor of the plaintiff, he does not seek to reverse it, or bring it before the court for revision by his writ of error; and also that the defendant waived this defence by pleading over, and thereby admitted the jurisdiction of the court.

But, in making this objection, we think the peculiar and limited jurisdiction of courts of the United States has not been adverted to. This peculiar and limited jurisdiction has made it necessary, in these courts, to adopt different rules and principles of pleading, so far as jurisdiction is concerned, from those which regulate courts of common law in England, and in the different States of the Union which have adopted the common-law rules.

In these last-mentioned courts, where their character and rank are analogous to that of a Circuit Court of the United States; in other words, where they are what the law terms courts of general jurisdiction; they are presumed to have jurisdiction, unless the contrary appears. No averment in the pleadings of the plaintiff is necessary, in order to give jurisdiction. If the defendant objects to it, he must plead it specially, and unless the

From *U.S. Reports*, 1856. Opinion of the Supreme Court, December Term, 1856.

fact on which he relies is found to be true by a jury, or admitted to be true by the plaintiff, the jurisdiction cannot be disputed in an appellate court.

Now, it is not necessary to inquire whether in courts of that description a party who pleads over in bar, when a plea to the jurisdiction has been ruled against him, does or does not waive his plea; nor whether upon a judgment in his favor on the pleas in bar, and a writ of error brought by the plaintiff, the question upon the plea in abatement would be open for revision in the appellate court. Cases that may have been decided in such courts, or rules that may have been laid down by common-law pleaders, can have no influence in the decision in this court. Because, under the Constitution and laws of the United States, the rules which govern the pleadings in its courts, in questions of jurisdiction, stand on different principles and are regulated by different laws.

This difference arises, as we have said, from the peculiar character of the Government of the United States. For although it is sovereign and supreme in its appropriate sphere of action, yet it does not possess all the powers which usually belong to the sovereignty of a nation. Certain specified powers, enumerated in the Constitution, have been conferred upon it; and neither the legislative, executive, nor judicial departments of the Government can lawfully exercise any authority beyond the limits marked out by the Constitution. And in regulating the judicial department, the cases in which the courts of the United States shall have jurisdiction are particularly and specifically enumerated and defined; and they are not authorized to take cognizance of any case which does not come within the description therein specified. Hence, when a plaintiff sues in a court of the United States, it is necessary that he should show, in his pleading, that the suit he brings is within the jurisdiction of the court, and that he is entitled to sue there. And if he omits to do this, and should, by any oversight of the Circuit Court, obtain a judgment in his favor, the judgment would be reversed in the appellate court for want of jurisdiction in the court below. The jurisdiction would not be presumed, as in the case of a common-law English or State court, unless the contrary appeared. But the record, when it comes before the appellate court, must show, affirmatively, that the inferior court had authority, under the Constitution, to hear and determine the case. And if the plaintiff claims a right to sue in a Circuit Court of the United States, under that provision of the Constitution which gives jurisdiction in controversies between citizens of different States, he must distinctly aver in his pleading that they are citizens of different States; and he cannot maintain his suit without showing that fact in the pleadings.

This point was decided in the case of *Bingham v. Cabot*, (in 3 Dall., 382,) and ever since adhered to by the court. And in *Jackson v. Ashton*, (8 Pet., 148,) it was held that the objection to which it was open could not be waived by the opposite party, because consent of parties could not give jurisdiction.

It is needless to accumulate cases on this subject. Those already referred to, and the cases of *Capron v. Van Noorden*, (in 2 Cr., 126) and *Montalet v. Murray*, (4 Cr., 46,) are sufficient to show the rule of which we have spoken. The case of *Capron v. Van Noorden* strikingly illustrates the difference between a common-law court and a court of the United States.

If, however, the fact of citizenship is averred in the declaration, and the defendant does not deny it, and put it in issue by plea in abatement, he cannot offer evidence at the trial to disprove it, and consequently cannot avail himself of the objection in the appellate court, unless the defect should be apparent in some other part of the record. For if there is no plea in abatement, and the want of jurisdiction does not appear in any other part of the transcript brought up by the writ of error, the undisputed averment of citizenship in the declaration must be taken in this court to be true. In this case, the citizenship is averred, but it is denied by the defendant in the manner required by the rules of pleading, and the fact upon which the denial is based is admitted by the demurrer. And, if the plea and demurrer, and judgment of the court below upon it, are before us upon this record, the question to be decided is, whether the facts stated in the plea are sufficient to show that the plaintiff is not entitled to sue as a citizen in a court of the United States. . . .

We think they are before us. The plea in abatement and the judgment of the court upon it, are a part of the judicial proceedings in the Circuit Court, and are there recorded as such; and a writ of error always brings up to the superior court the whole record of the proceedings in the court below. And in the case of the *United States v. Smith*, (11 Wheat., 172) this court said, that the case being brought up by writ of error, the whole record was under the consideration of this court. And this being the case in the present instance, the plea in abatement is necessarily under consideration; and it becomes, therefore, our duty to decide whether the facts stated in the plea are or are not sufficient to show that the plaintiff is not entitled to sue as a citizen in a court of the United States.

This is certainly a very serious question, and one that now for the first time has been brought for decision before this court. But it is brought here by those who have a right to bring it, and it is our duty to meet it and decide it.

The question is simply this: Can a negro, whose ancestors were imported into this country, and sold as slaves, become a member of the political community formed and brought into existence by the Constitution of the United States, and as such become entitled to all the rights, and privileges, and immunities, guarantied by that instrument to the citizen? One of which rights is the privilege of suing in a court of the United States in the cases specified in the Constitution.

It will be observed, that the plea applies to that class of persons only whose ancestors were negroes of the African race, and imported into this country, and sold and held as slaves. The only matter in issue before the court, therefore, is, whether the descendants of such slaves, when they shall be emancipated, or who are born of parents who had become free before their birth, are citizens of a State, in the sense in which the word citizen is used in the Constitution of the United States. And this being the only matter in dispute on the pleadings, the court must be understood as speaking in this opinion of that class only, that is, of those persons who are the descendants of Africans who were imported into this country, and sold as slaves.

The situation of this population was altogether unlike that of the Indian race. The latter, it is true, formed no part of the colonial communities, and never amalgamated with them in social connections or in government. But although they were uncivilized, they were yet a free and independent people, associated together in nations or tribes, and governed by their own laws. Many of these political communities were situated in territories to which the white race claimed the ultimate right of dominion. But that claim was acknowledged to be subject to the right of the Indians to occupy it as long as they thought proper, and neither the English nor colonial Governments claimed or exercised any dominion over the tribe or nation by whom it was occupied, nor claimed the right to the possession of the territory, until the tribe or nation consented to cede it. These Indian Governments were regarded and treated as foreign Governments, as must so as if an ocean had separated the red man from the white; and their freedom has constantly been acknowledged, from the time of the first emigration to the English colonies to the present day, by the different Governments which succeeded each other. Treaties have been negotiated with them, and their alliance sought for in war; and the people who compose these Indian political communities have always been treated as foreigners not living under our Government. It is true that the course of events has brought the Indian tribes within the limits of the United States under subjection to the white race; and it has been found necessary, for their sake as well as our own, to regard them as in a state of pupilage, and to legislate to a certain extent over them and the territory they occupy. But they may, without doubt, like the subjects of any other foreign Government, be naturalized by the authority of Congress, and become citizens of a State, and of the United States; and if an individual should leave his nation or tribe, and take up his abode among the white population, he would be entitled to all the rights and privileges which would belong to an emigrant from any other foreign people.

We proceed to examine the case as presented by the pleadings.

The words "people of the United States" and "citizens" are synonymous terms, and mean the same thing. They both describe the political body who, according to our republican institutions, form the sovereignty, and who hold the power and conduct the Government through their representatives. They are what we familiarly call the "sovereign people," and every citizen is one of this people, and a constituent member of this sovereignty. The question before us is, whether the class of persons described in the plea in abatement compose a portion of this people, and are constituent members of this sovereignty? We think they are not, and that they are not included, and were not intended to be included, under the word "citizens" in the Constitution, and can therefore claim none of the rights and privileges which that instrument provides for and secures to citizens of the United States. On the contrary, they were at that time considered as a subordinate and inferior class of beings, who had been subjugated by the dominant race, and, whether emancipated or not, yet remained subject to their authority, and had no rights or privileges but such as those who held the power and the Government might choose to grant them.

It is not the province of the court to decide upon the justice or injustice, the policy or impolicy, of these laws. The decision of that question belonged to the political or law-making power; to those who formed the sovereignty and framed the Constitution. The duty of the court is, to interpret the instrument they have framed, with the best lights we can obtain on the subject, and to administer it as we find it, according to its true intent and meaning when it was adopted.

In discussing this question, we must not confound the rights of citizenship which a State may confer within its own limits, and the rights of citizenship as a member of the Union. It does not by any means follow, because he has all the rights and privileges of a citizen of a State, that he must be a citizen of the United States. He may have all of the rights and privileges of the citizen of a State, and yet not be entitled to the rights and privileges of a citizen in any other State. For, previous to the adoption of the Constitution of the United States, every State had the undoubted right to confer on whomsoever it pleased the character of citizen, and to endow him with all its rights. But this character of course was confined to the boundaries of the State, and gave him no rights or privileges in other States beyond those secured to him by the laws of nations and the comity of States. Nor have the several States surrendered the power of conferring these rights and privileges by adopting the Constitution of the United States. Each State may still confer them upon an alien, or any one it thinks proper, or upon any class or description of persons; yet he would not be a citizen in the sense in which that word is used in the Constitution of the United States, nor entitled to sue as such in one of its courts, nor to the privileges and immunities of a citizen in the other States. The rights which he would acquire would be restricted to the State which gave them. The Constitution has conferred on Congress the right to establish a uniform rule of naturalization, and this right is evidently exclusive, and has always been held by this court to be so. Consequently, no State, since the adoption of the Constitution, can by naturalizing an alien invest him with the rights and privileges secured to a citizen of a State under the Federal Government, although, so far as the State alone was concerned, he would undoubtedly be entitled to the rights of a citizen, and clothed with all the rights and immunities which the Constitution and laws of the State attached to that character.

It is very clear, therefore, that no State can, by any act or law of its own, passed since the adoption of the Constitution, introduce a new member into the political community created by the Constitution of the United States. It cannot make him a member of this community by making him a member of its own. And for the same reason it cannot introduce any person, or description of persons, who were not intended to be embraced in this new political family, which the Constitution brought into existence, but were intended to be excluded from it.

The question then arises, whether the provisions of the Constitution, in relation to the personal rights and privileges to which the citizen of a State should be entitled, embraced the negro African race, at that time in this country, or who might afterwards be imported, who had then or should afterwards be made free in any State; and to put it in the power of a single State to make him a citizen of the United States, and endue him with the full rights of citizenship in every other State without their consent? Does the Constitution of the United States act upon him whenever he shall be made free under the laws of a State, and raised there to the rank of a citizen, and immediately clothe him with all the privileges of a citizen in every other State, and in its own courts?

The court think the affirmative of these propositions cannot be maintained. And if it cannot, the plaintiff in error could not be a citizen of the State of Missouri, within the meaning of the Constitution of the United States, and, consequently, was not entitled to sue in its courts.

It is true, every person, and every class and description of persons, who were at the time of the adoption of the Constitution recognised as citizens in the several States, became also citizens of this new political body; but none other; it was formed by them, and for them and their posterity, but for no one else. And the personal rights and privileges guarantied to citizens of this new sovereignty were intended to embrace those only who were then members of the several State communities, or who should afterwards by birthright or otherwise become members, according to the provisions of the Constitution and the principles on which it was founded. It was the union of those who were at that time members of distinct and separate political communities into one political family, whose power, for certain specified purposes, was to extend over the whole territory of the United States. And it gave to each citizen rights and privileges outside of his State which he did not before possess, and placed him in every other State upon a perfect equality with its own citizens as to rights of person and rights of property; it made him a citizen of the United States.

It becomes necessary, therefore, to determine who were citizens of the several States when the Constitution was adopted. And in order to do this, we must recur to the Governments and institutions of the thirteen colonies, when they separated from Great Britain and formed new sovereignties, and took their places in the family of independent nations. We must inquire who, at that time, were recognised as the people or citizens of a State, whose rights and liberties had been outraged by the English Government; and who declared their independence, and assumed the powers of Government to defend their rights by force of arms.

In the opinion of the court, the legislation and histories of the times, and the language used in the Declaration of Independence, show, that neither the class of persons who had been imported as slaves, nor their descendants, whether they had become free or not, were then acknowledged as a part of the people, nor intended to be included in the general words used in that memorable instrument. . . .

Racial Restrictions in the Law of Citizenship

Ian F. Haney Lopez

The racial composition of the U.S. citizenry reflects in part the accident of world migration patterns. More than this, however, it reflects the conscious design of U.S. immigration and naturalization laws.

Federal law restricted immigration to this country on the basis of race for nearly one hundred years, roughly from the Chinese exclusion laws of the 1880s until the end of the national origin quotas in 1965.[1] The history of this discrimination can briefly be traced. Nativist sentiment against Irish and German Catholics on the East Coast and against Chinese and Mexicans on the West Coast, which had been doused by the Civil War, reignited during the economic slump of the 1870s. Though most of the nativist efforts failed to gain congressional sanction, Congress in 1882 passed the Chinese Exclusion Act, which suspended the immigration of Chinese laborers for ten years.[2] The Act was expanded to exclude all Chinese in 1884, and was eventually implemented indefinitely.[3] In 1917, Congress created "an Asiatic barred zone," excluding all persons from Asia.[4] During this same period, the Senate passed a bill to exclude "all members of the African or black race." This effort was defeated in the House only after intensive lobbying by the NAACP.[5] Efforts to exclude the supposedly racially undesirable southern and eastern Europeans were more successful. In 1921, Congress established a temporary quota system designed "to confine immigration as much as possible to western and northern European stock," making this bar permanent three years later in the National Origin Act of 1924.[6] With the onset of the Depression, attention shifted to Mexican immigrants. Although no law explicitly targeted this group, federal immigration officials began a series of round-ups and mass deportations of people of Mexican descent under the general rubric of a "repatriation campaign." Approximately 500,000 people were forcibly returned to Mexico during the Depression, more than half of them U.S. citizens.[7] This pattern was repeated in the 1950s, when Attorney General Herbert Brownwell launched a program to expel Mexicans. This effort, dubbed "Operation Wetback," indiscriminately deported more than one million citizens and noncitizens in 1954 alone.[8]

Racial restrictions on immigration were not significantly dismantled until 1965, when Congress in a major overhaul of immigration law abolished both the national origin system and the Asiatic Barred Zone.[9] Even so, purposeful racial discrimination in immigration law by Congress remains constitutionally permissible, since the case that upheld the Chinese Exclusion Act to this day remains good law.[10] Moreover, arguably racial discrimination in immigration law continues. For example, Congress has enacted special provisions to encourage Irish immigration, while refusing to ameliorate the backlog of would-be immigrants from the Philippines, India, South Korea, China, and Hong Kong, backlogs created in part through a century of racial exclusion.[11] The history of racial discrimination in U.S. immigration law is a long and continuing one.

As discriminatory as the laws of immigration have been, the laws of citizenship betray an even more dismal record of racial exclusion. From this country's inception, the laws regulating who was or could become a citizen were tainted by racial prejudice. Birthright citizenship, the automatic acquisition of citizenship by virtue of birth, was tied to race until 1940. Naturalized citizenship, the acquisition of citizenship by any means other than through birth, was conditioned on race until 1952. Like immigration laws, the laws of birthright citizenship and naturalization shaped the racial character of the United States.

Birthright Citizenship

Most persons acquire citizenship by birth rather than through naturalization. During the 1990s, for example, naturalization will account for only 7.5 percent of the increase in the U.S. citizen population.[12] At the time of the prerequisite cases, the proportion of persons gaining citizenship through naturalization was probably somewhat higher, given the higher ratio of immigrants to total population, but still far smaller than the number of people gaining citizenship by birth. In order to situate the prerequisite laws, therefore, it is useful first to review the history of racial discrimination in the laws of birthright citizenship.

The U.S. Constitution as ratified did not define the citizenry, probably because it was assumed that the English common law rule of *jus soli* would continue.[13] Under *jus soli*, citizenship accrues to "all" born within a nation's jurisdiction. Despite the seeming breadth of this doctrine, the word "all" is qualified because for the first one hundred years and more of this country's history it did not fully encompass racial minorities. This is the import of the *Dred Scott* decision.[14] Scott, an enslaved man, sought to use the federal courts to sue for his freedom. However, access to the courts was predicated on citizenship. Dismissing his claim, the United States Supreme Court in the person of Chief Justice Roger Taney declared in 1857 that Scott and all other Blacks, free and enslaved, were not and could never be citizens because they were "a subordinate and inferior class of beings." The decision protected the slave-holding South and infuriated much of the North, further dividing a country already fractured around the issues of slavery and the power of the national government. *Dred Scott* was invalidated after the Civil War by the Civil Rights Act of 1866, which declared that "All persons born . . . in the United States and not subject to any foreign power, excluding Indians not taxed, are declared to be citizens of the United States."[15] *Jus soli* subsequently became part of the organic law of the land in the form of the Fourteenth Amendment: "All persons born or naturalized in the United States, and subject to the jurisdiction thereof, are citizens of the United States and of the state wherein they reside."[16]

Despite the broad language of the Fourteenth Amendment—though in keeping with the words of the 1866 act—some racial minorities remained outside the bounds of *jus soli* even after its constitutional enactment. In particular, questions persisted about the citizenship status of children born in the United States to noncitizen parents, and about the status of Native Americans. The Supreme Court did not decide the status of the former until 1898, when it ruled in *U.S. v. Wong Kim Ark* that native-born children of aliens, even those permanently barred by race from acquiring citizenship, were birthright citizens of the United States.[17] On the citizenship of the latter, the Supreme Court answered negatively in 1884, holding in *Elk v. Wilkins* that Native Americans owed allegiance to their tribe and so did not acquire citizenship upon birth.[18] Congress responded by granting Native Americans citizenship in piecemeal fashion, often tribe by tribe. Not until 1924 did Congress pass an act conferring citizenship on all Native Americans in the United States.[19] Even then, however, questions arose regarding the citizenship of those born in the United States after the effective date of the 1924 act. These questions were finally resolved, and *jus soli* fully applied, under the Nationality Act of 1940, which specifically bestowed citizenship on all those born in the United States "to a member of an Indian, Eskimo, Aleutian, or other aboriginal tribe."[20] Thus, the basic law of citizenship, that a person born here is a citizen here, did not include all racial minorities until 1940.

Unfortunately, the impulse to restrict birthright citizenship by race is far from dead in this country. Apparently, California Governor Pete Wilson and many others seek a return to the times when citizenship depended on racial proxies such as immigrant status. Wilson has called for a federal constitutional amendment that would prevent the American-born children of undocumented persons from receiving birthright citizenship.[21] His call has not been ignored: thirteen members of Congress recently sponsored a constitutional amendment that would repeal the existing Citizenship Clause of the Fourteenth Amendment and replace it with a provision that "All persons born in the United States . . . of mothers who are citizens or legal residents of the United States . . . are citizens of the United States."[22] Apparently, such a change is supported by 49 percent of Americans.[23] In addition to explicitly discriminating against fathers by eliminating their right to confer citizenship through parentage, this proposal implicitly discriminates along racial lines. The effort to deny citizenship to children born here to undocumented immigrants seems to be motivated not by an abstract concern over the political status of the parents, but by racial animosity against Asians and Latinos, those commonly seen as comprising the vast bulk of undocumented migrants. Bill Ong Hing writes, "The discussion of who is and who is not American, who can and cannot become American, goes beyond the technicalities of citizenship and residency requirements; it strikes at the very heart of our nation's long and troubled legacy of race relations.[24] As this troubled legacy reveals, the triumph over racial discrimination in the laws of citizenship and alienage came slowly and only recently. In the campaign for the "control of our borders," we are once again debating the citizenship of the native-born and the merits of *Dred Scott.*[25]

Naturalization

Although the Constitution did not originally define the citizenry, it explicitly gave Congress the authority to establish the criteria for granting citizenship after birth. Article I grants Congress the power "To establish a uniform Rule of Naturalization."[26] From the start, Congress exercised this power in a manner that burdened naturalization laws with racial restrictions that tracked those in the law of birthright citizenship. In 1790, only a few months after ratification of the Constitution, Congress limited naturalization to "any alien, being a free white person who shall have resided within the limits and under the jurisdiction of the United States for a term of two years."[27] This clause mirrored not only the de facto laws of birthright citizenship, but also the racially restrictive naturalization laws of several states. At least three states had previously limited citizenship to "white persons": Virginia in 1779, South Carolina in 1784, and Georgia in 1785.[28] Though there would be many subsequent changes in the requirements for federal naturalization, racial identity endured as a bedrock requirement for the next 162 years. In every naturalization act from 1790 until 1952, Congress included the "white person" prerequisite.[29]

The history of racial prerequisites to naturalization can be divided into two periods of approximately eighty years each. The first period extended from 1790 to 1870, when only Whites were able to naturalize. In the wake of the Civil War, the "white person" restriction on naturalization came under serious attack as part of the effort to expunge *Dred Scott.* Some congressmen, Charles Sumner chief among them, argued that racial barriers to naturalization should be struck altogether. However, racial prejudice against Native Americans and Asians forestalled the complete elimination of the racial prerequisites. During congressional debates, one senator argued against conferring "the rank, privileges, and immunities of citizenship upon the cruel savages who destroyed [Minnesota's] peaceful settlements and massacred the people with circumstances of atrocity too horrible to relate."[30] Another senator wondered "whether this door [of citizenship] shall now be thrown open to the Asiatic population," warning that to do so would spell for the Pacific coast "an end to republican government there, because it is very well ascertained that those people have no appreciation of that form of government; it seems to be obnoxious to their very nature; they seem to be incapable either of understanding or carrying it out."[31] Sentiments such as these ensured that even after the Civil War, bars against Native American and Asian naturalization would continue.[32] Congress opted to maintain the "white person" prerequisite, but to extend the right to naturalize to "persons of African nativity, or African descent."[33] After 1870, Blacks as well as Whites could naturalize, but not others.

During the second period, from 1870 until the last of the prerequisite laws were abolished in 1952, the White-Black dichotomy in American race relations dominated naturalization law. During this period, Whites and Blacks were eligible for citizenship, but others, particularly those from Asia, were not. Indeed, increasing antipathy toward Asians on the West Coast resulted in an explicit disqualification of Chinese persons from naturalization in 1882.[34] The prohibition of Chinese naturalization, the only U.S. law ever to exclude by name a particular nationality from citizenship, was coupled with the ban on Chinese immigration discussed previously. The Supreme Court readily upheld the bar, writing that "Chinese persons not born in this country have never been recognized as citizens of the United States, nor authorized to become such under the naturalization laws."[35] While Blacks were permitted to naturalize beginning in 1870, the Chinese and most "other non-Whites" would have to wait until the 1940s for the right to naturalize.[36]

World War II forced a domestic reconsideration of the racism integral to U.S. naturalization law. In 1935, Hitler's Germany limited citizenship to members of the Aryan race, making Germany the only country other than the United States with a racial restriction on naturalization.[37] The fact of this bad company was not lost on those administering our naturalization laws. "When Earl G. Harrison in 1944 resigned as United States Commissioner of Immigration and Naturalization, he said that the only country in the world, outside the United States, that observes racial discrimination in matters relating to naturalization was Nazi Germany, 'and we all agree that this is not very desirable company.' "[38] Furthermore, the United States was open to charges of hypocrisy for banning from naturalization the nationals of many of its Asian allies. During the war, the United States seemed through some of its laws and social practices to embrace the same racism it was fighting. Both fronts of the war exposed profound inconsistencies between U.S. naturalization law and broader social ideals. These considerations, among others, led Congress to begin a process of piecemeal reform in the laws governing citizenship.

In 1940, Congress opened naturalization to "descendants of races indigenous to the Western Hemisphere."[39] Apparently, this "additional limitation was designed 'to more fully cement' the ties of Pan-Americanism" at a time of impending crisis.[40] In 1943, Congress replaced the prohibition on the naturalization of Chinese persons with a provision explicitly granting them this boon.[41] In 1946, it opened up naturalization to persons from the Philippines and India as well.[42] Thus, at the end of the war, our naturalization law looked like this:

The right to become a naturalized citizen under the provisions of this Act shall extend only to—

> (1) white persons, persons of African nativity or descent, and persons of races indigenous to the continents of North or South America or adjacent islands and Filipino persons or persons of Filipino descent;
>
> (2) persons who possess, either singly or in combination, a preponderance of blood of one or more of the classes specified in clause (1);
>
> (3) Chinese persons or persons of Chinese descent; and persons of races indigenous to India; and
>
> (4) persons who possess, either singly or in combination, a preponderance of blood of one or more of the classes specified in clause (3) or, either singly or in combination, as much as one-half blood of those classes and some additional blood of one of the classes specified in clause (1).[43]

This incremental retreat from a "Whites only" conception of citizenship made the arbitrariness of U.S. naturalization law increasingly obvious. For example, under the above statute, the right to acquire citizenship depended for some on blood-quantum distinctions based on descent from peoples indigenous to islands adjacent to the Americas. In 1952, Congress moved towards wholesale reform, overhauling the naturalization statute to read simply that "[t]he right of a person to become a naturalized citizen of the United States shall not be denied or abridged because of race or sex or because such person is married."[44] Thus, in 1952, racial bars on naturalization came to an official end.[45]

Notice the mention of gender in the statutory language ending racial restrictions in naturalization. The issue of women and citizenship can only be touched on here, but deserves significant study in its own right.[46] As the language of the 1952 Act implies, eligibility for naturalization once depended on a woman's marital status. Congress in 1855 declared that a foreign woman automatically acquired citizenship upon marriage to a U.S. citizen, or upon the naturalization of her alien husband.[47] This provision built upon the supposition that a woman's social and political status flowed from her husband. As an 1895 treatise on naturalization put it, "A woman partakes of her husband's nationality; her nationality is merged in that of her husband; her political status follows that of her husband."[48] A wife's acquisition of citizenship, however, remained subject to her individual qualification for naturalization—that is, on whether she was a "white person."[49] Thus, the Supreme Court held in 1868 that only "white women" could gain citizenship by marrying a citizen.[50] Racial restrictions further complicated matters for noncitizen women in that naturalization was denied to those married to a man racially ineligible for citizenship, irrespective of the woman's own qualifications, racial or otherwise.[51] The automatic naturalization of a woman upon her marriage to a citizen or upon the naturalization of her husband ended in 1922.[52]

The citizenship of American-born women was also affected by the interplay of gender and racial restrictions. Even though under English common law a woman's nationality was unaffected by marriage, many courts in this country stripped women who married noncitizens of their U.S. citizenship.[53] Congress recognized and mandated this practice in 1907, legislating that an American woman's marriage to an alien terminated her citizenship.[54] Under considerable pressure, Congress partially repealed this act in 1922.[55] However, the 1922 act continued to require the expatriation of any woman who married a foreigner racially barred from citizenship, flatly declaring that "any woman citizen who marries an alien ineligible to citizenship shall cease to be a citizen."[56] Until Congress repealed this provision in 1931,[57] marriage to a non-White alien by an American woman was akin to treason against this country: either of these acts justified the stripping of citizenship from someone American by birth. Indeed, a woman's marriage to a non-White foreigner was perhaps a worse crime, for while a traitor lost his citizenship only after trial, the woman lost hers automatically.[58] The laws governing the racial composition of this country's citizenry came inseverably bound up with and exacerbated by sexism. It is in this context of combined racial and gender prejudice that we should understand the absence of any women among the petitioners named in the prerequisite cases: it is not that women were unaffected by the racial bars, but that they were doubly bound by them, restricted both as individuals, and as less than individuals (that is, as wives).

Notes

1. U.S. COMMISSION ON CIVIL RIGHTS, THE TARNISHED GOLDEN DOOR: CIVIL RIGHTS ISSUES IN IMMIGRATION 1–12 (1990).

2. Chinese Exclusion Act, ch. 126, 22 Stat. 58 (1882). *See generally* Harold Hongju Koh, *Bitter Fruit of the Asian Immigration Cases,* 6 CONSTITUTION 69 (1994). For a sobering account of the many lynchings of Chinese in the western United States during this period, *see* John R. Wunder, *Anti-Chinese Violence in the American West, 1850–1910,* LAW FOR THE ELEPHANT, LAW FOR THE BEAVER: ESSAYS IN THE LEGAL HISTORY OF THE NORTH AMERICAN WEST 212 (John McLaren, Hamar Foster, and Chet Orloff eds., 1992). Charles McClain, Jr., discusses the historical origins of anti-Chinese prejudice and the legal responses undertaken by that community on the West Coast. Charles McClain, Jr., *The Chinese Struggle for Civil Rights in Nineteenth Century America: The First Phase, 1850–1870,* 72 CAL. L. REV. 529 (1984). For a discussion of contemporary racial violence against Asian Americans, *see* Note, *Racial Violence against Asian Americans,* 106 HARV. L. REV. 1926 (1993); Robert Chang, *Toward an Asian American Legal Scholarship: Critical Race Theory, Post-Structuralism, and Narrative Space,* 81 CAL. L. REV. 1241, 1251–58(1993).
3. Act of July 9, 1884, ch. 220, 23 Stat. 115; Act of May 5, 1892, ch. 60, 27 Stat. 25; Act of April 29, 1902, ch. 641, 32 Stat. 176; Act of April 27, 1904, ch. 1630, 33 Stat. 428.
4. Act of Feb. 5, 1917, ch. 29, 39 Stat. 874.
5. U.S. COMMISSION ON CIVIL RIGHTS, *supra,* at 9.
6. *Id. See* Act of May 19, 1921, ch. 8, 42 Stat. 5; Act of May 26, 1924, ch. 190, 43 Stat. 153.
7. U.S. COMMISSION ON CIVIL RIGHTS, *supra,* at 10.
8. *Id.* at 11. *See generally* JUAN RAMON GARCIA, OPERATION WETBACK: THE MASS DEPORTATION OF MEXICAN UNDOCUMENTED WORKERS IN 1954 (1980).
9. Act of Oct. 2, 1965, 79 Stat. 911.
10. Chae Chan Ping v. United States, 130 U.S. 581 (1889). The Court reasoned in part that if "the government of the United States, through its legislative department, considers the presence of foreigners of a different race in this country, who will not assimilate with us, to be dangerous to its peace and security, their exclusion is not to be stayed." For a critique of this deplorable result, *see* Louis Henkin, *The Constitution and United States Sovereignty: A Century of Chinese Exclusion and Its Progeny,* 100 HARV. L. REV. 853 (1987).
11. For efforts to encourage Irish immigration, *see, e.g., Immigration Act of 1990, § 131, 104 Stat. 4978 (codified as amended at 8 U.S.C. § 1153 (c) [1994]). Bill Ong Hing argues that Congress continues to discriminate against Asians. "Through an examination of past exclusion laws, previous legislation, and the specific provisions of the Immigration Act of 1990, the conclusion can be drawn that Congress never intended to make up for nearly 80 years of Asian exclusion, and that a conscious hostility towards persons of Asian descent continues to pervade Congressional circles." Bill Ong Hing,* Asian Americans and Present U.S. Immigration Policies: A Legacy of Asian Exclusion, *ASIAN AMERICANS AND THE SUPREME COURT: A DOCUMENTARY HISTORY 1106, 1107 (Hyung-Chan Kim ed., 1992).*
12. Louis DeSipio and Harry Pachon, Making Americans: Administrative Discretion and Americanization, *12 CHICANO-LATINO L. REV. 52, 53 (1992).*
13. CHARLES GORDON AND STANLEY MAILMAN, IMMIGRATION LAW AND PROCEDURE § 92.03[1][b] (rev. ed. 1992).
14. Dred Scott v. Sandford, 60 U.S. (19 How.) 393 (1857). For an insightful discussion of the role of Dred Scott *in the development of American citizenship,* see *JAMES KETTNER, THE DEVELOPMENT OF AMERICAN CITIZENSHIP, 1608–1870, at 300–333 (1978);* see also *KENNETH L. KARST, BELONGING TO AMERICA: EQUAL CITIZENSHIP AND THE CONSTITUTION 43–61 (1989).*
15. Civil Rights Act of 1866, ch. 31, 14 Stat. 27.
16. U.S. Const. amend. XIV.
17. 169 U.S. 649 (1898).
18. 112 U.S. 94 (1884).
19. Act of June 2, 1924, ch. 233, 43 Stat. 253.
20. Nationality Act of 1940, § 201(b), 54 Stat. 1138. See generally *GORDON AND MAILMAN,* supra, *at § 92.03[3][e].*
21. Pete Wilson, Crack Down on Illegals, *USA TODAY, Aug. 20, 1993, at 12A.*
22. H. R. J. Res. 129, 103d Cong., 1st Sess. (1993). An earlier, scholarly call to revamp the Fourteenth Amendment can be found in PETER SCHUCK and ROGER SMITH, CITIZENSHIP WITHOUT CONSENT: ILLEGAL ALIENS IN THE AMERICAN POLITY (1985).
23. Koh, supra, *at 69–70.*
24. Bill Ong Hing, Beyond the Rhetoric of Assimilation and Cultural Pluralism: Addressing the Tension of Separatism and Conflict in an Immigration-Driven Multiracial Society, *81 CAL. L. REV. 863, 866 (1993).*
25. Gerald Neuman warns against amending the Citizenship Clause. Gerald Neuman, Back to *Dred Scott? 24 SAN DIEGO L. REV. 485, 500 (1987).* See also *Note,* The Birthright Citizenship Amendment: A Threat to Equality, *107 HARV. L. REV. 1026 (1994).*
26. U.S. Const. art. I, sec. 8, cl. 4.
27. Act of March 26, 1790, ch. 3, 1 Stat. 103.
28. KETTNER, supra, *at 215–16.*
29. One exception exists. In revisions undertaken in 1870, the "white person" limitation was omitted. However, this omission is regarded as accidental, and the prerequisite was reinserted in 1875 by "an act to correct errors and to supply omissions in the Revised Statutes of the United States." Act of Feb. 18, 1875, ch. 80, 18 Stat. 318. See *In re Ah Yup, 1 F.Cas. 223 (C.C.D.Cal. 1878) ("Upon revision of the statutes, the revisors, probably inadvertently, as Congress did not contemplate a change of the laws in force, omitted the words 'white persons.' ").*
30. Statement of Senator Hendricks, 59 CONG. GLOBE, 42nd Cong., 1st Sess. 2939 (1866). See also *John Guendelsberger,* Access to Citizenship for Children Born Within the State to Foreign Parents, *40 AM. J. COMP. L. 379, 407–9 (1992).*
31. Statement of Senator Cowan, 57 CONG. GLOBE, 42nd Cong., 1st Sess. 499 (1866). For a discussion of the role of anti-Asian prejudice in the laws governing naturalization, see generally *Elizabeth Hull,* Naturalization and Denaturalization, *ASIAN AMERICANS AND THE SUPREME COURT: A DOCUMENTARY HISTORY 403 (Hyung-Chan Kim ed., 1992)*
32. The Senate rejected an amendment that would have allowed Chinese persons to naturalize. The proposed amendment read: "That the naturalization laws are hereby extended to aliens of African nativity, and to persons of African descent, and to persons born in the Chinese empire." BILL ONG HING, MAKING AND REMAKING ASIAN AMERICA THROUGH IMMIGRATION POLICY, 1850–1990, at 239 n.34 (1993).
33. Act of July 14, 1870, ch. 255, § 7, 16 Stat. 254.
34. Chinese Exclusion Act, ch. 126, § 14, 22 Stat. 58 (1882).
35. Fong Yue Ting v. United States, 149 U.S. 698, 716 (1893).
36. Neil Gotanda contends that separate racial ideologies function with respect to "other non-Whites," meaning non-Black racial minorities such as Asians, Native Americans, and Latinos. Neil Gotanda, "Other Non-Whites" in American Legal History: A Review of *Justice at War, 85 COLUM. L. REV. 1186 (1985). Gotanda explicitly identifies the operation of this separate ideology in the Supreme Court's jurisprudence regarding Asians and citizenship. Neil Gotanda,* Asian American Rights and the "Miss Saigon Syndrome," *ASIAN AMERICANS AND THE SUPREME COURT: A DOCUMENTARY HISTORY 1087, 1096–97 (Hyung-Chan Kim ed., 1992).*
37. Charles Gordon, The Racial Barrier to American Citizenship, *93 U. PA. L. REV. 237, 252 (1945).*
38. . MILTON KONVITZ, THE ALIEN AND THE ASIATIC IN AMERICAN LAW 80–81 (1946) (citation omitted).
39. Act of Oct. 14, 1940, ch. 876, § 303, 54 Stat. 1140.
40. Note, The Nationality Act of 1940, *54 HARV. L. REV. 860, 865 n.40 (1941).*
41. Act of Dec. 17, 1943, ch. 344, § 3, 57 Stat. 600.
42. Act of July 2, 1946, ch. 534, 60 Stat. 416.

43. Id.
44. Immigration and Nationality Act of 1952, ch. 2, § 311, 66 Stat. 239 (codified as amended at 8 U.S.C. 1422 [1988]).
45. Arguably, the continued substantial exclusion of Asians from immigration not remedied until 1965, rendered their eligibility for naturalization relatively meaningless. "[T]he national quota system for admitting immigrants which was built into the 1952 Act gave the grant of eligibility a hollow ring." Chin Kim and Bok Lim Kim, Asian Immigrants in American Law: A Look at the Past and the Challenge Which Remains, *26 AM. U. L. REV. 373, 390 (1977).*
46. See generally *Ursula Vogel,* Is Citizenship Gender-Specific? *THE FRONTIERS OF CITIZENSHIP 58 (Ursula Vogel and Michael Moran eds., 1991).*
47. Act of Feb. 10, 1855, ch. 71, § 2, 10 Stat. 604. Because gender-based laws in the area of citizenship were motivated by the idea that a woman's citizenship should follow that of her husband, no naturalization law has explicitly targeted unmarried women. GORDON AND MAILMAN, supra, *at § 95.03[6] ("An unmarried woman has never been (statutorily* barred from naturalization.").
48. PRENTISS WEBSTER, LAW OF NATURALIZATION IN THE UNITED STATES OF AMERICA AND OTHER COUNTRIES 80 (1895).
49. Act of Feb. 10, 1855, ch. 71, § 2, 10 Stat. 604.
50. Kelly v. Owen, 74 U.S. 496, 498 (1868).
51. GORDON AND MAILMAN, *supra* at § 95.03[6].
52. Act of Sept. 22, 1922, ch. 411, §2, 42 Stat. 1021.
53. GORDON AND MAILMAN, *supra* at § 100.03[4][m].
54. Act of March 2, 1907, ch. 2534, § 3, 34 Stat. 1228. This act was upheld in MacKenzie v. Hare, 239 U.S. 299 (1915) (expatriating a U.S.-born woman upon her marriage to a British citizen).
55. Act of Sept. 22, 1922, ch. 411, §3, 42 Stat. 1021.
56. *Id.* The Act also stated that "[n]o woman whose husband is not eligible to citizenship shall be naturalized during the continuance of the marriage."
57. Act of March 3, 1931, ch. 442, §4(a), 46 Stat. 1511.
58. The loss of birthright citizenship was particularly harsh for those women whose race made them unable to regain citizenship through naturalization, especially after 1924, when the immigration laws of this country barred entry to any alien ineligible to citizenship. Immigration Act of 1924, ch. 190, § 13(c), 43 Stat. 162. *See, e.g.,* Ex parte (Ng) Fung Sing, 6 F.2d 670 (W. D. Wash. 1925). In that case, a U.S. birthright citizen of Chinese descent was expatriated because of her marriage to a Chinese citizen, and was subsequently refused admittance to the United States as an alien ineligible to citizenship.

BROWN et al. v. BOARD OF EDUCATION OF TOPEKA et al.

347 U.S. 483 (1954)

MR. CHIEF JUSTICE WARREN delivered the opinion of the Court.

These cases come to us from the States of Kansas, South Carolina, Virginia, and Delaware. They are premised on different facts and different local conditions, but a common legal question justifies their consideration together in this consolidated opinion.[1]

In each of the cases, minors of the Negro race, through their legal representatives, seek the aid of the courts in obtaining admission to the public schools of their community on a nonsegregated basis. In each instance, they had been denied admission to schools attended by white children under laws requiring or permitting segregation according to race. This segregation was alleged to deprive the plaintiffs of the equal protection of the laws under the Fourteenth Amendment. In each of the cases other than the Delaware case, a three-judge federal district court denied relief to the plaintiffs on the so-called "separate but equal" doctrine announced by this Court in *Plessy v. Ferguson*, 163 U.S. 537. Under that doctrine, equality of treatment is accorded when the races are provided substantially equal facilities, even though these facilities be separate. In the Delaware case, the Supreme Court of Delaware adhered to that doctrine, but ordered that the plaintiffs be admitted to the white schools because of their superiority to the Negro schools.

The plaintiffs contend that segregated public schools are not "equal" and cannot be made "equal," and that hence they are deprived of the equal protection of the laws. Because of the obvious importance of the question presented, the Court took jurisdiction.[2] Argument was heard in the 1952 Term, and reargument was heard this Term on certain questions propounded by the Court.[3]

Reargument was largely devoted to the circumstances surrounding the adoption of the Fourteenth Amendment in 1868. It covered exhaustively consideration of the Amendment in Congress, ratification by the states, then existing practices in racial segregation, and the views of proponents and opponents of the Amendment. This discussion and our own investigation convince us that, although these sources cast some light, it is not enough to resolve the problem with which we are faced. At best, they are inconclusive. The most avid proponents of the post–War Amendments undoubtedly intended them to remove all legal distinctions among "all persons born or naturalized in the United States." Their opponents, just as certainly, were antagonistic to both the letter and the spirit of the Amendments and wished them to have the most limited effect. What others in Congress and the state legislatures had in mind cannot be determined with an degree of certainty.

An additional reason for the inconclusive nature of the Amendment's history, with respect to segregated schools, is the status of public education at that time.[4] In the South, the movement toward free common schools, supported by general taxation, had not yet taken hold. Education of white children was largely in the hands of private groups. Education of Negroes was almost nonexistent, and practically all of the race were illiterate. In fact, any education of Negroes was forbidden by law in some states. Today, in contrast, many Negroes have achieved outstanding success in the arts and sciences as well as in the business and professional world. It is true that public school education at the time of the Amendment had advanced further in the North, but the effect of the Amendment on northern States was generally ignored in the congressional debates. Even in the North, the conditions of public education did not approximate those existing today. The curriculum was usually rudimentary; ungraded schools were common in rural areas; the school term

From *U.S. Reports*, 1954. Opinion of the Supreme Court, 1954.

was but three months a year in many states; and compulsory school attendance was virtually unknown. As a consequence, it is not surprising that there should be so little in the history of the Fourteenth Amendment relating to its intended effect on public education.

In the first cases in this Court construing the Fourteenth Amendment, decided shortly after its adoption, the Court interpreted it as proscribing all state-imposed discriminations against the Negro race.[5] The doctrine of "separate but equal" did not make its appearance in this Court until 1896 in the case of *Plessy v. Ferguson, supra,* involving not education but transportation.[6] American courts have since labored with the doctrine for over half a century. In this Court, there have been six cases involving the "separate but equal" doctrine in the field of public education.[7] In *Cumming v. County Board of Education,* 175 U.S. 528, and *Gong Lum v. Rice,* 275 U.S. 78, the validity of the doctrine itself was not challenged.[8] In more recent cases, all on the graduate school level, inequality was found in that specific benefits enjoyed by white students were denied to Negro students of the same educational qualifications. *Missouri ex rel. Gaines v. Canada,* 305 U.S. 337; *Sipuel v. Oklahoma,* 332 U.S. 631; *Sweatt v. Painter,* 339 U.S. 629; *McLaurin v. Oklahoma State Regents,* 339 U.S. 637. In none of these cases was it necessary to reexamine the doctrine to grant relief to the Negro plaintiff. And in *Sweatt v. Painter, supra,* the Court expressly reserved decision on the question whether *Plessy v. Ferguson* should be held inapplicable to public education.

In the instant cases, that question is directly presented. Here, unlike *Sweatt v. Painter,* there are findings below that the Negro and white schools involved have been equalized, or are being equalized, with respect to buildings, curricula, qualifications and salaries of teachers, and other "tangible" factors.[9] Our decision, therefore, cannot turn on merely a comparison of these tangible factors in the Negro and white schools involved in each of the cases. We must look instead to the effect of segregation itself on public education.

In approaching this problem, we cannot turn the clock back to 1868 when the Amendment was adopted, or even to 1896 when *Plessy v. Ferguson* was written. We must consider public education in the light of its full development and its present place in American life throughout the Nation. Only in this way can it be determined if segregation in public schools deprives these plaintiffs of the equal protection of the laws.

Today, education is perhaps the most important function of state and local governments. Compulsory school attendance laws and the great expenditures for education both demonstrate our recognition of the importance of education to our democratic society. It is required in the performance of our most basic public responsibilities, even service in the armed forces. It is the very foundation of good citizenship. Today it is a principal instrument in awakening the child to cultural values, in preparing him for later professional training, and in helping him to adjust normally to his environment. In these days, it is doubtful that any child may reasonably be expected to succeed in life if he is denied the opportunity of an education. Such an opportunity, where the state has undertaken to provide it, is a right which must be made available to all on equal terms.

We come then to the question presented: Does segregation of children in public schools solely on the basis of race, even though the physical facilities and other "tangible" factors may be equal, deprive the children of the minority group of equal educational opportunities? We believe that it does.

In *Sweatt v. Painter, supra,* in finding that a segregated law school for Negroes could not provide them equal educational opportunities, this Court relied in large part on "those qualities which are incapable of objective measurement but which make for greatness in a law school." In *McLaurin v. Oklahoma State Regents, supra,* the Court, in requiring that a Negro admitted to a white graduate school be treated like all other students, again resorted to intangible considerations: " . . . his ability to study, to engage in discussions and exchange views with other students, and, in general, to learn his profession." Such considerations apply with added force to children in grade and high schools. To separate them from others of similar age and qualifications solely because of their race generates a feeling of inferiority as to their status in the community that may affect their hearts and minds in a way unlikely ever to be undone. The effect of this separation on their educational opportunities was well stated by a finding in the Kansas case by a court which nevertheless felt compelled to rule against the Negro plaintiffs:

> "Segregation of white and colored children in public schools has a detrimental effect upon the colored children. The impact is greater when it has the sanction of the law; for the policy of separating the races is usually interpreted as denoting the inferiority of the negro group. A sense of inferiority affects the motivation of a child to learn. Segregation with the sanction of law, therefore, has a tendency to [retard] the educational and mental development of negro children and to deprive them of some of the benefits they would receive in a racial[ly] integrated school system."[10]

Whatever may have been the extent of psychological knowledge at the time of *Plessy v. Ferguson,* this finding is amply supported by modern authority.[11] Any language in *Plessy v. Ferguson* contrary to this finding is rejected.

We conclude that in the field of public education the doctrine of "separate but equal" has no place. Separate educational facilities are inherently unequal. Therefore, we hold that the plaintiffs and others similarly situated for whom the actions have been brought are, by reason of the segregation complained of, deprived of the equal protection of the laws guaranteed by the Fourteenth Amendment. This disposition makes unnecessary any discussion whether such segregation also violates the Due Process Clause of the Fourteenth Amendment.[12]

Because these are class actions, because of the wide applicability of this decision, and because of the great variety of local conditions, the formulation of decrees in these cases presents problems of considerable complexity. On reargument, the consideration of appropriate relief was necessarily subordinated to the primary question—the constitutionality of segregation in public education. We have now announced that such segregation is a denial of the equal protection of the laws. In order that we may have the full assistance of the parties in formulating decrees, the cases will be restored to the docket, and the parties are requested to present further argument on Questions 4 and 5 previously propounded by the Court for the reargument this Term.[13] The Attorney General of the United States is again invited to participate. The Attorneys General of the states requiring or permitting segregation in public education will also be permitted to appear as *amici curiae* upon request to do so by September 15, 1954, and submission of briefs by October 1, 1954.[14]

It is so ordered.

NOTES

1. In the Kansas case, *Brown v. Board of Education,* the plaintiffs are Negro children of elementary school age residing in Topeka. They brought this action in the United States District Court for the District of Kansas to enjoin enforcement of a Kansas statute which permits, but does not require, cities of more than 15,000 population to maintain separate school facilities for Negro and white students. Kan. Gen. Stat. § 72-1724 (1949). Pursuant to that authority, the Topeka Board of Education elected to establish segregated elementary schools. Other public schools in the community, however, are operated on a nonsegregated basis. . . .

In the South Carolina case, *Briggs v. Elliott,* the plaintiffs are Negro children of both elementary and high school age residing in Clarendon County. They brought this action in the United States District Court for the Eastern District of South Carolina to enjoin enforcement of provisions in the state constitution and statutory code which require the segregation of Negroes and whites in public schools. . . .

In the Virginia case, *Davis v. County School Board,* the plaintiffs are Negro children of high school age residing in Prince Edward County. They brought this action in the United States District Court for the Eastern District of Virginia to enjoin enforcement of provisions in the state constitution and statutory code which require the segregation of Negroes and whites in public schools. . . .

In the Delaware case, *Gebhart v. Belton,* the plaintiffs are Negro children of both elementary and high school age residing in New Castle county. They brought this action in the Delaware Court of Chancery to enjoin enforcement of provisions in the state constitution and statutory code which require the segregation of Negroes and whites in public schools. . . .

2. technical footnote deleted.
3. technical footnote deleted.
4. technical footnote deleted.
5. technical footnote deleted.
6. technical footnote deleted.
7. technical footnote deleted.
8. technical footnote deleted.
9. technical footnote deleted.
10. technical footnote deleted.
11. K. B. Clark, Effect of Prejudice and Discrimination on Personality Development (Midcentury White House Conference on Children and Youth, 1950); Witmer and Kotinsky, Personality in the Making (1952), c. VI; Deutscher and Chein, The Psychological Effects of Enforced Segregation: A Survey of Social Science Opinion, 26 J. Psychol. 259 (1948); Chein, What are the Psychological Effects of Segregation Under Conditions of Equal Facilities?, 3 Int. J. Opinion and Attitude Res. 229 (1949); Brameld, Educational Costs, in Discrimination and National Welfare (MacIver, ed., 1949), 44-48; Frazier, The Negro in the United States (1949), 674-681. And see generally Myrdal, An American Dilemma (1944).
12. technical footnote deleted.
13. technical footnote deleted.
14. technical footnote deleted.

"Is Racial Integration Essential to Achieving Quality Education for Low-Income Minority Students, In the Short Term? In the Long Term?"

This is Part 2 of a symposium begun in [P&R's] *July/August issue with contributions by Elaine Gantz Berman, Phyllis Hart/Joyce Germaine Watts, Lyman Ho & PRRAC Board member Kati Haycock. Here PRRAC Board member john powell adds [his] thoughts on the subject. We welcome additional commentary.*

john a. powell

". . . My schooling gave me no training as the oppressor, as an unfairly advantaged person, or a person in a damaged culture... At school, we were not taught about slavery in any depth; we were not taught to see slave holders as damaged people. Slaves were seen as the only group at risk of being dehumanized. My schooling followed the pattern which Elizabeth Minnich has pointed out: whites are taught to think of their lives as morally neutral, normative, and average, and also ideal, so that when we work to benefit others, this is seen as work that will allow 'them' to be more like 'us.'" — Peggy McIntosh, "White Privilege: Male Privilege."

The roles of segregation and integration have been central to understanding and maintaining or destabilizing white privilege. Much of the discussion about integration and segregation has been fought out with poignant focus on school and education. This is understandable, in that school plays a central role in the formation of the American citizenry. Common schools are the crucible of American identity. They are the place where our children spend a tremendous portion of their lives, where their values and identities are shaped. In my discussion about integration and segregation, however, I will start, not with schools or even housing, but by rethinking what we mean by integration and segregation and how our misunderstanding of these limits our imagination and practice with respect to racial issues in this country. What I am suggesting, then, is that our collective conceptual error has important implications for the movement towards a racially just society, a racial democracy. Recognition of this error should play an important role in our thinking about integration and segregation in the educational context.

Integration is Not Cultural Assimilation

Today, there is requestioning of the relative benefits of integration and segregation. Despite this questioning, much of the discussion around these issues remains largely unreflective. The debate about the relative merits of integration and segregation has a long, rich history in the Black community. The pros and cons of each approach were thoughtfully and often sharply debated by W.E.B. Du Bois and Booker T. Washington at the turn of the century. Washington's posited that Blacks should rely upon themselves for self-help, whereas Du Bois thought the most talented Blacks should learn from whites, and then bring these attributes back to the Black community. Much of today's discussions draws on some of the ideas raised by Washington and Du Bois without the benefit of the depth of thought they used to support their conclusions.

Scholars and others have not been clear about what we mean by the words integration and segregation.

In order to deepen the discussion today, it is important to give pause and reflect on what integration and segregation mean in contemporary terms and what the implications for these two strategies are in the 21st Century. Part of the difficulty is that scholars and others have not been clear about what we mean by the words integration and segregation. Indeed, I would suggest that in recent times the debate has not focused on integration and segregation, but assimilation and segregation. The attack on integration, then, has largely not been an attack on integration but an attack on assimilation.

Assimilation is problematic because it is a product of racial hierarchy. Although there have been many distinct versions of assimilation and segregation, both of these concepts have been framed primarily by the dominant white society and operate under the implicit assumption that there is something wrong with the racial "other." The less extreme assimilationist would *fix* the racial other by acculturating him or her to the dominant culture. The more extreme assimilationist position is that the racial other must intermarry into the dominant race and cease to be. In either scenario, the voice of the minority is either ignored or eliminated.

The white segregationist shares this belief in white racial hierarchy. The segregationist also believes there is something defective about the racial other. But unlike the assimilationist, the run-of-the-mill segregationist takes the position that the racial other must prove that he or she has been fixed or

From *Poverty & Race*, September/October 1996, pp. 7-10, 16-18, 20-23.

modified before segregation can end. A more extreme segregationist view is that the racial other cannot be fixed, and affiliation with any of them will diminish and contaminate whites. The idea that one drop of African blood contaminates white blood is closely associated with this view. Both assimilationists and segregationists are disturbed by the otherness of the racial other. The extreme segregationist is also concerned about the other as well as otherness.

One may protest that this is the position only of the dominant society. What about racial minority groups that want to segregate themselves from the dominant society? While theoretically one can imagine that a racial minority might, for positive reasons, want to segregate itself despite openness from the dominant society, this is simply not the history of racial politics in the United States. Indeed, when Washington called for self-segregation, it was in part because he accepted the position that Blacks were unfit and must prove themselves to whites before segregation could end. The reality is that many African-Americans have adopted segregation as an accommodation and protection from white racism. While this is understandable, from a self-survival point of view, the problem is that it does not destabilize white hierarchy and it also has very little practical benefit. When one looks at middle-class Blacks who choose to live in Black neighborhoods, among the prevalent reasons cited is the desire to have space to retreat from white racism and the frustration of dealing with whites in the workplace. This does not mean that there are not positive things about the Black community or Black culture. This is another variation of the assimilationist position. What I am suggesting is that when one examines the roots of segregation, either self-imposed or imposed by the dominant society, white racism is central to understanding it.

Social interaction is constitutive of the individual and the collective identity of the community. Assimilation envisions the absorption of minorities into the mainstream. Real integration is measured, however, by the transformation of institutions, communities and individuals. Real integration involves fundamental change among whites and people of color, as people and communities. Segregation is not just the exclusion of people, but also the limitation of their opportunities and economic resources. It creates and maintains a culture of racial hierarchy and subjugation. Integration, as a solution to segregation, has broader meaning: it refers to community-wide efforts to create a more inclusive society, where individuals and groups have opportunities to participate equally in their communities. Inclusion give us tools to build democratic communities, the ability to approach complex issues from a multitude of perspectives. Integration, then, transforms racial hierarchy. Rather than creating a benefactor-beneficiary distinction along lines of race and class, true integration makes it possible for all groups to benefit from each other's resources. Homogeneous education fails to prepare students of all races for a multicultural society. Integrated education necessarily implies a curriculum that respects and values cultural difference, while building a community of equals.

Many African-Americans have adopted segregation as an accommodation and protection from white racism.

Although I cannot do justice to this issue in a short article, it is important to consider the situation of Native Americans. There is a strong feeling among American Indians that if they integrate, they will lose their culture and be overwhelmed by the dominant society. The discussion about segregation and assimilation in many ways is not germane for Native Americans. First of all, the issue of segregation and assimilation is a discussion that takes place within a nation. The debate for Native Americans is about how to build or maintain a nation within a nation. Native Americans have not been pushing to be part of this nation, but rather to preserve their own nation. If they cannot maintain their nation, it is likely that these other issues will become more important. In addition, when one asserts that Native Americans or other groups that are not allowed to segregate may lose their culture and identity, one is essentially making a claim that if not allowed to segregate, a group may be forced to assimilate. Given the two alternatives, maybe segregation is more desirable.

But this is not the issue that Blacks face in large numbers. While it may be possible for a few African-Americans to assimilate, that is not possible for large numbers. Blacks in the United States are unassimilable—what one writer calls "the designated other." This leads us to segregation or something else.

Before considering something else, I want to assert that segregation is morally, pragmatically and ontologically flawed. It is morally flawed because it cannot be reconciled in our society with the fundamental value of equal respect and dignity of all people. It is pragmatically flawed in that it can never produce equal life chances for whites and "others." It is ontologically flawed in that it damages and distorts the identity of all members of the racist society where segregation is practiced.

Problems Caused Segregation

Segregation prevents access to wealth accumulation by residents of isolated, poor communities of color, thereby establishing barriers to market participation. Lack of educational opportunities, poor job accessibility and declining housing values in isolated, low-income communities are symptoms of the problem. Further, racial and economic segregation damages the whole metropolitan region, including both the urban cores and the suburbs. Segregation geographically polarizes metropolitan communities along lines of race, income and opportunity, and separates urban centers from the surrounding suburbs. The experience of attending desegregated schools is likely to increase participation in desegregated environments in later life. When students attend integrated schools, they are more likely to attend desegregated colleges, live in integrated neighborhoods, work in integrated environments, have friends of another race and send their children to integrated schools. Conversely, students from segregated schools are more likely to avoid interactions with other races and generally conduct their lives in segregated settings. As Peggy McIntosh points out in her article, "White Privilege: Male Privilege," her schooling as a white attending an all-white school led to strained interactions in the workplace as an adult. Once she entered an integrated work space, she realized she wouldn't be able to get along if she asked her non-white co-workers to adapt to her world view. One thing is clear to me: that racial neutrality or "color blindness" is more likely to work toward maintaining the status quo than destabilizing it.

Toward Incorporation

Traditionally, desegregation in education has meant either removing formal barriers or simply placing students in physical proximity to one another. These remedies are limited. Segregation is not just the exclusion of people, but also the limitation of their opportunities and economic resources. Properly conceived, integration is transformative for everyone involved. Integration embraces a multi-cultural concept of social interaction. Much of the focus on the benefits of integration has been on how integration will benefit Blacks and other "others." What has been missing is an understanding of how integration, as well as segregation, affects us all. If we are to be successful at integration, we move much closer to David Goldberg's notion of incorporation. He asserts that, "incorporation, then, does not involve extension of established values and protections over the formerly excluded group . . . [T]he body politic becomes a medium for transformative incorporation, a political arena of contestation, rather than a base from which exclusions can be more or less silently extended, managed, and manipulated." Incorporation allows the views and experiences of both the dominant group and minority groups to meet, informing and transforming each other. With incorporation, no experience is the exclusive one. In this respect, incorporation clearly differs from assimilation and desegregation models. The ultimate goal of integration is this transformative incorporation Goldberg describes.

Building a Participatory Democracy

If we accept this reconstituted way of of viewing integration, it provides a positive strategy for how to start thinking about integration in relationship to schools as well as a critical perspective on how integration in the past has failed.

Real integration is measured by the transformation of institutions, communities and individuals.

Most of the efforts of the past and even today are half-hearted, leaving students de facto segregated or token assimilated. Too often the assumption is that if we can fix the other by having them go to schools with whites without addressing the underlying assumption of white privilege, including cultural privilege, we have successfully integrated. In assessing integration efforts, we too often look at the racial composition of a school, and not at what happens in the school. But if we look at integration in the way suggested above, it requires that we look at what goes on in school as well as outside of school. It requires that we link housing, school, employment and cultural opportunities. Linking housing and education policies, rather than focusing solely on integrating schools, directs attention to the importance and benefits of racial integration in multiple settings. By contrast, the approach of desegregating schools in isolation from other important institutions disregards the significance of building and strengthening communities. A qualitative analysis of the social effect of integration makes clear that achieving broad integration remains a central goal in, and a necessary step toward, making a fully participatory democracy a reality. The social value of integration embodies the founding ideals of this country. Making it possible for everyone to participate actively in our democracy should be a fundamental goal woven into the fabric of the nation's public policies. Another necessary element of participation is for residents to feel connected to the community as valued members of the polity. Segregated society has continued to exclude community members, even when formal rights to participate exist. The school setting provides both academic and social tools for participating in society. The less formal environment of our neighborhoods and social circles provides equally important tools for everyday life. Integration of both schools and housing demonstrates for all of us how the practice of living and learning together can inform our understanding of the world.

The Legacy of *Brown*

More than forty years ago, the Supreme Court, in *Brown v. Board of Education,* recognized the unique harm experienced by Black students forced to attend racially segregated schools. The Court declared the circumstances unacceptable. Today, after a half-hearted effort at best, most American schools remain segregated. While the explicitly segregationist policies of the *Brown* era seldom exist today, a more subtle network of social and institutional barriers persist, working to maintain segregation in our schools and communities. Desegregated schools may be the only institutions in which African-Americans and Latinos students have access to the abundance of college and employment contacts that whites and wealthy students take for granted. William Julius Wilson and other social scientists have noted that the greatest barrier to social and economic mobility for inner-city Blacks is their isolation from the opportunities and networks of the mostly white and middle-class society. School desegregation has a profound impact on Blacks' ability to acquire knowledge that would enhance their academic and occupational success via social contacts and integrated institutions. Integration can be a tough concept to embrace when one considers that it cannot claim many examples. Integration has been attacked by both ends of the political spectrum. In 1995, in his concurring opinion in *Missouri v. Jenkins,* Justice Clarence Thomas noted that "[I]t never ceases to amaze me that the courts are so willing to assume that anything that is predominantly Black must be inferior." Several Afrocentrists recall early attempts at integration that resulted with assimilation. The implications of assimilation have appropriately been criticized by a number of scholars.

The Link Between Housing and Education

The spatial isolation of minority poor students concentrates the education disadvantages inherent to poverty. Racial segregation, moreover, denies all students the benefits of an integrated education. For parents fortunate enough to be able to choose where they live, their selection is often determined by the quality of public education for their children. America's metropolitan areas increasingly have become characterized by a poor minority core, with a white, middle-class suburban ring. More often than not, the public schools considered best are in the middle-class and upper-middle class neighborhoods. Negative perception about urban schools contribute to the unwillingness of white families to move to urban neighborhoods. Part of the reason urban schools have a poor reputation is, of course, because they are segregated by race and class. The two most commonly expressed concerns about integration are "white flight" and mandatory busing, both of which can weaken communities, resulting in the drive for many school districts to return to neighborhood schools. The return to neighborhood schools, for which many policy makers are now calling, may, in fact, maintain or increase the racial segregation of communities that are isolated by race and class. Integrating schools while simultaneously creating greater housing opportunities makes true integration the goal, while it recognizes the social and economic barriers to integration. Building more integrated communities seems possible and desirable when people of different racial and economic groups begin to recognize that, without ignoring their differences, they share many goals and concerns. When housing and school policies work together, integrated communities maintain a stable, yet diverse, population.

Integration requires that we link housing, school, employment and cultural opportunities.

john powell, Secretary of PRRAC's Board, is on the faculty of the University of Minnesota Law School, where he directs the Institute on Race & Poverty (415 Law Ctr., 229 19th Ave. S., Minneapolis, MN 55455, 612/625-5529, E-mail: irp@gold.tc.umn.edu). Peggy McIntosh's 1988 article, "White Privilege: Male Privilege," is Working Paper #189 from the Wellesley College Center for Research on Women, Wellesley, MA 02181, 617/283-2500.

Resources

When ordering items from the Resources Section, please note that most listings direct you to contact an organization other than PRRAC. Prices include the shipping/handling (s/h) charge when this information is provided to PRRAC. "No price listed" items often are free.

When ordering items from PRRAC: SASE = self-addressed stamped envelope (32¢ unless otherwise indicated). Orders may not be placed by telephone or fax. Please indicate which issue of P&R *you are ordering from.*

When we fill SASE orders, we enclose a contributions envelope; please—especially if you are a frequent user of our service—try to send us some needed operating funds. Thank you.

Race/Racism

• ***All That We Can Be: Black Leadership & Racial Integration the Army Way,*** by Charles Moskos & John Sibley Butler (224 pp., 1996, $24), is available from Basic Books, 800/242-7737.

• **"An Empirical Test of the Cultural Capital Hypothesis,"** by James Johnson, Elisa Jayne Bienenstock & Jennifer Stoloff, appeared in the Spring 1995 issue of *The Review of Black Political Economy.* The 21-page article uses data from the Multi-City Survey of Urban Inequality to show that cultural influences are not significant when statistical controls for human capital variables are incorporated into the model. Reprints may be available from Prof. Johnson, Dept. Geography, Univ. N. Carolina, Chapel Hill, NC 27599.

• ***Bell Curve* Bibliography:** Prof. Chandler Davidson of the Rice Univ. Sociology Dept. (6100 Main St., Houston, TX 77005-1892, 713/527-4831, E-mail: soc@rice.edu) has prepared a ca. 275-item bibliography of commentary on the Charles Murray-Richard Herrnstein opus. Also check out a new Princeton Univ. Press book, *Inequality by Design: Cracking the Bell Curve Myth,* by Claude Fischer, Michael Hout, Martin Sanchez Jankowski, Samuel Lucas, Ann Swidler & Kim Voss, all of the UC-Berkeley Sociology Dept.—318 pp., $14.95 from the Press, 41 William St., Princeton, NJ 08540, 609/258-5165. (Reminder: PRRAC also has a ca. 300-page packet of the texts of *Bell Curve* reviews, commentaries, etc. $15 to cover copying/mailing costs.)

• **"Black Church Burnings in the South"** is a 32-page, June 1996 report of a 6-month preliminary investigation prepared for the Ctr. for Democratic Renewal. Available (possibly free) from CDR, PO Box

50469, Atlanta, GA 30302, 404/221-0025, E-mail: cdr@igc.apc.org.

• ***Connect*** is the new bi-monthly newsletter of the Internatl. Movement Against All Forms of Discrimination & Racism. Organizational HQ is 3-5-11 Roppongi, Minato-ku, Tokyo 106 Japan, tel: (81-3) 3586-7447. The US Committee is at 467 Grandview Terr., Leonia, NJ 07605, 201/592-0350.

• ***Critical Race Theory: The Key Writings that Formed the Movement,*** eds. Kimberle Crenshaw, Neil Gotanda, Gary Peller & Kendall Thomas (494 pp., 1995), is available ($30) from The New Press, 450 W. 41 St., NYC, NY 10036, 212/629-8811.

• ***Federal Title VI Enforcement to Ensure Nondiscrimination in Federally Assisted Programs*** (677 pp., June 1996) is available (free) from the US Civil Rights Commn. (202/376-8110, Vanessa Williamson).

• **"Inclusive Practices Program Report"** provides data on foundations' and corporate giving programs' progress in increasing the number of racial minorities & women on their staffs. Contact the Council on Foundations, 1828 L St. NW, Wash., DC 20036, 202/466-6512.

• ***Modern Capital of Human Rights? Abuses in the State of Georgia*** (214 pp., 1996), challenging Atlanta's Olympics application statement that "for many," the city is "the modern capital of human rights," is available (no price listed) from Human Rights Watch, 485 Fifth Ave., NYC, NY 10017-6104. The report is one of a series on the US, and among the topics covered are police abuse, the death penalty, race and drug law enforcement, treatment of prisoners & children in confinement.

• ***Native American Directory: Alaska, Canada, US*** (800+ pp.) covers Native organizations, government agencies, museums, cultural centers, arts & crafts dealers, pow-wows, etc. $65.95 from Native Amer. Coop., PO Box 27626, Tucson, AZ 85726-7626.

• ***Race & Ethnic Relations 96/97*** (6th ed.), ed John Kromkowski (288 pp., 1996), contains 57 articles (31 of which are new), broken into 9 categories, including "Race & Ethnicity in the Amer. Legal Tradition," "Immigration," "Hispanic/Latino Americans," "Asian Americans," "African Americans." Contact Dushkin Pub. Group, 25 Kessel Ct., Madison, WI 53711-6227.

• ***Race, Poverty & American Cities,*** eds. (PRRAC Board Chair) John Charles Boger & Judith Welch Wegner (614 pp., 1996), contains 17 essays, by John Calmore, Peter Dreier, Ann Markusen, William L. Taylor, James Rosenbaum, George Galster, James Johnson, Jr., Chester Hartman, Michael Stegman and others. $19.96 (representing a 20% discount) for *P&R* readers, from Univ. N. Carolina Press, 800/848-6224.

• **"Race Relations in America"** is a 84-page, 1996 booklet, prepared by Mary von Euler, available (no price listed) from the Americans for Democratic Action Educ. Fund, 1625 K St. NW, #210, Wash., DC 20006, 202/785-5980, E-mail: adaction@ix.netcom.com.

• **"Seeing Race,"** an interview with Univ. of Mich. anthropologist Lawrence Hirschfeld (author of the 1996 MIT book *Race in the Making: Cognition, Culture & the Child's Construction of Human Kinds*), appeared in the June 1996 *Michigan Today.* Available from us with a SASE.

• **"The Affirmative Action Debate"** is a 19-page (+ Apps.), Sept. 1996 "Talking Back" Framing Memo, available (possibly free) from The Advocacy Inst., 1707 L St. NW, #400, Wash., DC 20036, 202/659-8475, E-mail: aiinfo@advocacy.org.

• **"The 1996 Latino Election Handbook"** (25 pp. $15) and "The 1996 Directory of Latino Elected Officials" (224 pp., $33) are available from the Natl. Assn. of Latino Elected & Appointed Officials. The former, from NALEO's LA office, 3409 Garnet St., LA, CA 90023, 213/262-8503; the latter, from their DC office, 514 C St. NE, Wash., DC 20002, 202/546-2536.

• **The Natl. Hispanic Council on Aging** has several publications: "In Triple Jeopardy: Aged Hispanic Women - Insights & Experiences," ed. Marta Sotomayor (148 pp., ? date, $18.95); "Culture & Tradition: Los Ancianos Latinos - A Health Promotion & Disease Training Manual," in Spanish & English ($10); "Elderly Latinos: Issues & Solutions for the 21st Century," eds. Marta Sotomayor & Alejandro Garcia (142 pp., 1993, $18.95 + s/h); "Empowering Hispanic Families: A Critical Issue for the '90s," ed. Marta Sotomayor (240 pp., 1991, $15.95). The Council is at 2713 Ontario Rd. NW, Wash., DC 20009, 202/745-2521.

• **"The October National Month of Resistance"** ("to the racists & women haters, to the gay-bashers & welfare slashers, to the prison builders & executioners") is being organized by Refuse & Resist, 305 Madison Ave., #1166, NYC, NY 10165, E-mail: refuse@calyx.com.

• **"The X in La Raza — an 'anti-book',"** by Robert Rodriguez (120 pp., 1996), part 2 to an article he wrote 15 years ago titled "Who Declared War on the Word Chicano?," is available ($12) from the author, a nationally syndicated columnist, at PO Box 7905, Albuquerque, NM 87194-7905, 505/248-0092, E-mail: XXXROBERTO@COL.COM.

• **Two UN Reports on US Racism:** "Report by Mr. Maurice Glélé-Ahanhanzo, Special Rapporteur on contemporary forms of racism, racial discrimination, xenophobia and related intolerance on his mission to the USA from 9 to 22 October 1994, submitted pursuant to Commission on Human Rights Resolutions 1993/20 and 1994/64" (44 pp.) and the US Government's January 16, 1995, Response are both available (no price listed) from the Meiklejohn Civil Liberties Inst., Box 673, Berkeley, CA 94701, 510/848-0599.

• ***Viva la Causa: 500 Years of Chicano History*** is a 60-minute, 2-part educational video, in English, based on the bilingual book of the same title edited by Elizabeth Martinez. The video alone is $37.50 indivs., $52.50 insts.; the book, $18; a Chicano History Teaching Kit, with a 70-page "Curriculum Guide for Elementary & Secondary School Teachers," the video and book, is $112.50, from SouthWest Organizing Project, 211 10th St. NW, Albuquerque, NM 87102, 505/247-8832.

• ***When Democracy Works*** is a new video, by Catherine Saalfield, showing the interconnectedness among 3 right-wing policy initiatives: California ballot anti-affirmative action and anti-immigrant initiatives; Colorado's anti-gay Amendment 2; and David Duke's bid for office in Louisiana. Contact Aubin Pictures, 22 Prince St., #427, NYC, NY 10012, 212/330-8220, E-mail: aubinpics@aol.com.

• **"Who's Planning the Future of the Bay Area? An Analysis of Latino Representation on Bay Area Commissions & Boards,"** by Roxanne Figueroa (14 pp., 1996), is available (likely free) from the Latino Issues Forum, 785 Market St., 3rd flr., SF, CA 94103, 415/284-7227. The report finds severe underrepresentation of Latinos, even though by the year 2010 1.6 million Latinos will reside in the 9 Bay Area counties.

• ***Wrong for All the Right Reasons: How White Liberals Have Been Undone by Race,*** by Gordon MacInnes (236 pp., 1996, $21.95), is available from NYU Press, 800/996-6987.

• **"Paul Robeson Week for Racial & Ethnic Harmony,"** sponsored by the DC Student Coal. Against Racism, will be held **Oct. 19-26.** Inf. from DC SCAR, PO Box 18291, Wash., DC 20036, 202/310-2930, E-mail: dcscar@igc.apc.org.

• **The Mauricio Gaston Inst. for Latino Comm. Dev. & Public Policy** has a Fall speakers series. Remaining events: Carol Hardy-Fanta on "Latino Political Representation in Mass.: Lessons from 4 Cities" **(Oct. 15)**; Michael Massagli on "Racial Residential Preferences: Underpinnings of Amer. Apartheid in Gtr. Boston" **(Oct. 22)**; Jim Campen on "Trailing the Pack: Hispanics & Mortgage Lending in Mass." **(Nov. 12)**; Elena Letona Milles & Esterla Barreto Cortez on "The Nature of Comm. Participation in Latino Comm. Agencies" **(Nov. 19)**; Peggy Levitt & Christina Gomez on "Does Race Matter? The Dominican Experience in Mass." **(Dec. 3)**. All lectures are 12-2; call 617/287-5790 for the U. Mass.-Boston location.

• **"Visions of the Future: The Information Revolution & People of Color,"** sponsored by the Univ. of MD Afro-American Studies Prog., will be held **Oct. 24-25** at the Univ. Confirmed speakers include Robert E. Johnson & Kweisi Mfume. Further inf. from Vivianne Hardy Townes, 301/405-1158, E-mail: secr@bss2.umd.edu.

• **The Natl. MultiCultural Inst.** has a workshop & conf. **Nov. 14-17** in DC. Inf. from the Inst., 3000 Conn. Ave. NW, #438, Wash., DC 20008-2556., 202/483-0700, E-mail: ncmi@ncmi.org.

Poverty/Welfare

• **"The ABCs of Welfare Reform: A Guide to the Personal Responsibility & Work Opportunity Reconciliation Act of 1996,"** by Candace Sullivan & Jule Sugarman (51 pp., Sept. 1996), is available ($22.50) from the Ctr. on Effective Services for Children, PO Box 27412, Wash., DC 20038-7412, 202/785-9524.

• **"Directory of Low Income Orgs. Working on Welfare,"** listing over 60 orgs. in 29 states, is available (free to low-inc. orgs. & advocacy orgs.) from the Ctr. on Social Welfare Policy & Law, 275 Seventh Ave., #1205, NYC, NY 10001-6708, 212/633-6967.

• ***Economic Security for All: How to End Poverty in the US,*** by Wade Hudson (320 pp., 1996), is available (free, but donations solicited to defray costs of book production; cost = $13/copy for printing + mailing) from the Econ. Security Proj., 509 Ellis St., SF, CA 94109, 415/749-0591, E-mail: whudson@igc.apc.org. Web edition: http://www.igc.apc.org.esp.

• **"Poverty & Death in the US — 1973 & 1991,"** from *Epidemiology* 1995; 6:490-497, which we noted in a previous issue of *P&R,* contained a significant calculation error. Contact co-author Nancy Krieger (Harvard School of Public Health, 677 Huntington Ave. Boston, MA 02115, 617/432-1571, E-mail: nkrieger@hsph.harvard.edu) for a copy of the published letter that pointed out the error & the authors' reply; a corrected version of the full manuscript will be published in the *Internatl. J. of Health Services.*

• **"Poverty Reduction & the World Bank: Progress & Challenges in the 1990s"** (142 pp., 1996) is available (no price listed) from The World Bank, 1818 H St. NW, Wash., DC 20433, 202/477-1234. According to the report, *1.31 billion* people, more than one-fifth of the world's population, live on less than a dollar a day, a figure that is increasing.

• **Summaries & Analyses of the New Welfare Law:** a listing of these is available from the Coalition on Human Needs, 1000 Wisconsin Ave. NW, Wash., DC 20007, 202/342-9726, E-mail: HN0079@handsnet.org.

• ***The Journal of Poverty: Innovations on Social, Political & Economic Inequalities*** is a new, refereed biannual, eds. Keith Kilty, Virginia Richardson & Elizabeth Segal, first issue to appear Spring 1997. Subs. $21.60/indivs. $28.80/insts., $45/libs. Free sample to libraries & faculty with library recommendation authorization, from Haworth Press, 10 Alice St., Binghamton, NY 13904-1580, 800/342-9678.

• ***The Low Income Consumer: Adjusting the Balance of Exchange,*** by Linda Alwitt & Thomas Donley of Depaul Univ., is a new Sage Publication book (PO Box 5084, Thousand Oaks, CA 91359-9924).

• **The Natl. Dialogue on Poverty,** a project of the Natl. Assn. of Comm. Action Agencies, has available a Summary Report of its April 1996 Natl. Policy Forum on Poverty. The 19-page report is available (possibly free) from NACAA, 1100 17th St. NW, #500, Wash., DC 20036, 202/265-7546, E-mail: nacaa@ix.netcom.com.

• **"The New Welfare Law,"** by David Super, Sharon Parrott, Susan Steinmetz & Cindy Mann (32 pp.); "The Timeline for Implementing the New Welfare Law," by Jocelyn Guyer, Cindy Mann & David Super (16 pp. + tables); "The Depth of the Food Stamp Cuts in the Final Welfare Bill" (5 pp.) are new publications from the Ctr. on Budget & Policy Priorities, 820 First St. NE, #510, Wash., DC 20002, 202/408-1056. Contact them for prices and 1996 publications list.

• ***Top Heavy: A Study of the Increasing Inequality of Wealth in America,*** by Edward Wolf (new updated ed., 112 pp., 1996, $7.95), is available from The New Press, 800/233-4830.

• **"Welfare Myths: Fact or Fiction? Exploring the Truth About Welfare"** (46 pp.) is available ($10) from the Ctr. on Social Welfare Policy & Law, 275 Seventh Ave., #1205, NYC, NY 10001-6708.

• **"Welfare Waivers Implementation - States Work to Change Welfare Culture, Community Involvement & Service Delivery"** is a July 1996 GAO report (GAO/HEHS-96-105), available (free) from USGAO, PO Box 6015, Gaithersburg, MD 20884-6015, 202/512-6000.

• **World Day to Overcome Extreme Poverty** will be held **Oct. 17**, sponsored by the Fourth World Movement. A commemoration will be held at 6:30 pm on the West Front of the US Capitol. Inf. from FWM, 7600 Willow Hill Dr., Landover, MD 20785-4658, 301/336-9489.

Community Organizing

• **A Critical Review** of (ex-PRRAC Board member) Gary Delgado's "Beyond the Politics of Place: New Directions in Community Organizing in the 1990s," by Mike Miller, Exec. Dir. of Organize Training Ctr., is available ($10) from OTC, 442A Vicksburg St., SF, CA 94114. Delgado's 99-page, 1994 document is available ($10) from the Applied Research Ctr., 1322 Webster St., Oakland, CA 94612.

• **"Social Psychological Perspectives on Grassroots Organizing,"** ed. Michele Wittig & B. Ann Bettencourt, is a special 220-page, 1996 issue of the *Journal of Social Issues,* $21 from J.S. Canner & Co., 10 Charles St., Needham Heights, MA 02194, 617/449-9103. . . .

Families/Children/ Women

• **"Call to Action: An Oakland Blueprint for Youth Development"** (80 pp., June 1996) is available (likely free) from the Urban Strategies Council, 672 13th St., Oakland, CA 94612, 510/893-2404, E-mail: council@urbanstrat.com.

• **Domestic Violence/ Welfare Reform** is the theme of a special 363-page, 1996 issue (vol. 30, no. 3) of *Clearinghouse Review.* Contact the Clearinghouse, 205 W. Monroe St., 2nd flr., Chicago, IL 60606-5013, 312/263-3830.

• **"Financing Early Childhood Facilities: Investment Strategies for California's Low-Income Communities,"** the final report of a Calif. Task Force, is available ($28) from the Natl. Econ. Dev. & Law Ctr., 2201 Broadway, #815, Oakland, CA 94612, 510/251-2600.

• **The Comm. Against Anti-Asian Violence** has called for a boycott of shoe & accessory manufacturer Kenneth Cole, claiming the company tolerates sexual & racial harassment of women of color in their workplace—a complaint about which has been filed with EEOC. More. inf. from the Committee, 191 E. 3rd St., NYC, NY 10009, 212/473-6485.

• **The Foundation for Child Development,** under its Neighborhood Research Grants Program, is disseminating the final reports on pilot efforts to develop measures & methods for evaluating comprehensive community-change initiatives that include a focus on young children & families. To receive these reports (which apparently are free), contact Barbara Leahy at the Foundation, 345 E. 46 St., NYC, NY 10017, 212/697-3150.

• **"Women Connecting Beyond Beijing"** is a new workshop series from the Center for Concern, "enabling local groups to work on local concerns within a global framework and to become a part of the global efforts to create a better future for all." Facilitator's packets ($15), Participant's workbooks ($3) + 15% s/h from the Ctr., 3700 13th St. NE, Wash., DC 20017, 202/635-2757.

• **"Sisters & Daughters Betrayed: The Sex Trade of Women & Girls"** is a **Oct. 17-18** conf., in Reno, sponsored by The Global Fund for Women & The Circle Against Sex Trafficking. Inf. from the Circle, 1525 Foothill Rd., Gardnerville, NV 89410, 702/782-6050.

• **"Dangerous Intersection: Feminist Perspectives on Population, Immigration & the Environment,"** co-sponsored by the Union Theological Seminary, will be held **Oct. 25-26** in NYC. Inf. from Andrea Smith, 212/802-8246. . . .

Housing

• **"$30,000,000 and Counting"** (77 pp., June 1996) is a summary of housing discrimination lawsuits compiled for the Natl. Fair Housing Alliance by the Fair Housing Ctr. of Met. Detroit. $6 from the Ctr., 1249 Washington Blvd., #1312, Detroit, MI 48226, 313/963-1274.

• **"Balancing Acts: The Experience of Mutual Housing Assns. & Comm. Land Trusts in Urban Neighborhoods"** & "Hands-On Housing: A Guide Through Mutual Housing Assns. & Comm. Land Trusts for Tenants & Organizers" are available (prices not listed) from Victor Bach, Comm. Service Soc. of NY, 105 E. 22 St., NYC, NY 10010, 212/254-8900.

• **"Building Public-Private Partnerships to Develop Affordable Housing,"** ed. Fred Cooper (114 pp.), is available (free) from HUD Comm. Connection, 800/998-9999. The guidebook summarizes the experience of 4 natl. intermediaries (Comm. Bldrs., Enterprise, LISC, Natl. Dev. Council), an overview by Rick Cohen & a foreword by James Rouse.

• **"Examining the Relationship between Housing, Education & Persistent Segregation"** (63 pp. + maps, Summer 1996) is a preliminary report, focussing on the Twin Cities, available (possibly free) from the Inst. on Race & Poverty, Univ. of MN Law School, 229 19th Ave. S., Mpls, MN 55455, 612/625-8071, E-mail: irp@gold.tc.umn.edu. The Institute's director and principal investigator on the project, PRRAC Board member john powell, is soliciting comments on the preliminary report.

• **"Expanding Housing Choices for HUD-Assisted Families"** is the first in a series of biennial reports to Congress on the Moving to Opportunity Demonstration, evaluating the impact of a program (in the Baltimore, Boston, Chicago, LA and NY metro areas) "to help low-income families move from public and assisted housing in high-poverty inner-city neighborhoods to better housing, education & employment opportunities in low-poverty communities." Copies of the 31-page, May 1996 report are available (probably free) from Dep. Asst. Sec. Margery Turner, HUD/PD&R, Wash., DC 20410-6000.

• **"Federal Policy in Transition: A National Briefing Book on Housing, Economic & Comm. Dev."** is available ($75) from the Natl. Low Income Housing Coal., 1012 14th St. NW, #1200, Wash., DC 20005, 202/662-1530 x234.

• **"HMDA Works"** is a new software package for analyzing local mortgage lending patterns. Contact Becky Reilly, Ctr. for Comm. Change, 1000 Wisconsin Ave. NW, Wash., DC 20007, 202/352-0567, E-mail: HN0280@handsnet.org.

• ***HUD Manual:*** The 1996 Supplement to this reference work and to *HUD Housing Programs: Tenants' Rights* are available from the Natl. Housing Law Project, 2201 Broadway, #815, Oakland, CA 94612, 510/251-9400. Contact them for prices and other related manuals.

• **"New Jersey Tenants Organizing Handbook"** (36 pp., 1996) is available ($9) from the NJ Tenants Org., 389 Main St., Hackensack, NJ 07601, 201/342-3775.

• **The Federal Housing Finance Board's 1995 Report on the Low-Income Housing & Comm. Dev. Activities of the Federal Home Loan Bank System** is available (likely free) from the Board, 1777 F St. NW, Wash., DC 20006, 202/408-2500.

• **"The Lessons of *American Apartheid:* The Necessity & Means of Promoting Residential Racial Integration,"** by (former PRRAC Board member) Florence Roisman, appeared in the Dec. 1995 *Iowa Law R.* Free reprints from Maureen McGovern, Widener Univ. School of Law, 4601 Concord Pike, Wilmington, DE 19803, 302/477-2137.

• **"The Persistent Racial Gap: Milwaukee's Mortgage Lending Market During the 1990s"** is available (no price listed) from the Fair Lending Coalition, 414/344-2885. A related study, "Survey of Small Business Lending in Denver," by Frank Ford, is available (no price listed) from the Denver Comm. Reinvestment Alliance, 303/556-2824.

• **"The State of the Nation's Housing: 1996"** (36 pp.) is available, possibly free, from the Jt. Ctr. for Housing Studies, Harvard Univ., 79 JFK St., Cambridge, MA 02138, 617/495-7908.

• **"Mount Laurel: What Lessons Have We Learned?"** is (likely was, given our late mailing date) a conf., **Oct. 3-4**, at Seton Hall Univ. Law School. Inf. from Prof. Tracy Kaye at the Law School, One Newark Ctr., Newark, NJ 07102-5210, 201/642-8455. A copy of the study that formed the basis for this conference, "The Impact of the Mt. Laurel Initiatives: An Analysis of the Characteristics of Applicants & Occupants," by Naomi Bailin Wish & Stephen Eisdorfer (88 pp. + Apps., August 1996), is available (no price listed) from Dr. Wish, Ctr. for Public Service, Seton Hall Univ., Duffy Hall, 400 S. Orange Ave., S. Orange, NJ 07079, 201/761-9510. The August 1996 report is still in draft form, but a final version should be available shortly.

• **The Natl. Assn. of Affordable Housing Lenders** is holding its 1996 E. Reg. Conf., **Oct. 10-11** in NYC. Inf. from NAAHL, 1050 17th St. NW, #950, Wash., DC 20036, 202/861-5770.

• **National Neighbors** is sponsoring a series of confs. exploring natl., reg. and local issues of discriminatory housing & lending: **Nov. 4** in Seattle; **Nov. 7** in Boston; **Nov. 16** in Cinn.; **Nov. 21-22** in Miami; **Dec. 4** (tent.) in Albuquerque. Inf. from Jill Mittelhauser at NN, 733 15th St. NW, #540, Wash., DC 20005-2112, 202/628-8899, E-mail: natlnbrs@essential.org.

• **The 1996 Natl. Housing Conf.** will be held **Nov. 7-8** in LA. Inf. from the Conf., 815 15th St. NW, #711, Wash., DC 20005, 202/393-5772.

• **"A Time of Change"** is the 15th annual network conf. of the Enterprise Fdn., **Dec. 3-7** in Miami. Inf. from the Fdn., Box 1170, Columbia, MD 21044-0170.

Immigration

• **"Human Rights Abuses Along the US Border with Mexico Persist Amid Climate of Impunity"** is a 37-page, April 1995 report available ($5) from Human Rights Watch/Americas, 485 Fifth Ave., NYC, NY 10017-6014, 212/972-8400.

• **"Impacts of Medicaid Managed Care on Immigrants & Refugees: A Best Practices Review with Policy Recommendations"** (68 pp., 1996) is available (no price listed) from the Chicago Inst. on Urban Poverty, 208 S. LaSalle St., #1818, Chicago, IL 60604, 312/629-4500.

• ***Network News*** is the newly revived quarterly newsletter of the newly revived Natl. Network for Immigrant & Refugee Rights, headed by PRRAC Board member Cathi Tactaquin. Sub. inf. from the Network 310 8th St., #307, Oakland, CA 94607, 510/465-1984, E-mail: nnirr@lgc.apc.org.

• ***Remembering the American Dream: Hispanic Immigration & National Policy,*** by Roberto Suro (125 pp., 1996, $9.95), is available from The Brookings Inst., 800/552-5450, 202/797-6258.

• **"Taxes Paid by Illinois Immigrants"** (35 pp., May 1996), a technical paper by The Urban Inst., & "Estimated Costs of Providing Welfare & Education Services to the Native Born & to Immigrants in Illinois," (the latter by Rob Paral, 36 pp. + Apps., May 1996), are available ($6.50 each) from The Latino Inst., 228 S. Wabash, 6th flr., Chicago, IL 60604, 312/663-3603.

• **"The End of Health Care for Immigrants?,"** by Dong Suh, a 10-page, June 1996 report on "the impact of pending [now enacted] immigration benefit disqualifications on Asian & Pacific Islander American health & the health of the public," is available (likely free) from the Asian & Pacific Islander American Health Forum, 116 New Montgomery St., #531, SF, CA 94105, 415/541-0866.

• ***Watching America's Door: The Immigration Backlash & the New Policy Debate,*** by Roberto Suro (80 pp., 1996, $9.95), is available from the Brookings Inst. 800/552-5450, 202/797-6258.

• **"When the 'Coloreds' are Neither Black nor Citizens: The U.S. Civil Rights Movement & Global Migration,"** by PRRAC Board member Bill Tamayo, appeared in the May 1995 *Asian Law Journal.* Reprints of the 32-page article may be available from the author, 11 Christopher Dr., SF, CA 94131. . . .

Court grows critical when race, law intersect

The majority now rejecting bias remedies

Tony Mauro and Tom Watson
USA TODAY

For the third time this month, the Supreme Court on Thursday said it was tired. Tired, that is, of the traditional approaches to remedying the national problem of race discrimination.

On June 12, the court's conservative majority voiced dissatisfaction with affirmative action and school desegregation. On Thursday, it was race-based redistricting that got the court upset.

Using race as the primary reason for creating a district, to enhance chances of electing a minority candidate, violates the constitutional guarantee of equal treatment of all races under the law, the court said.

That pronouncement, which throws hundreds of congressional, state and local districts nationwide into turmoil, must have given pause to retired Justice Harry Blackmun, who was in the courtroom Thursday to hear it.

It was 17 years ago that Blackmun penned the simple formulation that describes the underlying theory of the approach to civil rights that the current court is repudiating. "In order to get beyond racism, we must first take account of race," Blackmun wrote.

Under that banner, the court embraced affirmative action, which takes race into account by giving minorities preferences in contracts and employment. It endorsed special measures for minority students in schools and it encouraged remedies under the Voting Rights Act aimed at boosting the voting power of minorities.

But now, riding the same wave that brought the Republican majority to Congress last fall, the court seems to be saying that racial preferences are an idea whose time has passed.

In Baton Rouge, La., one of the areas affected by Thursday's ruling, opinion seems as divided as it is within the court.

A.J. Lord, owner of A.J.'s Restaurant, agrees it is important to have minorities in Congress. But he also believes other things are just as important, such as having members of Congress represent cohesive districts.

Louisiana's 4th District was drawn to create a majority-minority district, but it is so far-flung, says Lord, that many voters don't know who their congressman is.

"At some point, you have to weigh your objectives to elect black candidates to office, or have proper representation of a district," says Lord. "It's a balancing act and there's no easy solution."

Frank Ransburg, a political scientist at Southern University, a historically black school in north Baton Rouge, says abolishing the district now represented by Rep. Cleo Fields, who is black, would reverse important civil rights gains.

"There are some people in the state who don't feel that blacks should be allowed to fully participate in the political process," Ransburg says.

Most liberals say the court is too hasty in declaring the problem of racial bias solved, and that race-conscious remedies are no longer needed.

"The three decisions reflect unfortunate judicial resistance to reasonable efforts toward racial inclusiveness," says Harvard law professor Laurence Tribe. "The combined effect is to turn the clock back on an effort that is not yet completed."

The Rev. Jesse Jackson: "The court has authorized the country to unravel the legal fabric of social justice and inclusion that has been woven together over the last 41 years."

Jackson has special words of contempt for Justice Clarence Thomas, the court's only black justice, who was part of the 5-4 majority in all three cases. "It is especially painful that a descendant of slaves, in effect, stabbed Dr. (Martin Luther) King . . . in the back, and is paving the way back toward slavery," Jackson says.

The idea of drawing districts to pull in pockets of minority voters developed in the last two decades in response to a political truth: Black candidates are rarely elected in districts where whites form the majority of the population.

"There are thousands of redistricting plans in the South and throughout the country in

How they voted on the cases

The justices continued their conservative march Thursday. But they didn't always agree.

Georgia redistricting

▶ **Against:** Chief Justice William Rehnquist and justices Anthony Kennedy, Antonin Scalia, Clarence Thomas and Sandra Day O'Connor

▶ **For:** Justices John Paul Stevens, David Souter, Ruth Bader Ginsburg and Stephen Breyer

Louisiana redistricting

▶ Set aside for technical reasons in a unanimous ruling

Other racially drawn districts may be challenged

The Supreme Court's ruling Thursday against a black-majority congressional district in Georgia is expected to prompt court challenges to similar racially drawn districts across the USA. Opponents say the districts, often oddly shaped, reduce the power of white voters. Georgia's 11th District and Louisiana's 4th District were both challenged in cases that went to the high court, but justices did not rule on the Louisiana case because the plaintiffs no longer live in the district. Also Thursday, the court agreed to hear arguments against three minority-majority districts in Texas and to rehear arguments against the black-majority 12th District in North Carolina. All of the districts were created after the 1990 Census to comply with the federal Voting Rights Act's mandate to increase minority political representation.

Georgia's 11th District

In September 1994, a federal appeals court ruled in favor of white voters who said in a lawsuit that it was unconstitutional to draw a district specifically to provide more black voters. The district is represented by Rep. Cynthia McKinney, a second-term Democrat and the first black woman elected to Congress from Georgia.

GEOGRAPHY
The district sweeps southeast from Atlanta suburbs 250 miles to Savannah. It includes parts of 22 counties, but 60% of the population is in three urban counties: De Kalb (east of Atlanta), Richmond (Augusta) and Chatham (Savannah). Between the urban pockets are miles and miles of agricultural acreage that was once Georgia's cotton belt but is now mainly corn, soybean and peanut farms.

DEMOGRAPHICS
Blacks are 64% of the population, and 60% of the registered voters, in this district of 586,195 people. It is one of three black-majority districts in the state. Comparing the district to Georgia by race:

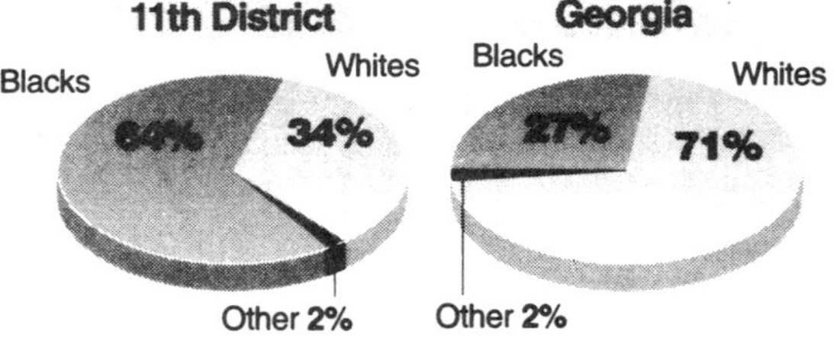

Sources: USA TODAY research by Barbara Hansen, Mark Pearson and Brian O'Connell; *Politics in America; Congressional Quarterly*, U.S. Census Bureau, *Congressional Districts in the 1990s, a Portrait of America.*

Louisiana's 4th District

The district has been redrawn by the state twice since the 1990 Census. For the 1992 election, it zigzagged through all or parts of 28 parishes and five of the states largest cities to get its black majority. In December 1993, a federal three-judge panel threw out that plan. In 1994, the Louisiana Legislature redrew the district. The federal court again rejected the plan. The Supreme Court accepted the case in 1994. Democrat Rep. Cleo Fields, first elected in 1992 in the 'Z' district, was re-elected in 1994 in the redrawn district.

North Carolina's 12th District

In 1993, the Supreme Court used this black-majority district to rule that racial gerrymandering might violate the rights of white voters. The case was sent back to a lower court for further study. That court ruled last year that the 12th District was constitutional. Democrat Melvin Watt, in his second term, represents the district of 552,386 people.

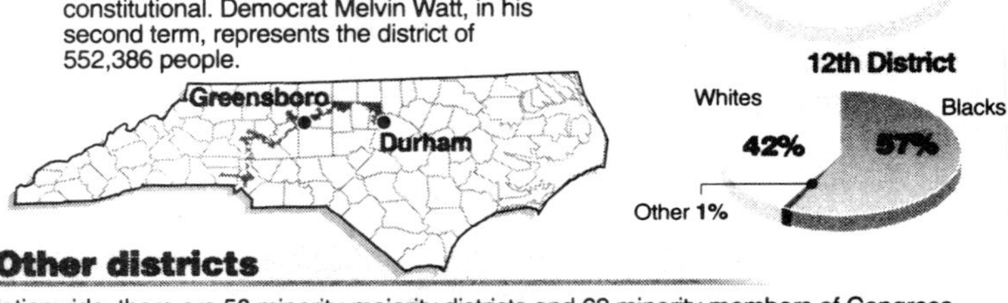

Other districts

Nationwide, there are 58 minority-majority districts and 62 minority members of Congress. Experts say these 18 districts could be at risk because of Thursday's ruling: Alabama's 7th; Arizona's 2nd; Florida's 3rd, 17th, 18th and 23rd; Georgia's 2nd and 11th; Illinois' 4th; Louisiana's 4th; New York's 12th; North Carolina's 1st and 12th; South Carolina's 6th; Texas' 18th, 29th and 30th; and Virginia's 3rd.

By Cliff Vancura, USA TODAY

which racial fairness was taken into account," says Lauglin McDonald of the American Civil Liberties Union. "All of these plans are presumed to be unlawful."

Others in the civil rights movement are more optimistic, especially after the court announced later Thursday that it would take up two new redistricting cases in the fall on related issues of race.

"They've muddied the waters, but they haven't yet turned 180 degrees," says Elaine Jones of the NAACP Legal Defense and Education Fund. "The issue has just begun."

Clinton administration civil rights chief Deval Patrick, whose department reviews redistricting plans under the Voting Rights Act, says, "It would be a tragedy if these decisions led to the resegregation of American democracy."

New Tolerance in the South or Old Power of Incumbency?

Blacks Won in Five Redrawn Mostly White Districts

Michael A. Fletcher

Washington Post Staff Writer

JACKSONVILLE, Fla.—Hundreds of Rep. Corrine Brown's supporters anxiously journeyed to Tallahassee in February for the trial that would decide the fate of Brown's majority-black congressional district and, many thought, her political future.

More than a century of Florida political history had taught the Democrat's defenders that she would likely lose her seat if the court overturned her majority-black district. But this time, history proved to be a poor teacher. Brown lost the trial but easily won reelection in her new, mostly white district. That success was duplicated by four other black congressional incumbents in the South whose predominantly black districts were overturned by the courts.

Their stunning success has opened a new front in the heated battle over black election districts, which civil rights advocates have long championed as the only way to ensure black representation in Congress and other elective bodies because of their historic tendency of whites to turn their backs on black candidates.

Opponents of racial gerrymandering are hailing the results of a major breakthrough in the tortured racial politics of the South. They call the victories of the black incumbents unassailable proof that racially polarized voting is fast becoming a vestige of the past.

"These results strongly vindicate the belief that black candidates can win in majority-white districts," said Clint Bolick, litigation director for the conservative Institute for Justice, a public interest law firm that has opposed "majority-minority" election districts.

But civil rights advocates are far more cautious about declaring victory over racism at the polls. They say majority-black districts made it possible for black candidates to be elected in the first place and demonstrate their ability to serve constituents of all races. Once in office, civil rights advocates say, these candidates reaped the advantages of incumbency.

"For someone to look at these results and claim that America has become a colorblind society overnight, despite everything we know, that is an amazing contention," said Theodore M. Shaw, associate director-counsel for the NAACP Legal Defense and Education Fund.

What the results show "may not be what those who are falling over themselves to say we've reached a colorblind society claimed," he continued. "The fact is incumbency is a powerful, powerful tool. It gives you the ability to raise money and get your message out."

While the reasons are hotly debated, there is no doubt that the surprising performances of the black congressional candidates who won reelection in newly redrawn districts are shattering old assumptions about racial voting patterns, especially in the South.

Besides Brown, outspoken liberal Cynthia McKinney (D-Ga.) won in a 65 percent white district outside Atlanta, with 59 percent of the vote. Sanford Bishop (D-Ga.) cruised to victory with 54 percent of the vote, in a district that is more than 60 percent white. And in Texas, black Democrats Eddie Bernice Johnson and Sheila Jackson Lee won easily in congressional districts that no longer have black majorities.

The only redistricted black member of Congress who did not recapture his or her seat was Rep. Cleo Fields (D-La.), who chose not to run for reelection.

Such an outcome appeared remote when white voters and conservative activists began filing lawsuits challenging the majority-black congressional districts created after the 1990 census to comply with the Voting Rights Act. The new districts had resulted in several states with significant black populations, including Florida, South Carolina, Alabama, North Carolina and Virginia, electing their first black members to Congress since Reconstruction. They also were a major reason that the number of blacks in the House increased by 17 in 1992.

"For the most part, blacks have been elected to Congress only because of the creation of majority-minority districts," said J. Gerald Hebert, a lawyer who has represented black officeholders in redistricting lawsuits.

But in lawsuits, plaintiffs have argued that the districts—some of which twisted and turned for hundreds of miles to absorb enough blacks to build a majority—corrupted the notion of equal opportunity by making race the predominant factor in determining their boundaries. Some activists have argued that such districts widen America's racial divide by making representatives responsible only to members of a single race.

When the challenges succeeded in several states, some activists predicted that the ranks of black congressional members would be decimated. They also said that the damage eventually would extend to state and local offices.

But the victories by the black incumbents, coupled with the election of Julia Carson (D), a black woman chosen to represent a majority-white district in Indiana, have caused opponents of the new districts to refine their arguments.

"I won because of the majority-minority district I used to represent, not in spite of it," McKinney said. "The majority-black district gave voters the opportunity to elect someone like me, who had only $38,000 to spend against a well-funded establishment candidate in the Democratic primary four years ago. . . . [It] enabled me to develop a track record, name recognition and the local and national contacts necessary to raise the nearly $1 million I spent to win" in the new district.

Bishop, a moderate to conservative Democrat who did not speak out against his redrawn district, sees his reelection both as an affirmation of his work in Congress and as evidence that old racial prejudices are slowly dying.

"Maybe incumbency hurts or helps, but he feels that there is something else going on as well," said Selby McCash, Bishop's communications director. "He feels like it is a new day in the South."

McCash said that while Bishop prevailed in a predominantly white district, a white state senator won reelection over a popular black opponent in an overlapping majority-black district. Those results, he said, offer further proof that race is diminishing as a factor in the minds of many voters.

Similar claims have been made here in Jacksonville, where Brown is just the latest black candidate to find success among white voters. Two years ago, mostly white Jacksonville elected a black sheriff—the equivalent of a police chief—whose candidacy enjoyed broad biracial support. Also, a popular black state senator and several members of the City Council enjoy significant white support, according to local political figures.

"Clearly this is a place where minority leadership is playing a role in moving us forward," said Paul McCormick, a Jacksonville political consultant.

But others are cautions about using these examples to proclaim victory over racially polarized voting.

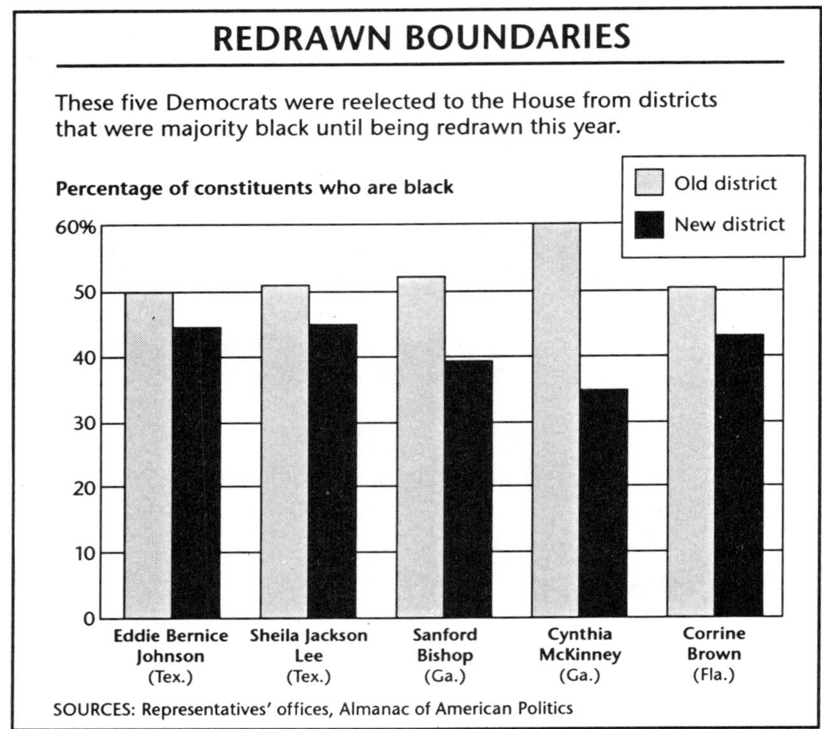

THE WASHINGTON POST

Brown's reelection was built on a foundation laid during four years in Congress and 10 years in the state legislature. Campaign literature trumpeted her service to senior citizens and veterans. She bragged about her ability to extract money for road improvements. Colorful billboards, featuring a beaming Brown with an American flag scarf draped over her shoulders, declared, "Corrine Cares!"

"I felt like I could let the work I've done speak for me," Brown said. "But I sincerely do not believe I could have won if I did not have the opportunity to serve."

In the end, the vote still went largely along racial lines. Brown swept more than 95 percent of the vote in many predominantly black precincts, which was virtually identical to the margin enjoyed by President Clinton. Meanwhile, she earned roughly a third of the white vote running against a white lawyer, Preston Fields, who has never held political office.

"Even though she won in a district that has changed, it is clear that we still have racially polarized voting," said Glenel Bowden, Brown's district director.

Similar patterns were apparent in preliminary voting analyses in McKinney's and Bishop's races. In both districts, the black candidate won almost unanimous support from black voters while winning about a third of the white vote—results that some analysts find less than encouraging.

"I think drawing any conclusions about these results is vastly premature," said Allan J. Lichtman, an American University history professor who has been an expert witness in 60 voting rights cases. "Those people who are so quick now to generalize about black opportunities didn't have a word to say when blacks were losing white districts all these years."

Proposition 209 Is a Blueprint for Court Fights, Scholars Say

■ **Politics:** *Legal experts disagree on where and how widely its social impact would be felt. But they are certain it would raise issues that might take years to resolve.*

BETTINA BOXALL

TIMES STAFF WRITER

At a mere 23 lines, Proposition 209 is one of the shortest and simplest initiatives on next week's ballot. But if the measure passes, its reach will be long. From voluntary school desegregation programs to police hiring to the awarding of contracts, Proposition 209 could cut a broad swath through the public sector.

Legal scholars say its precise impact is in many ways impossible to predict because the initiative raises a host of questions that will probably take years of court battles to resolve.

But interviews with professors from the state's leading law schools and lawyers representing state agencies point to a broad array of programs and policies that could run afoul of the initiative, which bans local and state government-sponsored affirmative action for women and minorities.

"This is a major reshaping of public institutions in the state," said UC Berkeley law professor Dan Rodriguez.

The measure could do much more than eliminate obvious affirmative action preferences, such as giving women or minorities extra consideration in public hiring or college admissions.

For example, the independent state legislative analyst's office says the future of UC's Mathematics, Engineering and Science Achievement (MESA) mentoring and study program would be in doubt because the 25-year-old project targets minority students at the elementary through university levels and tries to draw them into math and science fields.

Under 209, dozens of privately endowed scholarship funds in the UC system could be subject to legal challenge because they are limited to women or particular ethnic groups, according to the UC general counsel.

Voluntary magnet and school desegregation programs will be vulnerable to the extent that they take students' race into account, according to the state Education Department's general counsel.

The legislative analyst's office predicts that a police department could be challenged for launching a recruiting drive specifically aimed at women or minorities.

Proponents do not dispute that 209 will affect a variety of programs. But they argue that much affirmative action can simply be refashioned to replace race and gender considerations with some other factor, such as socioeconomic background.

"We'll see a new thinking in the way government approaches affirmative action," said Yes on 209 spokeswoman Jennifer Nelson.

Opponents have seized on 209's effect on such outreach efforts as MESA in arguing that the initiative will do far more than the public realizes, gutting programs that have helped women and minorities get into everything from medical school to contracting.

Compared with many of the tortuously long initiatives on the state ballot, Proposition 209 appears readily understandable.

The proposed constitutional amendment bars state and local governments from discriminating or granting "preferential treatment" on the basis of race, ethnicity, national origin or gender in public contracting, employment and education.

> *'The concept of a preference is extremely vague. It will require some judicial interpretation to figure out what preferential treatment means.'*
>
> *EVAN CAMINKER*
>
> *UCLA law professor*

But just what is preferential treatment?

In interviews with The Times, 11 constitutional and discrimination law experts—who have not been in the forefront of campaigning for either side—

From the *Los Angeles Times,* October 31, 1996, pp. B1, B4.

generally agreed that the term is not that well defined legally.

"The concept of a preference is extremely vague," UCLA law professor Evan Caminker said. "It will require some judicial interpretation to figure out what preferential treatment means."

A number of practices involving efforts such as recruiting and outreach may or may not survive, depending on how they are run and how narrowly or broadly judges interpret the initiative.

"The language isn't clear," UCLA law professor Julian Eule said. "There's an awful lot of leeway here about what courts are going to do."

Both Caminker and Eule question the measure's constitutionality.

'It's an attempt to use a bypass of the ordinary legislative process to undo the gains minorities have achieved. When it is used to reassert majority rule—and the entire goal of the Constitution is to prevent, and create checks against, pure majority preferences—that's deeply constitutionally problematic.'

JULIAN EULE

UCLA law professor

"It's an attempt to use a bypass of the ordinary legislative process to undo the gains minorities have achieved," Eule said. "When it is used to reassert majority rule—and the entire goal of the Constitution is to prevent, and create checks against, pure majority preferences—that's deeply constitutionally problematic."

But others interviewed said 209 should pass constitutional muster, particularly because it includes a nondiscrimination clause. "I'd be quite surprised if it was found to be unconstitutional," said UC Berkeley law professor Robert Post.

Another point of contention revolves around Clause C of the initiative.

More than 110 California law professors signed a statement that the provision could weaken California's unusually strict sex discrimination laws because it permits the government to consider "bona fide qualifications based on sex which are reasonably necessary" in public employment, contracting and education.

Now, women cannot be discriminated against unless there is a "compelling need." Clause C, the argument goes, would amend the state Constitution to allow gender discrimination if it is "reasonably necessary"—a lower standard.

A majority of legal scholars interviewed reject that interpretation, however.

"I don't see that it is going to change sex discrimination law," said Stanford University law professor Tom Grey.

He and others say Clause C applies only to the initiative and does not amend other sections of the Constitution. Still, Grey added, "there's no guarantee of how courts will construe the language. It's open to the other reading."

Gauging the initiative's impact is further complicated by a provision exempting court orders or consent decrees in force when the measure goes into effect.

A number of existing gender- and race-based affirmative action programs adopted under court order would therefore be preserved, such as the Los Angeles Police Department's hiring goals for women and minorities.

Education will perhaps feel the greatest impact if Proposition 209 becomes law.

The initiative would spell the end of race and gender preferences in public college admissions and hiring—although University of California regents stole that thunder when they voted last year to stop using race, gender or ethnicity as criteria in admissions as of Jan. 1, 1997, and in hiring and contracting beginning last January.

The policy change will result in a significant drop in the number of Latino, African American and Native American students admitted, while the enrollment of white and Asian students will rise, according to a UC report.

Beyond admissions, a number of longstanding programs could also be affected.

Public university scholarships restricted to women or minorities would be illegal, according to UC Berkeley professor Jesse Choper.

Terry Colvin, spokesman for the UC president's office, said the UC general counsel believes that racial, ethnic and gender preferences would have to be dropped from about $28 million in financial aid programs, including $7 million in privately endowed scholarships targeting groups, such as Portuguese men or undergraduate women at UC Berkeley.

Several legal scholars, including Stanford law professor John Donohue, said that under a broad reading of the initiative, funding for a women's center or an African American culture center on a public campus could be challenged.

Joseph Symkowick, general counsel of the State Department of Education, said magnet schools—which offer enriched programs to attract a diverse student body—would be threatened in their present form because many of them take race into account in admitting students.

The enrollment criteria would have to be changed, undercutting magnet programs' primary purpose: integration.

Similarly, Symkowick said voluntary desegregation programs, including busing and remediation efforts, would violate 209 because of their racial considerations.

There is a twist, however: Many existing magnet and involuntary school desegregation programs would be saved because they are under court order.

Richard Mason, general counsel for the Los Angeles Unified School District, said he believes most of the district's desegregation efforts,' including magnet programs, would continue unchanged because they stem from a 1981 court order.

Given that loophole, Symkowick predicted advocates in many school districts will attempt to preserve voluntary desegregation programs by seeking a federal court order.

The initiative would also end racial or gender preferences in public hiring and contracting.

State goals to award a certain percentage of public contracts to women- and minority-owned businesses would probably be eliminated, according to the legislative analyst's office.

A number of experts said that if a police department trying to diversify its force was considering two equally qualified applicants—one an African American woman and one a white man—the woman could not be chosen on the basis of her race and gender.

But what could a public agency do to diversity its pool of applicants, to make sure minorities and women apply? Could a police department or school district encourage Latinos or Asians to apply?

THE SPIN BILL BOYARSKY

Minorities' Political Muscle Is Growing

You wouldn't know it from recent rhetoric, but even in the vitriolic atmosphere of Campaign '96, I think the political clout of African Americans, Asian Americans and Latinos is growing.

The growth is slow, sometimes imperceptible—but significant when you keep in mind that minorities are almost a majority in California, and already a majority in Los Angeles County.

The current crop of speeches and commercials paints a picture of minorities on the run: Asian Americans tarred with a broad brush in the political contribution controversy; Asians and Latinos targets of anti-immigrant propaganda; leaders of all three groups expressing fear over the Proposition 209 campaign to eliminate state affirmative action programs.

I know a lot of people may not agree with me. Asian Americans correctly note their absence from state and national positions of political power as well as from the top rungs of the corporate ladder. The same is true for African Americans and Latinos.

But you have to look at demographic trends and the inevitable changes they bring. And you've got to glean some of your information from the business pages as well as from the political news.

Putting all this together, you get a different picture than the snapshot offered by the conventional wisdom. I see minorities on the move—into the broad middle class that dominates the American political process, with a substantial number into professions and business ownership.

Latinos are the most visible example of what I think is coming in a big way. In 1991, there were just four Latinos in the Assembly. There are now 10 and after next week's election, there will be probably be between 12 and 15. These lawmakers are, for the most part, from middle-class suburbia, with a different outlook and approach than minority lawmakers of a generation ago.

It was in 1970, a full generation ago, that I was introduced to minority politics in Los Angeles.

The inner city was the arena. Blacks and Latinos, all of them liberal Democrats, dominated the show. Campaigns were hymns of praise to the War on Poverty and the comprehensive—and complex—social welfare system bring created in Sacramento and Washington.

The campaigns climaxed in huge rallies in East and South L.A. The Sunday trip to South L.A. churches was on the schedule of every Democratic presidential, Senate and gubernatorial candidate.

Today's politics have little relation to those times. President Clinton's new conservatism has pushed the inner city toward the bottom of his agenda and inner-city lawmakers are angry. That was clear one night last week at a candidates forum in Inglewood featuring state Sen. Theresa Hughes, (D-Los Angeles) and her Republican opponent, Cliff McClain.

"Coming over here, I saw a man literally eating barbecue out of a garbage can," Hughes told me after she spoke. "I'm sure the president doesn't see that, isolated by his Secret Service." Or as Genethia Hayes, who heads the Southern Christian Leadership Conference here, put it a few days later: The Democratic Party no longer considers itself "the party of the poor, the downtrodden."

Of course, a growing number of minority group members no longer count themselves among the poor and downtrodden, either.

The improvement hasn't been broad or deep enough for some. "It will take more than 30 years to undo the damage of 300 years," said African American commentator Karen Grigsby Bates. Still, you can see signs of greater buying power each night on the Fox, UPN and WB television networks, which have sitcoms with black casts, targeted to the African American TV audience and the advertisers who want to appeal to them.

Statistics fill out the story. Last year, according to the research firm Target Market News, personal income for blacks rose to $325 billion form $304.5 billion in 1994. Black households spent $10.8 billion last year on new cars and trucks, a 156% increase from the year before. Black and Latino home ownership increased at a slightly higher rate than for whites. Latino-owned businesses generate about $12 billion a year in annual revenue in Southern California and provide about 110,000 jobs.

I say that greater political power eventually goes along with more economic power. That's evident in the case of Latinos, and their move to the suburbs.

"Latinos are maturing politically and economically," said state Sen. Richard Polanco, (D-Los Angeles), an architect of the Latino legislative election effort. And they are winning in suburban districts where Latinos are a minority.

This effort holds the greatest hope for increasing minority power. If the Democrats reclaim the Assembly, the party will choose the speaker. And if the Assembly Latino delegation rises to 15, it's possible for a Latino lawmaker to put together the 21 votes needed to become the Democratic caucus's choice for the top job.

These trends will change politics in California. Not immediately, perhaps, but in the next few years.

That will certainly happen if the minorities, often at odds, form coalitions. They did that this year when Latinos, African Americans and Asian Americans worked together against what they consider the danger of Proposition 209. Attorney Angela Oh, a Korean community leader, said she expects cooperation to continue. "This will bring coalitions together that have not worked together in the past," she said.

Because all these changes are happening at a fairly plodding rate, they don't find their way into political discussions that deal with racial minorities in simplistic terms.

But as the minorities become the majority, these demographic and economic shifts will shape California's future. As writer Bates said, "America in general and California specifically is starting to run out of white folks."

"Whether that constitutes a preference, I don't think anyone can tell you," Post said.

State hiring practices have already been revised by Gov. Pete Wilson, who last year rolled back some state affirmative action programs. As a result, the state Civil Service system stopped considering race and gender in its hiring, said Ted Edwards, affirmative action manager at the State Personnel Board.

State departments nonetheless retained hiring goals and timetables as a way of "monitoring" work force composition, said Edwards, who predicted that they would survive 209 because they do not factor into the ultimate hiring decision.

The legislative analyst's office is not so sure.

"We're pretty confident that hiring goals and timetables would be gone" because they create a dynamic that favors "underrepresented" groups, said Robert Turnage, of the legislative analyst's office.

Six law professors, including UCLA's Jonathan Varat and UC Hastings law professor Joseph Grodin, a retired state Supreme Court justice, said it is conceivable 209 could be used to challenge maternity benefits at public agencies that do not offer comparable paternity benefits.

The extent to which 209 would limit future court orders is another murky area.

The legal experts say that under the federal supremacy doctrine, federal judges in California would not be bound by Proposition 209. Similarly, they said, state judges invoking federal law could continue to order affirmative action as a remedy for discrimination.

But Linda Hamilton Krieger, acting law professor at UC Berkeley, predicted that things would be different for judges deciding cases under state law.

"It really ties judges' hands in the future in ways that I think people may not realize," Krieger said.

Even a judge who finds a government agency guilty of serious discrimination under state law would not be able to direct the agency to correct the situation with specific hiring goals and timetables outlawed by 209, she said.

Although uncertainty abounds in discussions of Proposition 209, there is one safe bet. There will be lawsuits aplenty.

"I think it's going to create a tremendous amount of litigation," Stanford law professor Barbara Babcock said.

The long retreat back to 'separate-but-equal'

Jeff Jacoby

Jeff Jacoby is a columnist for the Boston Globe. *His e-mail address is jacoby @globe.com*

BOSTON—In 1896, Supreme Court Justice John Marshall Harlan penned the greatest dissent in the history of American jurisprudence. In 1996, every Democrat in the California Assembly voted against a resolution commemorating Harlan's masterpiece.

That is the preposterous corner into which opponents of the California Civil Rights Initiative—the ballot initiative, known as Proposition 209, that would ban state discrimination on the basis of race or gender—have painted themselves.

The case that occasioned Harlan's dissent was *Plessy v. Ferguson*. At stake were the racist Jim Crow laws of the Old South. In what would prove the most toxic judicial decision since *Dred Scott*, eight of the high court's justices concluded that state-sponsored racial segregation was lawful.

They ruled that the 14th Amendment—despite guaranteeing "equal protection of the laws" to every citizen—did not prohibit "distinction based on color." It was the ruling white supremacists had hoped for, and it crushed any chance of civil rights for the next 60 years.

Only Juctice Harlan protested.

"Our Constitution is colorblind," he wrote in angry dissent, "and neither knows nor tolerates classes among citizens. In respect of civil rights, all citizens are equal before the law . . . The law regards man as man, and takes no account of his surroundings or of his color when his civil rights . . . are involved."

Harlan stood alone in 1896, but the seed he planted germinated. Decades later, when the NAACP Legal Defense Fund launched its litigation strategy to end racial segregation, Harlan's dissent in *Plessy* was its wellspring and inspiration.

Moral validity

In 1948, for example, the NAACP sued the University of Oklahoma, which claimed the right to exclude blacks from its law school as long as the state created a "separate but equal" non-white law school. In pursuing the case up to the Supreme Court, the NAACP's chief litigator, Thurgood Marshall, insisted on a principle that could have come right from Harlan's dissent. "Classifications and distinctions based on race or color," he argued, "have no moral or legal validity in our society."

Six years later, in *Brown v. Board of Education*, the Supreme Court held unanimously that "in the field of public education, the doctrine of 'separate-but-equal' has no place." Harlan was long gone, but his words had borne fruit at last. "His lonely dissent," the *New York Times* observed, had finally "become in effect . . . a part of the law of the land."

Yet in the four decades that followed, a new array of racial preferences, quotas and set-asides was enshrined into law. In the name of tearing down discrimination, a new edifice of discrimination was built up. More than ever before, public benefits today are conferred or withheld on the basis of race and ethnicity.

So when California Assemblyman Bernie Richter offered a resolution earlier this year to mark the centennial of the Harlan dissent, urging Californians to beware "the damage that racism and discrimination can cause," every Democrat in the chamber votes no. Better to turn their backs on Harlan's great moral teaching, they decided, than to do anything that might help Proposition 209.

The proposition passed anyway on Election Day, and were he alive at this hour, Harlan would rejoice. It embodies his profoundest conviction—that the law may not play favorites. Its language could not be more clear: "The state," Prop 209 commands, "shall not discriminate against, or grant preferential treatment to, any individual or group on the basis of race, sex, color, ethnicity or national origin in the operation of public employment, public education or public contracting."

Lord knows what the pro-quota forces would do to Harlan if he were still around to insist on equality under the law. In campaigning against the measure, they took the lowest of roads. Non-white supporters of Proposition 209 were tarred as "Uncle Toms" and "traitors." Anti-209 students at a California State University campus invited neo-Nazi David Duke to "defend" the initiative.

The opponents of color-blind law did not even scruple to insult a young widow who allowed the Yes on 209 campaign to tell her story in a radio ad. The woman's name is Janice Camarena. Her story is one Justice Harlan would have recognized.

On January 19, 1994, Ms. Camarena showed up for the 11 a.m. session of English 101 at San Bernardino Community College. She and another woman were the only white students in the class; as soon as the instructor noticed them, the two women were ordered to leave. That session of English 101, it turned out, was reserved for blacks only.

A century earlier, Homer Plessy had boarded a train in New Orleans. He was the only black passenger in the car; as soon as the conductor noticed him, Plessy was ordered to leave. That railway car, it turned out, was reserved for whites only.

Discrimination by race is discrimination by race. There is no moral difference between whites-only trains and blacks-only classrooms. Call it "separate-but-equal" or call it "affirmative action"—any law that metes out different treatment to different races is pernicious. What happened to Janice Camarena is as poisonous as what happened to Homer Plessy. Justice Harlan would have understood.

Immigration and the American Experience

The ever-growing influx of strangers to the Americas during the eighteenth and nineteenth centuries could have been perceived by its indigenous peoples as the intensification of conflict into the final stage of their conquest. Africans brought in bondage might have viewed the opening of America to the "wretched refuse" of Europe as a strategy designed to exclude them from prosperity and as a threat to their full enfranchisement.

To the European and Asian immigrant, America represented freedom from the constraints of state-bound societies whose limits could not be overcome except through emigration. Yet this historical pathway to liberty, justice, and opportunity came to be perceived as a "tarnished door" when the deep impulses of exclusion and exclusivity came to the fore. The victims were aliens who, ironically, achieved the American promise but were denied the reward of acceptance and incorporation into the very culture they helped to fashion. The following articles describe the immigrant experience and raise once again the issues that every large-scale multiethnic regime must address: How can unity and diversity be channeled into political, economic, and cultural well-being?

The history of immigration law does not champion American ethnic groups. Immigration laws include the Chinese Exclusion Acts of the 1880s, the National Origins Quota System of the 1920s, the Mexican Repatriation Campaign of the 1950s, and the McCarran-Walter Act in 1952. A new era began with the inclusiveness of the mid-1960s. The findings of the 1990 U.S. Census indicate a range of demographic, economic, and social indicators in this most recent era of immigration in the United States. Both the immediate impact of present-day newcomers and the changes in America that can be attributed to the conflicts and contributions of previous immigrants appear to be facets of nearly every contemporary social issue.

The U.S. Census documents the consequences of decades and generations of immigration. The Census enables us to discern the spectrum of American ethnicities and the regional patterns of ethnic settlement. The stories of new immigrants are aspects of a worldwide drama. The European and American contexts discussed in this unit provide perspectives on immigrant adjustment and their reception in various regimes and cultures.

The ongoing issue of cultural formation through language and the political artifices used to heighten or diminish ethnicity as a political factor are explored. The movement of people induces change and growth that poses great potential for well-being and economic development. Nevertheless, the influx of persons and cultures requires awareness of our cultural diversity and common humanity as well as energy, mutual openness to talent, and participation of all in the experience of being and becoming Americans.

Full employment and social-economic mobility in countries from which persons are coming to the United States would decrease incentives for migration. Political and religious freedom in other countries would negate another cause for the movement of people from oppressive regimes to democratic and liberal societies.

Changes in the U.S. immigration laws in 1965 contributed to the growing number of Central American, South American, and Asian immigrants who have entered the country. The flow of population also includes persons who have entered without governmental authorization. Extreme violence and political turmoil have contributed to the number of refugees seeking asylum in the United States.

As the unit articles make clear, immigration not only impacts on the receiving country but also affects nations that lose the talents, skills, and loyalty of disaffected migrants. Immigration, moreover, contributes to an already-complex process of intergenerational relationships and the socialization of persons whose experiences of profound cultural change are intensified by competition, patterns of settlement, options for mobility, and the consciousness of ethnic traditions that conflict with dominant cultural and educational institutions.

Michael Piore's assessment of children born to immigrant workers suggests an interesting lens through which the following articles may be read. Dr. Piore writes:

> There is nothing in the immigration process that ensures that this second generation will be able to move up to the higher level jobs toward which they aspire. Indeed, historically industrial societies appear consistently to disappoint the expectations of the second generation in this regard. That disappointment has in turn been the source of enormous social tensions. The sit-down strikes in the late thirties which sparked the industrial unions movement in the United States may in large measure be attributed to the reaction of the children of pre–World War I European immigrants to their labor market conditions. Similarly, the racial disturbances in Northern urban ghettos in the middle and late 1960s may be looked upon as a revolt of the black migrants against a society bent upon confining them to their parents' jobs.

UNIT 2

As a guide for your own study, the U.S. Commission on Civil Rights has noted that increased immigration raises the following issues for both recent arrivals and Americans by birth:

Employment: The areas of occupation selected by or imposed upon various ethnic populations trace ethnic group mobility strategies and ethnic succession in the workplace, especially in manufacturing, hospitals, restaurants, and maintenance and custodial positions. Some ethnic populations appear to have greater numbers of highly educated persons in professional or semiprofessional positions.

Institutional and societal barriers: The job preferences and discrimination against the ethnic enclave and persons in small communities that are isolated from mainstream English-speaking society suggest the value of second-language competencies. Mutual accommodation is required to minimize the effect of inadequate language skills and training and difficulties in obtaining licenses, memberships, and certification.

Exploitation of workers: The most common form is the payment of wages below minimum standards. Alien workers have been stereotyped as a drain on public services. Such scapegoating is insupportable.

Taking jobs from Americans: Fact or fiction?: The stunning fact is that immigrants are a source of increased productivity and a significant, if not utterly necessary, addition to the workforce as well as to the consumer power that drives the American economy.

Looking Ahead: Challenge Questions

A decade ago, American national policy advisers discussed the claims of irredentist populations as an ethnic/political issue of comparison between Poland and Germany and the United States and Mexico. How has the globalization of the economy—NAFTA and the European Union—changed the relationships among states and their perceptions of one another?

On December 10, 1996, the Mexican government passed a law to allow dual citizenship to persons living in the United States. What does this policy portend for the relationship between Mexico and the United States? Should statehood for northern Mexico become an option? At present, is this law of citizenship a threat to or an opportunity for ethnic group relations?

Why do periods of economic crisis appear to exacerbate tensions and strain relations among ethnic groups?

The clustering of ethnic populations in various regions of America has produced patterns that are worth pondering. Discuss the meaning of the American ethnicities found in each region. The southern quadrant of the country reveals an especially interesting and unique cluster in the largest 25 ethnic groups. What do these data indicate?

What remedies for language diversity are acceptable in a democratic society? Is the argument about stereotypic language compelling? Prescriptive? Misleading? Why?

How fruitful is discussion of immigration issues as if they were a matter of protecting American borders?

A Nation of Immigrants

It's a politician's bromide—and it also happens to be a profound truth. No war, no national crisis, has left a greater impress on the American psyche than the successive waves of new arrivals that quite literally built the country. Now that arguments against immigration are rising again, it is well to remember that every single one of them has been heard before.

Bernard A. Weisberger

Bernard A. Weisberger, a contributing editor to this magazine, writes the "In the News" column.

The uproar over Zoë Baird has subsided by now, and readers with short memories may profit by a reminder that she was forced to withdraw as President Clinton's first nominee for Attorney General because she and her husband had hired two "illegal aliens" for babysitting and housekeeping chores. The episode put immigration into focus as a "live" topic for op-ed and talk-show manifestoes before it faded, only to return to the headlines when Clinton embraced the Bush administration's policy (which he had denounced during the campaign) of turning back boatloads of Haitian refugees before they reached the Florida shore. But in June of 1993 the front pages carried the tragic story of a freighter, ironically named the *Golden Venture,* that ran aground just outside New York City. Its hold contained a crowd of Chinese workers being unlawfully smuggled into the United States, a crude practice supposedly long obsolete. Ten of them drowned trying to swim ashore. Later in the summer several hundred more "illegal" Chinese, California-bound, were intercepted and imprisoned aboard their ships until the U.S. government persuaded Mexico to take them in and ship them back. So it is that immigration regularly returns to the news. It always has. It always does.

The question of what our policy toward the world's huddled masses should be is especially topical at this moment. The Statue of Liberty still lifts her lamp beside the golden door, but in a time of economic downturn, there is no longer an assured consensus that the door should be kept open very far. Restrictionism is back in fashion. For every journalistic article like that of *Business Week* in July 1992, which notes that "the U.S. is reaping a bonanza of highly educated foreigners" and that low-end immigrants "provide a hardworking labor force to fill the low-paid jobs that make a modern service economy run," there is another like Peter Brimelow's in the *National Review*. His title tells it all: "Time to Rethink Immigration?" The burden of his argument is that America has admitted too many immigrants of the wrong ethnic background (he himself is a new arrival from Britain), that neither our economy nor our culture can stand the strain, and that "it may be time to close the second period of American history [the first having been the era of the open frontier] with the announcement that the U.S. is no longer an 'immigrant country.'" In short, we're here; you foreigners stay home. Nor are journalists the only voices in the debate. Last August California's governor Pete Wilson got media attention with a proposal to amend the Constitution so as to deny citizenship to an entire class of people born in the United States, namely, those unlucky enough to be the children of illegal immigrants.

If, as I have, you have been "doing" immigration history for many years, you've heard the restrictionists arguments before and expect to hear them again. And you are under the obligation to answer back, because what is at stake in the argument is nothing less than the essential nature of the United States of America. We are different. We aren't the only country that receives immigration or that has to deal with resentment directed toward "aliens." The popularity in France of Jean-Marie Le Pen's National Front party and the surge of anti-foreign (and neo-Nazi) "Germany-for-Germans" violence in Germany are evidence of that. It's also true that in a world of swift intercontinental travel and instant global communication, immigration policy cannot really be made by separate governments as if they lived in a vacuum. Such problems as there are demand multinational solutions.

Only America takes special pride in describing its nationality as independent of race or blood.

Nevertheless and notwithstanding, the United States of America is different. Immigration is flesh of our flesh, and we need to be reminded of that. Some sneer at the statement that we are a nation of immigrants as a cliché; all nations, they assert, are made up of mixtures of different peoples. So they are, as new tribes and races displaced old ones by conquest or by random migration. But the United States was created by settlers who arrived from elsewhere, who deliberately and calculatedly invited and urged others to follow them, and who encouraged the process in ways that were unique. Of course, countries like Canada and Australia depended on immigration for survival and success, but only the United States made the acquisition of citizenship swift and simple; only the United States made it a matter of principle to equalize the conditions of new citizens and old; only the United States takes special pride in describing American nationality as, by definition, independent of race and blood—as something that is acquired by residence and allegiance regardless of birthplace or ancestry.

Confirmation of that statement is in the record, and the record needs to be reviewed. It is not a flawless one. Of course the people of the United States have not always extended an equal welcome to all races; of course there have been spasms of hostility like the current wave—in the 1790s, in the 1850s, in the 1920s. They are also part of the record, but on the whole the record is exceptional and ought to be known and understood before any new major changes in policy are made.

Every Passover Jews the world over sit down to the Seder table to retell the story of Exodus from Egypt in order to pass on to their children and renew in themselves their sense of who, what, and why they are. There was a time when the Fourth of July was an occasion for re-creating the days of the American Revolution, in order to serve the same purpose for Americans. (I hope that it makes a comeback, despite the assaults of a misguided "multiculturalism.")

Now is the proper occasion for retelling the immigration story. So let us begin at the beginning, with the statement that offends the new exclusionist.

In the Beginning: 1607–1798

"We are a nation of immigrants." It's a politician's generality at an ethnic picnic, a textbook bromide swallowed and soon forgotten. It is also, as it happens, a profound truth, defining us and explaining a good part of what is extraordinary in the short history of the United States of America. There is no American ancient soil, no founding race, but there is a common ancestral experience of moving from "there" to "here." Among the founders of this nation who believed that they were agents of destiny was an English preacher who said in 1669, "God hath sifted a nation that he might send choice grain into this wilderness." The grain has arrived steadily and from many nations. "Americans are not a narrow tribe," wrote Herman Melville; "our blood is as the flood of the Amazon, made up of a thousand noble currents all pouring into one."

We begin arbitrarily with a seventeenth-century English migration that produced the First Families of Virginia (founded in 1607) and Massachusetts's Pilgrim Fathers (1620). Arbitrarily because already in 1643 Isaac Jogues, a French Jesuit missionary visiting New Amsterdam, said he heard eighteen languages spoken in that seaport town, which probably included Mediterranean and North African dialects and the Hebrew of a small settlement of Sephardic Jews.

But the stock planted in the 1600s was basically English. In the eighteenth century it turned "British" as Scots and Irish arrived in significant numbers, then partly European through an influx of Germans, and African, too, through the thousands of involuntary black immigrants brought in on the hell ships of the slave trade.

Those initial colonial migrations to "British North America" illustrate forces that are still at work in 1993. The names, faces, and languages change, but the basics remain. Immigrants are pushed out of their original homes by war, upheaval, misery, and oppression. They are pulled toward America by the promise of economic betterment and a chance to breathe free. Sometimes they are lured by promoters who want their passage money or their labor and skills. Sometimes they have come in legal or actual bondage.

But whenever and wherever they have come, they have changed what they found. That was clear from the moment that seventeenth-century England sent the first immigrant wave. The land was ripe for mass exodus. Civil, religious, and class war raged from beginning to end of the century, encompassing in their course the execution of one king and the expulsion of another. Major changes in the economy drove small farmers off their subsistence plots in favor of sheep. "The people . . . do swarm in the land as young bees in a hive," said one clergyman. "The land grows weary of her inhabitants," said another—by name John

Immigration helped bring on the Revolution, and gave it a surprising new meaning.

Winthrop, soon to move with fellow Puritans to a place called Massachusetts Bay.

The London government planted colonies to help house-clean the surplus population. Some started under the rule of private corporations that looked for gold and silk and settled for the profits in fish, fur, and tobacco. Some were begun by like-minded religious seekers, some by individuals to whom the king gave huge tracts of wilderness to turn into profitable agricultural estates. All needed people to thrive, and got them. Some 378,000 Englishmen and women left for the Western Hemisphere during the century; 155,000 wound up on mainland North America. They came on the *Mayflower*; they came in groups brought over by colonial proprietors who got so many extra acres of land per head of immigrant. They came as indentured servants, under bond to work a term of years. Some came in fetters at the request of unchoosy colonial administrators, like the governor of Virginia who asked London in 1611 for "all offenders out of the common gaols condemned to die." There may have been, over the decades, as many as 50,000 of such "fellons and other desperate villaines."

They brought the imprint of England in their baggage. Without stinting other contributions, there isn't any question that constitutional self-rule, Protestant individualism, capitalism, and the work ethic were hammered into the national character in the seventeenth-century English. And yet English with a difference. "They ate the white corn-kernels parched in the sun," Stephen Vincent Benét wrote in 1943, "and they knew it not, but they'd not be English again." Autocratic rule was modified almost at once because London was far away—and freedom attracted new settlers. Virginia demanded and got a representative assembly in 1624; all the other colonies followed in due course.

It was an age of religious rigidity, but state-imposed conformity had to bend to the needs of settlement. In 1632 King Charles I gave his supporter Cecilius Calvert, Lord Baltimore, the future state of Maryland (named for the Catholic queen). Calvert saw to it that his fellow Catholics, under heavy pressure back home, were tolerated within its borders. In the 1680s a different king bestowed yet another colony on William Penn. The Quaker Penn opened Pennsylvania not only to other members of the Society of Friends but to "dissenters" of every description. In different colonies intolerance rose and fell, but more often fell as population grew and spread. "Here," reported New York's governor in 1687, "be not many of the Church of England, few Roman Catholics, abundance of . . . singing Quakers, ranting Quakers, Sabbatarians, Anti-Sabbatarians, some Anabaptists, some Independents, some Jews; in short, of all sorts of opinions there are some, and the most part none at all."

By the start of the eighteenth century, that latitude, along with virgin land and prospering towns, was exerting a magnetic force outside England itself: in France, where, in 1685, the king revoked an edict that had protected his Protestant subjects, thereby sending thousands of Huguenots—thrifty, skilled traders and artisans—to settle in America; in the many little German princedoms plagued by war, taxes, and rack rents, so that altogether there were some 225,000 colonists of German stock on the Revolution's eve, including groups like the Mennonites (ancestors of the Amish) and Moravians.

They spread through several colonies, but those in Pennsylvania became known as the Pennsylvania Dutch (a corruption of *Deutsch*), and their clannish ways at least once exasperated the usually tolerant Benjamin Franklin. "Why should the Palatine *Boors*," he asked (the Rhenish Palatinate was a German region that furnished many new Pennsylvanians), "be suffered to swarm into our Settlements, and by herding together, establish their Language and Manners to the Exclusion of ours? Why should *Pennsylvania*, founded by the *English*, become a Colony of *Aliens*?"

There was no language problem with the "Ulster" Irish or Scots Irish. These Scots, deliberately planted in the northern counties of Ireland in the 1600s to help subdue the native Catholics, were busy and productive farmers until, in 1699, English landowners got the door slammed on competitive agricultural imports. The ensuing distress sent as many as 12,000 a year of the Ulstermen and women to the colonies. They poured into the frontier regions, carrying with them strict Calvinism and a distaste for both Indians and speculators who cornered huge tracts to sell at high prices. It was, in their eyes, "against the laws of God and nature that so much land should be idle while Christians wanted it to labor on and raise their bread." They were the ancestors of such as Daniel Boone and Andrew Jackson.

The end of the French and Indian War in 1763 spurred a rush of migration to the now-secure colonial frontiers and the growing seaboard towns of Boston, New York, Philadelphia, Charleston. From 1763 to 1775 some 221,000 newcomers arrived: 55,000 Ulstermen, 40,000 Scots, 30,000 English, 12,000 Germans and Swiss—and 84,500 chained Africans. Perhaps a third of all the colonists in 1760 were either born abroad or had parents who were. The English government, once worried about overpopulation, now feared depopulation even more and cracked down on large landowners' seductive invitations to immigrants. Thus the charge in Jefferson's bill of particulars showing that the king sought an absolute tyranny over the colonies: "He has endeavoured to prevent the Population of these states; . . . obstructing the Laws for Naturalization of Foreigners; refusing to pass others to encourage their Migrations hither, and raising the Conditions of new Appropriations of Lands."

Immigration helped bring on the Revolution, and to give it a surprising new meaning. By 1782 the former English colonies were separate states, linked by common interests and a common culture that was more than simply English. Michel Guillaume Jean de Crèvecoeur, a French immigrant, put it this way: "What then is the American, this new man? He is either an European, or the descendant of a European, hence that strange mixture of blood, which you will find in no other country. I could point out to you a family whose grandfather was an Englishman, whose wife was Dutch, whose son married a French woman, and whose present four sons have now four wives of different nations. . . . Here individuals of all nations are melted into a new race of men, whose labours and posterity will one day cause great changes in the world. . ."

The immigrant generals and soldiers who fought on the American side in the Revolution (like Gen. Frederick Mühlenberg, the German-trained Lutheran pastor who would become the first Speaker of the House) would have agreed. So would Tom Paine, the English immigrant author of *Common Sense*, which, in 1776, called on the future United States to become an "asylum for mankind."

But when the Constitutional Convention came to consider naturalization laws and residence requirements for officials, a different point of view was evident. Even a sturdy democrat like Virginia's George Mason did not "chuse to let foreigners and adventurers make laws for us & govern us." Pierce Butler of South Carolina—born in Ireland—believed that aliens brought in "ideas of Government so distinct from ours that in every point of view they are dangerous." Gouverneur Morris, a gifted master of sarcasm from New York, applauded generosity to foreigners but counseled "a moderation in all things. . . . He would admit them to his house, he would invite them to his table . . . but would not carry the complaisance so far as to bed them with his wife."

Compromise prevailed; no person may be a representative who has not been a citizen seven years, or become a senator with less than nine years' citizenship. Presidents must be American-born. The issue blew up again in 1798 during stormy confrontations between Jefferson's Republicans and conservative Federalist opponents who feared an infiltration of radical immigrants full of dangerous ideas hatched by the French Revolution, then in full career. A Federalist-dominated Congress passed the Alien and Sedition Acts of 1798, which allowed the President to expel foreigners whom he deemed dangerous on suspicion of treasonable activities. Jefferson called the measure "worthy of the 8th or 9th century," and when he and his supporters won the election of 1800, they let it die without renewal.

Young Republic, 1815–60

Jefferson's optimistic vision of an always enlightened and open-minded America has survived as a hotly contested influence on the land. But his expectation that the nation would remain permanently agrarian was totally wrong. Half a century after he left the White House, steam power had transformed the country. Inventors and investors proved the truest American radicals. Steamboats and rail lines crisscrossed a Union that spread to the Pacific and boasted more than thirty states. Mills, mines, factories, distilleries, packinghouses, and shipyards yearly churned out millions of dollars' worth of manufactured goods.

And it was linked to mass immigration. Immigrants furnished much of the labor that made the productive explosion possible and many of the consumers who made it profitable. The same industrializing processes that were at work and opened jobs here uprooted millions in Europe whose handicrafts became obsolete or whose land fell into the hands of those who could farm more "efficiently." Two decades of Napoleonic warfare, followed by three more of suppressed democratic and nationalist revolution, created a new reservoir of suffering from which emigration offered an escape.

America was a major beneficiary. Europe's growing cities and new overseas dominions beckoned, but the United States was the special promised land as the nineteenth century took its dynamic course. Fewer than 8,000 immigrants per year landed on American shores between 1783 and 1815, but 2,598,000 came in the next forty-five years: 1,500,000 in the 1840s and 3,000,000 in the 1850s. The pre–Civil War period of immigration belonged predominantly to 1,500,000 Germans and 2,000,000 Irish. It was the Irish whose transplantation was most shadowed in tragedy. Unbelievably, Ireland—only a few hours by water from the very center of the modern world in England—was stricken by the oldest of Biblical scourges, famine.

Irish migration had begun early. The rich English absentee landlords who ruled the country left their peasant tenants to feed themselves on the potatoes grown on tiny plots. A visitor declared that "the most miserable of English paupers" was better off. Irish Catholics and Irish nationalists were equally despised and frustrated. There was little future, and thousands, early in the century, migrated to the United States to find pick-and-shovel jobs on the growing network of turnpikes, canals, and railroads. But in 1845 the stream of opportunity seekers was turned into a flood of refugees. The potato crop, smitten by a fungus, failed in three successive years. Mass starvation was the result. In the hovels inhabited by the "Paddies," rats gnawed on unburied bodies while others in their death throes looked on, too weak to move. "All with

To their contemporaries, the Germans seemed a model minority, the Irish a problem minority.

means are emigrating," wrote one official; "only the utterly destitute are left behind."

Victims of the "Great Hunger" were not through with their torments when they boarded filthy, overcrowded, and underprovisioned ships, where, said one witness, it was "a daily occurrence to see starving women and children fight for the food which was brought to the dogs and pigs that were kept on deck." En route 10 to 20 percent of them died of disease. In the United States, lacking capital and prepared only for low-level employment, they were crammed into the new urban slums. Some were housed, according to an investigation committee, nine in a room in windowless and waterless cellars, "huddled together like brutes without regard to age or sex or sense of decency."

It was a little better for the Germans. Many were professionals and scholars with some capital, political refugees rather than disaster victims. Some came in groups that pooled their money to buy cheap Western lands, and these founded towns like New Ulm in Minnesota or New Braunfels in Texas. So many of them became Texans, in fact, that in 1843 the state published a German edition of its laws. An American reporter visited a German farm in Texas in 1857. "You are welcomed," he told readers, "by a figure in a blue flannel shirt and pendant beard, quoting Tacitus, having in one hand a long pipe, in the other a butcher's knife; Madonnas upon log-walls; coffee in tin cups upon Dresden saucers; barrels for seats to hear a Beethoven's symphony on the grand piano."

German farmers spread through Illinois, Michigan, Missouri, Iowa, and Wisconsin. German brewers, bookbinders, butchers, musicians, and other craftspeople settled cohesively and proudly in cities from New York to New Orleans, St. Louis to Cincinnati. In 1860, 100,000 New York Germans supported twenty churches, fifty German-language schools, ten bookstores, five printing establishments, and a theater, in neighborhoods known collectively as *Kleindeutschland* (little Germany). To contemporaries the Germans seemed a model minority, the Irish a problem minority—a kind of generalizing that would, in time, be transferred to other peoples.

Besides these two major groups, there were Danes, Norwegians, and Swedes arriving in increasing numbers from the 1850s onward; French-Canadians moving into New England textile factories to replace Yankee workers of both sexes; Dutch farmers drifting to western Michigan; and in 1849 Chinese who had heard of the California gold strikes and came for their share of the "Golden Mountain," as they called America—only to be crowded out of the mining camps by mobs and restrictive laws and diverted into railway labor gangs, domestic service, restaurants, and laundries.

The immigrants helped push the United States population from 4,000,000 in 1790 to 32,000,000 in 1860. They built America by hand, for wages that were pittances by modern standards—$40 a month in Pennsylvania coal mines, $1.25 to $2 a day on the railroads—but tempting nonetheless. (In Sweden farmhands earned $33.50 *per year.*) They dug themselves into the economy and into the nation's not-always-kindly ethnic folklore. New England textile towns like Woonsocket and Burlington got to know the accent of French-Canadian "Canucks." So many Swedes became Western lumbermen that a double-saw was called a "Swedish fiddle." Welsh and Cornish copper miners in Michigan's Upper Peninsula, were known as Cousin Jacks.

There were exceptions to the geographical stereotypes—Dutch settlements in Arizona, a Swedish nucleus in Arkansas, a Chinese community in Mississippi—and Irishmen in Southern cities like Mobile and New Orleans, where they were employed on dangerous jobs like levee repair because they were more expendable than fifteen-hundred-dollar slaves.

American culture shaped itself around their presence. Religion was a conspicuous example. The Church of Rome in America was turned inside out by the Irish, whose sheer numbers overwhelmed the small groups of old-stock English and French Catholics from Maryland and Louisiana. The first American cardinal, John McCloskey, was the son of a Brooklyn Irishman. The second, James Gibbons, an Irish boy from Baltimore. German and Swiss Catholic immigrants added to the melting-pot nature of their church in the United States before the Civil War—and the Poles and Italians were yet to come.

German and Scandinavian Lutheran immigrants—free of state and ecclesiastical authorities—developed strong local leaders and new, secessionist bodies, like the German-dominated Missouri Synod and the Scandinavian Evangelical Lutheran Augustana Synod. Both of these were theologically conservative groups. On the other side Isaac Mayer Wise, a German immigrant rabbi, became the patriarch of Reform Judaism in America, to save the faith, in his words, from "disappearance" into "Polish-cabalistical . . . supernaturalism." All the "immigrant churches" in the United States built their own networks of social service agencies, parochial schools, and ministerial training seminaries without state help, blending the faith of their fathers with an American style of independent congregational activism. In the house of God, too, the American was a "new man."

Ethnic politics took root in immigrant-crowded city wards. Nowhere was it stronger than among the gregarious Irish, whose neighborhood saloons became political clubhouses. The Society of St. Tammany was an old-stock New York City association founded in 1789 to promote Jeffersonian ideas. Fifty years later the Irish had so infiltrated it that a writer quipped: "Ask an Irishman, and he will probably tell you that St. Tammany was a younger brother of St. Patrick who emigrated to America for the purpose of taking a city contract to drive all Republican reptiles out of New York." Patronage jobs handed out by the machine made Irish cops a stereotype for the rest of the century.

But the lower-class Irish in particular stung an American elite long steeped in anti-popery. Anti-immigrant feelings began to rise in the 1840s and focused especially on the Irish, who, like poor people before and after them, were denounced for not living better than they could afford. "Our Celtic fellow citizens," wrote a New York businessman, "are almost as remote from us in temperament and constitution as the Chinese." Bigotry can always find excuses and weapons. The handiest one in the 1840s was anti-Catholicism.

In 1834 a Boston mob burned a convent. Ten years later there were riots in Philadelphia after a school board ruled that Catholic children might use the Douay version of the Bible in school. "The bloody hand of the Pope," howled one newspaper, "has stretched itself forth to our destruction." A few years after that, anti-Catholic and anti-foreign feelings merged in a nativist crusade called the Know-Nothing movement. Its goal was to restrict admission and naturalization of foreigners, and among its adherents was Samuel F. B. Morse, the father of telegraphy, who cried aloud: "To your posts! . . . Fly to protect the vulnerable places of your Constitution and Laws. Place your guards. . . . And first, shut your gates."

Know-Nothings had some brief success but little enduring impact. Their drive got strength from a generalized anxiety about the future of the country on the eve of the Civil War. But Know-Nothingism cut across the grain of a venerable commitment to equal rights, and no one put his finger on the issue more squarely than Abraham Lincoln when asked in 1855 whether he was in favor of the Know-Nothing movement: "How could I be? How can any one who abhors the oppression of negroes, be in favor of degrading classes of white people? Our progress in degeneracy appears to me to be pretty rapid. As a nation, we began by declaring that *'all men are created equal.'* We now practically read it, 'all men are created equal, *except negroes.*' When the Know-Nothings get control, it will read, ' all men are created equal, except negroes, and *foreigners and catholics.*' When it comes to this I should prefer emigrating to some country where they make no pretence of loving liberty—to Russia, for instance, where despotism can be taken pure, and without the base alloy of hypocrisy."

Three years later, on the Fourth of July, 1858, in debating with Stephen A. Douglas, Lincoln returned to the theme. What could the Fourth mean, he asked, to those who were not blood descendants of those who had fought in the Revolution? His answer was that in turning back to the Declaration of Independence, they found the sentiment "We hold these truths to be self-evident, that all men are created equal," that they "feel . . . and that they have a right to claim it as though they were blood of the blood, and flesh of the flesh of the men who wrote that Declaration and so they are. That is the electric cord . . . that links the hearts of patriotic and liberty-loving men together. . ."

Lincoln was unambiguous. There was no exclusively American race entitled to claim liberty by heredity. What held the nation together was an *idea* of equality that every newcomer could claim and defend by free choice.

That concept was soon tested to the limit with Lincoln himself presiding over the fiery trial. Foreign-born soldiers and officers served the Union in such numbers and with such distinction that the war itself should have laid to rest finally the question of whether "non-natives" could be loyal. It didn't do that. But it paved the way for another wave of economic growth and a new period of ingathering greater than any that had gone before.

High Tide and Reaction: 1885-1930

After 1865 the United States thundered toward industrial leadership with the speed and power of one of the great locomotives that were the handsomest embodiment of the age of steam. That age peaked somewhere in the 1890s. By 1929 the age of electricity and petroleum was in flower. And the United States was the world's leading producer of steel, oil, coal, automobiles and trucks, electrical equipment, and an infinite variety of consumer goods from old-fashioned overalls to newfangled radios. The majority of Americans lived in supercities, their daily existence made possible by elaborate networks of power and gas lines, telephone wires, highways, bridges, tunnels, and rails.

And the foreign-born were at the center of the whirlwind. Expansion coincided with, depended on, incorporated the greatest wave of migration yet. In the first fourteen years after the Civil War ended yearly immigration ranged from 318,568 in 1866 to 459,803 in 1873, slumping during the hard times of 1873–77, and rebounding to 457,257 in 1880.

Then came the deluge: 669,431 in 1881; 788,992 in 1882. Seven times between 1883 and 1903 the half-million total was passed. The million mark was hit in 1905 with 1,026,499—and exceeded six times between that year and 1914. The all-time peak came in 1907: 1,285,349.

All told, some 14,000,000 arrived at the gates between 1860 and 1900; another 18,600,000 followed between 1900 and 1930. Almost all of them came from Europe, a transoceanic transplantation unmatched in history.

The "old" Americans—that is, the children of immigrants who had arrived earlier—watched the influx with feelings that ran from pride to bewilderment and alarm, for the "new" immigration was not from traditional sources. Until 1890 most new arrivals were from familiar places: the British Isles, Germany, the Scandinavian countries, Switzerland, the Netherlands. But now it was the turn of southern

Chicago once had more Germans than any of Kaiser Wilhelm's cities except Berlin and Hamburg.

and eastern Europe to swarm. Of the roughly 1,280,000 in the record-setting 1907 intake, 260,000 were from Russia, which then included a goodly portion of Poland. Another 285,000 were from Italy. Almost 340,000 were from Austria-Hungary, a doomed "dual monarchy" that included much of the future Yugoslavia and Czechoslovakia and another part of Poland. About 36,000 were from Romania, Bulgaria, and what was left of the Ottoman Turkish Empire in Europe. There were modest numbers of Greeks and Portuguese.

These new immigrants were palpably different. There were Eastern Orthodox as well as Roman Catholics, and Orthodox Jews. There were, at a time when ethnic labels were taken with great seriousness, Magyars, Croats, Slovenes, Slovaks, and people generally grouped as "Slavs" and "Latins" and sniffed at in suspicion and disdain. In 1875 *The New York Times* said of Italians that it was "hopeless to think of civilizing them, or keeping them in order, except by the arm of the law." A Yankee watching Polish farm workers was struck by their "stolid, stupid faces." An American Jewish journal, offended by the beards, side curls, and skullcaps of Polish greenhorns, wondered what could be done with these "miserable darkened Hebrews."

The immigration patterns had shifted with the course of modern European history. A rising demand for political independence in central Europe fed political turbulence. Russian nationalism spawned anti-Semitic outbursts and hard, impoverishing economic restrictions on Jews. Southern Italy was overwhelmed by agricultural poverty that was increased by policies of industrialization and modernization that favored the north. Europe was full of hopeful seekers of streets paved with gold.

And there were voices to entice them. The immigration bureaus of Western states distributed literature in several languages touting opportunities within their borders. Railroad companies with land grants wooed Russian and German farmers to come out and buy (on long-term credit) tracts on the Great Plains. The Great Northern line—which James J. Hill built without land grants—offered fares as low as thirty-three dollars to any point on the tracks that ran from Minnesota to Oregon, plus sweet deals on acquiring and moving machinery, livestock, lumber, fencing. Steamship companies were in the hunt too. Modern technology had reduced the dreaded transatlantic passage to ten or twelve days instead of months. Steerage accommodations were far from clean or comfortable, but they cost as little as twenty-five dollars, and passengers were no longer likely to die on the way.

So the immigrants came. For the most part this was an urban migration. Millions went to the middling-sized red-brick towns dominated by the factory chimney and whistle. More millions went to the big cities, where they grunted and sweated in the creation of the skyscrapers, the bridges, the subways and trolley lines, the sewer and lighting systems—the guts of the metropolis. Or where, if they did not swing a pick or scrub floors, they sold groceries to those of their countrymen who did.

In the 1890s Chicago had more Germans than any of Kaiser Wilhelm's cities except Berlin and Hamburg; more Swedes than any place in Sweden except for Stockholm and Göteborg; more Norwegians than any Norwegian town outside of Christiana (now Oslo) and Bergen. Of some 12,500 laborers modernizing New York State's Erie Canal, fully 10,500 were Italians rounded up on the docks by Italian-speaking padrones and furnished to construction companies at so much per head. By 1897 Italians made up 75 percent of New York City's construction workers. Jews already dominated the town's once-German garment industry.

In Pennsylvania in 1900 almost 60 percent of white bituminous coal miners were foreign-born. In three anthracite coal mines in a single county, more than three-quarters of the work force was Slavic. Twenty-five languages were spoken in the textile mills of Lawrence, Massachusetts.

Ethnic monopolies of particular lines of work were established. In 1894 all but one of New York City's 474 foreign-born bootblacks were Italian, and Greeks dominated the confectionery business in Chicago until past the end of World War II.

For most, life in the golden land was potentially promising but actually brutal. Wages hung at or below the cost of living and far below the cost of comfort. Some parts of Chicago had three times as many inhabitants as the most crowded sections of Tokyo or Calcutta. A New York survey taker found 1,231 Italians living in 120 rooms. Single toilets and water faucets were shared by dozens of families. Uncollected garbage piled up in alleys. Privacy and health were equally impossible to maintain, and pulmonary diseases raged through the tenement "lung blocks."

Settlement-house workers took up residence in the worst neighborhoods, trying to teach the rudiments of hygiene. The American public school took on a new role. Authorities

In the 1890s, old New England families rallied to form the Immigration Restriction League.

regarded it as their mission to teach immigrant children not only basic skills but civic responsibility, respect for the flag, and the proper use of the toothbrush. In fact, the schools did produce millions of competent citizens. One alumna, Mary Antin, said that born Americans should be grateful for their role in "the recruiting of your armies of workers, thinkers, and leaders." But the precedent of having schools serve as agents of social policy—in this case of assimilation—would later haunt overburdened teachers and administrators.

The urban center of gravity of the new immigrants made it harder for them to be accepted. Most "native" Americans were encountering the basic problems of the big city—crowding, crime, graft, corruption, disease—for the first time. It was all too easy for them to associate these evils with the immigrants, who seemed always to be at the center of this or that dilemma. Sympathetic men and women like Jane Addams, Emily Balch, Hutchins Hapgood, and Horace M. Kallen did their best to explain immigrant culture to their fellow old-stock Americans and to guide the newcomers in acceptable American ways.

The immigrants themselves did not take on the role of clay awaiting the potter's hand. They organized their own newspapers, theaters, social clubs, night classes, and self-help societies. These, while keeping the old-country languages and folkways alive, steadfastly preached and practiced assimilation and urged members and readers to rush into citizenship and respectability, which the great majority of them did. Single men skimped and struggled to bring over families. Families sacrificed to send children to school. And the children found different paths to Americanization. Some joined political machines and parties; some worked in the union movement; others forged their own steps to success in business. (And some never graduated beyond the streets and dead-end jobs.)

Regardless of what they did, they were caught in the center of a steadily sharpening American debate over the "immigrant problem" that began in the early 1890s. It was a reprise of earlier nativist struggles. As early as 1882 Congress was prevailed upon to exclude Chinese from entry and citizenship. In the 1890s an Immigration Restriction League was formed. Its leaders were from old New England families who shared the fears of the writer Thomas Bailey Aldrich that through our "unguarded gates" there was pouring a "wild motley throng" of "Men from the Volga and the Tartar steppes."

Would the America of the future be populated, one restrictionist asked, by "British, German and Scandinavian stock, historically free, energetic, progressive, or by Slav, Latin and Asiatic races, historically down-trodden, atavistic and stagnant?" The call for an end to unchecked immigration was echoed by labor leaders like the AFL's Samuel Gompers (a Dutch-born Jewish immigrant from England in 1863), who complained that the "present immigration" consisted of "cheap labor, ignorant labor [that] takes our jobs and cuts our wages."

Bit by bit, curbs were imposed—first on immigrants with contagious diseases or serious criminal records, then on those who were "professional beggars" or anarchists or prostitutes or epileptics. In 1906 President Theodore Roosevelt got Congress to establish a commission to study the "problem." Chaired by the Vermont senator William Paul Dillingham, it labored for four years to produce a massive report that loaded the guns of a restrictionism based on invidious distinctions between the "old" and "new" immigrations. Among other things it marshaled data to "prove" that the most recent immigrants were "content to accept wages and conditions which . . . native Americans . . . had come to regard as unsatisfactory." It stated that "inherent racial tendencies" rather than poverty explained miserable immigrant living conditions and went on to say many other uncomplimentary things about the great-grandparents of some fifty million of today's Americans.

No action was taken on the report when it appeared in 1910. But racist feeling was on the rise. The Ku Klux Klan was revived in 1915. A hysterical drive for 100 percent Americanism during World War I and the Red scare immediately afterward fed a popular belief articulated by one congressman: "We get the majority of the communists, the I.W.W.'s, the dynamiters, and the assassins . . . from the ranks of the present-day immigrant."

In 1924 Congress passed the Johnson-Reed Act, which remained the cornerstone of national immigration policy for the next forty-one years. Starting in 1929, there would be an overall yearly limit of 150,000 on immigrants from outside the Western Hemisphere. The 150,000 was to be divided into quotas, assigned to nationalities in the proportion that they bore, by birth or descent, to the total population as of 1920.

What that meant was clear. The longer a national group had been here, the more of its descendants were in the population and the larger would be its quota. When the first shares were announced, half of all places were reserved for British residents, whereas only 5,802 Italians, 6,524 Poles, and 2,784 Russians could be admitted. Groups like Syrians or Albanians fared worse, with fewer than 100 places per year. And Asians were excluded altogether.

The national origins quota system of 1924 was a landmark, ending centuries of open admission. It was also a victory for ethnic stereotyping. Yet it was not without its ironies. For one thing, it did not impose limits on a Hispanic ingathering from Mexico and Puerto Rico that was just gaining steam. Nor did it deal with the internal migration of Southern blacks into Northern cities. Anglo-Saxon superiority was therefore left unprotected on two fronts.

And in the next and newest phase of the story, covering the final years of the twentieth century, there were dramatic changes in the "racial" composition of immigration that went far beyond anything that the Immigration Restriction League could possibly have anticipated.

The Third World Comes to the United States: 1965–90

Like a good many pieces of social policy legislation, the Johnson-Reed Act began to be outdated from the moment it took effect. One of its objectives—cutting down on immigration overall—was brutally affected by the Great Crash. In the deepest year of the Depression, 1933, only 34,000 immigrants arrived to take their chances in a shuttered and darkened economy.

The totals did not rise dramatically in the next seven years, but they were important weather vanes of change. Fascist and Communist dictators, and World War II, gave new meaning to the word *refugee* and a new scale to misery. Millions of victims of history would soon be knocking at our closed gates.

First came those in flight from Hitler, primarily Jews. Their claim to asylum was especially powerful, considering the savagery that they were fleeing (and no one suspected yet that extermination would be the ultimate threat). This was a special kind of exodus, heavy with intellectual distinction. Thousands of scientists, engineers, doctors, lawyers, teachers, and managers were hit by the Nazi purge of independent thinkers in every part of German life. "Hitler shakes the tree," said one American arts administrator, "and I collect the apples." The choicest apples included such men and women as Bruno Walter, George Szell, Lotte Lenya, Paul Klee, Thomas Mann, and Hannah Arendt in the arts and philosophy. In the sciences the lists included the physicists and mathematicians Edward Teller, Leo Szilard, Eugene P. Wigner, and Enrico Fermi (in flight from Mussolini's Italy) who shared in the creation of the atom bomb. The weapon was first proposed to the American government by the superstar of all the refugees, Albert Einstein.

World War II came—and more signals of change. In 1943 the sixty-one-year-old-Chinese Exclusion Act was repealed, because China was now an American ally. The gesture was small, and the quota tiny (105), and it could hardly be said to mark the end of anti-Asian prejudice when 112,000 American citizens of Japanese descent were behind barbed wire. But it was a beginning, a breach in the wall. The horrible consequences of Hitler's "racial science" were so clear that the philosophy of biological superiority underlying the national origins quota system received a fatal shock.

So the groundwork was laid for the future admission of nonwhite immigrants from the crumbling European empires in Africa and Asia—especially when, as it turned out, many of them were highly educated specialists.

Then the Cold War produced its worldwide tragedies and shake-ups, its expulsions and arrests and civil wars and invasions in China, Cuba, Korea, Indochina, the Philippines, Indonesia, Malaysia, Central Africa, the Middle East, Central America. A world in conflict was a world once more ready to swarm.

And in the United States an economic boom was reopening the job market. Attitudes toward immigration were changing as well. The children of the great 1890–1914 migration had come of age. They were powerful in the voting booths; political scientists credited them with a major role in supporting the New Deal. And the best-selling writers and dramatists among them were delving the richness of their experience in a way that wiped out the stereotypes of the old restrictionism.

So the walls began to crumble. First there were special enactments to clear the way for the wives and children of servicemen who had gotten married while overseas. Some 117,000 women and children entered under a War Brides Act of 1945—5,000 of them Chinese. In 1948 came the Displaced Persons Act, spurred by the misery of millions of homeless Eastern Europeans who had survived deportations, forced labor, bombings, and death camps. These were countries with the smallest national origins quotas. Congress did not repeal them, but it permitted borrowing against the future, so that at the end of the act's four-year life, for example, Poland's quota was mortgaged by half until 2000, and Latvia's until 2274. About 205,000 refugees entered under this law.

An attempt to overhaul the system in 1952 got entangled in the fear-ridden climate of McCarthyism, and the resulting McCarran-Walter Act kept the national origins quotas. Harry Truman vetoed it as "utterly unworthy of our traditions and ideals . . . our basic religious concepts, our belief in the brotherhood of man." It was passed over his veto, but time was on his side. Special emergency relief acts admitted refugees from China's civil war and Hungary's failed anti-Soviet uprising. Those who left Castro's Cuba needed no special relief, since there were as yet no limits on migration within the hemisphere, but they did get special help with resettlement. All told, in the 1950s immigration added up to some 2,500,000.

"Hitler shakes the tree," said one American arts administrator, "and I collect the apples."

It was a quality migration, lured by the promise of American wages and the consumer goods made visible in the films and television shows that America exported. And jet travel now put the promised land only hours away. Foreign governments ruefully watched their elites disappearing into the "brain drain" to the United States. Between 1956 and 1965 approximately 7,000 chemists, 35,000 engineers, 38,000 nurses, and 18,000 physicians were admitted. Between 1952 and 1961 Britain lost 16 percent of its Ph.D.s, half to the United States. Comparable losses were even more critical for developing states in the Third World or small European countries.

Yet there was still room at the bottom, for workers in the "service industries" and especially in the harvest fields of the Southwest. In 1951 growers got Congress to enact "temporary worker" programs that brought in thousands of Mexican braceros. Many who received green cards remained without authorization, joining imprecise numbers of illegal immigrants known as wetbacks after presumably swimming the Rio Grande to elude the Border Patrol. There were legal ways to stay too.

All we need is a gringuita
So that we can get married
And after we get our green card
We can get a divorce
Long live all the wetbacks.

So ran a popular Mexican ballad. Authorized and undocumented Mexicans alike became part of an enlarging Hispanic population, fed by migrants from Central America and the Caribbean. Great numbers of Puerto Ricans were part of it, but they did not count as immigrants because of the island's special status.

In 1965 the patched old system was finally discarded, and a brand-new act was passed. It mirrored the equal-rights spirit of the 1960s, modified by the political compromises that float bills through the riptides of congressional debate. The national origins quotas vanished, but there was no return to the wide-open days. Instead new quotas were established with three primary targets: reuniting families, opening the gates to refugees, and attracting skill and talent.

The new act mandated an annual limit of 170,000 immigrants from outside the Western Hemisphere, and 120,000 from within. These 290,000 were to be admitted under seven "preference" quotas. First and second preferences—40 percent of the total—were saved for unmarried grown sons and daughters of citizens and legally admitted alien residents. (Spouses, minor children, and parents of citizens came in free.) The third preference, 10 percent, went to "members of the professions and scientists and artists of exceptional ability." The fourth, 10 percent, went to adult *married* children of U.S. citizens, and the fifth, 24 percent, to brothers and sisters of citizens. The sixth, 10 percent, was held for "skilled labor in great demand" and "unskilled workers in occupations for which labor is in short supply," and the final preference, 6 percent, was for specifically defined refugees.

As Lyndon Johnson said when he signed the act at the base of the Statue of Liberty in October 1965, the new law was not "revolutionary." Yet, he added, it "repairs a deep and painful flaw in the fabric of American life. . . . The days of unlimited immigration are past. But those who come will come because of what they are—not because of the land from which they sprung."

The Immigration Act of 1965 was born in the year of Great Society programs and the Voting Rights Act. It fulfilled some of its authors' expectations and also carried some surprises—perhaps because 1965 was itself a turning-point year that also witnessed urban race riots and the first heavy and expensive commitments to combat in Vietnam. Johnson was wrong in one respect: The law's effects *have* been revolutionary, and are still with us every day. The twenty-five years of its existence have produced a major demographic turnaround.

Europe, the prime provider of new Americans for three centuries, fell off to little more than a 10 percent share of total immigration. The bulk of it now comes from Asia and the Western Hemisphere. In the decade from 1961 to 1970 some 3,321,000 immigrants arrived, and 1,123,000, less than 40 percent, were of European origin. Of 4,493,000 newcomers in the period 1971–80, only about 801,000 were Europeans. Between 1981 and 1990, when immigration totaled 7,338,000, the European contribution was only 761,550.

What of the other 85 to 90 percent? Of the 1,588,000 arrivals in the 1980s, 1,634,000 came from Asia (somewhat over one-third), 1,930,000 from North and South America, and 80,779 from Africa. The five major contributing nations were, in order, Mexico (640,300), the Philippines (355,000), Cuba (265,000), Korea (268,000), and China, both mainland and Taiwan (237,800).

Of the roughly 7,300,000 legal immigrants of 1981–90, 2,700,000 came from Asia, 3,600,000 from the Americas. The leaders—with numbers rounded—were Mexico at 1,656,000, the Philippines at 549,000, Vietnam with

281,000, the two Chinas with 98,000 and 346,000, and Korea with 334,000. Other heavy contributors were the Caribbean nations, with together 872,000; India with about 250,000, Laos at 112,000, Iran with some 116,000, Central America (Costa Rica, El Salvador, Guatemala, Honduras, Nicaragua, and Panama) with 468,000, and African nations with 177,000.

The rising Third World totals had two sources. One was the nature of the 1965 law itself, especially the fifth-preference brother-and-sister quota. Legally admitted and naturalized immigrants brought in their siblings, who went through the same cycle and then brought in *their* kin, and so on in a family tree of ever-spreading branches. When Congress endorsed family reunification, it had in mind the American 1950s model of two parents and two or three children. What it got was extended clans of Asians and Latins.

The other root of Third World influx was the bloody history of the 1970s and 1980s. The fall of Cambodia and South Vietnam in 1975 unleashed floods of refugees who were a special responsibility of the United States. Within the first six months we admitted some 130,000, and many more thousands under special quota exemptions in succeeding years. By 1990, counting their children born here, some 586,000 people of Indochinese origin were living in the United States.

The refugee problem was worldwide. It raised issues of what countries should share the burdens of admission. It sharpened agonizing questions of when repatriation might be justified: when a family was actually fleeing for its life and when it was only looking for a chance to go where air-conditioned cars and color television sets were the visible rewards of hard work (as if both motives could not coexist).

Congress made its own tentative answer with the first major modification of the 1965 law, the Refugee Act of 1980. It set up new offices within the federal government for handling refugee affairs and reshuffled the quota system. The old seventh (refugee) preference with its 17,400 slots was abolished in favor of an annual quota of up to 50,000 refugees that could be exceeded for "grave, humanitarian reasons" by the President in consultation with Congress. The overall limit was dropped to 270,000 as a tradeoff. A refugee was officially defined as a person who could not go home again by reason of a "well-founded fear of persecution" on the basis of race, religion, nationality, or political opinion.

And as if to mock the effort to set boundaries around social revolutions, President Carter's signature was hardly dry on the act when 125,000 new Cuban refugees were knocking at the gates, released by Castro through the port of Mariel. Carter declared that he would admit them with open arms and an open heart, a sentiment not fully shared by some residents of the South Florida communities where the *Marielitos* at first clustered.

Society had changed greatly since the unstructured and unsupervised days of mass arrivals at Ellis Island (long deserted and shuttered). The newest refugees did not find unskilled jobs and low-rent tenements waiting for them. It was the age of big government and bureaucratic organization. With the U.S. Treasury providing funds, and church and social service agencies the personnel, programs were launched to help with health care, schooling, and other roads to citizenship. Until the immigrants dispersed themselves around the country, they were lodged in temporary camps, some of them former Army bases. What had been left between 1890 and 1914 to friends, families, padrones, *landsleit*, and political machines was now managed under guidelines set in Washington.

Washington's welcome was not universal. Cold War politics infiltrated refugee policy in the 1980s. Refugees from Communist nations were welcomed, but those from countries officially deemed "democratic," like El Salvador, got shorter shrift. So did those who were "merely" trying to escape harsh but non-Communist regimes or grinding poverty, like the Haitians. The Immigration and Naturalization Service held thousands of them in detention while their petitions for asylum were suspiciously reviewed. Nonetheless, thousands of Central Americans managed to escape the net and find work—usually low-paid and menial—and to melt into the underground economy of the Hispanic communities in Florida and New York.

General statements about this newest great migration are dangerous because it is tempting to lump its members together by race and nationality, as the old Dillingham Report did, rather than by class, education, experience, income, or other categories. To describe Colombian dentists and Mexican cotton pickers as "Hispanics" or Korean chemical engineers and Pakistani nurses' aides as "Asian" suggests nonexistent similarities.

But some broad observations fit most of the new immigrants: They get to this country swiftly and by air, they quickly fall into the consumerist culture familiar to them through television at home, and they are quickly integrated into the bureaucratic structure of entitlements that characterize life in the United States today.

Beyond that, all-embracing descriptions strain the facts. The Vietnamese, for example, include English-speaking professionals who worked for American corporations, Catholics educated during the period of French control, and people from the bottom rung: in the words of one writer, "cosmopolites, bourgeois provincials, and dirt-poor peasants . . . gifted intellectuals, street-wise hustlers and unworldly fisherfolk and farmers." The Koreans most visible to New Yorkers are the hardworking grocers who seem to have taken over the retail fruit and vegetable business completely from the Italians. But a survey shows that more than a third of all Koreans in the United States have completed four years of college.

Recent years have witnessed a new restrictionism, but it is based on some very old alliances.

Filipino immigrants are found in hospitals, as doctors and nurses and sometimes behind the counter in the basement cafeterias; Indians in the newsstands of New York City and likewise doing advanced biochemical or genetic research in its university laboratories. Middle Eastern Arabs, both Christian and Muslim, are heavily concentrated in Detroit, and many work in the American auto industry at both shop and managerial levels. Israeli and Soviet Jewish immigrants—some of them jobless Ph.D.s—drive taxis in Washington, Los Angeles, Chicago, and New York—and work as engineers in defense industries in the Southwest. Puerto Ricans, other Latinos, and Chinese fill the places in New York's declining garment industry once held by Italians and Jews.

Within the communities of Cambodians, Peruvians, Ecuadorians, Iranians, Russians, Israelis, Irish, and Puerto Ricans the old saga goes on as children learn new ways and move to new, unexpected disruptive rhythms. But in education the effect of the new immigration has been dramatically different from what it was prior to World War I. Then the public schools were on the rise and confident of their power and duty to unify *all* children behind the undisputedly correct symbols and rites of Americanism.

In the mood of the 1970s, however, things changed. Emphasis on ethnic pride and the power of the civil rights revolution dictated a new approach. Immigrant children were no longer to be thrown into English-speaking classrooms to sink or swim. Instead bilingual programs would help them in transit to a new system without their being stigmatized as stupid because they could not understand the teacher. Going further, some educators argued that preparing children for a multicultural society required exposure to many "life-styles" and building the self-esteem of "minority" students through appreciation of their own languages, customs, and cultures. So some states mandated bilingual (usually Hispanic-English) programs into the curriculum at every level.

Whatever the virtues of the theory (debatable in the light of evidence), bilingualism provoked a strong counterreaction, and by 1990 some organizations were insisting that new immigrants were not working hard enough to learn the common tongue that was so valuable a social binding agency. An English-only drive got under way to designate English, by constitutional amendment, if necessary, as the *official* language of the United States.

In actual fact, Spanish (and other language) newspapers, television stations, religious congregations, and social clubs were a re-enactment of what had gone before. In the early 1900s there had been a vigorous immigrant press, which, in time, died out. But the English-only movement drew strength from a sense of increasing discomfort over the increasing numbers of immigrants, a reawakening of the old idea that a "flood" of "unassimilated" newcomers was pouring in.

A new restrictionism was born, featuring some familiar alliances. Middle- and upper-class taxpayers believed that the immigrants, concentrated in certain areas, were a burden on schools, hospitals, and welfare and law-enforcement agencies. On the other hand, there were workers who were convinced that the immigrants took away low-level jobs that were rightfully theirs or depressed wages by working in sweatshops or permitting the employment of their underage children. Black Americans tended especially to believe that material assistance that had been denied to them was going to the refugees. They were now the bypassed "old Americans."

Resentment was fed by the widespread admiration of the academic and business success of Asian Americans, who were, in great numbers, advancing up the professional scale. They were described by some sociologists as a "model minority"—their delinquents and failures overlooked while the spotlight fell on those who succeeded.

A dread of the unknown and uncountable hovered over lawmakers. Undocumented aliens came in from the Mexico in annual numbers estimated from a few hundred thousand to many millions a year. The oft-repeated statement that we were "losing control of our borders" had a powerful psychological kick in a time of multiple American troubles. Had we, in fact, reached the limit our power to offer asylum? Was there truth in what Sen. Alan Simpson said in 1982: "We have to live within limits. The nation wants to be compassionate but we have been compassionate beyond our ability to respond"?

The evidence of the actual economic effect of immigration is inconclusive. The contribution of immigrant specialists to a high-tech economy has to be considered. Every working-age, well-trained immigrant who enters the country becomes a free resource, not schooled at American cost—a dividend from the brain drain. Even the "low-end" immigrants, including the "illegals" (or undocumented), may contribute as much in sales and other taxes and in purchasing power as they take out in services and schooling. The case has also been made that the undocumented aliens, fearful of discovery, rarely claim benefits due them. Thousands of employers likewise insist that without immigrants they could not staff the service industries or harvest the fields.

And the falling American birthrate suggests to some economists the possibility of labor shortages in the next century. They say that we can easily absorb half a million or so legal immigrants annually, perhaps more—though of what kind and for how long are left to debate.

But while debate went on, Congress did make a second change in the 1965 law. The Simpson-Mazzoli Act of 1986 tried to deal with two much-disputed issues. One was how to identify and count the unmeasured number of undocumented aliens already in the country without intrusive violations of civil liberties. The other was how to enforce immigration limits without a gigantic and costly expansion of the hard-pressed Immigration and Naturalization Service. The solution to the first problem was dealt with through an amnesty for pre-1982 immigrants; the second, by turning employers into enforcement agents. They would be "sanctioned" by fines if they hired undocumented aliens. The bill sparked bitter controversy in its career in three separate Congresses before final passage. Mexican-American organizations, for example, argued that employers, rather than risk sanctions, would simply refuse to hire Hispanic-looking or -sounding men and women. Employers complained about the cost and difficulty of checking credentials. But in the end a coalition for passage was established. It is still too early to tell how well the law is working.

It is not too early, however, to make some general predictions about the future course of the peopling of America. Immigration on the current scale, plus natural increase, will over time change the character of the people who inhabit these United States. Hispanic-descended men and women alone now constitute a little more than 22,000,000 in a population of about 248,000,000. By 2010 they are expected to number 39,300,000 in an overall population of about 282,000,000. In other words, their increase will account for 28 percent of the total population growth in that period. Another set of census projections for the period from 1990 to 2025 sees the white population declining from 84.3 to 75.6 percent, the black population percentage rising from 12.4 to 14.6, and the percentage of "other races" almost doubling, from 3.4 to 6.5. In some urban areas where the current crop of new immigrants clusters, the terms *nonwhite* and *minority* are no longer synonyms; in Los Angeles County, for example, only 15 percent of public school children are white.

We began with a reference to the many-tongued New York that Isaac Jogues found in 1643. It is appropriate to return for a look some 350 years afterward. The old tale continues. "Young Immigrant Wave Lifts New York Economy," runs a recent story in *The New York Times*. The paper found that the 2,600,000 foreign-born residents of the city (about one-third of the total population) had a positive effect. Their addition to the ranks of workers, small business owners, and consumers had probably kept New York from becoming "boarded up." No fewer than eighteen countries had sent 5,000 or more people to the hard-pressed metropolis from 1980 to 1986. At least 114 languages are spoken in the city's school systems. In one Queens school a sign directs visitors to register in English, Chinese, Korean, and Spanish. Among those photographed or interviewed for the article were a Serbian-speaking garment worker, a Romanian technician in a hematology laboratory, and an Albanian building owner who began as a superintendent.

And as in New York, so also in the other great cities of America in the 1990s—in Los Angeles (44 percent of adults foreign-born) and Miami (70 percent foreign-born), in Chicago, Dallas, Boston, in the ten largest cities of the land where increases in immigrant population offset the economic impact of the loss of other residents—and in the neighborhoods across the country where the new immigrants are working and raising their American children. For them the streets may not be paved with gold, but the dreams still glisten. What memories they will give their children, what gods they will worship, what leaders they will follow, what monuments they will create are all part of history yet to be written. It seems safe to say that, like the English, Scots, Irish, Germans, Swedes and Finns, Greeks, Poles, Italians, Hungarians, and Russians before them, they will neither "melt" into some undistinctive alloy nor, on the other hand, remain aloof and distinct from one another. Some kind of functional American mosaic will emerge. It is the historic way; the great Amazon that Melville described as America's noble bloodstream flows on undisturbed, into a new century.

Part 1

American Ethnicities and the Politics of Inclusion

John A. Kromkowski

Table 1

National Index of Ethnic Variety: Self-Identification of Census Respondents

1990 Rank	Ancestry Group	Number	Percent	1990 Rank	Ancestry Group	Number	Percent
	Total population	248,709,873	100.0	43	Asian Indian	570,322	0.2
1	German	57,947,374	23.3	44	Canadian	549,990	0.2
2	Irish	38,735,539	15.6	45	Croatian	544,270	0.2
3	English	32,651,788	13.1	46	Vietnamese	535,825	0.2
4	Afro American	23,777,098	9.6	47	Dominican	505,690	0.2
5	Italian	14,664,550	5.9	48	Salvadoran	499,153	0.2
6	American	12,395,999	5.0	49	European	466,718	0.2
7	Mexican	11,586,983	4.7	50	Jamaican	435,024	0.2
8	French	10,320,935	4.1				
9	Polish	9,366,106	3.8	51	Lebanese	394,180	0.2
10	American Indian	8,708,220	3.5	52	Belgian	380,498	0.2
				53	Romanian	365,544	0.1
11	Dutch	6,227,089	2.5	54	Spaniard	360,935	0.1
12	Scotch-Irish	5,617,773	2.3	55	Colombian	351,717	0.1
13	Scottish	5,393,581	2.2	56	Czechoslovakian	315,285	0.1
14	Swedish	4,680,863	1.9	57	Armenian	308,096	0.1
15	Norwegian	3,869,395	1.6	58	Pennsylvania German	305,841	0.1
16	Russian	2,952,987	1.2	59	Haitian	289,521	0.1
17	French Canadian	2,167,127	0.9	60	Yugoslavian	257,994	0.1
18	Welsh	2,033,893	0.8				
19	Spanish	2,024,004	0.8	61	Hawaiian	256,081	0.1
20	Puerto Rican	1,955,323	0.8	62	African	245,845	0.1
				63	Guatemalan	241,559	0.1
21	Slovak	1,882,897	0.8	64	Iranian	235,521	0.1
22	White	1,799,711	0.7	65	Ecuadorian	197,374	0.1
23	Danish	1,634,669	0.7	66	Taiwanese	192,973	0.1
24	Hungarian	1,582,302	0.6	67	Nicaraguan	177,077	0.1
25	Chinese	1,505,245	0.6	68	Peruvian	161,866	0.1
26	Filipino	1,450,512	0.6	69	West Indies	159,167	0.1
27	Czech	1,296,411	0.5	70	Laotian	146,930	0.1
28	Portuguese	1,153,351	0.5				
29	British	1,119,154	0.4	71	Cambodian	134,955	0.1
30	Hispanic	1,113,259	0.4	72	Syrian	129,606	0.1
				73	Arab	127,364	0.1
31	Greek	1,110,373	0.4	74	Slovene	124,437	0.1
32	Swiss	1,045,495	0.4	75	Serbian	116,795	0.0
33	Japanese	1,004,645	0.4	76	Honduran	116,635	0.0
34	Austrian	864,783	0.3	77	Thai	112,117	0.0
35	Cuban	859,739	0.3	78	Asian	107,172	0.0
36	Korean	836,987	0.3	79	Latvian	100,331	0.0
37	Lithuanian	811,865	0.3	80	Pakistani	99,974	0.0
38	Ukranian	740,803	0.3				
39	Scandinavian	678,880	0.3	81	Nigerian	91,688	0.0
40	Acadian/Cajun	668,271	0.3	82	Panamanian	88,649	0.0
41	Finnish	658,870	0.3	83	Hmong	84,823	0.0
42	United States	643,561	0.3	84	Turkish	83,850	0.0

Table 1 and Table 3 from *America's Choice: The Election of 1992,* edited by William Crotty, Chapter 11, pp. 130-132. © 1992 by Dushkin/McGraw•Hill. All other data retrieved from the U.S. Census Bureau, 1990.

1990 Rank	Ancestry Group	Number	Percent
85	Israeli	81,677	0.0
86	Guyanese	81,677	0.0
87	Egyptian	78,574	0.0
88	Slavic	76,931	0.0
89	Trinidad & Tobagonian	76,270	0.0
90	Northern European	65,993	0.0
91	Brazilian	65,785	0.0
92	Argentinean	63,176	0.0
93	Dutch West Indian	61,530	0.0
94	Chilean	61,465	0.0
95	Samoan	55,419	0.0
96	Eskimo	52,920	0.0
97	Australian	52,133	0.0
98	Costa Rican	51,771	0.0
99	Assyrian	51,765	0.0
100	Cape Verdean	50,772	0.0
101	Sicilian	50,389	0.0
102	Luxemburger	49,061	0.0
103	Palestinian	48,019	0.0
104	Basque	47,956	0.0
105	Albanian	47,710	0.0
106	Indonesian	43,969	0.0
107	Latin American	43,521	0.0
108	Western European	42,409	0.0
109	Icelander	40,529	0.0
110	Venezuelan	40,331	0.0
111	Maltese	39,600	0.0
112	Guamanian	39,237	0.0
113	British West Indian	37,819	0.0
114	Barbadian	35,455	0.0
115	Bolivian	33,738	0.0
116	Afghanistan	31,301	0.0
117	Ethiopian	30,581	0.0
118	Celtic	29,652	0.0
119	Bulgarian	29,595	0.0
120	Malaysian	27,800	0.0
121	Estonian	26,762	0.0
122	Prussian	25,469	0.0
123	Cantonese	25,020	0.0
124	Iraqi	23,212	0.0
125	Belizean	22,922	0.0
126	Bahamian	21,081	0.0
127	Jordanian	20,656	0.0
128	Macedonian	20,365	0.0
129	Ghanian	20,066	0.0
130	Moroccan	19,089	0.0
131	South African	17,992	0.0
132	Alsatian	16,465	0.0
133	Tongan	16,019	0.0
134	Aluet	15,816	0.0
135	Amerasian	15,523	0.0
136	Uruguayan	14,641	0.0
137	Sri Lankan	14,448	0.0
138	Eurasian	14,177	0.0
139	Flemish	14,157	0.0
140	North American	12,618	0.0
141	Bangladeshi	12,486	0.0
142	Pacific Islander	11,330	0.0
143	Grenadian	11,188	0.0
144	South American	10,867	0.0
145	Polynesian	10,854	0.0
146	Okinawan	10,554	0.0
147	Central American	10,310	0.0
148	German Russian	10,153	0.0
149	Liberian	8,797	0.0
150	Burmese	8,646	0.0
151	New Zealand	7,742	0.0
152	Soviet Union	7,729	0.0
153	Middle Eastern	7,656	0.0
154	US Virgin Islander	7,621	0.0
155	Basque, Spanish	7,620	0.0
156	Carpath Russian	7,602	0.0
157	Fijian	7,472	0.0
158	Antigua	7,364	0.0
159	Manx	6,317	0.0
160	Basque, French	6,001	0.0
161	Hong Kong	5,774	0.0
162	Vincent/Grenadine Islander	5,773	0.0
163	Tirol	5,748	0.0
164	Rom	5,693	0.0
165	Central European	5,693	0.0
166	Nova Scotian	5,489	0.0
167	Paraguyan	5,415	0.0
168	Newfoundland	5,412	0.0
169	Bermudan	4,941	0.0
170	Cypriot	4,897	0.0
171	Kenyan	4,639	0.0
172	Sierra Leon	4,627	0.0
173	Saxon	4,519	0.0
174	Saudi Arabian	4,486	0.0
175	Charnorro	4,427	0.0
176	Bavarian	4,348	0.0
177	Azorean	4,310	0.0
178	Belorussian	4,277	0.0
179	Eritrean	4,270	0.0
180	Yemeni	4,011	0.0
181	Northern Irish	4,009	0.0
182	Cornish	3,991	0.0
183	West German	3,885	0.0
184	Moravian	3,781	0.0
185	Ruthenian	3,776	0.0
186	Sudanese	3,623	0.0
187	Mongolian	3,507	0.0
188	St. Lucia	3,415	0.0
189	Micronesian	3,406	0.0
190	Algerian	3,215	0.0
191	Windish	3,189	0.0
192	Khmer	2,979	0.0
193	Kitts/Nevis Islander	2,811	0.0
194	Ugandan	2,681	0.0
195	Nepali	2,516	0.0
196	Singaporean	2,419	0.0
197	Cypriot, Greek	2,197	0.0

Source: 1990 CP-S-1-2, Detailed Ancestry Groups for States.

Table 2

Regional Indexes of Ethnic Variety for 1980 and 1990 Censuses

1990 Rank	Ancestry group	Number	Percent	1980 Rank	Ancestry group	Number	Percent
	NORTHEAST	50,809,229	100.0		NORTHEAST	49,135,283	100.0
1	German	9,928,722	19.5	1	Irish	9,753,664	19.9
2	Irish	9,420,118	18.5	2	German	9,359,415	19.0
3	Italian	7,503,740	14.8	3	English	8,174,976	16.6
4	English	5,873,052	11.6	4	Italian	6,929,876	14.1
5	Norwegian	3,869,395	7.6	5	Afro American	3,506,942	7.1
6	Afro American	3,658,088	7.2	6	French	3,377,762	6.9
7	Polish	3,499,502	6.9	7	Polish	3,342,944	6.8
8	French	2,637,321	5.2	8	Scottish	1,873,429	3.8
9	Welsh	2,033,893	4.0	9	Russian	1,333,813	2.7
10	Spanish	2,024,004	4.0	10	Dutch	1,133,936	2.3
11	Russian	1,292,472	2.5	11	Puerto Rican	1,057,461	2.2
12	Puerto Rican	1,289,858	2.5	12	Hungarian	700,947	1.4
13	American	1,275,211	2.5	13	Swedish	659,486	1.3
14	Scottish	1,088,462	2.1	14	Spanish	613,844	1.2
15	Dutch	1,020,383	2.0	15	American Indian	583,046	1.2
16	French Canadian	973,230	1.9	16	Portuguese	512,768	1.0
17	Scotch-Irish	772,250	1.5	17	Austrian	412,653	0.8
18	Slovak	759,264	1.5	18	Welsh	411,161	0.8
19	American Indian	754,051	1.5	19	Ukranian	402,054	0.8
20	Swedish	669,531	1.3	20	Slovak	388,964	0.8
21	Hungarian	564,216	1.1	21	Greek	388,120	0.8
22	Portuguese	563,801	1.1	22	French Canadian	363,347	0.7
23	Chinese	374,410	0.7	23	Lithuanian	350,308	0.7
24	Ukranian	374,282	0.7	24	Czech	336,994	0.7
25	Lithuanian	325,523	0.7	25	Norwegian	226,477	0.5

1990 Rank	Ancestry group	Number	Percent	1980 Rank	Ancestry group	Number	Percent
	MIDWEST	59,668,632	100.0		MIDWEST	58,865,970	100.0
1	German	22,477,450	37.7	1	German	20,244,888	34.4
2	Irish	9,643,261	16.2	2	English	11,538,184	19.6
3	English	7,293,707	12.2	3	Irish	10,572,753	18.0
4	Afro American	4,875,147	8.2	4	Afro American	3,506,942	6.0
5	Polish	3,468,832	5.8	5	French	3,488,677	5.9
6	French	2,640,874	4.4	6	Polish	3,153,476	5.4
7	Italian	2,429,651	4.1	7	Scottish	2,307,293	3.9
8	American	2,204,709	3.7	8	Dutch	2,235,006	3.8
9	Dutch	2,123,623	3.6	9	Italian	1,995,424	3.4
10	Norwegian	2,000,129	3.4	10	Norwegian	1,899,306	3.2
11	American Indian	1,907,001	3.2	11	Swedish	1,847,564	3.1
12	Swedish	1,858,855	3.1	12	American Indian	1,575,595	2.7
13	Scottish	1,135,343	1.9	13	Czech	931,233	1.6
14	Scotch-Irish	1,078,883	1.8	14	Mexican	705,349	1.2
15	Mexican	1,021,049	1.7	15	Hungarian	587,175	1.0
16	Czech	671,371	1.1	16	Danish	571,292	1.0
17	Slovak	648,461	1.1	17	Russian	474,573	0.8
18	Danish	555,346	0.9	18	Welsh	445,719	0.8
19	Hungarian	504,619	0.8	19	Swiss	381,596	0.6
20	Welsh	493,214	0.8	20	Finnish	304,319	0.5

1990 Rank	Ancestry group	Number	Percent	1980 Rank	Ancestry group	Number	Percent
21	Russian	473,588	0.8	21	Slovak	303,041	0.5
22	French Canadian	436,548	0.7	22	Greek	233,474	0.4
23	Swiss	378,239	0.6	23	Lithuanian	222,638	0.4
24	Finnish	310,855	0.5	24	Belgian	217,021	0.4
25	Greek	255,780	0.4	25	Austrian	211,265	0.4

Note: Data are based on a sample and subject to sampling variability. Since persons who reported multiple ancestries were included in more than one group, the sum of the persons reporting the ancestry is greater than the total; for example, a person reporting "English-French" was tabulated in both the "English" and "French" categories. Changes were made to the wording of the question, respondent instructions, coding procedures, and tabulation categories between the 1980 and 1990 censuses. Questions concerning comparability may be directed to the Ethnic and Hispanic Branch, Population Division, Bureau of the Census.

Source: 1990 CP-S-1-2, Detailed Ancestry Groups for States and PC80-S1-10, Ancestry of the Population by State: 1980.

Table 3

Regional Indexes of Ethnic Variety for 1980 and 1990 Censuses

1990 Rank	Ancestry group	Number	Percent	1980 Rank	Ancestry group	Number	Percent
	SOUTH	85,445,930	100.0		SOUTH	75,372,362	100.0
1	German	14,630,411	17.1	1	English	19,618,370	26.0
2	Irish	12,950,799	15.2	2	Irish	12,709,872	16.9
3	Afro American	12,936,066	15.1	3	Afro American	11,054,127	14.7
4	English	11,375,464	13.3	4	German	10,742,903	14.3
5	American	7,558,114	8.8	5	French	3,532,674	4.7
6	American Indian	4,086,342	4.8	6	Scottish	3,492,252	3.9
7	Mexican	3,774,379	4.4	7	American Indian	2,928,252	3.9
8	French	2,964,481	3.5	8	Mexican	2,663,868	3.5
9	Scotch-Irish	2,616,155	3.1	9	Dutch	1,651,125	2.2
10	Italian	2,473,371	2.9	10	Italian	1,555,340	2.1
11	Dutch	1,780,043	2.1	11	Polish	943,536	1.3
12	Scottish	1,768,494	2.1	12	Spanish	705,594	0.9
13	Polish	1,361,537	1.6	13	Swedish	511,426	0.7
14	White	946,103	1.1	14	Russian	441,287	0.6
15	Swedish	671,099	0.8	15	Cuban	373,695	0.5
16	Spanish	614,708	0.7	16	Welsh	360,272	0.5
17	Acadian/Cajun	609,427	0.7	17	Czech	348,110	0.5
18	Cuban	594,106	0.7	18	Norwegian	253,799	0.3
19	Russian	545,671	0.6	19	Hungarian	239,786	0.3
20	Welsh	545,082	0.5	20	Greek	167,926	0.2
21	British	440,352	0.5	21	Danish	147,029	0.2
22	French Canadian	423,497	0.5	22	Swiss	143,636	0.2
23	Norwegian	369,485	0.4	23	Austrian	140,666	0.2
24	Hispanic	347,411	0.4	24	Puerto Rican	120,394	0.2
25	United States	341,677	0.4	25	French Canadian	104,725	0.1

1990 Rank	Ancestry group	Number	Percent	1980 Rank	Ancestry group	Number	Percent
	WEST	52,786,082	100.0		WEST	43,172,490	100.0
1	German	10,910,791	20.7	1	English	10,266,505	23.8
2	English	8,109,565	15.4	2	German	8,876,940	20.6
3	Irish	6,721,361	12.7	3	Irish	7,129,413	16.5
4	Mexican	6,648,726	12.6	4	Mexican	4,261,286	9.9
5	Afro American	2,307,797	4.4	5	French	2,493,133	5.8
6	Italian	2,257,788	4.3	6	Scottish	2,375,842	5.5
7	French	2,078,259	3.9	7	Afro American	1,898,272	4.4
8	American Indian	1,960,826	3.7	8	Italian	1,703,052	3.9
9	Swedish	1,481,378	2.8	9	American Indian	1,628,926	3.8
10	Scottish	1,401,282	2.7	10	Swedish	1,326,916	3.1
11	American	1,357,965	2.6	11	Dutch	1,284,432	3.0
12	Dutch	1,303,040	2.5	12	Spanish	1,161,484	2.7
13	Norwegian	1,258,552	2.4	13	Norwegian	1,074,257	2.5
14	Scotch-Irish	1,150,485	2.2	14	Polish	788,081	1.8
15	Polish	1,036,235	2.0	15	Danish	657,792	1.5
16	Filipino	991,572	1.9	16	Japanese	607,630	1.4
17	Spanish	919,916	1.7	17	Filipino	540,680	1.3
18	Chinese	826,760	1.6	18	Russian	531,759	1.2
19	Danish	738,508	1.4	19	Chinese	487,530	1.1
20	Japanese	722,700	1.4	20	Welsh	447,446	1.0
21	Russian	641,256	1.2	21	Portuguese	419,844	1.0
22	Hispanic	555,029	1.1	22	Swiss	279,231	0.6
23	Welsh	548,974	1.0	23	Czech	276,119	0.6
24	White	501,934	1.0	24	Hungarian	248,994	0.6
25	Portuguese	468,812	0.9	25	Scandinavian	208,799	0.5

Source: 1990 CP-S-1-2, Detailed Ancestry Groups for States and PC 80-S1-10, Ancestry of the Population by State: 1980.

Table 4

Ancestry of the Population in the United States: 1990

Ancestry group	1990 Census Number	Percent
Total population	248,709,873	100.0
EUROPEAN		
(excluding Hispanic groups)		
Alsatian	16,465	0.0
Austrian	870,531	0.4
Basque	47,956	0.0
Belgian	394,655	0.2
British	1,119,154	0.4
Cypriot	4,897	0.0
Celtic	29,652	0.0
Danish	1,634,669	0.7
Dutch	6,227,089	2.5
English	32,655,779	13.1
Finnish	658,870	0.3
French	10,320,935	4.1
German	57,985,595	23.3
Greek	1,110,272	0.4
Icelander	40,529	0.0
Irish	38,739,548	15.6
Italian	14,714,939	5.9
Luxemburger	49,061	0.0
Maltese	39,600	0.0
Manx	6,317	0.0
Norwegian	3,869,395	1.6
Portuguese	1,153,351	0.5
Scandinavian	678,880	0.3
Scotch-Irish	5,617,773	2.3
Scottish	5,393,581	2.2
Swedish	4,680,863	1.9
Swiss	1,045,495	0.4
Welsh	2,033,893	0.8
Albanian	47,710	0.0
Bulgarian	29,595	0.0
Carpath Russian	7,602	0.0
Croatian	544,270	0.2

Ancestry group	1990 Census Number	Percent
Czech	1,300,192	0.5
Czechoslovakian	315,285	0.1
Estonian	26,762	0.0
European	466,718	0.2
German Russian	10,153	0.0
Hungarian	1,582,302	0.6
Latvian	100,331	0.0
Lithuanian	811,865	0.3
Macedonian	20,365	0.0
Polish	9,366,106	3.8
Rom	5,693	0.0
Romanian	365,544	0.1
Russian	2,952,987	1.2
Serbian	116,795	0.0
Slavic	76,931	0.0
Slovak	1,882,897	0.8
Slovene	124,437	0.1
Soviet Union	7,729	0.0
Ukranian	740,803	0.3
Yugoslavian	257,994	0.1
Other European, n.e.c.	259,585	0.1
WEST INDIAN (excluding Hispanic groups)		
Bahamian	21,081	0.0
Barbadian	35,455	0.0
Belizean	22,922	0.0
Bermudan	4,941	0.0
British West Indies	37,819	0.0
Dutch West Indies	61,530	0.0
Haitian	289,521	0.1
Jamaican	435,024	0.2
Trinidad & Tobagoan	76,270	0.0
U.S. Virgin Islander	7,621	0.0
West Indian	159,167	0.1
Other West Indian, n.e.c.	4,139	0.0
CENTRAL AND SOUTH AMERICA (excluding Hispanic groups)		
Brazilian	65,875	0.0
Guyanese	81,665	0.0
Other Cen. & S. America,, n.e.c.	1,217	0.0
NORTH AFRICA AND SOUTHWEST ASIA		
Algerian	3,215	0.0
Arab	127,364	0.1
Armenian	308,096	0.1
Assyrian	51,765	0.0
Egyptian	78,574	0.0
Iranian	235,521	0.1
Iraqi	23,212	0.0
Israeli	81,677	0.0
Jordanian	20,656	0.0
Lebanese	394,180	0.2
Middle Eastern	7,656	0.0
Moroccan	19,089	0.0
Palestinian	48,019	0.0
Saudi Arabian	4,486	0.0
Syrian	129,606	0.1
Turkish	83,850	0.0
Yemeni	4,011	0.0
Other North African and Southwest Asian, n.e.c.	10,670	0.0
SUBSAHARAN AFRICA		
African	245,845	0.1
Cape Verdean	50,772	0.0
Ethiopian	34,851	0.0
Ghanian	20,066	0.0
Kenyan	4,639	0.0
Liberian	8,797	0.0
Nigerian	91,688	0.0
Sierra Leon	4,627	0.0
South African	17,992	0.0
Sudanese	3,623	0.0
Ugandan	2,681	0.0
African, n.e.c.	20,607	0.0
PACIFIC		
Australian	52,133	0.0
New Zealander	7,742	0.0
NORTH AMERICA		
Acadian	668,271	0.3
American	12,396,057	5.0
Canadian	560,891	0.2
French Canadian	2,167,127	0.9
Pennsylvania German	305,841	0.1
United States	643,602	0.3
Other North American, n.e.c.	12,927	0.0
OTHER GROUPS OR UNCLASSIFIED		
Other groups, n.e.c.	63,562,346	25.6
Unclassified or not reported	26,101,616	10.5

n.e.c. represents "not elsewhere classified"

Note: Data are based on a sample and are subject to sampling variability. Data for "Other Groups" include groups identified separately in the Race and Hispanic origin items. Since persons who reported multiple ancestries were included in more than one group, the sum of the persons reporting the ancestry group is greater than the total; for example, a person reporting "English-French" was tabulated in both the "English" and "French" categories.

Source: U.S. Department of Commerce, Bureau of the Census, Ethnic and Hispanic Branch, 1990 Census Special Tabulations.

Table 5

The Foreign-Born Population by Place of Birth for the United States: 1990

Place of Birth	1990 Census Number	Percent
Foreign-born persons	21,631,601	100.0
Europe	4,812,117	22.2
Austria	94,398	0.4
Belgium	41,111	0.2
Czechoslovakia	90,042	0.4
Denmark	37,657	0.2
Estonia	9,251	0.0
Finland	23,547	0.1
France	162,934	0.8
Germany	1,163,004	5.4
Greece	189,267	0.9
Hungary	112,419	0.5
Ireland	177,420	0.8
Italy	639,518	3.0
Latvia	26,380	0.1
Lithuania	30,344	0.1
Netherlands	104,216	0.5
Norway	46,240	0.2
Poland	397,014	1.8
Portugal	218,525	1.0
Romania	92,627	0.4
Spain	103,518	0.5
Sweden	57,166	0.3
Switzerland	43,991	0.2
United Kingdom	764,627	3.5
Yugoslavia	144,563	0.7
Other Europe	42,338	0.2
Soviet Union	336,889	1.6
Asia	5,412,127	25.0
Afghanistan	28,988	0.1
Burma	20,441	0.1
Cambodia	119,581	0.6
China	543,208	2.5
Hong Kong	152,263	0.7
India	463,132	2.1
Indonesia	50,388	0.2
Iran	216,963	1.0
Iraq	45,936	0.2
Israel	97,006	0.4
Japan	421,921	2.0
Jordan	33,019	0.2
Korea	663,465	3.1
Laos	172,925	0.8
Lebanon	91,037	0.4
Malaysia	34,906	0.2
Pakistan	93,663	0.4
Philippines	997,745	4.6
Saudi Arabia	17,312	0.1
Syria	37,654	0.2
Taiwan	253,719	1.2
Thailand	119,862	0.6
Turkey	65,244	0.3
Vietnam	556,311	2.6
Other Asia	115,438	0.5
North America	8,524,594	39.4
Canada	870,850	4.0
Caribbean	1,986,835	9.2
Antigua-Barbuda	12,452	0.1
Bahamas	24,341	0.1
Barbados	44,311	0.2
Cuba	750,609	3.5
Dominican Republic	356,971	1.7
Grenada	18,183	0.1
Haiti	229,108	1.1
Jamaica	343,458	1.6
Trinidad/Tobago	119,221	0.6
Other Caribbean	88,181	0.4
Central America	5,650,374	26.1
Belize	31,222	0.1
Costa Rica	48,264	0.2
El Salvador	472,885	2.2
Guatemala	232,977	1.1
Honduras	114,603	0.5
Mexico	4,447,439	20.6
Nicaragua	171,950	0.8
Panama	124,695	0.6
Other Central America	6,339	0.0
Other North America	16,535	0.1
South America	1,107,000	5.1
Argentina	97,422	0.5
Bolivia	33,637	0.2
Brazil	94,023	0.4
Chile	61,212	0.3
Colombia	303,918	1.4
Ecuador	147,867	0.7
Guyana	122,554	0.6
Peru	152,315	0.7
Uruguay	21,628	0.1
Venezuela	51,571	0.2
Other South America	20,853	0.1
Africa	400,691	1.9
Cape Verde	14,821	0.1
Egypt	68,662	0.3
Ethiopia	37,422	0.2
Ghana	21,714	0.1
Kenya	15,871	0.1
Morocco	21,529	0.1

Place of Birth	1990 Census Number	Percent
Nigeria	58,052	0.3
Senegal	2,369	0.0
South Africa	38,163	0.2
Other Africa	122,088	0.6
Oceania	122,137	0.6
Australia	52,469	0.2
Fiji	16,269	0.1
New Zealand	18,039	0.1
Tonga	11,040	0.1
Western Samoa	12,638	0.1
Other Oceania	11,682	0.1
Not reported	916,046	4.2

Note: The foreign-born population includes 1,864,285 persons who were born abroad of American parents. Data for foreign-born persons by place of birth, citizenship and year of entry is planned for 1993. The former Soviet Union is now referred to as the following geopolitical entities: Armenia, Azerbaijan, Byelarus, Georgia, Kazakhstan, Kyrgyzstan, Moldova, Russia, Tajikistan, Turkmenistan, Ukraine, and Uzbekistan.

Source: U.S. Department of Commerce, Bureau of the Census, Ethnic and Hispanic Branch, 1990 Census Special Tabulations.

Second part of article continues on page 59.

Part 2

Not Quite So Welcome Anymore

As reflected in a TIME poll, the public mood over immigration is turning sour again

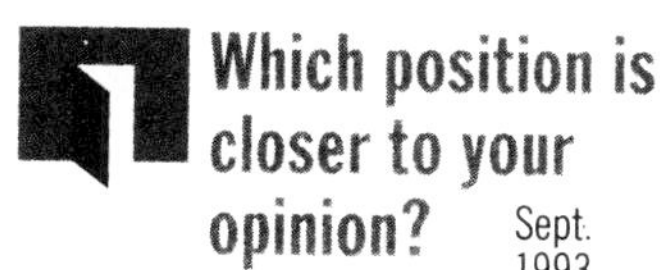

Which position is closer to your opinion?

	Sept. 1993	May 1985
Keep doors open to immigration	**24%**	**27%**
Strictly limit immigration	**73%**	**67%**

From a telephone poll of 1,108 adult Americans taken for TIME/CNN on Sept. 8-9 by Yankelovich Partners Inc. Sampling error is ±3%.

Are most immigrants coming into the U.S. legally or illegally?

	Poll answers	Actual breakdown 1992
Legally	**24%**	**76%**
Illegally	**64%**	**24%**

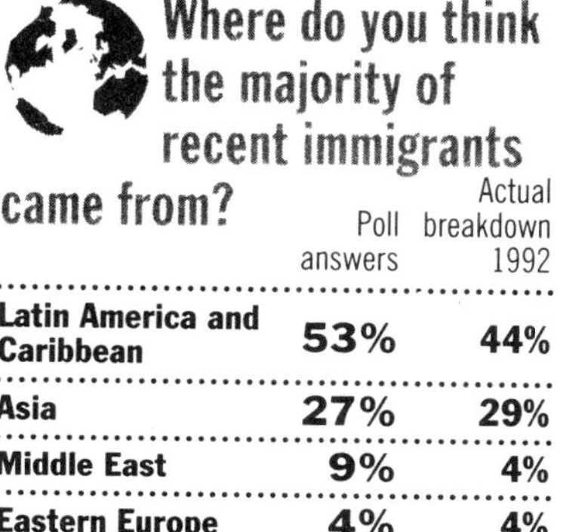

Where do you think the majority of recent immigrants came from?

	Poll answers	Actual breakdown 1992
Latin America and Caribbean	**53%**	**44%**
Asia	**27%**	**29%**
Middle East	**9%**	**4%**
Eastern Europe	**4%**	**4%**
Africa	**3%**	**3%**
India	**3%**	**4%**

Toward which group of recent immigrants do you feel most favorably and least favorably?

	Most favorable	Least favorable
Latin America and Caribbean	**22%**	**30%**
Eastern Europe	**20%**	**2%**
Asia	**18%**	**11%**
Africa	**6%**	**3%**
Middle East	**5%**	**26%**
India	**3%**	**2%**
None	**9%**	**10%**

BRUCE W. NELAN

AFTER NEW YORK'S WORLD TRADE Center is rocked by a thundering explosion, police round up a string of Arab immigrants as suspects, including an Egyptian radical who was admitted to the U.S. by mistake. Off the shore of New York's Long Island, a rusty tramp steamer called the *Golden Venture* runs aground, disgorging nearly 300 frightened Chinese trying to enter the country illegally; 10 die. Newly elected President Bill Clinton, reneging on a campaign promise, denies entry to Haitian boat people, then is blindsided by hostile public reaction when his first two choices for Attorney General turn out to have hired illegal immigrants as household help. When Texas border patrols mount a round-the-clock blockade along 20 miles of the Rio Grande, hundreds of Mexicans, many of whom commute illegally to day jobs in El Paso, angrily block traffic on a bridge between the U.S. and Mexico, chanting, "We want to work."

The incessant drumbeat of episodes like these has Americans increasingly concerned that their country is under siege and, in the popular phraseology, "has lost control of its own borders." In a study published last June, Bard College economist Dimitri Papadimitriou concluded that new laws were needed to head off "a bitter struggle between these new immigrants and disadvantaged segments of the U.S. population for increasingly scarce low-skill, low-wage jobs."

These sentiments recall a judgment voiced in a New York *Times* editorial: "There is a limit to our powers of assimilation, and when it is exceeded the country suffers from something very like indigestion." That observation was not made recently, however, but in May 1880, when anti-immigrant sentiment was also on the rise. Then too there was no effective limit on the number of immigrants entering the U.S. The hard fact is that when times are good, few worry about how many newcomers arrive; when times are tough, as they are now, cries of opposition invariably rise.

Many Americans are confused about whether the continuous inflow of immigrants makes the country stronger or weaker. Economic studies abound claiming that immigration spurs new businesses and new taxpayers. With no less conviction, others contend that immigrants and their children evade taxes and overburden local welfare, health and education systems. To compound the confusion, many Americans believe—wrongly—that more foreigners enter the country illegally than do legally. As the doubts grow, so does the potential for backlash. Polls show that almost two-thirds of Americans favor new laws to cut back on all immigrants and asylum seekers—legal as well as illegal. Though immigration is often regarded as a single issue, some distinctions are important:

▶ Legal immigrants. More than 1 million people are entering the U.S. legally every year. From 1983 through 1992, 8.7 mil-

> Once aliens enter the U.S., it is almost impossible to deport them, even if they have no valid documents. Thousands who enter illegally request asylum only if they are caught.

Would you favor changes in federal law to reduce the number of immigrants who enter the U.S. legally?

Favor	60%
Oppose	35%

Would you favor changes in federal law to reduce the number of immigrants who enter the U.S. illegally?

Favor	85%
Oppose	12%

How important is it for the Federal Government to track down illegal aliens living in the U.S.?

	Sept. 1993	May 1985
Extremely important	39%	36%
Somewhat important	41%	42%
Not worth the cost	18%	21%

Do these statements apply to immigrants who moved to the U.S. in the past 10 to 15 years?

	Yes
Are hardworking	67%
Are productive citizens once they get their feet on the ground	65%
Take jobs from Americans	64%
Add to the crime problem	59%
Are basically good, honest people	58%

lion of these newcomers arrived—the highest number in any 10-year period since 1910. A record 1.8 million were granted permanent residence in 1991. Because present law stresses family unification, these arrivals can bring over their spouses, sons and daughters: some 3.5 million are now in line to come in. Once here, they can bring in *their* direct relatives. As a result, there exists no visible limit to the number of legal entries.

►Illegal immigrants. This is what makes Americans almost unanimously furious. No one knows the numbers, of course, but official estimates put the illegal—or "undocumented"—influx at more than 300,000 a year currently and almost 5 million over the past 10 years.

►Asylum seekers. Until a few years ago, applications were rare, totaling 200 in 1975. Suddenly, asylum is the plea of choice in the U.S. and around the world, often as a cover for economic migration. U.S. applications were up to 103,000 last year, and the backlog tops 300,000 cases. Under the present asylum rules, practically anyone who declares that he or she is fleeing political oppression has a good chance to enter the U.S. Chinese are almost always admitted, for example, if they claim that China's birth-control policies have limited the number of children they can have.

Right now, once aliens enter the U.S., it is almost impossible to deport them, even if they have no valid documents. Thousands of those who enter illegally request asylum only if they are caught. The review process can take 10 years or more, and applicants often simply disappear while it is under way. Asylum cases are piling up faster than they can be cleared, with the Immigration and Naturalization Service falling farther behind every year. At her confirmation hearings at the end of September, Doris Meissner, Clinton's nominee as commissioner of the INS, conceded, "The asylum system is broken, and we need to fix it."

With pressure rising to do something about immigration, Clinton felt he had to get out and lead—if for no other reason than to head off draconian legislative proposals already in the works. The President put forward measures last July to tighten screening of potential immigrants abroad, speed deportations of phony asylum seekers and add 600 officers to the border patrol. "We will not," he declared, "surrender our borders to those who wish to exploit our history of compassion and justice."

The Administration has not, however, joined the national majority that now says it favors cutting back on legal immigration. Nevada Senator Harry Reid, a rising Democratic star in the immigration wars, has introduced a bill that would establish both an annual limit of 300,000 newcomers, including "immediate relatives," and a national identification card.

These measures, along with others from the House of Representatives, may come to life on Capitol Hill after the great debates on health care and the North

More than 100 million people around the world are currently displaced from their native land. Europe's xenophobia can only mean that more of them will want to come to the U.S.

Do you favor these proposals?

	Yes	No
Charge a small fee to each individual who crosses the border between the U.S. and Mexico or Canada in order to pay for tighter security at those borders.	70%	26%
Spend more federal tax money to tighten security at the border between the U.S. and Mexico.	65%	32%
Make it more difficult for people from other countries who claim they are the victims of persecution in their own countries to enter the U.S.	61%	35%
Require all U.S. citizens to carry a national ID card.	50%	48%
Stop providing government health benefits and public education to immigrants and their children.	47%	48%
Build a fence along the entire border between the U.S. and Mexico.	29%	68%

Would you favor a constitutional amendment to prevent children born here from becoming U.S. citizens unless their parents were also U.S. citizens?

Favor	49%
Oppose	47%

How much does the presence of illegal aliens in this country concern you?

	Sept. 1993	May 1985
Great deal	48%	43%
Somewhat	40%	44%
Not at all	12%	12%

American Free Trade Agreement are resolved. In fact, immigration questions already lurk beneath the surface of both these issues: should citizens carry a national medical identification card, and will the trade agreement lure more or fewer Mexicans north? Almost surely, Congress will try to reform immigration law again in 1994.

IMMIGRATION BACKLASH IS PARTICULARLY strong in New York, Florida, Texas and, most of all, California, which officials say contains more than half of all the illegal immigrants in the country. As the frequent bellwether of national changes, the state has already caught a low-grade fever from this issue. Governor Pete Wilson has won majority support for a proposed constitutional amendment that would prevent children born in the U.S. of illegal immigrants from automatically becoming citizens. Californians, more than most Americans, complain about special treatment for immigrants. TIME's poll indicates that 51% of Californians favor cutting off health benefits and public education to immigrants and their children, whereas nationally only 46% back such measures.

Because there is no national consensus, political leaders and activists stake out unpredictable and sometimes contradictory positions. Many liberals believe the doors should be open to all who seek new opportunities and hope to escape persecution. Other liberals argue that while open immigration policies are intrinsically good, they must be tempered to prevent newcomers from not only taking away American jobs but also competing with poor, ill-educated minorities already here.

Market-oriented conservatives still support immigration as a source of low-wage labor. But other conservatives call for immigration restrictions to halt the cultural transmogrification of American society. One of the most outspoken advocates for the latter is Daniel Stein, executive director of the Federation for American Immigration Reform, who favors a moratorium on all immigration, insisting that "nations do not have an unlimited capacity to absorb immigrants without irrevocably altering their own character"—an echo of a view enunciated more than a century ago.

But for all the hand wringing, American resistance falls far short of the hostility evident in Western Europe. Gangs of racist thugs in Britain engage in "Paki bashing." France has officially declared a target of "zero immigration." Germany insists it is "not a country of immigration," and neo-Nazis have taken the dictum literally enough to set fire to hostels for foreign workers and asylum seekers.

More than 100 million people around the world are currently displaced from their native land. Europe's xenophobia can only mean that more of them will want to come to the U.S. That is all the more reason for Americans to spend some time debating how many of them they are willing to take in. *—Reported by David Aikman/Washington and David S. Jackson/San Francisco*

(continued)

The Numbers Game

Altogether, the foreign born had a higher per capita income than the native born ($15,033 vs. $14,367) in 1989, but their median family income was almost $4,000 less than that of the native born ($31,785 vs. $35,508).

% of population under 18 that is foreign-born

- Los Angeles 21%
- San Francisco 19%
- Dade County (Miami) 18%
- New York City 12%
- Houston 10%
- Chicago 7%
- U.S. 3%

In 1976 there were 67 Spanish-speaking radio stations. Now there are 311, plus 3 Spanish-language TV networks and 350 Spanish-language newspapers.

Source: Market Segment Research, Inc.

Sources: Census Bureau, INS except where otherwise noted

32 MILLION PEOPLE IN THE U.S. (13%) SPEAK LANGUAGES OTHER THAN ENGLISH AT HOME.

Current Top 10 ancestry groups

		millions
1	German	58
2	Irish	39
3	English	33
4	African	24
5	Italian	15
6	Mexican	12
7	French	10
8	Polish	9
9	Native American	9
10	Dutch	6

IN 1940, 70% OF IMMIGRANTS CAME FROM EUROPE. IN 1992, 15% CAME FROM EUROPE, 37% FROM ASIA AND 44% FROM LATIN AMERICA AND THE CARIBBEAN.

JAPANESE AMERICANS marry non–Japanese Americans about 65% of the time, an out-marriage rate so high that since 1981 the number of babies born in the U.S. with one Japanese and one white parent has exceeded the number with two Japanese parents.

FOREIGN BORN AS A PERCENT OF TOTAL POPULATION

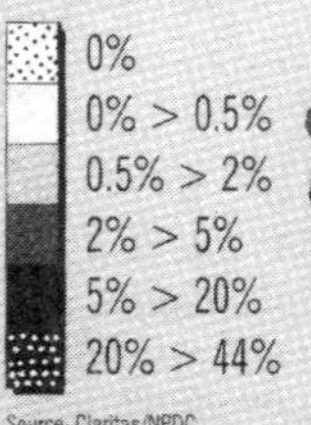

Source: Claritas/NPDC

The unemployment rate for the foreign born was 7.8% in 1990, compared with 6.2% for the native born.

Top 10 languages	Number of speakers in millions
1 English only	198.6
2 Spanish	17.3
3 French	1.7
4 German	1.5
5 Italian	1.3
6 Chinese	1.2
7 Tagalog	.8
8 Polish	.7
9 Korean	.6
10 Vietnamese	.5

In 1990 the population was: Anglo 76%, Black 12%, Latino 9%, Asian 3%. By 2050 the breakdown is projected to be: Anglo 52%, Black 16%, Latino 22%, Asian 10%.

% who eat these ethnic foods at least once a week	
Italian, other than pizza	39%
Mexican	21%
Chinese	18%
Cajun	5%
French	3%
Middle Eastern	3%
Indian	1%

Source: "Shopping for Health," Food Marketing Institute

Americans use 68% more spices today than a decade ago. The consumption of red pepper rose 105%, basil 190%.

Source: American Spice Trade Association

IN 1990 THERE WERE MORE EUROPEAN DESCENDANTS—including German, Irish, English, French, Dutch, Scots-Irish, Scottish, Swedish, Welsh and Danish, Portuguese, British and Swiss—living in California than in any other state. New York led in the number of Italians, Poles and Russians; Minnesota in Norwegians; Texas in Czechs; Pennsylvania in Slovaks; and Ohio in Hungarians.

Top 10 countries of origin for immigrants in fiscal year 1992	
Mexico	22%
Vietnam	8.0%
Philippines	6.3%
Soviet Union	4.5%
Dom. Republic	4.3%
China	4.0%
India	3.8%
El Salvador	2.7%
Poland	2.6%
United Kingdom	2.1%

More than 100 languages are spoken in the school systems of New York City, Chicago, Los Angeles and Fairfax County, Va.

Source: *Newcomers in American Schools*, Rand

The foreign-born population in 1990 totaled a record 19.8 million (8%), surpassing previous highs of 14 million in 1930 and 1980.

Since 1901, 30% of the U.S. Nobel prize-winners have been immigrants.

88% of African-born residents had a high school education or higher in 1990, compared with 76% of Asian-born, 57% of Caribbean-born and 77% of native-born.

Top 10 Christian religions

	% of population
1 Roman Catholic	26.2%
2 Baptist	19.4%
3 Protestant (no denomination supplied)	9.8%
4 Methodist	8.0%
5 Lutheran	5.2%
6 Christian (no denomination supplied)	4.8%
7 Presbyterian	2.8%
8 Pentecostal	1.8%
9 Episcopalian/Anglican	1.7%
10 Mormon/LDS	1.4%

Top 5 non-Christian religions

	% of population
1 Jewish	1.8%
2 Muslim/Islamic*	.5%
3 Buddhist*	.4%
4 Hindu*	.2%
5 Bahai	.01%

*Adjustments for undercounts due to language problems

Source: *One Nation Under God: Religion in Contemporary American Society* by Barry A. Kosmin and Seymour P. Lachman. Based on a telephone survey of 113,000 randomly dialed American households.

Seven out of 10 residents of Hialeah, Fla., are foreign-born. Other cities where more than half the population is foreign-born:

Miami, Fla. **60%**
Huntington Park, Calif. **59%**
Union City, N.J. **55%**
Monterey Park, Calif. **52%**
Miami Beach, Fla., Santa Ana, Calif. **51%** each

Is Latest Wave a Drain or Boon to Society?

Critics want to focus more on skills, less on family ties

Maria Puente

USA TODAY

What once were private mutterings that immigrants are more a drain than a benefit to society have become bold public pronouncements.

Many politicians and ordinary citizens now say legal immigrants should be admitted only if they have good job skills, not because they happen to have a sister living in New York.

Some even say immigrants, arriving at near-record levels, are radically changing the ethnic and cultural balance of the country—and the country needs to change back.

The question before Congress and the people has become: Are immigrants still good for the country?

In a computer analysis of data on the 2.2 million people who became legal immigrants in 1993–93, USA TODAY illustrates how newcomers have changed the nation, bringing new colors and languages, a new vibrancy and vigor.

But the analysis also documents how densely immigrants from a few countries have clustered in some cities, bringing strained public budgets, community tension and, often, few marketable job skills.

Using current proposals to restrict immigration as its framework, the computer analysis finds:

• If job skills replaced kinship as the basis for immigration, it would greatly alter who gets into the country. The immigrant stream would become more European and Asian, less Hispanic and Caribbean.

In 1993, for example, 52% of immigrants from Mexico—by far the largest immigrant group—identified themselves as laborers, excluding homemakers, retirees and students. That compared to 7% from China and 1% from India.

By contrast, 0.3% of Mexicans identified themselves as engineers, compared to 25% of Indians.

Overall, more than half the 1993 immigrants of working age report low-skilled or unskilled occupations.

• If immigration of extended families had been restricted in 1993, 85% of the 880,014 people admitted to the USA would have gotten in.

Indeed, the analysis underscores the overwhelming family character of immigration. In 1993, almost two-thirds of immigrants were admitted solely because they were related—either closely or in an extended fashion—to someone already here.

• If a small but growing minority of restrictionists gets its way, future immigrants would be far different from those who actually arrived.

In 1993, about 80% of legal immigrants were from Latino, Asian, African and Caribbean countries, and just a few countries dominated the stream: People from Mexico, China, the Philippines, Vietnam and the Dominican Republic made up nearly 40% of all immigrants.

By comparison, 97% of immigrants who came 100 years ago were European or Canadian.

• If immigrants came for jobs instead of kinship, they likely would be scattered across the USA.

Between 1991–93, however, the nation's immigrant clusters stood out. Selected ZIP codes in New York City, Los Angeles, Chicago, Miami and Houston together averaged 206,000 new immigrants a year.

The cumulative effect of all these trends, experts say, has pushed so many social buttons that a nation of immigrants is wondering whether it should remain one.

There is "uneasiness over the scale of immigration," Nathan Galzer, a Harvard professor and immigration expert, says in a recent essay. "When this coincides with bad economic conditions, a majority of Americans will say, 'There is too much immigration.' "

Here is one fact: If immigration continues at the current rate of about 800,000 a year, more than 8 million newcomers will have arrived between 1990 and 2000—the highest decade-long number since 1900–1910.

59% FAVOR 'BLENDING IN'

For 30 years, since the 1965 Immigration Act opened the nation's doors to immigrants from around the world, the country's political and social culture has assumed that immigration is a positive force.

Many Americans are not feeling so generous these days.

"Now we're coming at (immigration) from a new perspective—what's in the best interest of American *citizens*," says Rep. Lamar Smith, R-Texas, head of the House subcommittee on immigration.

His counterpart in the Senate, Alan Simpson, R-Wyo., echoes that view: "The national interest is the interest of the majority of Americans, not the interests of those seeking to come here or (their) relatives."

Smith and Simpson argue the United States should reduce overall numbers and admit only those "who will contribute to our economy and our society"—meaning those who are educated, job-skilled, English-speaking and quickly naturalized.

A USA TODAY/CNN/Gallup Poll of immigrants—the first comprehensive, national poll of its kind—finds many immigrants agree.

"If we are not selective on immigrants, it will expedite the deterioration of this country," says David Chen, 30, an insurance adjuster in New York who came from Taiwan. "They have to be self-supportive."

Immigrants and natives also are in agreement about the need for immigrants to assimilate: 59% of both groups say "blending in" is better.

Luis Llanos, 25, a Colombian who immigrated in 1986 and now lives in New York, says he's eager to fit in.

"Some (immigrants) say they don't like it here, but I say to them, 'Nobody brought you here, you don't have to be here,' " Llanos says.

But there is a viable, vocal coalition of immigrant advocates led by Sen. Ted Kennedy, D-Mass., who say they'll fight to preserve the traditional view of immigrants.

"We live in a diverse world," says Kennedy, sponsor of the 1965 law. "The genius of America has been to take different traditions and draw on them (to) enhance the country."

'SENSE OF LOSS OF CONTROL'

In part, the drive to change the immigration system is a consequence of public resentment of unchecked illegal immigration, now estimated at about 300,000 people a year.

Few politicians can ignore the overwhelming passage last year of Proposition 187 in California, which denies illegal immigrants access to benefits, schools and health services.

"There is this sense of loss of control," says Bill Ong Hing, an immigration expert at Stanford University. "I don't think we have (lost control), but there's a sense of that."

Add to that the uncertainty caused by the economic restructuring of the '90s, both in high and low level jobs.

In Atlanta, for example, seeing sizeable immigration for the first time, an undercurrent of tension has developed over fears about jobs.

Some "see immigrants as a threat to their job opportunities," says Jeffery Tapia, director of the Latin American Association. "When you're looking to survive, anyone who's a newcomer is seen as a threat."

But the impetus for change also may be based on a change in the immigrants themselves.

Today, Europeans make up just 18% of the immigrant stream, with 54% of newcomers from Asia, Africa and the Caribbean.

Most of these immigrants are not white, and some advocates say restrictionism is, at base, racism.

"A lot of their (arguments) are code words for, 'We don't want Mexicans or Asians,' " says Karen Narasaki of the National Asian Pacific American Legal Consortium.

A few restrictionists are blunt.

"Why this many? Why these particular immigrants? These questions are never addressed," says journalist Peter Brimelow, author of *Alien Nation,* a controversial book about "America's immigration disaster."

But these questions are being addressed by the national Commission on Immigration Reform, which this month called on Congress to cut immigration to 550,000 a year, largely by eliminating some categories of immigrants and reducing others.

Should immigration levels . . .

	All	Immigrants
Decrease	65%	30%
Stay the same	24%	44%
Increase	7%	15%

Should immigrants be encouraged to . . .

	All	Immigrants
Blend into American culture	59%	59%
Maintain own culture more	32%	29%
Both equally	4%	10%

Source: USA TODAY/CNN/Gallup Poll

By Cliff Vancura, USA TODAY

MANY WANT A 'TIME OUT'

Even assuming some change in immigration is necessary, there's no consensus on what kind. The various factions overlap on some important details but strongly disagree on others. Conservatives and liberals can be found on the same side:

• The *Alien Nation* faction argues there are too many immigrants and too many of the "wrong kind"—instead of skilled, white Europeans. They want a "time out" in immigration, and the highest priority to go to newcomers with skills.

Brimelow argues that immigration has changed the country "in a radical and rapid way unprecedented in history."

"Americans have the right to insist the government stop shifting the racial balance," he says.

Republican presidential candidate Patrick Buchanan supports this view, as do most restrictionist groups.

• Another faction argues that the system is mostly working, and the number of immigrants is acceptable, but that not enough is being done to "Americanize" them.

House Speaker Newt Gingrich is in this camp, along with GOP leaders Bill Bennett and Jack Kemp and many Democrats in Congress.

• Yet another faction favors even more generous immigration policies. Kennedy is a major voice here, along with a throng of advocacy groups. House Majority Leader Dick Armey, R-Texas, also is a philosophical ally.

"I'm hard-pressed to think of a single problem that would be solved by shutting off the supply of willing and eager new Americans," says Armey.

So far, President Clinton comes down somewhere in the middle, and backs the commission's proposals.

'WE HAVE TO DISCRIMINATE'

The profusion of immigration issues is bewildering, but these are some of the points of contention:

2. IMMIGRATION AND THE AMERICAN EXPERIENCE

The numbers. Because the commission is so influential, its recommendation for a relatively modest one-third reduction in the number of immigrants is likely to be adopted.

"Between the total restrictionists and the total open-border people, that's where we'll steer the boat," says Simpson.

Chain migration. The bulk of immigrants are spouses, children, grandchildren, siblings and parents of citizens or legal permanent residents. And once immigrants arrive, they may sponsor more relatives.

Wei Ming Wong, 41, an immigrant living in Los Angeles, can tick off 12 relatives who came to the USA thanks to one sister. "There is no one left" in Hong Kong, Wong says.

Cutting this chain migration is at the heart of the commission's proposals. It recommended immigration priority to go to nuclear families—spouses and minor children—and that the door be shut to siblings, their families and adult children.

These recommendations probably will be adopted by Congress.

Immigrant skills. Critics argue that immigration would best serve the nation if admissions were weighted on the basis of skills.

"We have to discriminate among people who want to come," says George Borjas, an economist at the University of California, San Diego, and a Cuban immigrant. "Choosing high-skilled workers is better."

Accepting that, the commission wants to eliminate 10,000 immigration slots now set aside for unskilled workers; Congress is likely to agree.

Immigrants and welfare. People cannot immigrate if they are likely to become a public charge. But courts have ruled that sponsorship "contracts" aren't enforceable.

Even advocates agree that's a huge loophole, and Congress is virtually certain to plug it. "We're going to look at sponsorship, set additional responsibilities," says Kennedy.

In addition, bills in Congress would cut off non-citizens from Supplementary Security Income—a program that provides aid to the poor and disabled. Non-citizens now make up about 30% of all SSI recipients.

The debate over all these aspects of immigration will begin in earnest this summer, and most experts are betting that the nation's door will close somewhat—but not entirely.

"The U.S. is largely what it is today because of our ability to draw and assimilate new peoples," says Arthur Helton, immigration expert at the Open Society Institute. "That has . . . resulted in displacement and conflict from time to time, but without it, we would not be America."

Solidarity Doesn't Mean Lost Identity

What unites the 263 million diverse people who make up America? The answer may be our character—that mixture of honesty and strength that Americans have always valued.

Stephen Goode

Surveying the 56 men from 13 colonies assembled in Philadelphia to draw up and ultimately sign the Declaration of Independence, John Adams, who later would succeed George Washington as president of the United States, despaired of them ever reaching consensus:

"Here is a diversity of religions, educations, manners, interest, such as it would seem almost impossible to unite in one plan of conduct," he confided in a letter to a friend.

Benjamin Franklin was of like mind, fearful that the colonists might not join together in the oncoming struggle with Great Britain. "We must all hang together," Franklin is said to have warned his fellow delegates when they were putting their names to the Declaration. "We must indeed all hang together, or assuredly we shall all hang separately."

What binds a diverse country like the United States — or, put another way, what holds together this nation of such great variety — has been a question that has been with the country from its inception, and one that continues to puzzle Americans today.

The cosmopolitan Franklin, a world-famous author who became the toast of France and Europe, said he found it odd that Americans could claim to be Rhode Islanders or Virginians first and Americans second. He argued there was a deeper unity, though he failed to define what it was, that made the people of the New World one people, and citizens of their colonies second. But many others have felt differently — and passionately so. Thomas Jefferson, for example, described himself as a Virginian and Adams wrote of himself as a man of Massachusetts.

In the 19th century, a divided nation fought a civil war — the bloodiest war of its history — unable to decide what might be agreed upon to bring the nation together, rather than allow it to fragment. And today — in the age of multiculturalism — Americans once again are apt to hear more about what divides them, rather than what brings them together. The United States — the nation that columnist Ben Wattenburg has called "the first universal nation" because its people come from everywhere — seems less universal than contentiously particular.

Black separatists argue that black Americans should go it alone. On campuses, African-American student centers are off limits to whites. And there are separatist movements among Hispanic Americans and Asian Americans, which argue that their peoples have no share in the American Dream. White-supremacist groups add their complaints that the same dream has been stolen from them and should be returned.

Nor does the social disorder end there. The old WASP leadership that once formed America's elite mostly is gone and the values of hard work and self-restraint that they professed are held up to ridicule by new generations that regard such qualities as narrow, self-destructive and unattractive. Ours has become an age in which deconstructionists have made it politically correct to deny that there is any such thing as an American core culture. In fact, Yale University refuses millions rather than instruct undergraduates in the character of that culture.

The French political writer Alexis de Tocqueville believed that such chaos always hovers near the center of a democracy. "Aristocracy made a chain of all the members of a community," from peasant to king, he wrote. "But democracy breaks that chain and severs every link of it."

> *Out of compassion, perhaps, public schools have emphasized minority cultures at the expense of core American values and ideals.*

What if anything unites the 263 million souls who now make up the United States? The question may have as many answers as there are Americans. Former Librarian of Congress Daniel J. Boorstin, author of the multivolume study *The Americans*, found deep in his scholarship that what Americans hold in common is "the ongoing search for a nation."

"The idea of the search is what holds us together," Boorstin tells **Insight**. "We are a people on a quest. We go and look for the kind of nation we want. The quest is the enduring American experiment. The meaning is in the seeking."

Boorstin sees Americans as always rallying around such goals — listed in the Declaration of Independence — as "life, liberty and the pursuit of happiness."

"Particularly the *pursuit*," he says.

Others prefer a less philosophical definition of citizenship. "It's a question of identifying with your friends in opposition to your enemies," says Thomas Fleming, editor of *Chronicles*, a monthly journal of opinion published by the Rockford Institute. "Your fellow citizens

The Idea of America

French aristocrat Alexis de Tocqueville visited the United States in the 1830s. The result was one of the masterpieces of writing about the young country, *Democracy in America*. An admirer of the American experiment, de Tocqueville nonetheless was deeply aware of the problems faced by the United States and nowhere more so than when he wrote about the necessity for citizens to have "ideas in common" they could turn to, despite the diversity of the people who inhabited the new country.

His words may be as appealing to Americans today as they were to Americans of more than a century and a half ago:

"Without ideas in common, there is no common action, and, without common action, there may still exist human beings, but not a social entity. In order for society to exist, and, even more, to prosper, it is then necessary that the spirits of all the citizens be assembled and held together by certain leading ideas; and that cannot happen unless each of them comes from time to time to draw his opinions from the same source, and unless each consents to receive a certain number of ready-made beliefs."

Alexis de Tocqueville *saw us whole.*

may not be the best people in the world ... but you will fight to defend them. [Nationality means] that I'm part of something and I don't have a choice."

He warns of efforts "to impose an artificial identity" — an overall Americanness — on people who don't share that identity because of regional, ethnic or other differences. To Fleming the idea that America is "dedicated to a proposition," be it universal equality or the pursuit of happiness, is both foolish and false. When he hears the word *proposition*, Fleming says, he thinks of "a guy trying to pick up loose women in a bar." That's a man "dedicated to a proposition," Fleming quips.

Somewhere between Fleming's skepticism and Boorstin's idealism, University of Alabama history professor Forrest McDonald argues "for a sense of Americanness that came with national identity," from the very beginning of the country, despite the fact of important, abiding regional loyalties. But he notes that "it wasn't until World War II that we ever fought a war as a totally united people."

McDonald tells **Insight** that among Americans today "there is a great deal more commonality than the media would have us believe." He cites the American intervention in Bosnia, which raised President Bill Clinton's approval ratings at a time when they had been falling. Even among the many who disapprove of him, says McDonald, the operative phrase is "rally around the leader."

McDonald thinks the things Americans hold in common have been around since the nation's founding. "They [the Founding Fathers] were very self-conscious about the magnitude of what they were undertaking, the shaping of history itself." And although they wouldn't have put it this way, says McDonald, "they were aware of the need to establish myths to hold the nation together."

Personal courage, honesty and the obligations of civic duty are values around which some of the myths developed, according to McDonald. And these virtues were subsumed under the word *character* — that mixture of truthfulness, solidity and steadfastness that the Founding Fathers believed essential to the citizenry of the new republic and on which its existence would depend, according to McDonald.

Historian Gordon S. Wood concurs in his 1979 classic, *The Creation of the American Republic*. "The essential question raised in debates Americans had with themselves in 1776 over the wisdom of independence was social: Were Americans the stuff republicans were made of?" wrote Wood.

Some have answered with a loud no, Americans didn't have that stuff — and probably still don't. Michael Lind, for example, a senior editor at the *New Republic* and author of *The Next American Nation*, sees racism as always corrupting and undermining our core myths, however potent they might be. "From the Founding Fathers all the way up until the mid-20th century, the American elite thought of America as an Anglo-Saxon or a white nation and they never really knew what to do with the nonwhites," he says. Lind looks for the emergence of a "liberal nationalism" in which loyalties in America transcend race and background.

For Lind, "Americans of different races share a common culture" that includes language. "There's a historic culture that makes you American," that includes "certain kinds of sports and holidays, folkways, and mores and manners and customs," but that's about it, according to Lind.

Nonetheless, Gordon Wood concluded that it was the question of character that was "surely the most important and most sensitive issue of all [for the Founding Fathers], for it involved ... the kind of people Americans were and wanted to be."

Wood doesn't stand alone. Walt Whitman, the great visionary poet of America, also saw character as central to American nationhood. "Sole among nationalities, these States have assumed the task to put in forms of lasting power and practicality ... the democratic republican principle," Whitman wrote. And that principle, he concluded, was "the theory of the development and perfection [of individual man] by voluntary standards, and self-reliance."

Facetiously, in a poem, Whitman asked Americans if their problems would be answered outside of their own character: "Were you looking to be held together by lawyers? Or by an agreement on paper?" No "living thing will so cohere," he answered.

Worried about a marked decline in the character of Americans in the first half of the 19th century, the people began a vast effort to improve it, according to Hoover Institution economist Thomas Sowell in his most recent book, *The Vision of the Anoint-*

ed. A public alarm sounded out in mid-century against "drunkenness, violence, and crime," he writes. This concern "led to massive campaigns against these social ills ... by numerous organizations at both local and national levels," a movement that included religious revivals, a temperance movement, and the creation of groups such as the Young Men's Christian Association and uniformed police departments, according to Sowell.

The result was "an all-out effort on many fronts against social degeneracy," an effort — private and nongovernmental — that paid off with a marked decline in alcohol consumption (down by 1850 to one-fifth of what it had been 20 years earlier!) and in crime rates across the board.

This great national search for character included the public-school system, creation of which began in the 19th century. The determination to develop character "was the reason the public schools were created," says Don Eberly, head of the Commonwealth Foundation, a Harrisburg, Pa., think tank. According to Eberly, "the ultimate purpose behind [public] education was to supply the nation with individuals capable of self-restraint and respect for others." This the schools did by giving students ample exposure to the stories of America's founding — and to tales whose overriding themes were always what makes solid citizens and people of strong character, according to Eberly. For him it's the anxiety over good character — and the lack of it — that concerns most Americans today and links them closely to their 19th-century counterparts.

"It's incivility in the streets and the lack of public manners at the shopping mall. It's the fact that private conduct is not governed by concerns for the social consequences. There's the avoidance of self-restraint," Eberly says. What people recognize is the absence of character because "everybody knows character in their neighbor when they see it," according to Eberly.

"You can get government out of things all you want," Eberly tells **Insight**, but it may not be big government that's at fault. "If the social institutions aren't working then things won't get better." The "American conversation is shifting toward" questions such as, "Are Americans still capable of self-governance?"

And Eberly claims "the ideology of unlimited personal liberation has really run its course." What's crashing, he says, "is the endless tolerance for every individual to fashion his or her own values." Change, he claims, is being felt in the schools where new curricula are being developed emphasizing character, and where more and more teachers, administrators, and (perhaps above all) parents realize "the alternative to some set of fundamental shared values is social chaos," says Eberly.

After winning consensus, *the time had come to sign the Declaration of Independence.*

Eberly sees any solution as one that first must be written in the hearts of men and women — a matter of character and not ideology. It is interesting that at the same time men of opinions as differing as those of the Library of Congress' Boorstin and Fleming of *Chronicles* regard rigid, doctrinaire ideology of any kind as dangerous and particularly un-American, primarily because they see such ideology as inhumane and as having no regard for the everyday life of individuals.

"The menace is ideology, the dogma of politics. It is a prison that makes [the American] experiment impossible," declares Boorstin. Moreover, it's contrary to the spirit of the Founding Fathers, "who had the courage to doubt that they had all the answers and made Amendment" to the Constitution possible, he says.

For Fleming, ideologies such as an advocacy of strong federal power is a notion that runs roughshod over regional loyalties, and is used "to subvert states' rights and destroy the powers of local communities." This undermines that delicate balance between the federal government's power and the power of the states and the people that should characterize American society.

He notes that "one of the reasons we live in a federal republic was because [the Founding Fathers] knew that nationhood on such a large scale was hard to maintain." Human beings think best in terms of where they live day-to-day.

And Fleming rightly warns, "The more we think in terms of that which is universal and abstract, the less we are able to shoulder the burdens of everyday life — taking care of our own family, being decent to your neighbor." Being good universally, he says, "is too big a moral burden for an individual to maintain."

A similar concern for the significance of roots is voiced by Alabama's McDonald, who deplores the almost universal ignorance of history among the young. Smart or dumb, "they know little or nothing about the past. They don't know where they are in space and time." If this is so, who can blame them for seeming lost?

What unites Americans indeed may be finally indefinable and impalpable, but nonetheless real. It may be what Abraham Lincoln called upon in his second inaugural address, delivered a month before his assassination and two months before the end of the Civil War.

Lincoln wanted Americans to find common purpose, despite the horrors of the war: "Though passion may have strained, it must not break our bonds of affection. The mystic chords of memory, stretching from every battlefield, and patriot grave, to every living heart and hearthstone, all over this broad land will yet swell the chorus of the Union, when again touched, as surely they will be, by the better angels of our nature."

Michael Rust contributed to this story.

Citizenship Is a Malleable Concept

BARBARA CROSSETTE

UNITED NATIONS

In an era of raw nationalism and turbulent migration across the globe, the debate over who belongs in a country and who doesn't is becoming more harsh. Just who has the right to be a citizen?

In the United States, a campaign to control immigration and limit citizenship is growing, with Republicans proposing that children born to illegal immigrants be denied citizenship and the right to free public education. Last month, erecting another barrier to citizenship, President Clinton signed a welfare law cutting benefits to immigrants, even those legally in the country.

In France, laws tightening conditions for French residence and citizenship have prompted protests and hunger strikes by Africans under deportation orders. And in the new countries of the former Soviet Union, drives to make language a criterion of citizenship have threatened to leave millions stateless, if not homeless.

Such cases illustrate that citizenship is far from a universally agreed upon concept. Rosemary Jenks, director of policy analysis at the independent Center for Immigration Studies in Washington, said methods of determining citizenship vary widely around the world, although countries rely on one of two basic criteria.

One becomes a citizen either by being born in the country or by descent—that is, by being born of a citizen or someone with citizen's rights, sometimes but not always a legal immigrant of that country. In 1993, the center found that only 12 of 38 nations surveyed granted birthright citizenship, among them the United States, Canada, India, New Zealand and Spain.

For immigrants, there are naturalization processes, though in most countries these are long, difficult and not automatic steps to citizenship. And in any case laws don't tell the whole story. Ms. Jenks said even countries with seemingly liberal statutes on the books give officials wide discretion to withhold citizenship for cultural or political reasons.

In Asia, as in Europe, the notion of citizenship may be rooted deeply in ethnicity and culture, closely related to long-established national boundaries. It can be hard to give up as well as obtain.

Reflecting his country's strong allegiance to heritage, Thailand's Prime Minister once told Thai-American children born in California that they must always think of themselves as Thais first. Indian-Americans, both citizens and immigrants, argue passionately in the letters columns of the New York newspaper India Abroad about how much they should or should not try to integrate into American life.

In Africa, ethnic identity runs thicker than national citizenship, reflecting the fact that the continent's national borders were put in place a mere hundred years ago by colonialists who drew lines on maps without reference to the people in them.

Countries have many ways to make sure outsiders stay outsiders.

"South Africa is perhaps the only country where we might see a real mosaic of ethnicities included in the concept of citizenship," said Thomas R. Lansner, a writer on Africa and a professor of international affairs at Columbia University. Elsewhere in Africa, passports may mean nothing as ethnically related people travel across boundaries to visit and trade, he said.

With at least one in every 21 people on Earth now on the move as a refugee or displaced person, tides of migration and explosions of nationalism are already rewriting citizenship, immigration and asylum laws. At the same time, people and governments are grasping for other ways to draw a line around themselves.

It can start with what you wear. In the Himalayan kingdom of Bhutan, a people of Tibetan descent threatened by an influx of Nepali-speaking outsiders decided some years ago to enforce the wearing of a traditional costume that was alien to ethnic minorities—a kind of visual identity card in the image of the majority. Similarly, Laos once required women to wear traditional sarongs to work in government offices.

In many places, new debates are under way over language, which can be a useful unifier of people or an unnecessary divider. In the United States, the most tolerant nation toward outsiders by far, rising immigration has prompted a movement to codify English as the national language.

Language Barrier

Arthur C. Helton, an international lawyer who directs migration programs at the Open Society Institute in New York, says language is a handy tool for governments "to include or exclude those it wishes from the community."

From the Baltics to Kazakhstan, many people—most but not all of them Russians—are being eliminated from participation in public life and sometimes barred from schools because they do not speak the new official language. Or their assimilation is made more difficult by the imposition of stringent language requirements.

Language campaigns can have disastrous unintended consequences, says a Sri Lankan poet, Anne Ranasinghe, who has been a citizen of three nations. Born a Jew in Germany, she fled to England, where she married a Sri Lankan and adopted his country, then Ceylon, as her own in 1952.

Four years later, the "Sinhala only" language policy gave the ethnic Sinhalese majority advantages over Tamils and all other minorities, be they Malay, European or Arab. Schoolchildren were divided linguistically, and people on an island where Buddhism, Hinduism, Islam and Christianity all flourished soon became conscious of religious differences. Tens of thousands have since died in ethnic warfare and terrorism.

"I don't believe in patriotism," Ms. Ranasinghe said. "I think it's dangerous. But on the other hand there has to be a certain concern for one's country. Here, we are now simply concerned with our own groups, religious communities or philosophical attitudes. Nobody cares for anyone else. We have lost the feeling of citizenship."

Held in War, Latins Seek Reparations

Japanese Descent, They Were Interned

TIM GOLDEN

SAN FRANCISCO, Aug. 28— They were pulled from schoolhouses in Colombia and Bolivia and from offices and stores around Lima, Peru. Warships carried them to the United States, and trains left them at desolate camps near places like Missoula, Mont., and Crystal City, Tex. Most of them remained there, under guard and behind fences, for years.

Although more than 2,000 of these Latin Americans of Japanese descent were deported to the United States in World War II, and forcibly interned on the orders of President Franklin D. Roosevelt, they have been little more than a footnote in this nation's history.

When the Federal Government began issuing apologies and reparations checks to Japanese-Americans held in the camps, most of those who came from Latin America were left out. Today, they began a campaign for redress. In a class-action suit filed in Federal district court in Los Angeles, hundreds of people uprooted from at least a dozen Latin American countries asked the United States Government for the same consideration it has given to Japanese-Americans under the Civil Liberties Act of 1988.

"Why are we left out?" asked Arthur Shibayama, a retired gas station owner from San Jose, Calif., who was deported from Peru as a boy, held for years in a Texas camp, and was then denied United States citizenship for years even though he had served in Europe as a soldier for the United States.

A demand for equal treatment 50 years after being uprooted and detained.

"We suffered at least as much as the Japanese-Americans, maybe more," Mr. Shibayama said. "I want the United States Government to take responsibility for the suffering that my family and my friends went through."

In addition to the formal apology and the reparations payments of $20,000 available to the Japanese-Americans interned in the camps, plaintiffs asked for punitive damages but did not specify any amount.

A spokesman for the Justice Department, Myron Marlin, said the Government would have no comment on the details of the lawsuit. But Mr. Marlin argued that in denying benefits to most of the internees who were brought to the camps from Latin America, the Clinton Administration was simply applying a law over which it has had no influence.

"Congress, in passing the law, determined that it would set up a requirement that people should have been citizens in order to get reparations," Mr. Marlin said, "That is the law that we are enforcing and administering today."

Little explanation was given for why the Latin Americans were mostly excluded as amends began to be made in 1990. But officials have argued in essence that those brought to the camps from abroad were illegal immigrants and therefore not entitled to the same rights as the Japanese-American internees, of whom there were about 100,000.

Mr. Marlin noted that any Japanese Latin American who was granted citizenship by 1952 was given it retroactively to the time they arrived in this country. About 150 such people had qualified for reparations, he said, and the office of redress administration, in the Justice Department, had searched for others.

One of the lawyers who filed the suit today, Robin S. Toma, described the Government's position as a perverse catch-22.

"The Government was not telling these people that they could apply for citizenship," said Mr. Toma, the son of Japanese-American internees. "They were telling them that they were being deported."

Of the 2,264 people of Japanese ancestry who were deported from Latin America, Mr. Toma said, nearly all of those who met the Congressional test were people who happened to have been helped by a single civil-rights lawyer in northern California. In 1952, the lawyer arranged for retroactive citizenship for scores of Latin Americans who were then facing deportation.

According to the 1982 report to Congress of a special commission that studied the Government's wartime internment policies in the preparation for the 1988 law, the Japanese Latin Americans were among about 3,000 Latin Americans from at least a dozen countries who were held [in] camps in the United States in World War II. The remainder were Latin Americans of German and Italian descent.

The arrest and transfer of Latin Americans to United States camps began, the report noted, as "a controlled, closely monitored deportation program to detain potentially dangerous diplomatic and consular officials." But the exercise quickly deteriorated into one in which prominent members of Japanese communities were rounded up and shipped off with no regard to their national loyalties.

With the encouragement of the Roosevelt Administration, Brazil, which had the largest Japanese population in Latin America, interned thousands of Japanese, In all, about 8,500 Latin Americans who had come from the Axis countries were held in 16 Latin nations.

The roughly 26,000 Japanese living in Peru became special targets. Although many of the country's Japanese immigrants had gone there as low-paid farm laborers at the turn of the century, they were the victims of cultural prejudices like those directed at Peru's Indian majority. Their success in business during an era of general economic difficulties deepened the resentment against them.

Libia Yamamoto, the sales manager for a charter bus company in San Francisco, recalled how the local constable in her hometown, Chiclayo, on Peru's northern coast, arrived one night in January 1943, apologizing sympathetically to her father, the well-known owner of a store on the local sugar plantation. Then the constable took her father away.

Nearly eight months later, the family was reunited in Crystal City, Tex., where Mrs. Yamamoto's parents were told that they and others would be deported to Japan in exchange for American civilians being held there.

The family managed to avoid joining the roughly 900 Japanese Latin Americans deported to Japan in such exchanges when her father became ill and was hospitalized. Over the years, Mrs. Yamamoto said, she entered classes for American citizenship and picked up application forms, only to have her efforts founder on one question: had she ever been deported from any country?

"I always got to that point," she said, "and I didn't have the right answer."

Indigenous Ethnic Groups

The contemporary issues of Native Americans as well as the descendants of all conquered indigenous peoples add their weight to the claims for cultural justice, equal protection, and due process in our hemisphere. As North and South America marked the 500th anniversary of Christopher Columbus's voyage of discovery, the indigenous peoples of the Americas explored their roots and new remedies for the conquest that turned many into a permanent underclass.

The following articles represent a cross section of the current experience of indigenous ethnic groups, their forced accommodation of a high-tech world, the environmental and cultural effects of rapid change, and the challenges to a renewal of their identifying traditions. The indigenous ethnic populations remember and invite us to recall their struggles, to find ways of shaping and sharing the new sense of pluralism offered within the American experience and the spiritual sources of ethnic identity that persons encounter as the legitimacy of ancient practices widens.

Indigenous ethnic communities have been plagued by a complex array of historical, social, cultural, and economic factors. As a result, in the late twentieth century, the traditions of indigenous ethnic groups have been renegotiated by yet another generation. The North and South American economies and pluralistic cultures are a challenging stage for their quest for self-sufficiency as well as their aspirations for the preservation of a unique cultural legacy. Current indigenous ethnic leaders challenge past perceptions. They find it increasingly difficult to strike a balance between traditional values and new demands. Native Americans' challenge of the American legal system is part of this current redefinition. Finally, however, they are challenging themselves to be themselves.

Novel approaches toward the peaceful reconciliation of conflict should be explored more thoroughly. For example, unlike conflict between ethnic groups in the United States, conflict between the United States and Native Americans is regulated by treaties. The struggle over claims regarding the rights of nations and the interests of the U.S. government and its citizens is no longer at the margin of public affairs. Does the definition of this conflict as an issue of foreign and not domestic policy provide a meaningful distinction? Should the claims of ethnic groups in defense of culture, territory, and unique institutions be honored and protected by law and public policy?

Ethnicity is built upon the truth and strength of a tradition. Senses of family and community, and an unwillingness to give up, have led to standoffs with many forces within America. In this light, this unit details ways in which an ethnic group retrieves its rights and heritage to preserve an ancient culture from amnesia and extinction.

The expansion and profitability of Native American gambling casinos, their attendant impact on state and local economies, and the tax exemptions enjoyed by these ventures appear to be headed toward contentions that may spill over into new issues of public order.

On the international level, the discussion of human and cultural rights of peoples guaranteed in the United Nations and the traditional mode of state sovereignty indicates that a fragile accommodation between indigenous people and the mainstream societies at whose margins they exist may be entering a new phase. Their unequal relationship began with the consolidation of large territorial political and economic regimes. Under scrutiny are personal rights and group rights, pluralistic realms that ensure transnational solidarity, and cultural and religious challenges to those in authority fueled by the passion for power at those intersections between modernity and tradition—the large-scale institutional versus the local and culturally specific community.

Looking Ahead: Challenge Questions

How should commitments to the self-determination of people be ensured and enforced? What levels of tolerance are assumed by the UN Working Group? What value conflicts, if any, are beyond compromise? How does gaming affect the work ethic?

What are the most compelling issues that face indigenous ethnic communities? Adoption? Economic? Culture?

What social, economic, and political conditions will affect the next indigenous ethnic generation?

Because of the strides of the current Native American community, will the next generation enter the middle class of America? Should that be a goal? Why?

What moral guides do American public and private bureaucratic systems have for addressing the challenges of fairness and impartiality? For group claims? For personal claims? For privacy?

UNIT 3

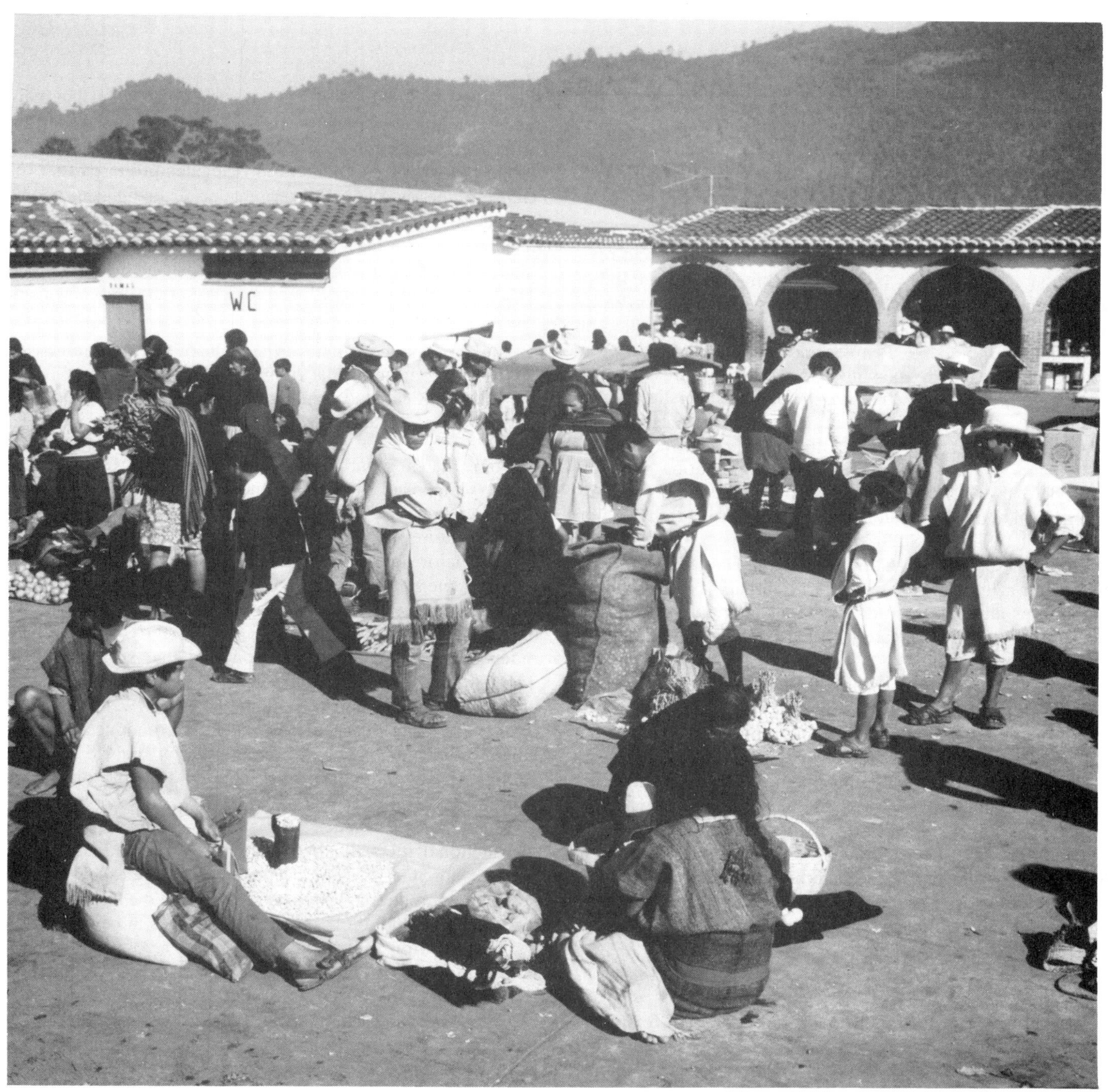

12th Session of UN Working Group on Indigenous Peoples

The Declaration Passes and the US Assumes a New Role

GLENN T. MORRIS

Glenn T. Morris is the Executive Director of the Fourth World Center for the Study of Indigenous Law and Politics, at the University of Colorado at Denver. He is also co-editor of the Fourth World Bulletin and Associate Professor of Political Science at CU-Denver.

After nearly nine years of debate, deliberation and revision, the United Nations Working Group on Indigenous Peoples (UNWGIP), at its 12th Session (25-29 July 1994), completed preparation of the Draft Declaration on the Rights of Indigenous Peoples and sent the document on to higher levels in the UN system. Over 160 indigenous peoples' organizations, forty two state members, nine specialized agencies of the United Nations, and dozens of interested non-governmental organizations, totaling nearly 800 individuals, participated in the 12th Session. The Declaration was forwarded to the UN Sub-Commission on Prevention of Discrimination and Protection of Minorities. At its 46th Session (in August 1994), the Sub-Commission agreed to transmit the Declaration to the UN Commission on Human Rights for discussion at its annual meeting in February 1995. For final adoption as an instrument of emerging international law, the Declaration must be ultimately be accepted by the UN General Assembly.

The 12th Session was notable for several important developments that this article reports in some detail. First, there was a significant debate about the Declaration's treatment of the right to self-determination; the ensuing discussion of the issue left momentous questions unresolved. Second, several other major issues that will have great bearing on the rights of indigenous peoples were postponed to future discussions in which they will be detached from the text of the Declaration. And third, the United States Government assumed a new and decidedly more dynamic role among the states that have actively participated in developing the Draft Declaration.

Self-determination

Discussion of the right to self-determination for indigenous peoples has always provoked passionate and oppositional controversy at Working Group sessions. In the initial drafts of the Declaration, the right was not mentioned explicitly at all. In subsequent drafts, at the insistence of indigenous peoples, the right was expressed, but was often accompanied by limiting language or provisions. At the 11th Session (1993), indigenous delegates proposed that reference to the right to self-determination for indigenous peoples should be modeled after the language already found in the International Covenant on Civil and Political Rights and the International Covenant on Economic, Social and Cultural Rights. That proposal was accepted, and Article 3 of the draft now reads:

> Indigenous peoples have the right of self-determination. By virtue of that right, they freely determine their political status and freely pursue their economic, social and cultural development.

Some states, notably the United States and Canada, have publicly opposed Article 3, and they can be expected to introduce dramatic revisions of it, or try to completely delete it in the future.

The major objection to self-determination stems from the fear by some states that explicit recognition of that right, in the language of the human rights covenants, will allow indigenous peoples and nations to exercise a right of political independence separate from the states that surround them. Through this exercise, states fear the dismemberment of their claimed territories and the emergence of new, independent indigenous states. This fear is especially pronounced in cases where indigenous enclaves are entirely surrounded by states or where indigenous territories contain valuable natural resources.

Most states assert that relations, especially territorial and jurisdictional relations, between themselves and indigenous peoples are internal, domestic matters that are beyond the scope of international law. The inclusion in the Declaration of a right that would allow indigenous peoples to be recognized to possess juridical character, with rights recognized in international forums, is viewed as an attack on the sovereignty and territorial integrity of current UN members.

Conversely, most indigenous peoples argue that they have never given their informed consent to be integrated into the states that came to surround them, that they have not been a party to the establishment of international legal principles to the present, and that they have been (and continue to be) denied the opportunity to decide for themselves their political status. In essence, they argue that they are in a state of internal colonial bondage, and they advocate an extension of international standards of decolonization to apply to their cases. In that regard, indigenous delegates have regularly stated that the right to self-determination is a major cornerstone of the Declaration, upon which other provisions of the document must rest.

Indigenous delegates have consistently argued that under the right to self-determination, complete independence is only one of several available options. They maintain that most indigenous peoples around the world do not aspire towards political independence, and would choose some variation of autonomy, short of independence, within the current state system. However, during the 12th Session, several states (Brazil, India, Myanmar) repeated their steadfast opposition to any recognition of a right to self-determination for indigenous peoples. Others, such as Denmark, expressed support for the self-determination provision.

Upon their arrival at the 12th Session, some indigenous representatives were surprised to find that the Declaration had been altered, without their consultation, from the form that had been concluded at the 11th Session. Of particular concern was the addition of Article 31, which recognizes "autonomy" or "self-government in internal and local affairs" as a specific form of the exercise of self-determination. Miguél Alfonso Martínez, the Latin American regional member of the Working Group and the author of Article 31, had reasoned that Latin American state governments were unlikely to accede to the open-ended interpretation of self-determination expressed in Article 3. He wrote and appended Article 31 to the Declaration in the hope that it would provide essential safeguards for Latin American indigenous peoples but not alarm the state governments of the region.

Serious discussion and disagreement developed over whether Article 31 would limit the right to self-determination expressed in Article 3. Some indigenous delegates (especially some Canadian and United States Indians, Native Hawaiians, Mapuches, Maoris, Nagas, and others) objected that the language of Article 3 was perfectly clear, and any attempt to modify the meaning (as they interpreted the intent of Article 31) might later be contrued as a limitation of the right to self-determination, that "autonomy" might result as the maximum (or at least the preferred) extent of the exercise of the right for indigenous peoples. They argued that Article 31 is therefore superfluous and should be deleted.

The opponents of Article 31 also suggested that certain states, notably the US and Canada, are hostile to Article 3 and can be expected to amend it significantly or even delete it from the Declaration, at future forums. If Article 3 is indeed eventually deleted, Article 31 will remain as the only articulation of what self-determination means. According to the opponents, Article 31, read alone, is an incomplete and inadequate protection of the right of self-determination for indigenous peoples.

The proponents of Article 31, on the other hand, maintained that the article should be read as an extension, not a limitation, of Article 3, and that local and regional autonomy would result as the *minimum* standard of self-determination that states must recognize for indigenous peoples. They suggested that for many indigenous peoples who must deal with states that fail to provide even minimal recognition of indigenous rights, Article 31 might provide a crucial safeguard against violations of fundamental human rights.

In future deliberations over the draft, the substance of the right to self-determination for indigenous peoples will remain of central importance. In the eyes of many indigenous peoples, the integrity of the entire instrument rests in the willingness of the international community to recognize the right of indigenous peoples to control their political, economic, social and cultural destinies. In contrast, the concerns of states over the freedom of indigenous peoples to exercise their right to self-determination is intimately linked to the belief that states possess a basic right to protect their own sovereignty and territorial integrity from competing indigenous claims. The ultimate success of the Declaration may therefore rest in the ability of the contending sides to assuage the fears of the other, by finding the common ground that satisfies the interests of all concerned.

Future Deliberations over the Declaration

According to modified UN rules of procedure, the discussion of the Draft Declaration at the Working Group level had been open to all UN members, all interested indigenous delegates, and all governmental and non-governmental organizations with an interest and a contribution to make to the efforts of the Working Group. With the conclusion of the Working Group's discussion, however, the Declaration was transmitted to the Sub-Commission and then to the Commission on Human Rights, where the procedures for participation are considerably more restrictive.

To participate at the Sub-Commission or the Commission, delegates must be credentialed by those respective bodies, and the application for credentialing must come through a non-governmental organization (NGO) that possesses consultative status within the UN Economic and Social Council (ECOSOC). To date, only twelve indigenous NGOs, primarily representing indigenous peoples of the Americas, have received consultative status.

During the 12th Session, both indigenous representatives and states expressed doubts that in future forums in which the Draft Declaration is discussed, indigenous peoples who are not affiliated with the recognized NGOs, or who are otherwise not credentialed, will be included in the discussions. This issue is of special concern to peoples from India and other parts of Asia and the Pacific, the Russian Federation, and Africa, because many of them are not currently members of credentialed NGOs.

The issue of who will be able to participate in future discussions becomes especially important when considering the probable course for the Declaration. According to a number of state observers at the 12th Session, once the Draft reaches the Commission on Human Rights, it will be sent to another working group, within the Commission itself. Unlike the discussions at the previous Working Group, which were directed by international legal experts (as opposed to delegates representing the interests of states), the Commission working group may well be directed by appointed delegates whose primary concern will be the protection of their governments' interests.

While the Draft is in the Commission's working group, it will be subject to a comprehensive review and reconsideration. Provisions that might seem problematic to states are susceptible to complete revision or removal. Indigenous representatives expressed concern that a limitation of their participation in this process may endanger the progress that has been made over the past ten years, and it may weaken the most important international legal instrument affecting indigenous peoples ever to appear.

Indigenous delegates have previous experience upon which to base their wariness. In 1989, during the debate over revision of International Labor Organization (ILO) Convention 107, only credentialed indigenous representatives could participate, and then only on a limited basis, while a number of important persons and perspectives were completely excluded. To many indigenous peoples, the ILO rules determining participation were totally arbitrary. Consequently, indigenous delegates now insist on more open participation at the Human Rights Commission and successive fora that deal with the Declaration.

Members of the Working Group itself have also recommended relaxation of the rules of procedure in the Human Rights Commission's discussion of the Draft. The Australian government promised that it would introduce a measure to allow indigenous participation, regardless of consultative status, and it proposed that any meetings of the Commission working group be convened immediately prior to the meeting of the Working Group on Indigenous Peoples, so as to maximize the opportunity for indigenous participation. Australia's proposals were endorsed by a few other countries, particularly Sweden, Denmark and Norway.

The Role of the US at the 12th Session and Beyond

The United States delegation to the 12th Session took a new and decidely more active role in the deliberations of the Working Group and the discussion of the Draft Declaration. Until the 1994 meeting, the United States has participated mostly as an observer, relying on the lead of countries such as Canada and Australia to fashion and advance the interests of state members at the Working Group.

For several years, some indigenous delegates to the Working Group have become convinced that the most prominent governments from English-speaking countries (Australia, Canada, New Zealand and the United States) have coordinated their participation in international forums concerned with indigenous peoples' rights. Rudolph Rÿser, Director of the Center for World Indigenous Studies, has charted a succession of joint meetings between those governments. According to Rÿser's analysis, Canada has played a particularly active role, one that is considered by many indigenous delegates to be especially hostile toward any expanded recognition of indigenous rights. Australia, conversely, has played a role that is publicly more sympathetic to indigenous claims, one that has even supported limited usage of terms like "peoples" and "self-determination." New Zealand and the United States, says Rÿser, have taken approaches that vary between those of Canada and Australia, while the US delegation's public posture has ranged from indifference to hostility.

Affirming Rÿser's analysis, the changing agenda of the United States has been revealed in an unclassified internal State Department memorandum of July 1993. In this document, State Department officials acknowledge that for the first dozen years of the Working Group's existence, the US "invested little effort in [it]." By 1993, however, the US attitude toward developments at the Working Group apparently had changed significantly. The memo explains that the Working Group and the Draft Declaration are now at a stage where it is important for the US to "try to shape the text [of the draft] to reflect US interests before it goes to the Commission [on Human Rights]."

Of major concern to the US is the question of what impact the application of the principles of collective rights and self-determination of indigenous peoples might have for the United States and international law. It is clear from the memo that the US opposes extending the right of self-determination, as it has been interpeted in the international human rights covenants, to indigenous peoples. The memo asserts that self-determination "is most commonly understood to mean the right to establish a sovereign and independent state, with separate personality under international law. Like many other countries, the United States could not accept the term in any contexts implying or permitting this meaning."

Addressing an issue closely related to self-determination, the State Department is critical of using the term "peoples" (with an "s" at the end) in conjunction with the word "indigenous." According to the memo, "the term [peoples] implies that such groups have the right to self-determination under international law." The document expresses concern about "the risks and uncertainties of extending the legal concept of self-determination to indigenous groups." It emphasizes that the recognition of indigenous collective rights expressed in the Draft Declaration is troublesome, because as a general rule, "the United States...does not recognize the existence of collective rights under international law..." and "we generally do not think it desirable to incorporate such rights into future legal instruments."

While the memo lends general support to the concept of a declaration for the protection of indigenous peoples, and while it even questions some basic assumptions about generally accepted notions in State Department circles (e.g., "recognizing carefully defined group rights need not *per se* be a BAD THING," and "should we oppose a tightly drawn treaty saying that a defined collective group has a defined legal right to practice their culture or religion opposable against their [sic] government?"), it also makes very clear that the security and integrity of the current state system is of preeminent importance.

The flavor of the 1993 memo was integrated into the US intervention at the 12th Session, where the use of the term "peoples" was deliberately avoided, and instead, the terms "people," "populations," "tribe," and "tribal," were used sixteen times. The delegation (led by Miriam Sapiro, from State's Legal Affairs Office, and John Crook, Counselor for Legal Affairs at the US Mission in Geneva) also provided further insight into the US position regarding indigenous self-determination. The memo suggests that US indigenous policy can be used as a working model for the effective implementation of indigenous rights on an international level, given that the essence and extent of self-determination for indigenous peoples should basically mean "self-governance and autonomy...within an existing state." Of course, this implies that US indigenous policy does not apply to "non-historic" or non-federally-recognized Indian nations, Alaskan or Hawaiian Natives, Chamorros, Samoans, or other indigenous peoples that have never been given any pretense whatsoever in the realm of "self-governance" or "autonomy."

Equally revealing of the true US policy, at unofficial meetings during the 12th Session, Crook and Sapiro made clear that the semantic debates over such terms as "people" versus "peoples" were less important to them than was some resolution of the substance of the right to self-determination itself. Sapiro asked several times, "What does Article 3 mean?" And at one session Crook even called the semantic debate "stupid." However, the term proved important enough that the US delegation has made a conscious, deliberate decision to refuse to use the term "peoples" at all. The apparent implication is that if the term self-determination can be interpreted, in any context, to recognize the right of indigenous peoples to independent political existence, then the United States will oppose it.

The current US position on the Declaration can be identified in a plank of the "Clinton-Gore Plan" (the campaign platform of 1992) and also in a statement by President Clinton on 29 April 1994, both of which affirmed "government-to-government" relationships between indigenous nations and the United States, while placing the treatment of indigenous self-determination solely within the domestic jurisdiction of the United States. Some indigenous delegates have observed that the use of the term "government-to-government" by the United States constitutes an attempt to reduce indigenous issues to "internal" status and to degrade the international (i.e., nation-to-nation) relationship that is embodied in the hundreds of treaties concluded between the US and various Indian nations. Others have observed that the quality of "self-determination" accorded to only the recognized "historic tribes" of the US is truncated by the language of the Indian Self-Determination and Education Act of 1975, which limits the exercise of self-determination to decisions concerning the allocation of appropriations distributed by the federal government.

Sapiro and Crook stated in the Session that the United States plans to play a more active role in the future of both the Draft Declaration and the Working Group. They appeared confident that the Draft would pass through the Sub-Commission in August 1994 (which it did), and that it would then be transmitted to a working group in the Commission on Human Rights, after February 1995. The delegation suggested that in future months very serious discussion and debate of the Draft will take place, especially over such controversial matters as collective rights, self-determination, control of territories and natural resources, and development matters, and that the US will play an active role in both the procedural and substantive aspects of these debates. The inference must be that, because the US and other states disagree with the wording of some key provisions of the Draft Declaration, significant changes might reasonably be expected at the Commission level.

In a briefing held in Washington DC, on 20 January 1995, John Shattuck, Assistant Secretary of State for Human Rights, reiterated that the US position regarding the Draft Declaration, at the February 1995 meeting of the UN Human Rights Commission, will be "supportive," and that the United States will follow Australia's lead in creating an open-ended working group within the Commission. Shattuck and his aides repeated that the US perceives human rights primarily pertaining to individuals, not to groups, that the US wants a clearer definition of "indigenous peoples," in order to determine to whom the rights in the Declaration apply. Shattuck also said that his office was committed to open discussions concerning the Declaration (to be held in the US), in various forums with indigenous groups and other NGOs.

The key features of US policy continue to be: that the US considers individuals and not groups to be the subject of human rights; that questions involving indigenous peoples are basically domestic matters to be negotiated between states and indigenous peoples; that the right to self-determination should be read more narrowly than it was in the past, and should not normally be read as a recognition of the right of independent political existence for indigenous peoples; and that any political and economic sovereignty rights of indigenous peoples are inferior and subordinate to the overarching sovereignty of existing states. Undoubtedly, the basic position of the United States on these questions will play an important and enduring role in the consideration of the Draft Declaration and in the future of the Working Group.

Whatever the role of the US in future deliberations of the Working Group, a serious amount of work remains unfinished and will have to be resolved in the coming years. These issues are, in summary, the scope and substance of the right of indigenous peoples to exercise self-determination, the international legal status of treaties between indigenous peoples and states, and the responsibilities of states and the United Nations in assuring that indigenous peoples and their territories are not sacrificed in the pursuit of national and international economic development.

(continued)

Indigenous Self-Determination and U.S. Policy

Commentary

As explained in the [first part] of this issue article, there has recently been a major shift in the posture of the United States Government regarding the Draft Declaration on the Rights of Indigenous Peoples and the UN Working Group on Indigenous Peoples (UNWGIP). Some have applauded the U.S. awakening in the indigenous-rights arena, replete with its dubious interpretation of the language of "self-determination," as a welcome and positive change. Unfortunately, we are unable to share that optimism.

In our view, the position shift should be viewed cautiously as perhaps the latest reflection of a long tradition in U.S. policy, which is characterized by massive contradictions of legal and moral obligations. American Indians, more than any other indigenous peoples, should understand the implications of U.S. posturing on human rights. The possibility or probability that the U.S. will support or promote the Draft Declaration on the Rights of Indigenous Peoples can and should be measured in relation to the attachment of the U.S. to other, comparable pieces of international legislation on human rights.

It should be understood that the Declaration on Indigenous Rights, even when finally concluded, will not create any immediately binding legal obligation on any state, because it is not a treaty. Subsequent to its adoption by the UN General Assembly, the Declaration may eventually be transformed into a Convention, just as the 1948 Universal Declaration on Human Rights was put into force in the form of two competing (or complementary) human-rights covenants, in 1976, but this development will take many years, if it happens at all. Present U.S. support for the Draft Declaration, therefore, can be understood to be virtually risk-free, as far as immediate legal obligations are concerned.

More importantly, the United States has consistently refused to participate in international human-rights institutions over the past fifty years. The U.S. Senate, which must ratify all treaties to which the country might become state-party, rejected all opportunities for the U.S. to accede to the 1948 Genocide Convention, until 1986. Similarly, it refused to ratify the 1966 International Covenant on Civil and Political Rights (which codifies that set of human rights expressed in the U.S. Bill of Rights itself), until 1992. Only last year, in 1994, did the Senate ratify the 1965 International Convention on the Elimination of All Forms of Racial Discrimination. But did ratification in these very few cases indicate that the United States would actually abide by the terms of the agreements? No, because whenever the Senate has ratified human-rights treaties, it has appended "provisions" and "reservations" that have made international laws subordinate to the laws of the United States. There is little reason to believe that the treatment of the Declaration on Indigenous Rights will be different.

The stated U.S. position should not be regarded as an insignificant policy change in an obscure area of international human-rights discourse, nor should it be viewed in isolation from the evidence of U.S. behavior when indigenous rights are obviously at stake. Rather, the policy statement should be viewed as intimately related to several other important foreign-policy areas that are implicated by past and present indigenous (or "nationality") conflicts around the globe. For example, the U.S. supported a Tibetan rebellion against Chinese occupation in the 1950s and 60s, but when President Nixon decided to play the "China card" against the USSR, in 1972, the Tibetans were abandoned to be slaughtered and exiled by the Chinese Army. Similarly, the U.S. supported Iraqi Kurds in their rebellion against Saddam Hussein, in 1973 (the prelude to the events of the Gulf War in 1991), but when U.S. interests in the region shifted, the Kurds, too, were abandoned to be slaughtered by the thousands. On the other hand, because of the strategic importance of Turkey, the U.S. virtually ignores the fate of Kurds in that country.

In another, similar policy contradiction, the U.S. supported and instigated Ukrainian secessionist rebellion against the USSR until 1991, when President Bush strangely attempted to persuade Ukraine *not* to seek independence, after all (of course, he was too late). Bush's address to the Ukrainians, in which he reversed forty-five years of policy to warn of the "excesses of suicidal nationalism," was labeled his "Chicken Kiev Speech" by *New York Times* columnist William Safire, marking the first evidence of a major dispute within the ranks of U.S. conservatives on indigenous nationality policy generally and the policy applied toward Russia, in particular.

It is difficult to underestimate the cynicism of U.S. policy on human rights. At the Vienna World Conference on Human Rights, in July 1993, President Clinton and Secretary of State Christopher swore before the world that the United States was prepared to join the International Covenant on Economic, Social and Cultural Rights. That promise could not have been less believable, considering the fact that the ESC Covenant has always been understood as the major human-rights statement of socialist regimes, led by the former USSR, and so it hardly could have been expected ever to gain approval in the Senate. Clinton and Christopher also preached human rights to the Chinese government and threatened to withhold Most-Favored Nation (MFN) trading privileges unless China reformed its behavior according to Western precepts of "democracy" -- and then reversed themselves, when China indicated that it was not about to be pressured on human-rights issues.

Meanwhile, within the U.S. itself, indigenous human-rights issues go largely unacknowledged and unaddressed by the public, because of the myth that the U.S. is the world's leader in observance of human rights. This myth probably explains why, though people in western Europe, Russia, and elsewhere are aware that President Clinton has refused to deal with the worldwide campaign to grant clemency to the American Indian political prisoner Leonard Peltier, Americans themselves hardly know his name. The illusion that the U.S. alone is the hegemonic arbiter of good and evil may account for its pursuit of the forced relocation of Diné on the Hopi Partitioned Lands, while it forbids the UNWGIP to discuss that issue, lest the U.S. scuttle that forum.

As a measure of the current U.S. foreign policy on rights of indigenous/nationality peoples, Chechnya is an illustrative case, since Russia remains the "centerpiece" of U.S. foreign policy in the post-Cold War era. U.S. reaction to Russia's most recent invasion of Chechnya (there have been several over the past 300 years) has been typically full of contradictions. Although members of the Clinton Administration have condemned Russia's brutal military *tactics* against the Chechens, there has been virtually no challenge to the legitimacy of the basic Russian claim over Chechen territory. President Clinton is clearly supporting Yeltsin's regime, in its attempt to fend off opponents, including the fascistic Vladimir Zhirinovsky, who has no sympathy for Chechens and wants to re-establish a Russian empire. The Clinton Administration believes that Yeltsin represents the best present hope that Russia will become a pro-Western capitalist enterprise. That hope is contingent on territorial integrity, however, and Chechen secession would probably seal Russia's doom, by tapping the wellspring of endemic separatism in the complex Russian Federation. Such separatism could bring on a period of chaos and, given the genuine possibility of a military coup, precipitate another Cold War.

The absence of official criticism and opposition from the U.S. Government has been matched in the U.S. mainstream media. The *New York Times*, for instance, has repeatedly supported Russia's suppression of Chechen self-determination and encouraged Washington to "quietly counsel [Yeltsin] to apply force carefully," because the Chechen claims "cannot be allowed to stand" (*NYT*, 14 December 1994). This, despite the *Times*' own acknowledgment that the Russians have, in the past, occupied Chechnya but never subdued it — because the Chechens have resisted and rebelled continually against Russian domination, twice earlier in this century.

The U.S. State Department (the agency that is constructing the policy on indigenous peoples' rights) agreed with the *Times*, giving Russian territorial claims and military actions higher legitimacy than those of the Chechens. State Department official Mike McCurry succinctly stated the U.S. position on 14 December 1994 (also later affirmed by President Clinton and Secretary of State Christopher) that "Chechnya is an integral part of Russia, and events in Chechnya, because of that, are largely an internal affair." Vice President Al Gore underlined the Administration's stance by saying that the US is "not going to challenge Russian territorial integrity [on the Chechen question]" (Associated Press, 9 January 1995).

As the *Times* concluded, the U.S. statements gave "Mr. Yeltsin a green light for military intervention" (NYT, 28 December 1994). Apparently, neither the U.S. nor the *Times* will object to the general principle of an established state invading a stateless people's territory. The feeble concern that they do raise is rather that the invasion was bungled — it was not done quickly or quietly or effectively enough, and it was not executed cleanly out of television camera range.

Ironically, Zbigniew Brezinski (Jimmy Carter's National Security Adviser), recently joined a few Republican members of Congress and a smattering of conservative newpaper editors in condemning U.S. policy for complicity in the denial of Chechen self-determination, in a column in the *Washington Post* (8 January 1995). Brezinski claims that Chechnya "could become the graveyard of America's moral reputation," because the U.S. refuses to come to the assistance of a "freedom-seeking" people that "dared to reach out for independence." His defense of the "helpless Chechens... who are not Russian and do not wish to be Russian," while laudable under normal circumstances, rings hollow when one recalls his lack of defense of the freedom-seeking Tibetans against China, or of the freedom-seeking East Timorese against Indonesia, and the pounding of the freedom-seeking Kurds by Iran, Iraq, and Turkey, during his watch at the White House. His commentary represents the depth of contradictory sentiments within both conservative ranks and the policy community at large.

In a most telling distortion in his column, Brezinski claims that the U.S. vilification of an indigenous or nationality struggle (of the Chechens), and justification of oppression (by the Russians) "has never happened before." In addition to the cases mentioned above, Brezinski seems to have forgotten the decades of U.S. opposition to the African National Congress, the IRA, the Eritreans, the PLO, the Polisario Front in the Western Sahara, and the Naga Nation struggling for its independence from India. The list of freedom-seeking peoples engaged in nationality and indigenous struggles that have been opposed by the United States could fill pages. It is precisely the United States' own history of opposition to self-determination struggles that should give pause to those who are watching the new U.S. agenda unfold on the indigenous-rights stage.

The justification applied by the U.S. to the Chechen case, that the survival of a state (Russia) and its territorial claims are more important than the survival of an indigenous people, can easily be observed in other serious cases at this very moment. The government of Myanmar (Burma) is waging a relentless and brutal military attack against the Karen Nation, killing hundreds and forcing tens of thousands of refugees to flee their homeland into Thailand. Not surprisingly, neither the United States, nor any other major power, has submitted any meaningful challenge to Myanmar's attacks. In November, just three months ago, the State Department claimed that it was taking a "conciliatory approach" toward the Burmese military regime, as far as human rights in general were concerned (especially the imprisonment of Nobel Peace Prize laureate Aung San Suu Kyi), but made no attempt to address the question of indigenous rights in particular. The U.S. maintains extensive trade relations with the Ne Win regime; the petroleum, natural gas, timber, weapons, and narcotics industries are all doing big business in Burma. Meanwhile, the U.S. supports, either actively or tacitly, the open relations between the Ne Win regime and China, Thailand, and Japan.

Rather than support the application of the principle of self-determination to the Chechens or the Karen—lest it set a precedent for other freedom-seeking peoples—the United States and other states of the world would prefer to protect the "sovereignty and territorial integrity" of the chauvinistic and human-rights-abusing governments of Russia and Myanmar out of political or economic expedience. Rather than examine the claims of the Karen or the Chechens, that they have never given their consent to be integrated into the Burmese or the Russian states, and that they have long-standing political and territorial claims of their own, the governments of the world side with the oppressor's invasion in the name of regional stability and order. Similar examples of expedience over principle can be cited from Chiapas to the Western Sahara, from Indonesia to Eritrea.

The self-determination of the peoples of Eritrea was ignored, even actively opposed, for over three decades by the major powers of the world, led alternately by the U.S. and the Soviet Union, in the interests of protecting Ethiopia's sovereignty. At the same time the U.S. was assuaging Israel's fear that the Red Sea might be completely bordered by states hostile to its existence. The Eritrean spirit of freedom prevailed despite prohibitive odds, surviving drought and over thirty years of military oppression from the Ethiopian government that was alternately supported by both the United States and the Soviet Union. Eritrea's seat in the United Nations, which can be celebrated as an enormous monument to the perseverance of the Eritrean people, should also serve as a constant source of shame to the world community that consistently rejected a legitimate claim of self-determination in favor of the territorial integrity claims of a corrupt Ethiopian government. Eritrea would still not be seated at the UN if it had to rely solely on the international community's embrace of high-sounding principles respecting the self-determination of peoples. Eritrea's seat would not exist had the Eritreans not mobilized the military might necessary to liberate their homeland and to defend and protect their claim to self-determination.

The lessons of the Chechens, the Karen, and the Eritreans should serve as important lessons to other indigenous peoples and nationalities. If the international community has a choice between the legitimacy of indigenous peoples' claims for territory, treaty rights, economic sustainability, or self-determination, versus the claims of a state, *any* state, for continued survival, indigenous peoples can be virtually certain that the statist claim will be supported consistently. For the United States, consolidating global hegemony is the preeminent national interest at this time. U.S. hegemony can be managed successfully only with a limited number of sovereign states in the system. The U.S., therefore, judges it imperative to forestall any possibility, real or imagined, of a wave of secessionism.

The United States clearly does not take international human-rights obligations seriously, despite its charade of being the world's bastion of respect for rights. Neither is it ever likely to accept the Declaration of Rights for Indigenous Peoples as a constraint on its own policy towards the indigenous peoples enclosed by its borders. At this point in history, there is no reason to believe that increased U.S. interest in indigenous peoples' rights is anything more than self-serving political posturing. The U.S. has made it clear that it opposes any meaningful recognition of the right to self-determination for indigenous peoples; it opposes any serious assertion of territorial or natural-resource control by indigenous peoples; it opposes recognition of the international standing of treaties between indigenous peoples and states; and its recommendation for the protection of indigenous rights rests solely within the domestic jurisdiction of the very states that have historically attacked, dismembered and sought to destroy indigenous peoples. Does this record bespeak an indigenous-rights policy that should be applauded?

American Indians in the 1990s

The true number of American Indians may be unknowable, but a rapidly growing number of Americans are identifying with Indian culture. The Anglo appetite for Indian products is creating jobs on poverty-plagued reservations. Gambling and tourism are the most lucrative reservation businesses. Meanwhile, the middle-class Indian's urge to "go home" is growing.

Dan Fost

Dan Fost is a contributing editor of American Demographics *in Tiburon, California.*

When Nathan Tsosie was growing up in the Laguna Pueblo in New Mexico, he was not taught the Laguna language. The tribe's goal was to assimilate him into white society.

Today, Tsosie's 9-year-old son Darren learns his ancestral language and culture in the Laguna schools. He speaks Laguna better than either of his parents. "They're trying to bring it back," says Darren's mother, Josephine. "I'm glad he's learning. I just feel bad that we can't reinforce it and really teach it."

The strong bonds American Indians still feel to their native culture are driving a renaissance in Indian communities. This cultural resurrection has not yet erased the poverty, alcoholism, and other ills that affect many Indians. But it has brought educational and economic gains to many Indians living on and off reservations. A college-educated Indian middle class has emerged, American Indian business ownership has increased, and some tribes are creating good jobs for their members.

The census counted 1,878,000 American Indians in 1990, up from fewer than 1.4 million in 1980. This 38 percent leap exceeds the growth rate for blacks (6 percent) and non-Hispanic whites (13 percent), but not the growth of Hispanics (53 percent) or Asians (108 percent).

The increase is not due to an Indian baby boom or to immigration from other countries. Rather, Americans with Indian heritage are increasingly likely to identify their race as Indian on census forms. Also, the Census Bureau is doing a better job of counting American Indians.

Almost 2 million people say that their race is American Indian. But more than 7 million people claim some Indian ancestry, says Jeff Passel at the Urban Institute. That's about 1 American in 35.

"A lot of people have one or more ancestors who are American Indian," says Passel. "There's a clear trend over the last three censuses for increasing numbers of those people to answer the race question as American Indian. But it doesn't tell you how 'Indian' they are in a cultural sense.

"The strength of this identification in places that are not Indian strongholds is transitory. If it becomes unfashionable to be American Indian, it could go down."

People who try to count American Indians employ many different means that often confound demographers. Tribes keep tabs on enrollment, but the rules vary on how much Indian blood makes one a member. Some tribes are not recognized by the federal government. Local health services may keep one set of records, while federal agencies like the Bureau of Indian Affairs will keep another. Some Indians are nomadic; Navajos, for example, may maintain three residences. Rural Indians can be hard to find, and minorities are always more prone to census undercounts. A growing number of mixed marriages blurs the racial boundaries even further.

"I don't know what an Indian is," says Malcolm Margolin, publisher of the

Reprinted with permission from *American Demographics*, December 1991, pp. 26-34.

INDIAN STATES

During the 1980s, Oklahoma replaced California as the state with the largest American Indian population. South Dakota dropped off the top ten list as New York moved into ninth place.

(population of the ten states with the largest American Indian populations, in thousands)

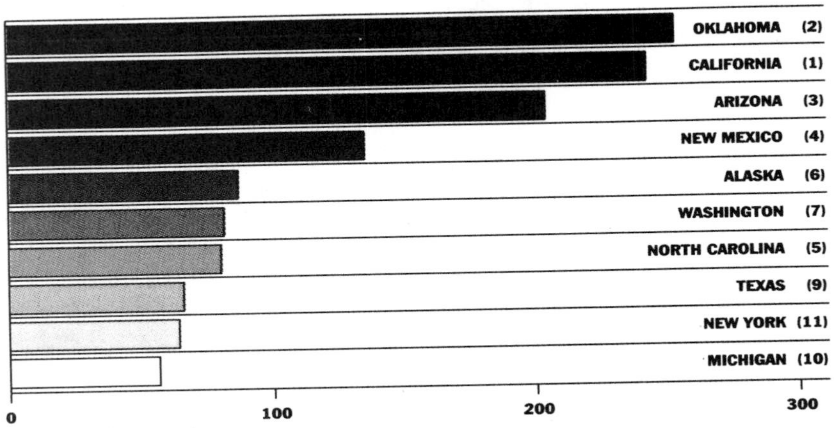

State	1980 rank
OKLAHOMA	(2)
CALIFORNIA	(1)
ARIZONA	(3)
NEW MEXICO	(4)
ALASKA	(6)
WASHINGTON	(7)
NORTH CAROLINA	(5)
TEXAS	(9)
NEW YORK	(11)
MICHIGAN	(10)

0 100 200 300

Note: 1980 ranks in parentheses.

Source: 1990 census

monthly *News from Native California*. "Some people are clearly Indian, and some are clearly not. But the U.S. government figures are clearly inadequate for judging how many people are Indian."

Even those who can't agree on the numbers do agree that Indians are returning to their roots. "In the early 1960s, there was a stigma attached to being American Indian," Passel says. These days, even Anglos are proud of Indian heritage.

IDENTIFYING WITH INDIANS

When white patrons at Romo's restaurant in Holbrook, Arizona, learn that their host is half Navajo and half Hopi, they frequently exclaim, "I'm part Cherokee!" The host smiles and secretly rolls his eyes. More *bahanas* (whites) are jumping on the Indian bandwagon.

"In the last three years, interest in Indian beliefs has really taken off," says Marzenda McComb, the former co-owner of a New Age store in Portland, Oregon. To celebrate the sale of her store, a woman performed an Indian smudging ritual with burnt cedar and an eagle feather. Most of McComb's customers were non-Indian.

Controversy often accompanies such practices. Some Indians bristle at the sharing of their culture and spiritual practices with whites. But others welcome people of any race into their culture. And many tribal leaders recognize that Indian art and tourism are hot markets.

Anglos are not the only ones paying more attention to Indian ways. Indian children are showing a renewed interest in their culture. Jennifer Bates, who owns the Bear and Coyote Gallery in California, says her 9-year-old son has taken an independent interest in Northern Miwok dance. "It's nice, knowing that we're not pushing it on him," she says. "He wanted to dance and make his cape. It's up to us to keep things going, and if we don't, it's gone."

The oldest generation of California Indians "grew up among people who recalled California before the arrival of whites," says Malcolm Margolin. These people have "something in their tone, their mood, their manners—a very Indian quality." Younger generations are more comfortable in the white world, he says, but they sense "something very ominous about the passing of the older generation. It's the sense of the younger generation that it's up to them."

The Zuni tribe is trying to revive ancient crafts by opening two tribal-owned craft stores—one in their pueblo in New Mexico, and one on San Francisco's trendy Union Street. The most popular items are fetishes—small stone carvings of animals that serve as good-luck charms. "After *Dances with Wolves* came out, we weren't able to keep the wolf fetishes in stock," says Milford Nahohai, manager of the New Mexico store.

JOBS ON RESERVATIONS

Many Indians on and off the reservation face a well-established litany of problems, from poverty and alcoholism to unemployment. Many tribal leaders say that only jobs can solve the problem. Promoting Indian-owned businesses is their solution.

The number of Indian-owned businesses increased 64 percent between 1982 and 1987, compared with a 14 percent rise for all U.S. firms, according to the Census Bureau. "A whole new system of role models is being established," says Steven Stallings, president of the National Center for American Indian Enterprise Development in Mesa, Arizona. "Indians see self-employment as a viable opportunity."

In boosting reservation-based businesses, Stallings aims to create sustainable, self-reliant economies. In some areas, 92 cents of every dollar earned on a reservation is spent outside the reservation, he says. Non-Indian communities typically retain as much as 85 cents.

Stallings's center hopes to start by attracting employers to Indian country. The next step is to add retail and service businesses that will "create a revolving economy on the reservation."

This strategy is at work in Laguna, New Mexico. The Laguna Indians were hit hard in 1982, when the price of uranium plummeted and the Anaconda Mineral Company closed a mine located on their reservation. But the Lagunas have bounced back with several enterprises, including Laguna Industries, a tribal-owned manufacturing firm that employs 350 people.

Laguna Industries' clients include the Department of Defense, Raytheon, and Martin Marietta. Its flagship product is a communications shelter that U.S. forces

INDIAN INDUSTRIES

American Indian specialty contractors had receipts of $97 million in 1987. But automotive and food-store owners may earn higher profits.

(ten largest industry groups in receipts for firms owned by American Indians and Alaska Natives)

rank	industry group	firms	receipts (in thousands)	receipts per firm (in thousands)
1	Special trade contractors	2,268	$97,400	$43
2	Miscellaneous retail	1,799	85,400	47
3	Agriculture services, forestry, and fishing	3,128	84,000	27
4	Automotive dealers and service stations	222	65,300	294
5	Food stores	301	54,300	180
6	Business services	2,532	48,600	19
7	Eating and drinking places	464	35,300	76
8	Construction	461	34,200	74
9	Trucking and warehousing	590	32,200	55
10	Personal services	1,719	26,500	15

Source: 1987 Economic Censuses, Survey of Minority-Owned Business Enterprises

INDIAN MARKETS

The 1990 census showed rapid increases among American Indians who live in large metropolitan areas. Some of the increases reflect an increasing willingness to declare one's Indian heritage.

(top ten metropolitan areas, ranked by American Indian, Eskimo, and Aleut population in 1990; and percent change in that population, 1980–90)

rank	metropolitan area	1990 population	percent change 1980–90
1	Los Angeles-Anaheim-Riverside, CA	87,500	5%
2	Tulsa, OK	48,200	41
3	New York-Northern New Jersey-Long Island, NY-NJ-CT	46,200	101
4	Oklahoma City, OK	45,700	82
5	San Francisco-Oakland-San Jose, CA	40,800	19
6	Phoenix, AZ	38,000	66
7	Seattle-Tacoma, WA	32,100	42
8	Minneapolis-St. Paul, MN-WI	24,000	49
9	Tucson, AZ	20,300	36
10	San Diego, CA	20,100	37

Source: 1990 census

used in the Gulf War. "It's pretty nice to see your own people getting involved in high-tech stuff," says welding supervisor Phillip Sarracino, 44.

Laguna Indians are given first priority for jobs at the plant, but several middle managers are white. Conrad Lucero, a plant group leader and former tribal governor, says that non-Indian supervisors are often retirees who lend their expertise until Indians can run things on their own.

"I have an 8-year-old daughter," says Sabin Chavez, 26, who works in the quality control division. "I'm hoping to keep this company going, so our kids can live on the reservation. It's a long shot, but we have to believe in long shots."

High morale at Laguna Industries is tempered by the risks of relying on the government. The Lagunas realize that their dependence on military contracts makes them vulnerable to cuts in the defense budget. And in August 1994, the tribe's right to bid on minority set-aside contracts will expire—partly because the business has been so successful.

"We have to be able to meet and beat our competitors on the open market," Lucero says. The Lagunas may succeed: Martin Marietta Corporation has already awarded Laguna Industries a contract based on price and not minority status, says Martin Marietta customer representative Michael King.

Laguna Industries has not solved all the tribe's problems, however. Tribal planner Nathan Tsosie estimates that unemployment runs as high as 35 percent on the reservation. Much of the housing is substandard, water shortages could impede future development, and alcoholism still tears Indian families apart. But Tsosie has an answer: "We just need to develop more. People leave the reservation to get jobs. If there were jobs here, they'd stay."

GAMBLING AND TOURISM

Indians bring some real advantages to the business world. The Lagunas show that a cohesive community can be organized into an efficient production facility. Other reservations have rich natural resources. But the biggest benefit may be "sovereignty," or the suspension of many local, state, and federal laws on Indian territory. Reservations have no sales or property tax, so cigarettes, gasoline, and other items can be sold for low prices. They can also offer activities not permitted off-reservation.

Like gambling.

"Bingo is a way for tribes to amass funds so they can get into other economic development projects," says Frank Collins, a Mescalero Apache from San Jose who specializes in development.

Bingo can be big business. One parlor on the Morongo reservation, just north of Palm Springs, California, draws 5,000 people a week and employs more than 140 people. The Morongo tribe's main objective is to develop as a major resort destination, says bingo general manager Michael Lombardi.

Lombardi won't say how much money bingo generates for the Morongos. He will

THE BEST STATES FOR

Indians in Business

This table shows how the states rank on the basis of business ownership among American Indians. States in the South may offer the most opportunity for American Indians, while midwestern states may offer the least.

The number of Indian-owned businesses in a state is not closely related to the business ownership rate. Business ownership rates are calculated by dividing the number of Indian-owned businesses by the number of Indians and multiplying by 1,000. The top-ranked state, Alaska, is one of only five states with more than 1,000 Indian-owned firms. But the state that ranks last, Arizona, has the seventh-highest number of Indian-owned businesses.

Statistical analysis also indicates that the pattern of business ownership among American Indians is not driven by the rate of growth in a state's Indian population during the 1980s, or by a state's overall level of business ownership.

There appear to be strong regional biases in patterns of Indian business ownership. The business ownership rate was 12.2 Indian-owned firms per 1,000 Indians in the South, 10.3 in the West, 9.6 in the Northeast, and only 7.4 in the Midwest.

One clue to a state's business ownership rate among Indians could be the share of its Indian population living on reservations. The lowest-ranking state, Arizona, contains seven of the ten most populated reservations in the U.S., including a large share of the huge Navajo reservation (1990 Indian population of 143,400 in Arizona, New Mexico, and Utah). South Dakota, ranking 47th, contains the large and economically troubled Pine Ridge, Rosebud, and Standing Rock reservations. Indians living on a reservation have limited entrepreneurial opportunities. Another factor that may be related to the Indian business rate is the state's general economic health: several states near the bottom of the ranking, Kentucky, Nebraska, and Michigan, have experienced weak economic growth during the 1980s.

But the most powerful predictor is probably the business skill of a state's Indian tribes. Third-ranking North Carolina is home to one branch of the Cherokee tribe, which has large investments in lumber and tourism. And Alaska may rank first because its native American, Eskimo, and Aleut population received billions of dollars in a federal land claim settlement. These data do not contain businesses owned by Eskimos or Aleuts. But many of Alaska's Indians live in isolated towns where small businesses have a captive, all-native audience.

—*William O'Hare*

William O'Hare is Director of Population and Policy Research Program, University of Louisville.

INDIAN OPPORTUNITY

(states with more than 100 American Indian-owned businesses in 1987, ranked by business ownership rate)

rank	state name	number of firms 1987	American Indian population 1987	business ownership rate*
1	Alaska	1,039	28,700	36.2
2	North Carolina	1,757	75,600	23.2
3	Texas	872	57,500	15.2
4	Virginia	188	13,300	14.1
5	Colorado	343	24,600	13.9
6	California	3,087	225,600	13.7
7	Louisiana	221	16,600	13.3
8	Massachusetts	132	10,700	12.4
9	Kansas	225	20,000	11.3
10	Florida	348	30,900	11.3
11	Maryland	123	11,300	10.9
12	Pennsylvania	139	12,800	10.8
13	Georgia	122	11,400	10.7
14	New Jersey	131	12,800	10.3
15	New Mexico	1,247	126,400	9.9
16	Illinois	182	19,600	9.3
17	Montana	405	44,700	9.1
18	Oklahoma	2,044	229,300	8.9
19	Oregon	306	34,500	8.9
20	North Dakota	208	24,300	8.6
21	Wisconsin	306	36,300	8.4
22	Ohio	149	17,700	8.4
23	Washington	602	72,300	8.3
24	Nevada	146	17,700	8.3
25	New York	425	54,800	7.8
26	Missouri	133	17,500	7.6
27	Minnesota	333	45,400	7.3
28	Michigan	304	50,900	6.0
29	South Dakota	267	49,000	5.5
30	Utah	109	22,700	4.8
31	Arizona	843	189,100	4.5

* *Number of American Indian-owned firms per 1,000 Indians.*

Source: Bureau of the Census, 1987 economic census, and author's estimates of 1987 Indian population

say that 113 reservations allow some form of gaming, and he attributes bingo's popularity to the effects of Reagan-era cutbacks in the Bureau of Indian Affairs budget. Lombardi says then-Secretary of the Interior James Watt told Indians, "Instead of depending on the Great White Father, why don't you start your own damn business?"

Indian culture also can create unique business opportunities. On the Hopi reservation in northern Arizona, Joe and Janice Day own a small shop on Janice's ancestral property. They swap elk hooves and cottonwood sticks, useful in Indian rituals, for jewelry, and baskets to sell to tourists.

The Days would like to credit their success to their shrewd sense of customer service. But they confess that the difference between profit and loss may be their wildly popular T-shirts, which read "Don't worry, be Hopi."

Not long ago, Hopis had to leave the reservation to go to school or find work. Today, the tribe has its own junior and senior high school and an entrepreneurial spirit. But small schools and small businesses won't keep people on the reservation. The Days still make a two-hour drive to Flagstaff each week to do their banking, laundry, and shopping. "The first Hopi you can get to build a laundromat is going to be a rich man," says Joe Day.

The Days lived in Flagstaff until their children finished high school. At that point, they decided to come "home." Janice's daughter is now an accountant in San Francisco, and she loves the amenities of the big city. "But who knows?" Janice says. "She may also want to come home someday. No matter where you are, you're still going to end up coming home."

THE URGE TO GO HOME

"Going home" may also mean renewing a bond with one's Indian heritage. While the population in 19 "Indian states" grew at predictable levels during the 1980s, the Urban Institute's Jeff Passel says it soared in the non-Indian states.

For example, Passel estimated the 1990 Indian population in Arizona at 202,000 (the 1980 population of 152,700, plus the intervening 58,600 births and minus the intervening 10,300 deaths)—a figure close to the 1990 census number (203,500). But in Alabama, a non-Indian state, Passel found a huge percentage increase that he could not have predicted. Alabama's Indian population grew from 7,600 in 1980 to 16,500 in 1990, a 117 percent increase. Higher birthrates, lower death rates, and migration from other states do not explain the increase.

Passel explains the gap this way: "The people who are Indians always identify themselves as Indians. They tell the census they are Indians, and they register their newborns as Indians." These people are usually found in the Indian states. "People who are part Indian may not identify themselves as American Indians. But they don't do that consistently over time."

Today, for reasons of ethnic pride, part-Indians may tell the Census Bureau they are Indian. At the hospital, they may identify themselves as white to avoid discrimination. This is most common in non-Indian states, which Passel generally defines as having fewer than 3,000 Indians in 1950.

"Instead of depending on the Great White Father, why don't you start your own damn business?"

California ranks second only to Oklahoma in its Indian population, but its mixture of tribes is unique in the nation. Some Indian residents trace their roots to native California tribes, says Malcolm Margolin. Others came west as part of a federal relocation program in the 1950s. In California cities, Cherokees, Chippewas, and other out-of-state Indians congregate in clubs.

"What has happened is the formation of an inter-tribal ethic, a pan-Indian ethic," Margolin says. "People feel that America has a lot of problems. That cultural doubt causes them to look for their ethnic roots, for something they can draw strength from. And for Indians, it's right there. It's ready-made."

THE GOOD, THE BAD, AND THE INTOLERABLE

Minority Group Rights

Will Kymlicka

WILL KYMLICKA is a professor of philosophy at the University of Ottawa.

Ethnocultural minorities around the world are demanding various forms of recognition and protection, often in the language of "group rights." Many commentators see this as a new and dangerous trend that threatens the fragile international consensus on the importance of individual rights. Traditional human rights doctrines are based on the idea of the inherent dignity and equality of all individuals. The emphasis on group rights, by contrast, seems to treat individuals as the mere carriers of group identities and objectives, rather than as autonomous personalities capable of defining their own identity and goals in life. Hence it tends to subordinate the individual's freedom to the group's claim to protect its historical traditions or cultural purity.

I believe that this view is overstated. In many cases, group rights supplement and strengthen human rights, by responding to potential injustices that traditional rights doctrine cannot address. These are the "good" group rights. There are cases, to be sure, where illiberal groups seek the right to restrict the basic liberties of their members. These are the "bad" group rights. In some cases, these illiberal practices are not only bad, but intolerable, and the larger society has a right to intervene to stop them. But in other cases, liberal states must tolerate unjust practices within a minority group. Drawing the line between the bad and the intolerable is one of the thorniest issues liberal democracies face.

I want to look at the relationship between group and individual rights in the context of the claims of indigenous peoples in North America. In both the United States and Canada, these peoples have various group rights. For example, they have rights of self-government, under which they exercise control over health, education, family law, policing, criminal justice, and resource development. They also have legally recognized land claims, which reserve certain lands for their exclusive use and provide guaranteed representation on certain regulatory bodies. And in some cases, they have rights relating to the use of their own language.

The situation of indigenous peoples is a useful example, I think, for several reasons. For one thing, they have been at the forefront of the movement toward recognizing group rights at the international level—reflected in the Draft Universal Declaration on Indigenous Rights at the United Nations. The case of indigenous peoples also shows that group rights are not a new issue. From the very beginning of European colonization, the "natives" fought for rights relating to their land, languages, and self-government. What has changed in recent years is not that indigenous peoples have altered their demands, but rather that these demands have become more visible, and that the larger society has started to listen to them.

Reflecting on this long history should warn us against the facile assumption that the demand for group rights is somehow a byproduct of current intellectual fashions, such as postmodernism, or of ethnic entrepreneurs pushing affirmative action programs beyond their original intention. On the contrary, the consistent historical demands of indigenous peoples suggests that the issue of group rights is an enduring and endemic one for liberal democracies.

Group rights, as I will use the term, refer to claims to something more than, or other than, the common rights of citizenship. The category is obviously very large and can be subdivided into any number of more refined categories, reflecting the different sorts of rights sought by different sorts of groups.

Two Kinds of Group Rights

For my purposes, however, the most important distinction is between two kinds of group rights: one involves the claim of an indigenous group against its own members; the other involves the claim of an indigenous group against the larger society. Both of these can be seen as protecting the stability of indigenous communities, but they respond to different sources of instability. The first is intended to protect a group from the destabilizing impact of internal dissent (that is, the decision of individual members not to follow traditional practices or customs), whereas the second is intended to protect the group from the impact of external decisions (that is, the economic or political policies of the larger society). I will call the first "internal restrictions" and the second "external protections."

Both are "group rights," but they raise very different issues. Internal restrictions involve intra-group relations. An indigenous group may seek the use of state power to restrict the liberty of its own members in the name of group solidarity. For example, a tribal government might discriminate against those members who do not share the traditional religion. This sort of internal restriction raises the danger of individual oppression. Group rights in this sense can be invoked by patriarchal and theocratic cultures to justify the oppression of women and the legal enforcement of religious orthodoxy.

Of course, all forms of government involve restricting the liberty of those subject to their authority. In all countries, no matter how liberal and democratic, people are required to pay taxes to support public goods. Most democracies also require people to undertake jury duty or to perform some amount of military or community service, and a few countries require people to vote. All governments expect and sometimes require a minimal level of civic responsibility and participation from their citizens.

But some groups seek to impose much greater restrictions on the liberty of their members. It is one thing to require people to do jury duty or to vote, and quite another to compel people to attend a particular church or to follow traditional gender roles. The former are intended to uphold liberal rights and democratic institutions, the latter restrict these rights in the name of orthodoxy or cultural tradition. It is these latter cases that I have in mind when talking about internal restrictions.

Obviously, groups are free to require respect for traditional norms and authorities as terms of membership in private, voluntary associations. A Catholic organization can insist that its members be Catholics in good standing, and the same applies to voluntary religious organizations within indigenous communities. The problem arises when a group seeks to use *governmental* power, or the distribution of public benefits, to restrict the liberty of members.

On my view, such legally imposed internal restrictions are almost always unjust. It is a basic tenet of liberal democracy that whoever exercises political power within a community must respect the civil and political rights of its members, and any attempt to impose internal restrictions that violate this condition is unjust.

External protections, by contrast, involve *inter*-group relations. In these cases, the indigenous group seeks to protect its distinct existence and identity by limiting its vulnerability to the decisions of the larger society. For example, reserving land for the exclusive use of indigenous peoples ensures that they are not outbid for this resource by the greater wealth of outsiders. Similarly, guaranteeing representation for indigenous peoples on various public regulatory bodies reduces the chance that they will be outvoted on decisions that affect their community. And allowing indigenous peoples to control their own health care system ensures that critical decisions are not made by people who are ignorant of their distinctive health needs or their traditional medicines.

On my view, these sorts of external protections are often consistent with liberal democracy, and may indeed be necessary for democratic justice. They can be seen as putting indigenous peoples and the larger society on a more equal footing, by reducing the extent to which the former is vulnerable to the latter.

Of course, one can imagine circumstances where the sorts of external protections demanded by a minority group are unfair. Under the apartheid system in South Africa, for example, whites, who constituted less than 20 percent of the population, demanded 87 percent of the land mass of the country, monopolized all the political power, and imposed Afrikaans and English throughout the entire school system. They defended this in the name of reducing their vulnerability to the decisions of other larger groups, although the real aim was to dominate and exploit these groups.

However, the sorts of external protections sought by indigenous peoples hardly put them in a position to dominate others. The land claims, representation rights, and self-government powers sought by indigenous peoples do not deprive other groups of their fair share of economic resources or political power, nor of their language rights. Rather, indigenous peoples simply seek to ensure that the majority cannot use its superior numbers or wealth to deprive them of the resources and institutions vital to the reproduction of their communities. And that, I believe, is fully justified. So, whereas internal restrictions are almost inherently in conflict with liberal democratic norms, external protections are not—so long as they promote equality between groups rather than allowing one group to oppress another.

The Group Rights of Indigenous Peoples

Which sorts of claims are indigenous peoples making? This is not always an easy question to answer. Self-government rights can be used either to secure external protections or to impose internal restrictions, and some indigenous groups use these rights in both ways.

But most indigenous peoples seek group rights primarily for the external protections they afford. Most groups are concerned with ensuring that the larger society does not deprive them of the resources and institutions necessary for their survival, not with controlling the extent to which their own members engage in untraditional or unorthodox practices. Under these circumstances, there is no conflict between external protections and individual rights. Groups that have these external protections may fully respect the civil and political rights of their own members. Indeed, many indigenous groups have adopted their own internal constitutional bills of rights, guaranteeing freedom of religion, speech, press, conscience, association, and a speedy and public trial.

In these cases, group rights supplement, even strengthen, standard human rights. Far from limiting the basic civil and political rights of individual Indians, they help to protect the context within which those rights have their meaning and efficacy. The long history of European-indigenous relations suggests that even if indigenous peoples have citizenship rights in the mainstream society, they tend to be politically impotent and culturally marginalized.

Some readers might think that I am underestimating the illiberal tendencies of indigenous groups. I have argued that many Indian communities are committed to respecting the rights of their individual members. Why then are most indigenous peoples in the United States opposed to the idea that their internal decisions should be subject to judicial review under the U.S. Bill of Rights?

This is an important question, which goes to the heart of the relationship between group and individual rights, and which is worth exploring in some depth. As part of their self-government, tribal councils in the United States have historically been exempted from the constitutional requirement to respect the Bill of Rights. Various efforts have been made by federal legislators to change this, most recently the 1968 Indian Civil Rights Act. According to this act, which was passed by Congress despite vociferous opposition from most Indian groups, tribal governments are now required to respect most (but not all) constitutional rights. However, there are still limits on judicial review of the actions of tribal councils. If a member of an Indian tribe feels that her rights have been violated by her tribal council, she can seek redress in a tribal court, but she cannot (except under exceptional circumstances) seek redress from the Supreme Court.

Indian groups remain strongly opposed to the 1968 Act, and would almost certainly resist any attempt to extend the jurisdiction of federal courts over Indian governments. Similarly, Indian bands in Canada have argued that their self-governing councils should not be subject to judicial review under the Canadian Charter of Rights and Freedoms. They do not want their members to be able to challenge band decisions in the courts of the mainstream society.

These limits on the application of constitutional bills of rights suggest that individuals or subgroups within Indian communities could be oppressed in the name of group solidarity or cultural purity. For example, concern has been expressed that Indian women in the United States and Canada might be discriminated against under certain systems of self-government, if these communities are exempt from the constitutional requirement of sexual equality. Demanding exemption from judicial review in the name of self government, for many people, is a smokescreen behind which illiberal groups hide their oppressive practices.

Before jumping to this conclusion, however, we should consider the reasons why groups that believe in individual rights would nonetheless be distrustful of judicial review. In the case of indigenous peoples, these reasons are, I think, painfully obvious. After all, the federal courts have historically accepted and legitimated the colonization and dispossession of Indian peoples and lands. Why should Indians trust the federal courts to act impartially now?

But there are other, more specific concerns. Many Indians argue that their self-government needs to be exempt from the Bill of Rights, not in order to restrict the liberty of women or religious dissidents, but to defend the external protections of Indians vis-à-vis the larger society. Their special rights to land, or to hunting, or to group representation, which reduce their vulnerability to external economic and political decisions, could be struck down as discriminatory under the Bill of Rights. Such protections do not, in my view, violate equality. On the contrary, a powerful case could be made that they promote equality, by protecting Indians from unjust majority decisions. But Indians rightly worry that the Supreme Court could take a different and more formalistic view of equality rights.

Indian leaders also fear that white judges might interpret certain rights in culturally biased ways. For example, traditional Indian forms of consensual political decision making could be seen as denying democratic rights. These traditional procedures do not violate the underlying democratic principle of the Constitution—namely, that legitimate authority requires the consent of the governed, subject to periodic review. However, they do not use the particular method for securing consent envisioned by the Constitution—namely, periodic election of representatives. Rather, they rely on time-honored procedures for ensuring consensual decision making. Indian leaders worry that white judges will impose their own culturally specific form of democracy, without considering whether traditional Indian practices are an equally valid interpretation of democratic principles.

It is often difficult for outsiders to assess the likelihood that self-government for an indigenous minority will lead to the suppression of basic individual rights. The identification of oppression requires sensitivity to the specific context, particularly when dealing with other cultures, and so it is not surprising that Indians would want these questions settled in a forum where judges are familiar with the situation.

Hence many Indian leaders seek exemption from the Bill of Rights, but at the same time affirm their commitment to basic human rights and freedoms. They endorse the principles, but object to the particular institutions and procedures that the larger society has established to enforce these principles. They seek to create or maintain their own procedures for protecting rights, specified in tribal constitutions (some of which are based on the provisions of international protocols).

Of course, not all Indian groups accept the commitment to respect individual rights. One example of internal restrictions concerns freedom of religion on the Pueblo reservation. Because they are not subject to the Bill of Rights, tribal governments are not required to obey its strict separation of church and state. The Pueblo have, in effect, established a theocratic government that discriminates against those members who do not share the tribal religion. For example, housing benefits have been denied to members of the community who have converted to Protestantism. In this case, self-government powers are being used to limit the freedom of members to question and revise traditional practices.

The Pueblo also use sexually discriminatory membership rules. If female members marry outside the tribe, their children are denied membership. But if men marry outside the tribe, the children are members. Here again, the rights of individuals are being restricted to preserve a communal practice (although there is some debate about whether this membership rule is in fact the "traditional" one, or whether it was adopted by the Pueblo at the behest of the American government, which hoped thereby to minimize its financial obligations).

In other cases, tribal governments have become profoundly undemocratic, governed by strongmen who ignore traditional ideals of consensus and govern by a combination of intimidation and corruption.

In these cases, not surprisingly, members of the Indian community often seek some form of outside judicial review. These cases put liberals on the horns of a serious dilemma. This is no longer a case of whites imposing "our" norms on Indians, who would prefer to live by "their" norms. The problem, rather, is that Indians themselves are deeply divided, not only about their traditional norms, but also about the ability of their traditional decision-making procedures to deal with these divisions. In some cases, reformers seeking federal judicial review may form a sizable minority, if not a majority, within their community. For example, the Native Women's Association of Canada, worried about the danger of sexual discrimination on their reserves, has demanded that the decisions of Aboriginal governments be subject to the Canadian Charter.

The Limits of Toleration

How should liberal states respond in such cases? It is right and proper, I think, for liberals to criticize oppressive practices within indigenous communities, just as we should criticize foreign countries that oppress their citizens. These oppressive practices may be traditional (although many aren't), but tradition is not self-validating. Indeed, that an oppressive practice is traditional may just show how deep the injustice goes.

But should we intervene and impose a liberal regime on the Pueblo, forcing them to respect the religious liberty of Protestants and the sexual equality of women? Should we insist that indigenous governments be subject to the Bill of Rights, and that their decisions be reviewable by federal courts?

It's important here to distinguish two questions: (1) Are internal restrictions consistent with liberal principles? and (2) Should liberals impose their views on minorities that do not accept some or all of these principles? The first is the question of *identifying* a defensible liberal theory of group rights; the second is the question of *imposing* that theory.

The first question is easy: internal restrictions are illiberal and unjust. But the answer to the second question is less clear. That liberals cannot automatically impose their principles on groups that do not share them is obvious enough, I think, if the illiberal group is another country. The Saudi Arabian government unjustly denies political rights to women or non-Muslims. But it doesn't follow that liberals outside Saudi Arabia should forcibly intervene to compel the Saudis to give everyone the vote. Similarly, the German government unjustly denies political rights to the children and grandchildren of Turkish "guest-workers," born and raised on German soil. But it doesn't follow that liberals outside Germany should use force to compel Germany to change its citizenship laws.

What isn't clear is the proper remedy for rights violations. What third party (if any) has the authority to intervene in order to force the government to respect those rights? The same question arises when the illiberal group is a self-governing indigenous community within a single country. The Pueblo tribal council violates the rights of its members by limiting freedom of conscience and by employing sexually discriminatory membership rules. But what third party (if any) has the authority to compel the Pueblo council to respect those rights?

Liberal principles tell us that individuals have certain claims that their government must respect, such as individual freedom of conscience. But having identified those claims, we now face the very different question of imposing liberalism. If a particular government fails to respect those claims, who can legitimately step in and force compliance? (By "imposing" liberalism, I am referring to forcible intervention by a third party. Noncoercive intervention is a different matter, which I discuss below.)

The attitude of liberals toward imposing liberalism has changed over the years. In the international context, they have become increasingly skeptical about using force to compel foreign states to obey liberal principles. Many nineteenth-century liberals thought that liberal states were justified in colonizing and instructing foreign countries. Woodrow Wilson defended the American colonization of the Philippines in 1902 on the grounds that "they are children and we are men in these matters of government and justice." Contemporary liberals, however, have abandoned this doctrine as both imprudent and illegitimate, and sought instead to promote liberal values through persuasion and financial incentives.

In the case of self-governing indigenous minorities, however, liberals have been much more willing to endorse coercive intervention. Many American liberals assume that the Supreme Court has the legitimate authority to overturn any decisions of the Pueblo tribal council that violate individual rights. They commonly assume that to have a "right" means not only that legislators should respect one's claim, but also that there should be a system of judicial review to ensure that respect. Moreover, this judicial review should occur at a country-wide level. That is, in addition to the various state and tribal courts that review the laws of state and tribal governments, there should also be a Supreme Court to which all governments within the country are answerable. Indeed, many American liberals often talk as if it is part of the very meaning of "rights" that there should be a single court in each country with the authority to review the decisions of all governments within that country.

This is a very particularist understanding of rights. In some liberal countries (for example, Britain), there is a strong tradition of respecting individual rights, but there is no constitutional bill of rights and no basis for courts to overturn parliamentary decisions that violate individual rights. (The same was true in Canada until 1982.) In other countries, there is judicial review, but it is decentralized—that is, political subunits have their own systems of review, but there is no single bill of rights and no single court to which all levels of government are answerable. Indeed, this was true in the United States for a considerable period of time. Until the passage of the Fourteenth Amendment, state legislatures were answerable to state courts for the way they respected state constitutions, but were not answerable to the Supreme Court for respecting the Bill of Rights.

It's easy to see why American liberals are committed to giving the Supreme Court such wide authority. Historically, this sort of judicial review, backed up by federal troops, was required to overturn the racist legislation of Southern states, which state courts had upheld. Given the central role federal courts have played in the struggle against racism, American liberals have developed a deep commitment to centralized judicial review. So when a question is raised about self-governing indigenous peoples, many liberals automatically support centralized review, even though these peoples were historically exempt from any such external intervention.

In short, contemporary liberals have become more reluctant to impose liberalism on foreign countries, but more willing to impose liberalism on indigenous minorities. This, I think, is inconsistent. Both foreign states and indigenous minorities form distinct political communities, with their own claims to self-government. Attempts to impose liberal principles by force are often perceived, in both cases, as a form of aggression or paternalistic colonialism. And, as a result, these attempts often backfire. The plight of many former colonies in Africa shows that liberal institutions are likely to be unstable when they are the products of external imposition rather than internal reform. In the end, liberal institutions can work only if liberal beliefs have been internalized by the members of the self-governing society, be it an independent country or an indigenous minority.

There are, of course, important differences between foreign states and indigenous minorities. Yet, in both cases, there is relatively little scope for legitimate coercive interference. Relations between the majority society and indigenous peoples should be determined by peaceful negotiation, not force. This means searching for some basis of agreement. The most secure basis would be agreement on fundamental principles. But if the two groups do not share basic principles, and cannot be persuaded to adopt the other's principles, they will have to rely on some more minimalist modus vivendi.

The resulting agreement may well exempt the indigenous minority from the Bill of Rights and judicial review. Indeed, such exemptions are often implicit in the historical treaties by which the minority entered the larger state. This means that the majority will sometimes be unable prevent the violation of individual rights within the minority community. Liberals have to learn to live with this, just as they must live with illiberal laws in other countries.

It doesn't follow that liberals should stand by and do nothing. An indigenous government that rules in an illiberal way acts unjustly. Liberals have a right, and a responsibility, to speak out against such injustice. Hence, liberal reformers inside the culture should seek to promote their principles through reason and example, and liberals outside should lend their support. Since the most enduring forms of liberalization are those that result from internal reform, the primary focus for liberals outside the group should be to support liberals inside.

Moreover, there is an important difference between coercively imposing liberalism and offering incentives for liberal reforms. Again, this is clear in the international arena. For example, the desire of former communist countries to enter the European Community (EC) has provided leverage for Western democracies to push for liberal reforms in Eastern Europe. Membership in the EC is a powerful, but noncoercive, incentive for liberal reform. Similarly, many people thought that negotiations over the North American Free Trade Agreement provided an opportunity for Canada and the United States to pressure the Mexican government into improving its human rights record.

There are many analogous opportunities for a majority to encourage indigenous peoples, in a noncoercive way, to liberalize their internal constitutions. Of course there are limits to the appropriate forms of pressure. Refusing to extend trade privileges is one thing, imposing a total embargo or blockade is quite another. The line between incentive and coercion is not a sharp one, and where to draw it is a much-debated point in the international context.

Finally, and perhaps most important, liberals can push for the development and strengthening of international mechanisms for protecting human rights. Some Indian tribes have expressed a willingness to abide by international declarations of rights, and to answer to international tribunals about complaints of rights violations within their communities. They accept the idea that their governments, like all sovereign governments, should be accountable to international norms. Indeed, they have shown greater willingness to accept this kind of review than many nation-states, which jealously guard their sovereignty in domestic affairs. Most Indian tribes do not oppose all forms of external review. What they object to is being subject to the constitution of their conquerors, which they had no role in drafting, and being answerable to federal courts composed entirely of non-Indian justices.

This shows, I think, that the assumption of American liberals that there must be one court within each country that is the ultimate defender of individual rights is doubly mistaken, at least in the case of indigenous peoples. History has proven the value of holding all governments accountable for respecting human rights. But the appropriate forum for reviewing the actions of self-governing indigenous peoples may skip the federal level, as it were. Many indigenous groups would endorse a system in which their decisions are reviewed in the first instance by their own courts and then by an international court. Federal courts, dominated by the majority, would have little or no authority over them.

These international mechanisms could arise at the regional as well as global level. European countries have agreed to establish their own multilateral human rights tribunals. Perhaps North American governments and Indian tribes could agree to establish a similar tribunal, on which both sides are fairly represented.

This isn't to say that federal intervention to protect liberal rights is never justified. In cases of gross and systematic violation of human rights, such as slavery, genocide, torture, or mass expulsions, there are grounds for intervening in the internal affairs of an indigenous group. A number of factors are relevant here, including the severity of rights violations within the community, the degree of consensus on restricting individual rights, and the ability of dissenting members to leave the community if they so desire. For example, whether intervention is justified in the case of an Indian tribe that restricts freedom of conscience surely depends on whether it is governed by a tyrant who lacks popular support and prevents people leaving the community or whether the tribal government has a broad base of support and religious dissidents are free to leave.

I should note that my arguments here do not just apply to indigenous peoples. They also apply to other national minorities—that is, other nonimmigrant groups whose homeland has been incorporated into a larger state through conquest, colonization, or the ceding of territory from one imperial power to another. Nonindigenous national minorities include the Québécois in Canada and Puerto Ricans in the United States. These groups differ from indigenous peoples in many ways, but in all these cases, the role of the federal courts in reviewing the decisions of self-governing minorities should be settled by negotiation, not imposition.

Cases involving immigrant groups are quite different. It is more legitimate to compel respect for liberal principles. I do not think it is wrong for liberal states to insist that immigration entails accepting the state's enforcement of liberalism, so long as immigrants know this in advance, and nonetheless choose to come.

Thinking Creatively about Rights

I've argued that the group rights sought by indigenous peoples need not conflict with human rights, and that the relationship between the two must be assessed carefully on a case-by-case basis. Even when the two do conflict, we cannot assume automatically that the courts and constitutions of the larger society should prevail over the self-governing decisions of the indigenous group. Indigenous peoples have good reasons, and sound legal arguments, to reject federal review of their self-government.

We should, however, think creatively about new mechanisms for enforcing human rights that will avoid the legitimate objections indigenous peoples have to federal courts. My aim is not to undermine human rights but rather to find fairer and more effective ways to promote them.

As Joseph Carens puts it, "People are supposed to experience the realization of principles of justice through various concrete institutions, but they may actually experience a lot of the institution and very little of the principle." This is exactly how many indigenous peoples perceive the supreme courts of Canada and the United States. What they experience is not the principle of human dignity and equality, but rather a social institution that has historically justified their conquest and dispossession.

Moreover, to focus exclusively on the danger of internal restrictions is often to miss the real source of injustice. The fact is that many indigenous groups feel compelled to impose internal restrictions because the larger society has denied them legitimate external protection. As Denise Réaume has noted, part of the "demonization" of other cultures is the assumption that they are naturally inclined to use coercion against their members. But insofar as some groups seem regrettably willing to use coercion to preserve traditional practices, this may be due, not to any innate illiberalism but to the fact that the larger society has failed to protect them. Unable to get protection for its lands and institutions, the minority turns to the only people it does have some control over, namely, its own members. This tendency does not justify internal restrictions, but it suggests that before we criticize a minority for imposing restrictions on its members, we should first make sure we are respecting its legitimate group rights.

Our goal, therefore, should be to find new mechanisms that will protect *both* the individual and group rights of indigenous peoples. We need to think about effective mechanisms, acceptable to indigenous peoples, for holding their governments accountable for the way individual members are treated. But we need simultaneously to think about effective mechanisms for holding the larger society accountable for respecting the group rights of indigenous peoples. Focusing on the former while neglecting the latter is counterproductive and hypocritical.

Many indigenous peoples have looked to the United Nations, and its draft declaration on indigenous rights, as a possible forum for pursuing these twin forms of accountability. Unfortunately, both the Canadian and U.S. governments have been reluctant to give any international body jurisdiction over the treaty rights, land claims, or self-government rights of indigenous peoples. Viewed in this light, the real obstacle to a more satisfactory balance of individual and group rights is not the refusal of indigenous peoples to accept external review, but rather the refusal of the larger society to accept restrictions on its sovereignty.

Canada Pressed on Indian Rights

Commission Urges Self-Rule for Tribes

Howard Schneider

Washington Post Foreign Service

OTTAWA, Nov. 21—Canada's governance of its aboriginal communities has failed and should be replaced by granting self-rule to as many as 80 separate Indian nations that would be provided with extensive land and resource rights, billions of dollars in extra aid and a new branch of Parliament to represent their interests, a blue-ribbon government commission reported today.

In a 4,000-page, $40 million report, the Royal Commission on Aboriginal People concluded that "Euro-Canada" had left the country's more than 800,000 Indians largely destitute, stripped of traditional lands and resources that should have been protected by treaty, and under immense pressure to assimilate into Western culture. The result: widespread poverty, high rates of alcoholism and teen suicide, and a growing potential for violence if Canada does not restructure the relationship with its original residents.

The commission suggested, in essence, that Canada start from scratch, renegotiating virtually every aspect of Indian governance and economics, and even soliciting the Queen of England to embody the new beginning in a royal proclamation. One issued in 1763, Indian leaders say, recognized their rights to independent government and came at a time of cooperation with European settlers, but later it was ignored during decades of domination and mistreatment.

"Some leaders fear that violence is in the wind," the commission stated in its summary. "What aboriginal people need is straightforward, if not simple: control over their lives in place of the well-meaning but ruinous paternalism of past Canadian governments."

The panel was established in 1991 by then-Prime Minister Brian Mulroney following a violent standoff between Mohawks and Quebec security officials. Mulroney appointed four of the commission's seven members from Indian communities and gave it a broad mandate to examine all aspects of Indian life. Its report came two years beyond its deadline, with tens of thousands of pages of testimony and reports collected, and with the distinction of being Canada's most expensive royal commission.

Indian leaders said the government should accept the commission's findings and begin implementing them immediately. "We call upon the government of Canada to deal with aboriginal peoples on a nation-to-nation basis, recognizing and encouraging the emergence of another order of government," said George Erasmus, a co-chairman of the commission.

But the impact of the document is uncertain. Its call for creation of dozens of self-governing nations is bound to echo in a country struggling to keep its European components—English- and French-speakers—unified. Within dozens of local communities, it will touch nerves as well. One recommendation, for example, would give Indian commercial fishermen priority over non-Indians during "times of scarcity"—an explosive issue in the struggling British Columbia salmon industry.

Likewise, the call for increased funding and a redistribution of land, timber, mineral, animal and other resources is likely to cause resentment throughout some parts of Canada; it was promptly criticized today by the Western-based Reform Party as a waste of money.

Indian Affairs Minister Ron Irwin all but ruled out extensive extra spending and many of the more comprehensive ideas included in the study. He said the current Liberal Party government supports Indian self-determination and wants to equitably settle land, resource and other issues in a way that will allow the communities to be economically independent—and is doing so on a case-by-case basis around the country. But that must be done, he said, within the constraints of a government struggling to balance its budget.

"Our aims are the same," he said of the government and the commission. "I don't know if it is going to come out" the way the panel recommended, with changes to the Canadian constitution and perhaps a dozen new independent tribunals established to renegotiate different aspects of Indian self-rule and resource claims.

But commission members and Indian leaders said it was time to abandon what they all a "project-by-project" approach that is neither quick nor comprehensive enough to address the problem. They want Canada to confront and correct an unpleasant part of its past—one they describe as including restrictions on Indian voting rights, prohibitions against free association and forced attendance by Indian children at boarding schools that were often the site of mental and physical abuse.

The price tag is steep in Canada's current fiscal climate—about $27 billion over the next 20 years. The commission contended that will be more than offset as Indian communities become economically successful, develop businesses using their land and resources, and stop having to rely on social services.

"We cannot escape the fact that we have built a great liberal democracy in part through the dispossession of aboriginal people and the imposition of our cultural norms," said Renee Dussault, a co-chairman of the commission. "The . . . sustained denial of this reality—manifested through the violation of agreements, the suppression of cultures and institutions, the refusal to live up to legal obligations—is the core of the problem. . . . Aboriginal people must have the opportunity and resources to exercise responsibility themselves."

The commission's 400 recommendations envision establishment of an extensive set of new institutions: a House of First Peoples to join the Parliament, an aboriginal university, parallel health and justice systems that would employ traditional methods of healing and curbing crime, and a panel, operating at arm's length from the government, to redistribute land and other resources in a way that recognizes historical Indian claims and forms a foundation for economic success. There would be between 60 and 80 such nations, established along historical, cultural and linguistic lines, with rights to establish governing institutions and norms.

Commission executive director Anthony Reynolds said it is a model similar to the one used in the United States, where tribes have developed businesses, including casinos, under their own rules and regulations. The commission report noted also that although Indians make up about 3 percent of Canada's population, they control less than 1 percent of the land, whereas U.S. tribes have land far in excess of the size of their population.

Amity in Indian Adoptions

John McCain

The writer, a Republican senator from Arizona, is chairman of the Senate Committee on Indian Affairs.

The adoption of Indian children has raised issues over the years that are charged with emotion and tragedy. As recently as two decades ago, inordinate numbers of Indian children were virtually kidnapped from their families and tribal communities and placed in foster and adoptive care.

Although these efforts sometimes were motivated by good intentions, the results often were tragic. Generations of Indian children were denied their rich culture and political heritage as Native Americans. The well-documented abuses from that era are horrifying. One study concluded that between 25 and 35 percent of all Indian children were torn from their birth families and tribes.

In 1978, Rep. Mo Udall and other leaders in Congress responded by enacting the Indian Child Welfare Act (ICWA) to prevent further abuses of Indian children. Under ICWA, adoptions of Indian children still could go forward, but the children's best interests were protected by involving Indian tribes in the welfare of their children.

Unfortunately, a new tragedy has emerged in recent years as ICWA has been implemented. This one has been borne by non-Indian adoptive families who, in a handful of high-profile cases, have had their adoptions of Indian children disrupted months and years after they received the child. In some cases, people facilitating the adoptions were accused of intentionally hiding from the courts, the adoptive families and the tribes the fact that the children involved were Indians covered by ICWA procedures. Some Indian tribes were accused of retroactively conveying membership on birth parents who wanted to change their minds long after the adoption placement was established with their voluntary consent.

In most cases, because Indian tribes typically were not made aware of an adoption until very late in the placement, tribes faced a tragic choice: Either intervene late in the proceeding and disrupt the certainty sought by the adoptive family and child, or stay out of it and lose all possibility of involvement in the life of the Indian child. The result has been great uncertainty and heartache on all sides. No matter the outcome in each of these cases, the Indian children have been the losers.

Several of these cases recently gained national attention. One involves the efforts of a non-Indian Ohio couple, Jim and Colette Rost, who have been trying to adopt twin daughters—now nearly 3 years old—placed with them at birth by an adoption attorney who failed to disclose that the children were Indians.

Last year some adoption advocates began to use cases such as these to build political support for sweeping amendments that would eviscerate ICWA. The Indian tribes believed they were under siege, battling distorted news stories about what ICWA does and does not do, while having to fend off efforts to weaken the law. By mid-1995 the rhetoric heightened, and positions hardened.

What happened next is a testament to how the most intractable of disputes can be resolved by voices of reason and people of goodwill.

Last summer, representatives on both sides left the battle lines to try to find common ground. Their initiative began a year-long process of negotiation between attorneys for non-Indian adoptive families and representatives of the Indian tribes to develop consensus amendments to ICWA.

What they achieved reflects a detailed, but not fragile, compromise. Its strength lies both in how it was developed and what it embodies. The attorney for the Rost family was involved in all the negotiations, along with representatives of the National Indian Child Welfare Association and the National Congress of American Indians (NCAI), the largest intertribal organization.

After extensive debate at its June, mid-year convention in Tulsa, NCAI endorsed the compromise. It also was endorsed by the American Academy of Adoption Attorneys and the Academy of California Adoption Attorneys. Many of my colleagues—including Sen. John Glenn (D-Ohio) and Rep. Deborah Pryce (R-Ohio)—who initially supported more far-reaching changes to the ICWA have indicated their support for this compromise.

Subsequently, several of us have introduced legislation that reflects the compromise. It has broad bipartisan support. Without trampling on tribal sovereignty and other fundamental principles in federal-Indian law, the bill amends the Indian Child Welfare Act to achieve greater certainty and speed in adoptions involving Indian children through new guarantees of early and effective notice in all cases. This is combined with new, strict time restrictions on both the right of Indian tribes to intervene and the right of Indian birth parents to revoke their consent to an adoptive placement. The bill would encourage early identification of the relatively few cases involving controversy and promote settlement of cases by making visitation agreements enforceable.

In exchange for guarantees of early notice, Indian tribes have agreed to language that will limit their right to intervene only to the earliest stages of an adoption placement, giving up their right under current law to intervene "at any point." If a tribe intervenes, it must certify to the state court that the child involved is a member, or eligible to be a member, of that tribe.

The Rosts's attorney has testified that prompt enactment of the compromise is likely to lead to an amicable settlement of the Rost case, ending further appeals of the recent court decision that allows the Indian twins to stay with the Rost family.

Those involved in the disputed cases believe the changes made by the compromise bill will prevent many future controversies. I share their view.

19. Amity in Indian Adoptions

Many times, Congress, with the very best of intentions, has passed laws which had unanticipated, adverse effects on the people they were intended to protect. The agreement we have reached on amendments to the Indian Child Welfare Act is intended to rectify ICWA's unintended consequences. The agreement respects the rights of Indians without risking the welfare of Indian children as a price of that respect. We need not impose on Indian children one or another deprivation—be denied your heritage or be denied a stable, secure home. These children, no less than any other children, deserve both cultural roots and loving parents. It is Congress's obligation to protect their rights to both by promptly enacting the agreement into law.

Dispute Over Indian Casinos in New Mexico Produces Quandary on Law and Politics

GEORGE JOHNSON

SANTA FE, N.M., Aug. 17—There was a time not long ago when a gambler here would have to travel 600 miles to Las Vegas, Nev., to wrestle with Lady Luck.

Now, within an hour's drive of Santa Fe, six Indian pueblos operate full-scale casinos. Altogether, 11 tribes statewide offer roulette, poker, blackjack and slot machines, as well as convenient automatic teller machines.

Allowing gambling to continue even though it is illegal.

There is one major problem. The casinos are operating in violation of Federal and state laws. More than a year after the State Supreme Court ruled that the gambling pacts that the tribes signed with Gov. Gary E. Johnson were illegal, a decision that two Federal judges have upheld, the casinos remain open.

No one apparently has the heart or stomach to shut them.

The gaming industry, employing 3,000 people and generating more than $200,000 million in revenue a year, may be the best thing to happen to New Mexico Indians in four centuries of Spanish and American dominance.

Last month, Judge Martha Vazquez of Federal District Court ruled against the casinos and then took the unusual step of staying her own decision, allowing the gambling to continue while the case is appealed.

"It's a vexing problem, a real paradox," said State Representative Max Coll, Democrat of Santa Fe and a leading opponent of casino gambling. "When it's obvious that something is illegal and continuing, it should be stopped."

The United States Attorney for New Mexico, John J. Kelly, who is in charge of enforcing Federal law on the reservations, says he is trying to avoid a direct confrontation while continuing to insist that the casinos are breaking the law. "The tribes are my neighbors, and I have a great deal of respect for them," Mr. Kelly said. "I know they'll do the right thing once we have a definitive judicial determination."

Last year two pueblos, Pojoaque north of here and Isleta south of Albuquerque, threatened to block highways through their land if they were forced to close the casinos.

Judge Vazquez's decision was met with tribal protests that compared gambling opponents with George Armstrong Custer and the gambling pacts with broken treaties.

At a news conference last month, according to The Albuquerque Journal, Gov. Jacob Viarrial of Pojoaque called Mr. Kelly an "Indian fighter and an Indian hater."

Under the Federal Indian Gaming Regulatory Act, tribes must sign agreements with their home states before opening casinos. Last July, the State Supreme Court overturned the agreements here because the Legislature had not approved them.

Mr. Kelly did not prosecute. He asked the tries and Legislature to negotiate new accords. But an anti-gambling coalition and political enemies of the Governor have blocked attempts to legalize the casinos.

In November, the State Supreme Court ruled that all gambling except for horse racing and the state lottery was illegal. Under some interpretations of the Indian gaming act, tribes can engage only in types of gambling allowed elsewhere in a state.

Mr. Johnson and the tribes had been relying on the fact that charities and fraternal organizations occasionally held so-called Las Vegas night fund-raising events. But the court ruled that those were illegal.

Mr. Kelly then ordered the casinos to close by January or face seizures of their equipment. Nine tribes sued in Federal Court, arguing that the pacts had been signed in good faith and had been approved by the Interior Secretary. That approval, critics contend, is simply a routine bureaucratic procedure.

Mr. Kelly extended the deadline, and the tribes agreed not to obstruct traffic and to close the casinos if the judge ruled against them.

Last month Judge Vazquez agreed that the pacts were illegal. That decision followed one by another Federal judge, John Conway, in June. In a case involving the Mescalero Apaches in southern New Mexico, Judge Conway also held that the gambling agreements were illegal.

Several tribes were preparing to close their casinos when Judge Vazquez stayed her order pending an appeal to the United States Court of Appeals for the 10th Circuit in Denver. To close the casinos, the judge said, would create hardships for the tribes, many of which had incurred debts and were using gambling profits to finance social programs.

The issues were so "serious, complex, and novel," she said, her decision might be overturned on appeal.

"It's an unusual situation we're in right now," Attorney General Tom Udall said. "Three courts have spent quite a bit of time analyzing this and come up with the same position."

At the request of Mr. Udall and Mr. Kelly, the circuit court has agreed to expedite the appeal and hear arguments, possibly as early as November. Mr. Udall, a Democrat who is often at odds with Mr. Johnson's Republican administration, said the gambling problems would not have arisen if Mr. Johnson had not been in such a hurry to sign the agreements with the tribes, which contributed $250,000 to his campaign.

In his first weeks in office, Mr. Johnson approved the agreements, which call for minimal state regulation in return for part of the proceeds.

"Johnson decided to give away the ranch," said Mr. Udall, son of former Interior Secretary Stewart L. Udall. "He really led the tribes down the primrose path. If Johnson had proceeded much more cautiously he could have come up with compacts everyone could live with."

Mr. Johnson's press secretary, Diane Kinderwater, said the Governor should be commended for quickly confronting a long-neglected problem. When he came into office, some casinos had been operating without agreements for years. Leaving regulation mostly to the tribes, she said, was consistent with Mr. Johnson's respect for Indian sovereignty.

Gov. Alex Lujan of the Sandia pueblo, a community of 500 just north of Albuquerque, said the tribes were caught in the middle of partisan squabbling. "Unfortunately," Mr. Lujan said, "this is a very political situation. If the Democrats and Republicans could just deal with the issue rather than bringing political affiliations into it, I think we would have valid compacts."

Like many other tribal leaders, Mr. Lujan said the gaming act gave too much power to the states. "Being a sovereign nation," he added, "our dealings should be directly with the United States Government."

Native-American Women in History

Nancy Shoemaker

Nancy Shoemaker teaches history at the State University of New York at Plattsburgh and is the editor of Negotiators of Change: Historical Perspectives on Native American Women *(New York: Routledge, 1995).*

Ironically, Native-American women figure prominently in traditional narratives of American history, but until recently women's experiences and perspectives have been largely excluded from research in Native-American history. Ask any schoolchild to name famous Native Americans from before 1850, and most likely you will hear of Pocahontas and Sacagawea. But pick up any book surveying American-Indian history, white-Indian relations in the United States, or the history of a particular tribe, and there will be little mention of either specific women or of women in general.

In the spirit of this uniting of two worlds and two peoples, Pocahontas's and Sacagawea's lives are often distorted to make a better story.

What exactly did Pocahontas and Sacagawea do to earn themselves a place in the pantheon of American-history heroines? Pocahontas was the daughter of the powerful Indian leader Powhatan, whose confederacy of different Indian nations in the Virginia region presented a significant challenge to the English colonists who settled at Jamestown in 1607. Pocahontas is remembered primarily for having saved Captain John Smith's life, an act which was probably part of a native captivity and adoption ritual but which endured in the narrative of American history because it implies that the conquered gladly assisted in their own conquest. Sacagawea became a historical figure for the same reason. As interpreter and guide to Meriwether Lewis and William Clark in their explorations of the Louisiana Purchase from 1804–1806, Sacagawea opened up the West to American settlement. At least that is how she has often been pictured in American popular culture, one arm extended, graciously directing Lewis and Clark to a landscape green with the promise of wealth. Although one Indian man, Squanto, was cast in that same role in the story of Pilgrim settlement of New England, Indian women seemed to fit this role much better, for the continents were themselves often depicted on maps and in promotional literature as gendered: the woman America, plump and naked except for a few leaves, embraced the iron-clad European conquistador and the "New World" and "Old World" melded into one.

In the spirit of this uniting of two worlds and two peoples, Pocahontas's and Sacagawea's lives are often distorted to make a better story. Most people trying to recall who Pocahontas was, want to marry her off to John Smith. In reality, she married another English colonist, John Rolfe, who was instrumental in making tobacco the enormously profitable mainstay of the Chesapeake economy. Similarly, Sacagawea, in a movie from the 1950s

From *OAH Magazine of History*, Summer 1995, pp. 10-14. © 1995 by the Organization of American Historians. Reprinted by permission.

starring Donna Reed, falls tragically in love with William Clark, but alas, must give him up because she is an Indian, and he is engaged to marry a white woman. Sacagawea's own story, as recounted in the journals of Lewis and Clark, seems much more tragic. A Shoshoni woman who as a girl had been captured by another Indian tribe, she was one of at least two wives of an abusive French fur trader named Charbonneau, the official guide hired by the exploring party. Popular renditions of these two women's lives get the details wrong, but the underlying reality may not have been all that different. Both Pocahontas and Sacagawea indeed married white men, and for that reason were well-placed to mediate the cultural and economic exchanges between Indians and Euro-Americans. Yet, as historian Clara Sue Kidwell has observed, it is difficult to discern Pocahontas's and Sacagawea's own motives, loyalties, and understandings of the historical events in which they participated.

It is equally difficult to know to what extent the histories of Pocahontas and Sacagawea can be generalized to shed light on Indian women's experiences in general. In other times and places, Indian women did become important go-betweens in the Indian and Euro-American cross cultural exchange. Sylvia Van Kirk's book, *Many Tender Ties*, a history of women in the beaver fur trade in Canada showed how crucial Indian women were to the success of the fur trade in its early years. Women processed furs, prepared foods such as pemmican (dried meat mixed with berries), and served as interpreters. And through their marital and sexual relationships with French and British fur traders, they linked their communities to Europeans in ways that both enhanced and complicated economic exchanges and political alliances. In later periods, Indian women continued to be important bicultural mediators, but may have felt increasingly divided by the competing interests of their own people and Euro-Americans. The Paiute woman Sarah Winnemucca, for instance, served as a scout and interpreter for the United States, but later wrote her autobiography and made speaking tours to bring attention to the injustices that had been committed against her people.

Sarah Winnemucca cannot be considered any more representative than Pocahontas or Sacagawea, but currently much of what historians know about Indian women's lives in the past comes from the stories of individual women. Especially useful are autobiographies. Most of these autobiographies of Indian women were dual-authored, either with anthropologists or with a popular mainstream writer. Whether the autobiography was part of an anthropologist's attempt to construct a life history that would also inform readers about culture as in the case of Nancy Lurie's *Mountain Wolf Woman*, or a popular writer's nostalgic rendering of how Indian life used to be, as in Frank Linderman's *Pretty-Shield* autobiographies can be useful documents for historians interested in understanding the changes in women's lives from their own perspective. Also, some autobiographies, *Pretty-Shield* and Gilbert Wilson's *Waheenee* for example, were originally published with a children's readership in mind, which means that they are very accessible to students.

The production of Indian women's autobiographies continues today. Wilma Mankiller, formerly principal chief of the Cherokee Nation, recently wrote an autobiography. And, Mary Crow Dog (now, Mary Brave Bird) has published two accounts of her life. Her *Lakota Woman* provides a glimpse into women's participation in the restless political struggles of the 1960s and 1970s, focusing on the American Indian Movement and the 1973 militant takeover of the hamlet of Wounded Knee, South Dakota. Despite the tremendous importance of women's autobiographies, historians still face the difficulty of connecting individual experience to the broader issues of native women's changing roles and attitudes.

Other than autobiographies, most of the documents available to historians were written by white men: explorers, government agents, and missionaries. And although these Euro-American recorders of Indian cultures often included some commentary on Indian women, their observations were loaded with assumptions and expectations about what they thought Indians and women were supposed to be. Euro-American accounts of Indian cultures were especially critical of native women's work. Indian women either seemed to work too much or they did work which in Euro-American societies was defined as men's work. At the time of European contact, Indian women in tribes east of the Mississippi were largely responsible for the agricultural fieldwork. They grew the corn, squash, and beans. On the northwest coast, Indian women were active traders, much too shrewd and aggressive than their Euro-American trading partners wanted them to be. And throughout native America, women did much of the carrying. They brought wood and water into the village or camp, and in the case of Plains Indian women had charge of dismantling, packing, transporting, and re-erecting tipis. Euro-American men criticized Indian men for abusing "their women" by treating them like "squaw drudges" or "beasts of burden," a stereotype of Indian women much in contrast with the romanticized, "Indian princess" portrayals of Pocahontas and Sacagawea.

Euro-American descriptions of Indian politics imposed biases on the documentary record of a different nature. In the often detailed transcripts of Indian councils, why were women rarely mentioned? Is it because they were not there? Or, is it because Euro-American observers of the council did not notice they were there or did not think their presence was worth mentioning? In those cases where women did make their presence known in the political arena, Euro-Americans exaggerated women's political power and derided certain tribes, particularly the Iroquois, for being "petticoat governments" or "matriarchates," disorderly societies in which women ruled over men. While it is true that among the Iroquois clan mothers had the right to designate a chief's successor and remove or "dehorn" chiefs from office, Iroquois women did not rule over men.

Anthropologists and historians, who must rely greatly on a documentary record which for the most part excludes native women's voices, have been especially suspicious of how Euro-American descriptions of native societies portray them as having separate spheres: a public, male sphere of politics, diplomacy, war, and trade; and a private or domestic female sphere of childbearing, child rearing, food processing, and household management. In reading the historical record, one would learn that women's labor usually took place within the proximity of the village or camp. While tending to their children women worked in nearby cornfields or gathered nuts, berries, and other wild foods. They distributed food within the household, and were often said to own the houses. Men's work usually involved dealing with outsiders, and men were most often, but not always, the diplomats, traders, and warriors. Indian women do appear to have been most active in a private or domestic sphere, while men seemed to control the public sphere. But do the documents give this impression of gendered public and private space because Euro-American men imposed their own preferences about distinct male and female worlds on what they saw, heard, and noticed?

Much of the research in Indian women's history thus far has challenged the existence of public/male and private/female spheres in Indian societies by looking for Indian women in the public space and reconstructing a public role for them. Among different tribes in different time periods, there were some women chiefs, some women who spoke in council, some women who went to war, and some women who participated actively in trade with Euro-Americans. However, this literature produced by historians could just as easily be misrepresenting Indian women's experience in its eagerness to find Indian women in places which Euro-Americans defined as the locus of power. One could just as easily criticize the model of male/public and female/private by asking whether power resided only in the public sphere. Given the significance of the family, or clan, in native political systems, the private or domestic sphere may have been an important site for discussion and decision making about issues such as whether their people should go to war, move, or make alliances with other nations. In the Iroquois example, the political duties of clan mothers originated in the matrilineal clan structure of Iroquois politics, in which chiefs represented their clans in council. Although few tribes had such institutionalized political roles for women, women's significance within the family must have allocated them some influence on decisions affecting the larger community.

Instead of simply highlighting instances in which native women appeared in a public sphere, historians of Indian women's history and gender history are now bringing a more complex array of questions to their research. Much of this research has focused on the effects of Euro-American contact. Thus, historians researching United States Indian policy have shown how many government programs promoting Indian assimilation saw gender roles as crucially important to transforming Indian cultures. Indian women and men variously responded to these programs, sometimes with open resistance, sometimes by diverting the intent of the policies, and sometimes by selectively accepting certain aspects of the policies to fit more closely their traditional ideas about gender. The impact of missionization on Indian women is similarly being reconsidered. Historians used to believe that Indian women were more likely than men to reject Christianity because missionaries also sought to restructure native families to fit a nuclear, patriarchal model. However, historians are now acknowledging the diversity of women's responses to Christian missions and acknowledge that many Indian women did choose to become Christian. Many even became leaders of women's church groups, and thus helped shape how Christianity became incorporated in native communities.

Few historians have conducted research upon Indian women's history in the twentieth century, even though the political and economic resurgence of native communities in recent decades raises interesting questions about women's participation in tribal government, the post-World War II migration to cities, and economic transitions from farming and ranching to wage labor. In the twentieth century, Indian women have been tribal chiefs, political activists, housewives, weavers, educators, provisioners of health care and social services on reservations and in urban communities, nuns, novelists, artists, and ranchers. Of course, they have also been mothers, daughters, wives, grandmothers, and aunts.

Scholars have long recognized the great diversity in the histories of American-Indian tribes and the impossibility of generalizing about Navajos and Cherokees, Menominees and Lakotas. Gender adds another dimension to this diversity. Within tribes, the experiences of men and women differed. Moreover, women within tribal groups may also have had different experiences based on their age, family background, religion, educational and work experiences, and choices they have made about where to live and what kind of life to pursue. While the growing interest in American-Indian women's history will make summarizing that history increasingly difficult, it will also bring us closer to understanding what Pocahontas and Sacagawea were really all about.

Bibliography

Albers, Patricia and Beatrice Medicine. *TheHidden Half Studies of Plains Indian Women.* Lanham, Md.: University Press of America, 1983.

Bataille, Gretchen M. and Kathleen Mullen Sands. *American Indian Women: Telling Their Lives.* Lincoln: University of Nebraska Press, 1984.

Canfield, Gae Whitney. *Sarah Winnemucca of the Northern Paiutes.* Norman: University of Oklahoma Press, 1983.

Crow Dog, Mary, with Richard Erdoes. *Lakota Woman.* New York: Harper Collins, 1990.

Kidwell, Clara Sue. "Indian Women as Cultural Mediators." *Ethnohistory* 39 (Spring 1992): 97–107.

Linderman, Frank B. *Pretty-Shield: Medicine Woman of the Crows.* Lincoln: University of Nebraska Press, 1932.

Lurie, Nancy Oestreich. *Mountain Wolf Woman: Sister of Crashing Thunder; The Autobiography of a Winnebago Indian.* Ann Arbor: University of Michigan Press, 1985.

Mankiller, Wilma and Michael Wallis. *Mankiller: A Chief and Her People.* New York: St. Martin's Press, 1993.

Spittal, W.G. *Iroquois Women: An Anthology.* Ohsweken, Ontario: Iroqrafts, 1990.

Van Kirk, Sylvia. Many Tender *Ties: Women in Fur-Trade Society, 1670–1870.* Norman: University of Oklahoma Press, 1980.

Wilson, Gilbert L. *Waheenee.* Lincoln: University of Nebraska Press, 1981.

Hispanic/Latino Americans

The following collection of materials on Hispanic/Latino Americans is a composite of findings about ethnicities. The clustering of these ethnicities and nationalities, as well as their relationship to the Spanish language, seems to be sufficient evidence of the commonalities that constitute the shared expression of this complex of memory and contemporary politics. Yet the interchangeable use of "Hispanic" and "Latino" as nominative of their differentiation from the Anglo-American founding, and their social expression as they search for a cultural and political terrain, are but the surface of the process of intergroup dynamics in the United States.

The articles in this unit propose angles of vision that enable us to view the process of accommodation and change that is articulated in political practice, scholarship, advocacy, and art. The issues presented provocatively shift traditional perspectives from the eastern and midwestern mind-set toward the western and southwestern analysis of immigration to the United States.

The Immigration Act of 1965 induced a process not unlike the period of large-scale eastern and southern European immigration between 1880 and 1924. This immigration includes scores of various ethnic groups. Cultural/geographic descriptions are not the clearest form of ethnic identity.

Hispanic/Latino Americans are not a single ethnic group. The designation of various ethnic populations whose ancestry is derived from Spanish-speaking countries by the words "Hispanic" and "Latino" is a relatively recent phenomenon in the United States. The cultural, economic, and political differences and similarities of various Hispanic communities, as well as the wide dispersal of these communities, suggest the need for care in generalization about Hispanic American populations.

The realities of these groups—whether they are political refugees, migrant workers, descendants of residents settled prior to territorial incorporation into the United States, long-settled immigrants, recent arrivals, or the children and grandchildren of immigrants—present interesting and varied patterns of enclave community, assimilation, and acculturation as well as isolation and marginalization. Hispanic/Latino American linkages to other Latin countries, the future of their emerging political power, and their contributions to cultural and economic change within the United States are interesting facets of the Hispanic/Latino American experience.

The Hispanic/Latino experience is a composite of groups seeking unity while interacting with the larger arena of ethnic groups that constitute American society. Convergent issues that bridge differences, as well as those that support ideological and strategic differences, bode a future of both cooperation and conflict.

What issues bind Hispanic groups together? What values cause cleavages among Hispanic populations? What does bilingualism mean? Is bilingualism a freedom-of-speech issue? Is bilingualism a concern of non-Spanish-speaking persons in the United States? What are the implications of establishing an official public language policy?

Competition and conflict over mobility into mainstream leadership positions are aspects of American society that may be exacerbated by the misuse of ethnic indicators. Nonetheless, indicators of social cohesion and traditional family bonds are apparently noncompetitive and nonconflictual dimensions of robust ethnic experiences. Thus, fears that Hispanic/Latino Americans may not relish competitive pressures are assuaged by the capacities of family and community to temper the cost of any such failure. This complex dynamic of personal and group interaction is a fascinating and fruitful topic for a society seeking competitiveness and stronger community bonds. Cast in this fashion, the American dilemma takes on a new and compelling relevance.

Looking Ahead: Challenge Questions

How does attention to historical background and its expression in current culture promote both understanding and tolerance?

What strengths and weaknesses do strong bonds of ethnic communities possess?

In what respects is Hispanic/Latino American culture becoming part of mainstream American culture?

To what do you attribute the popularity of Mexican, Italian, and Chinese foods in the marketplace?

UNIT 4

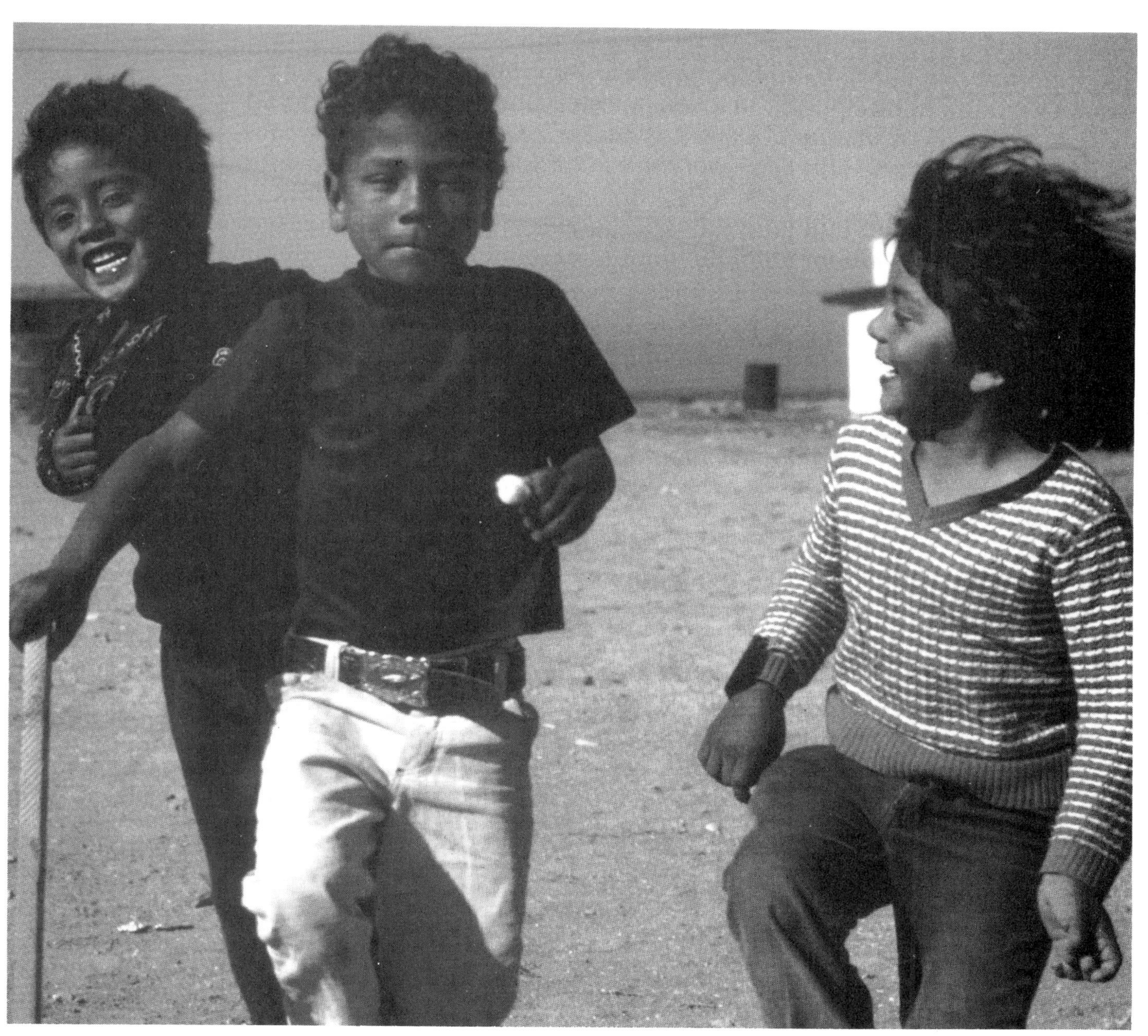

Specific Hispanics

SUMMARY Los Angeles, New York, Miami, Chicago, and Houston are well-known Hispanic markets. But just below the big five are dozens of smaller Hispanic centers. This first-ever look at 12 Hispanic groups reveals the top towns for Colombians, Brazilians, and others. The rapid growth of specific Hispanic groups is destined to attract attention from marketers.

Morton Winsberg

Morton Winsberg is professor of geography at Florida State University in Tallahassee.

Most marketers are familiar with the three biggest Hispanic-American groups. Since the U.S. census first counted Hispanics in 1970, those who identify Mexico, Puerto Rico, and Cuba as their country of origin have comprised about three-fourths of the total U.S. Hispanic population. Hispanics from other Latin-American nations and cultures are less well-understood, but they constitute one-quarter of an estimated $170 billion consumer market. And because Hispanics of all kinds often live together in small areas, each country of origin can form a visible and desirable target market.

Among all Hispanics, the share of Mexicans has fallen from 62 percent of all U.S. Hispanics in 1970 to 61 percent in 1990. The Puerto Rican and Cuban shares have remained at about 12 percent and 5 percent, respectively. Hispanic Americans who don't have origins in these three countries are a small share of the nation's total Hispanic population, but they have been growing. Their numbers grew by slightly more than 2 million between 1970 and 1990. Immigrants of the new wave have been fleeing civil wars in Nicaragua, El Salvador, Guatemala, and Colombia. Others come for jobs or to rejoin family members already here.

The 1970 and 1980 censuses identified just four categories of Hispanics: Mexican, Puerto Rican, Cuban, and "other." The 1990 census provides much more detailed information, identifying 12 nations of Hispanic origin, as well as "other" Central Americans and "other" South Americans. These data provide the first opportunity to understand where specific Hispanic groups live.

Many of the smaller Hispanic subgroups never show up on marketers' computer screens. Language barriers and the lack of large ethnic neighborhoods can make it hard to reach them with specially designed messages. Also, many Hispanic immigrants do not plan to become U.S. citizens or permanent residents. But rapid growth will inevitably lead more businesses to target Hispanic diversity. In ten years, America's Little Havanas will get a lot bigger.

Immigrants have always settled in America's largest cities, and today's immigrants are not much different.

BELOW THE BIG FIVE

Immigrants have always settled in America's largest cities, and today's immigrants are not much different. Six of the 12 Hispanic subgroups identified in the 1990 census have more than 80 percent of their populations in the nation's 20 largest cities, and 3 others have between 70 and 79 percent.

Mexican Americans are the only exception to the urban rule, because many of their ancestors never immigrated. Many Mexicans became U.S. citizens in the 19th century following the acquisition of Mexican territory by the United States. Almost all of this land was and still is rural or small cities. Many Mexicans who immigrated to the U.S. in recent years have settled in these same southwestern states. Here they normally reside in cities both large and small, as well as in rural areas.

Hispanics, like immigrants who came earlier, tend to concentrate in one or two major urban areas. New York City and Los Angeles early became a popular destination for Hispanics, but more recently, many have chosen Miami, Washington, D.C., and San Francisco. An example of an unusually high concentration of a Hispanic group in one city is the 77 percent concentration of people of Dominican origin in the New York urbanized area. Greater New York also has 60 percent of the nation's Ecuadorians and 44 percent of Puerto Ricans. Los Angeles has 49 percent of the nation's Guatemalans and 47 percent of its Salvadoreans. Miami is home to 53 percent of Cuban Americans.

Several U.S. places have Hispanic populations that rival or even surpass the largest cities in their countries of origin. New York's Puerto Rican population is now more than double that of San Juan. New York also has the second-largest urban population of Dominicans in the world, and the third-largest Ecuadorian population. The Mexican, Salvadorean, and Guatemalan populations of urban Los Angeles are surpassed only by those of their respective capitals: Mexico City, San Salvador, and Guatemala City.

The most exotic place where Mexicans cluster may be Bay City-Saginaw, Michigan.

Eighteen percent of all Hispanic Americans live in Los Angeles, and 12 percent live in New York. These two urban areas rank among the top-5 for 11 of the 12 Hispanic groups. Miami is on the top-5 list for 9 Hispanic groups, Washington, D.C., for 6, San Francisco for 5, and Houston and Chicago for 4.

The census also reveals many smaller areas with large and growing populations of specific Hispanics. For example, San Antonio and San Diego have the fourth- and fifth-largest Mexican-American communities in the nation, and Philadelphia has the third-largest Puerto Rican population. Tampa and Fort Lauderdale have the fourth- and fifth-largest concentrations of Cubans, and the Massachusetts areas of Boston and Lawrence have the third- and fourth-largest Dominican groups.

Chicago is the only midwestern urban area to come up on any of the top-5 lists, but it comes up a lot. Chicago has the country's second-largest Puerto Rican population, the second-largest Mexican population, and the third-largest Guatemalan and Ecuadorian populations. As a whole, Chicago has the fourth-largest Hispanic population of any urban area, at 4 percent of the national total.

TWELVE HISPANIC GROUPS

Laredo, Texas, is not big as urban areas go, with 99,258 people in 1990. But 94 percent of Laredo residents are Hispanic, and the overwhelming majority are of Mexican origin. The census count of Hispanics, also mainly Mexican, is 90 percent in Brownsville and 83 percent in McAllen, two other Texas border towns. Several border towns in other states have equally high shares of Mexican Americans.

Perhaps the most exotic place where Mexicans congregate in large numbers is in the Bay City-Saginaw metropolitan area in Michigan. Mexicans first came to Bay City-Saginaw to work on the local cucumber farms. The descendants of these farm laborers now hold urban jobs, many in the local foundries.

Puerto Ricans began immigrating to the U.S. after World War II, and now they are a significant presence in the industrial cities of New York and southern New England. When older residents of these cities had achieved middle-class status and moved to the suburbs, they left behind entry-level jobs in manufacturing and service, and low-cost housing. The Puerto Ricans who took those jobs established the barrios of New York City.

While less affluent Puerto Ricans came to the U.S. for jobs, many middle-class Cubans fled their native country for political reasons. Cubans soon became closely identified with southeastern Florida, but now they are found in several other Florida towns. In the university towns of Gainesville and Tallahassee, for example, many second-generation Cuban Americans live as students.

Dominicans are a major Hispanic force in New York City and several New England industrial towns. They are only 2 percent of the nation's 1990 Hispanic population, but they are 15 percent of Hispanics in New York, 22 percent in Providence, and 35 percent in Lawrence, Massachusetts. Dominicans are flocking to the Northeast for the same reason Puerto Ricans did several decades ago: jobs. Hondurans and Nicaraguans, who have also immigrated largely for economic reasons, are settling in more bilingual areas on the Gulf of Mexico.

Hondurans are most numerous in New York, Los Angeles, and Miami, and Nicaraguans are most common in Miami, Los Angeles, and San Francisco. But both groups are dwarfed by the enormous numbers of other Hispanics in these large urban areas, so their largest concentrations emerge in unexpected places. Although Hondurans are less than 1 percent of the nation's Hispanic population, they are 20 percent of Hispanics in New Orleans. Nicaraguans are also well-represented among New Orleans Hispanics, and they are visible in nearby Baton Rouge and Port Arthur. Salvadoreans are just 3 percent of the

Hispanics of all types cluster in New York a
Central Americans in San Francisco, Colomb

(top-five urbanized areas for H

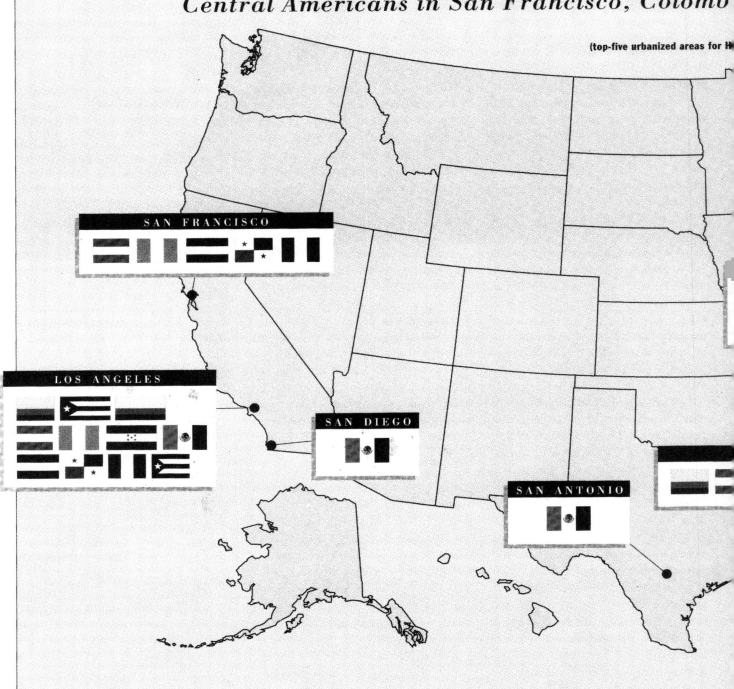

SAN FRANCISCO

LOS ANGELES

SAN DIEGO

SAN ANTONIO

OVER AMERICA

l Los Angeles. But you can also find lots of
ns in Chicago, and Peruvians in Washington.

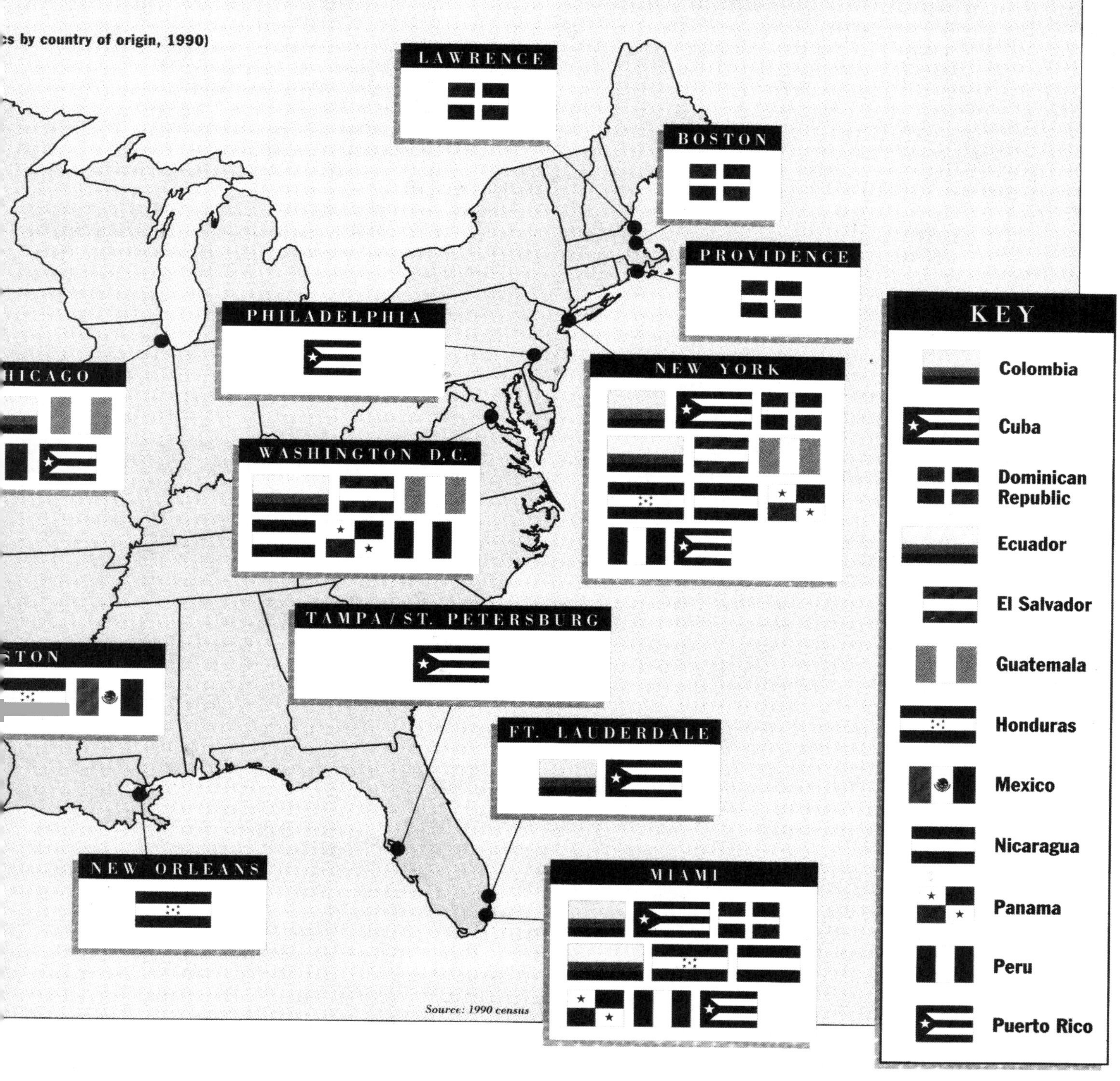

Little Quitos and Little

Mexico

top-five urbanized areas	population	share
U.S. total	13,393	100%
Los Angeles	3,066	23
Chicago	538	4
Houston	528	4
San Antonio	524	4
San Diego	414	3

El Salvador

top-five urbanized areas	population	share
U.S. total	565	100%
Los Angeles	265	47
New York	62	11
Washington, DC	52	9
San Francisco	43	8
Houston	39	7

Puerto Rico

top-five urbanized areas	population	share
U.S. total	2,652	100%
New York	1,178	44
Chicago	1,464	6
Philadelphia	107	4
Miami	68	3
Los Angeles	51	2

Dominican Republic

top-five urbanized areas	population	share
U.S. total	520	100%
New York	403	77
Miami	23	5
Boston	16	3
Lawrence, MA	12	2
Providence, RI	9	2

Cuba

top-five urbanized areas	population	share
U.S. total	1,053	100%
Miami	559	53
New York	154	15
Los Angeles	55	5
Tampa-St. Petersburg	32	3
Ft. Lauderdale	24	2

Colombia

top-five urbanized areas	population	share
U.S. total	379	100%
New York	152	40
Miami	53	14
Los Angeles	27	7
Ft. Lauderdale	12	3
Houston	10	3

nation's Hispanic population, but 25 percent of Hispanics in Washington, D.C.

Panamanians are perhaps the most geographically diverse of any Hispanic group. They are disproportionately represented in the local Hispanic population in towns near large military installations such as Fayetteville, North Carolina (Fort Bragg); Columbus, Georgia (Fort Benning); Clarksville, Tennessee (Fort Campbell); Killeen, Texas (Fort Hood); Seaside, California (Fort Ord); and naval installations in Norfolk, Virginia; and Tacoma, Washington. Many who identified their ethnic origin as Panamanian in the 1990 census were military personnel once stationed in the former Panama Canal Zone.

The affluent Connecticut town of Stamford is particularly attractive to South Americans.

People of South-American origin began moving in large numbers from New York City or coming directly from their homelands to coastal Connecticut towns during the 1980s, attracted to a growing number of service jobs that were not being filled by the local population. Housing was also more affordable than in New York City.

The affluent Connecticut town of Stamford is particularly attractive to South Americans. Its Hispanic population includes large proportions of Colombians,

San Juans

Mexicans are by far the largest Hispanic-American group, but 77 percent of Dominican Americans live in one urban area.

(top-five urbanized areas for Hispanics by country of origin, population in thousands; and share of segment, 1990)

Guatemala

top-five urbanized areas	population	share
U.S. total	269	100%
Los Angeles	133	49
New York	27	10
Chicago	15	6
San Francisco	11	4
Washington, DC	9	4

Peru

top-five urbanized areas	population	share
U.S. total	175	100%
New York	54	31
Los Angeles	27	15
Miami	16	9
Washington, DC	11	7
San Francisco	9	5

Nicaragua

top-five urbanized areas	population	share
U.S. total	203	100%
Miami	74	37
Los Angeles	37	18
San Francisco	25	12
New York	14	7
Washington, DC	8	4

Honduras

top-five urbanized areas	population	share
U.S. total	131	100%
New York	33	25
Los Angeles	24	18
Miami	18	14
New Orleans	9	7
Houston	5	4

Ecuador

top-five urbanized areas	population	share
U.S. total	191	100%
New York	115	60
Los Angeles	21	11
Chicago	8	4
Miami	8	4
Washington, DC	5	3

Panama

top-five urbanized areas	population	share
U.S. total	92	100%
New York	27	29
Miami	7	7
Los Angeles	6	6
Washington, DC	4	4
San Francisco	2	2

Source: 1990 census

Ecuadorians, and Peruvians. In nearby Norwalk, Colombians are 20 percent of the city's Hispanic population.

MARKETING ATTENTION

So far, few U.S. corporations have paid attention to the special needs of "other" Hispanics. Mainstream marketers "are resistant enough to work with Hispanic marketing in total," says Nilda Anderson, president of Hispanic Market Research in New York City. "They are not going to do focused marketing."

One problem is a lack of marketing information. Recent census results and private research have improved the data on smaller Hispanic groups, says Gary Berman, president of Market Segment Research in Coral Gables, Florida, but few data were available until the 1990s.

Another problem is that Hispanic immigrants are less likely than previous generations of immigrants to live in ethnic-specific neighborhoods. In Miami, for example, newly arrived Cubans are often neighbors to Nicaraguans, and Nicaraguans may live next to Venezuelans. The city's celebrated "Little Havana" neighborhood is defined by its Cuban-owned businesses, but census data do not show an extreme overrepresentation of Cubans living in the area adjacent to those businesses.

Whatever their nation of origin, most Hispanic immigrants quickly acquire two basic American tools: a car and a telephone. Miami's Cubans may go to Little Havana to shop, socialize, and eat, just as Miami's Nicaraguans go to the Sweetwater district to buy copies of *El Diario La Prensa* and loaves of *pan Nicaraguense*. But when the trip is over, they return to homes scattered all over the city.

Another problem is that many Hispanic immigrants are not interested in owning a home, buying a new car, or otherwise participating as full-fledged American consumers. New York City is home to about 10,000 foreign-born Brazilians, for example. But "most Brazilians are in New York only to save money for the return to Brazil," says Maxine L. Margolis, an anthropology professor at the University of Florida in Gainesville. In her book *Little Brazil*, Margolis tells the story of a local television news program called "TV Brasil." When it began, Brazilian-owned businesses were eager to sponsor it. But the ads failed to attract new customers, she says, because many Brazilians spend only what they must and save everything else.

Whatever their nation of origin, most Hispanic immigrants quickly acquire two basic American tools: a car and a telephone.

Perhaps the biggest problem is the size of "other" Hispanic groups. "TV Brasil's" producers tried to persuade the Coors Brewing Company to advertise by claiming that 200,000 Brazilians lived in New York City, according to Margolis. But Coors turned them down anyway, claiming that the market was too small.

These obstacles may scare most businesses away, but the few that do target "other" Hispanics are rewarded with a growing source of loyal customers. As the airline of Colombia, Avianca focuses its U.S. advertising on Colombians, says Alberto Gil, a marketing analyst for the airline in New York City. The city's five boroughs are home to about 86,000 Colombians, according to demographer Frank Vardy at the Department of City Planning.

Avianca advertising runs primarily on Spanish-language television, radio, and in newspapers circulated in New York. "We don't care so much about whether the [medium] has a high rating for all Hispanics, but for Colombians," he says. The airline gauges Colombians' interests by asking its customers to name their favorite publications, radio stations, and TV shows.

The airline also focuses on a 20-block area in North Queens that is the geographic heart of Colombian settlement in New York City. Travel agents in that neighborhood receive special attention from the airline, says Gil. "We are a symbol for [Colombians]," he says. "We are Colombia in the United States."

Colombian politicians are well aware that New York-based expatriates form a powerful voting bloc. In past elections, polling places for Colombian elections have been established at the Colombian consulate and in Queens, says Javier Castano, a reporter for the Spanish-language newspaper *El Diario*. Colombian presidential candidates occasionally travel to New York City at election time, and politicians from many countries buy advertising in *El Diario* and other New York media.

Immigrants follow well-worn paths when they come to the United States, and these paths do not change rapidly. If immigration from Latin America continues at its current rapid pace, America's Little Havanas, Little San Juans, and other Hispanic enclaves will eventually grow to the point where targeting "other" Hispanics makes sense to mainstream marketers. Investing small amounts of time and money on specific Hispanics today could yield big payoffs tomorrow.

—Additional reporting by Patricia Braus

Behind the Numbers This study examines 1990 Hispanic populations in urbanized areas, defined by the U.S. Census Bureau as "one or more places (central place) and the adjacent densely settled surrounding territory (urban fringe) that together have a minimum of 50,000 persons." In 1990, the census identified 397 urbanized areas. For more information, contact the author at (904) 644-8377 or the Census Bureau at (301) 763-4040.

The Ballad of Freddy Gonzalez

BY JOHN FLORES

The Navy names a battleship for a Hispanic Marine—28 years after his death in Vietnam

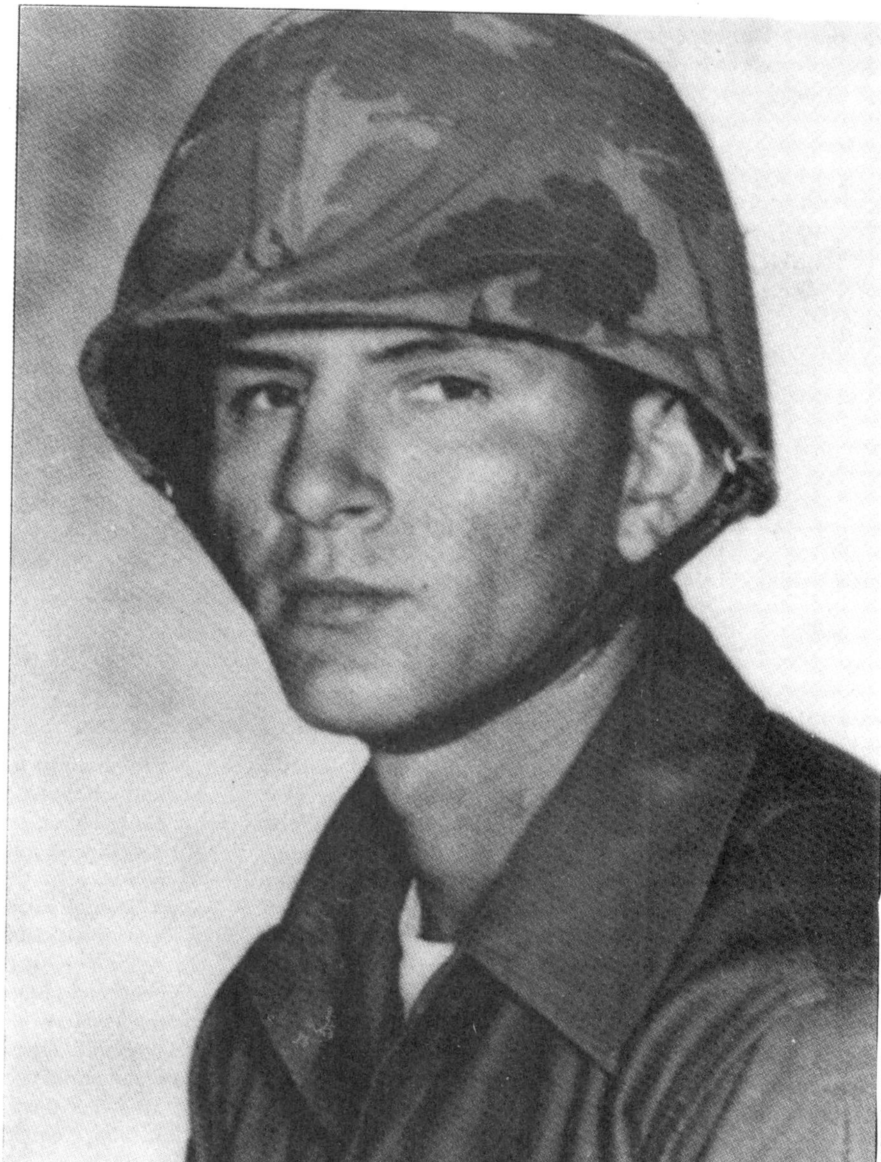

The Vietnam War, the longest in United States history, was also the most integrated. Hispanics were among the first Americans to arrive in Vietnam and among the last to leave. Thirteen Hispanics were awarded the Medal of Honor for their service in this conflict that altered forever the way the U.S. thinks of war.

One of the heroes of the Vietnam War, Medal of Honor recipient Alfredo Gonzalez, has been making the news this year. Nearly three decades after his death in Hue City, Vietnam, Marine Sergeant Alfredo "Freddy" Gonzalez resumed his battle watch October 12 at Naval Station Ingleside, near Corpus Christi, Texas. On that day, the Navy commissioned the *U.S.S. Gonzalez,* a guided-missile destroyer. It is the Navy's most advanced warship and the first modern destroyer named for a Mexican American.

Surviving members of his platoon in Vietnam still refer to Freddy as "Sergeant G." Their memories of him have not dimmed over

PHOTOGRAPHS COURTESY DOLIA GONZALEZ

the years. They came from cities and towns across the country to honor their friend and leader at both the February 1995 launch in Bath, Maine, and at the commissioning ceremony at Ingleside.

No less in the spotlight than the ship itself, with her buoyancy and charisma, is Freddy's mother, Dolia Gonzalez, 67. Dolia raised her son alone in Edinburg, Texas, on the modest salary of a waitress during the fifties and early sixties. It was a time when Mexican Americans were regarded as second-class citizens.

But things have changed for Dolia and many like her, whose parents came to the U.S. to find a better future. "We have what we have in this country today not just material things but better equality, because of people—men and women—who had the guts to forget about themselves and think of somebody else, something else, that has lasting meaning—this country. Our freedom," Dolia says. "Vietnam was a tragedy, and I lost my only child. But he died with the same spirit that people did in World War II, in defeating Hitler and the Japanese," she says. "We have to have people like him to keep this country alive."

Surviving members of his platoon in Vietnam still refer to Freddy (left) as "Sergeant G." Their memories of him have not dimmed over the years.

Born May 23, 1946, in Edinburg, Texas, Freddy enlisted in the Marine Corps soon after his graduation from high school in May 1965. He was killed February 4, 1968, at the St. Joan of Arc Catholic Church in Hue City, Vietnam, while serving his second tour of duty. The next year, Vice President Spiro T. Agnew awarded the Medal of Honor to Sergeant Gonzalez for the actions in Hue City that saved many of his fellow Marines. Dolia was there to receive the medal for her son, who was buried in Edinburg's Hillcrest Memorial Cemetery the day after the Hue City fighting ended in a Marine victory. He was the only Marine in the Tet Offensive combat to receive the award.

The Navy contacted Dolia a few months before the launching ceremony in Maine to ask her to be the ship's sponsor. She gladly accepted, and since that time she has been visited several times at her home in Edinburg by members of the ship's crew.

Dolia calls Freddy's Marine buddies and the ship crew members her "boys." Most of them call her "Mom." She likes the idea of having such an extended family, having lived so many years without Freddy.

Dolia still works as a waitress and is now employed at the old Echo Hotel in Edinburg. It was where Freddy and his friends had their high school proms and other parties. Today it is the central meeting place for city and county officials and the many Winter Texans who live in the Rio Grande Valley during the cold months.

Even after a long day at work, Dolia seems to defy the laws of age. She smiles easily, sitting in the living room of her modest home in the western part of Edinburg near the University of Texas–Pan American campus. Resting her tired legs on an ottoman after a six-hour day of walking the floor for her many customers, she smiles as she points to a picture of Freddy in his Marine uniform on the living room TV.

"I never had any problems with him when he was growing up," Dolia says fondly. "I'd even tell him to go out with his friends when he was in high school, but a lot of times he'd say no . . . that he wanted to spend time with me. You know, looking back, I think Freddy knew he wouldn't live a long time, so he wanted to spend time with me while he could."

She recounts stories of Freddy when he was a boy, working in the South Texas fields with her during the summertime. "One time, we were all working in a cotton field. Me, and my sister Jo, and Freddy. He would always carry a hoe and use it to kill snakes. He found a rattlesnake up ahead of Jo, and after he killed it he coiled it up again like it was alive," she says, laughing. "And when Jo saw it, she screamed and jumped up about two feet in the air and tried to run off. We all had a good laugh about that."

Anybody who knew Freddy remembers him, whether it was a classmate, friend, football coach, or commanding officer, and most of them attended the commissioning of the *U.S.S. Gonzalez.*

Former University of Texas football coach Fred Akers started his coaching career at Edinburg High School, and Freddy played for him during the 1964 season. "Freddy was a guy who didn't know how to quit. He played every second until the whistle blew," Akers says. "He was the kind of guy who, if you picked a fight with him and whipped him, he'd be waiting for you the next day."

Though patriotic, young Freddy wasn't perfect. He liked to party with friends and it got him into trouble a couple of times. Once, Akers recalls, Freddy and a group of football players smuggled beer into a McAllen drive-in, and the coach had to bail the boys out of jail.

Freddy felt so bad about that incident that he didn't eat for a couple of days. Dolia was worried, she says. "He moped around after that for a few days. He felt like a lot of guys looked up to him, and he let them down. I was starting to worry about him. Then one day he came home and asked, 'What's for supper?' That's when I knew everything was okay again," she says.

Robert Vela, now the athletic director for the Edcouch-Elsa School District near Edinburg, was one of Freddy's close friends. "We were in Little League together, and worked together in the fields, picking cotton," he says. "Freddy was the kind of friend who would take the shirt off his back and give it to you if he had to . . . but he didn't like showoffs or people with attitudes. One night we were playing basketball at Westside Park, and a guy we knew, a champion amateur boxer, came walking up with is boxing gloves hanging around his neck. He challenged anyone there to a fight."

Everybody knew the guy's reputation, and they all declined. All but Freddy. Vela continues, "Freddy, just being Freddy, he told the guy, 'Yeah, okay, I'll box you.' But Freddy was not a boxer. We were just street fighters. Pretty soon, this guy was taunting Freddy, smacking him in the face with jabs. He called Freddy a mamma's boy or something to that effect. Freddy just pulled the gloves off and threw them down. He jumped on the guy and started to pound him. We all had to pull him off the guy, and we never saw that guy around there again looking for a fight," Vela said.

After his first tour in Vietnam was over in February 1967, Freddy, now a corporal, wanted to be stationed with a Marine contingent at the Naval Air Station in Corpus Christi. His plan was to quietly serve the rest of his time stationed only two hours away from his girlfriend, his buddies, his mother, and the town he loved. But the Marines had other plans. Gonzalez, a trusted leader, was chosen as an instructor to prepare young Marines for guerrilla warfare.

He told friends he would never return to Vietnam. A few months later, Freddy learned of an ambush there in which an entire platoon was killed, including a group of men who had served under him. He felt responsible for the men, and felt the call of duty.

J.J. Avila, a childhood friend and former Edinburg High School teammate, was one of two Edinburg Marines who served as escorts for Dolia at Freddy's posthumous Medal of Honor ceremony. Having already served in the war himself, Avila says he tried to talk Freddy out of returning. "He called me over to his house to talk it over. I told him that he had done his duty, and he didn't need to go back. It wasn't his fault those guys died. But he had already made up his mind—I could see that—and there was no changing it," Avila says.

The war had divided the country because many Americans didn't believe United States troops should be fighting half a world away. Television brought the blood and brutality into the country's living rooms, fanning the flames of anti-war sentiment. Freddy was tormented, more than most Marines, by the thought of having to kill the Vietnamese. After all, he once told a friend, the Vietnamese worked the fields and lived simple lives, like most Hispanics from the Valley.

Torn between his conscience and his country, Freddy had to make a battlefield decision on the morning of February 4, 1968, at the St. Joan of Arc Catholic Church in Hue City, Vietnam. Few American troops were in the city—the old imperial and cultural capitol of Vietnam—when the communists broke a cease fire during Tet, the Vietnamese New Year. North Vietnamese troops, many dressed as civilians, infiltrated the city.

Freddy was serving as platoon sergeant with Company A, 1st Battalion, 1st Marines. His platoon was ambushed on its way into Hue in the Van Lrong Village. He maneuvered the platoon to safety, then knocked out enemy bunkers with hand grenades. He then took cover behind a nearby American armored vehicle and spotted a wounded Marine lying in the road ahead.

Colonel Marcus Gravel, commanding officer of the Marine division, detailed Freddy's actions in the 1975 dedication of an Edinburg elementary school named for him: "Without hesitation, he leaped from the tank and dashed into the street and returned with his injured comrade. Then, as the column moved against the enemy force, we were met by withering machine gun fire . . . again Freddy left his place of safety and assaulted the bunker, silencing it with hand grenades . . . Disregarding his own wounds, he told the corpsman who attempted to treat him to take care of the others."

Larry Lewis, from Chattanooga, Tennessee, was a rifleman in the platoon. He had come to Vietnam for the first time in September

1967 and had been under Freddy's command since that time. He was only a few feet away from Freddy when he was killed. "Our battalion had gotten split up. The resistance was just tremendous . . . demolition crews, mortar fire, rocket fire, machine guns, snipers," says Lewis. "By the time we got to Hue, Sergeant G at that time was probably one of the highest ranking [Marines]. Most of the officers were either killed or wounded."

Lewis was only a few feet away from Freddy in the schoolyard of the church. The platoon of about 35 men was pinned down, and Freddy told them to keep down out of the line of fire while he went on ahead to try to find a way to move the men. Lewis followed him, against orders, to give him cover. He watched Freddy grab an armload of small anti-tank rockets and enter the area of the church where the North Vietnamese Army were most heavily entrenched. Freddy began firing the rockets at the enemy troops. After hitting all the visible positions and silencing fire, Lewis says he thought Freddy had neutralized all the enemy positions. One last rocket came out of the rubble, Lewis says.

"I was on the second floor of the building. He was directly below me. I saw the rocket hit him. He took a direct hit. It was hard to believe that he was hit. I went down there and laid him on a door. His heart was still beating when I got him, but he died pretty soon after that," Lewis says.

Freddy died beside the bullet-riddled statue of Saint Joan of Arc.

"Prior to that, he was almost like Houdini. It seemed like he was everywhere all at the same time. I remember that he carried a twelve-gauge shotgun, a big bag of grenades, and a forty-five pistol . . . He was always there in the front, never in the back, waiting. He was always there for us," Lewis says.

Because he took out so many enemy positions with the hand grenades and rockets, Freddy saved the lives of the men in his platoon. What he did that day is indelibly etched in each man's mind.

Gonzalez is one of many Hispanics who died in the war. Statistics on casualties are hard to come by, but what is known is that Hispanics served and died far beyond their fair share. Nearly 20 percent of Vietnam casualties (those listed on the Vietnam Veterans Memorial) were men with Hispanic surnames. At the time, U.S. citizens classified as "Hispanic" constituted a much smaller proportion of the total population—roughly 5 percent. Puerto Rico alone sent 58,000 troops. Even noncitizens gave of themselves: In *Soldados: Chicanos in Viet Nam,* Charley Trujillo notes that there was a component of "*soldados* who were born in Tijuana, Mexicali, Piedras Negras, and many other places in Mexico who served in Viet Nam—green cards and all."

During the era of disillusionment with the war after the Tet Offensive, Hispanics, like most Americans, had little enthusiasm for the conflict. For most Hispanic activists, anti-war sentiment didn't become a major concern until the final months of 1969, when the Brown Berets steered the movement more in the direction of war protest. As the nation was torn, so were many of its fighting men, including Freddy Gonzalez.

More than two decades after the stormy protests, the war has been put in much clearer perspective. It is through stories like that of Freddy Gonzalez that the nation heals old wounds and gains a clearer understanding of sacrifice, duty, and honor, the codes most soldiers live by. All these years later, fellow Tejano hero and Vietnam Medal of Honor recipient Roy Benavidez says, "I ask myself again and again if it would have been worth it to my family if I had been killed and my body never returned. The answer is yes! . . . Our duty as survivors is to pass on the pride in the noble sacrifice made by our child, parent, spouse, or buddy." It is to this feeling, this solidarity, that the families of those sacrificed turn for comfort.

Robert Alaniz of Edinburg was one of Freddy's friends. He agrees with Freddy's mother and with Benavidez that despite the misguided policies behind U.S. troop involvement in Vietnam, Freddy did not die in vain. "One of the things that really stands out for me is that I had just received a letter from Freddy and he wrote that he had been assigned to the new kids who had just gotten to Vietnam, and he would train them. A few days later, I heard the bad news," says Alaniz. Freddy's letter was clear in its assertion that "He wanted to help the country. He wanted to get in the middle of it and try to end this thing," Alaniz remembers.

Dolia Gonzalez has placed her headstone beside Freddy's in the Hillcrest Memorial Cemetery where Freddy was buried. She still misses him and takes comfort in knowing she'll be buried beside him someday.

On October 12, 1996, at Corpus Christi Bay, Dolia entrusted her son's memory to the world. After 28 years, in the form of a battleship, he is once again on duty, this time to patrol the world's oceans with the most advanced missile systems yet devised.

Once again, his mother was there, bidding Freddy a tearful farewell.

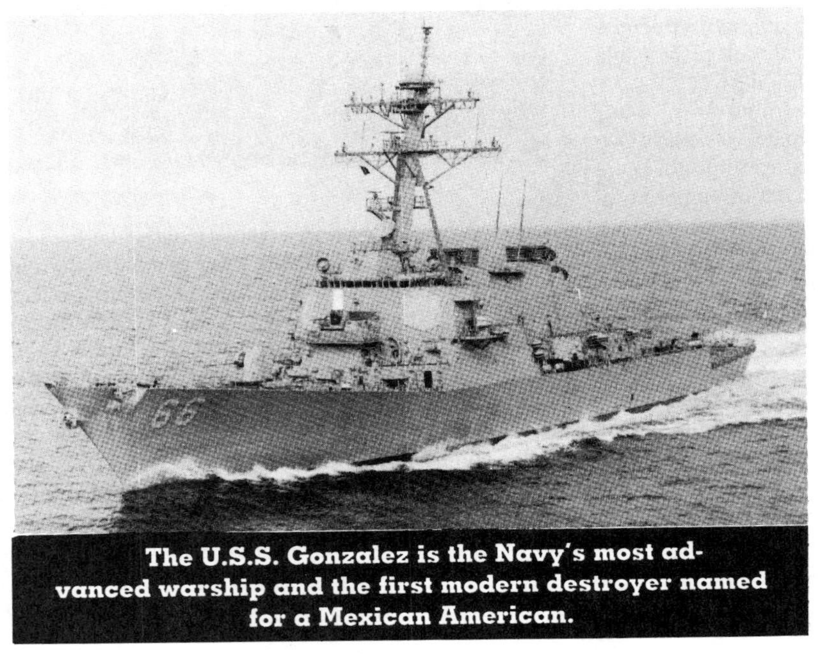

The U.S.S. Gonzalez is the Navy's most advanced warship and the first modern destroyer named for a Mexican American.

BAITING IMMIGRANTS

HEARTBREAK for Latinos

BY MERCEDES LYNN DE URIARTE

Twenty-one-year-old Gina Cardenas could hardly wait for summer to begin. Long hours of work, study, and persistence had paid off. First she won a prestigious fellowship including a paid internship as a metro reporter at a mid-sized Midwestern newspaper. Then she was accepted to an exchange program at one of Mexico's best-known universities, where, among other things, she would study Spanish.

But next came the notice from the U.S. State Department. Its Houston Passport Agency questioned her right to a passport. Cardenas is the daughter of naturalized immigrant parents. She was born in the United States with the assistance of a midwife at home in Brownsville, a Texas border town.

The agency asked her to supply a "combination of early public documents created at the time of your birth." These included an "attending midwife's report; prenatal and postnatal notes created by the midwife of your mother regarding her pregnancy and delivery; a certified copy of baptismal certificate; your parents' tax, rent, or employment records created at the time of your birth which indicated their U.S. residency; elementary-school records showing your name, date, and place of birth and indicating your parents' address or any other document established in your infancy or early childhood that indicates your place of birth."

Mercedes Lynn de Uriarte, who was born in the United States and raised in Mexico, has a Ph.D. in American Studies. She teaches journalism and Latin-American and Mexican-American Studies at the University of Texas at Austin. She is a former editor and writer at the Los Angeles Times, where she worked during the immigrant-bashing campaigns of the 1970s and 1980s. She writes frequently, both as a journalist and an academic, on cross-cultural issues.

Cardenas said her first reaction to the notice from the U.S. Passport Agency was one of disbelief. "I mean, this is my own government," she says. "I'm an American!" But her efforts to convince government bureaucrats of this fact dragged on for months. At the last minute, her papers came through, allowing her to participate in the program. But not before she had endured significant harassment.

Cardenas was not alone. This year, several other students who were U.S. citizens born to immigrant parents found their government reluctant to certify their citizenship with a passport.

In addition, as a result of Governor Pete Wilson's tirades against illegal aliens and the subsequent passage of Proposition 187, hundreds of California students brought here as babies by parents without government papers—youngsters who have lived here all their lives—found themselves ejected from universities. Most of these students worked full time to pay for their educations in an effort to leave behind economic hardship and gang pressures. Many were forced out just weeks before graduating.

"It is both shortsighted and heartbreaking," says Cristina Bodinger-de Uriarte, a sociology professor at California State University, Los Angeles, an urban campus with one of the most diverse populations in the nation. "Suddenly, within weeks of graduation, students were notified that unless they paid out-of-state tuition, they must leave school. Students who had worked full-time jobs for four or five years in order to finance their education and escape poverty were penalized. They were already stretched to the financial limit.

"Some of my best students were in tears for days—then they simply disappeared from the student body," she says.

Bodinger-de Uriarte says she does not understand the reasoning behind this push-out policy. "They are mistaken if they believe that these youngsters will return to other countries. Most of them speak no other language, have lived nowhere else, and identify with this country."

The push-out policy is aimed not just at students without documents. It extends to legal immigrants, as well. Regardless of high grades or outstanding accomplishments, regardless of their potential in a country increasingly dependent on global commerce, these students will find it far more difficult to get federally subsidized loans and grants.

According to student advisers who work in foreign-study programs, Spanish-surnamed students are having more and more trouble obtaining government documents. "I cannot remember any other period of time when there was so much trouble with official papers," says Helena Wilkins, who has worked in the University of Texas's study-abroad program for seven years.

Norma Madrid, who captured a prestigious business internship in Spain, also struggled to get proper documents. "She received the same inquiry as Gina did," says Wilkins. "And there was no reason for it. She was an American citizen. Norma badgered the passport people for months trying to get the matter straightened out. Finally, the passport came through."

Another student who almost lost her chance to study abroad was of Indian descent, says Wilkins, "but her name could have been mistaken for a Hispanic name. On the other hand, the government agency had all her paperwork and should have been able to realize that she was not Latina."

What these three students have in common, besides Hispanic-sounding names, are naturalized parents, all of whom had become citizens many years earlier.

Harassment of Latino students is but one component of an increasingly harsh national trend that includes Republican Presidential candidate Bob Dole's proposal to bar the children of undocumented immigrants from attending school.

"This is just the kind of policy that generates more desperation," attorney Peter Schey, executive director and president of the Center for Human Rights and Constitutional Law in Los Angeles, says of Dole's proposal. "We are in effect saying we'd rather see young people in gangs than in schools. This is legislated marginalization. It's the same sort of thinking that leads us into policies that deny immigrants a $20 inoculation, but pave the way toward health care that will later require spending $80,000 to remove a tubercular lung."

Actually, Dole's idea was tried and failed in the 1980s, when the state of Texas attempted to bar undocumented migrant children from classrooms. That effort led to a 1982 U.S. Supreme Court ruling that undocumented youngsters could not be denied a public education.

If a new effort to bar the children of immigrants were to succeed, the results for society at large would be disastrous. The current cost of U.S. illiteracy is already $200 billion annually if one takes into account its role in incarceration, unemployment, health, and welfare. Already, one in five adults—twenty-seven million—is functionally illiterate, according to the U.S. Department of Education. Most of those in prison today fall into this category, as do a significant percentage of the unemployed.

Republican politicians from Bob Dole to Pete Wilson have built political careers around promises to get tough on immigrants. In a pre-convention television commercial, the Republican National Committee launched a blatant attack on immigrants. As *The New York Times* reported, the ad opens with a shot of the border, and in case there is any misunderstanding, it has a sign saying MEXICO. The ad proceeds to show immigrants fleeing up the road under the glare of spotlights. "You spend $5.5 billion to support illegals," the ad screams, adding that "spending for illegals" is "up 12.7 percent under Clinton." The ad ends by urging voters to "tell President Clinton: Stop giving illegal benefits to illegals. End wasteful Washington spending."

The blame for immigrant-bashing can't all be placed on Republican politics, however. Bill Clinton has grown increasingly punitive in his policies and opportunistic in his portrayal of undocumented immigrants.

In response to the Republican ad, the Democratic National Committee released its own anti-immigrant ad. Clinton has boosted the number of border-patrol officers, brags the ad, while showing a picture of a brown-skinned man being handcuffed by a border-patrol agent. Another brown-skinned man is shown climbing down a wall with a rope, the *Times* reported, and then the ad shows "two gloved hands clutching a large chisel and trying to pry open a window."

In both the Republican and Democratic ads, Mexicans are portrayed as the only illegal-immigrant group. Thus an entire population is criminalized through visual images meant to incite anger and fear. What's more, the information in the ads is out of context and slippery.

U.S. Latinos should be wary of pledging allegiance to either party. Both seem equally prepared to generate hatred against those who look Mexican, Central American, or indigenous Latin American.

As the Democrats' commercial indicates, Clinton often links immigration to crime.

"As we have worked hard to bring the crime rate down all over America, we've made special efforts in our border communities, because we know we have special responsibilities there," he told San Diegans recently, citing increases in border-patrol agents in Arizona, California, and Texas. He described communities in the Southwest as "under siege" and pointed to the tough line taken by the Administration's Operation Gatekeeper.

In April the President signed anti-terrorism legislation that gives the INS sweeping new powers. One provision of the new law pushes due process aside, and allows for the hasty removal of foreign-born individuals who arrive at ports of entry without proper documentation. The decision is left to the immigration officer on duty, without court hearing or judicial review. The burden of proof of legal entry falls on immigrants. This provision fails to uphold international human-rights laws that were incorporated into the U.S. canon in 1980. Nor does it ensure the legal treatment of refugees protected under the U.N. convention relating to the status of refugees.

Clinton's decision to sign the welfare bill is a huge assault on legal immigrants, who will immediately lose food stamps and supplemental-security insurance.

"These proposals and enactments would strip away many of the already threadbare protections these people have," says Schey, who has successfully argued immigrant class-action suits before the U.S. Supreme Court. Schey says that the current anti-immigration movement is the most repressive in the past fifty years.

The crackdown on immigrants is based on political propaganda, not reality. Most undocumented individuals arrive on commercial carriers and overstay their visas or cross from Canada, according to the INS. Nevertheless, the United States disproportionately reinforces its southern border. The Clinton Administration recently proposed a $46 million increase for San Diego/Tijuana border control.

Most of the individuals who cross the southern border do not take jobs that Americans seek. A 1982 Reagan Administration initiative called Operation Jobs proved this point rather conclusively. For two weeks, beginning on April 26, 1982, dramatic TV visuals showed INS sweeps of workplaces in Fort Worth, Houston, San Francisco, Detroit, Newark, New York, Chicago, and Denver. It was one of the most extensive deportation efforts that the U.S. government had ever undertaken. Within five days, the INS seized 6,000 individuals. Local businesses felt the pinch immediately. In Los Angeles, merchants along Broadway, a main shopping thoroughfare for Latinos, reported a drop in sales of 30 to 80 percent. Subsequent newspaper reports revealed that the few Americans who took those vacated jobs quit within days because of brutal labor conditions. Two weeks after the raids, the press reported the deportees were once again at work.

Immigrants are not the drain on the social budget they are made out to be. Immigrants pay much more in taxes than they receive in education and social services. Over the course of their working lifetime, immigrants pay an average of $89,437 in state income and sales taxes, far more than the $62,600 it costs to educate a person from kindergarten through twelfth grade, according to a study released June 10 by the Tomás Rivera Center in Claremont, California.

The Urban Institute found that legal and illegal immigrants contribute $70.3 billion in tax payments into the system—but draw out only $42.9 billion in total services. Immigrants add billions more to the U.S. economy in consumer spending, the study found.

U.S. businesses have always depended on cheap foreign labor. The United States could not have become the wealthy industrialized leader of the early nineteenth century without both slave labor and European immigrant workers. The railroads were largely built by Chinese immigrants brought in by U.S. development barons for this purpose. Large-scale agricultural production still depends on Mexican workers today.

That's why the borders have remained porous. But in this era of downsizing and falling wages, border rhetoric plays well in Washington, and it's not the businesses that are being blamed, it's their workers.

Cracking down on migrant workers and their children does not address the root causes of immigration to the United States. The main reasons for the migration phenomenon we see around the world are flights for safety, job searches, and travel to reunite families, says attorney Schey.

"Yet never have our lawmakers sat down to develop a broad-based plan that would address these motivations," he says. "They have never targeted outflow nations. They have never effectively addressed oppressive regimes—indeed, we often support them, even when their citizens are immigrating in huge numbers. Consider our track record with Iran, Haiti, the Philippines, and El Salvador, to mention just a few."

Anti-immigrant movements throughout our history have ridden the crest of prejudice.

Jeremiah Jenks and W. Jett Lauck, former members of the United States Immigration Commission, observed this pattern in 1912: "Many persons, who have spoken and written in favor of restriction of immigration, have laid great stress upon the evils of society arising from immigration. They have claimed that disease, pauperism, crime, and vice have been greatly increased through the incoming of immigrants. Perhaps no other phase of the question has aroused so keen feeling, and yet perhaps on no other phase of the question has there been so little accurate information."

But backlash against immigrants seems to be ingrained in our culture. In 1882, the Chinese Exclusion Act provided the most obvious example. Its forerunner, an 1879 California statewide ballot that passed by a margin of 154,638 to 833, may have set a precedent for the exclusion act, which restricted Chinese immigration for more than fifty years, and for its contemporary counterpart, Proposition 187. The 1952 McCarran-Walter Act was another effort to control ethnic distribution. Among other provisions, it established a complicated procedure for admitting Asians, and set up a long list of conditions allowing for deportation. It also granted wide powers of search, seizure, and interrogation to INS agents.

These efforts have portrayed immigrants as criminals, economic parasites, or health risks. In recent years, those targeted most frequently have been Latinos. My own research indicates that over the last century, the U.S. press has exhibited a consistent negative bias against Latinos.

A rise in hate crimes since 1991 shadows the current anti-immigrant rhetoric. In 1994, the Los Angeles County Human Relations Commission reported a 23.5 percent rise in hate crimes against Latinos. Last November, the Coalition for Humane Immigrant Rights of Los Angeles released an eighteen-page report, "Hate Unleashed: Los Angeles in the Aftermath of 187," which documented 229 cases of "discrimination, denial of services, civil-rights violations, hate speech, and hate crimes" since the passage of Proposition 187.

Gina Cardenas is in many ways a prototypical immigrant success story. Her mother and father met and married in the United States. Both worked hard to give their four children opportunities they never had. Gina, the oldest, is the first in her family to go to college, the first to travel to the nation's capital, the first to receive scholarships. Like many other American children of immigrant parents, Cardenas is a profile of initiative and independence.

Now she is poised to contribute to her nation, pursuing her interest in international relations, and developing her foreign-language skills—valuable assets in the current, global economy. But her government has shown little interest in her contribution, and has treated her with suspicion because of her Mexican name.

Cardenas and thousands of other Latinos are caught in the maelstrom of anti-immigrant sentiment, which has cycled through our history for more than a century. The maelstrom swirls around U.S. economic needs, as the government responds to both urban and agricultural demands.

Today the nation faces major changes as technology retools the workplace, as demographics reconfigure the population, and as trade becomes globalized. These changes require discussion of public policies, including immigration.

But instead of looking for solutions, our leaders are carting out the old scapegoats.

From Out of the Shadows: Mexican Women in the United States

Vicki L. Ruiz

Beginning with the Coronado expedition of 1540, Spanish-speaking women migrated north decades, even centuries, before their European American counterparts ventured west. The Spanish colonial government, in efforts to secure its territorial claims, offered a number of inducements to those willing to undertake such an arduous journey. Subsidies given to a band of settlers headed for Texas included not only food and livestock, but also petticoats and stockings. Although some settlers would claim "Spanish" blood, the majority of people were *mestizo* (Spanish/Indian), and many colonists were of African descent.

Few women ventured to the Mexican North as widows or orphans; most arrived as the wives or daughters of soldiers, farmers, and artisans. Over the course of three centuries, they raised families on the frontier and worked alongside their fathers or husbands, herding cattle and tending crops. Furthermore, the Franciscans did not act alone in the acculturation and decimation of indigenous peoples, but recruited women into their service as teachers, midwives, doctors, cooks, seamstresses, and supply managers.

Women's networks based on ties of blood and fictive kinship proved central to the settlement of the Spanish/Mexican frontier. At times women settlers acted as midwives to mission Indians, and they baptized sickly or still-born babies. As godmothers for these infants, they established the bonds of *commadrazgo* between Native American and Spanish/Mexican women. However, exploitation took place *among* women. For those in domestic service, racial and class hierarchies undermined any pretense of sisterhood. In San Anttonio in 1735, Antonía Lusgardia Ernandes, a mulatta, sued her former employer for custody of their son. Admitting

The Spanish . . . offered a number of inducements to those willing to undertake such an arduous journey. Subsidies given to a band of settlers headed for Texas included not only food and livestock, but also petticoats and stockings.

paternity, the man claimed that his former servant had relinquished the child to his wife since his wife had baptized the child. The court, however, granted Ernandes custody. While the godparent relationship could foster ties between colonists and Native Americans, elites used baptism as a venue of social control. Indentured servitude was prevalent on the colonial frontier persisting well into the nineteenth century.

The history of Spanish/Mexican settlement has been shrouded by myth. Walt Disney's *Zorro*, for example, epitomized the notion of romantic California controlled by fun-loving, swashbuckling rancheros. As only three percent of California's Spanish/Mexican population could be considered rancheros in 1850, most women did not preside over large estates, but helped manage small family farms. In addition to traditional tasks, Mexican women were accomplished *vaqueras* or cowgirls. Spanish-speaking women, like their European American counterparts, encountered a duality in frontier expectations. While placed on a pedestal as delicate "ladies," women were responsible for a variety of strenuous chores.

Married women on the Spanish/Mexican frontier had certain legal advantages not afforded their European American peers. Under English common law, women, when they married, became *feme covert* (or dead in the eyes of the legal system) and thus, they could not own property separate from their husbands. Conversely, Spanish/Mexican women retained control of their land after marriage and held one-half interest in the community property they shared with their spouses. Interestingly, Rancho Rodeo de las Aguas, which María Rita Valdez operated until the 1880s, is now better known as Beverly Hills.

From *OAH Magazine of History,* Winter 1996, pp. 15-18. © 1996 by the Organization of American Historians. Reprinted by permission.

Life for Mexican settlers changed dramatically in 1848 with the conclusion of the U.S.-Mexican War, the discovery of gold in California, and the Treaty of Guadalupe Hidalgo. Mexicans on the U.S. of the border became second-class citizens, divested of their property and political power. Their world turned upside down. Segregated from the European American population, Mexican Americans in the barrios of the Southwest sustained their sense of identity and cherished their traditions. With little opportunity for advancement, Mexicans were concentrated in lower echelon industrial, service, and agricultural jobs. This period of conquest and marginalization, both physical and ideological, did not occur in a dispassionate environment. Stereotypes affected rich and poor alike with Mexicans commonly described as lazy, sneaky, and greasy. In European American journals, novels, and travelogues, Spanish-speaking women were frequently depicted as flashy, morally deficient sirens.

At times these images had tragic results. On 5 July 1851, a Mexican woman swung from the gallows, the only woman lynched during the California Gold Rush. Josefa Segovia (also known as Juanita of Downieville) was tried, convicted, and hanged the same day she had killed an Anglo miner and popular prize fighter, a man who had assaulted her the day before. Remembering his Texas youth, Gilbert Onderdonk recounted that in proposing to his sweetheart he listed the qualities he felt set him apart from other suitors. "I told her . . . I did not use profane language, never drank whisky, never gambled, and never killed Mexicans."

Some historians have asserted that elite families believed they had a greater chance of retaining their land if they acquired an Anglo son-in-law. Intermarriage, however, was no insurance policy. In 1849, María Amparo Ruiz married Lieutenant Colonel Henry S. Burton and five years later the couple purchased Rancho Jamul, a sprawling property of over 500,000 acres. When Henry Burton died in 1869, the ownership of Rancho Jamul came into question. After seven years of litigation,the court awarded his widow only 8,926 acres. Even this amount was challenged by squatters, and she would continue to lose acreage in the years ahead. Chronicling her experiences, Ruiz de Burton wrote *The Squatter and the Don* (1885), a fictionalized account of the decline of the ranching class.

Providing insight into community life, nineteenth-century Spanish language newspapers reveal ample information on social mores. Newspaper editors upheld the double standard. Women were to be cloistered and protected to the extent that some residents of New Mexico protested the establishment of co-educational public schools. In 1877 Father Gasparri of *La revista católica* editorialized that women's suffrage would destroy the family. Despite prevailing conventions, Mexican women, due to economic circumstances wrought by political and social disenfranchisement, sought employment for wages. Whether in cities or on farms, family members pooled their earnings to put food on the table. Women worked at home taking in laundry, boarders, and sewing while others worked in the fields, in restaurants and hotels, and in canneries and laundries.

In 1900, over 375,000 to 500,000 Mexicans lived in the Southwest. By 1930 this figure increased ten-fold as over one million Mexicanos—pushed out by revolution and lured in by prospective jobs—came to the United States. They settled into existing barrios and forged new communities both in the Southwest and the Midwest. Like their foremothers, women usually journeyed north as wives and daughters. Some, however, crossed the border alone and as single mothers. As in the past, women's wage earnings proved essential to family survival. Urban daughters (less frequently mothers) worked in canneries and garment plants as well as in the service sector. Entire families labored in the fields and received their wages in a single check made out to the head of household. Grace Luna related how women would scale ladders with one hundred pounds of cotton on their backs and some had to "carry their kids on top of their picking sacks!"

Exploitation in pay and conditions prompted attempts at unionization. Through Mexican mutual aid societies and progressive trade unions, Mexican women proved tenacious activists. In 1933 alone thirty-seven major agricultural strikes occurred in California. The Los Angeles Dressmakers' Strike (1933), the San Antonio Pecan Shellers' Strike (1938), and the California Sanitary Canning Company Strike (1939) provide examples of urban activism.

Like the daughters of European immigrants, young Mexican women experienced the lure of consumer culture. Considerable intergenerational conflict emerged as adolescents wanted to dress and perhaps behave like their European American peers at work or like the heroines they encountered in movies and magazines. Evading traditional chaperonage became a major preoccupation for youth. However, they and their kin faced the specter of deportation. From 1931 to 1934, over one-third of the Mexican population in the United States (over 500,000 people) were deported or repatriated. Discrimination and segregation in housing, employment, schools, and public recreation further served to remind youth of their second-class citizenship. In María Arredondo's words, "I remember. . . signs all over that read 'no Mexicans allowed.'"

Operating small barrio businesses, the Mexican middle-class at times allied themselves with their working-class customers and at times strived for social distance. The League of United Latin American Citizens (LULAC) represented a group that did both simultaneously. An important civil rights organization, with women's active participation, LULAC confronted segregation through the courts; however, only U.S. citizens could join. Conversely, El Congreso de Pueblos de Hablan Española (Spanish-speaking People's Congress) stressed immigrant rights. Indeed, this 1939 civil rights convention drafted a comprehensive platform which called for an end to segregation in public facilities, housing, education, and employment.

After World War II, Mexican women were involved in a gamut of political organizations from the American G.I. Forum to the Community Service Organization (CSO). An Alinsky-style group, CSO stressed local issues and voter registration. Two CSO leaders, Cesar Chávez and Dolores Huerta, forged the United Farm Workers (UFW) during the early 1960s, he as president, she as vice president. A principal negotiator, lobbyist, and strategist, Huerta relied on extended kin and women friends in the union to care for her eleven children during her absences. Although criticized for putting the union first, Dolores Huerta has had few regrets. As she told historian Margaret Rose, "But now that I've seen how good [my children] turned out, I don't feel so guilty." Family activism has characterized UFW organizing.

As part of global student movements of the late 1960s, Mexican American youth joined together to address continuing problems of discrimination, particularly in education and political representation. Embracing the mantle of cultural nationalism, they transformed a pejorative barrio term "Chicano" into a symbol of pride. "Chicano/a" implies a commitment to social justice and to social change. A graduate student in history at UCLA, Magdalena Mora, not only wrote about trade union struggles but participated in them as well. She organized cannery workers in Richmond, California and participated in CASA, a national immigrant rights group. An activist since high school, she died in 1981 of a brain tumor at the age of twenty-nine. The informal credo of the Chicano student movement: to return to your community after your college education to help your people. Magdalena Mora never left.

A layering of generations exist among Mexicans in the United States from seventh-generation New Mexicans to recent immigrants. This layering provides a vibrant cultural dynamic. Artists Amlia Mesa Bains, Judy Baca, and Yolanda López and writers Sandra Cisneros, Pat Mora, and Cherrie Moraga (to name a few) articulate the multiple identities inhabiting the borderlands of Chicano culture. Across generations, women have come together for collective action. Communities Organized for Public Service (San Antonio) and Mothers of East L.A. exemplify how parish networks become channels for social change. Former student activists María Varela and María Elena Durazo remain committed to issues of economic justice, Varela through a New Mexico rural cooperative and Durazo as a union president in Los Angeles. Whether they live in Chicago or El Paso, Mexican women share legacies of resistance. As Varela related, "I learned . . . that it is not enough to pray over an injustice or protest it or research it to death, but that you have to take concrete action to solve it."

Bibliography

de la Torre, Adela and Beatríz M. Pesquera, eds. *Building With Our Hands: New Directions in Chicana Studies*. Berkeley: University of California Press, 1993.

Del Castillo, Adelaida R. ed. *Between Borders: Essays on Mexicana/Chicana History*. Los Angeles: Floricanto Press, 1990.

Deutsch, Sarah. *No Separate Refuge: Culture, Class, and Gender on the Anglo-Hispanic Frontier in the American Southwest, 1880-1940*. New York: Oxford University Press, 1987.

Gutiérrez, Ramón. *When Jesus Came, the Corn Mothers Went Away: Marriage, Sexuality, and Power in New Mexico, 1500-1846*. Stanford: Stanford University Press, 1990.

Martin, Patricia Preciado. *Songs My Mother Sang to Me: An Oral History of Mexican American Women*. Tucson: University of Arizona Press, 1992.

Martínez, Elizabeth. *500 Years of Chicano History in Pictures*. Albuquerque: Southwest Voter Organizing Project, 1991.

Mora, Magdalena and Adelaida R. Del Castillo. *Mexican Women in the United States: Struggles Past and Present*. Los Angeles: UCLA Chicano Studies Research Center, 1980.

Orozco, Cynthia E. "Beyond Machismo, La Familia, and Ladies Auxiliaries: A Historiography of Mexican-Origin Women's Participation in Voluntary Associations and Politics in the United States, 1870-1990." In *Renato Rosaldo Lecture Series Monograph* Vol. 10. Tucson: University of Arizona Mexican American Studies and Research Center, 1992-93.

Ruiz, Vicki L. *Cannery Women, Cannery Lives: Mexican Women, Unionization, and the California Food Processing Industry, 1930-1950*. Albuquerque: University of New Mexico Press, 1987.

———. *From Out of the Shadows: A History of Mexican Women in the United States*. (forthcoming)

———. "Mascaras y Muros: Chicana Feminism and the Teaching of U.S. Women's History." In *New Viewpoints in U.S. Women's History*. Ed. Susan Ware. Cambridge: Schlesinger Library Publications, 1994.

Weber, Devra. *Dark Sweat, White Gold: California Farm Workers, Cotton, and the New Deal*. Berkeley: University of California Press, 1994.

Magazines, Latinos Find Themselves on the Same Page

Marie Arana-Ward

Washington Post Staff Writer

Want to take the fat out of your grandmother's chimichangas? Or find out how Latino kids do at Harvard? Maybe you'd like to know how to dress for success if you look more like Gloria Estefan than Christie Brinkley. If you do, where do you turn?

Suddenly, there's a wealth of choices.

In the space of one year, five new national magazines have stepped forward to answer those very questions. They are tailored to appeal to a newly recognized American consumer—an upwardly mobile Hispanic with a solid education, a steady job and a pocketful of cash. First came Washington's Latina Style early last year, then Si out of California, Latina out of New York and Moderna out of Texas. Just a few weeks ago the premiere issue of a close relative, People magazine's Spanish-language edition, People En Espanol, appeared on news racks across the country.

"Finally!" said Mirella Levinas, the Chilean American managing director of Washington's Cartier shop. "They've discovered us." By "us" she meant Latina females, a clear target for these magazines. "Latin women are different from other American women," Levinas said. "We feel different, and we like to keep that difference alive. These publications are a vehicle for that."

"The people in here are real Hispanics," said Clara Gonzales, a housekeeper from Rockville, flipping pages and pointing at the glossy pictures. "It's so nice to see them in a first-class magazine."

Full of attitude, color advertising and readership questionnaires, the fledgling publications are catering to a burgeoning market with a purchasing power of more than $250 billion a year. It's called the Latino middle class, and U.S. retailers are just beginning to fathom its potential.

The 1990 U.S. census was the first time Americans could choose to identify themselves as Hispanics, and 23 million did. Six years later, that figure would be closer to 32 million. And the count will increase exponentially. By 2040, according to census projections, Hispanics will number more than 80 million. One out of every four Americans will be a Hispanic.

While that means more poor Hispanics, it also means that more will be middle- and upper-class Americans.

"What we have here," said M. Isabel Valdes, president and founder of Hispanic Market Connections Inc., a research firm in Palo Alto, Calif., "is a population with annual family incomes greater than we thought."

In October, Pepperdine University research fellow Gregory Rodriguez published a ground-breaking study showing that during the 1980s the number of middle-class Latinos in Southern California grew 3½ times faster than the number of Latino poor. According to Rodriguez, half of all Southern California Hispanics own their own homes, the quintessential signal of middle-class status.

The Media Response

Landon Y. Jones Jr., managing editor of People magazine, said he had been lobbying for years for a Spanish-language edition to appeal to prosperous Hispanics. But the market he had in mind was Mexico—a territory already staked out by Newsweek's Spanish-language edition. It took the murder of the wildly popular singer Selena last April to awaken Jones to People's possibilities in the United States.

"I had never even heard of her," he said. "But when I learned that 50- to 60,000 people had attended her memorial service in Texas, I paid good attention." First, he put a Selena story on the cover of a special Southwest edition of People. It sold 442,000 copies in a single day. A memorial edition that followed sold a million copies.

"I had never seen a demand like that. It was bigger than any response we'd had for our special issued on Jackie or Audrey Hepburn," said Jones. "When I went back to the boardroom to propose a national Spanish-language edition of People, no one argued."

With an initial printing of 250,000 copies, People En Espanol is a quarterly publication that combines original articles in Spanish and Spanish translations from People's regular English-language edition. The contents, similarly, are a combination of Latino and mainstream subjects—a profile of Oprah Winfrey is followed by one of Gloria Estefan.

"There is a huge gap between the mainstream media and most Latinos," said Betty Cortina, the magazine's Cuban-born associate editor. "There is very little out there for them. Latinos want news about themselves, but they also want to know what's going on in this country. And they want it in Spanish."

Birth of a Partnership

"Well, maybe not entirely in Spanish," said Christy Haubegger, the publisher and founder of Latina, an unabashedly feminine magazine that is the product of a joint venture with Essence Inc., the African American publishing empire. Launched in May with 300,000 copies and with a second issue out this month, Latina is 70 percent English and 30 percent Spanish.

Haubegger sees a market entirely different from the one identified by Vanidades ("Vanities") or Buenhogar (Good Housekeeping) or Ser Padres (Parenting) or Cosmopolitan in Spanish, all of which have been around for years and see their readership as Spanish-speaking and largely foreign.

The U.S. Latino household Haubegger is targeting has more than one generation reading its pages: a Spanish-dominant grandmother, a bilingual mother and an English-dominant teenager. The magazine strives to appeal to all three. It's full of fashion and beauty advice, and with good reason: Market research shows that Hispanics buy more lipstick, more perfume and more shampoo than non-Hispanics.

Of Latina's staff of 19, hardly anyone is over 30. "Yes, our staff is young," Haubegger acknowledges, "but so are our readers." The median age for all Hispanics in the United States, in fact, is her age—28.

Here's how Haubegger sees her average reader: "She's in her twenties or thirties; bilingual; she either has or is working on her BA; she's the first woman in her family to work full time and raise kids too. Like most Latinos, she's part of a large family. Her parents speak mostly Spanish, her children mostly English. She's English-dominant, although she things Spanglish is fun. She's devoted to her family, but she's out to do things her way. She's going to redefine success. I want her to pick up Latina magazine as if she's picking up a mirror for the very first time."

Haubegger, born of a Mexican American teenage mother, was adopted as a baby by well-to-do German Americans in Houston. "Everyone immediately around me was blond and blue-eyed." She recounts how she never thought of herself as a real Hispanic until she was at Stanford Law School. There, she decided she wanted to do something about what she saw as a void in the American media. She echoes other Hispanic women when she described why:

"Nobody was paying attention to people who looked like me. There are still too few places where you can see our faces and read about our achievements. We Latinos ennoble this country with our blood and our sweat. I want to show this on the pages of our magazine."

Haubegger's commitment impressed Edward Lewis, founder and chief executive of Essence, when she came in for a 1993 interview, referred by one of his editors. He had been looking for a way to position his company with the growing Hispanic market, and he was struck "by the young woman's passion and integrity" and by her confidence that she could produce a magazine that captured the whole Hispanic spectrum.

"The real trick, as far as I was concerned, was to appeal to the Cuban in Miami, the Puerto Rican in New York, the Mexican in Texas and the Hispanic in Illinois, all at once. She felt there was a commonality, but I needed to be convinced."

Lewis asked her to write a business plan. Within months she presented one to his board and won their support—and a multimillion-dollar investment from the man who probably knew better than anyone else in the country what it means to publish for an ethnic readership. Lewis started Essence magazine in 1969; today it has a circulation of 1 million. One in 10 African American women reads it.

WHAT THEY EARN

While much attention has been given to the Hispanic poor, Census Bureau figures suggest that there is more dramatic growth higher on the income spectrum. Advertisers are beginning to focus on the spending habits of the wealthier sector.

Hispanic family incomes	1992 Number	1992 Percent	1982–1992 Absolute change	1982–1992 Percent change
$100,000+	119,000	2.3%	+83,000	230.5%
75,000–99,999	166,000	3.2	86,000	110.1
50,000–74,999	554,000	10.7	180,000	48.5
25,000–49,999	1,631,000	31.5	477,000	41.5
15,000–24,999	1,113,000	21.5	363,000	48.4
Under 15,000	1,589,000	30.7	677,000	74.2

SOURCE: Census Bureau

THE WASHINGTON POST

"I want to see these two communities—American blacks and Hispanics—come together," said Lewis. "If we trust each other and get politically involved, it will only be to the good."

The Independent

One publisher who's not new to the market is Alfredo Estrada, chief executive of Hispanic Publishing Corp. He has a new entry as well: Moderna—a lighthearted, frothy publication with articles such as "How to Make Your Man a Better Lover."

"I guess it's very chic to start a Hispanic magazine these days," said Estrada. "It's like Columbus discovering America. People tend to forget that some of us were here before they came." A Cuban-born graduate of Harvard and the University of Texas Law School, Estrada inherited his interest in publications from his father, who is now chairman of Vista, a Spanish-language tabloid magazine founded in 1985 and inserted in 26 Sunday newspapers around the country. The younger Estrada is publisher and founder of Hispanic Publishing, the umbrella company for Hispanic, Vista and now Moderna magazine. He began operations in Washington, and then moved to Austin, Tex., in 1994.

His new bilingual women's magazine is pitched to middle-income women ($35,000 to $45,000), ages 18 through 44. Its two issues so far have sold about 150,000 copies at national newsstands.

"We're not Time Warner and we're not Essence," he said. "We're littler, we're funkier. We moved to Texas to save on costs and because a great majority of our readers are here. This is not just a business for us. It's a personal mission. We're in it for the long haul."

One of his former employees already has jumped ship and gone into business for herself. Anna Maria Arias, Hispanic magazine's managing editor for five years, parted ways with Estrada when it came to deciding whom Moderna's target readers should be. "All my research suggested that the Latina readers we wanted were English-dominant. Just because you're a bilingual doesn't mean you can read all that well in Spanish. And I certainly felt Moderna didn't need to talk down to these women. I wanted an issue-oriented magazine with an emphasis on business and education."

Arias stayed behind in Washington and started her own magazine, Latina Style in early 1994. Launched in the spring of 1995, it's an all English-language, no-nonsense bimonthly that features Hispanic women leaders: the fashion designed Carolina Herrera; FBI Special Agent Juanita Benavides Leos; or Anita Perez Ferguson, president of the National Women's Political Caucus.

According to Arias, her readers have average household incomes of $60,000. They are overwhelmingly English-dominant "achievers" who are "integrated into the mainstream, but also rooted" in the Hispanic culture. Most are married Mexican-American working women with children. And two out of three live in Texas and California.

But there is one magazine that is shooting for something beyond the ranks of Middle America: Its name is Si, and it is a glossy, art nouveau, sleek high-fashion concept, whose writers and editors are among the best-known names in Hispanic American literature—Ana Castillo, Esmeralda Santiago, Francisco Goldman. Based in Los Angeles, Si is the brainchild of Joie Davidow, who founded L.A. Weekly in 1978 and L.A. Style in 1985. A non-Hispanic with a wide network of Latino friends and associates. Davidow said, "I guess I have an instinct for seeing market niches. When I sold L.A. Style to American Express in 1991, I began looking around for another project." A friend, Eileen Rosaly, started bombarding her with arguments for a Hispanic magazine.

"I told Joie, we're not reflected anywhere," said Rosaly. "We're absent. We're gigantic, invisible and affluent. 'Prove it to me,' she said. So I researched for three months and brought her the numbers."

Today, Davidow is Si's director and editor-in-chief, Rosaly is director of operations and Cecilia Alvear, an NBC producer, is editor-at-large. Si's circulation, according to advertiser estimates, is 50,000.

The Wanted Ads

Highbrow or low, one language or two, all of these magazines are competing for the same advertising dollar, struggling to convince advertisers of their vision and the vast buying power of their readers. "They're just not familiar with the culture," said Moderna's editor, Christine Granados. "And our sales calls end up being lessons." Certian companies have taken the lessons to heart: J. C. Penney, Neiman Marcus, Budweiser, Bacardi, Chrysler and Toyota, to name a few, have advertised in more than one of the new magazines, paying from $7,125 to $10,000 a page.

But so far, there's no successful model for a mass-market Hispanic magazine. And not for lack of trying. Just ask the former publisher of Mas ("More"), a general interest, glossy Spanish-language magazine published in the late 1980s by Univision, the highly popular Spanish-language TV network.

Univision had already demonstrated its ability to fuse culturally different Hispanics into one mega-audience for television, a medium with a strong, proven Latino consumer. So it had a great expectations when it launched Mas out of its headquarters in Miami. "We were as big an investment in the Hispanic reader as could be," said former publisher Roger Toll. "We had a newsstand circulation of 680,000. A full-page ad cost $20,000."

But when the Mexican media giant Televisa bought Univision from Hallmark in 1993, it took a look at Mas, decided that it was losing money and closed the magazine. "we were the Time magazine, the Vanity Fair, the Vogue of the American Hispanic," said Toll. But not big enough for a TV company.

Toll, who is now editor-in-chief of Snow Country, a ski magazine, is quick to add, "Of course, Latina and People En Espanol have big, smart publishers behind them. And that may be what it takes. . . . Someone committed to print."

"Everyone knows there is a huge Latino population in this country," said Mas's former editor, Enrique Fernandez, "That much is a reality. So, you ask me, is there an audience? Yes. Is there an appetite? Yes. Is there a business in Hispanic print? Well, that we don't know quite yet."

Indeed, producing a magazine for this niche market presents its own special problems—from finding the right images to using the right Spanish. Latina's Haubegger complains that it is very hard to locate experienced Hispanic models. The major modeling agencies don't represent more than a few. It's why you tend to see them again and again on these pages.

And merging the different dialects of Spanish takes considerable thought and effort. "We have a Puerto Rican editor, a Cuban and a Mexican," says People En Espanol's Betty Cortina. "We police each other as we edit, making sure that we maintain a high-level, slang-free Spanish. We're trying to bust the myth that everyone wants a different kind of Spanish."

Searching for Outlets

But even Time Warner is discovering that it has things to learn when it comes to this kind of publishing. Selena may have sold to Hispanic readers, but when People released a Spanish-language special on Princess Di, the audience response was only lukewarm. People printed 115,000 copies and sold only 30,000.

And then there are questions about trying to reach new heights with old methods. People Vice President Jeremy Koch said that whereas he's not worried about finding readers and advertisers for People En Espanol, he is less confident about distributors. New magazines are trying to wedge into antiquated patterns of Hispanic product distribution—through sales at Latino grocery stores or neighborhood stands. "There's an opportunity for us to be better than that," said Koch. "We've got the mainstream advertisers. We just need to break through to a bigger audience. And we won't be able to do that if we use the same old outlets. We're going to do it; we're committed to it. We just have to find out how."

One company that thinks it has found out the "how" of the Hispanic market is Honda, which has been advertising in Spanish-language venues for years and has current ads in Latina, Si and People en Espanol. According to Susan Wrede, advertising account director for Honda in L.A.'s Agencia de Orci, Hispanics spend more than $11 billion annually on new cars. Honda has fought hard to get its share of that market, Wrede says.

Honda has ads in the new publications, Wrede said, because it has been impressed with "the high quality of these glossies and their new level of editorial excellence." But above all, the company believes that this kind of advertising works. "Honda started targeting print ads to Hispanics back in 1989, when it was the number five car brand in that market," she said. "Today it is number one.

"When a magazine ad campaign produces that kind of climb, it tends to give you a whole lot of faith."

Ed Rensi, chairman of the National Hispanic Corporate Council Institute and president/CEO of McDonald's USA, appears to have a whole lot of faith too. "When we first got involved with the Hispanic market there wasn't much research available," he said at a November conference of U.S. corporations meeting to talk about Hispanic market opportunities. "But we plunged in."

"Today, no company that expects to remain competitive, that expects to expand globally and that expects to remain responsive to consumer needs can afford to ignore a market that is $300 billion strong and a permanent part of the business equation," Rensi said. "Over the next 15 years, the aggregate purchasing power of Hispanics is expected to triple to an estimated $965 billion. Let me ask you, who among us would ignore a market today that will grow that much tomorrow?"

African Americans

A 1988 *New York Times* editorial suggests an appropriate introductory focus for the following collection of articles about an ethnic group that traces its American ancestry to initial participation as "three-fifths" persons in the U.S. Constitution and to its later exclusion from the polity altogether by the U.S. Supreme Court's *Dred Scott* decision. The editors of the *Times* wrote in the article "Negro, Black and African American" (December 22, 1988):

> The archaeology is dramatically plain to older adults who, in one lifetime, have already heard preferred usage shift from *colored* to *Negro* to *black*. The four lingual layers provide an abbreviated history of civil rights in this century.

Renaming this ethnic group "African American" may produce the fresh vision needed to understand and transcend the deep racism that infects society. The following glimpses of the African American reality, its struggles for freedom, its tradition and community, its achievements, and the stresses of building bridges between worlds reveal a dense set of problems. More importantly, they suggest pieces of authentic identity rather than stereotype. Becoming a healthy ethnic society involves more than the end of ethnic stereotyping. The basis of ethnic identity is sustained by authentic portrayal of positive personal and group identity. The cultivation of ethnicity that does not encourage disdain for and self-hatred among members and groups is an important psychological and social artifice.

Progress on issues of race involves examination of a complex of historical, social, cultural, and economic factors. Analysis of this sort requires assessment of the deep racism in the American mentality—that is, the cultural consciousness and the institutions whose images and practices shape social reality.

Discrimination and prejudice based on skin color are issues rarely broached in mainstream journals of opinion. Ethnic and racial intermarriage and the influence and impact of skin hue within the African American community raise attendant issues of discrimination and consciousness of color. This concern began in eighteenth- and nineteenth-century laws and practices of defining race that shaped the mentalities of color consciousness, prejudice, and racism in America. Other dimensions of the African American experience can be found in this unit's accounts of African American traditions and experiences of self-help and the family. New perspectives on the civil rights era can be gained from reflective accounts of the many leaders who have influenced the direction of social change that reconfigured race and ethnic relations in America.

As this debate continues, patterns of change within African American populations compel discussion of the emerging black middle class. The purpose and influence of the historically black university, the reopening of the discussion of the separate-but-equal issue in the courts, and the renewed attention to Afrocentric education are clear evidence of the ambivalence and ambiguity inherent in the challenges of a multicultural society. Earlier dichotomies—slave/free, black/white, poor/rich—are still evident, but a variety of group relations based on historical and regional as well as institutional agendas to preserve cultural and racial consciousness have complicated the simple hope for liberty and justice that was shared by many Americans. Issues of race and class are addressed in this section. Various approaches to Afrocentrism are explained and contrasted.

Questions on the future state of American ethnic groups raise profound issues. For example, understanding of the changing structure of the African American family has stubbornly eluded researchers and parents who confront the realities of pride and prejudice. Does the continual discovery of prejudice and discrimination in corporations have implications for public policy? Should public policy sustain an ethnic model of family or direct the formation of family life that is consonant with public purposes and goals?

The civil rights movement has been over for more than 20 years, but many African Americans still face challenges in housing, employment, and education. Changing circumstances within the larger American society and the civil rights agenda itself have been affected by success and failure, and once-clear issues and solutions have taken on more complex structural, economic, and philosophical dimensions. The growing gap between blacks and whites in terms of education, financial status, and class, and the growing crime and death rates of young black men paint a daunting picture of past policies and of this population's future. According to scales of mortality, health, income, education, and marital status, African Americans have emerged as one of the most troubled segments of American society. These problems also foreshadow grave difficulties for the African American family in the years ahead.

To be sure, African Americans have made advances since the civil rights movement of the 1960s. They have made dramatic gains in education, employment, and financial status. Unfortunately, they still are portrayed as being part of an urban underclass when only one-third of their population is considered part of this group. While not all African Americans are poor, those who are poor are in desperate situations. Will help come from the African American population that now constitutes part of the middle and upper classes of American society?

UNIT 5

Scholarly differences of opinion concerning the composition of the urban underclass do not minimize the hardships that many endure. The growth of the underclass, its isolation from society, and society's inability to help it are tremendous obstacles that face our nation. Concrete strategies for improving this situation call upon both the public and the private sectors in areas of education, employment, and training. Suggestions for meeting future needs of this population and pragmatic policy responses also will help the general population.

Patent historical distortion and various forms of statistical evidence have been included in interpretations and rearticulations of race and ethnicity. The issues of race in the workplace and remedies for discriminating practices have been raised in the debate regarding the Civil Rights Act of 1991. Exploring ethnic and racial mobility and developing strategies that foster the breakdown of discrimination engage us in a web of baffling arguments and social, political, and institutional procedures.

Looking Ahead: Challenge Questions

What are the most compelling issues that face African American communities?

What social, economic, and political conditions have supported the expansion of an African American middle class?

What explains the persistence of an African American underclass?

Explore the impact of the O. J. Simpson trial on shaping consciousness of ethnic group identity.

In what respect is attention to education an answer to economic and social integration of African Americans?

Does the name "African Americans" augment the development of pluralism? Which view of Afrocentrism?

Discuss the influence of religion on the civil rights movement.

What effect will the Supreme Court's deemphasis on remedies for segregation and on other initiatives that use racial preferences have on race and ethnic relations?

What relevance does the Nation of Islam have to the public dialogue that shapes relationships among racial and ethnic populations?

Comment on the idea that attitudinal change founded on achieving middle-class status could extend to the diminishing of interest in and the relevance of being an African American.

Understanding Afrocentrism

Why Blacks Dream of a World Without Whites

GERALD EARLY

Gerald Early is director of the African and Afro-American Studies Program at Washington University in St. Louis.

The White man will never admit his real references. He will steal everything you have and still call you those names.

—Ishmael Reed, *Mumbo Jumbo* (1972)

Furthermore, no one can be thoroughly educated until he learns as much about the Negro as he knows about other people.

—Carter G. Woodson, *The Mis-Education of the Negro* (1933)

[Alexander] Crummell's black nationalism was marked by certain inconsistencies, but they derived from the inconsistencies and hypocrisy of American racism, rather than from any intellectual shortcomings on his part. It was impossible to create an ideology that responded rationally to an irrational system.

—Wilson Jeremiah Moses, *Alexander Crummell: A Study of Civilization and Discontent* (1989)

In a span of three weeks during the early spring semester of 1995, Angela Davis and bell hooks, two notable black leftist, feminist thinkers, visited the campus of Washington University in St. Louis, invited by different student groups. They were generally well received, indeed, enthusiastically so. But there was, for each of them during these visits, something of a jarring note, both involving black students.

Professor Davis, entertaining questions during a panel session after having spoken earlier on the subject of prison reform, was asked by a black woman student what she had to offer black people as a solution to their problems. The student went on to explain that she did not consider herself an African-American. She was simply an African, wishing to have nothing to do with being an American or with America itself. She wanted black people to separate themselves entirely from "Europeans," as she called white Americans, and wanted to know what Davis could suggest to further that aim.

Davis answered that she was not inclined to such stringent race separation. She was proud of being of African descent but wished to be around a variety of people, not just people like herself. Davis felt further that blacks should not isolate themselves but accept in partnership anyone who was sincerely interested in the cause of overthrowing capitalism, a standard and reasonable Marxist response to the "essentializing" of race in a way that would divert true political engagement "against the system." The student was visibly annoyed with the answer, which presumably smacked of "white" intellectualism.

Professor bell hooks, after her address on ending racism and sexism in America—love, I think, was the answer—was asked by a black woman student how feminism was relevant to black women. Hooks explained that feminism was not only for white women, that black women needed to read more feminist texts, even if some of them were racist. After all, Karl Marx was racist but he did give the world a brilliant analysis of capitalism. She had said in her speech how disappointed she was that her black women students at City College of New York were not inclined to embrace feminism, rejecting it as something white. She felt that these black women were unduly influenced by black male rappers who bashed feminism. The answer did not persuade or please the student.

Later that day, I heard many black undergraduates dismiss hooks's talk as not addressing the needs of black people, as being too geared to the white feminists in the audience. Some were disturbed that hooks would feel that they formed their opinions on the basis of listening to rap records. None of this was said, necessarily, with hostility, but rather with regret and a shade of condescension that only the young can so keenly and innocently express when speaking about the foolishness of their elders.

I recall a fairly recent incident where a black student, a very bright young woman, asked if, when doing research, one had to acknowledge racist books. I told her that a certain amount of objectivity was part of the discipline of being a scholar. Anger at unjust or inaccurate statements and assessments was understandable, but personalizing everything often caused a kind of tunnel vision where crude self-affirmation seemed to be the only fit end of scholarship. She responded that she would refuse to acknowledge racist sources, that if the book was racist, then everything it said was tainted and should be disregarded.

The attitudes of these students have been shaped by Afrocentrism, an insistence by a growing number of black Americans to see the world from an "African-centered" perspective in response to the dominant "European-centered" perspective to which they feel they have been subjected throughout their lives. Afrocentrism is many things and has many degrees of advocacy. It can range from the commercialism and pretense of the shallow holiday called Kwanza (no shallower, it should be said, than the commercialized celebration of Christmas) to the kente-cloth ads and nationalist talk that one finds in most black publications these days; from talk about racist European scholarship to a view that world culture is essentially African in origin and that Europeans are usurpers, thieves, and generally inferior. On the one hand, we have the recent cover story "Is Jesus Black?" in *Emerge*, an Afrocentric-tinged news magazine for the black middle class. The answer in this instance, of course, is clearly yes. (Obviously, this is grounds for competing claims between blacks and Jews; whatever can be said about Jesus' skin color or the religious movement that bears his name, there is no question that he was a Jew.) On the other hand, we have the first explicitly Afrocentric Hollywood Western in Mario Van Peebles's 1993 film *Posse*, a jumbled multicultural critique of white *fin de siècle* imperialism and the myth of how the West was won.

No doubt, Afrocentrists specifically and black folk generally found it to be a signal victory that in the recent television dramatization of the love affair between Solomon and Sheba, Sheba was played by a black actress and Solomon by a swarthy Hispanic. In the 1959 Hollywood film version of *Solomon and Sheba*, directed by King Vidor—who, incidentally, made the first all-black Hollywood film—Solomon was played by Yul Brynner and Sheba by Gina Lollobrigida. It is safe to say that the real Solomon and the real Sheba, if they ever existed, did not look remotely like any of the actors who ever played them. But whom we want them to look like is very important. The Afrocentrists will feel their triumph to be complete when black actors portray Beethoven, Joseph Haydn, Warren G. Harding, Alexander Hamilton, Hannibal, Abraham Lincoln, Dwight Eisenhower, Cleopatra, Moses, Jesus Christ and Saint Augustine. Many African-Americans are inclined to believe that any noted white with ambiguous ancestry must be black. They are also inclined to believe that any white with dark skin tones, one who hangs around blacks or who "acts black" in some way is truly black. At various times in my life, I have heard blacks argue vehemently that Madonna, Phoebe Snow, Keith Jarrett, Mae West, Ava Gardner and Dorothy Parker were black, even though they did not have a shred of evidence to support the claims. Blacks have always been fascinated by "passing," by the possibility that some whites are really black—"fooling old massa," so to speak.

AFROCENTRISM IS AN INTELLECTUAL MOVEMENT, A political view, a historically traceable evolution, a religious orthodoxy. It derives, in part, from Negritude and Pan-Africanism, which stressed the culture and achievements of Africans. Both movements were started by Africans, West Indians and African-Americans in response to European colonialism and the worldwide oppression of African-descended people. But Afrocentrism is also a direct offshoot of earlier forms of black nationalism, in which blacks around the world believed they had a special destiny to fulfill and a special consciousness to redeem. More important, Afrocentrism is a mood that has largely erupted in the last 10 to 15 years in response to integration or, perhaps more precisely, to the failure of integration. Many blacks who have succeeded in the white world tend to feel most Afrocentric, although I think it would be a mistake to see Afrocentrism purely as middle-class, since significant numbers of working-class blacks are attracted to some elements of it. The bourgeois, "midcult" element of Afrocentrism, nonetheless, is very strong. "Integrated" middle-class blacks see it as a demonstration of their race loyalty and solidarity with their brothers and sisters throughout the world, whether in American cities or on African farms. (It is worth noting the economic clout of the black middle class, which can be seen in the growing number of black Hollywood films and filmmakers, in new black magazines ranging from *Body and Soul* to *The Source* to *Upscale*, and in the larger audience for black books. It is the market power of this class that has given Afrocentrism its force as a consumer ideology.)

So the middle-class black, having had more contact with whites and their institutions, is expected to speak for and to other blacks. Afrocentrism, like Negritude and Pan-Africanism, is meant to be an ideological glue to bring black people together, not just on the basis of color but as the expression of a cultural and spiritual will that crosses class and geographical lines. As W.E.B. Du Bois wrote in 1940: "Since the fifteenth century these ancestors of mine and their other descendants have had a common history; have suffered a common disaster and have one long memory.... The real essence of this kinship is its social heritage of slavery; the discrimination and insults; and this heritage binds together not simply the children of Africa, but extends through yellow Asia and into the South Seas. It is this unity that draws me to Africa."

Louis H. Farrakhan, the head of the Nation of Islam, is probably the most familiar figure associated with Afrocentrism. (Muhammad Ali introduced Islamic conversion to an even bigger public, suffering greatly for his religious and political beliefs and becoming the most noted and charismatic dissident of his era. Ali's prodigious athletic abilities and his genial temperament succeeded in endearing him to the American public despite his religion. He never became a member of Farrakhan's sect.) Farrakhan is a fiery preacher, prone to making extreme statements, with a militant flair and a racist edge, that have the conviction of truth among some blacks. He especially exploits the idea that he is a heroic black man at grave risk for daring to tell the truth about the white man. (Malcolm X used this device effectively, too.) He is also a master demagogue who exploits the paranoia of his audience. But then, as a friend once said to me, "What black person isn't justified in being at least half-paranoid?"

Farrakhan has found three effective lines of entry among blacks, particularly young blacks, that draw on the Afrocentric impulse: First, that Islam is the true religion of black people. (This has led to a move among black Christian leaders to point out with great vehemence the African origins of Christianity, to make it, in effect, a black religion.) Second, that black people need business enterprise in their community in order to liberate themselves (an old belief among blacks, going back to at least the early part of the 19th century). And third, that Jews of European descent (what he calls "false Jews") are not to be trusted, a charge that exploits the current tension between blacks and Jews—and that Farrakhan has used to move into the black civil-rights establishment. All three positions enjoy remarkable support within the black middle class, a situation that has helped Farrakhan tap people's insecurities for his own purposes. The Nation of Islam may be famous for converting addicts and criminals, but above all, it wants, as all religions do, to win over the middle class, with its money, its respectability and its organizational know-how.

Whatever might be said of Farrakhan's importance as a political figure in the black community or in the United States, he is a minor figure in the development of Afrocentrism. His position in the history of Afrocentrism is similar to that of, say, Rush Limbaugh in the development of American conservatism. He is, like Limbaugh, a figure the media can use to give a sellable face and voice to a unique temper among a group of people. For both Limbaugh and Farrakhan represent an intense sentimentality in American life, a yearning for a fantasized, idealized past of racial grandeur and simplicity. This sentimentality appeals powerfully to the black middle class, which yearns for a usable, untainted past. This partly explains why Farrakhan and the Muslims can often be found speaking to black college students.

In thinking about the connection between class and nationalistic feelings, it should be recalled that in Harriet Beecher Stowe's 1852 novel, *Uncle Tom's Cabin,* the most light-complexioned blacks, the ones with the greatest skills, George, Eliza and Cassy, return to Africa at the novel's end to retrieve their degraded patrimony. It might be said that this is purely Stowe's own perverse vision, since some of the fiercest advocates for returning to Africa have been Martin Delany, Alexander Crummell and Marcus Garvey, all very dark men. Yet there is more than a little truth to the idea that class, caste and race consciousness are closely interwoven. Nationalism of whatever sort has almost always been an affair of a disaffected middle class. And until the 1920s, the black middle class in America was disproportionately made up of light-skinned people.

The paradox of the bourgeois aspect of Afrocentrism is that it rejects cosmopolitanism as being "white" or "Eurocentric." Yet Afrocentrism has no other way of seeing cosmopolitanism except on the "Eurocentric" model, so it tries to make Africa for black Americans the equivalent of what Europe is for white Americans: the source of civilization. Indeed, by trying to argue that Africa is the source of Western civilization, the Afrocentric sees the African, symbolically, as the mother of white Europe (just as the black mother, the mammy, is the mythic progenitor of the white South, or so Langston Hughes seemed to believe in his famous short story "Father and Son," which became his even more famous play, *Mulatto).* The African becomes, in this view, the most deeply cultured person on the planet, which matches his status as the oldest person on the planet, with the longest and deepest genetic history. In short, Afrocentrism becomes another form of the American apologizing for being American to people he imagines are his cultural superiors. Afrocentrism tries to mask a quest for American filiopiety behind a facade of African ancestor and culture worship.

IT WOULD BE EASY, ON ONE LEVEL, TO DISMISS AFROCENTRISM as an expression, in white workplaces and white colleges, of intimidated black folk who are desperately trying to find a space for themselves in what they feel to be alien, unsympathetic environments. Seen this way, Afrocentrism becomes an expression of the low self-esteem and inferiority that blacks feel most intensely when they are around whites; their response is to become more "black," estranged from the environment that they find so unaccepting of them. The greatest psychic burden of the African-American is that he must not only think constantly about being different but about what his difference means. And it might be suggested that Afrocentrism does not solve this problem but merely reflects it in a different mirror. There is a certain amount of truth to this, especially at a time when affirmative action, which promotes group identification and group difference, tends to intensify black self-consciousness. And black people, through no fault of their own, are afflicted with a debilitating sense of self-consciousness when around whites. When whites are in the rare situation of being a minority in a sea of blacks, they often exhibit an abject self-consciousness as well, but the source of that self-consciousness is quite different. The white is used to traveling anywhere in the world and having his cultural inclinations accommodated. The black is neither used to this nor does he realistically expect it. The European exults in his culture while the African is utterly degraded by his. That blacks should want to free themselves from the white gaze seems not merely normal but essential to the project of reconstructing themselves as a people on their own terms. And the history of blacks in the United States has been an ongoing project—tragic, pathetic, noble, heroic, misguided, sublime—of self-reconstruction.

NOT JUST ON THE BASIS OF COLOR BUT AS AN EXPRESSION OF CULTURAL WILL

When it comes to black folk in America, the white man wants to say that if you have one-thirty-second portion of black blood, a mere drop of black blood, then you are black, no matter what your skin color. But when it comes to the ancient Egyptians, it doesn't matter if they have a drop of black blood, and we know that they had at least one-thirty-second portion of African blood. It doesn't matter how much African blood they have, they are still white. The white man wants to have his cake and eat it too. When it's convenient, he wants you to be black and when it's convenient, he wants you to be white. Either you're a nigger, because he thinks you're nothing. Or you're white, if you have done anything he's bound to respect. The white man wants to control all the definitions of blackness.

—A conversation with an Afrocentric friend

Afrocentrism, like a good many nationalistic ideologies, might be called the orthodoxy of the book, or more precisely, the orthodoxy of the books. Afrocentrism is an attempt to wed knowledge and ideology. Movements like Afrocentrism, which feels both its mission and its authority hinge on the revelation of a denied and buried truth, promote a fervent scholasticism, a hermeneutical ardor among true believers for compilations of historical minutiae on the one hand, and for grand philosophical tracts on the other. The former might be best represented by George G. M. James's *Stolen Legacy*, published in 1954, the latter by Mustafa El-Amin's *Al-Islam, Christianity, and Freemasonry* and *Freemasonry, Ancient Egypt, and the Islamic Destiny*. These books were not written by professional historians or by college professors. The fact that several classic Afrocentric texts have been written by amateurs gives Afrocentrism its powerful populist appeal, its legitimacy as an expression of "truth" that white institutional forces hide or obscure. At the same time, this leaves it vulnerable to charges of being homemade, unprofessional, theoretically immature and the like. It is one of the striking aspects of Afrocentrism that within the last 20 years it has developed a cadre of academics to speak for it, to professionalize it, to make it a considerable insurgency movement on the college campus.

There are several texts that might be considered the literary and intellectual cornerstones of the Afrocentrism movement. Molefi K. Asante, professor and chair of African-American studies at Temple University in Philadelphia, is credited with inventing the name "Afrocentrism" or "Afrocentricity" (although currently the term "Africentrism" is on the rise in certain quarters, probably because there is a group of black folk who, for some reason, despise the prefix "Afro," as if the word "Africa" itself were created by the people of the continent rather than by Europeans). Asante's very short books, including *The Afrocentric Idea*, published in 1987, and *Afrocentricity: The Theory of Social Change*, published in 1980, are frequently the starting points for people seeking a basic explanation of this ideology. As defined by Asante, Afrocentrism seems to take the terms and values of Eurocentrism—intense individualism, crass greed, lack of spirituality, warlike inclinations, dominance and racism, dishonesty and hypocrisy—and color their opposites black, giving us a view of black people not terribly different from the romantic racism of Harriet Beecher Stowe and other whites like her in the 19th and 20th centuries. I cannot recount the number of "race sensitivity" meetings I have attended where blacks begin to describe themselves (or those they perceive to be Africans) as more spiritual, more family-oriented, more community-oriented, more rhythmic, more natural and less combative than whites. All of which is, of course, a crock of nonsense, largely the expression of wishes for qualities that blacks see as absent from their community life now. But, thanks to Asante, this has become the profile of the African in the Afrocentric vision.

Martin Bernal's massively researched two-volume *Black Athena* (published in 1987 and 1991) is a popular title in Afrocentric circles, in large measure because Bernal, a professor at Cornell, is one of the few white scholars to take Afrocentrism seriously—William Piersen, Robert Farris Thompson and Andrew Hacker, in decidedly different ways, are others—and one of the few to write an academic treatise in its defense that forces whites to take it seriously too. (The irony that blacks still need whites, in some measure, to sell their ideas and themselves to other whites is not entirely lost on those who have thought about this.)

Black Athena supports three major contentions of the Afrocentrists: 1) ancient Egypt was a black civilization; 2) the Greeks derived a good deal, if not all, of their philosophy and religion from the Egyptians; 3) European historiography has tried strenuously and with clear political objectives to deny both. Bernal's book provoked a scathing attack by Mary R. Lefkowitz, a professor at Wellesley, who characterizes Afrocentrism as a perversion of the historiography of antiquity and a degradation of academic standards for political ends. Lefkowitz has also battled with Tony Martin, a cultural historian, barrister and Marcus Garvey specialist, who began using and endorsing the Nation of Islam's anti-Semitic *The Secret Relationship Between Blacks and Jews* (Vol. 1) in his classes on slavery at Wellesley. Martin responded in 1993 with his own account of the dispute, *The Jewish Onslaught: Despatches from the Wellesley Battlefront*, which elaborates his claims of Jewish racism and the hypocrisy of academic freedom.

Maulana Karenga, professor and chair of black studies at California State University at Long Beach, created the black philosophical code called the Kawaida, which was the inspiration for Kwanza and the seven principles (Nguzo Saba) that the holiday celebrates. The code contains a bit of Marxism to create a "theoretical" ambiance. Karenga is also author of the popular *Introduction to Black Studies*, used by many colleges in their introductory courses, despite its rather tendentious manner, which he tries to pass off as sharp-minded Marxism, and the fact that the book is weak on a good many aspects of African-American life and culture.

Perhaps the most popular Afrocentric text is Chancellor Williams's *The Destruction of Black Civilization: Great Issues of a Race from 4500 B.C. to 2000 A.D.* (published in 1987), an account of his exhaustive research trips to Africa. Although not directly trained in the study of African history, Williams studied under William Leo Hansberry, a history professor at Howard University and probably the leading black American authority on Africa during the 1930s, 1940s and 1950s. Hansberry did path-breaking work in an utterly neglected field, eventually becoming known as "the father of African studies" in the United States. (Scholars, until recently, did not think Africa had a "history." The continent, especially its sub-Saharan regions, had an "anthropology" and an "archaeology," folkways to be discovered and remains to be unearthed, but never a record of institutions, traditions, political ideologies and complex societies.) Williams also did research on African history at Oxford and at the University of London, where, because of colonialism, interest in the nature of African societies was far keener than in the United States. His book *The Re-Birth of African Civilization,* an account of his 1953–1957 research project investigating the nature of education in Europe and Africa, calls for Pan-African education of blacks in Africa and around the world. Williams concluded that "European" and "Eurocentric" education was antithetical, both politically and intellectually, to African interests, a common refrain in Afrocentrist thought.

Most Afrocentric scholars at universities today genuflect at the intellectual altar of Cheikh Anta Diop, a Senegalese humanist and scientist who began his research into African history in 1946, as the battle against European colonialism in Africa was beginning. Diop saw his mission as undermining European colonialism by destroying the European's claim to a superior history. He was tenacious in demonstrating that Africa had a "real" history that showed that Africans were the product of civilizations and not of the jungle. This claim to history was a sign to the African that he was an equal player in the family of man, and was essential to any demand for independence.

For Diop, it was not enough to reconstruct African history; it was also necessary to depict a unified Africa, an idea that, whether myth or fact, was considered ideologically crucial by the Pan-African movement to overthrow European imperialism. Like every other oppressed people, the African could face the future only if he could hark back to some version of his past, preferably a past touched with greatness. This could be done only by running African history and civilization through Egypt, the only African civilization that impressed European intellectuals. As jazz and cultural critic Stanley Crouch suggested, Egypt is the only African civilization that has monuments, a physical legacy that indicates history as understood in European terms. Thus, for black people in Africa to be unified, for black people around the world to feel unified, ancient Egypt has to be a "black" civilization and serve as the origin of all blackness and, even more important, all whiteness. We know from scientific evidence that Africa is the place of origin for human life. If it is also true that Egypt is the oldest civilization from which Europeans borrowed freely (Bernal makes a persuasive argument for the influence of Egypt on European intellectuals through the 19th century), then Africans helped shape Western culture and were major actors in history, not bit players in the unfolding drama of European dominance.

Diop's doctoral dissertation, based on the idea that Egypt was African and that European civilization was largely built on Egyptian ideas, was rejected at the University of Paris in 1951. The story goes that he was able to defend his dissertation successfully only in 1960 when he was accompanied into the examination room by an army of historians, sociologists and anthropologists who supported his views, or at least his right as a responsible scholar to express them. By then, with African independence in full swing, his ideas had a political currency in Africa as an expression of Pan-Africanism. And no one supported the idea of a unified Africa more than Egypt's then-president, Gamal Abdel Nasser, probably the most powerful independent leader on the continent. Like Gandhi, Nasser called himself a black man, and he envisioned an Africa united in opposition to Israel and South Africa. It was a good moment for Diop to be saying what he was saying. At the 1956 Conference of Negro-African Writers and Artists in Paris, Diop was one of the most popular speakers, although black American James Baldwin was not much impressed with his thesis. (Admittedly, for Baldwin this was pretty new stuff.) For his part, Diop, a Marxist, thought the American delegation was blindly anticommunist and naively committed to the integrationist policies of the civil-rights movement.

Diop produced a number of volumes translated into English, some based on his dissertation. They include *The African Origin of Civilization: Myth or Reality, Civilization or Barbarism: An Authentic Anthropology* and *The Cultural Unity of Negro Africa.* For Diop, everything turned on establishing that ancient Egypt was a black civilization: "The history of Black Africa will remain suspended in air and cannot be written correctly until African historians dare to connect it with the history of Egypt." Moreover, Diop felt that the African could not remove the chains of colonialism from his psyche until he had a fully reconstructed history—in other words, until he had an unusual past. Diop was brilliant and clearly obsessed. His importance in the formation of African-American intellectual history does not depend on whether his historical theories are correct. (Although there is considerable debate about ancient Egypt—not surprising, since there is no documentation of the claim in the language of the people who lived there at the time—it is now conceded by virtually everyone that the Egyptians were a mixed-race people.) Diop's work transcends questions of historical accuracy and enters the realm of "belief." Much of what Diop wrote may be true (he had vast amounts of evidence to support his claims) but, as a Marxist, he was not motivated simply by the quest for positivistic, objective "truth." He wanted to use the supposed objectivity of scientific research for political ends.

DIOP BROUGHT TOGETHER THREE IMPORTANT elements in understanding the origins of Afrocentrism: first, the tradition of professional, politically motivated historical research that buttresses the claims of untrained, amateur historians; second, the explicit connection between knowledge of one's "proper" history and one's psychological and spiritual well-being; third, the connection between "proper" knowledge of one's history and the realization of a political mission and purpose. If European history functioned as an ideological and political justification for Europe's place in the world and its hope for its future, why shouldn't African history function in the same manner? This is the reasoning of the Pan-Africanists and Afrocentrists who see "proper" history as the version that is most ideologically and politically useful to their group. Diop's research supports the idea of a conspiracy among white historians to discredit or ignore black civilization. Without a "proper" knowledge of African history, Diop argues, blacks will remain politically impotent and psychologically crippled. These ideas have become the

"BLACK" CIVILIZATION AND SERVE AS THE ORIGIN OF ALL BLACKNESS

uncritical dogma of Afrocentrism. By the time Diop died in 1986, he had been virtually canonized by an important set of black American scholars who identified themselves as Afrocentric.

Diop is useful for Afrocentrism today not only because of his monumental research but because he was an African, thus linking Afrocentrism to Africa itself and permitting the black American to kneel before the perfect intellect of the "purer" African. But Diop's ideas about ancient black civilization in Egypt and the importance of fuller knowledge of its history had been advanced earlier by several African-American intellectuals, including W.E.B. Du Bois in his momentous book *Black Folk, Then and Now: An Essay in the History and Sociology of the Negro Race*, which appeared in 1939. Du Bois said he was inspired to write about the glories of the Negro past after hearing a lecture in 1906 at Atlanta University by the preeminent white anthropologist Franz Boas, debunker of racism and mentor of Zora Neale Hurston. Du Bois's work remains, despite the more richly researched efforts of Diop, Bernal and St. Clair Drake in *Black Folk Here and There* (published in two volumes in 1987 and 1990), the best and most readable examination of the subject. Indeed, his work must be seen in a larger historical context, dating back to the founding of the American Negro Academy in 1897, when he and other black intellectuals tried to organize themselves for the purpose of producing scholarship that defended the race and promoted race consciousness. Yet Du Bois's book is not the central work of the Afrocentric movement by a black American writer.

That book would be Carter G. Woodson's *The Mis-Education of the Negro*, originally published in 1933. Woodson, a Harvard Ph.D. in history who launched both the Association for the Study of Negro Life and History (1915) and Negro History Week (1926), was as obsessed with the reconstruction of the Negro past as Diop or Du Bois. He churned out dozens of books on virtually every aspect of African and African-American history. Some were wooden, opaque or just plain sloppy, and several are unreadable (even in the opinion of his assistant, the late, brilliant black historian Lorenzo Greene), indicating the haste with which they were composed. Even so, Woodson was a serious and demanding scholar. Greene thought of him, at times, as having the pious devotion of a Franciscan friar and the crotchety temper of an eccentric intellectual consumed by his work.

The Mis-Education of the Negro, although written by a man who endorsed Booker T. Washington and the Tuskegee method, was generally critical of black education. Black people, Woodson argued, were not being educated in a way that would encourage them to press their own political and economic interests or make them a viable social group in the United States. They were, in fact, being educated against their own interests, largely because their education was controlled by whites who saw advantage in giving blacks an inferior education. Moreover, Woodson made the explicit connection between "improper" education, including a lack of knowledge about the black past, and the psychological degradation of the Negro, his internalized sense of inferiority. In short, a white-controlled education led to Uncle Tomism and black sellouts, to a defective Negro who suffered from false consciousness, or, more precisely, "white" consciousness. Some of this argument was restated in black sociologist E. Franklin Frazier's seminal 1957 work, *Black Bourgeoisie*. The black middle class was almost exclusively the target of this indictment—a fact that prompted that class to romanticize certain aspects of black lower-class life, particularly its antisocial and criminal elements, in an effort to demonstrate its solidarity with "authentic" black experience. This was true with the Black Panthers in the late 1960s and it continues with rap music today. Another consequence is that the black middle class insists on a degree of race loyalty that sometimes thwarts any critical inquiry that does not promote race unity.

Much of Woodson's argument resonates with blacks today because it seems to endorse the idea of Afrocentric schools and especially the idea that knowledge of a glorious African past would give black youngsters self-esteem, reduce violence and criminality in black neighborhoods, and lead to the spiritual and political uplift of black people. This is why history is actually a less important discipline to the rise of Afrocentrism than psychology. After all, the reconstruction of black history was always connected with the reconstruction of the black mind, a mind that existed before the coming of the white man—or at least a mind that could be free of the white man and his image of what black people were.

In some ways, the rise of Afrocentrism is related to the rise of "black psychology" as a discipline. The Association of Black Psychologists was organized in 1968, a time when a number of black professional offshoots were formed in political and ideological protest against the mainstream, white-dominated versions of their organizations. Somewhat later came the *Journal of Black Psychology*, given impetus by the initial assaults against black intelligence or pointed suggestions of black genetic inferiority by Richard Herrnstein, Arthur Jensen and others in the early 1970s; this was also the time of the first wave of court challenges against affirmative action. The black psychology movement argued for new modes of treatment for black mental illness, the medical efficacy of using black history to repair a collectively damaged black psyche, and the destruction of "Eurocentrism" and the values it spawned—from the idealization of white standards of beauty to the scientific measurement of intelligence—as totally inimical to the political and psychological interests of black people. Rationality, order, individualism, dominance, sexual repression as well as sexual license, aggression, warmaking, moneymaking, capitalism itself—all soon became "white values."

That all of this happened during the era of Vietnam War protests, when white Western civilization was coming under withering intellectual attack from the radical left, is not without significance. Radical white intellectuals, who otherwise had no more use for a black epic history than a white one, found the black version useful as a weapon against "Eurocentrism," which, as a result of the Vietnam War, they held in utter contempt. In short, Jean-Paul Sartre and Susan Sontag were as instrumental, albeit indirectly, in the formation of Afrocentrism as, say, the Black Power movement of the late 1960s or the writings of African psychiatrist Franz Fanon, whose *The Wretched of the Earth* became the revolutionary psychological profile of the oppressed black diaspora. Also occurring at this time was the

THE RECONSTRUCTION OF BLACK HISTORY WAS ALWAYS CONNECTED WITH THE RECONSTRUCTION OF THE BLACK MIND, A MIND FREE OF THE WHITE MAN

movement on white college campuses to establish black studies programs, which provided a black intellectual wedge into the white academy. These programs, largely multidisciplinary, required an ideological purpose and mission to bind together the various disciplines, which is why many began to articulate some kind of Afrocentrism or, as it was called in the 1970s, "black aesthetic"—in other words, an ideological framework to give black studies a reason for being. When used to challenge the dominance of Western thought, Afrocentrism becomes part of a multicultural wave of complaint and resentment against the white man by a number of groups that feel they have been oppressed.

In an age of dysfunction and psychotherapy, no one can have greater claim to having been made dysfunctional by political oppression than the African-American, who was literally a slave; and no one can have a greater need for recourse to psychotherapy in the form of Afrocentrism. But what made the black psychology movement possible was the rise of the Nation of Islam, particularly the rise of Malcolm X.

The charismatic Muslim minister did two things. First, he forced the white mainstream press to take notice of black nationalism, Pan Africanism and the concept of African unity. Previously these ideas had been marginalized as ridiculous or even comic expressions of black nationalism, to be read by blacks in black barbershops and beauty salons as they thumbed through the Ripley's-Believe-It-or-Not-type work of the self-taught black historian J. A. Rogers (*One Hundred Amazing Facts About the Negro*, *Five Negro Presidents* and the like). Malcolm X revitalized the ideas of Marcus Garvey, the great black nationalist leader of the 1910s and 1920s, whose Universal Negro Improvement Association became, for a time, one of the most popular black political groups in America. Malcolm, like Garvey, felt that the Negro still needed to be "improved" but, unlike Garveyites, the Muslims did not offer costumes and parades but sober suits, puritanical religion, dietary discipline and no-nonsense business practices. Malcolm himself was also, by his physical appearance alone, a figure who would not be dismissed as a buffoon, as Garvey often was by both blacks and whites. According to Malcolm's *Autobiography,* his father had been a Garveyite as well as a wife beater who favored his lighter-skinned children. Malcolm's Islamic-based black nationalism, his sexual abstinence, which lasted from his religious conversion until his marriage a decade later, and his triumph over his own preference for lighter-skinned blacks and whites were all meant to demonstrate, vividly, how he superseded his father as a nationalist and how the Nation of Islam has superseded Garveyism.

Malcolm enlisted a body of enforcers, the feared Fruit of Islam, grim-faced men who, one imagines, were supposed to personify the essence of an unbowed yet disciplined black manhood. In this way, he dramatically associated black nationalism with a new type of regenerated black male. It was said in the black community, and may still be, that no one bothers a Muslim for fear of retribution from the Fruit of Islam. Certainly, there was a point in the development of the Fruit of Islam and the Nation itself in the 1960s and early 1970s (Malcolm was assassinated in 1965) when both were closely associated with racketeering and gangster activity. During this period, many East Coast mosques were among the most terrifying organizations in the black community.

Second, Malcolm, in his *Autobiography*, also managed to link the psychological redemption of the Negro with his reacquaintance with his history. The prison chapters of the *Autobiography* have become nearly mythic as a paradigm of black reawakening. Malcolm's religious conversion became, in a sense, the redemption of the black male and the rehabilitation of black masculinity itself. Lately, we have seen two major black male public figures who were incarcerated for serious crimes, Marion Barry and Mike Tyson, use the Malcolm paradigm to resuscitate their standing with the black public. The martyrdom of Malcolm gave this paradigm a blood-endorsed political heroism that has virtually foreclosed any serious criticism of either its origins or its meaning.

It is extraordinary to contemplate how highly regarded Malcolm X is in the black community today, especially in comparison with Martin Luther King. (When I wrote an article for *Harper's* that was critical of Malcolm X, I received three death threats.) Despite the fact that King's achievements were enormous—and that Malcolm left really nothing behind other than a book—King's association with integration, with nonviolence, even with Christianity has reduced him in the eyes of many blacks. When blacks in major cities, inspired by figures like Malcolm X and the romanticization of Africa that Malcolm's nationalism wrought, began to organize African-oriented celebrations, such as my aunts did in Philadelphia with the creation of the Yoruba-inspired Odunde festival in 1975, then Afrocentrism has succeeded not only in intellectual spheres but on the grass-roots level as well. Its triumph as the legitimation of the black mind and the black aesthetic vision was complete.

Afrocentrism may eventually wane in the black community but probably not very soon. Moreover, a certain type of nationalistic mood, a kind of racial preoccupation, will always exist among blacks. It always has, in varying degrees. Homesickness is strong among black Americans, although it is difficult to point to a homeland. What Afrocentrism reflects is the inability of a large number of black people to deal with the reality of being American and with the meaning of their American experience.

Stanley Crouch is right in pointing out that the Afrocentrist is similar to the white Southerner after the Civil War. To black nationalists, the lost war was the "war of liberation" led by black "revolutionaries" in the late 1960s, which in their imagination was modeled on the struggles against colonialism then taking place around the world. (The enslavement of the Africans, of course, was an earlier lost war, and it also weighs heavily on the Afrocentrist. He, like the white Southerner, hates the idea of belonging to a defeated people.) This imaginative vision of a restored and indomitable ethnicity is not to be taken lightly. In a culture as driven by the idea of redemption and as corrupted by racism as this one, race war is our Armageddon. It can be seen in works as various as Thomas Jefferson's *Notes on the State of Virginia*, David Walker's *Appeal to the Colored Citizens of the World*, Joseph Smith's *Book of Mormon*, D.W. Griffith's *Birth of a Nation* and Mario Van Peebles's *Posse.*

WHAT BLACKS DESIRE DURING THESE TURBULENT TIMES IS EXACTLY WHAT WHITES WANT: THE SECURITY OF A GOLDEN PAST THAT NEVER EXISTED

TODAY, AFROCENTRISM IS NOT A MATURE POLITICAL movement but rather a cultural style and a moral stance. There is a deep, almost lyrical poignancy in the fantasy of the Afrocentrist, as there is in the white Southerner's. What would I have been had I not lost the war? The Afrocentrist is devoted to his ancestry and his blood, fixated on the set of traditions that define his nobility, preoccupied with an imagined lost way of life. What drives the Afrocentrist and the white Southerner is not the expression of a group self-interest but concern with pride and honor. One group's myth is built on the surfeit of honor and pride, the other on the total absence of them.

Like the white Southerner, the Afrocentrist is in revolt against liberalism itself, against the idea of individual liberty. In a way, the Afrocentrist is right to rage against it, because liberalism set free the individual but did not encourage the development of a community within which the individual could flower. This is what the Afrocentrist wishes to retrieve, a place for himself in his own community. Wilson Jeremiah Moses, a black historian, is right: Afrocentrism is a historiography of decline, like the mythic epic of the South. The tragedy is that black people fail to see their "Americanization" as one of the great human triumphs of the past 500 years. The United States is virtually the only country where the ex-masters and the ex-slaves try to live together as equals, not only by consent of the ex-masters but by the demand of the ex-slaves. Ironically, what the Afrocentrist can best hope for is precisely what multiculturalism offers: the idea that American culture is a blend of many white and nonwhite cultures. In the end, although many Afrocentrists claim they want this blending, multiculturalism will not satisfy. For if the Euro-American is reminded through this that he is not European or wholly white, the African-American will surely be reminded that he is not African or wholly black. The Afrocentrist does not wish to be a mongrel. He wants, like the Southerner, to be pure.

Afrocentrism is intense now because blacks are in a special period of social development in a nation going through a period of fearsome transition. Social development, by its nature, is ambivalent, characterized by a sense of exchange, of gaining and losing. Afrocentrism, in its conservatism, is opposed to this ambivalence and to this sense of exchange. What blacks desire during these turbulent times is exactly what whites want: the security of a golden past that never existed. A significant number of both blacks and whites want, strangely, to go back to an era of segregation, a fantasy time between 1920 and 1955, when whites felt secure in a stable culture and when blacks felt unified and strong because black people were forced to live together. Afrocentrism wants social change without having to pay the psychic price for it. Perhaps many black folk feel that they have paid too much already, and who is to say they are not right.

The issue raised by Afrocentrism is the meaning and formation of identity, which is the major fixation of the American, especially the black American. In a country that relentlessly promotes the myth of self-reliance because it is unable to provide any sense of security in a cauldron of capitalistic change, identity struggle is so acute because so much is at stake. Afrocentrism may be wrong in many respects, and it certainly can be stifling and restrictive, but some of its impulses are right. In a culture where information and resources of knowledge are the main levers for social and economic advancement, psychological well-being has become increasingly important as, in the words of one scholar, "a social resource," just as "social networks of care and community support [have become] central features of a dynamic economy." Black folk know, and rightly so, that their individual identities are tied to the strength of their community. The struggle over black identity in the United States has been the struggle over the creation of a true black community here. What integration has done to the individual black mind in the United States is directly related to what it has done to the black community. This is the first lesson we must learn. The second is that perhaps many black folk cling to Afrocentrism because the black *American* experience still costs more, requires more courage, than white Americans—and black Americans—are willing to admit.

10 Most Dramatic Events In African-American History

Lerone Bennett Jr.

1. The Black Coming

A YEAR before the arrival of the celebrated *Mayflower*, 244 years before the signing of the Emancipation Proclamation, 335 years before *Brown* vs. *Board of Education*, a big, bluff-bowed ship sailed up the river James and landed the first generation of African-Americans at Jamestown, Va.

Nobody knows the hour or the date of the official Black coming. But there is not the slightest doubt about the month. John Rolfe, who betrayed Pochohontas and experimented with tobacco, was there, and he said in a letter that the ship arrived "about the latter end of August" in 1619 and that it "brought not anything but 20 and odd Negroes." Concerning which the most charitable thing to say is that John Rolfe was probably pulling his boss' leg. For no ship ever called at an American port with a more important cargo. In the hold of that ship, in a manner of speaking, was the whole gorgeous panorama of Black America, was jazz and the spirituals and the black gold that made American capitalism possible.* Bird was there and Bigger and King and Malcolm and millions of other Xs and crosses, along with Mahalia singing, Duke Ellington composing, Gwendolyn Brooks rhyming and Michael Jordan slam-dunking. It was all there, illegible and inevitable, on that day. A man with eyes would have seen it and would have announced to his contemporaries that this ship heralds the beginning of the first Civil War and the second.

As befitting a herald of fate, the ship was nameless, and mystery surrounds it to this day. Where did this ship come from? From the high seas, where the crew robbed a Spanish vessel of a cargo of Africans bound for the West Indies. The captain "ptended," John Rolfe noted, that he needed food, and he offered to exchange his cargo for "victualle." The deal was arranged. Antoney, Pedro, Isabella and 17 other Africans with Spanish names stepped ashore, and the history of Africans in America began.

And it began, contrary to what almost all texts say, not in slavery but in freedom. For there is indisputable evidence that most of the first Black immigrants, like most of the first White immigrants, were held in indentured servitude for a number of years and then freed. During a transitional period of some 40 years, the first Black immigrants held real property, sued in court and accumulated pounds and plantations.

This changed drastically in the sixth decade of the century when the White founding fathers, spurred on by greed and the unprotected status of African immigrants, enacted laws that reduced most Africans to slavery. And so, some 40 years after the Black coming, Black and White crossed a fatal threshold, and the echo of that decision will reverberate in the corridors of Black and White history forever.

2. The Founding of Black America

WHEN, on a Sunday in November 1786, the little band of Black Christians arrived at Philadelphia's St. George's Methodist Episcopal Church, the sexton pointed to the gallery. The Blacks paused and then started up the rickety stairs with downcast eyes and heavy hearts. To the leaders of this group, Richard Allen and Absalom Jones, this was the ultimate indignity—to be shunted from the first floor to the gallery in a church Black men had helped build.

The group had barely reached the top of the stairs when a voice from the pulpit said, "Let us pray." Without thinking, the men plopped down where they were—in the *front* of the gallery. Allen was praying as hard as he could when he heard loud voices. He opened his eyes and saw a white sexton trying to pull Absalom Jones from his knees.

"You must get up; you must not kneel down here!" the White sexton said.

"Wait until the prayer is over," Jones replied.

The voices echoed through the church, and people looked up and beheld the incredible scene of a Black Christian and a White Christian wrestling in the house of the Lord over the color of God's word.

"Get up!" the sexton said. "Get up!"

"Wait until the prayer is over," Jones replied wearily, "and I will not trouble you any more."

Four or five White Christians rushed to the sexton's aid, and the struggle spread over the gallery. Before the issue was resolved, the prayer ended. The Black men stood up then and, without a word, streamed out of the church in the first mass demonstration in Black American history.

Richard Allen added a mournful postscript:

". . . And they were no more plagued by us in the church."

They were no more plagued by Blacks in a lot of places. For the Philadelphia demonstration was the focal point of a national movement that created the foundations of Black America. On April 12, 1787, Richard Allen and Absalom

The Shaping of Black America

Reprinted with permission from *Ebony* magazine, February 1992, pp. 107-108, 110, 112, 114, 116.

Jones created the Free African Society which DuBois called "the first wavering step of a people toward a more organized social life."

Similar societies were formed in most major Northern cities. And on this foundation rose an intricate structure of independent Black churches, schools and cultural organizations. The movement climaxed in the 1820s and 1830s with the founding of Freedom's Journal, the first Black newspaper, and the convening of the first national Black convention.

3. *Nat Turner's War*

GOD was speaking, Nat Turner said later.

There was, he remembered, thunder and lightning and a "loud voice" in the sky. And the voice spoke to him, telling him to take up the yoke and fight against the serpent "for the time was fast approaching when the first should be last and the last should be first."

Nat Turner was numbered among the last. And although he was a slave in Southampton County, Va., it would be said of him later that he "made an impact upon the people of his section as great as that of John C. Calhoun or Jefferson Davis." A mystic with blood on his mind and a preacher with vengeance on his lips, he was an implacable foe of slaveholders. He had believed since he was a child that God had set him aside for some great purpose. And he decided now that God was calling him to rise up and "slay my enemies with their own weapons."

To this end, Turner, who was about 30 years old, chose four disciples and set his face towards Jerusalem, the county seat of Southampton.

On Sunday morning, Aug. 21, 1831, the disciples gathered on the banks of Cabin Pond on the property of Joseph Travis, who had married the widow of Turner's last master and who had therefore inherited Turner and death. Nat, who appreciated the value of a delayed and dramatic entrance, appeared suddenly late in the afternoon and announced that they would strike that night, beginning at the home of his master and proceeding from house to house, killing every man, woman and child.

At 1 a.m., Nat Turner and his army crept through the woods to the home of the luckless Joseph Travis. They were seven men, armed with one hatchet and a broadax. Twenty-four hours later, they would be seventy and at least fifty-seven Whites would be dead.

When, on Monday morning, the first bodies were discovered, a nameless dread seized the citizens. Men, women and children fled to the woods and hid under the leaves until soldiers and sailors arrived from Richmond and Norfolk. Some Whites left the county; others left the state.

Defeated in an engagement near Jerusalem, Turner went into hiding and was not captured until six weeks later. On Nov. 11, 1831, the short Black man called the Prophet was hanged in a field near the courthouse. Before climbing the gallows, he made one last prophecy, saying there would be a storm after his execution and that the sun would refuse to shine. There was, in fact, a storm in Jerusalem on that day, but Turner was not talking about the weather—he was predicting a major disturbance in the American psyche. The storm he saw came in the generation of crisis that his act helped precipitate.

4. *Free at Last!*

TO Felix Haywood, who was there, it was the Time of Glory when men and women walked "on golden clouds."

To Frederick Douglass, it was a down-payment on the redemption of the American soul.

To Sister Winny in Virginia, to Jane Montgomery in Louisiana, to Ed Bluff in Mississippi, to Black people all over the South and all over America, it was the Time of Jubilee, the wild, happy, sad, mocking, tearful, fearful time of the unchaining of the bodies of Black folks. And the air was sweet with song.

Free at last!
Free at last!
Thank God Almighty!
We're free at last.

W.E.B. Dubois was not there, but he summed the whole thing up in phrases worthy of the ages. It was all, he said, "foolish, bizarre, and tawdry. Gangs of dirty Negroes howling and dancing; poverty-stricken ignorant laborers mistaking war, destruction, and revolution for the mystery of the free human soul; and yet to these Black folk it was the Apocalypse." And he added:

"All that was Beauty, all that was Love, all that was Truth, stood on the top of these mad mornings and sang with the stars. A great human sob shrieked in the wind, and tossed its tears upon the sea—free, free, free."

Contrary to the common view, the emancipation of Blacks didn't happen at one time or even in one place. It started with the first shot fired at Fort Sumter. It continued during the war and in the Jubilee summer of 1865, *and it has not been completed.* For the slaves, who created the foundation of American wealth, never received the 40 acres of land that would have made freedom meaningful.

It was in this milieu that African-Americans embarked on a road called freedom. As the road twisted and turned, doubling back on itself, their enemies and their problems multiplied. But they endured, and endure.

5. *Booker T. Washington vs. W. E. B. DuBois*

THERE was a big parade in Atlanta on Wednesday, Sept. 18, 1895, and a huge crowd gathered in the Exposition Building at the Cotton States Exposition for the opening speeches. Several Whites spoke and then former Gov. Rufus Bullock introduced "Professor Booker T. Washington." The 39-year-old president of Tuskegee Institute moved to the front of the platform and started speaking to the segregated audience. Within 10 minutes, reporter James Creelman wrote, "the multitude was in an uproar of enthusiasm — handkerchiefs were waved . . . hats were tossed into the air. The fairest women of Georgia stood up and cheered."

What was the cheering about?

Metaphors mostly—and words millions of Whites wanted to hear. Washington told Blacks: "Cast down your buckets where you are." To Whites, he offered the same advice: "Cast down your bucket [among] the most patient, faithful, law-abiding and unresentful people the world has seen . . . ."

Suddenly, he flung his hand aloft, with the fingers held wide apart.

"In all things purely social," he said, "we can be as separate as the fingers, yet [he balled the fingers into a fist] one as the hand in all things essential to mutual progress."

The crowd came to its feet, yelling.

Washington's "Atlanta Compromise" speech made him famous and set the tone for race relations for some 20 years. One year after his speech, the Supreme Court rounded a fateful fork, endorsing in *Plessy* vs. *Ferguson* the principle of "separate but equal."

Washington's refusal to make a direct and open attack on Jim Crow and his implicit acceptance of segregation brought him into conflict with W.E.B. DuBois and a group of Black militants who organized the germinal Niagara Movement. At its first national meeting at Harpers Ferry in 1906, the Niagara militants said, "We claim for ourselves every single right that belongs to a freeborn American, political, civil, and social; and until we get these rights we will never cease to protest and assail the ears of America."

So saying, the Niagara militants laid the foundation for the National Association for the Advancement of Colored People which merged the forces of Black militancy and White liberalism.

6. *The Great Migration*

HISTORY does not always come with drums beating and flags flying.

Sometimes it comes in on a wave of silence.

Sometimes it whispers.

It was like that in the terrible days of despair that preceded the unprecedented explosion of hope and movement that is called The Great Migration.

This event, which was the largest internal migration in American history and one of the central events of African-American history, started in the cracks of history, in the minds and moods of the masses of Blacks, who were reduced to the status of semi-slaves in the post-Reconstruction period. Pushed back toward slavery by lynchings, segregation and the sharecropping systems, they turned around within themselves and decided that there had to be another way and another and better place. The feeling moved, became a mood, an imperative, a command. Without preamble, without a plan, without leadership, the people began to move, going from the plantation to Southern cities, going from there to the big cities of the North. There, they found jobs in wartime industries and sent letters to a cousin or an aunt or sister or brother, saying: Come! And they came, hundreds and hundreds of thousands. The first wave (300,000) came between 1910 and 1920, followed by a second wave (1,300,000) between 1920 and 1930, and third (500,000) and fourth (2,500,000) waves, even larger, in the '30s and '40s.

In the big cities of the North, Blacks emancipated themselves politically and economically and created the foundation of contemporary Black America.

7. *Brown vs. Board of Education*

THE marshal's voice was loud and clear.

"Oyez! Oyez! Oyez! All persons having business before the Honorable, the Supreme Court of the United States, are admonished to draw near and give their attention, for the Court is now sitting."

The marshal paused and intoned the traditional words:

"God save the United States and this Honorable Court!"

It was high noon on Monday, May 17, 1954, and the Supreme Court was crammed to capacity with spectators. Among the dozen or so Blacks present was Thurgood Marshall, chief counsel of the NAACP, who leaned forward in expectation.

Cases from four states (South Carolina, Virginia, Delaware, Kansas) and the District of Columbia were before the Court, which had been asked by Marshall and his associates to overturn the *Plessy* vs. *Ferguson* decision and declare segregation in public schools unconstitutional. All America awaited the long-expected decision which would come on a Monday. But which Monday? No one knew, and there was no sign on the faces of the justices that the issue was going to be settled on this day.

The Court disposed of routine business and announced decisions in several boring cases involving the sale of milk and the picketing of retail stores. Then Chief Justice Earl Warren picked up a document and said in a firm, quiet voice: "I have for announcement the judgment and opinion of the Court in No. 1—*Oliver Brown et al. v. Board of Education of Topeka*. It was 12:52 p.m. A shiver ran through the courtroom, and bells started ringing in press rooms all over the world.

Warren held the crowd in suspense, reviewing the history of the cases. Then, abruptly, he came to the heart of the matter:

"Does segregation of children in public schools solely on the basis of race, even though the physical facilities and other "tangible" factors may be equal, deprive the children of the minority group of equal educational opportunities?" Warren paused and said: "We believe that it does." The decision was unanimous: 9-0.

The words raced across the country and were received by different people according to their different lights. Southern diehards like Herman Talmadge issued statements of defiance and promised a generation of litigation, but the implications of the decision were so enormous that many Americans were shocked into silence and wonder. In Farmville, Va., a 16-year-old student named Barbara Trent burst into tears when her teacher announced the decision. "We went on studying history," she said later, "but things weren't the same and will never be the same again."

8. *Montgomery and the Freedom Movement*

IT was a quiet, peaceful day in Montgomery, Ala., the Cradle of the Confederacy—but it was unseasonably hot for December 1.

The Cleveland Avenue bus rolled through Court Square, where Blacks were auctioned in the days of the Confederacy, and braked to a halt in front of the Empire Theater. There was nothing special about the bus or the day; neither the driver nor the passengers realized that a revolution was about to begin that would turn America and the South upside down.

Six Whites boarded the bus at the Empire Theater, and the driver stormed to the rear and ordered the foremost Blacks to get up and give their seats to the White citizens. This was an ancient custom, sanctioned by the peculiar mores of the South, and it excited no undue comment. Three Blacks got up immediately, but Rosa Parks, a mild-mannered seamstress in rimless glasses, kept her seat. For this act of defiance, she was arrested. Local leaders called a one-day bus boycott on Monday, Dec. 5, 1955, to protest the arrest. The one-day boycott stretched out to 381 days; the 381 days changed the face and heart of Black America, creating a new leader (Martin Luther King Jr.), and a new movement. There then followed in quick succession a series of movements (the Sit-ins and Freedom Rides) and dramatic events (Birmingham, Selma, Watts, the March on Washington) that constituted Black America's finest hour and one of the greatest moments in the history of the Republic.

9. *Little Rock*

THE GIANT C-119 flying boxcars circled the field, like grim birds.

One by one, they glided into the Little Rock, Ark., airport and debouched paratroopers in full battle gear. There were, in all, more than 1,000 soldiers, Black and White; and they were in Little Rock to enforce the orders of a federal court. For the first time since the Reconstruction era, the United States of America was deploying federal troops to defend the rights of Black Americans.

Escorted by city police cars, a convoy of olive-drab jeeps and trucks sped to Central High School where a howling mob had prevented the enrollment of nine Black students. The troops deployed on the double to block all entrances to the schools, and signalmen strung telephone lines and set up command posts.

Wednesday morning, Sept. 25, 1957, dawned bright and clear, and nine Black teenagers gathered at the ranch-style home of Daisy Bates, president of the Arkansas NAACP. At 8:50 a.m., there was a rumble of heavy wheels. The teenagers rushed to the window.

"The streets were blocked off," Daisy Bates recalled later. "The soldiers closed ranks . . . Oh! It was beautiful. And the attitude of the children at that moment: the respect they had. I could hear them saying, 'For the first time in my life I truly feel like an American.' I could see it in their faces: Somebody cares for me—*America cares.*"

At 9:45, U.S. soldiers with drawn bayonets escorted six Black females and three Black males into Central High School, and the Rev. Dunbar H. Ogden, president of the Greater Little Rock Ministerial Association, said: "This may be looked back upon by future historians as the turning point—for good—of race relations in this country."

10. *Memphis and the Triumph of the Spirit*

THERE had never been a moment like this one.

Time stopped.
Everything stopped.

And every man and woman living at that terrible time would be able to tell you until the end of their time what they were doing and where they were on Thursday, April 4, 1968, when word came that Martin Luther King Jr. had been assassinated on the balcony of the Lorraine Motel in Memphis, Tenn.

The response in Black and White America was tumultuous. Performances, plays, meetings, baseball games were cancelled, and men and women walked aimlessly through the streets, weeping.

There were tears, rivers of tears, and there was also blood. For Black communities exploded, one after another, like firecrackers on a string. Some 46 persons were killed in uprisings in 126 cities, and federal troops were mobilized to put down rebellions in Chicago, Baltimore and Washington, D.C.

To counteract this fury, and to express their sorrow, Americans of all races and creeds joined forces in an unprecedented tribute to a Black American. President Lyndon B. Johnson declared a national day of mourning and ordered U.S. flags to fly at half-mast over U.S. installations at home and abroad. On the day of the funeral—Tuesday, April 9—more than 200,000 mourners followed King's coffin, which was carried through the streets of Atlanta on a wagon, borne by two Georgia mules.

Eighteen years later, the spirit and the truth of Martin Luther King Jr. triumphed when he became the second American citizen (with George Washington) to be celebrated in a personal national holiday.

Color Blind

Getting beyond race takes more than a program in the workplace. An excerpt from a new book by ELLIS COSE

IN "THE ETHICS OF LIVING JIM CROW," AN AUTOBIOgraphical essay published in *Uncle Tom's Children* in 1940, Richard Wright told of his first job at an eyeglass lens-grinding company in Jackson, Mississippi. He landed the job, in part, because the boss was impressed with his education, and Wright was promised an opportunity to advance. "I had visions of working my way up. Even Negroes have those visions," wrote Wright. But even though he did his best to please, he discovered, over time, that nobody was teaching him a skill. His attempts to change that only provoked outrage. Finally, a co-worker shook his fist in Wright's face and advised him to stop making trouble: "This is a white man's work around here, and you better watch yourself."

Such sentiments obviously would not be openly voiced in most companies today. The civil rights revolution has seen to that. Still, it seems that every so often we get ugly reminders—of which the Texaco imbroglio is the latest—that Jim Crow's spirit is not yet dead. In 1994, Denny's restaurant chain agreed—in a settlement with the Justice Department—to put a civil rights monitor on its payroll and to cough up $45 million in damages, after a slew of complaints alleging discrimination against customers and employees. The previous year Shoney's, another restaurant chain, settled a suit for over $100 million that alleged, among other things, that managers were told to keep the number of black employees down in certain neighborhoods.

People of color with training and experience are "treated like s—t in too many places on the job," said assistant labor secretary Bernard Anderson, whose responsibilities include the Office of Federal Contract Compliance Programs. Even within the labor department, said Anderson, he had seen racial prejudice. When a black colleague, a Rhodes scholar, appointed two other blacks with impeccable credentials to positions, "the black lawyers were very empowered and encouraged by all of this," recalled Anderson, but a number of the white lawyers . . . were just shaking in their boots." By and by, he said, a "poison pen memorandum" found its way around the department. The missive made insulting, scatological comments, questioned the credentials of the people who had been appointed, and declared that affirmative action had gone too far.

Resentment against minorities often surfaces in places where "diversity" or affirmative action programs are in place. And that resentment often breeds resistance that results not merely in nasty comments but in outright sabotage.

Some time ago, the black employees of a large, international corporation invited me to talk about a previous book, *The Rage of a Privileged Class,* at a corporate-wide event. In talking with my hosts, I quickly discovered that they were not merely interested in my insights. They wanted me to send a message to the management. They were frustrated because a corporate affirmative-action program, of which the management was extremely proud, was not doing them any good. Mid-level managers, it turned out, got diversity points for hiring or promoting minorities, but the corporation had defined minorities in such a way that everyone who was not a U.S.-born white man qualified. In other words, the managers got as much credit for transferring white men from Europe, Australia, and Canada as they did

From *Newsweek,* November 25, 1996, pp. 50, 53-56. Adapted from *Color Blind* by Ellis Cose.

for promoting African Americans. And that is exactly what they were doing, according to the black employees, who wanted me to let the management know, in a nice and subtle way, that such behavior was unacceptable.

I'm not sure what message the management ended up extracting from my speech, but I am sure that the frustrations those black employees felt are widespread—and that the cause lies less in so-called diversity programs than in the widespread tendency to judge minority group members more by color than by ability.

Some two decades ago, I received a brutal lesson in how galling such attitudes can be. At the time, I was a young (maybe twenty-one or twenty-two years old) columnist-reporter for the *Chicago Sun-Times*. Though I had only been in the business a few years, I was acquiring something of a regional reputation.I hoped to break into magazine writing by garnering a few freelance assignments from *Esquire* magazine, so I had made an appointment with one of its editors.

The editor with whom I met was a pleasant and rather gracious man, but what he had to say was sobering. He wasn't sure, he confided, how many black readers *Esquire* had, but was reasonably certain the number was not high. Since I had not inquired about his readership, the statement took me a bit by surprise. I had been a longtime reader of *Esquire*, and it had never previously occurred to me that I was not supposed to be, that it was not me whom *Esquire* had in mind as an audience—never mind as a contributor. I don't know whether the editor bothered to read my clippings, but then, the clips were somehow superfluous; the very fact that I had written them made them so. All the editor saw was a young black guy, and since *Esquire* was not in need of a young black guy, they were not in need of me. I left that office in a state of controlled fury—not just because the editor had rejected me as a writer, but because he had been so busy focusing on my race that he was incapable of seeing *me* or my work.

A nominal commitment to diversity does not necessarily guarantee an appreciably better outcome, as I came to see several years ago when I was approached by a newspaper publisher who was in the process of putting together his management team. He was interested, he said, in hiring some minority senior managers, so I gave him some names of people who might be likely candidates. Over the next several months, I watched as he put his team in place—a team, as it turned out, that was totally white. Only after he had largely assembled that group did he begin serious talks with some of the nonwhites I had recommended.

Do we have the vaguest idea how to create a society that is truly race neutral?

I don't doubt the man's sincerity. He did want to hire some minority managers, and eventually did so. But what was clear to me was that to him, minority recruitment meant the recruitment of people who couldn't be trusted with the organization's most important jobs. His first priority was hiring people who could do the work—meaning whites—and only after that task was complete would he concern himself with the window dressing of diversity.

Over the years, I have learned that affirmative action in theory and affirmative action in practice are two different things. In the real world it is much more than simply opening up an organization to people who traditionally have been excluded; it is attempting, usually through some contrived measures, to make organizations do what they don't do naturally—and it goes down about as easily as castor oil. Shortly after I announced my resignation as editor of the editorial pages of the New York *Daily News*, I took one of my white staff members out to lunch. He told me he had enjoyed working with me and was sorry to see me go. He had cringed when he heard that I was coming, he confided, for he had feared that I would be just another affirmative action executive, presumably incapable of doing the job competently. He admitted that he had been pleasantly surprised.

I was pleased but also saddened by his confession—pleased that he felt comfortable enough to tell me how he truly felt and saddened that the very fact that a person of color got a high-ranking job would lead him (as it had led so many before him) to question that person's credentials. Yet, having occasionally been the target of affirmative-action recruiters, I am fully aware that (whatever they may say in public) they don't always pay as much attention to credentials as to color. Therefore, I understand clearly why even the ostensible beneficiaries of such recruitment tactics may find affirmative action, as practiced by major corporations, distasteful and even offensive. A decade and a half ago, for instance, I received a call from an associate of an executive search firm who, after verbally tap dancing for several minutes, essentially asked whether I wished to be considered for a job as a corporate director of equal opportunity. I was stunned, for the question made no sense. I was an expert neither on personnel nor on equal-employment law; I was, however, black, which seemed to be the most important qualification. I laughed and told him that I saw my career going in another direction. Still, I wondered just how serious the inquiry could be, since I seemed (to me, at least) so unsuited for the position. Since then, I have received other calls pushing jobs that have seemed every bit as outlandish.

At one point, a man called to discuss the presidency of a major foundation. I confessed I didn't understand why he was calling me, and he assured me that the client was extremely interested in having me apply. The man's earnestness intrigued me enough that I sent him a resume. I never heard from him again, which confirmed, in my mind at any rate, that his interest was anything but genuine. I imagined him sitting in his office with a long list of minority candidates, from whom he would collect resumes and promptly bury them in a file, merely so that his clients would be able to say they had considered minorities. Indeed, when the foundation head was finally named (he was a white man with a long professional association with the foundation trustees), it was clear to me that the supposed search had been a sham. After one takes a few such calls, one realizes that the purpose is often defensibility ("Yes, we took a hard look at fifteen minority candidates, but none quite fit the bill") and that the supposed high-level position is merely bait to attract the interest of people who don't really have a shot—but in whom everyone must pretend they are interested because an affirmative-action program is in place.

It's logical to argue for the replacement of such shameful practices with something better—for some form of meritocracy. Yet affirmative-action critics who extol the virtues of a meritocracy generally ignore the reality of how a real-world so-called meritocracy works. If qualified, capable, and talent-

Twelve Steps Toward Racial Harmony

AMERICANS HAVE LITTLE ALTERNATIVE BUT TO ACCEPT THE POSSIBILITY THAT race will continue to divide us. Yet it is clear that society is more hospitable to minorities and more—racially—egalitarian than it was a few generations ago. There is every likelihood that it can become more so. Hence, we have to ask the question—if only as an experiment in thought: Do we have the vaguest idea how to create a society that is truly race neutral? The short answer, I suspect, is no. Otherwise we would be much further along the way than we are. Still, I believe we can get beyond such platitudes as "Let's just love one another," which is the verbal equivalent of throwing up our hands in noble resignation. Enumerating steps our society could take toward racial sanity is obviously not the same as putting America's racial goblins to rest. It is, however, a necessary prelude to moving the dialogue beyond the realm of reassuring yet empty platitudes. So what would some of those steps be?

1 **WE MUST STOP EXPECTING TIME TO SOLVE THE PROBLEM FOR US:** In "Guess Who's Coming to Dinner," there is a scene in which Sidney Poitier (who plays a physician in his thirties in love with a young white woman) turns, in a fit of rage, to the actor playing his father. Only when the older generation is dead, Poitier declares, will prejudice wither away. The sobering realization is that Poitier is now older than his "father" was then, and the problem, obviously, remains.

Time doesn't heal all wounds; it certainly doesn't solve all problems. It is often merely an excuse for allowing them to fester. Our problems, including our racial problems, belong to us—not to our descendants.

2 **WE MUST RECOGNIZE THAT RACE RELATIONS IS NOT A ZERO-SUM GAME**: The presumption that America is a zero-sum society, that if one race advances another must regress, accounts, in large measure, for the often illogical reaction to programs that aim to help minorities. Such thinking even explains some of the hostility between members of so-called minority groups. *Can only one person of color rise within a given organization?* One hopes not. *Does an increase in Latino clout portend a decline in blacks' well-being?* It shouldn't.

Unfortunately, we have too often reveled in political rhetoric that puts across the opposite message; and have too often rewarded those who exploit our anxiety and insecurities—as opposed to those who demonstrate the willingness and ability to harness our faith in each other and in ourselves.

3 **WE MUST REALIZE THAT ENDING HATE IS THE BEGINNING, NOT THE END, OF OUR MISSION:** Occasionally, I turn on my television and am greeted by some celebrity exhorting me to stop the hate. I always wonder about the target audience for that particular broadside. I suspect that it is aimed mostly at people who don't hate anyone—perhaps as a reminder of our virtue. I certainly can't imagine a card-carrying member of the local Nazi group getting so fired up by the message that he turns to the television and exclaims, "Yes, you're right. I must immediately stop the hate."

Stopping the hate does little to bring people of different races or ethnic groups together. Certainly, it's better than stoking hate, but discrimination and stereotyping are not primarily the result of hatred. If we tell ourselves that the only problem is hate, we avoid facing the reality that it is mostly nice, nonhating people who perpetuate racial inequality.

4 **WE MUST ACCEPT THE FACT THAT EQUALITY IS NOT A HALFWAY PROPOSITION:** This century has seen huge changes in the status of black Americans. It has also seen the growth of largely segregated school systems, the development and maintenance of segregated neighborhoods, and the congealing of the assumption that blacks and whites belong to fundamentally different communities. The mistake was in the notion that social, economic, and political equality are not interrelated, that it was possible to go on living in largely segregated neighborhoods, socialize in largely segregated circles, and even attend segregated places of worship and yet have a workplace and a polity where race ceased to be a factor. As long as we cling to the notion that equality is fine in some spheres and not in others, we will be clinging to a lie.

5 **WE MUST END AMERICAN APARTHEID**: Americans have paid much homage to Martin Luther King's dream of a society where people would be judged only by the content of their character—even as they have yanked children out of schools when a delicate racial balance tipped, or planted themselves in neighborhoods determinedly monochromatic, or fought programs that would provide housing for poor blacks outside of the slums. There is something fundamentally incongruous in the idea of judging people by the content of their character and yet consigning so many Americans at birth to communi-

ties in which they are written off even before their character has been shaped.

WE MUST REPLACE A PRESUMPTION THAT MINORITIES WILL FAIL WITH AN EXPECTATION OF THEIR SUCCESS: When doing research with young drug dealers in California, anthropologist John Ogbu found himself both impressed and immensely saddened. "Those guys have a sense of the economy. They have talents that could be used on Wall Street," he remarked. "They have intelligence—but not the belief that they can succeed in the mainstream." Somewhere along the line, probably long before they became drug dealers, that belief had been wrenched out of them.

Creating an atmosphere in which people learn they cannot achieve is tantamount to creating failure. The various academic programs that do wonders with "at-risk" youths share a rock-hard belief in the ability of the young people in their care. These programs manage to create an atmosphere in which the "success syndrome" can thrive. Instead of focusing so much attention on whether people with less merit are getting various slots, we should be focusing on how to widen—and reward—the pool of meritorious people.

WE MUST STOP PLAYING THE BLAME GAME: Too often America's racial debate is sidetracked by a search for racial scapegoats. And more often than not, those scapegoats end up being the people on the other side of the debate. "It's your fault because you're a racist." "No, it's your fault because you expect something for nothing." "It's white skin privilege." "It's reverse racism." And on and on it goes. American culture, with its bellicose talk-show hosts and pugnacious politicians, rewards those who cast aspersions at the top of their lungs. And American law, with its concept of damages and reparations, encourages the practice of allocating blame. Although denying the past is dishonest and even sometimes maddening, obsessing about past wrongs is ultimately futile.

Certainly, loudmouths will always be among us and will continue to say obnoxious and foolish things, but it would be wonderful if more of those engaged in what passes for public discourse would recognize an obvious reality: It hardly matters who is responsible for things being screwed up; the only relevant question is, "How do we make them better?"

WE MUST DO A BETTER JOB AT LEVELING THE PLAYING FIELD: As long as roughly a third of black Americans sit on the bottom of the nation's economic pyramid and have little chance of moving up, the United States will have a serious racial problem on its hands. There is simply no way around that cold reality. It is pointless to say that the problem is class, not race, if race and class are tightly linked.

During the past several decades, Americans have witnessed an esoteric debate over whether society must provide equality of opportunity or somehow ensure equality of result. It is, however, something of a phony debate, for the two concepts are not altogether separate things. If America was, in fact, providing equality of opportunity, then we would have something closer to equality of racial result than we do at present. The problem is that equality of opportunity has generally been defined quite narrowly—such as simply letting blacks and whites take the same test, or apply for the same job.

Equality of opportunity is meaningless when inherited wealth is a large determinant of what schools one attends (and even whether one goes to school), what neighborhoods one can live in, and what influences and contacts one is exposed to. *In Black Wealth, White Wealth,* sociologists Melvin Oliver and Tom Shapiro pointed out that most blacks have virtually no wealth—even if they do earn a decent income. Whites with equal educational levels to blacks typically have five to ten times as much wealth, largely because whites are much more likely to inherit or receive gifts of substantial unearned assets. This disparity is a direct result of Jim Crow practices and discriminatory laws and policies.

America is not about to adopt any scheme to redistribute resources materially. What Americans must do, however, if we are at all serious about equality of opportunity, is to make it easier for those without substantial resources to have secure housing outside urban ghettos, to receive a high-quality education, and to have access to decent jobs.

9 **WE MUST BECOME SERIOUS ABOUT FIGHTING DISCRIMINATION:** In their rush to declare this society colorblind, some Americans have leaped to the conclusion that discrimination has largely disappeared. They explain away what little discrimination they believe exists as the fault of a few isolated individuals or the result of the oversensitivity of minorities.

Making discrimination a felony is probably not a solution, but more aggressive monitoring and prosecution—especially in housing and employment situations—would not be a bad start. Just as one cannot get beyond race by treating different races differently, one cannot get beyond discrimination by refusing to acknowledge it. One can get beyond discrimination only by fighting it vigorously wherever it is found.

10 **WE MUST KEEP THE CONVERSATION GOING:** Dialogue clearly is no cure-all for racial estrangement. Conversations, as opposed to confrontations, about race are inevitably aimed at a select few—those who make up the empathic elite. Yet, limited as the audience may be, the ongoing discourse is crucial. It gives those who are sincerely interested in examining their attitudes and behavior an opportunity to do so, and, in some instances, can even lead to change.

11 **WE MUST SEIZE OPPORTUNITIES FOR INTERRACIAL COLLABORATION:** Even those who have no interest in talking about the so-called *racial situation* can, through the process of working with (and having to depend on) people of other races, begin to see beyond skin color. Conversation, in short, has its limits. Only through doing things together—things that have nothing specifically to do with race— will people break down racial barriers. Facing common problems as community groups, as work colleagues, or as classmates can provide a focus and reduce awkwardness in a way that simple conversation cannot.

12 **WE MUST STOP LOOKING FOR ONE SOLUTION TO ALL OUR RACIAL PROBLEMS:** Meetings on racial justice often resemble nothing so much as a bazaar filled with peddlers offering the all-purpose answer. The reality is that the problem has no single or simple solution. If there is one answer, it lies in recognizing how complex the issue has become and in not using that complexity as an excuse for inaction. In short, if we are to achieve our country, we must attack the enemy on many fronts.

Ellis Cose

ed minorities and women exist, they say, corporations will reward them because they will recognize that it is within their economic interest to do so. That may well be true. But it is also true that effective executives are trained, not born. They come about because companies make an investment in them, in their so-called human capital, and nurture their careers along—and if corporations only see the potential in white men, those are the people in whom the investments are likely to be made.

Our problems, including our racial problems, belong to us—not to our descendants

John Kotter, a Harvard Business School professor and author of *The General Managers*, discovered that effective executives generally benefited from what he called the "success syndrome." They were constantly provided with opportunities for growth: "They never stagnated for significant periods of time in jobs where there were few growth possibilities." The executives also, to be blunt about it, are often people of relatively modest intellectual endowment. They succeed largely because they are chosen for success.

A true meritocracy would do a much better job of evaluating and choosing a broader variety of people. It would challenge the very way merit is generally imputed and, in giving people ample opportunity to develop and to prove themselves, it would create a truly level playing field.

Simply eliminating affirmative action would not bring such a true meritocracy about. Indeed, a large part of the reason affirmative action is so appealing to so many people is that a meritocracy that fully embraces people of color seems out of reach; and affirmative action is at least one method to get people to accept the fact that talent comes in more than one color.

Yet, by its very nature, affirmative action is polarizing. Wouldn't it be better, argue a growing number of Americans, to let it die in peace? A chorus of conservative critics even invoke the dream of Martin Luther King Jr. to make the case.

King would probably be more astonished than anyone to hear that conservatives now claim him as one of their own, that they have embraced his dream of a color-blind world and invoke it as proof of the immorality and undesirability of gender and racial preferences. But even if he had a bit of trouble accepting his status as a general in the war against affirmative action, he would appreciate the joke. And he would realize that it is the fate of the dead to be reborn as angels to the living. King no doubt would be pleased to have new friends in his fight for justice, but he would approach them with caution. After sharing his disappointment over past alliances with people whose commitment to change did not match his own, King would address his new associates bluntly. "All right," he might say, "I understand why you oppose affirmative action. But tell me: What is *your* plan? What is *your* plan to cast the slums of our cities on the junk heaps of history? What is *your* program to transform the dark yesterdays of segregated education into the bright tomorrows of high-quality, integrated education? What is *your* strategy to smash separatism, to destroy discrimination, to make justice roll down like water and righteousness flow like a mighty stream from every city hall and statehouse in this great and blessed nation?" He might then pause for a reply, his countenance making it unmistakably clear that he would accept neither silence nor sweet nothings as an answer.

Alternative Afrocentrisms

THREE PATHS NOT TAKEN—YET

"Mercy mercy me, things ain't what they used to be," purled the late soul singer Marvin Gaye. For African Americans this truth cuts both ways. Jim Crow is dead the smiling black visages of Michael Jordan and Shaquille O'Neal adorn the walls of countless white boys and girls. But at the same time, a host of virulent social pathologies is devastating our cities. And the only strategy so far devised by black political leaders is one combining whiny importuning of outsiders with wishful mythologizing when among fellow blacks—a frantic attempt to build self-esteem even if it comes at the expense of truth, self-improvement, and interracial harmony.

It doesn't have to be this way. African Americans have an array of healthy and inspiriting traditions upon which to draw in the battle against despair and dependence. A full two generations ago, 1920s novelist Jessie Fauset brought to life characters who captured all of the contemporary dilemma. "It comes to every colored man," comments one of her protagonists, "when he thinks, 'I might just as well fall back; there's no use pushing on. A colored man just can't make any headway in this awful country.' Of course, it's a fallacy. And if a fellow sticks it out he finally gets past it, but not before it has worked considerable confusion in his life."

The forgotton Fauset is one of three African Americans profiled in the suite of essays that follows. The others are the famed educator Booker T. Washington and the novelist-folklorist Zora Neale Hurston. In very different ways, each embodies a tradition from which American blacks today might draw proud sustenance and strength, without resorting to historical distortions or group-against-group animosity.

Of our trio, only the practical, gritty Washington offered himself as a political leader. The irrepressible Hurston, a libertarian Republican, was an enthusiastic supporter of Senator Robert A. Taft for her party's presidential nomination, however. Fauset preferred art to politics; a friend and ally of NAACP leader W. E. B. DuBois, she occupied an anomalous position within that organization as a kind of tony Washingtonian (of the Booker T. variety).

Welfare checks and gerrymandered black congressional districts were of no interest to this trinity. Surveying the state of Potomac blacks during Reconstruction, Booker T. Washington fretted that "among a large class there seemed to be a dependence upon the Government of every conceivable thing.... How many times I wished then, and have often wished since, that by some power of magic I might remove the great bulk of these people into the country districts and plant them upon the soil, upon the solid and never deceptive foundation of Mother Nature, where all nations and races that have ever succeeded have gotten their start." Whatever one thinks of a policy of mass rustication for Black Americans (Tony Brown, in his provocative new book *Black Lies, White Lies,* continues to recommend it in 1995), the point is that neither Washington nor Hurston nor Fauset lack for boldness of vision or ambition.

The other thing they share is a common idea that African-American business, art, literature, and social institutions can prosper only through the efforts of their own race. This places the trio and their heirs outside the bounds of current polite debate. Washington, Hurston, and Fauset all disdained the enfeebling dependence on Great White Father State that current establishment liberals preach, but they would also scoff at the establishment conservative fantasy that a "colorblind society" is right around the corner—and perhaps even resist the desirability of such a society.

This doesn't imply anti-white animus; an emphasis on black enterprise, for instance, will actually lead to closer cooperation and understanding between the races. Booker T. Washington believed that the brickmaking program at Tuskegee Institute fostered racial harmony, for "in educating our students we were adding something to the wealth and comfort of the community. As the people of the neighborhood came to us to buy bricks, we got acquainted with them; they traded with us and we with them. Our business interests became intermingled. We had something which they wanted; they had something which we wanted. This, in a large measure, helped to lay the foundation for the pleasant relations that have continued to exist between us and the white people in that section."

This theme was taken up in the 1960s by Malcolm X, who said (in a sermon that Supreme Court Justice Clarence Thomas is fond of quoting): "The American black man should be focusing his every effort toward building his *own* businesses and decent homes for himself. As other ethnic groups have done, let the black people, wherever possible, however possible, patronize their own kind, and start in those ways to build up the black race's ability to do for itself. That's the only way the American black man is ever going to get respect."

This sentiment was distinctly unfashionable when Malcolm X uttered it, and Booker T. Washington's emphasis on self-help and mutual aid seemed positively anachronistic to the '60s civil-rights movement, with its single-minded pursuit of things political. In a 1987 profile by Juan Williams in *The Atlantic Monthly,* Clarence Thomas argued, "I don't see how the civil-rights people today can claim Malcolm X as one of their own. Where does he say black people should go begging the Labor Department for jobs? He was hell on integrationists. Where does he say you should sacrifice your institutions to be next to white people?"

Today, virtually no one except the odd Klansman defends state-mandated segregation. But state-mandated integration, the cornerstone of the last three decades of civil-rights law, is definitely under fire. And the failures of government programs erected under the aegis of "civil rights" are now manifest and massive: the relentlessly ugly and impersonal public housing projects in which the Negro proletariat is warehoused; the coercive experiments in busing and school integration that have waged war on working-class white neighborhoods while belittling black students (whose IQs will skyrocket, they are told, merely by rubbing shoulders with white urchins); the widely resented quotas that require corporate America to over-promote black professionals, irritating white professionals, while doing absolutely nothing for the kid on a Watts streetcorner.

Faced with this collapse of the 1960s program, many black Americans are suddenly casting about for alternative models and political allegiances. The new exemplars seem, at first glance, wildly incongruous—ranging from Malcolm X to Clarence Thomas to Louis Farrakhan to Colin Powell to Thomas Sowell to the Black Panthers. There are, however, a set of common beliefs among this group. Recall that Justice Thomas's two principal intellectual influences are Malcolm X and Sowell, and that he dallied with the Black Panthers in their early pre-violence phase, when they promoted neighborhood schooling and policing, community-funded lunches for kids, and the Second Amendment.

Quite apart from the lynch ropes placed around their necks by a livid civil rights establishment, there are other ties that bind black freethinkers today. Race pride, a fierce independence, a refusal to buy into the cheap sentimentalities that have debased our political currency: these are qualities shared by African-American iconoclasts of the 1990s. They are qualities found in Washington, Hurston, and Fauset too.

Such qualities explain seemingly inexplicable incidents like Zora Neale Hurston's denunciation of the *Brown v. Board of Education* decision: "The whole matter revolves around the self-respect of my people. How much satisfaction can I get from a court order for somebody to associate with me who does not wish me near them? . . . I regard the ruling of the United States Supreme Court as insulting rather than honoring my race." Or as Clarence Thomas told *Reason* in 1987, "You don't need to sit next to a white person to learn how to read and write."

Black is Beautiful. So said the slogans of the pride movement; yet too few black children absorbed that truth in its fullness. Some made the leap only weakly, and landed short in the swamp called "Unblack is Ugly."

One thing Booker T. Washington, Zora Neale Hurston, and Jessie Fauset had in common was a humanity that allowed them to celebrate the world of blackness without vandalizing either historical fact or the self-regard of their non-black fellow citizens. A second shared trait was their view that one cannot love America unless one first loves one's very own bit of the mosaic: South Carolinian, Methodist, black, whatever. These are real insights, grown rare today, especially joined together in the same person. We might yet recreate that wise combination, however—if we will study the ideas of these distinctive African-American greats and some of their pre-1960s brethren.

—*The Editors*

Booker T. Washington

by Elizabeth Wright

Booker T. Washington might have expressed the same ideas in different terms, but he probably would have agreed with the major theme of Joel Kotkin's recent book, *Tribes.* Kotkin selects five of America's immigrant ethnic groups to demonstrate how each—Jews, Chinese, Japanese, British, and Indians—achieved economic health primarily due to a tradition of strong ethnic ties.

In each case, cultural identity acted as a positive force, inspiring the trust and mutual dependence that were the catalysts for phenomenal success in business. Members of these groups not only expanded the American economic pie, but went on to create their own peculiar niches. Each group became, as Kotkin puts it, "embedded in the American economy."

"If every member of the race should strive to make himself the most indispensable man in his community, and to be successful in business, however humble that business might be, he would contribute much towards smoothing the pathway of his own and future generations."

At the turn of this century, a very similar idea ruled Washington's vision of the role of blacks in America. It was his determination that his people should create for themselves, "through the struggle toward economic success," an indispensable place in the American economy. He spoke of blacks "knitting our business and industrial relations" to those of others, so that the contribution of blacks would become "essential to the welfare of the republic."

In 1900, at the founding convention of the National Negro Business League, there was good reason to hope that these aspirations would come to fruition. After all, the purpose of the league was to help black men and women who had already achieved success in business to become even more effective entrepreneurs.

"It is easily seen," wrote Washington, "that if every member of the race should strive to make himself the most indispensable man in his community, and to be successful in business, however humble that business might be, he would contribute much towards smoothing the pathway of his own and future generations."

As a keen observer of the behavior of other ethnic groups, Washington reflected on their mutual cooperation, which eased the path to business success. At one point, he cautioned blacks that if they did not find their place in the economic scheme of things, there were sure to be more immigrants coming to the shores of America who would eagerly fill the void.

With resources scarce among blacks, Washington stressed all the more the critical importance of group solidarity. Independence and self-sufficiency could best be achieved when blacks, working cooperatively, would "gain knowledge, experience, and wealth within our own ranks."

By the time of this first convention of the League, thousands of blacks had already demonstrated their capacity to seize opportunities. Many engaged in the skilled trades, since every type of craft had been learned by the slaves. Later, blacks took advantage of the fact that most crafts businesses could be started with little capital.

As noted in a 1950 study, *The Negro in American Business*, "The Negro in the South was not only proficient as a carpenter, blacksmith, shoemaker, barber, tailor, and cook, but as a result of almost two-and-a-half centuries of slavery, up to the outbreak of the Civil War, the knowledge of these skills was concentrated almost exclusively in the hands of the Negroes, free and slave."

By the late eighteenth century, blacks were an economic presence in several cities. In Philadelphia, which was regarded as the largest and most important center of free black life in the country, a 1798 report showed that almost 25 percent of the black families used their property for business. The city was renowned for its excellent restaurants and caterers—both fields monopolized by blacks.

Success stories were common also in southern cities like Richmond, Norfolk, Charleston, Baltimore, and Washington, D.C. In Virginia, property ownership among free blacks doubled between 1830 and 1860, and in Tennessee, real estate owned by blacks tripled during the decade 1850–60. Before the end of slavery, Savannah had more free blacks and black businesses than any other municipality in Georgia, and there were many successful businesses in Macon. The wealthiest free black in Georgia was James Boisclair, who owned a popular saloon and the largest dry goods store in Dahlonega.

These blacks clearly understood the connection between the ownership of businesses and property and the ability to have greater control over what happened in their lives. Historian Juliet Walker points out: "In pre-Civil War America, even the absence of political freedom did not preclude the business participation of blacks as creative capitalists.... Antebellum blacks developed enterprises in virtually every area important to the pre-Civil War business community."

The very principle that protected property rights in general, including slave ownership, was what protected blacks' rights to own personal property. Walker writes, "It was the very sanctity of private property in American life and thought that allowed blacks, slave and free, to participate in the antebellum economy as entrepreneurs."

By the turn of the century, it was clear that a spirit of enterprise prevailed among large numbers of blacks. It was Washington's mission to find the methods to transmit this spirit to still greater numbers. He made an appeal to group identity, to the individual's responsibility to play his part in uplifting the race.

That it would take black helping black was a given. Self-help began with each person's willingness to commit himself to the discipline of work, no matter how modest the labor. Like others before and after him, Washington linked moral virtues to his "bootstraps" philosophy of self-help. The defining expression born in this period, that which exhorted blacks to live their lives so that each would become a "credit to the race," still rings in the latent memories of many.

Washington's teaching of capital development through work and thrift acknowledged the customs so characteristic of other economically successful groups. By emphasizing the impor-

Expectations, and role models, according to Booker T. Washington

It makes a great deal of difference in the life of a race, as it does in the life of an individual, whether the world expects much or little of that individual or that race. I suppose that all boys and girls born in poverty have felt at some time in their lives that the weight of the world was against them. What the people in their communities did not expect them to do, it was hard for them to convince themselves that they could do.

After I got so that I could read a little, I used to take a great deal of satisfaction in the lives of men who had risen by their own efforts from poverty to success. It is a great thing for a boy to be able to read books of that kind. It not only inspires him with desire to do something and make something of his life, but it teaches him that success depends upon his ability to do something useful, to perform some kind of service that the world wants.

—*"The Intellectuals and the Boston Mob" speech delivered in 1911*

tance of industriousness and sobriety he sought to link a homespun nationalism to a personal commitment to the ongoing improvement of the race.

If the legacy of slavery had its countless adverse consequences, then it was up to blacks to discover a positive legacy on which to capitalize and turn to their advantage. As a former slave, Washington was well acquainted with the humiliation of bondage, yet he had no patience with those who would replay the sins of the past. With all of its ambiguities, he still viewed America as a land of opportunity for blacks. He declared, "We should not permit our grievances to overshadow our opportunities." Yes, it was possible for blacks themselves to retrieve from the years of degradation the means for economic and moral uplift, and to find, through their own effort, "compensations for the losses suffered."

Washington's rational, optimistic message was fully appreciated by a great many blacks of the time. In 1899, when William Pettiford became head of the black-owned Alabama Penny Loan & Savings in Birmingham, he was determined that the bank should be a tool of instruction for Birmingham's blacks. His goal was to educate ordinary people in the principles of saving and thrift, to impart the importance of sacrificing today to build for tomorrow.

After a successful advertising campaign to recruit new depositors, Pettiford discovered that about 90 percent of his new customers had never before held bank accounts. Regarding it his duty to encourage the wise use of money, he set about educating all who walked through his bank's doors in finance and investment, while providing loans and other services. Pettiford claimed that by encouraging blacks to save and make prudent investments, "it has been possible to stimulate a wholesome desire among our people to become property owners and substantial citizens."

Penny Savings became well known for granting loans for home building and business development. The bank was praised also for the role it played in keeping the money of blacks "constantly in circulation in our immediate community." Washington called the operation of Penny Loan & Savings the best illustration of "how closely the moral and spiritual interests of our people are interwoven with their material and economical welfare." He praised Pettiford because he was "far-seeing enough to attempt to develop this wealth that is latent in the Negro people."

Just as honorable were those blacks who used financial clout to combat racism. Washington celebrated Harlem realtor Philip Payton, who attained national attention when he and other black realtors bought two apartment buildings in order to prevent the eviction of black tenants by bigoted white landlords. A newspaper editorial cited Payton's actions as an "unexpected and novel method of resisting race prejudice."

Her black characters are often prosperous doctors, caterers, and modistes. There is a staidness, a steadiness about them, but they are no Oreos. They are securely colored and securely American.

Payton's sense of responsibility epitomized all that Washington sought to teach. By acquiring wealth as Payton had done, blacks could slap bigotry in the face, and be prepared to move confidently into the future when legal restrictions were at last lifted. Throughout the worst days of Jim Crow constraints, Booker T. Washington never doubted that efforts to win full legal rights would eventually succeed. He said, "It is important and right that all privileges of law be ours, but it is vastly more important that we be prepared for the exercise of these privileges." This is why he saw in a healthy business class the key to the future. He held business men and women to a high standard, since he believed they had a unique responsibility to the race. On their success depended the building of a sound economic foundation upon which everything else would rest.

To people like Washington, the businessman was the ultimate black role model. "It was evident," he wrote "that the success of Negro businessmen was largely dependent upon, and would tend to instill into the mass of the Negro people, habits of system and fidelity in the small details of life, and that these habits would bring with them feelings of self-reliance and self-respect, which are the basis of all real progress, moral or material."

In turning obstacles and difficulties to advantage, claimed Washington, "the Negro businessman has a peculiar opportunity for service, an opportunity that is offered to no other class among the members of the race." He wanted all blacks to take pride in the race's business people. In referring to the perseverance required by black entrepreneurs to overcome what often seemed like insurmountable obstacles, he once reflected, "I was never more proud than I am today that I am a Negro. I am proud and grateful to be identified with a race which has made such creditable progress in the face of discouragement and difficulty."

The business successes of blacks during the eighteenth and nineteenth centuries were achieved before severe Jim Crow restrictions went into effect in the South. But even after such biased laws were in place, great numbers of blacks continued to found firms, turning sections of some cities into what historian John Sibley Butler describes as "entrepreneurial enclaves." Serious damage was done to black economic development by laws that prevented the expansion of their businesses beyond the limited borders of segregated black neighborhoods. But even greater damage was caused by the later arrival of a black leadership whose teachings were vastly different from those of people like Washington, Pettiford, and Payton. Suddenly blacks were guided to view their problems as beyond their abilities to resolve: to look outward, especially to government, for solutions; and to see themselves as objects of sympathy.

Washington's greatest fears came true. By the time of the legal victories in the 1960s, the earlier spirit of enterprise had been depleted, and a new civil rights vision redefined black missions and goals. The call to group solidarity now became a strategy primarily to coerce benefits from whites, or "the system." Even self-help was redefined as an initiative first requiring the input of whites.

The moral force of earlier leaders, who had galvanized tens of thousands of individuals to work toward economic independence and self-reliance, ceased to carry influence. Booker T. Washington's call for blacks to make themselves economically indispensable faded into a distant echo. Is it not time to listen once more?

Elizabeth Wright is editor of Issues & Views, *a quarterly publication on subjects affecting the black community (PO Box 467, New York, NY 10025).*

Jessie Fauset

by Bill Kauffman

For never let the thought arise
That we are here on sufferance bare;
Outcasts, asylumed 'neath these skies,
And aliens without part or share.

This land is ours by right of birth,
This land is ours by right of toil;
We helped to turn its virgin earth,
Our sweat is in its fruitful soil.

—James Weldon Johnson
from "*Fifty Years 1863–1913*"

The notion that African Americans are here on sufferance bare never once crossed the mind of Jessie Fauset, whose novels depicted a robust Negro middle class that was much more than George Babbitt in blackface.

Jessie Redmon Fauset was born in 1882 to a father who was a respected A. M. E. minister in Camden, New Jersey. The Faucets were on the fringe of stylish Old Philadelphia society; they were frayed gentility, polite and mannerly if occasionally behind on the grocery bill. ("There is no pride so strong, so inflexible, so complacent as the pride of the colored 'old Philadelphia'," wrote Fauset in *Comedy: American Style.)*

Hers was a close and loving family; she was raised, she later recalled, in a "very conservative, not to say very religious, household," and she grew up with a sense of the dignity of her race. Of course when the white world impinged young Jessie met the usual slights. At the Philadelphia High School for Girls "I happened to be the only colored girl in my classes . . . and I'll never forget the agony I endured on entrance day when the white girls with whom I had played and studied through the graded schools refused to acknowledge my greeting."

Upon graduation from Cornell, Jessie Fauset taught French for a dozen years at Washington, D.C.'s storied Dunbar High ("The Greatest Negro High School in the World"), named after the turn-of-the-century black American poet best remembered for his exclamation, "I know why the caged bird sings!"

Fauset chose W. E. B. DuBois as her mentor. He, in turn, recognized his protégé as a distaff member of the "talented tenth" whose efforts DuBois believed would uplift the race. We must, Jessie lectured the usually unlecturable DuBois, "teach our colored men and women *race* pride, *self*-pride, self-sufficiency (the right kind) and the necessity of living our lives, as nearly as possible, *absolutely*, instead of comparing them always with white standards."

Fauset wrote stories, reviews, and poetry for *The Crisis*, the NAACP flagship, before becoming full-time literary editor in October 1919. Though her own experiences of the richness of segregated black middle-class life kept her from swallowing whole the NAACP's integrationist panacea, she worked alongside the prickly DuBois for seven fruitful years. With sweetness and vigor she cultivated the flowering of Negro letters, for she shared in the delight expressed by her friend, the poet Countee Cullen: "Yet I do marvel at this curious thing: To make a poet black, and bid him sing!"

Jessie Fauset disdained literary politics and petty jealousies. As a wise older brother counsels in her first novel, *There Is Confusion* (1924), "Our battle is a hard one and for a long time it will seem to be a losing one, but it will never really be that as long as we keep the power of being happy.... Happiness, love, contentment in our midst, make it possible for us to face those foes without. 'Happy Warriors,' that's the ideal for us."

Fauset practiced what she preached. Her little kindnesses and generous praise encouraged the Harlem Renaissance of the 1920s. She was, arguably, the discoverer of Langston Hughes, who was forever grateful. ("I found Jessie Fauset charming—a gracious, tan-brown lady, a little plump, with a fine smile and gentle eyes . . . From that moment on I was deceived in writers, because I thought they would all be good-looking and gracious like Miss Fauset.") Even the *rouge et noir* bad boy Claude McKay said of Fauset: "All the radicals liked her, although in her social viewpoint she was away over on the other side of the fence."

Few people, it seemed, wanted to hear about Jessie's side of the fence. *There Is Confusion* was rejected by one publisher because, she was told, "White readers just don't expect Negroes to be like this." Her black characters are often prosperous doctors, caterers, and modistes: the sort who have, rather than are, domestic help. There is a staidness, a steadiness about them, but they are no Oreos. They are securely colored and securely American.

Her four novels frequently feature light-skinned Negroes who "pass" for white in a burlesque of the integrationist dream. "Emotionally, as far as race was concerned, she was a girl without a country," Fauset mourned for one such woman in her final novel, *Comedy: American Style* (1933). "Later on in life it occurred to her that she had been deprived of her racial birthright and that that was as great a cause for tears as any indignity that might befall man." "What is fundamentally important to mankind everywhere," Fauset understood, is "love of kind, love of home...love of race."

Jessie Fauset's ardent hope was that colored boys and girls be raised in the fullest knowledge of their birthright. In *There Is Confusion* Joanna comes home from school and asks plaintively, "Didn't colored people ever do anything, Daddy?" Her father then tells her "of Douglass and Vesey and Turner. There were great women too, Harriet Tubman, Phyllis Wheatley, Sojourner Truth, women who had been slaves, he explained to her, but had won their way to fame and freedom through their own efforts." She abhorred sugarcoating and counseled truth: "The successful 'Negro' novel must limn Negro men and women as they really are, with not only their virtues but their faults," she averred.

It was for the Joannas of America that Fauset and DuBois edited *The Brownies' Book*, an unprofitable monthly published from January 1920 until it folded two years later. This wholesome hodgepodge of homilies, lore, and biography was dedicated, Fauset rhymed:

> To children, who with eager look
> Scanned vainly library shelf, and nook,
> For History or Song or Story
> That told of Colored Peoples' glory.

The publication's purpose, declared the editors, was: "To make colored children realize that being 'colored' is a normal, beautiful thing. To make them familiar with the history and achievements of the Negro race. To make them know that other colored children have grown into beautiful, useful, and famous persons. To teach them delicately a code of honor and action in their relations with white children. To turn their little hurts and resentments into emulation, ambition, and love of their homes and companions. To point out the best amusements and joys and worthwhile things of life. To inspire them to prepare for definite occupations and duties with a broad spirit of sacrifice."

Fauset devoted her career to acts of ancestor worship, of recovery and restoration. She translated Haitian poets. When her sister died she endowed a "Helen Lanning Corner" in the public school in which Mrs. Lanning had taught; this room was "to contain books only about colored people, especially colored children." She sponsored similar rooms in other schools. In 1932 Fauset insisted, "No part of Negro literature needs more building up than biography.... It is urgent that ambitious Negro youth be able to read of the achievements of their race....There should be some sort of *Plutarch's Lives* of the Negro race. Someday, perhaps, I shall get around to writing it."

> **Hurston was suspicious of anyone, from Left or Right, who judged individuals by category. "The solace of easy generalization was taken from me, but I received the richer gift of individualism," she wrote.**

She didn't. A marriage—a happy, companionable union—intervened, and the illness of various relatives brought out the nurse in Jessie Fauset. She published no books between 1933 and her death in 1961. Unlike Zora Neale Hurston, Jessie Fauset has enjoyed no spectacular revival—nor, given the unfashionableness of her resolutely middle-class colored American subjects, is she likely to.

Yet she speaks to us still. The better Afrocentric curricula are Helen Lanning Corners. Renewed appreciation of such distinct cultural achievements as baseball's Negro Leagues is very much in the Fauset stream. Every Ohio boy reading Langston Hughes is her son: every black girl who feels a confident, bitterless pride in her race and her country is a daughter of Jessie Fauset.

Associate Editor Bill Kaufman is the author of Every Man a King, Country Towns of New York, *and* America First!

Old Philadelphian Jessie Fauset on black roots

He started out as a slave but he rarely thinks of that. To himself he is a citizen of the United States whose ancestors came over not along with the emigrants in the Mayflower, it is true, but merely a little earlier in the good year 1619. His forebears are to him quite simply early settlers who played a pretty large part in making the land grow. He boasts no Association of the Sons and Daughters of the Revolution, but he knows that as a matter of fact and quite inevitably his sons and daughters date their ancestry as far back as any. So quite as naturally as his white compatriots he speaks of his "old" Boston families, "old Philadelphians," "old Charlestonians." And he has wholesome respect for family and education and labor and the fruits of labor. He is still sufficiently conservative to lay a slightly greater stress on [the] first two of these four.

Briefly he is a dark American who wears his joy and rue very much as does the white American. He may wear it with some differences but it is the same joy and the same rue.

—from *The Chinaberry Tree,* 1931

Zora Neale Hurston

by David T. Beito

Zora Neale Hurston has been rediscovered. Her reputation shines much brighter today, in fact, than it ever did in her lifetime. A participant in the Harlem Renaissance as a folklorist and playwright, she became a best-selling novelist in the 1930s and 1940s. Less than two decades later, she died in obscurity and poverty. Her reputation languished until 1975 when Alice Walker, the author of *The Color Purple,* published a laudatory essay in *Ms.* Since then, Hurston has inspired a virtual cottage industry of books and articles. Her fiction has been embraced by assorted varieties of feminists, multiculturalists, and black nationalists. A kind of Zoramania has taken hold among the politically correct in particular.

There is no small amount of irony here. For Hurston subscribed to political views that would surprise many of her modern fans. She backed the Republican presidential primary bid of Robert Taft in 1952, condemned the Supreme Court's decision in *Brown v. Board of Education,* and implied that Eleanor Roosevelt had cynically manipulated black voters. If Hurston could participate in today's political debates, she would no doubt be consigned to a netherworld populated by the likes of Walter Williams, Thomas Sowell, and Anne Wortham.

The environment of Hurston's youth nurtured attitudes of individualism and self-reliance. She grew up in the all-black town of Eatonville, Florida, where her father, a former sharecropper and son of a slave, once served as mayor. Eatonville was the setting for Hurston's most famous novel, *Their Eyes Were Watching God* (1937). With much justification, *Saturday Review* put it "in the same category—with that of the William Faulkner, F. Scott Fitzgerald, and Ernest Hemingway—of enduring American literature." Not all the reviews were positive. Novelist Richard Wright, then a member of the Communist party, condemned the novel's implicit message that the lives of blacks could be appreciated apart from a focus on racist and capitalistic oppression. Alain Locke, a leader in the Harlem Renaissance, wondered when Hurston would take up the more legitimate task of "social document fiction."

Wright and Locke were right to be worried over Hurston's freethinking. While she never expressed a systematic political philosophy, Hurston's instincts, as reflected in her writings, were those of a libertarian. Her biographer, Robert E. Hemenway, has identified deep aversion to the then-fashionable model of "black pathology" as a major source for her views. Hurston found fault with the pathology model not only because it discounted the creative richness of black culture but because it gloried in victimization. It treated blacks as little more than cardboard cut-outs: "There is an over-simplification of the Negro. He is either pictured by the conservatives as happy, picking his banjo, or by the so-called liberals as low, miserable, and crying. The Negro's life is neither of these. Rather, it is in between, and above and below these pictures."

One of the most worrisome implications of the "black pathology" approach was that it gave social engineers an entree to "rescue" blacks from themselves. Hurston's comments on the role played by the welfare state in this process were prescient. Welfare, she charged, was "the biggest weapon ever placed in [the] hands of those who sought power and votes." It created a world that turned independent and prideful individuals into pawns of the "Little White Father" in Washington. "Once they had weakened that far," she concluded, "it was easy to go on and on voting for more relief, and leaving government affairs in the hands of a few."

Hurston was not a garden variety "black conservative," however. Her novels and nonfiction reveal what today would be called individualist feminism. Camille Paglia would have delighted her. In many ways, she resembled her contemporaries Rose Wilder Lane, Isabel Patterson, and Ayn Rand in personal and intellectual profile. All four women advanced an "Old Right" critique of the welfare state in the tradition of H. L. Mencken, Robert Taft, and Garet Garrett.

Hurston also shared an affinity with the isolationism of the Old Right. A now-restored chapter from the original manuscript of her autobiography *Dust Tracks on a Road* features a biting indictment of imperialism. She declared: "I do not mean to single out England as something strange and different in the world. We, too, have our Marines in China. We, too, consider machine gun bullets good laxatives for heathens who get constipated with toxic ideas of a country of their own." For Hurston, international big-power politics represented little more than a glorified scramble for "protection money."

Her individualism, however, unlike that of Lane, Rand, and Paterson, had to contend directly with the thorny question of race. Circumstances forced Hurston into an almost impossible dilemma. On the one hand, she deplored the imposed sorting of legal segregation. Hurston demanded "the complete repeal of all Jim Crow Laws in the United States once and for all, and right now." At the same time, she was not about to entrust New Deal liberals with the job. They were "racial cardsharps" who would use any pretext to fasten dependency on big government. Faced with limited alternatives, she proved willing to support segregationists, such as Senator Spessard Holland of Florida, as long as they opposed the common enemy of welfare-state liberalism. Hurston may have made wrong choices but she certainly was not any more "naive" than New Dealers who had once formed alliances with Senator Theodore Bilbo of Mississippi and other vitriolic racists for the "greater good" of FDR's programs.

Hurston was suspicious of anyone, from Left or Right, who judged individuals by category. "I found," she asserted, "that I had no need of either class or race prejudice, those scourges of humanity. The solace of easy generalization was taken from me, but I received the richer gift of individualism. . . . So Race Pride and Race Consciousness seem to me to be not only fallacious, but a thing to be abhorred."

In 1955, Hurston returned to the limelight by opposing the Supreme Court's decision in *Brown v. Board of Education.* She castigated the ruling as "forced association" and as an insult to black teachers who taught in segregated schools. "It is a contradiction in terms," she argued, "to scream race pride and equality while at the same time spurning Negro teachers and self-association." The narrow impact of the ruling, however, was not as important to her as the long-term implications for liberty. She feared that it was a "trial-balloon" that would be used as a precedent in a larger campaign to replace the Constitution with "government by administrative decree."

Neither assimilationist, nor accomodationist, nor nationalist, Hurston defies tidy categorization within black history. What distinguishes her is her ability to speak directly to the quest of individuals for freedom and self-reliance. This gives her writings a timeless quality, and a very broad appeal.

David T. Beito is an assistant professor of history at the University of Alabama.

Zora Neale Hurston describes the joy of blackness

But I am not tragically colored. There is no great sorrow damned up in my soul, nor lurking behind my eyes. I do not mind at all. I do not belong to the sobbing school of Negrohood who hold that nature somehow has given them a lowdown dirty deal and whose feelings are all hurt about it. Even in the helter-skelter skirmish that is my life, I have seen that the world is to the strong regardless of a little pigmentation more or less. No, I do not weep at the world—I am too busy sharpening my oster knife.

Someone is always at my elbow reminding me that I am a granddaughter of slaves. It fails to register depression with me. Slavery is 60 years in the past. The operation was successful and the patient is doing well, thank you. The terrible struggle that made me an American out of a potential slave said "On the line!" The Reconstruction said "Get set!"; and the generation before said "Go!" I am off to a flying start and I must not halt in the stretch to look behind and weep. Slavery is the price I paid for civilization, and the choice was not with me. It is a bully adventure and worth all that have paid through my ancestors for it. No one on earth ever had a greater chance for glory. The world to bet on and nothing to be lost. It is thrilling to think—to know that for any act of mine, I shall get twice as much praise or twice as much blame. It is quite exciting to hold the center on the national stage, with spectators not knowing whether to laugh or to weep.

—from "How It Feels to Be Colored Me"

Part 1

God and the Civil Rights Movement

Professor James M. Washington addresses Union Day '96 attendees

Following a luncheon in the Refectory, Union Day participants and attendees gathered in James Chapel for a lecture by Professor of Church History James M. Washington on "God and the Civil Rights Movement: A Retrospective, 1941–1968," the subject of his current research. He put forth a central question to which panelists would later respond: Can one do a religious history of the civil rights movement? Or, what was there religious about the civil rights movement?

"Union Theological Seminary is a good place to ask this kind of question,..." Washington said, quoting Paul Tillich's comment that "religion is the substance of culture and culture a form of religion." Yet, Washington says, when he hears that assertion, he must ask: "And? And? And?"

In describing the way African Americans have written and spoken about their pain and its connection to religious experience, Washington drew on Albert Jay Raboteau's *Slave Religion*. The book examines the experience of slaves and their grappling with the problem of evil as reflected in the question, "Could it be possible that the old god of the African continent had failed them?"

Washington identified "an implicit conflict between the philosophy of the Declaration of Independence and that of the Constitution."

"Not only is this a central theological question that has been addressed from a Black theological perspective, a Womanist perspective, and several other historical perspectives," Washington said, "It is a question in American society, as well." Washington identified "an implicit conflict between the philosophy of the Declaration of Independence and that of the Constitution." According to Washington, this tension came to a head in 1845, when many denominations in this country split over the issue of slavery.

The debate, Washington noted, was not just over the translation of the Greek word *doulas* as either slave or servant, but about the nature and destiny of this country and whether or not one could create a society that was truly under God. "By 1861, as the nation was on the brink of warfare," he said, "a Presbyterian minister cried out 'the stench of slaves long-since gone has finally reached the nostrils of God.' "

"The civil rights movement was not just a movement for social change. . . . It was a fight for the soul of America."

Washington, who grew up in Knoxville, Tennessee during the civil rights movement, says he has learned a great deal by reflecting on that experience from an historical perspective. "The civil rights movement was not just a movement for social change," he said, "It was a fight for the soul of America; a fight not simply about ideology but about whether or not people of conviction and values, people who had a firm belief that God somehow plays a part in human history, would have their prayers answered. These people uttered prayers, sang songs, engaged in the movement, not simply because they wanted freedom, but because they wanted to know the answer to the question: 'Is there a God?' They asked over and over again, 'Is God on our side?'

"In order for people—not just students—but indigenous people to do what they did, which was like going into guerrilla warfare in some communities, it had to be based on some strong religious conviction.

"The question is: 'How did we muster the courage to resist this form of oppression?'" Washington asked. "Those who have interpreted the Civil Rights movement are right when they insist that one has to see the movement in the context of the history of protest in the United States."

"The feeling that the presence of God must be linked somehow in struggle is one of the great legacies of the civil rights movement."

Washington pointed to the abolitionist movement and various attempts to defeat and oppose the system. "One of the more common rationales for putting forth the challenge and motivation," he observed, "was Christian idealism or Christian pacifism... which dovetailed with the social gospel movement itself and had its roots in biblical understanding of martyrdom. Indeed, one great misreading of *Uncle Tom's Cabin* has ignored the fact that what was seen as Tom's 'accommodationism' by those who do not read the text in the context of biblical narrative, was not 'accommodation,' but Tom as the paradigmatic Christian martyr...based on the conviction that without the shedding of blood, there can be no remission of sin.

"The idea that God plays some role in American history, as well as in the life of the church, was in crisis by the 1930s, partially because of the worldwide Depression, but partly because many were beginning to experience the 'death of God'.... What was clear, on the part of protesters and activists, whether motivated by Christian conviction or patriotism, was that somehow God plays a role in this (although) some used different words like transcendence, some purpose beyond themselves.

"The feeling that the presence of God must be linked somehow in struggle is one of the great legacies of the civil rights movement," Washington concluded. "What I am trying to do is write and research an interfaith and interdenominational history of this movement. What is clear to me, from a larger standpoint, is that the clouds of the 'death of God' movement that hung over the heads of people in the sixties was not just a formal debate among theologians but sometimes it was an experience on the street."

Washington ended his presentation with some words from the late Ralph Abernathy:"Lord, we don't have much money. But we have our bodies. This is what we offer on this day."

Part 2 of article continues on next page.

Josephites mark 125 years

■ **Service:** *The order of Catholic priests has staffed African-American parishes in Baltimore and other cities for over a century.*

Marilyn McCraven

Sun Staff

When Carl Stokes won a partial scholarship to Loyola High School in the 1960s, there was no way his family could make up the difference.

Not to fear: His parish priest, a Josephite at St. Francis Xavier in East Baltimore, made sure all expenses were covered.

"If you had the ability, they would make sure that you got all the tools and the educational opportunities to go to the next level," said Stokes, 46, a former Baltimore City councilman and lifetime member of St. Francis.

Stokes' story is one of many that will be shared as the Josephites celebrate their 125th anniversary today, with Cardinal William H. Keeler presiding at a 5 p.m. Mass at St. Francis Xavier Church, 1501 E. Oliver St., the country's oldest African-American Roman Catholic parish. A reception and banquet will follow at the Baltimore Convention Center.

The events mark the 1871 founding of St. Joseph's Society of the Sacred Heart in London, which sent white priests to Baltimore that same year to staff African-American Catholic parishes and schools. They assumed control of St. Francis Xavier and in 1892 became a separate American order to concentrate on their work among blacks, many of them freed slaves.

St. Francis Xavier spawned seven other parishes for African-Americans in Baltimore. St. Monica's and Sacred Heart are defunct, but still operating are St. Peter Claver in Sandtown-Winchester; St. Pius V in Harlem Park, which merged with St. Barnabas; and St. Veronica's in Cherry Hill. Christ the King in Dundalk was turned over to the archdiocese.

These were the only parishes blacks attended until the 1950s, when they felt accepted at Baltimore's other Catholic churches, said the Rev. Peter E. Hogan, the Josephite archivist.

Though in decline in recent years, the order has continued to play a significant role in education, housing, the rehabilitation of drug addicts and alcoholics and other pursuits, say local religious and civic leaders.

"Black Catholics have always seen the Josephites as somebody who could go to the pope and the bishops for us," said Sister Claudina Sanz, superior general of the 168-year-old Oblate Sisters, a group of African-American nuns founded here.

The Rev. Robert M. Kearns, the superior general of the Josephites, led the effort to raise money to build new and renovated homes under the Nehemiah project. His appeal to a variety of religious groups—synagogues and black and white Protestant churches—netted $2.2 million in pledges that leveraged millions more in federal, state and city dollars.

The groups promised to "rise up and build"—as the Old Testament prophet Nehemiah had urged—in the impoverished neighborhoods of Sandtown-Winchester and Penn North in West Baltimore. With the Enterprise Foundation as the developer, 300 houses have been built, 150 are to be built and 150 are to be renovated, Kearns said.

"The Josephites are to be commended for the leadership they've shown in their outreach to the oppressed in the city, especially through the Nehemiah project," said Rev. Douglas Miles of Baltimoreans United in Leadership Development, the church-based community group that initially lobbied the religious community for money for the project in 1986.

The Josephites sponsor the largest Head Start program in Maryland, with nearly 300 preschoolers at St. Veronica's.

A Josephite, Bishop John H. Ricard, oversees parishes serving 85,000 Catholics in Baltimore and is head of Baltimore-

From the *Baltimore Sun*, November 30, 1996, pp. 1A, 8A.

based Catholic Relief Services, the world's second-largest nonprofit provider of foreign aid.

Another Josephite, the Rev. Joseph Verrette, runs the state-funded Tuerk House in West Baltimore, a 28-day inpatient drug and alcohol treatment program for people with no health insurance.

But the shortage of priests has caused the order to curtail its projects. "We've pulled out of 26 parishes over the past 20 years" in the United States and the Bahamas, said the Rev. Eugene McManus, former Josephite superior general.

However, there are several new black priests, and they're working closely with an order of priests from Nigeria, which is sending missionaries to this country for long stints. Several Joesphite parishes in Baltimore remain "vibrant," said McManus.

St. Francis Xavier and St. Peter Claver have 800 registered families each, church officials say. Some St. Francis members travel from Washington and Pennsylvania to attend one of the three Sunday Masses, said the Rev. William Norvel, pastor at St. Francis Xavier.

"When I go there, I'm surrounded by people I've known since I was 5 years old," said Stokes.

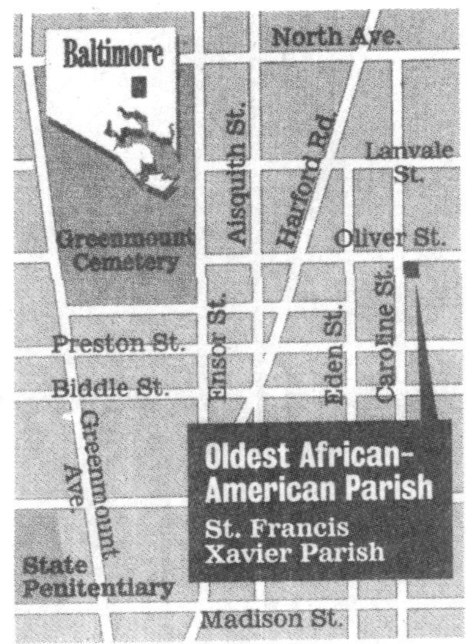

State Del. Kenneth C. Montague Jr. also credits the Josephites with helping to open the door to educational opportunities.

In 1960, Montague became the first African-American to attend Loyola High School. As a student at St. Peter Claver Elementary, he said, "One day they just came to me and said 'take this test and if you pass, you'll go to Loyola.'

"I never asked, but I'm sure [the Josephites]" were instrumental in making the opportunity available, said Montague, a University of Maryland Law School graduate.

The Josephites' national headquarters and residence are in a formidable brownstone in the 1100 block of N. Calvert St. downtown. Their retirement residence is on Lake Avenue near Roland Park.

In Baltimore, there are eight active priests, 10 administrators and 15 retired members. Many of the order's 125 active priests are in Deep South parishes in Texas, Louisiana and Mississippi.

Most Josephite priests and brothers are white, typically Irish-Americans from major East Coast cities, but most of their seminarians are black, said McManus, the former Josephite superior general. Despite the difference in race, the Josephites bond with African-Americans to the extent that some even refer to themselves as being black.

"I never thought of myself as white" after becoming a Josephite, said McManus, who still has a trace of his native Brooklyn, N.Y., accent. "Almost all of the people I worked with were black; I was working for black causes. I just thought of myself as black."

From Scottsboro to Simpson

ABIGAIL THERNSTROM & HENRY D. FETTER

ABIGAIL THERNSTROM is a senior fellow at the Manhattan Institute and author of *Whose Votes Count?* HENRY D. FETTER practices law in Los Angeles.

DEPRESSING episodes in American race relations come and go, but this one may stick. As we write, the news of the verdict in the O. J. Simpson trial is still fresh, though a new drama has quickly replaced the original one. Race—not crime and punishment—is its theme. And, while the long-running show that ended on the third of October was part soap, part sporting event (with an array of television pundits keeping score), this one is no fun at all. Unforgettable images have flitted across our television screen: of cheers, hugs, and high fives among black crowds; of racist graffiti in Brentwood, the white, traditionally liberal, upscale neighborhood in which O. J. and Nicole both lived. Are we two nations or one? The question—long a staple in the rhetoric of the left—must now be taken seriously.

A man confronted with overwhelming evidence of guilt has now gone free. It has happened before; it will happen again. But, from day one—a Friday evening in June of 1994—this was a tale like no other. Remember the opening act: a double-murder suspect on a leisurely cruise, with the police in tow and an armada of law-enforcement and media helicopters hovering overhead. Simpson—the product of a black ghetto, winner of the Heisman Trophy, National Football League star, and nationally known actor, sportscaster, and commercial spokesman—was a man on a jog from the law. Along the route taken by Simpson and a long-time friend, spontaneous crowds formed, chanting "Free the Juice." (The suspect had already become a victim.) Only at his Brentwood home was Simpson finally taken into custody. The charge was first-degree murder: His ex-wife, Nicole Brown Simpson, and Ronald L. Goldman, a waiter at a neighborhood restaurant, had been found dead in the blood-spattered courtyard of Nicole's condominium. Both had been stabbed repeatedly; Nicole's throat had been slashed through to the spinal bone.

Simpson quickly assembled a self-described "Dream Team" of lawyers, with Johnnie Cochran, Los Angeles's most prominent black attorney, as lead trial counsel, backed up by a nationally renowned battery of experts. Millions of dollars were available and committed to the defense. With a judge scrupulously attentive to the rights of the accused and the desires of the defense, the trial proceeded at a leisurely pace in a courtroom dominated by Cochran. Outside there quickly gathered a caravan of television trailers, mobile studios, and souvenir sellers, dubbed "Camp O. J.," all of whom set up shop for the year-long stay. Business in Simpson memorabilia boomed, and the flood of bestsellers spawned by the case still shows no signs of abating.

Simpson is not the most prominent American ever to be charged with murder. (That "honor" still belongs to Vice President Aaron Burr, charged with the killing of Alexander Hamilton.) And yet the trial was unique. The courtroom proceedings were televised live; in making their closing and other arguments, lead lawyers for the opposing teams often turned their gaze from the jurors to the cameras. Anyone with a computer and modem could read the daily transcripts. If print and broadcast tabloids were consumed by the case, much the same was true for National Public Radio, the *New Yorker,* and other "quality" media. Numerous law schools based courses on the case, although only Harvard believed that memoranda prepared by its first-term students warranted the trial judge's unsolicited attention. Every conceivable angle of the case was explored at length, including a not-uninteresting piece in a golf magazine which assessed the charges against Simpson in light of his "Jekyll and Hyde" conduct at the prominent Los Angeles country club at which he played. And, as the verdict came in, an estimated 100 million television viewers watched—an audience larger than that for the first night of the Gulf War, the resignation of Richard Nixon, or the Apollo 11 moon walk.

The cult of celebrity

Race is what makes the case significant, but it was actually fame that determined much of its handling by the authorities. Although he had been charged with two brutal murders, the police made no effort to take Simpson into custody, instead, negotiating a "surrender" at a time and place of his choosing, in a manner more akin to a prosecution for insider trading than a double homicide. Then, when he violated that agreement, the officers did not intervene by force; instead, they languidly escorted Simpson to his house and watched while he sat in his car for an hour, telephoned his mom, and drank a glass of orange juice.

Once in jail, the mantle of celebrity remained firmly in place. There, Simpson was allowed a privileged regimen that lasted until public disclosure reportedly curtailed it. He was allowed to sleep later than other inmates, shower more often, exercise or watch television during more "free" hours, receive hot meals at irregular hours, enjoy unlimited visits with his girlfriend, use a special pillow, and, on weekends, receive dozens of friends, who were listed on an extraordinarily lengthy "material witness" list. On Christmas day, he was the only inmate permitted to have visitors.

Considerations of celebrity informed the formal trial proceedings as well. Prospective jurors had to complete an unprecedented 60-plus-page questionnaire in which they were asked a mass of not especially pertinent questions that ranged far beyond those necessary to elicit prior knowledge, bias, or prejudice.

Where celebrities roam, the media follows, and trial Judge Lance Ito proved more than willing to lend his presence to the hoopla. Early on, he appeared in a week-long series of television interviews. He went out of his way to welcome into his chambers such celebrity figures as Geraldo Rivera and Larry King. A number of discharged jurors became part of the show. Appearing at press conferences and on television, talking about their experiences and offering opinions about the case, they became a regular adjunct to the proceedings in court. After the verdict, jurors who lasted emerged on Oprah Winfrey and other shows. Money for talking was theirs for the asking.

Bit players in the drama attained their 15 minutes and more of fame, most notably Kato Kaelin, the unemployed actor who lived in O. J. Simpson's guest house and baby-sat for Nicole. After giving equivocal and inarticulate testimony in court, Kaelin became the host of a Los Angeles radio program; initial reviews were quite favorable. Meanwhile, his old, soft-core porn films turned up on various cable networks.

Then too, the televised trial opened up new career paths for lawyers, a notoriously frustrated group. Whereas lawyers may have once aspired to judgeships, their star is now fashioned on that ne plus ultra of contemporary life: the talk-show host. They became sportscasters, recruited in droves to provide instant analyses of the trial-as-Super-Bowl by a battalion of broadcast outlets, including E! (Entertainment) Network, otherwise best known for the Howard Stern Show. A number of the most prominent lawyer-sportscasters were elevated to full-time status as the new hosts of regularly scheduled programs having nothing to do with the trial or even the law—most notably, Gerry Spence, Leslie Abramson (defense lawyer for Eric Menendez in his televised trial and perhaps the first "star" created by this still relatively novel process), and CNN's two regular trial watchers, Greta Van Susteren and Roger Cossack. Two of the defense lawyers have found their new-found celebrity to be a useful vehicle for pitching screenplays that they had been toiling on, without success, before the trial. (They have now also begun work on a CBS drama series.) Whatever one thinks of the verdict, it is clear that at least these lawyers had a good trial.

But what made the often tawdry spectacle that enveloped the case most truly representative of the celebrity culture it exemplified was the lack of substance at its core. Who, after all, was Simpson? His great feats on the college and professional gridiron were almost 20 years in the past. His acting career had fizzled out after some embarrassing appearances in grade-B movies, and his life as a sportscaster was in eclipse; it had been almost a decade since he had appeared on ABC's prime-time Monday Night Football. As a corporate pitchman, most notably for Hertz, he had become the prototypical celebrity—someone famous for being famous, or what Daniel Boorstin has called "the human pseudo-event."

Indeed, nothing better illustrated Simpson's relative "obscurity" than the lack of attention paid, at the time, to his conviction for wife beating in 1989. In a culture that is rapacious for the most minor peccadilloes of the truly famous, the event passed almost without notice. And in the five years before the murder, the only extended mention of Simpson in the *Los Angeles Times* was in a 1993 piece marking the twenty-fifth anniversary of his Heisman Trophy. It was really not surprising that lead prosecutor Marcia Clark had never heard of Simpson until that day in 1994 when she was called by the police who needed help in applying for a warrant to search his home.

The race card

Simpson was rich and famous, and he wore his racial identity exceedingly lightly. He had black friends, but his life was not notable for involvement in black issues or causes. He lived in a largely white neighborhood, his murdered ex-wife was white, as is his former girlfriend. The black media had largely ignored his activities in recent years. Apart from a bit part in the television miniseries "Roots," almost two decades ago, it is hard to think of any connection between him and anything race-related. Booked for murder, however, he became a racial cause.

Black defendants in criminal cases are, alas, common enough, and, most of the time, the prosecutors have the upper hand. But celebrity status shifts the balance of power. All eyes are on highly visible black defendants—particularly all black eyes. Every move, from arrest to trial, is watched with deep suspicion. And, while in an earlier era authorities could ignore the deeply felt emotions stirred by such cases, in 1995—especially in Los Angeles—they cannot.

In the city of Rodney King, the authorities were from the outset on their racial toes. Despite the brutality of the crime, the apparently overwhelming evidence of Simpson's guilt, his flight from arrest, and a sordid history of domestic abuse and violence, the prosecutors chose not to seek the death penalty. Rather than try the case in the largely white locality where Simpson lived and the crime had been committed, the Los Angeles district attorney selected a downtown venue. A conviction by a mostly white jury drawn from the west side of Los Angeles would "lack credibility," he privately explained.

In the prosecution of Los Angeles police officers for the beating of Rodney King, the initial verdict of acquittal was viewed as lacking credibility because white jurors sat in judgment of the beating of a black man by whites. In the Simpson case, the logic was reversed: The victims are white, the defendant black, but racial fairness demands (the D.A. concluded) a heavily black jury.

The original jury consisted of six black women, two black men, two Hispanics, one white woman, and one juror who identified himself as half white and half Native American. (No white male was selected as either a juror or alternate.) Alternates replaced many of those initially selected, with the result that the final breakdown was one black man, eight black women, two white women, and one Hispanic man.

The panel was thus three-quarters black. Even for the Central Court House, this was unusual. The makeup of recent juries has been, on the average, 46 percent white, 25 percent black, 19 percent Latino, and 10 percent Asian. The pool of 900 from which the Simpson jurors were drawn was 40 percent white, 28 percent black, 17 percent Hispanic, and 15 percent Asian. How then did the final panel become 75 percent black? The prosecutors made scant use of a jury consultant, failed to exercise half of its peremptory challenges, ignored the question of race, and focused instead on picking women in the belief that they would listen with particular sympathy to the domestic-violence evidence.

It was a gamble, and it worked out badly. A mostly black jury was an invitation to racial mischief, readily accepted by the defense. The race card wasn't just played; it was "played from the bottom of the deck," as defense attorney Robert Shapiro lately acknowledged. In fact, Cochran's closing statement eerily echoed a defense attorney's final argument on behalf of the two white men accused of the brutal murder of a 14-year-old black youngster, Emmett Till, after he "wolf-whistled" at a white woman in 1955: "I am sure that every last Anglo-Saxon one of you has the courage to acquit these men."

There were actually two racial cards in Cochran's hand. In equating detective Mark Fuhrman with the LAPD and with Hitler, he brilliantly indicted the entire LAPD for the racism of a single individual and appropriated the Holocaust for his own ends. The suffering of blacks in Los Angeles in 1995 became the moral equivalent of that of Jews under the Third Reich. And he placed all those who sought Simpson's conviction (including the family of Ronald Goldman, conveniently Jewish) on the side of the Nazis. The Goldman parents and their son, not to mention Nicole Simpson and her family, were thus stripped of their moral standing as victims. In their place stood O. J., now a symbol of black suffering.

Cochran's appeal to racial solidarity was ugly—and perhaps unnecessary. Most members of the jury had apparently made up their minds before the closing arguments, as had the public outside the courtroom. After the preliminary hearing, about 60 percent of whites in a national sample said they believed Simpson to be guilty, and the same was true in March 1995, two months into the trial. For blacks, by contrast, 68 percent of those polled that March believed Simpson innocent, and the percentage expressing an opinion of actual guilt had declined from 15 percent in November to 8 percent four months later. At the end of the trial, 83 percent of blacks agreed with the verdict, while only 37 percent of whites did. Between the public at large and the jury, however, there was obviously one important difference. The racial split on the outside was not reflected in the final verdict of those on the inside, although with nine blacks on the jury and the threat of another riot (implicitly made by Cochran), perhaps a simple desire for self- and public-preservation made unanimity inevitable. Indeed, one of the white jurors has since stated her belief in Simpson's guilt.

The racial divide split television pundits as well; black commentators were almost uniformly cheerleaders for the defense, while the white attorneys were more balanced in their views. Reactions to Cochran were similarly divided. He was hailed in the black community as "our new Joe Louis." In August, he gave the keynote speech at the annual convention of the National Association of Black Journalists and, a month later, stole the spotlight from both President Clinton and General Colin Powell at a conference of the Congressional Black Caucus attended by 5,000 participants. After the verdict, former Los Angeles mayor Tom Bradley called him a "national hero."

White perceptions of Cochran's style have, let us say, not been as favorable.

Two races, two views

Two nations, separate and unequal, was the Kerner Commission's description in 1968. The inequality has been dramatically reduced (the good news that the media largely ignores). The median income of black married couples with children is only somewhat less than that for all American families; 12 percent of all college students are now black—a figure proportionate to the black population.

It's the sense of separation—quite a different matter—that is truly worrisome. The Simpson polling data was a wake-up call, but ominous signs had been flickering on the landscape for some time. In a 1970 Harris poll, 64 percent of blacks said that the Black Panthers gave them a sense of pride. In a 1989 ABC/*Washington Post* survey, 26 percent of blacks signed on to the notion that the majority of whites shared the racist views of the Ku Klux Klan, with another 25 percent of blacks believing that at least one-quarter of whites were in the KKK camp. A 1993–1994 Black Politics Survey found that 50 percent of African-American respondents thought a separate black political party was a fine idea.

After a grand jury dismissed Tawana Brawley's totally groundless 1988 claim that she had been kidnapped and raped by a gang of white men, including a couple of policemen, 73 percent of white New Yorkers understood that she had fabricated the entire story, while only 33 percent of blacks did. Gallup Organization and other analyses indicate that up to 40 percent of African Americans believe that some sort of white conspiracy accounts for the scourge of drugs, guns, or AIDS in black inner-city neighborhoods—and, even more ominously, that educated blacks hold views that are as conspiratorial as those of the uneducated. Virulently anti-white voices like that of Khalid Muhammad and Leonard Jeffries are regularly heard on college campuses because that is where they find a sympathetic audience.

The National Association of Black Social Workers has declared that "black children should not be placed with white parents under any circumstances." In recent years, the percentage of blacks who approve of interracial marriage has been dropping, while white acceptance has been going up. Likewise, some data from Detroit suggest that black enthusiasm for integrated neighborhoods has been declining. In the years from 1978 to 1992, Detroit's whites increasingly accepted having black neighbors, but blacks became less willing to live in predominantly white parts of the metropolitan area.

"It's a black thing, you wouldn't understand" was the slogan on a T-shirt popular among black youth a few years back. In many of the nation's urban schools, racially divisive messages permeate Afrocentric and other curricular materials. Racially determined perspectives are much celebrated. Fundamental differences between whites and blacks are emphasized; agreement is viewed as racially and culturally coercive. It's no wonder that race consciousness is rising. We've been hard at work encouraging it, and not only in our schools. Every affirmative-action policy delivers the message that white folks and black folks really are not the same, that blacks have much to gain from that perceived difference, that color consciousness is the ticket to success. The Simpson acquittal is affirmative action gone over the cliff: Such racial double standards have now infected juries and perverted the administration of justice, a tragic denouement to the half-century-old quest to eliminate bias against blacks in the legal system.

The Simpson acquittal was not unique. No one knows how often black jurors have cast a racial protest vote in the face of overwhelming evidence that a black defendant is guilty. Courts do not keep records indicating the breakdown of juries by race. But, in the Bronx, black defendants are acquitted in felony cases almost one-half of the time—nearly three times the national rate. In Washington, D.C., 95 percent of defendants are black, as are 70 percent of the jurors; in 29 percent of all felony trials last year, the accused went free. In addition, post-verdict letters and statements in a number of cases draw a clear picture of jury nullification. Thus a Baltimore jury that included eleven blacks refused to convict Davon Neverdon of murder last July, despite the presence of four eyewitnesses; the lone Asian-American juror blew the whistle. In Washington in 1990, an all-black Jury acquitted Darryl Smith of murder; a subsequent letter from an anonymous juror to the court said a minority on the panel who "didn't want to send any more Young Black Men to Jail" had swayed the rest.

A sense of racial grievance infecting the criminal justice system—whatever its source—is not benign. The result is a heightened distrust of the law, the vital foundation upon which justice, order, and racial harmony depend. Color-blind justice is the American ideal; color-consciousness is its enemy and, as the Simpson case highlights so starkly, seems to be on the increase. From such color-conscious justice, there is, of course, no appeal—no redress. Acquittals (unlike convictions) are the end of the legal road, except in those rare instances in which federal prosecutors can start anew.

From Scottsboro to Simpson

Interviewed for a symposium in a September 1994 issue of *Ebony,* author Nikki Giovanni described the Simpson case as Scottsboro redux. Johnnie Cochran, in his closing remarks, also referred to the Scottsboro nine. There is a similarity, but it is not the one that either Giovanni or Cochran is likely to have in mind. In both the Scottsboro and O. J. cases, jurors were asked to go beyond the evidence in the interest of broader societal purposes. "Show them, show them that Alabama justice cannot be bought and sold with Jew money from New York" was the 1933 "send-a-message" appeal, one that was just as successful as Cochran's.

But there the similarity ends. Recall the Scottsboro facts: On a March morning, nine black youths were rousted from a freight train in northern Alabama by a hastily assembled posse and accused of rape by two white women. After a narrow escape from lynching, the nine, ranging in age from 13 to 20, were rushed to trial in a Scottsboro courtroom within two weeks of the arrest. Represented by an unprepared out-of-state counsel who had no more than a half-hour consultation with his clients, eight of the defendants were summarily convicted and sentenced to death by all-white juries who deliberated within earshot of large crowds surrounding the courthouse, cheering each guilty verdict. After seven subsequent trials, two reversals by the Supreme Court, and a recantation by one of the two women, five of the men served varying prison terms, the last released only in 1950.

No leisurely police escort, phone calls to mom, calming sips of orange juice, black jurors, celebrated black attorney, or solicitous judge for the Scottsboro nine. In that case, the duly authorized legal process made a mockery of due process, surely something that cannot be said about the Simpson trial, whatever its other flaws. And yet, such ludicrous comparisons have real currency. With the Republican ascendancy in Congress, Jesse Jackson regularly refers to the end—once again—of Reconstruction, while Representative Charles Rangel has equated today's conservatives with yesterday's KKK.

The rhetoric of racial grievance carries a high cost. The views of Jackson, Rangel, and other black leaders help shape the perceptions of ordinary blacks, raising the level of despair and anger, inviting just the sort of hunger for retribution that was on display in the post-verdict days. "I think he did it," said a black Los Angeles musician. "But I don't think he's guilty. There is an unpaid debt in black history, and we [pulled] for O. J. because of past injustices to blacks." Among African Americans, it was clearly a widely held view—or at least so it seems from media reports.

"It was a great day for African Americans," a former Simpson juror said on the day of the verdict. That "great day" was followed by another: an unprecedented rally of black masses led by an extremist messenger of separation and bigotry. Whites and blacks ever more apart: it's a black catastrophe and an American tragedy. The storm warnings are up; we ignore them at our peril.

Asian Americans

The following collection of articles on Asian Americans invites us to reflect on the fact that the United States is related to Asia in ways that would seem utterly amazing to the worldview of the American founders. The expansion of the American regime across the continent, the importation of Asian workers, and the subsequent exclusion of Asians from the American polity are signs of the tarnished image and broken promise of refuge that America extended and then revoked. The Asian world is a composite of ethnicities and traditions ranging from the Indian subcontinent northeastward to China and Japan. The engagement of the United States beyond its continental limits brought American and Asian interests into a common arena now called the Pacific Rim. The most recent and perhaps most traumatic episode of this encounter was the conflict that erupted in 1941 at Pearl Harbor in Hawaii. Thus, examining the Asian relationship to America begins with the dual burdens of domestic exclusion and war.

The cultural roots and current interaction between the United States and Asia form a complex of concerns explored in this unit's articles. Understanding the cultural matrices of Asian nations and their ethnicities and languages initiates the process of learning about the Asian emigrants who for many reasons decided to leave Asia to seek a fresh beginning in the United States.

The population growth of Asian Americans since the immigration reform of 1965, the emergence of Japan and other Asian nations as international fiscal players, and the image of Asian American intellectual and financial success have heightened interest in this ethnic group in the United States. The variety of religious traditions that Asian immigrants bring to America is another dimension of cultural and moral importance. In what respect are non-Judeo-Christian-Islamic faith traditions issues of consequences? This aftermath of conflict and resulting analysis have riveted attention to the ethnic factor.

The details of familial and cultural development within Asian American communities compose worlds of meaning that are a rich source of material from which both insights and troubling questions of personal and group identity emerge. Pivotal periods of conflict in the drama of the American experience provide an occasion for learning as much about ourselves as about one of the newest clusters of ethnicities—the Asian Americans.

One of the first large-scale interactions between the United States and Asia was with the Philippine Islands and its populations. This experience of war and empire and the attendant century-long process of military and defense relationships as well as the exportation of institutions and cultural change have forged a unique international-intercultural symbiosis. The role of the ethnic Chinese diaspora and the emergence of economic strength and political change in Asia suggest the globalization of the ethnic factor. Even the name of this American ethnic population has changed, as has its relationship to the islands and its ancestry. There is new politicization of the future of both an Asian homeland and the diasporic remnant. Its aspiring leaders are fashioning a new consciousness that is meaningful for its time and is inspiring actions that will articulate a most worthy future.

Looking Ahead: Challenge Questions

The public passions generated during World War II have subsided, and anti-Japanese sentiment is no longer heard. Is this statement true or false? Why?

Under what circumstances and toward which nations could the snarls of ethnic hatred be renewed?

What impact did Asian Americans have on the presidential elections? Are attitudinal and institutional obstacles to inclusion such as contributions from persons associated with foreign interests and corporations simply matters of law or are they symptoms of prejudices and fears of ethnic politics?

How can inclusiveness as an American value be taught? What approaches are most promising?

UNIT 6

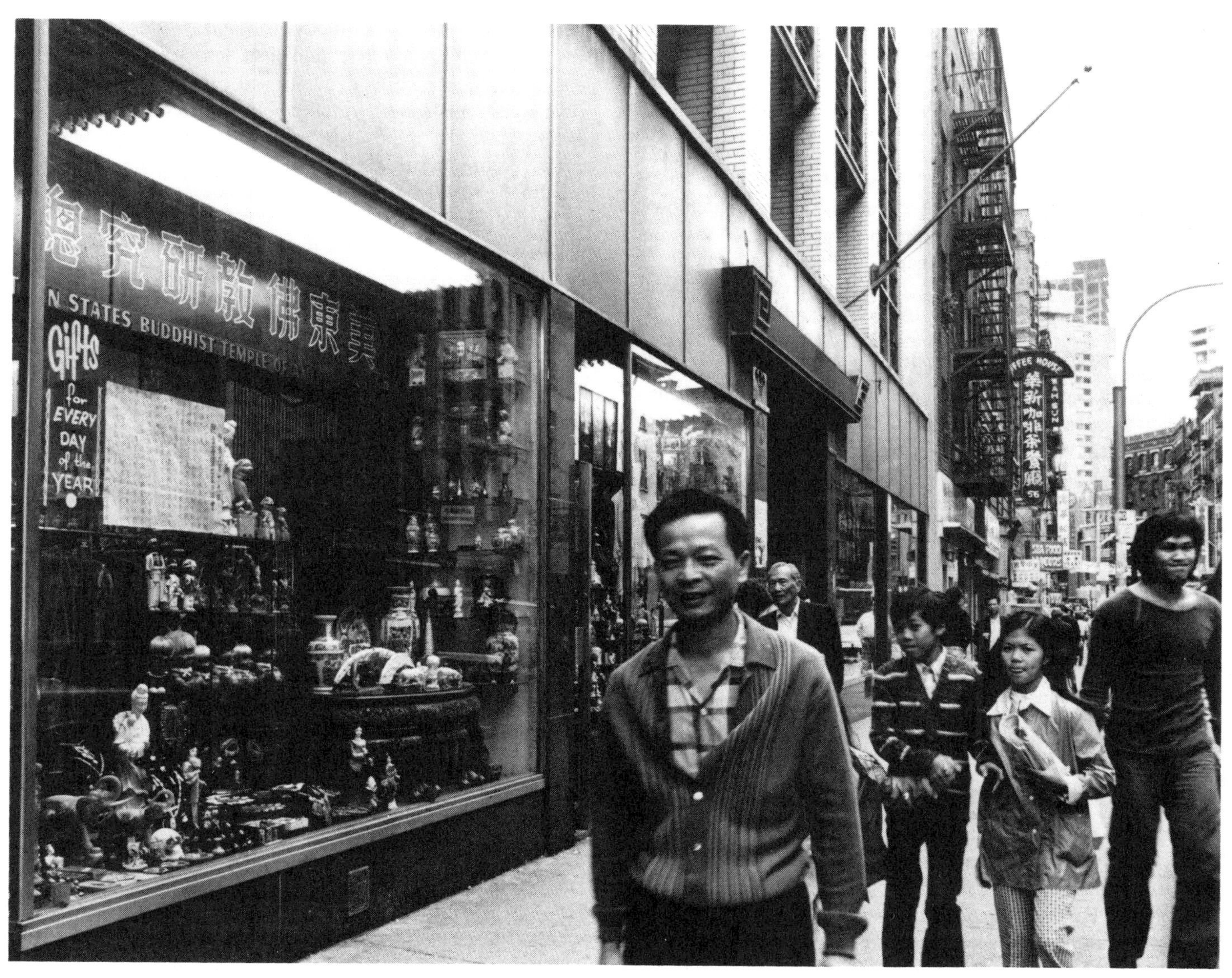

Misperceived Minorities

'Good' and 'bad' stereotypes saddle Hispanics and Asian Americans

Pamela Constable

Washington Post Staff Writer

Richard Lopez, 29, a fourth-generation Mexican American businessman from San Bernardino, Calif., grew up in what he called a "Brady Bunch" suburb, and learned Spanish only to communicate with his great-grandmother. He is mystified when Hispanic newcomers complain of discrimination and angry when whites assume he needed special help to move up in American society.

"Nobody ever put a roadblock in front of me. I earned my way into college, and it offended me when people asked if I was receiving affirmative action," he says in a telephone interview. "I think a lot of the whining about discrimination is blown out of proportion. The biggest thing holding a lot of Mexicans back here is their resentment against those who succeed."

Ray Chin, 46, an insurance agent in New York's Chinatown, spent his teenage years washing bathrooms and delivering groceries in the city after his parents fled Communist China in the 1950s. Today he has earned the stature that often leads Asian Americans to be called the "model minority," a phrase he views as more curse than compliment.

"Yes, we can successfully join the mainstream, but once we reach a certain level, we're stifled by that glass ceiling," Chin says amid the din of a crowded Chinese restaurant. "People think we Asians can take care of ourselves, and they don't see the need to help us. But it's not true. We are still not included in things and we have to work three times harder to get to the same level as our co-workers."

No matter how much personal success they achieve, Hispanics and Asian Americans say they must fight stereotypes that can undermine their confidence or limit their potential. Whether "negative" or "positive"—the lazy, welfare-dependent Hispanic or the shy, technically oriented Asian American—such perceptions can be equally harmful and unfair, members of both groups say.

Worse, they say, is that ethnic minorities in the United States sometimes come to accept others' stereotypes about them, even when the facts and their experiences do not support those biases. For that reason, they may remain extremely sensitive to discrimination even when they have matched or surpassed white Americans in income and education.

Such contradictions—both in the views of other Americans toward Hispanics and Asian Americans and, at times, in the views of those groups about themselves—appeared throughout a nationwide telephone poll of 1,970 people conducted by The Washington Post, the Kaiser Family Foundation and Harvard University.

Yet there is also enormous diversity of opinion and experience within these two ethnic categories, other surveys and interviews show. The perceptions of Hispanics and Asian Americans about their opportunities and obstacles vary dramatically depending on their class, community and country of origin.

"It's very misleading to talk about the views of whites versus the views of minority groups like Latinos, because you cannot assume commonalty within those groups at all," says Rodolfo de la Garza, a professor of government at the University of Texas in Austin. He says it is crucial to know what language people speak, where they were born and how long they had been in the United States to accurately assess their views.

In a recent nationwide survey of 1,600 Hispanics by the Tomas Rivera Center in Claremont, Calif., for example, 71 percent of Hispanics from Central America said they believe that U.S. society discriminates against Hispanics, but only 42 percent of Cuban Americans agreed. Just over half of Mexican American respondents, by far the largest group of Hispanics in the United States, shared that view.

Poverty rates vary widely within both the Hispanic and Asian American communities, often depending on when, and from what country, members emigrated. In Los Angeles, unemployment is only 4 percent among Korean Americans, who flocked to the United States in the 1960s, but it is 21 percent among newly arrived Cambodian refugees. In New York, 32 percent of Dominican Americans are poor, but only 11 percent of Colombian Americans are.

For Hispanics or Asian Americans who live in the cocoon of urban ethnic enclaves, it may take a foray into other regions to make them appreciate the prejudice faced by others. Juan Santiago, 30, an office manager in the Bronx, N.Y., whose parents emigrated from the Dominican Republic, says he never experienced discrimination growing up in his heavily Dominican neighborhood. Then he went out to New Mexico as a foreman on a construction job.

"All the workers were Mexican, and the white owners had no respect for them. The work was very hard, the pay was

From *The Washington Post National Weekly Edition,* October 23–29, 1995, pp. 10-11.

HOW HISPANICS, ASIANS SEE THEMSELVES AND HOW OTHERS SEE THEM

Poll respondents were given a list of things some people have mentioned as reasons for the economic and social problems that some Hispanics and Asian Americans face today and were asked if each one is a major reason for those problems.

Is this a major reason for Hispanics' problems?	Hispanics who said 'yes'	Whites who said 'yes'	Blacks who said 'yes'	Asians who said 'yes'
Lack of jobs	68%	42%	74%	53%
Language difficulties	66%	56%	59%	59%
Lack of educational opportunities	51%	46%	63%	53%
Breakup of the Hispanic family	45%	28%	38%	22%
Past and present discrimination	43%	31%	58%	29%
Lack of motivation and an unwillingness to work hard	41%	25%	19%	32%

Those polled were asked the same question about Asians:

Is this a major reason for Asians' problems?	Asians who said 'yes'	Whites who said 'yes'	Blacks who said 'yes'	Hispanics who said 'yes'
Language difficulties	44%	44%	52%	37%
Lack of jobs	34%	31%	46%	43%
Past and present discrimination	20%	24%	41%	31%
Lack of educational opportunities	17%	18%	31%	31%
Breakup of the Asian family	14%	16%	27%	35%
Lack of motivation and an unwillingness to work hard	10%	22%	23%	20%

Polling data comes from a survey of 1,970 randomly selected adults interviewed in August and September, including 802 whites, 474 blacks, 352 Asian Americans and 252 Hispanics. The minority groups were oversampled to obtain large enough subsamples to analyze reliably. Margin of sampling error for the overall results is plus or minus 3 percentage points. The margins of sampling error for the four subsamples ranged from 4 percentage points for the white subsample to 7 percentage points for the Hispanic subsample. Sampling error is only one of many potential sources of error in public opinion polls.

SOURCES: Washington Post/Kaiser Family Foundation/Harvard University survey

THE WASHINGTON POST

very low, and there was no overtime," he recounts. "They tried to exploit me, too, but I knew my rights and I wouldn't let them. Until, then, I never really understood what discrimination was."

BUT LIFE INSIDE ETHNIC GHETTOS ALSO CAN CONFINE and isolate, discouraging immigrants from joining American society at large and reinforcing others' misperceptions about them. In interviews, many foreign-born Hispanics and Asian

Americans said they cling to immigrant communities, speaking to bosses and salesclerks in their native tongues and rarely meeting white Americans.

Yu Hui Chang, 35, a waitress in lower Manhattan, N.Y., says she and her husband work 12 hours a day in Chinese restaurants and rarely see their young son. Speaking through an interpreter in the cramped office of a Chinatown labor union, the Shanghai-born woman says she feels trapped in her community but is determined to succeed in her new country.

"It is very hard to be a woman in Chinatown," says Chang, who emigrated in 1982. "My life is nothing but working, working all the time. In China, I thought America was full of gold, and I still have the dream of taking that gold back home, but I can never save any."

Like Chang, the great majority of Asian Americans and Hispanics who responded to the Post/Kaiser/Harvard poll said they believe strongly in the American dream, but 46 percent of Asian Americans and 55 percent of Hispanics said they are farther from achieving it than they were a decade ago.

Both groups singled out hard work and family unity as keys to success here, and both singled out the same major obstacles: lack of good jobs, crime and violence, high taxes and the gap between their incomes and the rising cost of living. All agreed that learning English is crucial.

"You have to learn the language of the enemy to survive," says Juan Garcia, a Dominican-born man who manages a discount clothing shop in Washington Heights, a largely Hispanic section of Manhattan. "I've been here 13 years and my English is still poor, so I can't always defend myself," he adds in Spanish, describing his humiliation at being turned away from a fast-food counter when he could not explain his order.

Nonetheless, Garcia says he would not want to give up the comforts of American life. His son, 16, is studying computers and dreams of becoming a doctor. "Once you become civilized, you don't want to go back to a village with no lights or running water," he says.

Nationwide, the poll suggested that Asian Americans as a group think they have done much better economically than Hispanics think they have done. Asian Americans also have a far more optimistic view of their chances for success. Eighty-four percent of Asian Americans guessed that the average Asian American is at least as well off as the average white American, and 58 percent said they have the same or better chance of becoming wealthy.

Hispanics, on the other hand, tended to be more pessimistic and to believe others' critical views of them. In the poll, 74 percent of Hispanics said the average Hispanic is worse off than the average white, and 41 percent cited low motivation and unwillingness to work as a reason for their lack of advancement. Yet studies show that Hispanics have an unusually high level of participation in the work force.

"We are very susceptible to what others think about us, so we absorb those negative stereotypes in defiance of the facts," says Cecilia Munoz, Washington director of the National Council of La Raza, a Hispanic advocacy group. A 1994 survey by the council found that Hispanics have been most often depicted on TV and in films as "poor, of low status, lazy, deceptive, and criminals."

In the Post/Kaiser/Harvard poll, only one-quarter of white Americans cited unwillingness to work as a major obstacle for Hispanics; many more agreed with Hispanics that language problems and lack of educational opportunities are their biggest problems. In assessing the status of Asian Americans, whites cited only language difficulties as a major problem, suggesting that whites believe that Asian Americans face fewer barriers than Hispanics face.

More Hispanics say they thought they face the most discrimination as a group, but despite their relative economic success, more Asian Americans say they and their relatives and friends had experienced prejudice personally.

A majority of both groups agree that minorities should work their way up without special government help but also insist that government should protect their rights, for example by enacting tougher laws against workplace discrimination. And in interviews, many Hispanics and Asian Americans expressed deep concerns about a rising tide of anti-immigrant feeling.

Some specialists say the recent political furor over illegal immigrants has exacerbated a false impression that hordes of foreigners are arriving on U.S. shores. In the poll, the respondents guessed that 65 percent of Hispanics in the United States were born in foreign countries. According to the National Council of La Raza, only 33 percent of Hispanics were born in foreign countries.

"I see many Latinos trying to distance themselves from their roots as they react to the wave of anti-immigrant sentiment," says Harry Pachon, who directs the Tomas Rivera Center. "But I keep asking, how does an Anglo driving down the street pick out which Latino is native-born, which is a refugee, which is undocumented?"

IN OTHER WAYS, THE POLL SUGGESTED THAT MOST respondents are not especially hostile to either ethnic minority. Three-quarters said it "wouldn't make much difference" to the country if the number of Hispanics or Asian Americans were to increase significantly. Less than one-quarter said it would be a "bad thing" if either group were to grow substantially.

Yet the perception of growing xenophobia has created tensions between foreign-born and more established Hispanics and Asian Americans. Even in a community such as Jackson Heights, in Queens, N.Y., where Korean, Cuban, Vietnamese and Colombian immigrants live in tolerant proximity, second-generation residents expressed concern in interviews that illiterate or illegal newcomers are creating a negative image of all ethnic minorities.

"People have this idea that we are coming here in industrial quantities to invade America and go on welfare. The truth is that most of us were born here, we are working hard or going to school," says Mario Vargas, 22, a college student whose parents emigrated from Colombia. "But these days, the stereotypes are making it harder for the rest of us."

NEIGHBORING FAITHS

HOW WILL AMERICANS COPE WITH INCREASING RELIGIOUS DIVERSITY?

DIANA L. ECK

Diana L. Eck, Ph.D. '76, professor of comparative religion and Indian studies, chairs the Committee on the Study of Religion in the Faculty of Arts and Sciences and is also director of the Pluralism Project. The project's multimedia CD-ROM, On Common Ground: World Religions in America, *will be published in early 1997 by Columbia University Press. Eck's most recent book is* Encountering God: A Spiritual Journey from Bozeman to Banaras *(Beacon Press, 1993). This article is slightly adapted from Eck's 1996 Phi Beta Kappa Oration, delivered during Commencement week.*

I first came to Harvard as a student of the culture and religions of India. I was fascinated by India's many religious traditions—the interrelations, tensions, and movements of Hindu, Buddhist, Jain, Muslim, and Sikh traditions over many centuries in a complex culture. But never did I imagine as I began teaching here in the late 1970s that the very interests that drew me to India would lead me in the 1990s to the study of the United States. So how is it that a scholar of comparative religion and Indian studies has spent the past five years studying America—furtively at first, fearful to be treading on the territory of some of Harvard's most distinguished scholars, then unapologetically, flagrantly, even zealously?

That intellectual passage from India to America began here at Harvard. The circumstances that drove me to study America raise important issues—for Harvard, for the United States, and perhaps for the world. They are issues all of us will encounter in a world shaped by a new geopolitical and a new "georeligious" reality.

For me, this journey began in the academic year 1989–90. Suddenly the contextual ground under my own feet as a scholar and teacher began to shift. In the past, I had always had several students from India in my classes on India, but in that year, their numbers increased. Only now, they were not from India, but were Indian Americans, born and raised in San Antonio, Baltimore, or Cleveland. They were, as I discovered, the children of the first generation of immigrants who had settled in America after the passage of the 1965 immigration act. That historic event finally removed the legal legacy of racism that had been built into immigration legislation from the first Chinese exclusion act in 1882 to the Johnson Reed Act in 1924, which effectively barred Asian immigrants for four decades. The 1965 policy opened the door again for immigration from Asia and from other parts of the world.

There were Muslims from Providence, Hindus from Baltimore, Sikhs from Chicago, Jains from New Jersey. They represented the emergence in America of a new cultural and religious reality.

As a scholar of India, I had taken note of the effects of the new immigration on that country, the so-called "brain drain," as thousands of Indian professionals, doctors, and scientists left India for the United States. I have to admit, however, that I had never stopped to think what this would mean for the United States until the children of this first generation of Indian immigrants reached college age and enrolled in my classes at Harvard that year. There were Muslims from Providence, Hindus from Baltimore, Sikhs from Chicago, Jains from New Jersey. They represented the emergence in America of a new cultural and religious reality.

From *Harvard Magazine*, September/October 1996, pp. 38-44.

Some came from very secular families and knew little of their Indian heritage. Others had grown up in the new Hindu or Muslim culture of temples and Islamic centers their parents had begun to establish here in the United States. Some had been to Muslim youth leadership camps, organized by the Islamic Society of North America. Some had been to a Hindu summer camp at Rajarajeswari Pitha in the Poconos, or to a family Vedanta camp at Arsha Vidya Gurukulam in Saylorsburg, Pennsylvania. Some were involved as founding members of the Jain Youth of North America. Straddling two worlds, critically appropriating two cultures, they lived in perpetual inner dialogue between the distinctive cultures of their parents and grandparents and the forceful, multiple currents of American culture. In their own struggles with identity lay the very issues that were beginning to torment the soul of the United States.

The new questions that arose were not only those that underlay the foreign cultures requirement of the Core Curriculum—how we might understand some "other" civilization so different from our own. Other questions pushed themselves to the fore: What does it mean to speak of "our own" culture? Who do "we" mean when we say "we?" How are "difference" and "otherness" defined, and by whom? The word "multicultural" signaled the fact that every dimension of American culture had become more complex. Racial issues became multisided, with Hispanic and Latino, Korean and Filipino, Chinese and Indian perspectives. Religious diversity shattered the paradigm of an America the sociologist Will Herberg had confidently described as a "three religion country"—Protestant, Catholic, and Jewish. By the 1990s, there were Hindus and Sikhs, Buddhists and Jains. There were more Muslims than Episcopalians, more Muslims than Presbyterians, perhaps soon more Muslims than Jews.

The sons and daughters of the first generation from South Asia rose at Harvard to become some 5 percent of the Harvard undergraduate population. In the spring of 1993, when that first class graduated, I slipped into the balcony at Memorial Church for the Baccalaureate service and sat with the families of Mukesh Prasad and Maitri Chowdhury, the first marshals of the Harvard and Radcliffe graduating classes that year—both Hindus. Maitri recited a hymn from the Rig-Veda in ancient Sanskrit. It was a new Harvard. It had happened in four years.

The Puritans founded Harvard College to provide an educated Christian ministry for the churches. Before Judah Monis, a Sephardic Jew, was hired to teach Hebrew in 1722, he publically converted to Christianity. But both Judah Monis and Cotton Mather would be astounded at Harvard in the 1990s—its Chinese and Korean Christian fellowships, its diverse and vibrant Jewish community, its rapidly growing Islamic Society. In December 1994, the newly founded Harvard Buddhist Community observed the Buddha's Enlightenment Day for the first time ever at Harvard. There in the Divinity School's Braun Room, beneath the august portraits of a long lineage of divinity deans, some 50 Harvard students from a dozen Buddhist lineages sat on rows of square zabutons, listening to Pali, Tibetan, and Vietnamese chanting and rising, one by one, to make offerings of incense.

What has happened at Harvard has happened at major universities throughout the country. In the 1990s, universities have become the microcosms and laboratories of a new multicultural and multireligious America. It is not uncommon to have Hindu and Jew, Muslim and Christian in a single rooming group. These changes in university demographics have come not from abroad, but from the rapidly changing cultural and religious landscape of the United States. Harvard's issues, America's issues, have become, increasingly, a fresh recasting of many of India's issues, the world's issues: race, culture, religion, difference, diversity, and whether it is possible to move from diversity to pluralism.

I knew in 1990 that my own teaching context had radically changed and the scope of my academic work would have to change, too. Increasingly, it became clear to me that the very shape of traditional fields of study was inadequate to this new world. In my field, those of us who study Buddhism, Islam, or Hinduism all earn our academic stripes, so to speak, by intensive study in Japan, Egypt, or India, doing language studies, textual editions and translations, fieldwork. And those who study religion in America focus largely on the Protestant mainstream, or perhaps on Catholics, or American Judaism—but not on American Buddhism, not on the Muslims of America, not on the Sikhs of America. And those historians who focus their work on what has become known as ethnic studies are curiously silent about the religious traditions of America's ethnic minorities—the old Islamic traditions of the African slaves, the old Chinese temples in Montana and Idaho, or the early Sikh communities in California's Imperial Valley.

The Muslim Community Center on New Hampshire Avenue in Silver Spring, Maryland.

IN 1991, THE PLURALISM PROJECT AT HARVARD SET OUT TO STUDY multireligious America, beginning right here in Boston. Our research seminar visited the mosque in Quincy built in the shadow of the great cranes of the shipyards by Lebanese immigrants who came early in the century, and we found that there were some 20 other mosques and Islamic centers that are part of the Islamic Council of New England—in Dorchester, Wayland, Cambridge. We went to the spectacular new Sri Lakshmi temple in Ashland, a temple designed by Hindu ritual architects with tall towers decorated with the images of the gods and consecrated with the waters of the Ganges mingled with the waters of the Mississippi, the Colorado, and the Merrimack rivers. We visited half a dozen other Hindu communities in Boston, and two Sikh gurdwaras in Millis and Milford, and a Jain temple in Norwood, housed in a former Swedish Lutheran church. We found a dozen Buddhist meditation centers, with their respective Tibetan, Burmese, Korean, and Japanese lineages of instruction. And we visited the temples of the Cambodian Buddhists in Lowell and Lynn, the Vietnamese in Roslindale and Revere, the Chinese in Quincy and Lexington. Eventually, we published *World Religions in Boston*, a documentary guide to a city whose Asian population had doubled in 10 years, now a multireligious city.

It was clear that what was true of Boston might well be true of many other American cities. So the Pluralism Project sent a research team of students, multiethnic and multire-

Stupa containing relics of the Buddha, presented as a gift from Thailand to the Jodo Shinshu Buddhist Mission of North America in 1935. The stupa is built on the roof of the Buddhist Church of San Francisco on Pine Street.

ligious, to study "hometown" America, fanning out across the United States every summer for three years. We were guided by three kinds of questions. First, who is here now in the 1990s? How many Hindu temples are there in Chicago? How many mosques in Oklahoma City? How many Buddhist temples in Houston? Second, how are these traditions changing as they take root in American soil? And third, how is America changing as Americans of many religions begin to appropriate this new multireligious reality and come to terms once again with our foundational commitment to religious freedom and, consequently, religious pluralism?

We found many remarkable developments. For example, Buddhist communities widely separated in Asia are now neighbors in Los Angeles, Seattle, and Chicago—Vietnamese, Cambodian, Thai, Chinese, Japanese, Korean, and Tibetan Buddhists. Here in America, these Buddhist communities are just beginning to know one another and to meet the distinctive communities of "new Buddhists"—Americans of all races who have come to Buddhism through its meditation practices and its ethics. The Buddhist Sangha Council of Southern California, the Buddhist Council of the Midwest, the Texas Buddhist Association are evidence of the beginning of a new "ecumenical" Buddhism. There are American Buddhist newspapers and magazines, feminist Zen sitting groups, exemplary Buddhist AIDS hospice projects. Today Buddhism is an American religion.

We visited communities that represent the entire spectrum of Islam in America: African American communities, Muslim immigrants from Syria and Lebanon whose forebears came in the early 1900s, and new immigrant Muslims from Africa and South Asia. All of them are in the process of working out what it is to be both Muslim and American. They gather in huge annual conventions in Dayton or in Kansas City to discuss the Muslim family in America or the American public schools. The Islamic Medical Association tackles ethical issues in medical practice, while the Washington-based American Muslim Council facilitates Islamic participation in the American political process.

We found that most of the new religious institutions are invisible. The first generation of American mosques could be found in places like a former watch factory in Queens, a U-Haul dealership in Pawtucket, Rhode Island, a gymnasium in Oklahoma City, and a former mattress showroom in Northridge, California. There were Hindu temples in a huge warehouse in Queens, a former YMCA in New Jersey, or a former Methodist church in Minneapolis. Most of the Vietnamese Buddhist temples of Denver, Houston, and Orange County were in ranch-style homes. Because of the invisibility of these first-generation religious institutions, many Americans, understandably, have remained quite unaware of these new communities.

The past decades, however, have also seen the beginnings of a striking new visible landscape. There are new mosques and Islamic centers in Manhattan and Phoenix, rising from the cornfields outside Toledo and from the suburbs of Chicago and Houston. There are multimillion-dollar Hindu temples, like the Sri Venkateswara temple in Pittsburgh, the Bharatiya Temple in the northern suburbs of Detroit, the spectacular Sri Meenakshi Temple south of Houston, the Ganesha temple in Nashville, and dozens of others. The Buddhists have made a striking architectural imprint, with, for example, the huge Hsi Lai temple in Hacienda Heights, California, and the Jade Temple in Houston. In the western Chicago suburb of Bartlett, the Jains have built a large new temple. To the north in Palatine is a striking new hexagonal gurdwara of the Sikhs.

There are some neighborhoods where all this is visible in short compass. For example, driving out New Hampshire Avenue, one of the great spokes of Washington, D.C., into Silver Spring, Maryland, just beyond the Beltway there is a stretch of road a few miles long where one passes the new Cambodian Buddhist temple with its graceful, sloping tiled roof, the Ukrainian Orthodox Church, the Muslim Community Center with its new copper-domed mosque. Farther along is the new Gujarati Hindu temple called Mangal Mandir. The many churches along the way also reveal the new dimensions of America's Christian landscape: Hispanic Pentecostal, Vietnamese Catholic, and Korean evangelical congregations sharing facilities with more traditional English-speaking "mainline" churches.

THE DIVERSITY OF NEW HAMPSHIRE AVENUE, HOWEVER, IS NOT simply a curiosity for a Sunday drive. What it represents has profound implications for every aspect of American public life. What is happening to America as all of us begin to renegotiate the "we" of "We, the people"? That "we" in the United States is increasingly complex, not only culturally and racially, but also religiously What will this religious diversity mean for American electoral politics, for the continuing interpretation of "church-state" issues by the Supreme Court, for American public education and the controversies of school boards, for hospitals and health-care programs with an increasingly diverse patient population, and for colleges and universities with an increasingly multireligious student body? While many Americans are only dimly aware of the changing religious landscape, the issues this new diversity has raised are already on the agenda of virtually every public institution, including Harvard.

New Hampshire Avenue dramatizes the new diversity, but building a pluralist society from that diversity is no easy matter in a world in which the "politics of identity" is busy minting our identities in smaller and smaller coins, and in a world in which religious markers of identity are often presumed to be the most divisive of all differences. American public debate is charged with the power of these issues. Some say such a multicultural and multireligious society is impossible. Their voices have been raised at each and every stage of American immigration—too many Catholics, too many Jews, too many Chinese and Japanese. Those voices are present today, and some of the most extreme have called for the repeal of the 1965 immigration act. Others have insisted there is simply too much *pluribus* and not enough *unum*. And still others would insist that this is a secular society, so why make a point of looking at religious differences at all?

But to ascertain how we—all of us—are doing in this new struggle for America's soul, we have to look not only at race, not only at ethnicity, but at religion. The history of prejudice and stereotype demonstrates that religious insignia and institutions often become key markers of "difference." The persistent attacks on synagogues and Jewish graveyards provide ample testimony to the tactics of hatred. So does the long and continuing history of racist attacks on black churches. Religious insignia, religious markers of identity, and religious institutions come to stand in a public way for the very heart of the community and often become the most visible targets for bigotry and violence.

And so it is as America's new immigrants become increasingly visible as religious minorities. In New Jersey, the dot or *bindi* on the forehead, worn by many Hindu women, stood for the strangeness of the whole Indian immigrant community in the eyes of a racist group calling themselves the "Dotbus-

Above: The Hindu Sri Lakshmi temple in Ashland, Massachusetts. Above left: Priests circle the temple with water to be used in the consecration ceremony, the "mahakumbhabhishekam," in May 1990.

ters." Those who beat Navroze Mody to death in 1987, shouting "Hindu, Hindu, Hindu," did not know or care whether he was a Hindu, but conflated race, religion, and culture in one cry of hatred.

The Pluralism Project has documented the ways in which today's minority religious communities have experienced the violence of attacks on their visible religious institutions. In February 1983, for example, vandals broke into the newly constructed Hindu-Jain Temple in Pittsburgh and smashed all the white marble images of the Hindu deities. The sacred scripture of the Sikhs, housed on a side altar, was torn to pieces. "Leave!" was written across the main altar. In 1993, the temple of a tiny Cambodian Buddhist community in Portland, Maine, was vandalized with an axe, its doorjambs hacked, its doors broken, the contents of the Buddha hall strewn in the front yard, and the words "Dirty Asian Chink, Go Home!" written on the walls. In September 1994, a nearly completed mosque in Yuba City, California, was burned to the ground, leaving its dome and minaret in the ashes of a fire that the sheriff deemed to be arson. There are dozens of these incidents every year, some of them now documented by such groups as the Council on American-Islamic Relations, but most of them noted only in the pages of local newspapers.

The documentary register of acts of violence is easier to assemble than the register of new initiatives of cooperation and understanding, for violence is still deemed more "newsworthy" than cooperation. Yet assembling the evidence of new patterns of interreligious encounter, cooperation, and relationship is also important in discerning how the "we" is being reconfigured in multireligious America. For example, on April 2, 1993, a groundbreaking in Sharon, Massachusetts, brought Jews, Christians, and Muslims together from the Greater Boston area. There on a hillside overlooking the fields of a former horse farm, rabbis and priests, imams and Muslim leaders each turned a shovel of earth for the new Islamic Center of New England. Two weeks later, across the country in Fremont, California, Saint Paul's United Methodist Church and the Islamic Society of the East Bay broke ground together for a new church and a new mosque, to be built side by side on the same property. They named their common access road "Peace Terrace," and they are now next-door neighbors. "We want to set an example for the world," said one of the Muslim leaders.

All across America, there are new interreligious councils—in cities like Tulsa, Oklahoma, and Lincoln, Nebraska. The Interreligious Council of Southern California supported the appointment of a Buddhist chaplain in the California State Senate and backed the Sikhs in their petition to the Los Angeles Police Department to be allowed to wear the turban while serving as policemen. The Interfaith Conference of Metropolitan Washington, D.C., brought people of all religious communities together in March 1994 in the wake of the Hebron massacre. Because of new relationships of trust, the head of the Washington board of rabbis offered prayers right there on New Hampshire Avenue at the Muslim Community Center.

The public symbolic acknowledgment of America's diversity is also becoming more visible. In April 1990, for example, the city council of Savannah, Georgia, issued a proclamation in which Islam was recognized as having been "a vital part of the development of the United States of America and the city of Savannah." On June 25, 1991, for the first time in history, a Muslim imam, Siraj Wahaj of Brooklyn, opened a session of the U.S. House of Representatives with prayer. On February 20, 1996, at the end of the month of Ramadan, Hillary Clinton welcomed Muslims to the White House for the first Eid celebration ever to take place there. She said, "This celebration is an American event. We are a nation of immigrants who have long drawn on our diverse religious traditions and faiths for the strength and courage that make America great."

There on a hillside overlooking farm fields, rabbis and priests, imams and Muslim leaders each turned a shovel of earth for the new Islamic Center of New England.

The sacred Hindu thread ceremony, the "upanayana," at Sri Venkateswara Temple, Bridgewater, New Jersey.

A FEW YEARS AGO, MY HARVARD COLLEAGUE SAMUEL HUNTINGTON, a distinguished political scientist, wrote of the deep religious currents that so profoundly shape the great civilizations of the world.* In the new post-Cold War era, he predicted that "civilizational identity" will have a major role in the coming political realignment. He contended that the Confucian, Islamic, and Hindu worlds will be forces to reckon with in the geopolitical arena and he foresees a "clash of civilizations." But where exactly are these worlds and civilizations, we might ask, with Hindus in Leicester, Durban, Toronto, and Houston? With huge mosques in Paris, London, Chicago, and Toledo? One of the decisive facts of the 1980s and 1990s has been the tremendous migration of peoples from one nation to another, both as immigrants and as refugees. Every part of the globe is experiencing the demographic changes of these migrations. Today, the Islamic world is no longer somewhere

*Samuel P. Huntington, "The Clash of Civilizations?" *Foreign Affairs*, volume 72, number 3 (summer, 1993).

Today, the Islamic world is no longer somewhere else, in some other part of the world; instead Chicago, with its 50 mosques and nearly half a million Muslims, is part of the Islamic world.

else, in some other part of the world; instead Chicago, with its 50 mosques and nearly half a million Muslims, is part of the Islamic world. America today is part of the Islamic, the Hindu, the Confucian world. It is precisely the interpenetration of ancient civilizations and cultures that is the hallmark of the late twentieth century. *This* is our new georeligious reality. The map of the world in which we now live cannot be color-coded as to its Christian, Muslim, or Hindu identity, but each part of the world is marbled with the colors and textures of the whole.

The plurality of religious traditions and cultures challenges people in every part of the world today, including the United States, which is now the most religiously diverse country on earth. Diversity we have—here in America and here at Harvard. It is not an ideology invented by the multicultural enthusiasts of the left. It is the new reality of our society. Diversity we have. But what is pluralism? First, pluralism is not diversity alone, but the energetic engagement with that diversity. Diversity can and has meant the creation of religious ghettoes with little traffic between or among them. In this new world of religious diversity, pluralism is not a given, but an achievement. In the world into which we now move, diversity without engagement, without a fabric of relationship, will be increasingly difficult and increasingly dangerous.

Second, pluralism will require not just tolerance, but the active seeking of understanding. Tolerance is a necessary public virtue, but it does not require Christians and Muslims, Hindus, Jews, and ardent secularists to know anything about one another. Tolerance is simply too thin a foundation for a world of religious differences. It does nothing to remove our ignorance of one another, and leaves in place the stereotype, the half-truth, the fear that underlie old patterns of division and violence. In the world into which we now move, our ignorance of one another will be increasingly costly.

And finally, pluralism is not simply relativism. The new paradigm of pluralism does not require us to leave our identities and our commitments behind, for pluralism is the encounter of commitments. It means holding our deepest differences, even our religious differences, not in isolation, but in relationship to one another. The language of pluralism is that of dialogue and encounter, give and take, criticism and self-criticism. In the world into which we now move, it is a language we will have to learn.

Whether in India or America, whether on New Hampshire Avenue or at Harvard University, the challenge for all of us today is how to shape societies, nations, neighborhoods, and universities that now replicate and potentially may reconfigure the differences that have long divided humankind.

Above: Masjid Al-Khair in Youngstown, Ohio. Above left: New construction supervised by Phramaha Prasert Kavissaro, abbot at Wat Buddhanusorn, a Thai Buddhist temple in Fremont, California.

THE CHINESE DIASPORA

PETER KWONG

Hundreds of years before there was any talk of an "Asian miracle," vast numbers of Chinese left their homeland in search of fortune abroad. Most, from southern China, traveled first to the area that is now Laos, Myanmar, and Vietnam, then farther afield, into what is now Thailand, Indonesia, and Malaysia. The California gold rush lured some, while economic growth in Latin America beckoned others. Often they left China out of desperation—because of land shortages, wars, famines, or intrusive governments. Many left home with little except their dreams of returning as wealthy men.

Now the wealth created by the ethnic Chinese consists of a great deal more than the Chinatowns of major cities. The Chinese businessmen who live across Southeast Asia have been the driving force behind the region's economic explosion. In Thailand ethnic Chinese make up 10 percent of the population but control 81 percent of the market value of listed companies. In Indonesia they compose 3.5 percent of the population but control 73 percent of such capital. Most of Asia's estimated one hundred billionaires are ethnic Chinese.

Some of these tycoons have also transformed parts of North America. For example, the moneyed elite from Hong Kong own sizable portions of San Francisco's downtown area and reside in large Mediterranean-style mansions in the hills surrounding the city. In the mid-1980s, they began investing in Canada, where the government has promised permanent residence to people who have a net worth of at least a half-million Canadian dollars and who are willing to invest significant sums in the Canadian economy. From 1985 to 1994, a little over 9.7 percent of all immigrants to Canada were businesspeople, and by 1994 more than half of those usually affluent immigrants came from either Taiwan or Hong Kong. By the end of 1994, according to one estimate, ethnic Chinese had added a net worth of $15 billion to Canada's economy. Toronto and Montreal both benefited from this movement of overseas Chinese capital, and Vancouver, partly because of its location and climate, has been particularly blessed by some of East Asia's wealthiest investors, who now control 25 percent of its most expensive and prestigious neighborhood, the West End.

When the totals are added up, overseas Chinese are said to control more than $2.5 trillion of wealth. For perspective, compare that with the 1995 gross domestic product in Japan of $5.1 trillion, or the figure for the United States of $7.2 trillion.

In a sense, many of these Chinese have fulfilled their ancestors' dreams of coming home rich. The entrepreneurs who fared so well in Asia and North America have been fueling mainland China's double-digit growth since free-market reforms opened its economy in 1979. By 1993, 69 percent of direct foreign investment in China, totaling $47.5 billion, came from ethnic Chinese in Hong Kong. Taiwan, according to China, had by 1993 put up $6.4 billion, or 9.3 percent of total foreign investment in the mainland economy. (The true figure is likely to be much higher.)

The recent success of Chinese expatriates has been so stunning that businesspeople everywhere are searching for explanations, much like when pundits speculated on the successes of Japan in the 1970s and 1980s. Was the secret ingredient teamwork? Company loyalty? A stronger work ethic? Now economic theorists are studying Chinese culture and history, and Confucius has become the patron saint of entrepreneurs and developing economies worldwide. The overseas Chinese,

Powerful overseas Chinese are investing in China, to be sure. But it's not just out of love of ancient homeland. It's business.

Reprinted with permission from *Worldbusiness*, May/June 1996, pp. 26-31.

long the outcasts of Asia, are now the international business community's model citizens.

Ask Casey K. C. Foung why the majority of investors who fueled and have capitalized on the Asian boom are of Chinese descent, and he has a simple answer. "When Asian countries sought foreign investment to develop, Western capital was not there," says Foung, a New York resident who is the founder of Arch Associates, a medium-size quilt-making firm with extensive operations in China. "When China decided to open, the only capital came from the overseas Chinese. China would have preferred infusion from high-tech American and European corporations, but the West was reluctant to venture in without legal guarantees: property rights, tax laws, price deregulation, international arbitration. Overseas Chinese capital took the risk."

Members of the Chinese "diaspora" come from a 600-year tradition of enterprising fortune seekers who escaped China's strict government controls in order to ply their trades. Most of them came from two southeastern provinces, Guangdong and Fujian, on the cultural periphery of the Chinese empire. Operating in their new homelands without the protection of China's government, they readily adapted to different trading systems and governing styles and established import-export businesses through commercial networks, often made up of Chinese who spoke the same dialect.

For more than 300 years, ethnic Chinese around Asia controlled rice mills, light manufacturing, and money lending. They owned plantations, oil mills, timber industries, manufacturing concerns, and the bulk of small retail shops selling staples. They thereby made themselves indispensable to the various indigenous populations and later to the imperialists who ruled them. "The Chinese," wrote T. M. Ward, a British physician stationed in Malacca in 1827, "are the most enterprising, the most opulent, the most industrious and the most determined in pursuit of wealth."

British, Dutch, and French colonial rulers recognized this indispensability and capitalized on it, giving the ethnic Chinese throughout Asia special status as go-betweens, especially during the nineteenth century, colonialism's peak. Their businesses also provided the most reliable and readily available tax revenue for colonial governments, and because of that these governments barred the Chinese from all but their traditional trading occupations.

Understandably, the non-Chinese who lagged behind economically were often resentful, accusing their Chinese residents of dominating their economies by dubious means and unfair practices. After World War II, postcolonial nationalist governments in the region generally became hostile to Chinese residents, and after the fall of the nationalists in 1949, suspected them of having ties to the communists. Almost without exception, the ethnic Chinese experienced severe persecution and restrictions. In Thailand and Indonesia, they were forced to assimilate by adopting local names. In Malaysia, the government set up impediments through occupational, educational, and other quotas favoring ethnic *bumiputras*, or "sons of the soil." There have been periods of intense racial violence, such as in Malaysia in the 1960s and 1970s, and in Indonesia in 1965.

Because of the centuries of persecution, overseas Chinese have developed a deep-rooted sense of insecurity and impermanence. "We'll be here as long as there's money to be made," is a frequent refrain of theirs throughout Asia. This outlook, not unlike that of an illegal street vendor ready to roll up his merchandise and disappear before the police arrive, is reflected in the way in which many smaller overseas Chinese businesses operate. They favor gutsy investments in industries such as garment manufacturing, shoes, toys, textiles, plastics, and electronics, while spreading their investments around the world in order to minimize risks from political or economic collapse in their own fields. Deals are often marked by access to reliable, timely information and quick action, both of which are made possible by far-flung business networks forged along the lines of kinship and common dialects—as well as by the family structure of the businesses themselves.

"When it's all in the family, things are more flexible; there is more trust," says the director of a publicly traded real estate company in Hong Kong. (Like many overseas Chinese business executives, the executive shuns publicity, asking to remain anonymous.) "There isn't so much of a corporate

FOLLOW THE MONEY

Foreign direct investment in China, 1979–1994, in billions of dollars

Hong Kong	**$67.3**
Taiwan*	**9.8**
United States	**6.1**
Japan	**5.3**
Singapore	**2.7**

*Analysts estimate that the Chinese government may underreport Taiwanese investment in China by as much as 50 percent because a large percentage of Taiwanese money is invested in China via Hong Kong companies.

Source: *Statistical Yearbook of China 1995* and *Overseas Chinese Business Networks in Asia*

hierarchy. People genuinely work for the family's interests, not to prove themselves and climb the corporate ladder. Traditionally, decisions are made more quickly. There's no need to jump through the hoops of board meetings and shareholders' meetings."

Of course, there is nothing peculiarly *Chinese* about these networks or patriarchal family businesses. "Just look at the Rockefeller family," says a Chinese American with a master's degree in business from Columbia University who once worked for a major United States corporation. He is now helping to restructure his family's manufacturing business, which has operations in Asia, North America, and Latin America. "There is nothing ethnic about it. American businesses start out small, too, and they have the same family-oriented structure. But as the business grows, accountability and reporting become more and more important. Westerners don't know much about the Chinese, so they like to romanticize them. And they are wrong!"

Says Peter Li, a Hong Kong–born sociology professor at the University of Saskatchewan: "The West has not been paying attention [to ethnic Chinese business development], and when it finally did, it was surprised and felt locked out. When you don't know what's going on, you look for all sorts of cultural explanations. This happened to the Jews as well."

The crudest, most commonly expressed cultural explanation is that Chinese people succeed because of their work ethic: Chinese entrepreneurs are the very embodiment of diligence and thrift. Herman Kahn, the founder of a United States think tank, the Hudson Institute, observed as early as 1979 that so-called neo-Confucian societies create dedicated, motivated, responsible, and educated individuals with an enhanced sense of commitment, organizational identity, and loyalty to various institutions. These societies, Kahn argued, are superior to those of the West in the pursuit of industrialization, affluence, and modernization.

There are overseas Chinese who promote this characterization as well. Wang Gungwu, a prominent Indonesian-born historian and a retired vice chancellor of the University of Hong Kong, has observed many ethnic Chinese striving to embrace their historic culture. For example, dozens of conferences on the overseas Chinese have been held in Hong Kong, Taiwan, Singapore, the United States, France, and the Netherlands, with numerous panels discussing such matters as the role of Chinese culture in business.

Mainland China too invites overseas experts to seminars and conferences, on such topics as "Socialism with Chinese Characteristics," or on the capitalist reforms instituted by Deng Xiaoping. Overseas Chinese parents previously uninterested in Chinese culture are now pushing their children to learn the Chinese language and study their heritage in order to be in a better position to exploit the new opportunities proliferating through ethnic ties. For example, during a 1989 conference on Confucianism held in China, China's president, Jiang Zemin, appealed to overseas Chinese to show support for China's precious cultural heritage. The overseas Chinese have, at times, answered such calls, such as when they donated $700,000 for the reconstruction of a shrine to the Yellow Emperor (the mythical ancestor of all Chinese people) in central China.

AT HOME ABROAD

Population and percentage of ethnic Chinese in selected countries

Country	Chinese population	% of total population
Taiwan	20,370,000	97.0%
Myanmar	7,805,000	17.5
Indonesia	6,552,000	3.5
Hong Kong	6,174,000	98.0
Thailand	5,800,000	10.0
Malaysia	5,510,000	29.0
Singapore	2,079,000	77.0
United States	1,645,500	0.7
Philippines	1,200,000	2.0
Vietnam	1,000,000	1.4
Canada	587,000	2.2
Macao	446,200	97.0
Cambodia	250,000	2.5
Japan	110,000	0.9
Laos	50,000	1.3

Sources: *Overseas Chinese Business Networks in Asia,* by the East Asia Analytical Unit of the Australian Department of Foreign Affairs and Trade; 1990 United States Census; 1991 Canadian Census; United States State Department; World Bank

One of neo-Confucianism's top promoters is Singapore's senior minister, Lee Kuan Yew. Lee is a former Anglophile, who is proud of his Cambridge University education. His is a well-ordered society, buttressed by Lee's interpretation of neo-Confucianism. He has been outspoken among those attributing Asian successes to "Asian values," often a euphemism for strong rulers, obedient citizens, and hard work. Lee argues that democracy as understood and practiced in the West, is not conducive to rapid economic growth and that Asians strongly desire that kind of growth.

This new love of Confucianism—by people in business, no less—is strange. In the Confucian world, merchants were always frowned upon because their main motivation was profit instead of learning. And although China's ruling bureaucracies historically colluded with merchants to control the peasant population, and merchants were sometimes allowed to elevate their status by paying off officials, merchants were generally kept at the very bottom of the Confucian social ladder.

Starting in the late nineteenth century, every Chinese leader who attempted to pull China out of the backwardness and misery of the feudal age saw Confucianism as a curse. Getting rid of its pervasive, stultifying influence was critical, they thought, if China was to emerge as a modern nation in the twentieth century.

Coastal traders from southern China in the 1700s and 1800s sailed across the South China Sea to escape the restrictions placed on them by the Confucian state. They went as far as they could from the seat of Confucian authority—Beijing—in pursuit of the freedom to trade and make a profit. All the Asian economic miracles have so far occurred on the periphery of China's Confucian civilization: Japan, South Korea, Taiwan, Hong Kong, Singapore, and now the special economic zones in coastal China. These booming areas are very much heirs to the old colonial treaty ports, areas that were the most exposed to the influences of Western civilization in the nineteenth and twentieth centuries.

"I'm successful not because I'm Chinese," says Casey Foung, the New York–based executive. "I'm not Chinese. I grew up an American in the United States, and had to learn Chinese late in life. I am successful precisely because I am American, bringing American know-how to the Chinese. Americans can be helpful in Chinese economic development, and they can take advantage of their knowledge of marketing, advertising, international finance. The Chinese are so new to this that they can use any help they can get. That's precisely what I did."

Foung's vision contrasts dramatically with other theories about why members of the Chinese diaspora have been so successful and in turn what it takes to be successful in China and the rest of Asia. If success is implicitly attributed to membership in an exclusive group, doesn't that mean that competition is unfairly stacked against people who aren't of that group? Overseas Chinese businesses *do* help one another, pool their resources, and feed one another information within their business networks. But too frequently, all that is distilled into a simple cultural explanation: To do business with the Chinese, you have to be Chinese. At the very least, Westerners feel they need *guanxi*, connections to break into the networks of this alien culture, or a Chinese mediator who can provide such connections.

"Old-boy" networks based on college affiliation, club memberships, or ethnicity are common in the United States and elsewhere, but knowing the right people can be even more important in an environment where the legal system is weak, as in China. In this sense, men such as Singapore's Lee cannot claim to share in China's socialist values, so Confucian culture becomes a form of *guanxi*. For example, at the Second World Chinese Entrepreneurs Convention in Hong Kong in 1993, Lee enthusiastically hobnobbed with some of the top overseas Chinese businesspeople, such as Hong Kong's Li Ka-shing, the head of Hutchison Whampoa, and Malaysia's Robert Kuok, who controls Shangri-La Hotels and Resorts, stressing that *guanxi* is an important advantage of the overseas Chinese that they should put to use as they compete against Western rivals for business opportunities in China. *Guanxi*, Lee said, will be useful for about twenty years, until China develops a legal system that will assuage foreign investors.

One businessman, who as a college student in the United States in the 1960s was a Maoist but is now an investor in chemical factories in China, doesn't underestimate the importance of having an understanding of language and culture that overseas Chinese might bring to the negotiating table. But their expertise often boils down to something far more vulgar than a deep knowledge of China's history, language, or literature. "When you operate in Asia, you are talking about doing business in areas where there are no written laws," he says. "Doing business means dealing with officials and bureaucrats at all levels and bribing them to leave you alone. The real advantage for Chinese expatriates is that the officials expect you to understand that. They find it easier to open their mouth to ask for bribes openly."

The overheated economy of the mainland is still hobbled by a myriad of bureaucratic restraints. All new ventures there require commercial permits; licenses to buy, own, sell, or lease property; land-use permits; construction permits; licenses to import raw materials; permission to exchange currency—the list goes on and on. "Doing business in China is a constant problem," says a manufacturer from Taiwan who recently set up a factory in the city of Changchun, in the northern province of Jilin. "First you spend a lot of money to obtain licenses. Then you entertain local officials. You pay high rents, you bribe [your way] around housing regulations—it cost us a mint just to wine and dine the officials in charge. It took six months to get the operating license, then another three months to get the land permit to build the factory. Doing business in China is not just about the business operation: You are really dealing with people. Without a legal system, you have to satisfy all the people in charge. And although they won't let you do business unless their palms are greased, the officials in charge find it difficult to tell you exactly what they want with people they don't know."

Overseas Chinese entrepreneurs in Asia are accustomed to this kind of bribery, which is prevalent throughout the region. Executives from United States companies, on the other hand, are not. In fact, the Foreign Corrupt Practices Act makes bribery illegal. One Chinese American consultant was hired by a major United States telecommunications company to make a bid for a cable television channel license in China's Sichuan province. Unable to offer any sweet deals, he didn't get the contract. Most of the mainland contracts go to overseas Chinese companies from Hong Kong and Taiwan, although the Japanese and the Germans have been quick to catch on to the realities of doing business in China. The only reason the Japanese don't get more business deals in China is that many Chinese still hate them on account of the Japanese occupation of China more than fifty years ago.

There may be advantages for ethnic Chinese, but businesspeople don't *have* to be Chinese to be successful in China. Westerners can succeed if they understand the bribery system there and are willing to cultivate personal trust with officials. "It's really no big deal for most businesses," the ex-Maoist chemical executive says. "You are only asked to do double accounting. If the cost of a product is $1,000, your invoice should say $1,100. Once the bill is paid, you and the official split the $100. It's no skin off your back. The poor Chinese people are paying for it anyway." After a pause, he adds, "I wish that capitalism would eliminate this corrupt feudal Chinese system—though I feel funny saying this."

Western observers have noted, with a dose of derision, Hong Kong's obsession with the cellular telephone. But the standard phone greeting in Hong Kong these days shows that there is more going on than just idle chatter. Instead of the traditional Chinese "Have you eaten?" comes the rather more modern "What's your game these days?" That constant, obsessive search for the latest business opportunity fits perfectly with the ever-shifting nature of global business. Globalization has meant that, more often than not, goods are not produced in single factories but in several places around the world. For example, a computer's parts may be constructed in various cities around Asia, assembled in Shenzhen, tested and packaged near Boston, and sold in Paris.

The traditional, family-based system is remarkably well suited for fast movement within these subcontracting setups, constantly taking advantage of shifting labor costs, while in a typical Western corporation the hierarchical chain of command makes major changes difficult. "For the Americans, every contract is scrutinized by hundreds of lawyers and bickered over by various departments," says the Hong Kong real estate executive. By the time the cumbersome decision-making machinery reacts, the opportunities in the flexible new markets have already been detected by smaller, more agile firms, and are long gone.

In the 1970s and 1980s, for example, while the West focused its attention on competition from Japan, other parts of Asia presented a host of new business opportunities. Though many Southeast Asian national economies were enjoying an even faster rate of growth than Japan's, Western firms were reluctant to venture into what they considered to be risky markets. Overseas Chinese businesses were already there, however: They detected the new opportunities and took full advantage of them.

The global marketplace has also seen these ethnic Chinese family businesses begin to modify the age-old structures based on family, clan, and home village, in favor of the same rational business organizations that businesspeople of any other ethnic group would establish. Deals such as the one in which Li Ka-shing bought Canada-based Husky Oil in 1987 and the one in which Thailand's Chinese-owned Charoen Pokphand teamed up for a time with the United States giant Wal-Mart to open discount stores throughout China are examples of how business for the diaspora has evolved.

As China has tried to become a modern, industrialized country, the various reformers and revolutionaries have lobbied the overseas Chinese communities for material support. Attributing their mistreatment in foreign lands at least partly to China's backwardness and degraded international status, the overseas Chinese wanted to help transform China, and a few of them became very nationalistic and patriotic. The father of Chinese nationalism and the founder of the Republic of China, Sun Yat-sen, was himself a scion of an overseas Chinese family. In the 1940s the overseas Chinese became heavily embroiled in the civil war, as both the communists and the nationalists competed for their loyalty. Their involvement culminated in 1949 when many returned to China to help the revolutionary government's cause; among them were hundreds of Chinese Americans and some 250,000 Chinese Indonesians. Unfortunately, many encountered a miserable fate because of their bourgeois Western backgrounds. Branded traitors and capitalists because of their relatives still abroad, their family property was confiscated during the Cultural Revolution, and they were imprisoned. Some tried to escape, and many died.

Those who survived joked bitterly about their predicament by calling themselves the "dead *huaqiao*" [the dead overseas Chinese] in contrast to the "living *huaqiao*," their compatriots who had remained abroad and prospered.

Ever since the mainland Chinese government began to allow capitalism to flower in the 1980s in an effort to modernize, it has tried to enlist the help of the overseas Chinese. In doing so it has even been willing to admit that some excesses were made during the Cultural Revolution, and as a gesture of goodwill it has returned confiscated property to expatriate families and praised them copiously for their patriotism and their contributions to the betterment of China.

Although they may be enjoying some of the benefits, the overseas Chinese have learned to keep their distance from the mainland. Their loyalties do not lie with the Chinese nation-state but rather with the profits that can be made there, through special economic zones where their investments are protected and they are free to move their capital. At the same time, ethnic Chinese around the world are watching how China deals with Taiwan and Hong Kong. For many of them who might have been sold on the "We are all Chinese" pitch, the saber rattling of recent months has been sobering. Many Hong Kong and Taiwan residents hold foreign passports, obtained either through investment in Canada, the United States, or Australia or through their children's foreign citizenship abroad. Although overseas Chinese claim that all they need is freedom to make money, they like to send their children to Western universities and establish a foothold in an English-speaking country. They regard their assets in countries such as the United States as an insurance policy against potential instability in Southeast Asia or on mainland China.

"In the United States there really is a respect for law," says Andrew Kwan, a United States citizen who owns an insecticide factory near Beijing. "That's very attractive for us. My family is here; we have a house. A lot of us would not be willing to give up our foreign passport to go back to China."

Overseas Chinese businesspeople whose professional and private interests are truly global are called astronauts by their less fortunate compatriots because, for example, they live in California and do business in Asia. They will invest in China if that is where the money is to be made, but if the labor costs there increase and productivity levels off, they are just as likely to turn to Vietnam to set up fertilizer plants, to India to set up joint ventures in electronics, or to Bangladesh, Fiji, Mauritius, or Guatemala to set up garment factories. Increasingly, they are joining the transnational world of capitalism developed under European domination, where national borders lose meaning and national identity is neither a hindrance nor an asset. It is increasingly a world in which "Chineseness" also means very little. As Ien Ang, a Chinese scholar born in Indonesia to Chinese parents and raised in Holland, says: "I am inescapably Chinese by descent. I am only sometimes Chinese by consent. When and how is a matter of politics."

It is ultimately political questions such as whether China attacks Taiwan or crushes the spirit and laws of Hong Kong that will determine if overseas Chinese continue to invest in China and profit from its seemingly boundless opportunities. Even Singapore's Lee Kuan Yew, a great champion of the cultural pull of Confucianism, admits that ethnicity will take a backseat to the pressures of realpolitik. "We are ethnic Chinese," Lee has said, "but we must be honest with ourselves and recognize that at the end of the day, our fundamental loyalties are to our home, not to our ancestral country. To think otherwise is not realistic. It will only lead to grief when our interests fail to coincide."

Peter Kwong, the director of Asian American Studies at Hunter College in New York City, is the author of The New Chinatown. *Dusanka Miscevic, a writer and historian, also contributed to this article.*

Asian-Indian Americans

SUMMARY

The Asian-Indian population of the U.S. is affluent and growing. Asian Indians often work as professionals and entrepreneurs. Marketers divide the group into three segments, but all Indians are keenly interested in financial security, good value, and shopping around. Although Asian Indians assimilate easily into U.S. culture, the best way to reach them is to support their communities and traditions.

Marcia Mogelonsky

Marcia Mogelonsky is a contributing editor of American Demographics.

Imagine a rapidly growing ethnic group of almost 1 million people who are generally well-educated and wealthy. Best of all, they speak English. Some may call this a marketer's dream. It also happens to be the general profile of Asian-Indian Americans, a segment of the population worth a closer look.

The number of Asian Indians immigrating to the United States increased rapidly after 1965, when amendments to the Immigration and Nationality Act made it possible for them to enter the country in greater numbers than ever before. Although the first sizable group of Asian Indians arrived in this country between 1907 and 1914, the population today is still primarily first-generation immigrants.

Although immigration data have been available for decades, the U.S. decennial census did not enumerate the Asian-Indian population separately from a miscellaneous category of "other Asians" until 1980. Furthermore, the population fluctuates as temporary residents arrive and leave as students, management trainees, and visiting technology specialists. As of 1990, however, the Asian-Indian population in the United States numbered 815,000, up 111 percent from 387,000 in 1980. While the increase may look small when measured against the 819 percent increase for Cambodians or the 1,631 percent increase in the Hmong population, it is impressive when compared with the 4 percent increase in non-Hispanic whites or 13 percent increase among blacks. Pakistani and Bangladeshi populations in the United States are much smaller, but have been growing even faster. The Pakistani population increased fivefold in the 1980s, from 16,000 to 81,000. Almost 12,000 people identified themselves as Bangladeshi in the 1990 census, up from a miniscule 1,300 in 1980.

Asian Indians are an especially strong presence in Middlesex-Somerset-Hunterdon, New Jersey.

Reprinted with permission from *American Demographics,* August 1995, pp. 32-39.

Asian-Indian Country

More than three-quarters of Asian-Indian Americans live in ten states.

(top-ten states with largest Asian-Indian populations in 1990, population in 1990 and 1980, and percent change 1980-90)

1990 rank	state	1990 population	1980 population	percent change 1980-90
1	California	159,973	59,774	167.6%
2	New York	140,985	67,636	108.4
3	New Jersey	79,440	30,684	158.9
4	Illinois	64,200	37,438	71.5
5	Texas	55,795	23,395	138.5
6	Florida	31,457	11,039	185.0
7	Pennsylvania	28,396	17,230	64.8
8	Maryland	28,330	13,788	105.5
9	Michigan	23,845	15,363	55.2
10	Ohio	20,848	13,602	53.3
	TOTAL U.S.	815,447	387,223	110.6

Source: U.S. Census Bureau

Asians Indians traditionally have flocked to the Northeast, and primarily the urban portions of New York and New Jersey. But California led the states in 1990, with almost 159,000 Asian-Indian residents, up from 60,000 in 1980. Wyoming boasts the smallest population of Asian Indians—240—but it is also the first state in the nation to elect an Asian Indian to its legislature, Republican Nimi McConigley. Throughout the U.S., well-educated Asian Indians are assuming positions of power.

As with most recent immigrant groups, Asian Indians tend to live in and around major metropolitan areas. New York City, home to more than 106,000 Asian Indians in 1990 (1.2 percent of the city's population), had the largest population. It is followed by Chicago (54,000), Los Angeles-Long Beach (44,000), and Washington, D.C. (36,000). Asian Indians are an especially strong presence in Middlesex-Somerset-Hunterdon, New Jersey. They accounted for 2.3 percent of its population in 1990, the largest concentration of any metro area. They also made up 2.1 percent of the population of the Jersey City metro.

PROFESSIONALS AND ENTREPRENEURS

In many cases, the first wave of an immigrant group consists of affluent people. Asian Indians are a classic example of this rule. Among Asian Indians in the work force in 1990, 30 percent were employed in professional specialty occupations, compared with 13 percent of all U.S. employees. Twenty percent of foreign-born Indian professionals are physicians, 26 percent are engineers, and 12 percent are post-secondary teachers, according to the Washington, D.C.-based Center for Immigration Studies. Asian Indians are slightly overrepresented among managerial and sales/technical/clerical workers, and underrepresented among service and blue-collar workers, according to the 1990 census.

"The earlier immigrants came because of their qualifications. They had no trouble getting green cards or professional posts," says Dr. Madhulika Khandelwal of the Asian/American Center at Queens College in Flushing, New York. Indeed, foreign-born Indian professionals are highly qualified: more than 67 percent hold advanced degrees. And 21 percent of the 14,000 American-born Asian Indians aged 25 and older hold post-bachelor's degree accreditation.

"The more recent immigrants differ in two ways," says Khandelwal. "The professionals among them, those with master's degrees or even medical degrees or doctorates, are not always able to find jobs in their chosen professions in this country. They are faced with a choice—staying in India and working as professionals, or emigrating to America and working in trade or service jobs that may not suit their qualifications." This second wave also includes lower-middle-class Indians who tend to work in service industries, usually with members of their extended families, says Khandelwal.

United States immigration policy is based on family reunification, so it is not surprising that the qualifications of immigrants have changed over the past decade, according to the Center for Immigration Studies. Many find positions in family-run businesses or work in service industries such as taxi driving until they make enough money to pursue more lucrative ventures. More than 40 percent of New York City's 40,000 licensed Yellow Cab drivers are South Asian Indians, Pakistanis, and Bangladeshis. But most see their taxi-driving phase as a transitional period to acclimatize them to the U.S. and to give them the money they need to get started.

Many Asian Indians are self-employed. The number of Asian-Indian-owned businesses increased 120 percent between 1982 and 1987, according to the latest available Survey of Minority-Owned Business Enterprises released by the Census Bureau. Dollar receipts for these businesses increased 304 percent in the same five-year period.

"Asian Indians dominate in some trades, such as convenience and stationery stores," says Eliot Kang of the New York City-based Kang and Lee Advertising, which specializes in marketing to Asian minorities.

Kang points out that Asian-Indian retailers get an edge on competitors by pooling their resources and forming associations, which enables them to buy in bulk

Indian Density

India is home to almost 1 billion, but much of the country is still rural.

(population per square kilometer of states in India, 1991)

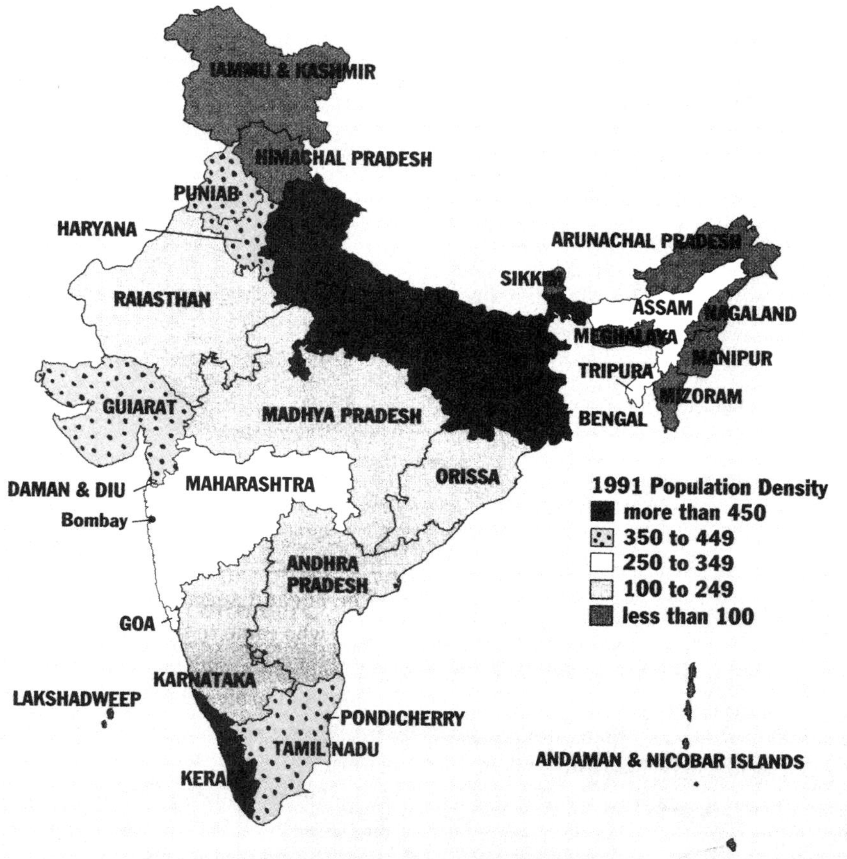

INDIA'S BIGGEST

Ten Indian states have more than 40 million residents.

state	population	state	population
Uttar Pradesh	139,112,287	Madhya Pradesh	66,181,170
Bihar	86,374,465	Tamil Nadu	55,858,946
Maharashtra	78,937,187	Karnataka	44,977,201
West Bengal	68,077,965	Rajasthan	44,005,990
Andhra Pradesh	66,508,008	Gujarat	41,309,582

Sources: ML Infomap Private Ltd., New Delhi, India (boundary file); Demosphere International, Falls Church, VA (population statistics); ArcView 2, ESRI, Redlands, CA (mapping software).

and sell at lower prices. "Large family networks and family financing give these businesses a chance to grow and expand. And because so many family members are involved, Asian-Indian businesses can flourish in labor-intensive service industries."

"Asian Indians dominate in some trades, such as convenience and stationery stores."

The Census Bureau tallied close to 30,000 Asian-Indian-owned service businesses in 1987. Retail establishments ran a distant second, at slightly more than 9,000. Asian-Indian ownership of hotels and motels is the standout example of Indian penetration into the service segment. In 1994, 7,200 Asian-Indian owners operated 12,500 of the nation's 28,000 budget hotels and motels, according to the Atlanta-based Asian American Hotel Owners Association.

ONE MARKET, THREE SEGMENTS

The median income for Asian-Indian households is $44,700, versus $31,200 for all U.S. households, according to the 1990 census. Not all Asian Indians are affluent, however. Dr. Arun Jain, professor of marketing at the State University of New York in Buffalo, divides the market into three distinct segments. The first, the majority of whom immigrated in the 1960s, is led by a cohort of highly educated men who came to this country because of professional opportunities. Most are doctors, scientists, academics, and other professionals who are now in their 50s and at the peak of their earning potential. Jain estimates that their average annual income may top $100,000. The wives of these high-powered professionals usually do not work outside of the home and are not highly educated. These wo-

Asian Indians may save at least 15 percent of their income.

men may have no more than a high school education, and a good portion do not speak English fluently, says Jain. Among this group, the majority of children are in college or about to marry and start families of their own.

The second segment includes immigrants who came to the U.S. in the 1970s. Like the first segment, the men are highly educated professionals. Yet unlike the first wave, many are married to highly educated women who work outside of the home. Their children are college-bound teenagers.

The third segment is made up of relatives of earlier immigrants who have been sponsored by established family members in this country. They are often less well-educated than members of the first two segments. This is the group most likely to be running motels, small grocery stores, gas stations, or other ventures. In this group, Jain also includes the majority of Asian-Indian Ugandans who fled that regime in the 1980s and have established themselves in this country.

Lifestyle and generational differences set the three groups apart, at least to some extent. People in the first segment are thinking about their children's marriages, while those in the second are about to put their children through college. Men in the first segment may be looking toward retirement, while the men and women in the third group are trying to establish themselves in successful businesses.

Generational distinctions are only part of the story, however. India has nearly 1 billion residents separated into 25 states and 7 union territories, speaking 15 official languages. "We are like Europe," says Pradip Kothari, president of the Iselin, New Jersey-based Indian Business Association, a not-for-profit organization linking the more than 60 small businesses that flourish in this heavily Indian enclave of Middlesex County.

SECURITY AND VALUE

Linguistic, nationalistic, and generational differences may divide the Indian population, but they share a number of underlying principles and goals. Jain points out that all Asian Indians place great value in education. "Indians will do anything to further their children's education," he says.

Financial security is also important. Saving money is a major part of Indian culture, and targeted saving—for education or retirement—is especially emphasized. Jain estimates that the savings rate among Asian Indians in the U.S. is higher than the national average of 5 percent; he places it as high as 15 to 20 percent, similar to the rate in India. Asian-Indian Americans also place a high value on inheritance and prize investments that guarantee a secure future for children and grandchildren.

"When Indians get together, they will discuss such things as CD rates and which banks are offering the best value," says Eliot Kang of Kang and Lee Advertising. "They are savvy, informed, and conscious of getting value for their investments. They will compare and weigh information carefully and thoroughly before making a commitment."

Jain points out that investment bankers and financial institutions who reach out to this market stand to make substantial gains, particularly those in Asian-Indian communities. "We rely on local banks for local transactions," adds Pradip Kothari. "Because there are no foreign banks in New Jersey, we are forced to rely on Indian banks in New York City for international transactions. But we invest locally. We try to buy CDs at a bank that is interested in our community."

Asian Indians also find security in well-defined property and life insurance. "Indians love insurance," says Jain. "And they tend to buy policies with cash value." He points out another motivation for insurance companies to pursue this market. "Indians tend to carry little disability insurance. This is especially true of professionals who may be self-employed."

Asian-Indian merchants in the Oak Tree Road area of Iselin, New Jersey, favor Metropolitan Life and New York Life because these companies participate in

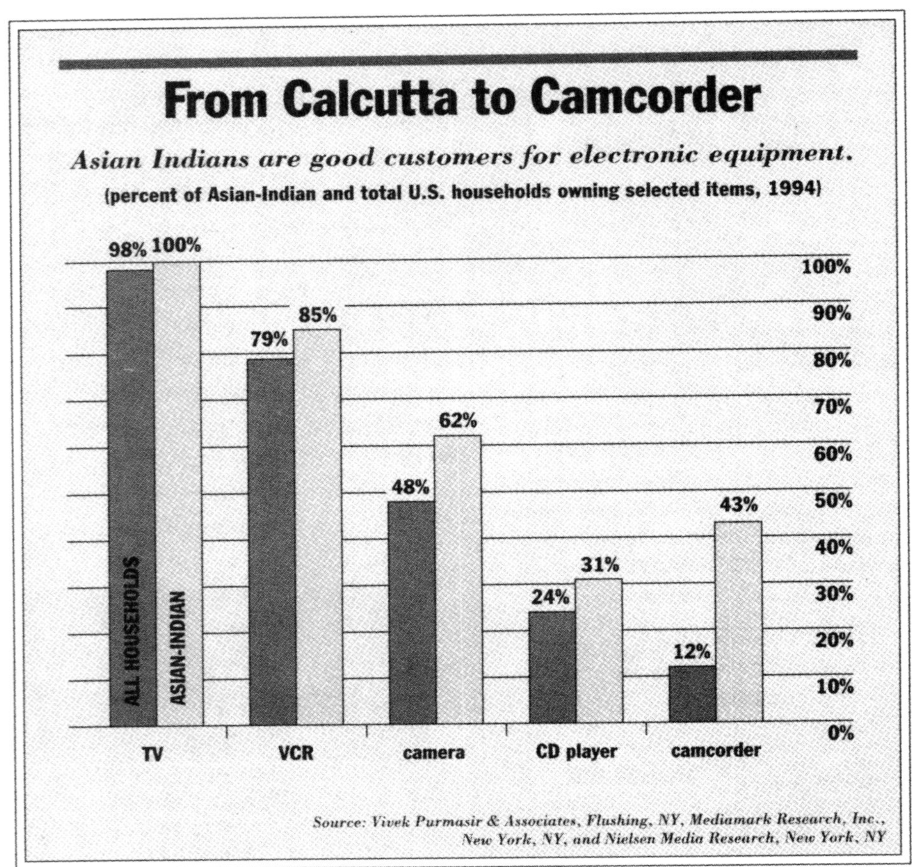

THE INDIAN TOWER OF BABEL

Asian-Indian immigrants to the U.S. share the same mother country, but this doesn't mean they understand each other. India's constitution recognizes a total of 15 official languages, and a recent Indian census tabulated more than 500 mother tongues spoken within the nation's boundaries. These languages are similar to regional accents in the U.S., because they give clues to an Asian Indian's regional origin. This may in turn point to other cultural differences, such as religion or food preferences.

The languages of India are members of the Indo-Aryan branch of Indo-European, the family to which the majority of western languages belong. While some Indian languages are spoken by millions of people, others are common only to a handful. Each Indian state has its own official language or dialect, but residents may speak a host of other dialects, which form a sort of chain link with each other. This means that although neighbors who speak different dialects may understand each other, those who live a few dialects apart may not.

Almost 70 percent of Asian Indians aged 5 and older enumerated in the 1990 U.S. census reported speaking a language other than English at home.

The U.S. has 330,000 Hindi speakers, and a sizable number speak Gujarathi, Panjabi, Bengali, or Marathi. Some language groups are microscopic, however, such as the 18 people who speak Bihari and presumably hail from the northeastern Indian state of Bihar, where it is the official language. Fortunately for them, all 18 speak English well, as do the vast majority of all Asian Indians in the U.S.

Marketers don't necessarily need to speak 500 Indo-Aryan languages. But they do need to be aware of the diversity among their Asian-Indian customers.

—*Marcia Mogelonsky*

SPEAKING IN INDIAN TONGUES

English may be the only common language spoken by Asian-Indian Americans.

(five Indian languages spoken by largest numbers of Americans, number speaking language in U.S. in 1990, and Indian/Pakistani states where languages are spoken)

language	number of speakers in U.S.	Indian/Pakistani states where language is spoken
Hindi (Urdu)	331,484	Uttar Pradesh, Madhya Pradesh, Bihar, Haryana, Delhi, Rajasthan, Punjab, Himachal Pradesh, West Bengal, and Maharashtra, India
Gujarathi	102,418	Gujarat, Bombay district of Maharashtra, India
Panjabi	50,005	Punjab, northwest frontier province and Karachi, Pakistan; Haryana, Delhi, and Ganganagar district of Rajasthan, India
Bengali	38,101	Bangladesh, West Bengal, Tripura, and Assam, India
Marathi	14,755	Maharashtra and eight adjoining districts in three older states of India

Source: U.S. Census Bureau

the community, says Kothari. Metropolitan Life was a major sponsor of the local Navaratri, a religious festival that attracted some 100,000 participants from around New Jersey, New York, and even further afield. "It didn't take a lot. One of the chief executives of the company attended the festival, and the company took out a series of ads in the souvenir program. Now we feel that we should reward the company for taking an interest in us."

Indians do not have a "throw-away" mentality, says Jain. They expect value for their money and buy things with an eye to quality and durability. "Some West-

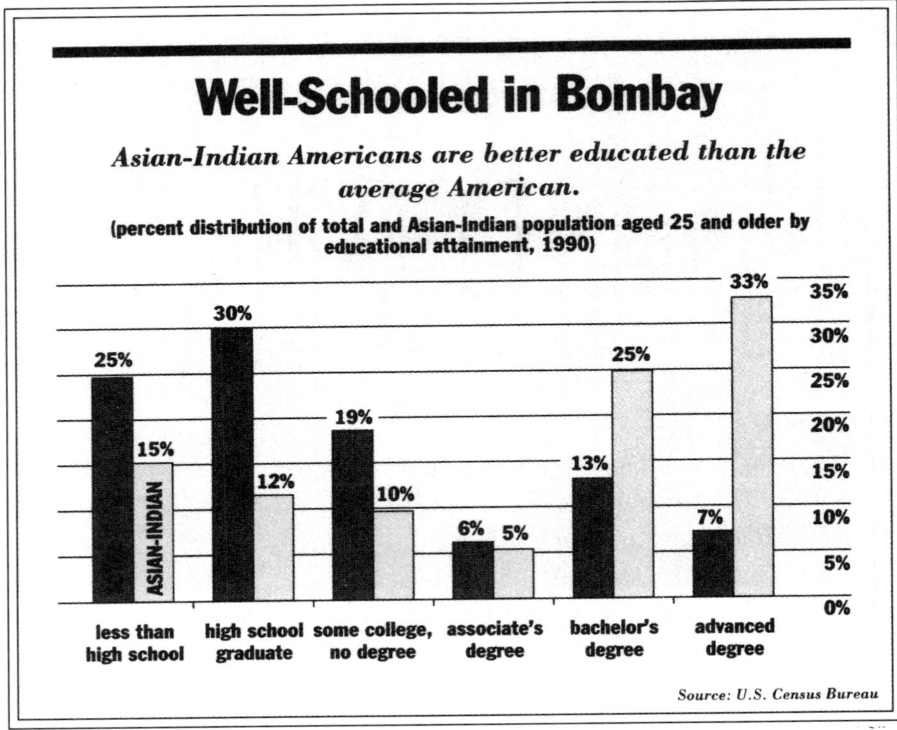

Asian Indians expect value for their money. They shop for quality and durability.

erners may think it strange to see a doctor or engineer standing in line at a department store to get a broken appliance repaired. They may think, 'Wouldn't it be easier just to buy a new one?' But that is not the Indian way," says Jain.

Seeking value goes beyond durable goods. Many Asian Indians run up large long-distance telephone bills talking to extended family in India, so they actively price-shop among both major and smaller long-distance companies. These telecommunications companies are perhaps the most active in marketing directly to Asian Indians, with Indian-theme advertisements, Indian-language services, and highly competitive rates.

ASSIMILATING EASILY

The children of Asian-Indian immigrants set the tone for many purchases made outside the local Indian communities, especially for clothing and food. Second generation and "generation one-and-a-halfers," as Bryn Mawr College assistant dean Sonya Mehta describes Indians who came to the U.S. when they were young, may feel more American than Indian.

Asian-Indian children, like most second-generation Americans, are straddling two cultures. While they are as Americanized as their schoolmates, they are strongly influenced by their parents' tradition and religion. They may listen to American pop music and watch American movies, but they are also comfortable with the popular music and movies of India. They also tend to follow the ways of their elders when it comes to such traditions as marriage and child-rearing.

This dual existence has found an outlet in a flourishing subculture of Indo-American magazines like *Masala*, *Onward*, and *Hum*. The magazines feature articles on drug use and prostitution among young Asian-Indian Americans, but they also review Indian art and dance exhibitions. Advertisers include long-distance telephone companies, airlines, Indian restaurants, and matchmaking/dating services.

Children in Asian-Indian American households carry a lot of weight when it comes to non-Indian food purchases. "My kids want American food. They don't like Indian food," says Pradip Kothari's wife Nandini. "And they want specific things—McDonald's, Coke, and things like that." SUNY Buffalo's Arun Jain points out that many Indian women, especially those who may not be particularly English-literate or educated in Western traditions, are not familiar with many products found in the typical supermarket. He suggests that food manufacturers and retailers could enhance sales to this group by offering hints on how to adapt products to Indian recipes and the Indian palate, through cooking courses on cable TV or recipes in ethnic newspapers.

While children may influence food shopping choices, parents—especially fathers—are the primary decision-makers for most major purchases. Couples shop together, but the husband maintains veto power over purchases, according to Jain. This is especially true for older, less-wealthy shoppers. Even when husband and wife are both professionals, it is not unusual for the man to dominate purchase decisions.

The children of older Indian immigrants are now beginning to marry and start families of their own. Many proud parents are willing to spend a large amount of money on parties, gifts, honeymoons, and even down payments for houses or condominiums. At the same time, many of these parents are about to retire. This is another reason for parties and the myriad goods and services associated with them—banquet halls, caterers, printers, and other service providers. Asian Indians sometimes seek such services from other Indians who understand their culture, but not always. "Indians do not necessarily want to deal with other Indians," says Jain. "What they want is credibility, respect, and good service. Indians will patronize stores with good service."

Jain sees a burgeoning opportunity for the travel and tourism industries as this older generation reaches its retirement years. "Most people go to India to see their families, but as they age, there is less reason to travel, since there are fewer people left to visit in the old country. This is the time for Indian empty nesters to see the United States," Jain says. And while most non-Indians may assume that the only foreign trips Indians make are back to their home country, Nandini Kothari points out that her family does so only once every three or four years. "We go to see our families, but we don't go too often. It's usually too hot, the kids don't enjoy it, and there are so many family obligations that we don't get much of a chance to rest. We prefer to go to the Caribbean for our vacations."

REACHING ASIAN INDIANS

Although 68 percent of Asian Indians aged 5 and older speak a language other than English, only 21 percent do not speak English very well. Should marketers go out of their way to reach a group that has little problem accessing the information and advertisements already out there? "Most definitely," says Jain.

"If you want to win Asian-Indian customers, you have to participate in their communities," says Pradip Kothari. "You don't have to spend a lot of money for name recognition—a little goes a long way." Rajiv Khanna, president of the New York City based India-America Chamber of Commerce, a national organization with more than 300 members, agrees. "Become involved with organizations such as ours. Advertise in community newspapers and on Indian cable TV. Network with Indian groups; sponsor Indian cultural events."

"If you want to win Asian-Indian customers, you have to participate in their communities."

One way to contact Asian-Indian consumers is to get on the information highway. "The Internet is a wonderful resource for keeping informed about business affairs," says Bryn Mawr dean Sonya Mehta, who points out that there are more than a dozen newsgroups for Asian-Indian subscribers on the Net (see "Taking It Further").

Asian Indians also keep tabs on each other and informed about news at home through a host of Indian newspapers and magazines published in the U.S. The choices range from the 25-year-old weekly *India Abroad* to an array of glossy monthly magazines with cultural and business features. Iselin, New Jersey, has local cable TV geared to its large Asian community, and cable offerings on such networks as TVAsia, Eye on Asia, and Vision of Asia offer programming of interest to the market. Local radio programming is also important to Asian Indians as a vehicle for disseminating information about Indian culture and events.

"Targeted media are available," says SUNY Buffalo's Jain. "There are even specialty mail-order lists that target Asian Indians. But even more important than media advertising is the power of word of mouth. Indians talk to each other; they share information, recipes, news. They remember companies and organizations that sponsor Indian events. Reaching key opinion leaders will guarantee that your product or service quickly reaches the entire market."

TAKING IT FURTHER

For more information about the demographics of Asian Indians, see "Asian and Pacific Islanders in the U.S.: 1990, CP-3-5," available from the Government Printing Office at (202) 512-1800. Immigration data are available from the Immigration and Naturalization Service; telephone (202) 376-3066. *The Statistical Record of Asian Americans* ($105) is published by Gale Research, Inc.; telephone (313) 961-2242. *Foreign-Born Professionals in the United States*, by Leon F. Bouvier and David Simcox, is available from the Center for Immigration Studies; telephone (202) 466-8185. India-Net is an online communication service for people of Indian origin residing outside of India; for more information, contact Gaurang Desai, gdesai@megatest.com. Info-India is a volunteer-written digest of Indian newspapers; contact Vishal Sharma, vishal@spetses.ece. ucsb.edu. Prakash reviews about 60 Indian publications a day; contact Arvind Sitaram, asitaram@us.oracle.com. The Worldwide Indian Network lists useful documents for Indians in the U.S.; contact Biswanath Halder, bhalder@lynx.dac.neu.edu.

The Ethnic Legacy

Ethnicity is often associated with immigrants and with importation of culture, language, stories, and foods from foreign shores. Appalachian, western, and other regional ethnicities are evidence of multigenerational ethnic cultural development within the American reality. The persistent, ongoing process of humanity expressed in unique and intriguing folkways, dialect languages, myths, festivals, and foods displays another enduring and public dimension of ethnicity. As this unit's articles illustrate, ethnic experiences may be less foreign and alien than most imagine them to be.

The contributions and concerns of various ethnic immigrant groups over many generations provided a deep weave and pattern to the material and social history of America. Today we see a consciousness of ethnic tradition, exasperation and anger about stereotypes, and efforts to institutionalize attention to groups. Change and ethnicity are not contradictory, for each generation creates anew its ethnicity, which, alongside other affinities, affiliations, and loyalties, helps to guide our interactions. Present concerns of ethnic groups include language, preservation of neighborhoods, ethnic studies, and the rearticulation of historical claims to fairness, justice, and equity.

Perhaps the most obvious oscillation between celebration of achievement and concern about fairness is seen in the legacies of ancestry-conscious persons and groups. Should such populations be denied their distinctiveness through absorption into the mass of modernity, or can their distinctiveness accompany them into mainstream modern American identities? Their ethnicity is not a form of diminished existence; they are "Americans Plus"—Americans with a multicultural affinity and competencies in more than one culture.

The winds of political change in Ireland and England, the Middle East, and Eastern and Central Europe reveal the saliency of ethnicity and the varied textures of group relations. In America the ongoing affinity of ethnic populations to the nations of their origins is expressed in subtle as well as obvious ways. These articles explain the transmission of ethnic tradition in music and suggest linkages between religion and ethnicity. The story of the interaction of ethnicity and religion is curiously exposed in the etymology of the Greek word ethnikos (*i.e.,* the rural, Gentile, or pagan people of the ancient Mediterranean world). Though such philological roots no longer drive our principal understanding of ethnicity, the experience of social affinity and cultural affiliation elaborated in the following articles about ethnics deepens our awareness and understanding of ethnicity—a changing yet persistent aspect of human identity and social cohesiveness.

Looking Ahead: Challenge Questions

How does the ethnicity of an earlier era suggest the tension between worlds of meaning discussed in this section?

Comment on the idea that the legacy of multiple ancestral origins and ethnic identities of European Americans from an earlier era in America argues for the passing relevancy and their marginality to the central ethnic issues of our time.

What is a central ethnic issue? By what criteria do we decide the importance and preferential protection of one ethnic group vis-à-vis another group?

What lessons can be learned from the immigration and settlement experiences of Eastern and Southern Europeans?

UNIT 7

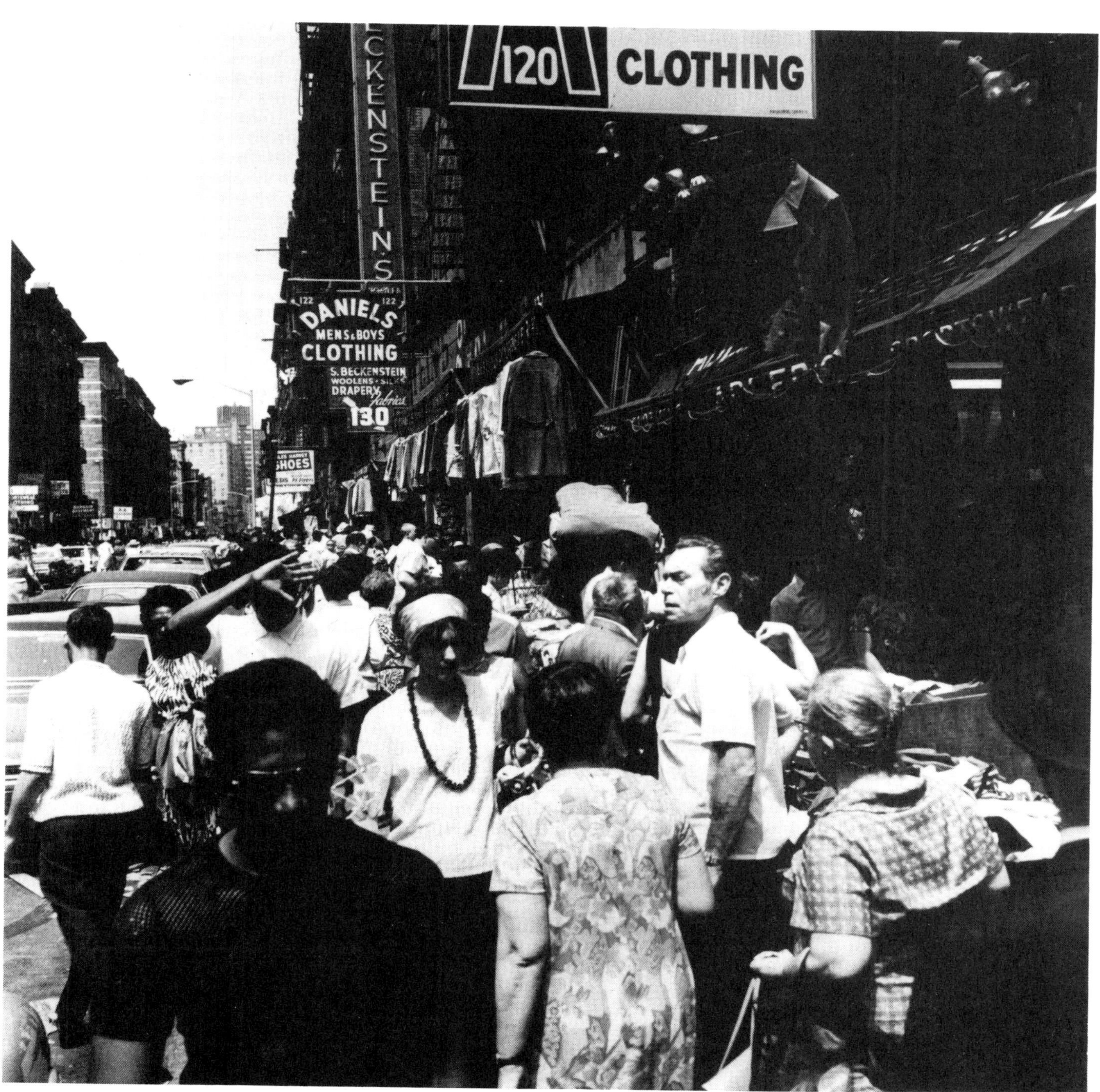

120
CLOTHING
BECKENSTEIN'S
DANIELS
MENS & BOYS
CLOTHING
S. BECKENSTEIN
WOOLENS • SILKS
DRAPERY
Fabrics
130
SHOES

THE NEW ETHNICITY

Michael Novak

The word "ethnic" does not have a pleasing sound. The use of the word makes many people anxious. What sorts of repression account for this anxiety? What pretenses about the world are threatened when one points to the realities denoted and connoted by that ancient word? An internal history lies behind resistance to ethnicity; such resistance is almost always passional, convictional, not at all trivial. Many persons have tried to escape being "ethnic," in the name of a higher moral claim.

There are many meanings to the word itself. I have tried to map some of them below. There are many reasons for resistance to the word "ethnic" (and what it is taken to represent). Rather than beginning with these directly, I prefer to begin by defining the new ethnicity.

The definition I wish to give is personal; it grows out of personal experience; it is necessitated by an effort to attain an accurate self-knowledge. The hundreds of letters, reviews, comments, invitations, and conversations that followed upon *The Rise of the Unmeltable Ethnics* (1972) indicate that my own gropings to locate my own identity are not isolated. They struck a responsive chord in many others of Southern and Eastern European (or other) background. My aim was—and is—to open up the field to study. Let later inquiry descern just how broadly and how exactly my first attempts at definition apply. It is good to try to give voice to what has so far been untongued—and then to devise testable hypotheses at a later stage.

The new ethnicity, then, is a movement of self-knowledge on the part of members of the third and fourth generation of Southern and Eastern European immigrants in the United States. In a broader sense, the new ethnicity includes a renewed self-consciousness on the part of other generations and other ethnic groups: the Irish, the Norwegians and Swedes, the Germans, the Chinese and Japanese, and others. Much that can be said of one of these groups can be said, not univocally but analogously, of others. In this area, one must learn to speak with multiple meanings and with a sharp eye for differences in detail. (By "analogous" I mean "having resemblances but also essential differences"; by "univocal" I mean a generalization that applies equally to all cases.) My sentences are to be read, then, analogously, not univocally; they are meant to awaken fresh perception, not to close discussion. They are intended to speak directly of a limited (and yet quite large) range of ethnic groups, while conceding indirectly that much that is said of Southern and Eastern Europeans may also be said, *mutatis mutandis,* of others.

I stress that, in the main, the "new" ethnicity involves those of the third and fourth generation after immigration. Perhaps two anecdotes will suggest the kind of experience involved. When *Time* magazine referred to me in 1972 as a "Slovak-American," I felt an inner shock; I had never referred to myself or been publicly referred to in that way. I wasn't certain how I felt about it. Then, in 1974, after I had given a lecture on ethnicity to the only class in Slavic American studies in the United States,* at the City College of New York, the dean of the college said on the way to lunch, "Considering how sensitive you are on ethnic matters, the surprising thing to me was how

*This Slavic American course—in a happy symbol of the new ethnicity—is housed in the Program of Puerto Rican Studies, through the generosity of the latter.

From *Further Reflections on Ethnicity* by Michael Novak, published by Jednota Press, 1977. Originally from *Center* magazine, July/August 1974, pp. 18-25.

The new ethnicity is a fledgling movement, not to be confused with the appearance of ethnic themes on television commercials, in television police shows, and in magazines.

American you are." I wanted to ask him, "What else?" In this area one grows used to symbolic uncertainties.

The new ethnicity does not entail: (a) speaking a foreign language; (b) living in a subculture; (c) living in a "tight-knit" ethnic neighborhood; (d) belonging to fraternal organizations; (e) responding to "ethnic" appeals; (f) exalting one's own nationality or culture, narrowly construed. Neither does it entail a university education or the reading of writers on the new ethnicity. Rather, the new ethnicity entails: first, a growing sense of discomfort with the sense of identity one is *supposed* to have—universalist, "melted," "like everyone else"; then a growing appreciation for the potential wisdom of one's own gut reactions (especially on moral matters) and their historical roots; a growing self-confidence and social power; a sense of being discriminated against, condescended to, or carelessly misapprehended; a growing disaffection regarding those to whom one had always been taught to defer; and a sense of injustice regarding the response of liberal spokesmen to conflicts between various ethnic groups, especially between "legitimate" minorities and "illegitimate" ones. There is, in a word, an inner conflict between one's felt personal power and one's ascribed public power: a sense of outraged truth, justice, and equity.

The new ethnicity does, therefore, have political consequences. Many Southern and Eastern European-Americans have been taught, as I was, not to be "ethnic," or even "hyphenated," but only "American." Yet at critical points it became clear to some of us, then to more of us, that when push comes to shove we are always, in the eyes of others, "ethnics," unless we play completely by their rules, emotional as well as procedural. And in the end, even then, they retain the power and the status. Still, the stakes involved in admitting this reality to oneself are very high. Being "universal" is regarded as being good; being ethnically self-conscious raises anxieties. Since one's whole identity has been based upon being "universal," one is often loathe to change public face too suddenly. Many guard the little power and status they have acquired, although they cock one eye on how the ethnic "movement" is progressing. They are wise. But their talents are also needed.

The new ethnicity, then, is a fledgling movement, not to be confused with the appearance of ethnic themes on television commercials, in television police shows, and in magazines. All these manifestations in the public media would not have occurred unless the ethnic reality of America had begun to be noticed. In states from Massachusetts to Iowa, great concentrations of Catholics and Jews, especially in urban centers, have been some of the main bastions of Democratic Party politics for fifty years. The "new politics," centered in the universities, irritated and angered this constituency (even when, as it sometimes did, it won its votes). Thus there is a relation between the fledgling new ethnicity and this larger ethnic constituency. But what that relationship will finally be has not yet been demonstrated by events.

Those who do not come from Southern or Eastern European backgrounds in the United States may not be aware of how it feels to come from such a tradition; they may not know the internal history. They may note "mass passivity" and "alienation" without sharing the cynicism learned through particular experiences. They may regard the externals of ethnic economic and social success, modest but real, while never noticing the internal ambiguity—and its compound of peace and self-hatred, confidence and insecurity.

To be sure, at first many "white ethnics" of the third generation are not conscious of having any special feelings. The range of feelings about themselves they do have is very broad; more than one stream of feeling is involved. They are right-wingers and left-wingers, chauvinists and universalists, all-Americans and isolationists. Many want nothing more desperately than to be considered "American." Indeed, by now many have so deeply acquired that habit that to ask them point-blank how they are different from others would arouse strong emotional resistance.

For at least three reasons, many white ethnics *are* becoming self-conscious. As usual, great social forces outside the self draw forth from the self new responses. First, a critical mass of scholars, artists, and writers is beginning to emerge—the Italians, for example, are extraordinarily eminent in the cinema. Second, the prevailing image of the model American—the "best and the brightest" of the Ivy League, wealthy, suave, and powerful—has been discredited by the mismanagement of war abroad, by racial injustice at home, and by attitudes, values, and emotional patterns unworthy of emulation internally. The older image of the truly cultured American is no longer compelling. Many, therefore, are thrown back upon their own resources.

Finally, the attitudes of liberal, enlightened commentators on the "crisis of the cities" seem to fall into traditional patterns: guilt vis-a-vis blacks, and disdain for the Archie Bunkers of the land (Bunker is, of course, a classy British American name, but Carroll O'Connor is in appearance undisguisably Irish). The national media present to the public a model for what it is to be a "good American" which makes many people feel unacceptable to their betters, unwashed, and ignored. Richard Hofstadter wrote of "the anti-intellectualism of the people," but another feature of American life is the indifference—even hostility—of many intellectuals to Main Street. In return, then, many people respond with deep contempt for experts, educators, "limousine liberals," "radical chic," "bureaucrats"—a contempt whose sources are partly those of class ("the hidden injuries of class") and partly those of ethnicity ("legitimate" minorities and unacceptable minorities). The national social class that prides itself on being universalist has lost the confidence of many. Votes on school bond issues are an example of popular resistance to professionals.

In my own case, the reporting of voting patterns among white ethnic voters during the Wallace campaigns of 1964 and 1968 first aroused in me ethnic self-consciousness. Descriptions of "white backlash" often put the blame—inaccurately I came to see—upon Slavs and other Catholic groups. The Slavs of "South Milwaukee" were singled out for comment in the Wallace vote in Wisconsin in 1964. First, South Milwaukee was not distinguished from the south side of Milwaukee. Then, it was not noted that the Slavic vote for Wallace fell *below* his statewide average. Then, the very heavy vote for Wallace in outlying German and British American areas was not pointed out. Finally, the strong vote for Wallace in the wealthy northeastern suburbs of Milwaukee was similarly ignored. It seemed to me that those whom the grandfathers called "hunkies" and "dagos" were now being called "racists," "fascists," and "pigs," with no noticeable gain in affection. Even in 1972, a staff advisory in the Shriver "trip book" for a congressional district in Pittsburgh called the district "Wallace country," though the Wallace vote in that district in 1968 had been twelve per cent, and the Humphrey vote had been fifty-eight per cent. I obliged the staff member to revise his account and to call the district "Humphrey country." It is one of the most consistently liberal districts in Pennsylvania. Why send this constituency the message that it is the enemy?

Jimmy Breslin was once asked by an interviewer in *Penthouse* how, coming out of Queens, he could have grown up so liberal. Actually, next to Brooklyn, there is no more liberal county in the nation. A similar question was put to a liberal journalist from the Dorchester area, in Boston. The class and ethnic bias hidden in the way the word "liberal" is used in such interviews cries out for attention.

One of the large social generalizations systematically obscured by the traditional anti-Catholicism of American elites is the overwhelmingly progressive voting record in America's urban centers. The centers of large Catholic population in every northeastern and north central state have been the key to Democratic victories in those states since at least 1916. The hypothesis that Catholics have been, second only to Jews, the central constituency of successful progressive politics in this century is closer to the facts than historians have observed. (Massachusetts, that most Catholic of our states, stayed with McGovern in 1972.) The language of politics in America is, however, mainly Protestant, and Protestant biases color public perception. Protestant leadership is given the halo of morality and legitimacy, Catholic life is described in terms of negatively laden words: Catholic "power," "machine politics," etc.

"Become like us" is an understandable strategy, but in a nation as pluralistic as the United States, it is shortsighted.

There are other examples of odd perception on the part of American elites with respect to Catholic and other ethnic populations. The major institutions of American life—government, education, the media—give almost no assistance to those of "white ethnic" background who wish to obey the Socratic maxim: "Know thyself." One of the greatest and most dramatic migrations of human history brought more than thirty million immigrants to this land between 1874 and 1924. Despite the immense dramatic materials involved in this migration, only one major American film records it: Elia Kazan's *America! America!* That film ends with the hero's arrival in America. The tragic and costly experience of Americanization has scarcely yet been touched. How many died; how many were morally and psychologically destroyed; how many still carry the marks of changing their names, of "killing" their mother tongue and renouncing their former identity, in order to become "new men and new women"—these are motifs of violence, self-mutilation, joy, and irony. The inner history of this migration must come to be understood, if we are ever to understand the aspirations and fears of some seventy million Americans.

When this part of the population exhibits self-consciousness and begins to exert group claims—whether these are claims made by aggregated individuals or claims that are corporate—they are regularly confronted with the accusation that they are being "divisive". ("Divisive" is a code word for Catholic ethnics and Jews, is it not? It is seldom used of others: white Southerners, Appalachians, Chicanos, blacks, native Americans, prep-school British Americans, or others who maintain their own identity and institutions.) Earl Raab writes eloquently of this phenomenon in *Commentary* (May, 1974): "Modern Europe . . . never really accepted the legitimacy of the corporate Jew—although it was at its best willing to grant full civil rights to the individual Jew. That, for the Jews, was an impossible

The fact of American cultural power is that a more or less upper-class, Northeastern Protestant sensibility sets the tone, and that a fairly aggressive British American ethnocentricity, and even Anglophilia, govern the instruments of education and public life.

paradox, a secular vision of Christian demands to convert . . . [And] it is precisely this willingness to allow the Jews their separate identity as a group which is now coming into question in America." Individual diversity, yes; group identity, not for all.

The Christian white ethnic, like the Jew, actually has few group demands to make: positively, for educational resources to keep values and perceptions alive, articulate, and critical; negatively, for an equal access to power, status, and the definition of the general American purpose and symbolic world. Part of the strategic function of the cry "divisive!" is to limit access to these things. Only those individuals will be advanced who define themselves as individuals and who operate according to the symbols of the established. The emotional meaning is: *"Become like us."* This is an understandable strategy, but in a nation as pluralistic as the United States, it is shortsighted. The nation's hopes, purposes, and symbols need to be defined inclusively rather than exclusively; *all* must become "new men" and "new women." All the burden ought not to fall upon the newcomers.

There is much that is attractive about the British American, upper-class, northeastern culture that has established for the entire nation a model of behavior and perception. This model is composed of economic power; status; cultural tone; important institutional rituals and procedures; and the acceptable patterns of style, sensibility, and rationality. The terse phrase "Ivy League" suggests all these factors. The nation would be infinitely poorer than it is without the Ivy League. All of us who came to this land—including the many lower-class British Americans, Scotch-Irish, Scandinavians, and Germans—are much in the debt of the Ivy League, deeply, substantially so.

Still, the Ivy League is not the nation. The culture of the Ivy League is not the culture of America (not even of Protestant America).

Who are we, then, we who do not particularly reverberate to the literature of New England, whose interior history is not Puritan, whose social class is not Brahmin (either in reality or in pretense), whose ethnicity is not British American, or even Nordic? Where in American institutions, American literature, American education is our identity mirrored, objectified, rendered accessible to intelligent criticism, and confirmed? We are still, I think, persons without a public symbolic world, persons without a publicly verified culture to sustain us and our children.

It is not that we lack culture; it is not that we lack strength of ego and a certain internal peace. As Jean-Paul Sartre remarks in one of his later works, there is a distinction between one's identity in one's own eyes and one's identity in the eyes of others. In the United States, many who have internal dignity cannot avoid noticing that others regard them as less than equals, with a sense that they are different, with uncertainty, and with a lack of commonality. It is entirely possible that the "melting pot" would indeed have melted everyone, if those who were the models into which the molten metal was to be poured had not found the process excessively demanding. A sense of separate identity is, in part, induced from outside-in. I am made aware of being Catholic and Slovak by the actions of others. I would be sufficiently content were my identity to be so taken for granted, so utterly normal and real, that it would never have to be self-conscious.

The fact of American cultural power is that a more or less upper-class, Northeastern Protestant sensibility sets the tone, and that a fairly aggressive British American ethnocentricity, and even Anglophilia, govern the instruments of education and public life. Moreover, it is somehow emotionally important not to challenge this dominant ethnocentricity. It is quite proper to talk of other sorts of social difference—income, class, sex, even religion. To speak affirmatively of ethnicity, however, makes many uneasy. Some important truth must lie hidden underneath this uneasiness. A Niebuhrian analysis of social power suggests that a critical instrument of social control in the United States is, indeed, the one that dares not be spoken of.

In New York State, for example, in 1974 the four Democratic candidates for the office of lieutenant governor (not, however, for governor) were named Olivieri, Cuomo, La Falce, and Krupsak. It was the year, the pundits say, for "ethnic balance" on the ticket. But all four candidates insisted that their ethnicity was not significant. Two boasted of being from *upstate*, one of being a *woman*, one of being for "the *little* guy." It is publicly legitimate to be different on any other account except ethnicity, even where the importance of ethnic diversity is tacitly agreed upon.

If I say, as I sometimes have, that I would love to organize an "ethnic caucus" within both the Democratic Party and the Republican Party, the common reaction is one of anxiety, distaste, and strained silence. But if I say, as I am learning to, that I would love to organize a "caucus of workingmen and women" in both parties, heads quickly nod in approval. Social class is, apparently, rational. Cultural background is, apparently, counter-rational.

Yet the odd political reality is that most Americans do not identify themselves in class terms. They respond to cultural symbols intimate to their ethnic history in America. Ethnicity is a "gut issue," even though it cannot be mentioned. A wise political candidate does not, of course, speak to a longshoreman's local by calling its members Italian American and appealing to some supposed cultural solidarity. That would be a mistake. But if he speaks about those themes in the cultural tradition that confirm their own identity—themes like family, children, home, neighborhood, specific social aspirations, and grievances—they know he is with them: he does represent them. In order to be able to represent many constituencies, a representative has to be able to "pass over" into many cultural histories. He may never once make ethnicity explicit as a public theme; but, implicitly, he will be recognizing the daily realities of ethnicity and ethnic experience in the complex fabric of American social power.

According to one social myth, America is a "melting pot," and this myth is intended by many to be not merely descriptive but normative: the faster Americans—especially white ethnic Americans—"melt" into the British American pattern, the better. There is even a certain ranking according to the supposed degree of assimilation: Scotch Irish, Norwegians, Swedes, Germans, Swiss, Dutch, liberal or universalist Jews, the Irish, and on down the line to the less assimilated: Greeks, Yugoslavs, Hungarians, Central and East Europeans, Italians, Orthodox Jews, French Canadians, Portuguese, Latins and Spanish-speaking. . . . (The pattern almost exactly reflects the history and literature of England.).

Now it was one thing to be afraid of ethnicity in 1924, in confronting a first and second generation of immigrants. It is another thing to be afraid, in 1974, in confronting a third and fourth generation. Indeed, fears about a revival of ethnicity seem to be incompatible with conviction about how successful the "melting pot" has been. Fears about a "revival" of ethnicity confirm the fact that ethnicity is still a powerful reality in American life.

What, then, are the advantages and disadvantages in making this dangerous subject, this subterranean subject, explicit?

The new ethnicity notes many significant differences besides those based upon race, and defines political and social problems in ways that unite diverse groups around common objectives.

The disadvantages seem to be three. The first one on everyone's mind is that emphasis on ethnicity may work to the disadvantage of blacks. It may, it is said, become a legitimization of racism. It may "polarize" whites and blacks. Nothing could be further from the truth. Those who are concerned about the new ethnicity—Geno Baroni (Washington), Irving Levine (New York), Barbara Mikulski (Baltimore), Ralph Perrotta (New York), Steve Adubado (Newark), Otto Feinstein (Detroit), Stan Franczyk (Buffalo), Kenneth Kovach (Cleveland), Edward Marciniak (Chicago), and others—have given ample proof of their concern for the rights and opportunities of black Americans. Many got their start in the new ethnicity through their work among blacks. The overriding political perception among those concerned with the new ethnicity is that the harshness of life in the cities must be reduced by whites and blacks together, especially in working-class neighborhoods. Present social policies punish neighborhoods that integrate. Such neighborhoods should be rewarded and strengthened and guaranteed a long-range stability.

But fears about ethnicity require a further two-part response. Racism does not need ethnicity in order to be legitimated in America. It was quite well legitimated by Anglo-American culture, well before white ethnics arrived here in significant numbers, well before many white ethnics had ever met blacks. Indeed, there is some reason to believe that, while racism is an international phenomenon and found in all cultures, the British American and other Nordic peoples have a special emotional response to colored races. Not all European peoples respond to intermarriage, for example, with quite the emotional quality of the Anglo-Saxons. The French, the Spanish, the Italians, and the Slavs are not without their own forms of racism. But the felt quality of racism is different in different cultures. (It seems different among the North End Italians and the South Boston Irish of Boston, for example.)

In America, racism did not wait until the immigrants of 1880 and after began to arrive. Indeed, it is in precisely those parts of the country solely populated by British Americans that the conditions of blacks have been legally and institutionally least humane. In those parts of the country most heavily populated by white ethnics, the cultural symbols and the political muscle that have led to civil-rights and other legislation have received wide support. Liberal senators and congressmen elected by white ethnics—including the Kennedys—led the way. Even in 1972, both Hamtramck and Buffalo went for George McGovern. McGovern's share of the Slavic vote was fifty-two per cent. Nixon won the white Protestant vote by sixty-eight per cent.

It will be objected that white ethnic leaders like Frank Rizzo of Philadelphia, Ralph Perk of Cleveland, and others are signs of a new racism on the part of white ethnics in the Northern cities, of a retreat from support for blacks, and of a rising tide of anti-"crime" and antibusing sentiment. The proponents of the new ethnicity perceive such developments as a product of liberal neglect and liberal divisiveness. The proponents of the new politics talk well of civil rights, equal opportunity, economic justice, and other beautiful themes. But the new politics, in distinguishing "legitimate" minorities (blacks, Chicanos, native Americans) from "less favored" minorities (Italians, Slavs, Orthodox Jews, Irish, etc.), has set up punitive and self-defeating mechanisms. The new politics has needlessly divided working-class blacks from working-class whites, in part by a romance (on television) with militance and flamboyance, in part by racial discrimination in favor of some against others, not because of need but because of color.

The second part of this response is that the politics of "the constituency of conscience" (as Michael Harrington, Eugene McCarthy, and others have called it)--the politics of the liberal, the educated, the enlightened—is less advantageous to blacks than is the politics of the new ethnicity. The new politics is less advantageous to blacks because it is obsessed with racial differences, and approaches these through the ineffectual lenses of guilt and moralism. Second, it is blind to cultural differences among blacks, as well as to cultural differences among whites; and sometimes these are significant. Third, it unconsciously but effectively keeps blacks in the position of a small racial minority outnumbered in the population ten to one.

By contrast, the new ethnicity notes many other significant differences besides those based upon race, and defines political and social problems in ways that unite diverse groups around common objectives. In Chicago, for example, neither Poles nor Italians are represented on the boards or in the executive suites of Chicago's top 105 corporations in a higher proportion than blacks or Latinos—all are of one per cent or less.* In Boston, neither white ethnics nor blacks desire busing, but this highly ideological instrument of social change is supported most by just those affluent liberals—in such suburbs as Brookline and Newton—whose children will not be involved.

The new ethnic politics would propose a strategy of social rewards—better garbage pickup, more heavily financed and orderly schools, long-range guarantees on home mortgages, easier access to federally insured home improvement loans, and other services—for neighborhoods that integrate. As a neighborhood moves from, say, a ten per cent population of blacks to twenty per-cent or more, integration should be regulated so that long-range community stability is guaranteed. It is better long-range policy to have a large number of neighborhoods integrated up to twenty or thirty per-cent than to encourage—even by inadvertence—a series of sudden flights and virtually total migrations. Institutional racism is a reality; the massive migration of blacks into a neighborhood does not bring with it social rewards but, almost exclusively, punishments.

There are other supposed disadvantages to emphasis upon ethnicity. Ethnicity, it is said, is a fundamentally counter-rational, primordial, uncontrollable social force; it leads to hatred and violence; it is the very enemy of enlightenment, rationality, and liberal politics. But this is to confuse nationalism or tribalism with cultural heritage. Because a man's name is Russell, or Ayer, or Flew, we would not wish to accuse him of tribalism on the ground that he found the Britons a uniquely civilized and clear-headed people, thought the Germans ponderous and mystic, the French philosophically romantic, etc. A little insular, we might conclude, but harmlessly ethnocentric. And if it is not necessarily tribalistic or unenlightened to read English literature in American schools, just possibly it would be even more enlightened and even less tribalistic to make other literatures, germane to the heritage of other Americans, more accessible than they are.

The United States is, potentially, a multiculturally attuned society. The greatest number of immigrants in recent years arrives from Spanish-speaking and Asian nations. But the nation's cultural life, and its institutions of culture, are far from being sensitive to the varieties of the American people. Why should a cultural heritage not their own be imposed unilaterally upon newcomers? Would not genuine multicultural adaptation on the part of all be more cosmopolitan and humanistic? It would be quite significant in international affairs. The Americans would truly be a kind of prototype of planetary diversity.

Some claim that cultural institutions will be fragmented if every ethnic group in America clamors for attention. But the experience of the Illinois curriculum in ethnic studies suggests that no one school represents more than four or five ethnic groups (sometimes fewer) in significant density. With even modest adjustments in courses in history, literature, and the social sciences, material can be introduced that illuminates inherited patterns of family life, values, and preferences. The purpose for introducing multicultural materials is neither chauvinistic nor propagandistic but realistic. Education ought to illuminate what is happening in the self of each child.

What about the child of the mixed marriage, the child of *no* ethnic heritage—the child of the melting pot? So much in the present curriculum already supports such a child that the only possible shock to arise from multicultural materials would appear to be a beneficial one: not all others in America are like him (her), and that diversity, as well as homogenization, has a place in America.

The practical agenda that faces proponents of the new ethnicity is vast, indeed. At the heights of American

---

*Cf. "The Representation of Poles, Italians, Latins, and Blacks in the Executive Suites of Chicago's Largest Corporations." The Institute of Urban Life, 820 North Michigan Avenue, Chicago, Illinois 60611.

economic and social power, there is not yet much of a melting pot. Significant ethnic diversity is manifested in the proportion of each group studying in universities, on faculties, in the professions, on boards of directors, among the creators of public social symbols, and the like. In patterns of home ownership, family income, work patterns, care for the aged, political activism, authoritarianism, individualism, and matters of ultimate concern, group differences are remarkable. About all these things, more information is surely needed. Appropriate social policies need to be hypothesized, tried, and evaluated.

Ethnic diversity in the United States persists in the consciousness of individuals, in their perceptions, preferences, behavior, even while mass production and mass communications homogenize our outward appearances. Some regard such persistence as a personal failure; they would prefer to "transcend" their origins, or perhaps they believe that they have. Here two questions arise. What cultural connection do they have with their brothers and sisters still back in Montgomery, or Wheeling, or Skokie, or Pawtucket? Second, has their personal assimilation introduced into the great American superculture fresh streams of image, myth, symbol, and style of intellectual life? Has anything distinctively their own—formed in them by a history longer than a thousand years—been added to the common wisdom?

The new ethnicity does not stand for the Balkanization of America. It stands for a true, real, multicultural cosmopolitanism. It points toward a common culture truly altered by each new infusion of diversity. Until now, the common culture has been relatively resistant to internal transformation; it has not so much arisen from the hearts of all as been imposed; the melting pot has had only a single recipe. That is why at present the common culture seems to have become discredited, shattered, unenforceable. Its cocoon has broken. Struggling to be born is a creature of multicultural beauty, dazzling, free, a higher and richer form of life. It was fashioned in the painful darkness of the melting pot and now, at the appointed time, it awakens.

Italian Americans as a Cognizable Racial Group

Dominic R. Massaro

Dominic Massaro is a Justice of the Supreme Court of New York. A "Grande Ufficiale della Repubblica Italiana," he is chairman emeritus of The Conference of Presidents of Major Italian-American Organizations. In 1991 his treatise, Cesare Beccaria—The Father of Criminal Justice: His Impact on Anglo-American Jurisprudence *(Prescia: International UP, 1991), garnered Italy's International Dorso Prize. Justice Massaro is the representative of the American Judges Association to the United Nations.*

Italian Americans are a cognizable racial group for purposes of the scope and application of civil rights laws. This view is confirmed by the sophistication of sociological definition and historical evidence, which is grounded in legal analysis and judicial interpretation. There are a number of citations, quotes, and references to which I will allude, including a limited amount of previous scholarship. Let me note at the onset that Italian Americans, more often than not, take umbrage at being defined as a minority group. Yet, a review of the relevant case law suggests that in no other manner can they hope for success in advancing legal claims that allege discrimination on the basis of national origin. Traditionally, civil rights legislation has provided virtually no protection against this form of discrimination. But the decision in *Scelsa v. the City University of New York* (CUNY) decided last November in Federal District Court in Manhattan—hereinafter referred to as *Scelsa*—accents the slow but steady erosion of the artificial distinction between "race" and "national origin" that has heretofore given rise to ethnic minorities, including Italian Americans, receiving "different treatment under the law, as written or applied."

As an aside, you should be aware of what lies behind my view of *Scelsa*. In my position [as] Human Rights Commissioner, and in response to a growing number of complaints, I threatened mandamus against CUNY in November 1971; that is, I mandated that it release a statistical breakdown of Americans of Italian descent employed throughout the university system. Twenty years later, while on the bench as a non-partisan choice, I was invited to chair the Legislative Advisory Committee on Urban Public Higher Education. The Committee's central charge was to investigate and suggest redress for discrimination against Italian Americans at CUNY. Its final report, rendered 12 September 1991, contained a series of recommendations utilizing the special expertise of CUNY's Italian American Institute aimed at "underscor[ing] the University's commitment to the richness of diversity." Within a year, as the *Scelsa* Court observed that CUNY sought "to sever the outreach, counseling and research aspects of the Institute . . . [and] shunt aside its Director."

However, what I found particularly disturbing was that, despite two intervening decades, only negligible changes had been made to remedy the woeful underrepresentation of Italian Americans in the work force. The release of these earlier statistics became the underpinning for critical reportage, academic study, the designation of Italian Americans as an affirmative action category by CUNY (the so-called Kibbee Memorandum), and legislative inquiry. The latter culminated in public hearings and provided the backdrop for the establishment of the John D. Calandra Italian American Institute of CUNY in 1979.

From a purely legal perspective, *Scelsa* presents us with a precedent-making judicial grant of extraordinary relief to Italian Americans; not only did the case galvanize Italian-American organizations, it placed the Italian American Legal Defense and Higher Education Fund that handled the action in the forefront of civil rights activity. By its very nature, injunctive relief is an extraordinary remedy; it is grounded in equity; that is, it is responsive to the demands of justice and right conscience. The manner in which it was granted and the fact that it was granted by the *Scelsa* Court is significant. A colleague stated it rather succinctly; namely, that the decision "is a delight to those who are sympathetic to the plaintiffs' position and a nightmare to those favoring the defendants."

The petitioner, Dr. Joseph V. Scelsa, filed the action in both an individual and representative capacity (as director of the Calandra Institute). As dual plaintiff, he sought to bar CUNY from accomplishing three things: (l) "from employment discrimination against Italian Americans";

This article first appeared in *Italian Americans in a Multicultural Society,* edited by Jerome Krase and Judith N. DeSena, 1994, pp. 44-55.

(2) "from relocating the Institute and transferring its operations to several different units of CUNY"; and (3) from removing him as the Institute's director. At the heart of his brief was the averment of discrimination in employment on the basis of national origin. The statutory prohibition against this type of discrimination is specifically proscribed by Title VII of the Civil Rights Act of 1964. Notwithstanding, the prohibition has been largely ignored by the courts and rarely used with success by plaintiffs seeking redress on this ground.

The *Scelsa* Court granted all three requests (or prayers as we say) by way of a preliminary injunction *pendente lite;* that is, pending trial, it barred CUNY from acting so as to prevent the further perpetration of a perceived wrong(s) until such time as the underlying issues are resolved. It concluded that the plaintiffs (Dr. Scelsa and the Institute) had "shown a balance of hardships tipping decidedly in their favor" and "irreparable harm" would otherwise follow. Significantly, the Court allowed Dr. Scelsa, equating his position as director of the Calandra Institute with representation of the Italian-American community of New York City, to cross the litigation threshold to test the merits of the case. In doing so, the Court relied not only on the so-called "disparate impact" theory of Title VII, wherein a discriminatory effect may be shown vis-à-vis employment patterns, but, *sua sponte*: by its own initiative, it also invoked Section 1981 of the Civil Rights Act of 1866, our nation's first civil rights statute for jurisdictional purposes.

This Reconstruction era statute is far wider in scope than Title VII. It concerns the right to make and enforce both private and public contracts and provides broad federal remedies for the enjoyment of all benefits of a contractual relationship. The Court noted that "in grant-[ing injunctive] relief to which the party in whose favor it is rendered is entitled," it may do so on such grounds "even if the party has not [specifically] demanded such relief in the party's pleading." Section 1981 was not pleaded in the moving papers. But the Court raised CUNY's two-decade-old awareness of Italian-American nonrepresentation and the university's pledge(s) to address and seek to correct this imbalance to the level of a contractual relationship with the Italian-American community. It noted:

> A Section 1981 violation may be established not only via presentation of evidence regarding defendant's affirmative acts but also by evidence regarding defendant's omission where defendant is under some duty to act. . . . The Court must find that CUNY's current policy represents either an attempt to renege on the promises of the past or, by denying that such promises were ever made or intended to be kept, a reaffirmation of the original findings of discrimination against an under-representation of Italian Americans that motivated the original Kibbee Memorandum. . . .

Cited by the *Scelsa* Court is a case entitled *St. Francis College v. Al-Khazraj,* which was decided by the United States Supreme Court five years earlier in 1987. This also is significant. Due to the representative conferral granted to Dr. Scelsa because of the Calandra Institute's wider purposes, the citation espouses, on a stage even larger than employment, an opportunity for Italian Americans as a group to redress harms arising out of national origin discrimination. Discrimination on the basis of national origin has always been, and sadly continues to be, a destructive force in American society. As such, it is indistinguishable from racial discrimination. Notwithstanding, modern day civil rights legislation expressly prohibiting discrimination based on "race, color, religion, sex or national origin," has not been interpreted either administratively or judicially to afford protection to these victims of national origin discrimination. The clear and unambiguous language set forth in Title VII as advanced in *Scelsa* states that failure by an employer because of national origin "to hire . . . or otherwise to discriminate against any individual with respect to his compensation, terms, conditions, or privileges of employment" is an unlawful employment practice. Yet the Act has a history of selective enforcement and it would appear that claims of national origin discrimination—either dismissed on procedural grounds or on the merits—have met with failure. A review of the regulations charting compliance with Title VII reveal that, notwithstanding the clear reference to "national origin," redress has primarily been defined within the context of racial classification for governmental purposes. Neither racial minorities nor ethnic minorities (including Italian Americans) have "melted" into Anglo conformity. Sociologists generally agree that thus far in the American saga, "acculturation" and not "structural assimilation" has proven to be the norm; and the diversity inherent in "cultural pluralism" has persisted well into the third, even the fourth generation. Public policy misconception of the process continues to ignore this reality, and the legal definition of minority continues for practical purposes to be synonymous with skin color.

In light of this, no governmental compilation of ethnic data is either required or taken; thus, legal writers rightly contend that is all but impossible to prove the existence of discrimination based on national origin. Therefore, Italian Americans who are victims of discrimination must try to prove their case without the benefit of officially compiled statistics—an overwhelming task given essential Title VII procedural requirements. The need for statistical analysis in order to fulfill the initial legal burden of going forward to establish what we term a *prima facie* case was noted in *Scelsa;* nor did CUNY, despite good faith promises extracted in the 1970s to do so, maintain ongoing data on Italian-American recruitment and employment for affirmative action purposes. However, and in view of this failure, two statistical studies compiled by the plaintiff, Calandra Institute, were deemed "the best available evidence" by the Court. The *Scelsa* Court went further. By adopting the conception of race set forth in *St. Francis College* under the 1866 law, it eased the way toward addressing not only employment but an array of civil rights violations alleging national origin discrimination against Italian Americans by CUNY.

The Civil Rights Act of 1866 was an enabling statute for the Thirteenth Amendment. This post-Civil War enactment intended to confer the equality "enjoyed by white citizens" of the time—the white majoritarian Anglo or Nordic "race" then populating the country, the standard control group, if you will—upon all other persons and in all respects. The Supreme Court's decision in *St. Francis College,* relying on the 1866 Act, significantly expanded the definition of "race" for purposes that can find and have found expression in the modern day search for equal protection under the law by those claiming national origin discrimination.

In *St. Francis College,* the Court held that a white person may be protected from racial discrimination. It based its holding on a broad construction of the original intent of Section 1981 of the 1866 Act. Section 1981 of the Act states: "All Persons . . . shall have the same right . . . to make and enforce contracts . . . and to the full and equal benefit of all laws and proceedings. . . ." The Court rejected the counter argument that a Caucasian was barred from suing other Caucasians under the statute. Instead, relying heavily on the legislative history of Section 1981 and on the general conception of race during the nineteenth century when the statute was enacted, it observed:

> [It] may be that a variety of ethnic groups . . . are now considered to be within the Caucasian race. The understanding of "race" in the nineteenth century, however was different. Plainly, all those who might be deemed Caucasian today were not thought to be of the same race at the time Section 1981 became law.

In support of this reasoning, the Court examined two strands of evidence from the nineteenth century: dictionary and encyclopedia definitions of "race" and the legislative history of Section 1981. In considering nineteenth-century definitions of race, Webster's dictionary of 1877 proved insightful: "[t]he descendants of a common ancestor; a family, tribe, people or nation, believed or presumed to belong to the same stock." The Court also listed "races" found in nineteenth-century encyclopedias: the *Encyclopedia Americana* (1858) and the *Encyclopedia Britannica* (1878) that *inter alia* referred to "Italians" and various other ethnic "races." Similarly, a review of the legislative history of Section 1981 proved convincing to the Court. It too was "replete with references to the universality of its application"; that is, to all ethnic "races." This, combined with the nineteenth-century concept of race as illustrated by reference materials of the period, formed the foundation for the Court's holding:

> Based on the history of Section 1981, we have little trouble in concluding that Congress intended to protect from discrimination identifiable classes of persons who are subjected to intentional discrimination solely because of their ancestry or ethnic characteristics. Such discrimination is racial discrimination that Congress intended Section 1981 to forbid, whether or not it would be classified as racial in terms of modern scientific theory.

The Court's opinion specifically rejected reliance on genetics and/or physical characteristics:

> It is clear from our holding that a distinctive physiognomy is not essential to qualify for Section 1981 protection.

In making this finding, the Court defined the word "race" in its sociological, perhaps sociopolitical, rather than biological sense. "Race" in the sociological sense considers the concept that people differ from each other not primarily because of physical attributes, but because of differences rooted in culture. A review of the legislative history of the Act reveals that its supporters intended that its protection be liberally construed, encompassing the civil liberties of all persons without distinction as between race and national origin. Interestingly, the Court's research disclosed that only in this century have "races" been divided physiognomically, that is, "Caucasoid," "Mongoloid" and "Negroid," footnoting that many modern biologists and anthropologists . . . criticize [these] classifications as arbitrary and of little use in understanding the viability of human beings."

The *Scelsa* Court found that "[d]iscrimination on the basis of national origin is encompassed within the scope of activities prohibited by Section 1981." Italian Americans have benefited from this revised standard on a number of occasions prior to *Scelsa,* although not with the same potential for a sweeping remedy. The District of Maine in *DeSalle v. Key Bank of Southern Maine* in 1988 was the first Court to hold that Italian Americans are an identifiable class entitled to maintain an action under Section 1981 for purposes of discrimination. In *DeSalle,* the plaintiff had sued his former employer, alleging breach of contract and violation of civil rights on the basis of his Italian heritage. In accordance with *St. Francis College,* the Court held that discrimination based on a plaintiffs ancestry was actionable as a civil rights claim under Section 1981. The Court highlighted the references in *St. Francis College* to various ethnic "races." It concluded:

> The definition of race in the nineteenth century, when the legislative sources for Section 1981 were enacted, differed from the definition prevalent today; not all Caucasians were considered of the same race. . . . Section 1981 was designed to protect identifiable classes of persons, such as Italo-Americans, "who are subjected to intentional discrimination solely because of their ancestry or ethnic characteristics. . . ."

In one of the few cases where a plaintiff prevailed on the merits is a 1989 national origin discrimination case. The Ninth Circuit, which is based in San Francisco, held in *Benigni v. City of Hemet* that Italian Americans are protected against discrimination for purposes of a companion Section 1982 of the 1866 Act, which concerns the right to hold property. The plaintiff, an owner of a restaurant, had obtained a jury verdict claiming that the defendant's police officers had discriminatorily harassed his business and customers forcing him to sell his business at a loss. The Court of appeals, in upholding the verdict, agreed:

> Elements of an intentional discrimination claim . . . are present in this case because the evidence tends to show the discriminatory effect of greater law enforcement activity at [the plaintiffs business] than at other bars, and the discriminatory intent of singling out Benigni based on his Italian ancestry.

The Court cited *St. Francis College* for the interrelated proposition: "targets of race discrimination for purposes of Section 1981 include groups that today are considered merely different ethnic or national groups.

In another context, the Supreme Court has ruled that peremptory challenges in jury selection may not be used to further racially discriminatory motives. Under existing case law, a defendant must establish that he is "a member of a cognizable racial group" to make a *prima facie* or initial showing of discriminatory peremptory challenges. In 1989, *United States v. Biaggi* treated the issue. A motion to set aside a verdict on the ground that the prosecution had used its peremptory challenges discriminatorily to exclude Italian Americans from the jury was brought. In his moment of defeat, Mario Biaggi, the senior United States Congressman from New York City, provided yet another service to an Italian-American constituency that extended well beyond the confines of his congressional district. Relying on characteristic Italian names ending in vowels to make the claim, it was argued that the prosecution had exercised certain peremptory challenges solely to strike potential Italian-American jurors. The Court held that Italian Americans constitute a "cognizable racial group" for purposes of raising objections to this form of challenge. The *Biaggi* decision followed two strands of reasoning: The first traced the meaning of "racially cognizable group"; the second traced the meaning of this term in light of *St. Francis College*. As to the first strand, the Court found:

> Italian Americans are "recognizable" and "distinct." and appear to have been "singled out for different treatment under the laws, as written or applied. . . ." Italian Americans share a common ancestry in Italy, a common cultural and religious heritage here and there, and they often still share a common language. They are identifiable, in part, by their characteristic last names. The Court takes judicial notice that Italian Americans are considered in this district to be a recognizable and distinct ethnic group, commonly identified by their last names and by their neighborhoods. These qualities are sufficient to render Italian Americans no less cognizable than the other groups who have already been recognized for equal protection purposes.

The Court referred to three criteria useful in finding Italian Americans a cognizable racial group. They "(1) are definable and limited by some clearly identifiable factor; (2) share a common thread of attitudes, ideas or experiences; and (3) share a community of interests, such that the group's interests cannot be adequately represented if the group is excluded from the jury selection process."

Limiting its holding to the Eastern District of New York, which is based in Brooklyn, the Court held that Italian Americans satisfy these criteria to make "a sufficient showing to categorize [themselves] as cognizable." Moreover, it provided a detailed and illuminating discussion of its reasons for taking judicial notice of Italian Americans' cognizability:

> These observable, distinguishable names constitute a clearly identifiable factor separating Italian Americans from most other ethnic groups. These names emanate from Italian ancestors who immigrated to this country and who constitute a discrete resource from which Italian-American heritage has been passed down.
>
> Italian Americans share a common experience and background in their links to Italian families, Italian culture, and Italian group loyalties, and often share the same religious and culinary practices. The Court takes judicial notice that Italians have been subject to stereotyping, invidious ethnic humor and discrimination. (" . . . Italians . . . continue to be excluded from executive, middle-management, and other job levels because of discrimination based upon their religion and/or national origin"). . . . Like any group recently emigrated from a cohesive nation, Italian Americans share numerous common *threads* of attitudes, ideas, and experiences, often including largely intertwined family relations in the country of origin. Finally, Italian Americans have a community of interest; they generally share certain cherished values received through generations of Italian civilization and religion, including values relevant to moral culpability. Across the board exclusion of this group could not but impair the representation of these interests in juries.

Having concluded that Italian Americans are a cognizable racial group, the Court recounted *St. Francis College's* review of the nineteenth-century scholarly definitions of race and the legislative history of the 1866 Act. As to this second strand of reasoning, it found that the [l]egislative history of post-Civil War statutes provides corroborative support for the view that, at that time, "races" included "immigrant groups" coming from each foreign nation and, further, "[i]t can therefore be confidently concluded that . . . *cognizable racial groups* include[s] a variety of ethnic and ancestral groups subject to intentional discrimination, including Italian Americans."

The *Biaggi* decision has since been cited with approval. Although the Court did accept the prosecution's racially neutral explanations for exercising the peremptory challenges, and denied the motion to set aside the guilty verdict, the decision is still crucial. It admirably recognizes discrimination against Italian Americans in various aspects of American society. Additionally, it highlights for us that as an ethnic group, "Italian Americans are also shielded by the [Fourteenth Amendment's] equal protection clause's prohibition against discrimination because of ancestry."

In sum, Section 1981 grounds for seeking relief in cases of national origin discrimination illustrate a definite trend; namely, an expanded equal protection jurisprudence where race can be and, in fact, has been equated with ethnicity, or national origin. The Section provides an effective vehicle where injustice or inequity prevails against ethnic minorities. Moreover, Section 1981 filings are neither limited to the employment arena nor burdened with detailed procedural requirements that are a prerequisite to filings under modern-day civil rights legislation. Ethnics who have suffered discrimination as a result of their national origin in any area, would be well served in seeking judicial solicitude by alleging discrimination based on "race" under this statute—either alone or in conjunction with other statutory remedies.

In seeking social justice where right or entitlement within a sphere of cultural pluralism is denied, servitude in any form is alien to the espousal of a philosophy based on mutual respect and tolerance for differences. Indeed, it has been argued that the theory of Anglo conformity is inherently discriminatory: it requires assimilation into a majoritarian culture and inferentially emarginates other legitimate forms of cultural expression. Section 1981 relief, as we have seen from a reading of *Scelsa,* provides a wide avenue to redress this form of coercion. At the very least, it should suffice to assist plaintiffs who allege national origin discrimination in crossing the litigation threshold to test the merits of their cause before the Courts.

WORK CITED

Scelsa v the City University of New York, 806 F.Supp. 1126 (S.D.N.Y., 1992).

St. Francis College v. Al-Kharaj, 481 U.S. 604 (1987).

DeSalle v Key Bank of Southern Maine, 685 F. Supp. 282 (D. Me., 1988).

Benigni v. City of Hemet, 879 F. 2d 472 (9th Cir., 1989).

United States v. Biaggi, 673 F. Supp. 96 (E.D.N.Y., 1989).

Greek-Americans in the Political Life of the United States

John Brademas

On June 12, 1984, I addressed the Propeller Club of the United States in Athens, Greece. With headquarters in Washington, D.C., and seventeen thousand members in one hundred clubs worldwide, the Propeller Club brings together leaders of the maritime industry interested in promoting better understanding among nations. As the first native-born American of Greek origin elected to Congress, I decided to discuss the increasing participation of Greek-Americans in the political life of the United States.

Having while in Congress been deeply involved in the foreign policy struggle that followed the August 1974 invasion of the Republic of Cyprus by Turkish military forces equipped with arms supplied by the United States, I also spoke of the continuing problem of Cyprus.

At this writing, twenty-two thousand Turkish troops, in violation of international law, and of resolutions of the United Nations, remain on Cyprus. In July 1985, the first "government" of the "Turkish Republic of Northern Cyprus" assumed office, thereby underscoring the continuing refusal of the government of Turkey to remove its military forces. Like his predecessor, President Carter, President Reagan, while claiming to work through the United Nations and other diplomatic channels for a solution to this ongoing crisis, has been unwilling to press Turkey to take serious steps for a fair and peaceful resolution of the Cyprus problem. Beyond the terrible injustice done to the people of this small island republic who have been driven from their homes, the impasse continues to poison both Greek-American and Greek-Turkish relations and thus threaten the effectiveness of the NATO Alliance.

As THE SON of a Greek immigrant, I naturally feel at home in the land of my father's birth. After all, every one of us of Greek origin takes a special pride in that fact. We remember what the great poet Constantine Cavafy said of King Antiochus:

> ... He was the best of all things, Hellenic—
> mankind has no quality more precious:
> everything beyond that belongs to the Gods.

Yet because I am not only a Hellene but an American, I want to discuss today the role that Americans of Greek descent play in the politics of the United States.

We all know that in the early part of this century, thousands of Greek men and women emigrated to America. My own father, Stephen Brademas, at the age of twenty-one, left Calamata to make his way eventually to northern Indiana, where he met my mother, a schoolteacher. Stephen and Beatrice Brademas settled down and raised their family in the town of South Bend, Indiana.

Estimates differ, but the most reliable are that about two and a half million people who were either born in Greece or are of Greek descent live in the United States, with substantial Greek communities in Boston, Chicago, Detroit, San Francisco and New York. In New York City, there are 300,000 Greek-Americans; in Astoria, in the Borough of Queens, nearly 100,000, the largest Hellenic community outside Greece. After early years of struggle, most Greek-Americans have moved into the ranks of middle-income families, with a healthy percentage enjoying upper-income status.

Over the years, Americans of Greek Origin have been prominent in science, business, education, the arts, the media and public life. In medicine, for example, the Greek-American contribution is represented by Dr. George Papanicolaou, who invented the Pap smear test for cervical cancer, and Dr. George Cotzias, who developed L-dopa, the drug used in treating Parkinson's disease; in business, by the president of Mobil Corporation, William Tavoulareas; shipping executive George P. Livanos; the Gouletas family of realtors; in education, by my fellow university president, Peter Liacouras, who heads Temple University; in the arts, by the painter Theodoros Stamos, the conductor Dimitri Mitropoulos, the theater director Elia Kazan, the filmmaker George Lucas, the actors John Cassavetes, Alex Karras and Telly Savalas, the singer Maria Callas; and in journalism and writing, Nicholas Gage, author of the best-selling book *Eleni*.

The Greek Immigrant Experience

Important as the achievements of our compatriots in all these areas have been, I want to focus today on the participation of Greek-Americans in public life. First, you must understand that Greeks were in significant ways different from other ethnic groups who came to the United States. Few in number, they rarely congregated in permanent ghettos. By avoiding the hardships of large, overcrowded, working-class neighborhoods, they were not compelled to organize politically either for individual gain or community protection.

Like all immigrants, our people initially worked for someone else, but eventually most succeeded in owning their own businesses. As independent entrepreneurs, they rarely looked to government jobs or public assistance, and they stood apart from the growing political influence of the trade union movement. This commercial independence was augmented by the social isolation stemming from the inward aspect of the Greek-American community—the preoccupation with family, church and local social clubs. Finally, an obsessive preoccupation during the 1920s and 1930s with the politics of the Old Country tended to dissipate the political energies of Greeks living in the United States.

Political Involvement

It would be a mistake, however, to say that political life was completely dormant for Greek-Americans. Viewing politics as a civic obligation, our people voted proudly and regularly, with a few Greek-Americans emerging into the public limelight. Two of the most prominent were George Vournas, the great AHEPA (American Hellenic and Progressive Association) leader, and Charles Maliotis of Massachusetts, a close friend of the Kennedys and of two Speakers of the United States House of Representatives, the late John W. McCormack and the present Speaker, Thomas P. O'Neill, Jr.

In the subsequent rise of Greek-Americans in American politics, certain events and personalities stand out as important symbols. One was Mike Manatos, who in 1961 became the first Greek-American on the White House staff, where he served both Presidents Kennedy and Johnson. In later years, his son Andrew was an Assistant Secretary of Commerce. Here I must also mention Peter Peterson, first Greek-American to hold a cabinet post, as Secretary of Commerce. Another symbol was George Christopher, who, in 1955, was elected Mayor of San Francisco, first Greek-American to lead a big city. In the years since, Greek-Americans have served as mayors in cities coast to coast: Saint Paul, Minnesota; Gary, Indiana; Savannah, Georgia; Syracuse, New York; Hartford, Connecticut; Annapolis, Maryland; and Lincoln, Nebraska. George Athanson served longer as Mayor of Hartford than any other person, while Lee Alexander, Mayor of Syracuse for fourteen years, is chairman of the National Conference of Democratic Mayors.

In 1958, I became the first native-born American of Greek origin ever to serve in either chamber of Congress when, on my third attempt, I was elected to the United States House of Representatives. Actually, the first Hellene elected to Congress was Miltiades Miller, who was born in Greece, came to America and served one term in the House of Representatives in the late nineteenth century. I regret to have to tell you that he was a Republican!

It would not be until 1966 that I would be joined in Congress by other Greek-Americans. That year, however, marked the beginning of an escalation of political victories by Americans of Greek descent that continues until today. In 1966, Peter Kyros of Maine and Nick Galifianakis of North Carolina were elected to Congress, and Spiro Agnew of Maryland became the nation's first Greek-American governor. In 1968, Agnew was designated by Richard Nixon to be Vice-President and overnight the name Spiro became a household word. Also that year Gus Yatron of Pennsylvania was elected to Congress, bringing the number of Greek-Americans in the House of Representatives to four.

Two years later, Paul Sarbanes of Maryland, son of immigrants from Laconia, Greece, was elected to the House and in 1972, L. A. "Skip" Bafalis of Florida also became a Congressman.

In 1974, Michael Dukakis, son of a highly respected Greek immigrant physician, was elected Governor of Massachusetts, a position to which he was again elected last year, while in 1974, Paul Tsongas went to the U.S. House of Representatives from the same state.

In 1976, Congressman Sarbanes of Maryland set a precedent when he was elected the nation's first United States Senator of Greek origin. You may be interested in this sidelight: Paul Sarbanes, Mike Dukakis and I have in common more than our Greek heritage. All three of us are Democrats, all graduates of Harvard and all of us studied at Oxford University as Rhodes Scholars. Let me here interject that there is no abler Governor in the United States than Mike Dukakis nor a finer member of the United States Senate than Paul Sarbanes. Both of these men are exceptionally intelligent, have now had several years of experience in high public office and are nonetheless relatively young. In my judgment, they will both be increasingly important figures on the national scene.

In 1978, Paul Sarbanes was joined in the Senate by Paul Tsongas, while Nicholas Mavroules was elected to the House of Representatives and Olympia Bouchles Snow of Maine became the first Greek-American woman elected to Congress.

In 1980, having served twenty-two years in Congress, I was defeated in my bid for reelection. My district had become over the years more conservative, unemployment was high and Ronald Reagan won in my area by a landslide over President Jimmy Carter.

But the elections of 1982 brought two more Greek-Americans to Washington—Congressmen Mike Bilirakis of Florida and George Gekas of Pennsylvania.

My brief survey has focused on persons elected to national office and so does not include hundreds of Greek-Americans in state and municipal posts or in staff positions on Capitol Hill.

Let me here observe that the preoccupation with small business, which forty years before had kept early immigrants from involvement in politics, developed during the 1960s and 1970s into a useful vehicle for influencing public opinion. Greek-Americans have also generally been treated more favorably by the press and the public than other ethnic groups. These factors have meant that Greek-Americans are often in positions in business and the professions that give them an opportunity for meaningful exposure to the public—and for political action.

Greek Americans and Cyprus

This combination of more and more Greek-Americans winning elections to office, growing economic strength in the small business community and the professions and public respect for persons of Greek origin helped make possible their effective political participation in the events following the invasion of Cyprus in 1974 by Turkey.

This is not the place to rehearse the tragic events of nearly a full decade ago. Let me make just a few observations here. As you know, the American political system is based on a constitutional separation of powers. We do not have a parliamentary system of government in which the legislature must customarily support the executive branch. Even today, on such issues as Central America, you will observe how members of Congress of President Reagan's own party oppose him.

In the American democracy, Congressmen and Senators have an independent and often powerful influence on the conduct of foreign policy. This arrangement often frustrates Presidents, of both parties, but it is the American way of governing. We certainly had an example of such influence by Congress in the Cyprus crisis.

You will all recall the invasion, in mid-August of 1974, of the sovereign Republic of Cyprus by some forty thousand Turkish troops equipped with weapons supplied by the United States. Under our law, no country receiving American arms is permitted to use them for other than defensive purposes. Moreover, U.S. law says that if American arms are used by recipient nations for aggression, all further arms *must* be immediately terminated. The law, to reiterate, *mandates* a halt to further shipments.

Because the then Secretary of State, Henry Kissinger, refused to enforce the clear requirement of American law and halt additional arms to Turkey, several of us in Congress acted. We insisted that the laws of our country be enforced and we, therefore, organized an effort to impose an arms embargo on Turkey. Beyond my own work, the leaders of this movement were then Congressman Sarbanes and the late Benjamin Rosenthal in the House of Representatives and Senator Thomas Eagleton of Missouri in the Senate.

A Question of Law and Principle

Although there was much talk of a "Greek lobby," the truth is that there were only a handful of Americans of Hellenic origin in Congress at the time. That we were able to win this struggle was in large measure due to the effectiveness of our argument, namely, that the laws of the land must be respected, even by Presidents and Secretaries of State. You will also recall that these events occurred only a few days and weeks following the resignation of President Nixon, in effect, for his failure to obey the law.

There was another reason for our effectiveness in winning the Turkish arms embargo fight in 1974, and that was the public support for our cause generated across the country by Americans of Greek and Armenian origin and by our friends. I shall not here describe the legislative battles over the last nine and a half years on the arms embargo on Turkey and the occupation of Cyprus. You and I know that the embargo was finally lifted, and we know, too, that there has still been no resolution of the Cyprus tragedy. The struggle for justice for the people of that beleaguered island nation therefore continues.

My point here, however, is that the issue of Cyprus produced a remarkable demonstration of political action on the part of the Greek-American community and its friends. We were effective. New organizations were created by these events and older ones made more politically conscious.

For example, the American Hellenic Institute, led by Washington attorney Eugene Rossides, and the United Hellenic American Congress, organized by Chicago businessman Andrew Athens, helped focus these political efforts. Members of AHEPA and other Greek-American societies intensified their activities while leaders like George P. Livanos and others gave strong support every step of the way. What Greek-Americans discovered from the Cyprus crisis, then, was that well-organized political action, combined with able leadership and the right issue, could significantly affect national policy.

As you are all aware, both the recent unilateral declaration of independence by Turkish Cypriots and the proposals of the Reagan Administration on military aid to Greece and Turkey have provoked renewed criticism by Congress on the part of both Democrats and Republicans. Ironically, ten years after the invasion and occupation of Cyprus, we must still be concerned over the fate of that small, democratic country.

The question of Cyprus continues to trouble not only Americans of Greek origin but all Americans who care about the rule of law in the conduct of our nation's foreign policy.

POLISH AMERICANS AND THE HOLOCAUST

Rev. John T. Pawlikowski, O.S.M., PhD.

I am most grateful for the opportunity to present the 1994 Fierdorczyk lecture. The topic suggested to me, Polish Americans and the Holocaust, is one surrounded with great possibilities for enhanced understanding but considerable controversy as well. Since I have found members of Polonia, as well as the general American community, fairly unacquainted with the details of the Polish story of victimization during the Nazi era I shall begin my narrative with a brief account of that story. Following that I would like to turn my attention, and yours, to some contemporary implications of the Holocaust for Polish Americans, in particular for their relations with Jewish Americans with whom they share a patrimony of victimization.

The Nazi Invasion of Poland: Its Goals and Impact

On September 1, 1939, Poland was invaded by one of the world's strongest and most modern armies. Over 1,800,000 soldiers, representing the elite of the German army, took part in the campaign against it. The German army was vastly superior to any counter-force Poland could mount in its defense because of its tremendous fire-power and mobility enhanced by its motorization. On September 3, 1939, in fulfillment of their treaty obligations to Poland, Great Britain and France declared war on Nazi Germany. The war had been transformed into an allied effort. Though this Franco-British declaration was of great political significance, it had little immediate impact on the military situation. Fighting alone and basically unaided, Poland had to confront more than two thirds of the combined German forces.

From the very outset of the German invasion of Poland, it was apparent that the Nazis were not engaged in a conventional war to defeat the Polish military nor even to subdue the state politically. Instead, as the contemporary Polish-American historian Richard Lukas puts it, ". . . the Germans waged war against the Polish people, intent on destroying the Polish nation."[1] This is an extremely crucial point, one that is often overlooked in writings on Polish victimization under the Nazis. Poles were not killed first and foremost as individual dissenters, whether religious or political. Nor did the Nazi leadership wish only to conquer Poland in a military or political sense. Rather, the Polish nation as nation fell victim to the same basic ideology which eventually turned its attention with even greater fury to the annihilation of the entire Jewish population of Europe.

The Nazi theory of racial superiority totally dehumanized the Polish people. In the Nazi perspective, Poles were considered untermenschen (subhumans) who lived on land coveted by the superior German race. Poland was not simply to be defeated and occupied, the primary goal of the subsequent Nazi invasions of other Western European countries. "The aim is not the arrival at a certain line," declared Hitler, "but the annihilation of living forces."[2]

Even prior to the actual invasion of Poland, Hitler had authorized on August 22, 1939, killing, "without pity or mercy all men, women, and children of Polish descent or language. Only in this way," he insisted, "can we obtain the living space we need."[3] And the person placed in charge of implementing Hitler's Polish "plan," Heinrich Himmler, said outright that "all Poles will disappear from the world. . . . It is essential that the great German people should consider it as its major task to destroy all Poles."[4]

From the above quotations it becomes amply evident that key Nazi operatives, including Hitler himself, seriously contemplated the total extermination of the Polish population in due time. Whether they would have carried out this plan fully if they had been given the opportunity is a matter of conjecture at best. The annihilation of Jews is a fact, not merely a possibility. But on the level of theory, in trying to understand where the Poles fit into the Nazi victimization scheme, no other conclusion can be drawn except that they belong with Jews, Gypsies, and the mentally and physically incapacitated as candidates for eventual total extinction in the gradual emergence of the new Aryan humanity.[5]

Once Poland was firmly under Nazi control, the country was divided into two separate zones. All of western Poland, including the regions of Poznania, Pomerania and Silesia, and sections of central and southern Poland were formally annexed to the Reich. The remaining Polish territories not annexed outright into Germany were set up for administrative purposes as an occupation region and assigned the name "General Government."

The Nazi policy of imposed "Germanization" in the annexed territories relied upon four strategies: a campaign of wide-spread and unmitigated terror; expropriation of land and possessions; deportations; and enslavement. The terror, designed to be harsh enough to mute all possible resistance, began immediately after the invasion in 1939. Virtually every city, town and village in western Poland witnessed wholesale massacres and executions of the leading citizenry. In the city of Bydgoszcz, for example, some 10,000 people perished, out of a population of 140,000, during the first four months of occupation. But even the regions designated as falling under the "General Government" were subjected to much the same treatment.

The terror employed by the Nazis to pacify the Polish population included an extensive use of torture. One of the most notorious sites was the training school for the Gestapo at Fort VII in Poznan. Famous as an institute of sadism, Fort VII drew its victims from the ranks of the clergy, university professors and politicians. It experimented with every conceivable form of torture, from massive beatings to the inflation of prisoners' intestines to the point of bursting.

The Nazi policy of destroying the Polish nations focused strongly, but not exclusively, upon eliminating anyone with even the least political and cultural prominence. But the Nazis had a wide definition of those falling under the rubric of "elite." The category included teachers, physicians, priests, officers, people in business, landowners, writers and extended even to anyone who had completed secondary school. As a result, millions of Poles qualified for liquidation in the Nazi effort to reduce Poland to a nation of indentured servants in the first instance and, perhaps in due time, to wipe it off the map completely.

Hitler gave the initial approval and then turned over direction of the Polish campaign to Himler's SS and the police forces. The SS lost little time in implementing his order. In November, 1939, they arrested almost two hundred professors and fellows of the Jagiellonian University in Cracow, one of Europe's oldest centers of higher learning, as well as the faculty of the Polytechnic. Those seized were all sent to Sachsenhausen, where many perished. The incident caused great concern throughout Europe. The Nazis thus decided to speed up the process of removing the Polish professors from the scene. Taking advantage of the preoccupation of world opinion with military operations in the West in the Spring of 1940, the Nazis launched a massive program to exterminate the Polish intelligentsia living in the General Government region under the code name of "extraordinary purification action." At least six thousand were murdered on the spot; several thousand others were arrested and sent to the newly established Auschwitz concentration camp.

It is important to underline at this point the centrality of the Auschwitz camp in the Nazi plan to destroy Poland and why, as a result, it retains such central symbolic value for contemporary Poles. Originally opened as a camp for German prisoners of war, Auschwitz was quickly transformed into the principal camp for Polish victims even though Poles were also sent to Stutthof, Dachau, Ravensbruck, Sachsenhausen, Mauthausen and Neuengamme. Poles remained the majority of the inmates at Auschwitz until 1942, when Jews assumed that dubious distinction. For Poles, the Auschwitz camp remains a vital link in their collective memory of facing the threat of national, not just political, extinction.

In the course of the controversy over the Carmelite convent at the Auschwitz site, significant mistakes were made on all sides.[6] Surely the first critical misstep was taken on the Catholic side when approval was granted for the erection of the Carmelite convent at the camp without any consultation with the Jewish community. Intended or not, this unilateral move left the distinct impression within the Jewish community that Catholics considered Auschwitz their sacred shrine alone. This was bound to provoke deep and quite understandable feelings of hostility among Jews, especially the survivor community and the members of families whose relatives had perished at Auschwitz. But as the controversy became public and grew more intense, some European Jewish leaders in particular spoke about Auschwitz as though it was the exclusive domain of their community. Some seemed to lack any basic information about the historical origins of the camp as a place of incarceration for German political prisoners and its early role as the central execution site in the Nazi plan to annihilate the elite of Polish society.[7] Mr. Stanislaw Krajewski, a Polish Jew who serves as the American Jewish Committee's representative in Warsaw, has written of the problem of mutual misunderstanding. He admits that "most Poles do not recognize the exceptional character of the project to wipe out the Jewish people and either poorly understand or altogether ignore the Jewish significance of Auschwitz." But he likewise insists that people in the West, including Jews, simply do not appreciate the depth of Polish suffering at Auschwitz: "The historical fact is that the Nazis tried to crush the Polish nation; they not only introduced bloody terror but began to murder Polish elites and destroy Polish culture. The Auschwitz camp was used also for this purpose, and during its first two years of existence, this was its main function."[8] I might add at this point that even Western Christians, with extensive experience in Christian-Jewish dialogue, frequently reveal insufficient awareness of the profound (and enduring) impact of the Nazi era on Polish national life.

Returning to the narrative of the Nazi attack on the Polish nation, we find various tactical shifts in the campaign of extermination against the Polish elite. But the main thrust of the campaign, reduction of the nation to a condition of servitude, continued unabated throughout the war, even when personnel and equipment were needed much more urgently on the war front itself. This took a heavy toll on the Polish people, not only physically but psychologically as well. The Nazis, for example, committed troops to the work of museum destruction in Poland at a time when the absence of reserves on the frontlines was beginning to impinge upon the Nazi war machine. Such activities clearly show that the Nazis envisioned far more than merely the military defeat of Poland. They literally wished to wipe out its cultural identity, preparing perhaps for the time in the future when the people itself might vanish as well.

By the time the war had ended and the Nazis defeated, Poland had suffered the loss of forty-five percent of its physicians and dentists, fifty-seven percent of its attorneys, over fifteen percent of its teachers, forty percent of its professors, thirty percent of its technicians, and nearly twenty percent of its clergy. The majority of its journalists also disappeared. While these statistics are considerably lower than the ones for the Jewish community, and probably lower than those for the Gypsy community as well (though not all categories would be applicable to this community), it still represents a substantial destruction of the "carriers" of the Polish cultural, intellectual, political and religious traditions.

The Nazi effort to annihilate the Polish intelligentsia was part of a systematic program to destroy Polish culture. Education was a particular focus of the Nazi plan. The Nazis hoped eventually to transform Poland into an "intellectual desert." The Nazis denied Polish young people the right to a secondary and university education. Most primary schools were forced to use German as their language of instruction. Polish universities were often occupied by military and civil authorities, and their libraries and laboratories were pillaged. State, municipal, and ecclesiastical archives suffered the same fate.

Polish art and history also became the targets of the Nazi effort to eradicate Polish national self-identity. Major art museums were generally stripped of their collections, with many going to Germany (including some to Hitler himself). After the war only thirty-three of the one hundred seventy-five pre-war art museums had sufficient collections remaining to reopen for public viewing. Museums that were left untouched usually were used by the Nazis to demonstrate alleged German influences on Polish culture. History books were largely confiscated by the Nazis and teachers forbidden to make reference to the nation's past and the persons who shaped it. Monuments, busts, memorials, and inscriptions of Polish heroes, including Kosciuszko, Chopin, and Piłsudski were removed. In Warsaw the Nazis even planned to erect a monument to the victory of the Third Reich in the exact place where the monument to King Zygmunt III was located. This was thus a plan of total national annihilation, *a plan the Nazis enacted in Poland alone of all their occupied territories*.

Hitler understood that the attack on Polish culture would remain incomplete unless Poland's cities took on a German character. The change in this direction began with a change of names—Gdynia became Gotenhafen, Lódz was called Litzmannstadt, Rzeszów was renamed Reichshof. Street names were also Germanized. Hitler hoped eventually to reduce Warsaw to a German provincial town of 100,000–200,000 people. This plan was never realized, however, because of the increasing drain on Nazi resources as the war went on. Cracow, however, which became the center of the General Government, did take on a very German flavor with a large transplanted German population.

Himmler and his chief assistant in the Polish campaign, General Hans Frank, launched a program to expel Poles from certain areas of the country (e.g., the Lublin region) and replace them with German peasants. By and large, these programs proved unsuccessful. But they were very painful for the affected people, sometimes involving the abductions of children from their parents who in some instances were sent to the Reich to be raised as "Germans" and in others were assigned to medical experimentation centers. Racial factors played an important role in determining where a person, especially a child, was sent. Auschwitz and other camps were the lot of many of those displaced.

Because of the close ties between the Catholic church and Polish nationalism over the centuries, the Nazis realized they would have to break the back of the church if their plan of national annihilation was to succeed. When the Nazis partitioned Poland after the invasion, they seriously undercut the church's own territorial structures by dividing up historic dioceses. Thus weakened, the Polish church, especially in the annexed areas, lost most of its hierarchy and clergy: Wrocław, 49.2 percent; Chełmo, 47.8 percent; Lódz, 36.8 percent; and in Poznan, 31.1 percent. Overall 1,811 Polish diocesan priests perished under the Nazis out of the total of 10,017 in 1939. Many church buildings were also destroyed. In Poznan, for example, only two out of the pre-war thirty churches remained at the end of the war.

Polish Catholics, in addition to suffering the internal destruction of their church, also felt abandoned by the Catholic leadership. The Holy See basically followed a policy of reserve even after it received strong appeals from Polish bishops to denounce Nazi atrocities against Polish Catholics as well as in the case of the Third Reich's "euthanasia campaign" and the Italian attack against Greece. The London-based Polish government-in-exile also frequently expressed discontent with the Vatican's unwillingness to denounce the Nazi atrocities against the Polish nation in a more public and detailed fashion.

Richard Lukas addresses this issue in his writings on the Nazi era. He recognizes the practical difficulties the Vatican faced with respect to Poland, in part due to the flight of Cardinal Hlond from the country which caused great disruption in the Polish church. He likewise acknowledges that Pius XII's rather cold reception of Hlond in Rome is considered by Poles one saving feature of the overall papal approach to their national suffering under the Nazis. Yet, for Lukas, the balance sheet does not read well, an evaluation he supports with references to concrete reactions by Poles during the period.

"In the face of the.persecution of the church of Poland," says Lukas, "the Vatican pursued a timid, reserved attitude."[9] This was likely the result of a constellation of forces—a sentimentality about Poland on Pius' part, a tinge of Germanophilism, and fears that public denunciations would make matters worse for the Poles. It was not until June 2, 1943, that the Pope finally issued the long awaited statement denouncing the attack against Poland. Just as in the case of the Jews, Pius XII shied away from explicit condemnation of the Nazis.

The 1943 statement, which admittedly did ease Polish-Vatican tensions to some degree, was an effort to counteract the wide-spread criticism that had grown up within clerical ranks because of the Vatican's seeming hesitancy on the Polish question. There were even Polish voices calling for the severing of ties with the Vatican. Some Poles, according to Lukas, were so upset at Rome that they left church at the mention of Pius' name. The Jesuits of Warsaw were so concerned about the situation that they published a defense of Vatican activities in behalf of Poland. And Catholic historian Fr. John Morley, who also raises the Polish question and sees Vatican inaction as resulting from the primacy accorded by the Holy See to its relations with Germany, relates how Rome explicitly instructed its nuncios on ways to counter the mounting dissatisfaction with its approach to Poland.[10]

The political opposition forces in Poland were also highly critical of Pius' stance. An underground organ published by the Polish Socialists accused the Pope of "walking hand in hand with the Hitlerite . . . Fascists." *Glos Pracy*, another underground newspaper, declared that the Pope had shut himself up in the Vatican without bothering to defend his own people. And the Polish Minister of Interior said that "the people would be relieved by official news about the protest of the Holy See and the Polish government, given the flagrant and never hitherto-experienced persecution of the church in Poland."[11]

Contemporary Implications of Polish Victimization Under the Nazis

As we reflect today on the continuing significance of the determined effort by the Nazis to reduce Poland to perpetual servitude by totally destroying its national identity, and perhaps even, if the possibility had presented itself, to eradicate the population as such, the first responsibility that looms large is remembrance. Nobel prize author Elie Wiesel has said that to forget the victims of the Holocaust is to kill them a second time. Yet, I must candidly say, that in working on Holocaust-related issues in scholarly and public circles for well over two decades my judgment must be that both Polonia and Poland itself has fared poorly up till now in this duty of remembrance. We have been far more vocal in criticizing Jews for not including remembrance of Polish victims in programs under their auspices than we have been active as a community in organizing our own. My own efforts over the years to generate interest within Polish organizations in this regard has generally met no response. While it may be quite proper to criticize the exclusion of Polish victims in public Holocaust ceremonies in particular, such criticism will inevitably lose its force unless it is accompanied by internal efforts from within Polonia and within Poland. For that reason I was pleased to read several months ago in *Zgoda*, a call by PNA President Edward J. Moskal for enhanced commemoration of the Polish victims of the Nazis coupled with a willingness to extend blame for the failures in this regard to the Polish community as well.[12] My fervent hope is that this plea by President Moskal will be taken seriously and implemented by Polish religious groups, fraternal organizations, and academic associations.

Let me add here that in addition to remembering the Polish victims, we must also pay greater honor to the Polish righteous, especially the heroic members of *Zegota*, the only group in Nazi occupied Europe dedicated specifically to saving Jews. I am well aware of some of the political complications with respect to certain members of this movement. But we must put that aside and honor them here in North America as well as in Poland for their courage during the war itself. So far the only film or video that I know of on *Zegota* was produced by a Jewish film maker from Washington, Sy Rotter. Where are the Polish efforts in this regard?

At this point let me introduce an issue which has produced considerable controversy within Polonia, namely, the presentation of Polish victimization and the Polish righteousness in the new U.S. Holocaust Memorial Museum in Washington, D.C. As a member of the federal Holocaust Commission since its creation by Congress in 1980, I feel quite justified in standing before you and saying that the initial goals for this museum with respect to Poland have been realized to a significant extent. The stories of Polish victimization, as well as of Polish rescue efforts, have been fully integrated into the museum's main exhibit. They are not just off somewhere in a side room. And the stories are told with fundamental accuracy. While some legitimate questions have been raised about certain portions of the text, and while I certainly believe the exhibit needs amplification and expansion, the museum graphically portrays the Nazi attack on the Polish nation, depicts the incarceration and extermination of the "elites," and even includes (prominently displayed) one of the key texts regarding future Nazi plans for mass annihilation of Poles. And the special exhibit on Zegota, as well as the official lists of Righteous from Yad Vashem in Israel, clearly give visitors (the vast majority of whom are non-Jewish) an understanding of the extent to which Poles attempted to rescue Jews under the most trying of conditions.

Clearly there are issues in the Museum (e.g. the Kielce pogrom) that need further review. I am committed to such an effort, along with additional Polish representatives on the Council who President Clinton will hopefully soon appoint. I look forward to continued collaboration with interested Polish academics and groups, such as the Holocaust Education Committee of the Kosciuszko Foundation in New York, who have proven so helpful in generating materials and testimonies from Polish survivors. The witness of Joseph Wardzala of Derby, CT, for example, in recording his personal testimony of prison life under the Nazis for the Museum is vital for preserving the story of Polish victimization for future generations. So is the witness of Ambassador Władysław Bartoszewski, a leading figure in *Zegota* and now Polish Ambassador in Vienna, who was honored along with *Zegota* at a public ceremony at the Holocaust Museum on March 22nd.

All is not perfect in terms of the Polish story at the Holocaust Museum. But it is far better than many have made it out to be in public comments in the press. I might add that a recent professional poll of Museum visitors which included a question on attitudes towards Poles and Poland revealed little or no "anti-Polish" feeling among such visitors.

The second major implication I see for Polonia and Poland today from a reflection on the Holocaust is the importance of cultural preservation and enhancement. This does not mean that I advocate cultural isolationism on the part of Poles or Polish Americans. Quite the contrary. I am totally in support of my colleague Dr. Thaddeus Gromada, Director of the Polish Institute of Arts and Sciences, who insisted, in a major address at the Shrine in Doylestown, PA in September 1992, on efforts to integrate the authentic Polish and Polish-American experience into the mainstream of American culture.[13] But we have seen from the example of the Nazi period that destruction of a culture goes hand-in-hand with the physical disappearance of a people. Polish culture served during the Nazi era, as well as the subsequent Communist era, as a powerful bulwark against annihilation by extermination or assimilation. Neither Poles nor Polish Americans today can afford to enter new partnerships in an increasingly pluralistic Europe and America without firm roots in our own culture. We must be prepared to bring something substantial to these new partnerships.

The third implication of the Holocaust concerns the much-debated issue of Church-State relations. This remains a central constitutional question for Poland today and we are facing it anew, albeit in somewhat different ways, here in the United States. Considerable study has been done by Protestant and Catholic scholars on this issue. Some, such as Professor Gordan Zahn, have emphasized how the desire on the part of the German Catholic Church to maintain its Concordat with Hitler muffled its original prophetic critique of Nazism developed by the German Bishops at their Fulde meeting in 1934. For Zahn, one lesson of the Holocaust for the churches is the importance of maintaining a distance from the state for the sake of the church's own integrity.

As Poles and Polish Americans continue to weigh the complex issues involved in church-state relations today in both our countries, the Holocaust can teach us that it seems in the best interests of the Church itself to keep a distance from the state. Official recognition may well mean official cooperation which can easily degenerate into co-option by the state authorities for their own ends, thereby muting the Church's prophetic mandate in any society. In light of the Holocaust experience it is important for Poles to listen to such voices as Jerzy Turowicz, Józef Tischner and Bishop Józef Zycinski, who in varied ways have urged restraint with respect to the Church's direct role in public affairs.[14] And Polish Americans should support such a perspective in Poland rather than giving encouragement to the forces of excessive religio-nationalism. The Polish American community can also assist Poles in better understanding the American experience in Church-State separation, even though they recognize that no simple transfer of perspective is possible or desirable. As in other central areas of Polish national life, Poland must be allowed to be Poland even though it can surely profit from contact with the U.S. experience. I have in fact found many Poles significantly interested in such interchange on the Church-State question, as a number of recent colloquia, including one sponsored by the Marshall Foundation to which I was invited, bear witness.

The final implication of the Polish experience of the Holocaust that I would like to raise this evening is that of *solidarity*. On one of the walls of the Holocaust Museum in Washington we have a portion of the famous quote attributed to Lutheran Pastor Niemoller who eventually died for his opposition to Hitler. Pastor Niemoller said, if I may paraphrase his remarks, that when the Nazis came for the trade unionists, the homosexuals, the Communists, the Jews, and the Catholics, he did not protest because he was not identified with any of these groups. And when the Nazis finally came for him, there was no one left to protest.

Niemoller's statement serves as a powerful reminder for all peoples today, including Polish Americans, of two basic realities. The first is the critical importance of establishing networks of intergroup bonding and support in times of relative social tranquility. There is little hope of developing such ties in times of acute social crisis if they have not been nurtured in more peaceful moments. And we never know when and where such can suddenly become vital. Only recently two U.S. cities, Billings, Montana and Eugene, Oregon have experienced sudden challenges from neo-Nazi elements. Both have responded in exemplary fashion. One lesson that emerges from a study of the Holocaust for Polish Americans (and I dare say for Poles as well) is that the Polish nation stood pretty much alone when it was attacked by the Nazis in 1939. The nation was more or less abandoned by the Western countries, despite certain military alliances that existed on paper, and even to a significant degree by the Vatican.

This abandonment has generated decades of anger within Polonia. I do not wish to suggest that this anger has been without any foundation. But I do want to urge Polish Americans to take a second look at the matter, to see whether a certain exaggerated nationalism which in turn bred isolationism might not have contributed to the relative lack of effective alliances in the inter-war period.

Poles in Poland will need to re-examine the nation's set of alliances in this new hopeful, yet potentially threatening, era in Europe. It is not my role to enter into that discussion here. But Polish Americans will also need to seriously re-examine their ties to other groups in our society. Clearly, establishing effective relationships with key minority groups, especially Hispanics and African Americans with whom Polish Americans often share the urban landscape, becomes an important priority. Equally so do ties with American Jewry given the historic linkage between the two communities stemming from Poland itself. While Polish-Jewish relations have been marked by tensions on numerous occasions here in America,[15] we have also witnessed reasonably successful efforts to build lasting coalitions, both in several local communities such as New York, Chicago, Buffalo and Milwaukee and through the National Polish American-Jewish American Council based in Chicago. Through these channels Poles and Jews have begun not merely to discuss and study our past mutual history, but, as we continue this process, to work cooperatively for mutual support of each other's social agendas as well as joint action on issues of importance to both our communities (e.g. foreign aid legislation). Such efforts need expanded support both from the leadership of American Polonia as well as from the grass roots. The Holocaust has taught both Poles and Polish Americans that safety exists only in solidarity with others.

The second implication emerging from the more general notion of solidarity is the importance of standing up for the basic rights of all people. Poles must answer the challenge of discrimination whether directed against them or others. When any one group is singled out for attack, the poison inevitably enters the bloodstream of society and begins to claim other victims as well. This is crystal clear in the Holocaust. The experience of victimization under the Nazis, then, should place Polish Americans in the forefront of the struggle for human rights and human equality for all. The day on which Polonia becomes identified with opposition to human rights and human equality is the day on which it has lost all sense of its own victimization under the Nazis.

Responding to the Holocaust in the constructive ways I have suggested above, particularly the commitment to improve bonding with the Jewish community with whom we share a history of Nazi victimization, will not prove easy. But I know from my own experience of my grandmother's very human and personal interaction with Polish Jews in the Logan Square neighborhood of Chicago where I was reared, as well as from my experience of seeing firsthand the profound welcome accorded the first group of Israelis to revisit Poland in twenty years (a professional dance company), Jews and Poles both have roots in the soil of Poland that can never be totally erased. It will take the courage and tenacity of the soldiers who tried to defend Poland against impossible military odds and the partisans who kept the spirit of freedom alive; it will take the resolve of the courageous men and women of Zegota. We should not expect it to be otherwise. Nothing worthwhile ever is.

Notes

1. Richard C. Lukas, *Forgotten Holocaust: The Poles Under German Occupation 1939–1944.* Lexington, KY: The University Press of Kentucky. 1986.
2. Cf. Eugeniusz Duraczynski, *Wojna i Okupacja: Wrzesien 1939–Kwiecien 1943.* Warsaw: Wiedza Powszechna, 1974, 17. Also Jewry 1933–1945. New York: Schocken, 1973, 163; 193 and Leon Poliakov, *Harvest of Hate: The Nazi Program for the Destruction of the Jews of Europe* (New York: Holocaust Library, 1979), 263.
3. Cf. Janusz Gumkowski and Kazimierz Leszczynski, *Poland under Nazi Occupation.* (Warsaw: Polonia Publishing House, 1961), 59.
4. Cf. Karol Pospieszalski, *Polska pod Niemieckim Prawem.* (Poznan: Wydawnictwo Instytutu Zachodniego, 1946), 189.
5. For a discussion of the elimination of the handicapped and the Gypsies relative to the extermination of the Jews, cf. Sybil Milton, "The Context of the Holocaust," *German Studies Review,* 13:2 (May 1990), 269–283.
6. Cf. John T. Pawlikowski, "The Auschwitz Convent Controversy: Mutual Misperceptions," in Carol Rittner and John K. Roth (eds.), *Memory Offended: The Auschwitz Convent Controversy.* (New York, Westport, CT., London: Praeger, 1991), 63–73. Also cf. Wladyslaw T. Bartoszewski, *The Convent at Auschwitz.* (New York: George Braziller, 1990).
7. John T. Pawlikowski, "The Auschwitz Convent Controversy," 65.
8. Cf. Stanislaw Krajewski, "Carmel at Auschwitz: on the Recent Polish Church Document and Its Background," *SIDIC 22* (1989), 16.
9. Richard Lukas, *Forgotten Holocaust,* 16.
10. John Morely, *Vatican Diplomacy and the Jews During the Holocaust: 1939–1943.* (New York: Ktav, 1980), 140; 146.
11. Cited in Richard Lukas, *Forgotten Holocaust,* 16–17.
12. Edward J. Moskal, "The Polish Victims of the Holocaust," *Zgoda* (February 15, 1994), 5.
13. Thaddeus V. Gromada, "Polish Americans and Mainstream America," unpublished lecture, Polish Apostolate Seminar, Our Lady of Czestochowa Shrine, Doylestown, PA, September 27, 1992, 4.
14. Cf. John T. Pawlikowski, "The Holocaust: Its Implications for Contemporary Church-State Relations in Poland," *Religion in Eastern Europe,* XIII:2 (April 1993), 1–13 and "Katolicyzm a zycie publiczne najnowsze doswiadczenia amerykanskie," *WIEZ* 35:2 (Luty 1992), 93–110. Also cf. Part IV, "The Church," in Janine R. Wedel, (ed.), *The Unplanned Society: Poland During and After Communism.* New York: Columbia University Press, 1992, 188–219.
15. The tension over the Auschwitz convent situation is certainly not the first instance of Polish-Jewish controversy in the United States. For an earlier example, cf. Andrzej Kapiszewski, "Polish-Jewish Conflicts in America During the Paris Peace Conference: Milwaukee as a Case Study," *Polish American Studies,* XLIX:2 (Autumn 1992), 5–18.

Jerusalem Journal

A Riddle: What Is Catholic, Jewish and Stateless?

SERGE SCHMEMANN

JERUSALEM, Nov. 24—In 1990, Regina and Alexander Deriev and their son, Denis, took advantage of the new religious freedoms in the Soviet Union and were baptized into the Roman Catholic Church. In 1991, they immigrated to Israel.

That combination in itself would not make the Derievs different from many other Soviet immigrants in Israel. It is common knowledge here and a source of some resentment among Israelis that tens of thousands of the immigrants—the exact figure is impossible to ascertain—have questionable Jewish credentials.

Some are Christians, while some others have little or no Jewish ancestry, and many of those who are Jewish have little interest in observing Jewish customs and law.

The difference is that Mrs. Deriev, a Jew by birth, insisted when they arrived in Israel on telling authorities that she is Christian, instead of simply maintaining that she is a non-believer as many other Soviet immigrants have done. That thrust the Derievs smack into the heart of the fundamental Israeli debate over who is a Jew, and for five years it left them in a singular state of limbo.

Last Friday, the Israeli High Court rejected the Derievs' application for citizenship, noting that the Law of Return, which governs the right of Jews to settle in Israel, excludes Jews who have adopted another faith. Under the law, spouses and immediate family of someone who is accepted as Jewish are allowed to qualify for Israeli citizenship.

The country from which the Derievs came, the Soviet Union, no longer exists. So they cannot be deported, and they cannot go to some other country because they have no passports. Kazakstan, where they last lived when it was part of the Soviet Union, will not take them back because they are not Kazaks. Russia will not take them because they are not Russians—Mr. Deriev, a non-Jew, is Ukranian and Mrs. Deriev, by Russian standards, is still a Jew. Ukraine would not take them because Mr. Deriev does not speak Ukrainian.

The Derievs have been living in a small, one-bedroom apartment in an Arab suburb of Jerusalem. Mr. Deriev works as an engineer recording liturgical music and their son attends an Arab Christian school.

Back in 1991, when the Derievs decided to emigrate, they had no idea it would be like this. In the Soviet Union, being Jewish was a matter of nationality—like being Ukranian, Chechen or Russian—and had nothing to do with religion. In fact, the Russian language, unlike English or Hebrew, has separate words for Jewish nationality—"Yevrei"—and the Jewish religion—"Iudeistvo."

So Mrs. Deriev—who like many other Soviet Jews had never practiced Judaism, but whose nationality was listed in their passport as Jewish—did not think she was changing her nationality, much less betraying her heritage, when she adopted Catholicism. Nor would most Soviet Jews. In fact, the father of Yuli Edelstein—a former Soviet refusenik who is now Minister of Absorption and thus charged with bringing Jews to Israel—is a Russian Orthodox priest in Russia.

"My father and mother were both Jewish in their passports, but they were staunch Communists, and never put any significance on being Jewish," Mrs. Deriev said. "In fact, my father was a professor of Marxism-Leninsim."

A FAMILY SINKING IN RELIGIOUS AND ETHNIC QUICKSAND.

"I was different—I wrote things the authorities didn't like. The K.G.B. kept tabs on me, my poetry was never published, and I was only accepted into the Union of Writers with 'glasnost' "—the new policy of openness introduced by Mikhail Gorbachev after 1985.

But Mrs. Deriev's poetry did attract the attention of Joseph Brodsky, the exiled poet, and he urged her to leave the Soviet Union. Israel seemed a logical choice. The Derievs were living in the remote Kazakstan city of Karaganda, the Soviet Union was falling apart, thousands of Soviet Jews were leaving and many of their friends were already in Israel.

"We presumed that Israel was a Western, democratic country, where I would finally be published," Mrs. Deriev said.

So Mr. Deriev went to distant Moscow to fill out the forms at the Dutch Embassy, which represented Israeli interests at a time when there were no diplomatic relations.

"The form had blanks for 'nationality' and 'faith,' and I asked the Israeli official what I should put for my wife, if she's Jewish and Catholic," Mr. Deriev said. "He said for 'faith,' put either 'Jewish' or 'non-believer.' I put 'non-believer.' "

On arrival in Israel, Mrs. Deriev was given another form. On this one, she put "Catholic." "I thought it was shameful to hide my faith," she said. "It was the only important choice I ever made, and I didn't hide it even from my father."

What Mrs. Deriev did not appreciate at the time was that the issue she raised went to the very identity of the state of Israel. Ever since the founding by secular Zionists—many of them socialists from Russia—the question of who is a Jew has reappeared in countless forms and disputes.

Under Jewish religious law, a Jew is defined as a person whose mother is a Jew. But the Law of Return was drafted to grant Israeli citizenship to those who would have been persecuted as Jews under the Nazis and so was extended to the grandchildren of a Jew. The exception was those who deliberately adopted another faith.

These rules, however, mingled religious and civil definitions in a way that gives rise to endless disputes. Thus a Russian immigrant who is recognized as a Jew for purposes of citizenship may not be recognized as a Jew by the Orthodox rabbis, a conflict that has already created problems with marriages and burials, which are controlled by the Orthodox rabbinate.

Another conflict to which American Jews are particularly sensitive is the resistance of Israeli Orthodox rabbis to recognizing conversions performed by Reform or Conservative rabbis in the United States. Thus an American converted to Judaism in the United States could be judged ineligible to settle in Israel.

In Mrs. Deriev's case, one twist is that she had immigrated first and converted later, she would have had far fewer problems. Once she had received her citizenship, she would have been free to convert to Christianity.

The Derievs' lawyer, Lynda Brayer, is in fact a South African Jew who was baptized into the Catholic Church after she was already in Israel. Her practice is in human-rights law.

"The only reason they're in trouble is that they didn't lie," Mrs. Brayer said.

Mrs. Brayer said she believed that the Derievs were victims of a fundamental clash between the Israeli Government's historic effort to bring as many Jews as possible into Israel and the determination of the rabbis to maintain as much control as possible over the purity of the arrivals.

Her argument before the High Court was that the Israeli official in Moscow who told applicants to put "Jewish" or "non-believer" on their application forms did so deliberately, to bring in as many immigrants as possible while the doors were open. She declared that Israel was therefore bound to accept the Derievs.

By contrast, immigrants from the United States would have had to submit to a thorough check by religious authorities before being allowed to make aliyah, as Jewish immigration to Israel is called.

Her next step, Mrs. Brayer said, will be to seek refugee status for the Derievs, so they could at least settle in another country.

The Ethnic Factor: International Challenges for the 1990s

The process of better understanding the multiethnic character of America and the world involves the coordinated efforts of formal and informal education, which are influenced by public and private institutions and the community-based voluntary associations that are the building blocks of society. This collection of articles addresses resistance to the challenges that are embedded in passionately held and politically potent traditions of ethnic opposition. The persistence of confusion, uncertainty, insensitivity, and violence toward and between ethnic groups is a sobering and stunning fact. Strategies for dealing with the tension and reality of bias are examined in this unit. Hatred and prejudice are frequently based on conscious manipulation of powerful images that profoundly shape personal and group identity. Exploring other societies is often a way of gaining fresh perspective on the American reality; differences and commonalities of the situations described in this unit are worth pondering.

Examination, for example, of the legacy of the civil rights laws crafted during the 1960s and the process of shaping a society grounded in exclusionary habits and institutions involves assessment on many levels—the social, the political, the ideological, and the economic. Even on the most basic level of public perception, most agree that progress has been made toward a society of equality and social justice, with increased hopes for decreased segregation in schools and neighborhoods. Yet disparities of these views among ethnic and racial groups indicate that uniformity and a shared sense of the past and present are not generally common. Attempting to overcome such gulfs of misunderstanding before they lead to more serious forms of conflict is among the great challenges of the present.

Since the breakup of the Soviet empire, ethnicity has reoriented the international arena. New national claims as well as the revival of ancient antagonisms are fragmenting Europe. War, the systematic expression of conflict, and its aftermath are also occasions for the use and misuse of ethnically charged political rhetoric. The presence of a politically relevant past and the invocation of religious warrants for group conflict have indicated the need for new approaches to peacekeeping and educational strategies for meeting and transcending group differences. The critiques challenging multiculturalism, the educational controversy regarding which should be the dominant expressions of our human commonality, and the various values and virtues found in all ethnic traditions pose challenges for economically and socially turbulent times. Whether these moments are crises of growth or decline will be measured by a host of indicators. Which of these indicators are the most salient is, of course, another question, whose answer depends on our selective invocation of historical materials and ethnic symbols as guides for contemporary analysis.

Ethnic relations have erupted into warfare in Africa, where conflicts have shattered emerging states and thus challenged the hopeful myth of postcolonial renewal as well as the racial/ethnic myth of black solidarity. But Africa's emerging countries are not alone: The Middle East, Central Europe, Canada, and the Balkans are additional venues of destructive conflict. Each of these simmering cauldrons—not melting pots—illustrates the stakes and consequences of unresolved conflict and distrust concerning land, religion, culture, leadership, and economic production and distribution. Each also shows the rewards and recognitions that fuel human passions, ambitions, and the will to dominate and to govern the affairs and destinies of various peoples that cohabit contiguous regions. Thus, the dramas of regional ethnic struggle and the growth of worldwide ethnic challenges to the constitution of human order itself are increasingly marked by episodes of blatant bigotry and intolerance. Fanaticism and zealotry impose themselves on the stage of history, which is rushing toward a new millennium. The threshold of hope that it promises for those who can recover and embrace the mystery of diversity waits to define the human condition in the twenty-first century.

UNIT 8

Looking Ahead: Challenge Questions

International events frequently affect the United States. In what ways can such events affect ethnic populations?

Explain how the relationship of ethnic Americans to changes and challenges in the world arena provides strength or liability to American interests. Does conflict between ethnic interests and national interests present real or imaginary fears about our activities in international affairs? Explain.

How will increased immigration, technological advances, and a more competitive world market affect the relationships between ethnic groups?

Is the American military becoming a society unto itself? Has the end of the military draft isolated military society from the American mainstream? Is national service a duty of citizenship?

Should the claims of ethnic groups in the United States in defense of culture, territory, and unique institutions be honored and protected by law and public policy? Why?

Resurgence of Ethnic Nationalism in California and Germany: The Impact on Recent Progress in Education

José Macias

University of Texas at San Antonio

In a comparative study, the author examines the recent passage of California's "anti-illegal immigrant" Proposition 187, and the resurgence of hostility toward resident "foreigners" in Germany, as forms of ethnic nationalism resulting in exclusionary movements directed toward Mexicans, and Turkish and other non-German groups, respectively. Historical analysis and data from educational ethnographic studies reveal the interrelationship of historically constructed racial or ethnic ideology, intergroup experience, and education. Schools, while recent targets of exclusionary social movements, are still key sites for an education in new ways of thinking about racial and ethnic-group relations.

> *California, 1994:* The results of the Fall general elections included the passage of Proposition 187 by a large majority of the California electorate. The state referendum proposed to withhold virtually all government services and benefits to "illegal" immigrants in the state, including support to families with dependent children, most health care, and all education to children of undocumented immigrant parents. Its proponents argued that this population does not legally qualify for the aforementioned benefits and services, and that they are too costly a burden for the taxpaying citizens of this country's largest state. Although implementation has been blocked by a series of court orders, a redefinition of ethnic group relations and the open persecution of undocumented Mexicans and other suspects was clearly established in the state, region, if not the whole of the United States. [Macias 1995:4–5]

> *Germany, 1992:* During the course of fieldwork in September, a colleague and I sat in a restaurant in Mainz, discussing a variety of topics related to my comparative research project—migration, education, and integration of ethnic groups in Germany, as well as related "hot" topics including German reunification, the European Community, guestworkers, and the like. Midway through our main course a sudden flash of light and a deafening thud from the front of the building interrupted the tranquil evening. We were later to learn—after the initial shock, confusion, and arrival of the police squad cars—that we had just witnessed a violent attack by a German "redneck" on the Syrian restaurant in which we were dining. Fortunately no one was injured in this incident, there was minor damage to the property, and we were able to continue, as our conversation turned to the escalating German hostility and violence toward foreign residents of Germany that has been reported in recent years by the media and German government itself. [field notes]

In this article, I examine the growing phenomenon of ethnic group conflict, particularly the return of open hostility directed by a majority population toward minority ethnic groups. Two cases are the basis for this discussion: California, with its Proposition 187, the anti-illegal-immigrant referendum; and Germany, a country marked by growing hostility toward its foreign residents in recent years. One purpose here is to compare and contrast these two situations to search for the common underlying dynamics in which sociopolitically weak, "foreign" ethnic groups have been singled out for societal persecution, scapegoating, and exclusion. Another objective is to examine the role of education both as part of the discourse, as well as a potential, albeit partial solution in this kind of group conflict.

Two methodological threads are intertwined here. First, I take a diachronic perspective to outline some fundamental historical elements of the two cases over time (Brubaker 1990; Macias 1990, 1993). This approach assumes that complex phenomena follow from a series of events that need to be taken into account as part of an explanation of the present. The second line is ethnographic, in which I draw on data from two projects carried out over the last several years. From 1987 to 1991, I conducted fieldwork to study the educational experiences of Mexican immigrant students moving into a U.S. school system and within a transnational migrant stream (Macias 1990). While the overall study involved fieldwork in immigrant communities and schools in both Mexico and the United States, the data reported here depict the California situation before the current backlash.

The Mexico-U.S. project naturally involved a review of a comparative body of cases on migration, and the role of education for the integration of foreign

From *Anthropology & Education Quarterly,* Vol. 27, No. 2, June 1996, pp. 232-252.

groups in receiving nation states. Out of these, the case of Turkish guestworkers and "foreigners" in Germany presented several similarities to Mexican immigrants in the United States. Armed with a few key contacts and German language fluency, I decided to develop this comparative study, and between 1990 and 1993 I conducted fieldwork in Berlin, Hamburg, and Frankfurt. But nobody had foreseen in the late 1980s, when I was still planning the work, Gorbachev and the collapse of the Communist Bloc, the fall of the Berlin Wall, and German reunification. And few were prepared for the open return of hostility toward guestworkers and other non-Germanic ethnic populations of a kind that had not been seen since the end of World War II. The dramatic escalation of this hostility was widely documented during the fieldwork period and added a critical focus to my inquiry.

Ethnographic data presented here came from similar sources in both sites: school and classroom observations; interviews with teachers, program specialists, and school administrators; and documents describing relevant policies and programs. German fieldwork activities also included home-family observations and interviews, and interviews with government and community agencies that served guestworker and other ethnic communities.

California Ethnic Nationalism: Territorial Displacement and Structural Exclusion

The two events described in the opening of this article are each grounded in histories that can help us understand the similar evolution and common meaning of current phenomena apparently separated by geography, culture, and nation. For instance, Proposition 187 can be understood as a form of ethnic nationalism in which the majority ethnic group singled out undocumented immigrants, who represent a "foreign" ethnic group, as the source of California's recent socioeconomic problems, and who then were defined as "not belonging" in the society of which they have been a part for a century and a half. These two assumptions cleared the way for an official exclusionary movement against illegal residents, which culminated in the success of Proposition 187. But for Mexicans, the main group targeted, this is not a new experience. They know their own history in the United States, including their periodic subjection to this kind of treatment since the arrival of the United States in the Southwest.

California ethnic nationalism, as exemplified by Proposition 187, is grounded in the earliest contact between Northern European Americans and previously settled American Indians and Mexicans. The early 19th century marks the beginning of substantial contact between whites and the settled people of the Southwest. In the 1800s the "Indian problem" was being resolved through U.S. government policies of territorial displacement, cultural destruction, and genocide—a treatment that ultimately resulted in the relegation of small numbers of surviving American Indians onto a reservation system. This treatment of American Indians had been politically and morally justified by the ideology of U.S. Manifest Destiny:

> Manifest Destiny had its roots in Puritan ideas, which continue to influence Anglo-American thought to this day. . . . Anglo-Americans believed that God had made them custodians of democracy and that they had a mission. . . . Their destiny made manifest was to spread the principles of democracy and Christianity to the unfortunates of the hemisphere. [Acuna 1988:13]

But while Manifest Destiny was largely successful in the removal of American Indians, Mexicans presented another kind of problem.

When people from the United States reached Mexico in the early 1800s, they found a people struggling toward nationhood after its 300-year legacy of Spanish colonial rule. As a nation left destitute and politically chaotic from centuries of Spanish plundering and dominance, the government not only allowed but invited U.S. Americans to help Mexicans settle their northern territories (Acuna 1988). From present-day Utah to Texas, and in New Mexico, Arizona, Nevada, and California, the newcomers came in contact with Spanish creoles, Indians, and the numerically dominant mestizos, all citizens of the young Mexican nation.

But the Mexican policy of open borders and peaceful cooperation met its demise when the new settlers and their government quickly turned to Manifest Destiny and the supremely grounded right to appropriate all territory to the Pacific Ocean. To make a very long story very short, the United States pressured, threatened, made war, and then assumed this control through the Treaty of Guadalupe Hidalgo and the annexation of the northern territories of the weakened Mexican nation. Mexicans resisted this forced incorporation through both political and violent means, but to no avail. Under the new regime, U.S. Americans systematically abrogated the treaty, illegally appropriated most Mexican land-holdings, and relegated Mexicans to the lowest ranks of the political economy and social order (Acuna 1988).

Since that time, Mexicans have been subjected to a "love-hate" relationship with U.S. society. When in favor with the dominant majority, Mexicans are welcomed, employed as a needed labor force, and are allowed to make their lives peacefully in the United States. But at other times, they have been singled out for persecution, blamed for society's problems, and targeted for deportation. For example, through the early 20th century, the U.S. border with Mexico was open, and Mexicans crossed it freely, back and forth. Mexicans in this period, as today, were the largest non-European ethnic group involved in the development of the U.S. Southwest. Their skills and labor ensured the building of the transcontinental railroad, helped mine the region's natural resources, made farming a lucrative enterprise, and made ranching a traditional hallmark of U.S. American culture. In fact, the entire "cowboy" culture—for example, horses, leather, livestock, rodeos, the barbecue, chili, and the guitar-strumming, singing cowboy—was taken from the already existing Mexican "charro" subculture and ensured the successful adaption of U.S. Americans to the harsh and expansive West. But by the early 1900s a deep anti-immigrant sentiment permeated the national mood, with the most severe actions coming in the form of the Chinese Exclusion Act (Takaki 1993). With restrictions now also established for Mexicans, European immigrants came under the more generous quotas reserved for them.

A brief period of interest in Mexicans and other "Latins" took place in the 1920s and 1930s within U.S. popular culture. The oversexed "Latin lover," the saucy "hot señorita," and the uncouth "Mexican bandit" epitomize the type of superficial, romantic, and negative images that dominated the cinematic, printed, and other popular media of that period. But the Mexican masses remained exotic and foreign enough to still be relegated to the lowest ranks of society and its institutions. Another flip-flop in relations occurred after the 1929 Wall Street crash that marked the beginning of the Great Depression. In 1930 Herbert Hoover began a program of deportation of Mexicans in which thousands were "repatriated" to Mexico without due process, many as legal citizens and residents of the United States. Thus, government policy to the effect that Mexicans "do not belong" in the United States coincided with a peak in immigration, economic decline, and the negative stereotyping of certain groups selected for scapegoating as the source of the nation's problems. Through the 1950s, conditions for Mexicans in the Southwest did not change substantially. For instance, Mexicans were allowed to hold only agricultural, manual labor, and service jobs that paid substandard wages under the poorest of working conditions. Those who broke this pattern often capitalized on their light skin color, changed their names, or otherwise managed to pass the barrier of being Mexican. While illegal, segregation in housing and education was systematic and effective. Their treatment at the hands of the U.S. public ranged from stereotyping to violent attack. Mexicans rejected these conditions as they have resisted their oppression since the intrusion of the United States a century and a half ago. Labor strikes were a common form of protest, as were legal challenges to school segregation. A few local victories were won, but with little systematic change.

World War II and its aftermath included a few expressions of "normal relations" between U.S. Americans and Mexicans. A labor shortage in that period led to the importation of temporary workers from Mexico through the Bracero Program, an international agreement that lasted through the 1950s. After its conclusion, many braceros who had decided to stay and work were periodically rounded up and deported by the Immigration and Naturalization Service. The societal lot of Mexicans remained marginal as a result of their systematic exclusion from opportunities for economic mobility, political power, and the education that would lead to these.

Since the 1960s, some measure of social progress has resulted from the initiatives of the Civil Rights movement, but a period of regression began in the early 1980s with two trends: (1) the return of a fundamental "American" social ideology and politics, with Californian Ronald Reagan its banner carrier and (2) a dramatic rise in illegal immigration from Mexico and other nations experiencing economic and political hard times. The present period thus represents a cyclical resurgence of a complex of dominant group beliefs about and behavior toward Mexicans that has taken place against the backdrop of U.S. national development, and within a history of intimate, conflictual experiences between the two groups.

The Cycle of Mexican Educational Exclusion, Inclusion, and Back

The chaotic World War I era marked a period of large-scale migration to the United States. Europe's conflict of empires and nations caused waves of displaced humanity to land on U.S. shores, while in America the aftermath of the 1916 Mexican Revolution pushed hundreds of thousands of Mexican nationals across the border. While reaping the benefit of abundant, cheap labor, the nation also faced the task of integrating millions of newcomers into society. Thus, systematic public schooling came to be offered to Mexicans and other immigrant groups, just as the sociopolitical ideology of "Americanization" gained dominance.

Americanization was grounded in a set of ideas current at that time. For instance, nationalistic fervor had resulted in the ethnic conflicts of World War I, but if everyone were uniformly "American," with a common national identity and loyalty, we could avoid political conflict. Also, a common socialization for work and citizenship would benefit immigrants and society. Moreover, the popular "melting pot" idea held that immigrants should give up their cultures, languages, and all other foreign attributes.

Americanization thus became the dominant policy for immigrant education. Throughout the Southwest, Mexican children attended Americanization schools to receive English instruction, citizenship training, and preparation for work. The latter curriculum stressed non-skilled job training, for example, home economics and factory work. Citizenship involved a dose of U.S. history and saluting the flag. English instruction used the "sink or swim" method and the explicit rejection of Spanish.

Beyond its logic, however, the rhetoric of Americanization was both contradictory and extreme in practice. For instance, Americanization schools or classrooms were implemented by public school districts but were segregated from "regular" ones and, thus, were inequitable in terms of resources and quality. In addition, lack of contact and interaction with peers in mainstream schools precluded a full socialization experience that would enhance students' skills and competencies in society. Since the main purpose of this program was to teach "American" cultural values and behavior, the incorporation of students' cultural knowledge and skills never was a consideration. Moreover, the informal, personal treatment given students reinforced the formal program, and teachers regularly meted out verbal humiliation and corporal punishment to students for speaking Spanish, for their ethnic behavior, for their physical appearance, in other words, for being Mexican. Ideally, Mexicans were to give up all traces of their foreign heritage in order to become "American." This brand of education was designed to culturally assimilate Mexican children, bring them under control, while preparing them to continue in the lowest strata of the socioeconomic order.

Mexican parents resisted this treatment. Individuals sometimes petitioned local schools to allow their children into the regular program; other times they took group action. The documentary film *The Lemon Grove Incident* depicts a classic case of school segregation in the 1930s wherein a Mexican community takes legal action against the local school district and wins (Espinosa 1982). A California court ruled for the parents who claimed that their children's segregated school provided an inferior education and deprived them of necessary opportunities due to all Americans. But change was slow, and Mexicans remained largely excluded from education for decades.

An upturn in the educational cycle aptly describes the progress that followed the Supreme Court school desegregation ruling of 1954. By the mid-1960s federal government policies and programs were in place that represented the first good-faith attempts to provide equitable education for ethnic minorities. For instance, programs began to address inequity and the special needs of children with social, cultural, and linguistic "disadvantages." Furthermore, the education profession generally jumped on the ethnic-minority education bandwagon and developed more inclusive philosophies, curricula, and instructional strategies. In the 1970s and 1980s "cultural difference," "learning styles," and "bilingual and multicultural education" became standard jargon in the educational lexicon.

Ironically, California was until recently in the vanguard of most initiatives to improve the schooling of ethnic minority students. For instance, port-of-entry programs specifically targeted students newly arrived in the United States. A typical example was the Newcomers Program, which I observed in the large Central Valley city of Vintageland.[1] Beginning in the late 1970s, Vintageland School District experienced a great influx of Mexican immigrants, as well as refugees from several Asian nations among its student population. These students came with distinct cultural backgrounds, limited English skills, and diverse educational backgrounds (Macias 1990, 1993).

Officially, the Vintageland program provided these newcomers with an English as a Second Language (ESL) program and a basic curriculum to prepare them for regular classrooms. But Mrs. Weiss, the program's director, added that "we provide a warm, comfortable, secure environment . . . [and] give confidence. . . . Students learn what school is about, . . . and they get one semester of credit." Moreover, the program maintained working ties with other key agencies, regularly referring students and their families for appropriate medical, dental, or social services. The program managed in these ways to mainstream and respond to the needs of its migrant, immigrant, and refugee student body.

Another example of California educational leadership was in Orchardtown, a rural community I studied on the southernmost margins of the San Francisco Bay Area. Although rapid growth and modernization has come in the form of new shopping centers and increased commuter traffic along the nearby state highway, the still viable, old downtown preserves Orchardtown's small-town feel. With agriculture still the base of the economy, much of the local population and labor pool is comprised of Mexicans, the only group in the area willing to fill this economic niche. A part of this population is settled, but a large cohort follows the seasonal migrant workstream that brings them here from April through October for work in the tomato, spinach, and other field harvests. Families represent more than one migration pattern: some former migrants have settled in the community, and others traverse Texas, Arizona, and other states; some migrate between Mexico and the United States, and others are new arrivals from Mexico. These migrant families bring about 300 school-age children with them, a number that increases by another hundred in summer.

Educators in Orchardtown School District generally knew much about the migrant experience, particularly the low-income and family stresses that detract from students' schooling. The district addressed the educational needs of students in various ways, including a dual-language emphasis, curricular rigor, and special attention to the socioeconomic and cultural situation of the students. Mary Paz, principal of Morningside Elementary, said the district philosophy holds that "kids can learn" and considers language difference a strength. The "real factor," she added, is good teachers and how they implement these ideas.

Ms. Rogelio is one of these teachers whose classroom at one school is made up of mostly "kids from Mexico" who receive "some bilingual content instruction everyday." For example, Rogelio teaches social studies in Spanish and math in English on one day and then switches languages on the next. Every school in the district had at least two classrooms that implemented a bilingual or ESL program. Another third-grade teacher, Tina Pulido, says that students with Mexican schooling tend to bring high levels of Spanish language competence: "When we write stories, the Mexican kid has a sense of what a story is: . . . organized sentences." Pulido asserts that students' advanced grounding in Spanish is generalizable to other academic subjects, although her observation does not apply to students who've had little schooling, or a poor experience in Mexico or in the United States. But positive assessments of students' skills such as these heighten teachers' expectations.

High expectations, in turn, appear to drive a general emphasis on a strong curriculum. Angela Rogelio related that her own "success hypothesis" requires that students have a quality schooling that includes a good curriculum, appropriate instruction, and appreciation of students' cultural heritage. Martin Sosa is a 7th-and-8th-grade math teacher at Rancho San Jose Junior High School who supports rigor in the curriculum. Sosa also claims that students who come with schooling from Mexico are well prepared in mathematics, with "good comprehension and problem solving skills." The point is that Sosa also tends to "push" his math curriculum to all students, since he says that even the average students are ready to handle it.

Roberto Gomez is director of the district's migrant education program, which attends to the particular needs of migrant students. Eligibility for the program requires evidence that the student's parents must move during the school year because of employment in an agriculturally related job. There has been no requirement for proof of citizenship or legal residence status; it has not been the responsibility of school personnel to verify if students or families are "legal" or "illegal."

The migrant program supports schooling in a variety of ways. Migrant students, for example, are monitored through a national system, as they move across state lines, between school districts, and through local migrant programs. For students and parents, participation in the migrant program provides information and helps facilitate entry into each new school situation. Those who periodically leave for Mexico remain eligible for the program upon their return. Meanwhile, an "individual service contract" may be drawn up between program personnel and the student, who agrees to a plan of study while away. Students are able to receive credit and keep up this way.

Parents benefit in various ways through their involvement in the program. Director Gomez says that the Mexican parents have little knowledge of U.S. schools. Through program meetings, classroom visits, and other involvement, parents receive information, suggestions, and encouragement to help their children succeed in school. Gomez believes this kind of support is especially important because the parents, as former migrant students themselves, may have little schooling in either country. Families typically hear about the migrant program and other school services through relatives and other personal sources. But one evening, I attended a multifaceted informational program that had been organized at Rancho San Jose Junior High. The well-publicized program drew about 150 parents, their children, and school personnel. "Noche Ranchera" was opened by a faculty music ensemble playing traditional Mexican music. The principal gave a brief welcome, after which the curriculum coordinator gave an overview of the school curriculum and special programs. Then another faculty member explained the district's testing program and alerted the audience to some approaching schoolwide testing dates. Then a series of activities related to the topic of parental support followed: a teacher's brief speech, a parent small-group activity, and an emotional testimonial by Martin Sosa, who shared his personal journey from migrant student to teacher and spoke of the support given him by his parents and teachers. The evening was interspersed with music throughout and appeared to succeed as an educational, social, and cultural program.

The foregoing examples illustrate some of the ways that California schools and educators have recently served students of Mexican and other immigrant origins. School-level personnel, in particular, supported these improvements not only because they work closely with students and families but also because they understand the pedagogical bases of the policies and programs that they are putting into practice. Ostensibly, a growing interest in diversity and effective schooling for ethnic-minority students would seem to characterize the education camp, if not California society as a whole. But suddenly, the direct impact of Proposition 187 would simply rid the schools of "illegal" immigrant students, making irrelevant the question of what kind of schooling they should receive. Local districts are free to make their own improvement efforts, but this is less feasible with shrinking budgets and a growing hostility from outside.

What, then, accounts for the sudden flip-flop in which California voters singled out immigrants for their illegal status and moved to deny them education? Politics is a key element in the turn of events. Public educational policies are always determined within a wider public discourse that is ultimately a political one. In California, the discourse around a number of socioeconomic problems found a political target in "illegal immigrants," their children, and state programs that provided them with benefits. While the problems have been around since the mid-1980s, the discourse escalated and finally took on a life of its own as a political, election-year movement, with education a "logical," easy target.

Recent trends within education also figured here: Since the early 1980s widespread criticism of the entire education system has dominated the public discourse, and since that time, we have been in a "back-to-basics" cycle that stresses mathematics, science, and literacy. Although nobody can disagree with the necessity of these subjects, this push deemphasizes, by default, improvement efforts in history, geography, languages, arts, and music. These are subjects in which teachers might find it relatively more straightforward to develop multicultural curricula and, concurrently, to use it as a means of including Mexican students in the instructional process. Thus, both California's serious economic downturn, in an epoch when simple politics played well and when education needed reforming anyway, and the rise of interethnic hostilities, including immigrant bashing, are elements that all came together in the form of Proposition 187.

German National Development and Racial Ideology

Germany presents another case of contemporary ethnic conflict that has received wide media coverage. Reports of harassment and violence directed toward guestworkers, refugees, and other resident foreigners, the rise of neo-Nazi groups, and a shift to nationalist, anti-foreigner politics are instantly interpreted as a resurgence of Nazi Germany, and easy comparisons to other situations are tempting. But prior to any comparisons, the German case must be seen within its own historical development.

Through World War II, Germany harbored an image of itself as an ethnically homogeneous nation, even if contrary to historical evidence (Sauer 1992). But the postwar period left a critical need for labor and led to the undeniable ethnic diversification seen in Germany today. In the 1950s Germany entered into agreements with a succession of European nations to import *gastarbeiter* (guestworkers) for the postwar economic boom (Castles 1986). Among the first to arrive were workers from Italy, Spain, and Portugal; others from Yugoslavia, Greece, and Turkey followed. Initially imported as temporary labor, by the 1970s many of these "foreigners" had brought or started families and were permanently settled in Germany (Castles 1985). Today, the Turks are the largest of these guestworker groups, numbering 1.8 million. Furthermore, since the mid-1980s increasing numbers of political refugees from around the world have taken advantage of Germany's asylum policy, the most liberal in all of Europe, to contribute to the exponential growth of the foreigner population.

Actively recruited and legally admitted by the German state, these groups have been accepted by much of the German citizenry, but continual barriers have prevented their full incorporation in German society. These barriers have included widespread cross-cultural misunderstanding, social discrimination, and residential segregation. Other barriers to full integration take the form of myriad governmental laws and policies that regulate entry and legal status, work and economic opportunities, and education and social benefits (O'Brien 1988). By the mid-1970s the German government reacted to a dramatic rise in the number of all foreigners by implementing a program for encouraging and paying Turks and other guestworkers to return to their homelands (Körner and Mehrlander 1986; Penninx 1986). The remigration policy generally failed. This population has worked, settled, and had families in Germany, with their second- and third-generation children possessing little knowledge of or experience with Turkey (Körner and Mehrlander 1986). But by the end of the 1980s "the German mood towards immigrants [had] soured. . . . Guestworkers in Germany in 1989, particularly Turks, [were] the subject of widespread hostility and a growing anti-immigrant political party" (Tomasi, Tomasi, and Miller 1989). That was just before the fall of the Berlin Wall. Now Germany's pressures from global economic competition, European integration and, since 1990, national reunification all have aggravated even more ethnic group tension and hostility toward foreigners.

Germany apparently has had considerably less experience with non-Germanic ethnic groups, in contrast with the United States, whose experience with racial and ethnic diversity was underway for two centuries before its existence as a nation. So, are today's observations simply a modern resurgence of the Nazi era, which is often explained away as an aberration in German history, as "Hitler's doing"? Or does a longer historical view perhaps help explain both that era and the present?

The German case reveals a set of assumptions and beliefs that crystallized in the nation-building era of 19th-century Europe. One strand in this thought derived from German Romanticism, a genre exemplified by Goethe, Schiller, and other philosophers and writers of the 18th and 19th centuries. A key part of the Romantic vision was the idealization of the natural domain: the cosmos, the natural environment, and humanity. This view pointed to nature for both practical teachings and moral guidance in human affairs. Then Darwin, with his theory of biological evolution, arrived by the middle of the 19th century. The idea of a natural hierarchy of the species in which *Homo sapiens* ruled superior, while controversial among the general populace (it challenged creation theories of the universe), provided the spark for a social darwinism built upon both Darwin's science and the idea of essential nature from German Romanticism.

German writers, thinkers, and social critics quickly attributed an ethical quality to nature. For instance, the idea that the more developed, superior species supersede and dominate the less evolved, inferior forms was evidence of the wisdom of nature to ensure the "survival of the fittest." By extension, human races also were judged to have evolved in a hierarchy, as evidenced in each group's achievements and the domination of one superior group over all others.

Thus Darwinism provided a scientific rationale for a number of assumptions that were incorporated into a romantic vision of a German race by not only the literati but also the social thinkers of the 19th-century nation-building era:

> The aesthetic and socio-historical idiom of German Romanticism was perfectly suited to the elaboration of the ethnocultural conception of nationhood. The celebration of individuality as *Einzigkeit* or uniqueness . . . of unconscious, organic growth . . . of the vitality and integrity of traditional, rooted folk cultures: . . . all of these themes were easily transported from the domain of aesthetics and cultural criticism to that of social philosophy. [Brubaker 1990:391]

German Romanticism and its philosophy had peaked at a critical time of historical transformation, and its seductive images were appropriated for the political task of nation building:

> In the social and political thought of Romanticism . . . nations are conceived as historically rooted, organically developed individualities, united by a distinctive *Volkgeist* and by its infinitely ramifying expression in language, custom, law, culture and the state. (Brubaker 1990:391]

Thus a number of related concepts, including German organic kinship, racial purity, and cultural superiority were first introduced into the German social consciousness and contributed a racial element to Germany's national ideology.

Within this historically constructed ideology, racial assumptions have defined who is and who is not German. A racial group is biologically related; thus kinship or blood ties determine who is German. The idea of racial and ethnic boundaries was extended to political boundaries and membership: "What is specific about the concept of the German nation . . . lies in the fact that it is constructed biologically. German nationals are defined by their origin; one can only be born a German" (Rathzel 1990:41).

Since 1913 until only recently, German citizenship has been legally based in the principle of jus sanguinis, or blood-kinship (Brubaker 1990). For decades, an explicit racial ideology formed part of the dominant group's social philosophy, politics, and institutional treatment of ethnic groups defined as not belonging to the German nation. The semantic category *Ausländer* (foreigners) separates those who do not "belong" from the dominant, majority German ethnic group. It was this very principle—Germany for Germans only—that supported the takeover by the National Socialists (Nazis) before World War II, as they justified ethnic cleansing as a solution to broader economic, political, and international crises (Burleigh 1991).

Today we see in Germany the resurgence of ethnic hostilities not seen since the 1940s. A reactionary social climate and the popularity of nationalistic, anti-foreigner politics have resulted in physical violence toward German residents in guestworker or refugee statuses. While only a very small minority of Germans is actually involved in these actions, historically minded observers cannot help but see these current hostilitiy toward Turks and other ethnic groups as a resurgence of old, stable patterns of German thinking and behavior (O'Brien 1988). Many Germans agree with this view, as they openly debate this crisis and ask themselves what kind of folk and society they want to be.

The Schooling of Foreigners, the Reeducation of Germans

Some indications are that many Germans have decided to redirect their nation's history to become a more inclusive society. For instance, large public demonstrations against racism and xenophobia have been organized in Berlin, Frankfurt, and other German cities. The Green Party and other political organizations also are working against blatant anti-foreigner politics, while the national leadership has recently taken an aggressive stance against the proliferation of extremist, neo-Nazi groups. In settings ranging from neighborhood and workplace to family, many other Germans have assumed personal responsibility for speaking out and acting concretely on these critical issues.

In all of this, education, schools, and educators appear to be key actors resisting the past and working for progressive change. This was not always the case, because German education has been marked by systematic neglect, discrimination, and exclusion of Turks and other foreigners, even into the 1980s. Turkish-German bilingualism has undergone intensive study, but no systematic initiatives have begun to address the critical issues inherent in language transition and loss, and their impact on school achievement (Pfaff 1981, 1991). Structural barriers to schooling remain, while research has documented the segregation of educational opportunity for foreigner children who, by the secondary level, cluster "at the lowest level—*the Hauptschule*—and remain there" (Baker et. al. 1985:219) to receive preparation for unskilled and semiskilled jobs (Gitmez and Wilpert 1987). The last set of issues to gain notice have been the personal experiences of students living between two worlds: the dilemma of choosing between two sets of cultural values and beliefs, the crisis of identity, or the decision whether to wear traditional or modern clothes (Saydam 1990; Springer 1992). But in Berlin and Hamburg, I interviewed and observed administrators and teachers who felt a responsibility to address issues of diversity and inclusion in their professional roles. High in the educational hierarchy are administrators such as Herr Schmidt, a Hamburg School Board administrator and also the German national representative to the education task force of the European Community. In response to the shortcomings of the past, state educational agencies now have offices to oversee policy and programs addressing the education of foreigners. The reality, says Schmidt, is that Germany is an immigration country responsible for the integration of children and youth through education. Since the late 1970s, states have responded variably through programs for newcomers, bilingual instruction, German as a second language, and vocational education.

Schmidt shared a vignette that captures the tension inherent in these attempts to reform the past. He explained that the *multikulturelle Gesellschaft* (multicultural society) is now "in" but that some theories about the multicultural society and intercultural education can be extreme. Then Schmidt told of one community in which multicultural enthusiasts insisted that Germans learn Turkish, and noted that these extreme supporters of intercultural education actually stimulated a right-wing reaction among those who countered, "We want this to be a German school."

But more successful attempts to initiate educational change can be found in progressive communities. The Hamburg suburb of Wilhelmsburg is known as a *Sozialsbrennpunkte* (social flashpoint). This is jargon for communities of both German and foreigner, working, or welfare families, who live in public housing located in areas with high levels of poverty, substance abuse, and crime. According to one teacher, families are typically afraid to let children out of their massive, impersonal high-rise apartments. At the same time, Wilhelmsburg is an historically "Red" workers' community with a population mixed along class and ethnicity, and a record of progressive action.

This progressive bent is often expressed in the attitudes and behaviors of administrators and teachers of the local *Grundschule* (elementary school). In an interview, the school principal indicated that integration is the main goal of education for the foreign students, who make up about 35 percent of her school's population. This is not a straightforward matter for Turks and other groups who suffer from stigma, discrimination, relative poverty, and related social disadvantages in Germany. The Turkish community's strong fear of losing its culture further points to the crucial role of education in providing an accepting and effective experience for Turkish students and their families.

The staff of this school explained that most of their students have grown up in Germany, unlike many newcomers at higher grade levels who are likely to have had formative experiences in Turkey or other countries of origin. But children come to school typically "not ready to learn," as the bleak neighborhood provides few stimulating environments, such as parks, museums, or wholesome recreational venues. The school's approach is to provide a safe, supportive, and enriching environment to all children, regardless of background. While staff claims to make no distinctions among students, I took note of some efforts they clearly are making on behalf of their foreign students. In the classroom, these include both the integration of culturally inclusive curricular content and bias-free instruction—elements of the typical Multi Kulti (multicultural education) approach.

Outside of school the staff takes advantage of the strong Turkish family and community systems (Gitmez and Wilpert 1987). For instance, in addition to the typical school-to-home notes and phone calls, individual teachers try to know and maintain personal contact with Turkish parents. Occasional invitations to Turkish homes are seen as opportunities to make contact, as are standing invitations by teachers for Turkish parents to visit the classroom or share a cultural activity with the class.

The director described a schoolwide project they had once organized. Wir Können Viel Zusammen Tun (We Can Do Much Together) was a parent-involvement program that, in addition to cooking, dancing, and other social activities, had as its goal consciousness raising to combat *Ausländerfeindlichkeit* (hostility toward foreigners). While the project had attendance problems due to parents' working, the need for child care, and Turkish parents' lack of facility in German, the effort had been made to change school relations with and within the community.

In one case, a teacher's interest in the community was great enough that he has become closely involved with a group of Turkish boys. Originally formed as a gang to protect against German skinheads who regularly invaded the community to beat up Turks and other foreigners, the group continues as a social club, with the German teacher acting as advisor and cultural facilitator to the Turkish adolescents. Here, progressive community attitudes attract educators who believe "they have a job to do," in one teacher's words, that is, to maximize their students' education.

In Berlin I found another site of progressive action in Frau Adler's second-grade classroom. This teacher is involved in a special Turkish bilingual, biliteracy project that has received state funding (Berlin is a city-state) for ten years. The project is in place through the collaborative efforts of a group of Free University of Berlin researchers and the school's administrators, teachers, and staff (personal communication, Carol Pfaff, 1991). The program is open to both Germans and Turks, but parents must request it.

While the ultimate goal is to teach German, Adler and the Turkish teacher who co-ops with her use what is termed *coordination* to teach both German fundamentals and Turkish basics in parallel fashion. Bilingual language instruction is the focus, but the team also teaches in the content areas. A parent-involvement component encourages the parents to come into class to cook, do arts and crafts, or other forms of cultural sharing.

While Adler admits that formal measures of achievement may not improve, she claims other benefits from this program. Children receive language training in two languages, their behavior improves, and they gain new attitudes. As second- or third-generation Turks in Germany, Adler's Turkish students know little about their own history and culture. Thus a critical benefit accrues to Turkish children as they hear and see their language used in class and as they see the involvement of their parents grow through the acceptance of Turkish language and culture. They gain a new consciousness and feeling about themselves, says Adler. But the German children benefit as well, she continues. The learning of a second language enhances their learning of German. And the German children gain another consciousness about languages, that is, that another language is just another system of communication, she adds. Adler's hope is that these new attitudes generalize to other forms of diversity with which children must be prepared to live in school and in society.

These examples are followed by a less than optimistic postscript, however. Schmidt notes that lack of resources have prevented the development of systematic improvements so far. Now with the *Sparpolitik* (budget-cutting policy) that has kicked in since reunification in 1990, state and local governments find it even more difficult to fund educational improvements. Moreover, in the current reactionary social climate, educators find it more difficult to carry out alone the changes needed to better include and school Turkish and other foreign children.

History, Ideology, Society: The Place of Education

Clearly, we need to learn more about each of the cases presented here, and to bear in mind that all things are not equal in any two situations. Still, we can begin to better understand the central problem from this kind of historical comparison. Within this view, three interrelated elements stand out in the California and German cases: ideology, experience, and education. In both cases, a resurgence of ethnocentrism, xenophobia, and nationalism can be linked to a standing ideology that rationalizes dominant-group exclusion and persecution of target groups (Arendt 1973). A particular set of beliefs has been constructed through internal processes of group development and refined over time through external contact with others. Historically, the Germanic people represented a number of different tribal heritages that needed a common identity and cohesion before a nation-state could be built. Race, a narrowly defined blood kinship, provided this organizing principle, which then came to function with other assumptions of group superiority and purity. These ideas have been part of Germany's legacy since its inception as a nation. The atrocities of World War II, the persecution, imprisonment, and genocide of unwanted groups, primarily the Jews, were the "logical" extreme expression of this ideology, and the events of today represent a return by some elements in Germany to that belief system, however modified in form.

In contrast to Germany's ideological "headstart," experience preceded ideology in the United States. For example, African slavery in the United States was initially justified on a Christian-heathen argument, but "race" became the rationale after slaves began to adopt Christianity (Takaki 1993). The enslavement of Africans and removal of American Indians provided the experiential ground in which the official policy of Manifest Destiny was cultivated to justify the territorial displacement and subjugation of Mexicans in the latter half of the last century. The standard cliché that "Americans only think through action and doing" applies, in that historical subjugation and exclusion of racial and ethnic groups became a key part of a definition of the United States as a nation. Although the development of racial or ethnic ideologies took different routes in Germany and the United States, the common point is that a similar complex of ideas has existed at some level in both places.

The identification of an ideology does not mean that a group goes about daily life thinking consciously about a related set of racist or ethnocentric beliefs, plotting how to act on them. Except for the most fundamental elements, most members of a group would not admit holding ideas that have received negative criticism in modern times. The longevity of these ideas depends on more subtle mechanisms including: the popular repackaging of imagery of Romanticism or of the Manifest Destiny of a chosen people with a great calling to fulfill; the official representation of historical events in favor of the dominant group, to the degree that the mistreatment of other groups never really happened or was not that bad, or that victim groups are actually the racists; or in the political revival of earlier, simple solutions to complex issues, a return to an idealized past when we had few problems, and "other" groups were easily dismissed by decree. Politics is clearly the arena to which elements of racial or ethnic thinking have returned, through the kind of nationalistic imagery, informational selectivity, and emotional persuasion in which politicians are skilled.

Beyond similar ideologies, other historical factors in each case have mediated their translation into practice. For example, the U.S. Constitution, with its principles of equality, democracy, and human rights, together with the concept of equal legal protection, is another way of thinking about the rights and recourse due to all, including members of minority groups. Thus, two competing ideologies have been in tension throughout U.S. history, with the result that systematic racial persecution and exclusion have been reduced over time, albeit gradually and largely through the efforts of the persecuted groups themselves. This tension has accounted in part for the periodic expression of the racial and ethnic system of thought, not only in the historical "love-hate" Mexican-U.S. relationship described earlier but in other phenomena such as racial segregation (after Emancipation), Americanization policy ("ethnic/language difference is bad"), or immigrant bashing ("get rid of them"). The manifestation of this ideology is thus cyclical, coming out at certain times in social discourse, in local and national politics, and in the treatment of target groups. In contrast, German society has been relatively less constrained in the practice of its racial beliefs. Ultimately, World War II and world condemnation were necessary to put an end to the Nazi atrocities. But an externally motivated change of behavior did not necessarily affect deeply seated German beliefs about permissible intergroup relations; they simply have been suppressed.

One way of summarizing these different conditions is that Germany has had the more explicit ideology but a shorter history of implementation and now faces external pressures to change. The United States, on the other hand, has applied a less-articulated exclusionary ideology over a longer period of time and with more groups. But the periodic return of exclusionary social phenomena appears to automatically force an internal examination of those historically grounded beliefs that are, by definition, in direct contradiction with essential democratic values. This does not imply an advantage in either nation's quest to redirect its history, for both internal dialogue and external opinion would appear to be important. On the other hand, internally motivated dialogue and change would seem to be minimum requirements, and a more solid basis for lasting resolutions.

The critical point of commonality in these cases is what dominant groups have come to believe about targeted ethnic groups and what is permissible behavior toward them. An education, in the broad sense, in certain beliefs, ideas, and behavior has formed the predispositions of both individuals and groups. But it follows equally that education, or reeducation, is thoroughly implied in the redirection of the habits of the past. The role of education in the present cases illustrates how schools actually have taken responsibility for implementing policies, programs, and strategies that constructively address the group divisions at issue here. The California and German schools studied here feature curricula that incorporate students' ethnic backgrounds, instruction that utilizes their cultural knowledge and linguistic skills, and educators' concerted attention to the material and social conditions faced by their students. The ends achieved through these school improvement efforts are the enhanced inclusion of all students in the educational process, and the new conceptions of race and ethnic group relations modeled through those efforts.

But we cannot assume that formal education can solve all the problems of ethnic group interaction in either California or Germany, especially when reactionary sociopolitical movements have targeted the best efforts of schools for easy solutions. The abundance of uninformed, political, and emotionally charged solutions suggests the potential and critical role of education beyond school fences. Although Proposition 187 surfaced in the political arena, its ideas obviously found support in many other places, including families, the workplace, and the media. Parents and families must somehow be supported in their task of caring for and socializing their children and helped to gain new understandings about human differences that should not matter, such as race, and actions that are unsupportable, such as negative stereotyping and discrimination. Education continues to be a great need in the workplace, despite recent advances. Several instances of racial or ethnic discrimination have been widely reported in the media recently, involving issues that range from verbal and physical harassment to problems of hiring, promotion, and pay. The backlash against affirmative action policy reminds us that lasting social progress is ultimately dependent on popular understandings that support that change.

Political and government leaders need to understand the key role they play in the resolution of racial and ethnic conflicts, and education can help. The preparation of informed leadership will depend on the accessibility of useful information about what the real problems are, about how schools can continue to be part of a constructive solution, and about how social policy and legislation are involved. A role for anthropologists is clearly implied in all of these potential educational sites.

But neither anthropologists, nor families, nor school teachers, nor politicians, acting alone, can turn an entire nation's history around. All must contribute to such a transformation based on education. That education must be based on dialogue, a sense of responsibility to resolve common societal problems, and knowledge of our common and group histories. Only when we begin to understand the present as directly linked to the past will we be in a position to explore new ways of thinking about intergroup relations in a free democracy.

José Macias is an associate professor in the Division of Bicultural Bilingual Studies at the University of Texas at San Antonio.

Notes

Acknowledgments. The research reported here was supported by the University Research Committee, the Department of Educational Studies, and the Ethnic Studies Program, all units of the University of Utah. The author gratefully acknowledges the assistance of Elizabeth Escalera-Bell in the preparation of the manuscript.

1. All community names and personal names are pseudonyms.

References Cited

Acuna, Rodolfo. 1988. A History of Chicanos, 3rd edition. New York: Harper and Row.

Arendt, Hannah. 1973. The Origins of Totalitarianism. New York: Harcourt, Brace, Jovanovich.

Baker, David, Yilmaz Esmer, Gero Lenhardt, and John Meyer. 1985. Effects of Immigrant Workers on Educational Stratification in Germany. Sociology of Education 58(October):213–277.

Brubaker, William R. 1990. Immigration, Citizenship, and the Nation-State in France and Germany: A Comparative Historical Analysis. International Sociology 5(4):379–407.

Burleigh, Michael. 1991. Racism as Social Policy: The Nazi "Euthanasia" Programme, 1939–1945. Ethnic and Racial Studies 14(4):453–469.

Castles, Stephen. 1985. The Guests Who Stayed—The Debate on "Foreigners Policy" in the German Federal Republic. International Migration Review 19(3):517–534.

1986. The Guest-Worker in Europe—An Obituary. International Migration Review 20(4):761–778.

Espinosa, Paul, dir. 1982. The Lemon Grove Incident. Film, VHS, 60 min. San Diego: KPBS-TV.

Gitmez, Ali, and Czarina Wilpert. 1987. A Micro-Society or an Ethnic Community? Social Organization and Ethnicity amongst Turkish Migrants in Berlin. *In* Immigrant Associations in Europe. John Rex, Daniele Joly, and Czarina Wilpert, eds. Pp. 86–125. Brookfield, VT: Gower.

Körner, Heiko, and Ursula Mehrlander. 1986. New Migration Policies in Europe: The Return of Labor Migrants, Remigration Promotion and Integration Policies. International Migration Review 20(3):672–675.

Macias, José. 1990. Scholastic Antecedents of Immigrant Students: Schooling in a Mexican Immigrant-Sending Community. Anthropology and Education Quarterly 21(4):291–318.

1993 Forgotten History: Educational and Social Antecedents of High Achievement Among Asian Immigrants in the U.S. Curriculum Inquiry 23(4):409–432.

1995 Proposition 187 and Racism. Ethnic Studies Program Newsletter [University of Utah] 2(2):4–5.

O'Brien, Peter. 1988. Continuity and Change in Germany's Treatment of Non-Germans. International Migration Review 22(3):109–134.

Penninx, Rinus. 1986. International Migration in Western Europe since 1973: Developments, Mechanisms and Controls. International Migration Review 20(4):951–972.

Pfaff, Carol W. 1981. Sociolinguistic Problems of Immigrants: Foreign Workers and Their Children in Germany. Review article. Language in Society 10:155–188.

1991 Turkish in Contact with German: Language Maintenance and Loss among Immigrant Children in Berlin (West). International Journal of the Sociology of Language 90:97–129.

Rathzel, Nora. 1990. Germany: One Race, One Nation? Race & Class 32(3):31–48.

Sauer, Paul. 1992. On the History of Jews in Southwest Germany. European Education 24(4):68–72.

Saydam, Onur. 1990. Turkish Children and Youth. Western European Education 22(1):80–85.

Springer, Monika. 1992. A Conversation with Turkish Female Students: "Every Sheep Is Hung by Its Own Leg." European Education 24(3):77–82.

Takaki, Ronald. 1993. A Different Mirror: A History of Multicultural America. New York: Little, Brown.

Tomasi, Silvano, Lydio Tomasi, and Mark Miller. 1989. IMR at 25: Reflections on a Quarter Century of International Migration Research and Orientations for Future Research. International Migration Review 23(3):393–402.

NO CANADA?

After the referendum, a chill descends on Montreal

Guy Lawson

Guy Lawson is a writer living in Toronto.

Love consists in this,
that two solitudes protect
and touch and greet each other.
—Rainer Maria Rilke

On a frigid Monday night last November, four weeks after Quebec's referendum on separating from the rest of Canada, I took a walk up Montreal's main north-south street, known to the city's French inhabitants as Boulevard St-Laurent and to its English inhabitants as St. Lawrence or, as some still call it, the Main. It is, by tradition, the segregation line of Montreal: east is French, west is English. The first blizzard of winter had hit town, and city workers were out with their plows. The snow was falling sideways. As I trudged past chic bistros, *la look grunge* bars, bilingual beggars (*"as-tu trente sous?"* followed by "buddy, can you spare some change?"), there were no visible traces of the latest crisis to tear through the city. During the referendum campaign, every lamppost had been covered with posters: WHY RISK YOUR JOB? the federalists asked; vote Yes to independence AND IT ALL BECOMES POSSIBLE, the separatists answered. But the morning after the vote the posters were gone, instant ephemera.

Most of the stores on the street were shabby and forlorn, low-rise buildings pocked with FOR RENT signs. *Plus ça change, plus c'est la même chose.* But in the quiet of the night and the slanting snow, St-Laurent seemed to me a cultural war zone, dividing a city stuck somewhere between the past and the present, between the enervating, centuries-old French-English conflict and the cosmopolitan society of today, between the last referendum and the next one.

I had come to Montreal in the final tense days before the vote on October 30 expecting to see a country, my country, die. When the campaign began in September the sovereigntist leader was Jacques Parizeau, the premier of Quebec, an oddly Anglophilic man from a wealthy Montreal family, with a taste for three-piece suits and pompous gestures. Parizeau promised voters that Quebec would have an economy the size of Austria's; that it would be Canada's equal, a full member of the North American Free Trade Agreement, a nation entire of itself. Federalists in Ottawa and Quebec City said that separation would have disastrous financial consequences: The Canadian dollar would plummet, the stock market would collapse, businesses would flee. In the last referendum on separation, in 1980, Premier René Lévesque had argued, as Parizeau was now doing, that Quebec could stand alone economically. It was an argument that failed to resonate, apparently; the separatists lost, 60 percent to 40 percent.

In 1995 Parizeau was certain that another appeal to the voters' financial interests would prevail, and his government confidently selected experts to report on the economic impact of sovereignty. But in the early weeks of the campaign the reports came back, and they were uncertain at best and entirely gloomy at worst. Trying to run on a platform at once culturally conservative—nothing will change; your language and way of life will be protected—and socially liberal—everything will change; together we will at last build a just society—the separatists trailed badly in the polls. Quebec's voters seemed unmoved by the whole idea of independence. Some federalists even talked of destroying the nationalist movement forever.

But on October 7 control of the campaign changed hands. Lucien Bouchard, the leader of the Bloc Québécois, the separatist party that held fifty-three of Quebec's seventy-five seats in the federal parliament in

Ottawa, became the de facto leader of the sovereigntists, and what had been under Parizeau a tedious discourse about passports and currency and deficits was transformed into a bitter struggle to forge a new nation. Bouchard had been a small-town lawyer and had learned to speak English late in life, but his American wife and his years as Canada's ambassador to France had given him a reputation, somewhat exaggerated, for sophistication and worldliness. A year earlier Bouchard had lost a leg in a near-death fight with necrotizing fasciitis, the flesh-eating disease, and his survival and recovery had come to symbolize the movement for independence. Bouchard dismissed the ominous economic reports with a wave of his hand. He ridiculed surveys showing that many voters were confused by the referendum question, which was artfully designed to imply that separation might not really mean separation. He ignored statements by Quebec's aboriginal people, who claim vast tracts of the province as their traditional land, that they would separate from Quebec if Quebec separated from Canada.

Parizeau was a technician; one of his few attempts at emotional symbolism was a mawkish poem to the Québecois nation that he had commissioned from a committee consisting of two lawyers, a sociologist, a journalist, and a folk singer. Bouchard, on the other hand, understood anger and the power of an image: In a televised address just prior to the referendum, Bouchard held up a Montreal tabloid newspaper from 1981. On the cover was a lurid color photograph of then Prime Minister Pierre Trudeau and current Prime Minister Jean Chrétien, both Francophone Quebecers, laughing at a news conference the morning after what separatists all know as the Night of the Long Knives. During constitutional negotiations in Ottawa, the story goes, while René Lévesque slept in his hotel bed, Trudeau and Chrétien (who was Trudeau's justice minister) cut a deal with Canada's other provincial premiers to create a new constitution. For Bouchard, the referendum was about Quebec's humiliation, and putting an end to it. The rallying cry of the separatists, *Maîtres chez nous* (masters in our own house), pricked the collective unconscious. Real and imagined Québecois history since the conquest of the French by the British in 1759 rose from the dead. A vote for Oui became a vote for "we."

With Bouchard leading the campaign, a solitary figure leaning resolutely on his cane as he shuffled from speech to speech, the separatist cause climbed steadily, inexorably, in the polls. What had been an obscure Canadian nonstory, just another chapter in an endless saga of debate and dispute, suddenly had become world news.

By the time I arrived in Montreal, the federalist campaign, bewildered by the hurricane of passion sweeping across Quebec, had fallen into desperate and frenzied confusion. At the Unity Rally staged in the center of the city three days prior to the referendum, more than 100,000 Canadians, mostly English-speaking, many bused in from other provinces, waved flags and NON signs stapled to the ends of hockey sticks. People of every skin color jostled and shoved, always politely, while politicians babbled incomprehensibly over the huge loudspeakers, the feedback punctuated by one recognizable word: "Canada! . . . Canada! . . . Canada!" And yet, despite their passion, not one of the federalists was able to say anything coherent about the country they were trying to save.

There were, by that point, two referenda being contested simultaneously in Quebec. Prime Minister Chrétien warned of the dire consequences of separation—unemployment, uncertainty, economic chaos. Separatists spoke of ancestry and identity, questions of the heart.

It was not that Oui voters did not believe Chrétien's threats. It was that they had heard them too often. The separatist supporters I talked with before the referendum accepted that independence would bring economic sacrifices and had in fact come to see those sacrifices as noble, a sacred duty. A generation or two would suffer, they said, but that suffering would be heroic, part of the long Québecois narrative of victimization and survival. Chrétien's realpolitik had nothing in common with Bouchard's appeal to the id. They were, quite simply, not speaking the same language.

The result of the vote on October 30 was 50.6 percent Non to 49.4 percent Oui, a margin of 54,288 votes out of almost 5 million. According to polls, 60 percent of Francophones voted for independence and 95 percent of Anglophones and Allophones—in the doublespeak of race and language in Quebec, "Allophone," from the Greek root "Allos," the Other, is the euphemism for those whose mother tongue is neither French nor English—voted against. October 30 was supposed to be a night of finality. But in his concession speech Lucien Bouchard declared the vote a moral victory for separatists and said that another referendum would be held soon. Premier Parizeau promised revenge and said, "We are beaten, it's true. But by what? Money and the ethnic vote."

Later that night, at 3:00 A.M., Bernard Landry, the deputy premier of Quebec, who was also the minister responsible for immigration, went to his Montreal hotel to check in. He walked up to the night clerk, a woman named Anita Martinez, took out his glasses, and stared at her name tag. Then he leaned across the counter and said, menacingly, that it was because of people like her, immigrants, that the Oui side had lost. "Why is it that we open the doors to this country so you can vote No?" Landry demanded. Martinez, shaking and crying, retreated to a back room. When another clerk, a Francophone, asked if she could help Landry "check in," he flew into a rage. A security guard had to be called. As Landry later explained to the *Montreal Gazette*, "In Quebec, we insist on using the correct [French] expression all the time, 'enregistrer.'" As for Martinez, Landry denied he'd blamed her or minorities for the loss. The conversation, he said, "was done in a cold tone and I never raised my voice."

A few days later, in a move that a provincial government spokesman said was completely unrelated to the referendum, Quebec cut the number of immigrants the province will accept in the future. Later still, former members of the 1960s nationalist terrorist group Front de Libération du Québec (FLQ) redubbed themselves the Mouvement de libération nationale du Québec and demanded a moratorium on immigration until the province becomes an "independent republic." It was reported in the English press that scrutineers appointed by the provincial government had rejected thousands of ballots in some predominantly English suburbs of Montreal because, it was said, the X's were too thick, too skinny, not at the right angle. And a few days after the vote, the government announced that four hospitals in Montreal, which provided service mostly for Anglophones and Allophones, were to be closed.

"I feel like they're waiting for me to leave," Sylvia Wilson said to me that Monday night in a Spanish restaurant on St-Laurent. "It's not in my day-to-day life. It's more abstract. 'You don't mean anything, we won't pay attention to you, you're not part of the vision.' It's like attrition or early retirement: we're not going to fire you, but could you please leave the company?"

Sylvia, a redhead with freckles, big black boots, and a torn gray sweater, works for a film production company in the city. As we talked, a Montreal Canadiens hockey game played on the TV behind the bar. Another of the ceaseless reminders of Montreal's poverty stopped by our table, a crooked-toothed waif in a stained parka. The money she collected from us would go to buy homeless kids clothes, food, and, she said with amazing honesty, cigarettes.

"I'm what they're supposed to want," Sylvia said. "I'm bilingual, I work in English and French." She is also the daughter of a *pure laine* (dyed-in-the-wool) Québecoise mother and an Anglophone father, a marriage she calls "incredibly brave" because of the lack of support her parents received from either community. Her life has been defined by the politics of language. As a child she remembers having "serious language confusion. In kindergarten, I was thinking in French and English at the same time. I didn't know if I was coming or going. I couldn't communicate." In the 1980 referendum, her mother was in favor of separation; her father, against. The household, she said, was "tense." Sylvia grew up on the west side of the city in the 1970s, when the separatist government of René Lévesque made French the only official language of Quebec. She witnessed the mass flight of Anglos from Montreal—more than 150,000 between 1976 and 1981, many of them members of the city's English elite.

When I asked her if she was going to leave Montreal, at first she said, "Those who are going to leave have left. The rest of us will stay." Ten minutes later, as she talked about the mess that is Montreal's economy, she said, "This is the first time I've considered moving for reasons that have nothing to do with my career. I like being a Canadian." Ten minutes after that, she sighed and said, "To leave Montreal for purely political reasons isn't what I'm like. I don't know. I am thinking about it."

It was the kind of confusion I found in every Anglophone and Allophone I met in Montreal. Defiance and uncertainty and displacement and free-floating anxiety. Madame Chu, the owner of a corner store in the east end, said that "sometimes French people get angry and yell at me when I serve a customer in English." She said she doesn't know what to do. She wants to leave, but she has a lease. The man who runs the delicatessen where I bought my newspapers every morning told me he has a degree in medicine from Lebanon, but that he'd never get a chance to practice in Montreal because he's not a Québecois. He would like to leave as well.

Dr. Barbara Rubin Wainrib, a clinical psychologist and adjunct professor who teaches Crisis and Trauma Intervention at McGill University, explained to me that "nothing's been done physically in Montreal to non-Francophones—the houses are still intact—but psychologically houses have been destroyed." When I met with her in a cafeteria on the McGill campus, Dr. Wainrib, a New Yorker who has lived in Montreal since the 1950s, was wearing a red blazer and white blouse, the colors of the Canadian flag. She handed me her study, the results of a questionnaire completed by 292 people who were asked about their emotional state in the two weeks prior to the referendum. Half reported sleep disturbances and nightmares, 72 percent said they'd felt angry and irritable, 65 percent said they were concerned about having to move somewhere else—what Dr. Wainrib called "the spontaneous flight response"—83 percent said they had financial concerns for themselves or their family because of the vote. She pointed to what she said was the most important column: half of her sample ticked the box describing the elements of having suffered actual trauma.

One woman wrote on the back of her questionnaire, "I can't describe to you the fear, despair, anger, depression I experienced. . . . My family has been here for 200 years. I felt that, no matter what happens, we of the minority, no matter what our race or ethnic origin, will suffer. Those of the visible minorities will be in an even worse position than so-called Anglophones. If they separate and the economy suffers, we will be blamed. If they can't separate we are still blamed. When there is cheating at the ballot box, lies by Bouchard on the podium, racial slurs that the majority doesn't immediately renounce, we are not safe."

I noticed that on the bottom of her survey Dr. Wainrib had asked, "Optional: Do you identify yourself as a Sovereigntist () or Federalist ()?" I asked her if any sovereigntists had replied and she said she didn't think so. I asked about the emotional responses to the referendum among Francophones and she said, "I don't know. I live and work on an Anglophone island." She pulled out the forms of a couple of Francophones who had answered. A woman wrote, "I am a French-speaking Québecoise and I was treated as a dog by my coworkers because I was not for the Yes. They made me feel that I did not belong in the French-speaking socety."

I watched the referendum results in an apartment in the Plateau District of Montreal at a kind of Super Bowl party for separatists: play-by-play analysis and computer graphics and catchy theme music beamed out of three televisions; beers were scattered on the coffee table beside a bowl with the stakes from a pick-the-winner pool. A dozen young Québecois, all but one of whom voted Oui, tilted forward in their seats as the early results came in. Marie-Claude Doré, a Oui, watched as Lac-St-Jean, her home region, a remote area in the northeast famous for its huge succulent blueberries and hell-or-high-water nationalism, reported 70 percent for independence. The excitement, early on, was palpable: Yes was ahead, 57 percent to 43 percent. But in the hyper-speed of electronic elections the lead quickly shrank: 56, 53, 51. When the tally reached a dead heat, Marie-Claude and her friends joined hands and said a silent prayer. The Yes percentage ticked up a few hundredths. They laughed. "It worked!" Then it ticked down again.

I kept a diplomatic silence as torpor settled in. Marie-Claude said what everyone was thinking: "It's Montreal." Quebec's only cosmopolitan city and Canada's only truly bilingual city, more than two-thirds Francophone, a sixth Anglophone, and a sixth Allophone, voted **65.5 percent against independence.**

Marie-Claude is, in many ways, a perfectly unremarkable young urban professional. Her black Volkswagen Jetta was parked outside on Rue St-Joseph, she works out at the YMCA, and she goes with her girlfriends for overpriced pasta at loud bistros. She has a bob of blonde hair that she gets streaked and curled, and, as a dentist, she has a patient but firm manner. But she's also a Québecoise from the small city of Chicoutimi, in Lac-St-Jean; her grandmother is a Bouchard. Quebec outside of Montreal is a vast wilderness dotted with homogeneously Québecois small cities and villages like Chicoutimi; in those regions the vote was 59 percent in favor of separation.

During the weeks leading up to the referendum, Marie-Claude wavered between voting Oui and not voting at all. To vote Non wasn't an option—it would be a vote against her people and her past. When I asked her why she finally voted Oui, she said, "I hear about the Night of the Long Knives and I'm angry about René Lévesque waking up that morning and being cheated—this feeling that things are always planned behind Quebec's back. I see a continuous line from the conquest by the English in 1759. From the beginning the relationship wasn't equal. You can still feel it. I think we still feel attacked—maybe even when it's not true. History is always there for us."

When she thought that the separatists were going to win she was elated. "I had so much energy to give to my country, to the new project." But at 10:20 on October 30 the announcement was made: the Oui side had lost. The party broke up. Shrugs and two-cheek kisses were exchanged. Tomorrow everything would be back to normal. What would have been a cataclysm for others had been a simple hope for Marie-Claude and her friends. I stole a glance at the sheet of paper with everyone's predictions in the pool and saw that more than half of them, including Marie-Claude, had bet against themselves.

Josh Freed, a Montreal humorist, was the co-editor and author, in 1984, of *The Anglo Guide to Survival in Quebec*, a satirical primer to the French east end of Montreal that had as its principal advice, "If you want to be spoken to in English in Montreal speak French badly—Francophones will immediately switch. But if you want to speak French, insist on speaking English." At a smoked-meat joint on St-Laurent, on another cold Montreal night, Freed was exhausted, his sense of humor, he said, sorely tested. "One of the horrible things about the referendum," Freed said, "is this weird calling up of your roots. I consider myself Jewish, bald, of Russian ancestry, a Quebecer, a Canadian, a Montrealer, and I've never really weighed the degree to which I'm one or the other. But in the weeks before the referendum, when it looked like the separatists might win, I found this Canadian root called up. It's very painful to feel these parts of yourself fighting. I didn't want to know I'm more Canadian than Quebecer."

Freed told me of the overwhelming reception he had received at a Chinese banquet after the referendum. "Suddenly, we're all ethnic together," he said. "The separatists have turned everyone who isn't **Québecois into a f - - - g family,** united in our opposition to them." He said he knows only one person who is actually leaving because of the referendum. "But I know a thousand who are talking about it," he said. "People are going to sell their houses, go liquid in a big way. I'd guess ten to twenty thousand a year are going to leave before the next referendum—which, of course, the separatists are counting on. It's one of the things that pisses me off. It's in their interest for us to leave."

Downtown, in the clique of skyscrapers at the foot of the city's Mont Royal, I met with a successful Anglophone businessman whom I had talked to on the phone. He had nervously told me, off the record, of death threats associates of his had received from separatist fanatics. In a large suite at the end of a hushed corridor, the businessman, expressing the latent fear of reprisals that is pervasive among non-Francophones, said he did not want to be identified. "A lot of business is being canceled, and a lot of business is being postponed. Companies are diversifying out of Quebec. There won't be public announcements. People have learned to slip out quietly so they don't upset their French customers."

The businessman, who was involved in organizing the Unity Rally in the last few days of the referendum, showed me a poster of an aerial shot of the crowd that day. "I can't tell you how many hard-nosed businessmen had tears in their eyes," he said. "It was the fear of loss of roots, of community, of friends and family, position in society, all at once.

"In my twenty-five-year career there have been six prolonged recessions because of politics in Quebec. This is not a sport. The turmoil causes consternation about the viability of doing business here." He lowered his voice. "But business won't be unprepared next time. There's serious money behind Montreal separating from Quebec. We'll set up a corridor to Ontario. Montreal has 65 percent of the gross provincial product and almost half the population. They can have the rest of Quebec."

The Sunday after the referendum, René-Daniel Dubois, a leading Québecois playwright, was the subject of a full-page interview in *Le Monde* of Paris. A former separatist, Dubois was one of the 40 percent of Francophones who voted Non. He likened the referendum to "a failed suicide." "The Québecois imagine that sovereignty will be their act of birth," he said. "Meanwhile, they do not define themselves as actors, but as victims of the hatred and wickedness of the others." Describing Quebec as a "'soft' totalitarian society," Dubois said, "The true alternative is this: to be the young man in the white shirt in front of the tank in Tiananmen Square, or to be the driver of the tank. Our myths tell us that we are the young man. The truth is that we are seated in the tank."

I met with Dubois on a Saturday in November, just before the closing night of the revival of his seventeen-part one-man play in French, *Don't Blame the Bedouins*. A stocky man with hair shaved to prickle length, wire-rimmed glasses, and a tobacco-rasp voice, Dubois told me that he was suffering "a kind of boycott. People scream at me, won't talk to me. Culture is always used symbolically in Quebec. Artists are only good if they can be used for nationalism." What was lost in the symbolism were real social problems, Dubois said. "Half the boys in Montreal don't finish high school, and Quebec has the highest youth suicide rate in the Western world. It's a catastrophe."

The audiences for his play, he told me, had been unusually small. The English-language daily, on the other hand, did a big spread on him, and Anglo columnists had quoted approvingly from his *Le Monde* interview. When I pointed out that he had been shunned by the French and bear-hugged by the English, Dubois shrugged. "What do you expect?"

A couple of weeks after the referendum I arranged to meet again with Marie-Claude and her friend Chantale. Over a *vrai* Québecois breakfast—bacon and eggs and potatoes and beans and toast and, for the second course, a plate of crepes swimming in maple syrup—they told me that Francophones who had voted Oui were depressed. They thought nothing had changed, that nothing *would* change. I asked them how they felt about Bernard Landry's behavior on the night of the referendum and the cut in immigration to Quebec and the fears of Anglophones and Allophones. They both looked at me with surprise. The stories hadn't been covered in the French media, they said.

"We are not in contact with Anglos, you know," Marie-Claude said, "except you."

I was, I realized, on the other side of a segregated city. The divide of Boulevard St-Laurent, the French-speaking and English-speaking neighborhoods of Montreal, the French and English press, meant that there were two versions of everything. When Bouchard spoke on television just before the referendum, the French version of his address summoned the spirits of the Night of the Long Knives; the terse, disjointed English version he delivered that same night talked of the future partnership between Quebec and the rest of Canada. There were two sets of facts here. If the facts were agreed upon, then there were two completely different interpretations of those facts.

How you saw what was happening in Quebec depended on your point of view. To Anglophones and Allophones, the Québecois are a dominant, even oppressive majority. But through Francophone eyes, the province is a tiny, embattled island in an invincible sea of English. The idea that the Québecois could ever oppress anyone seems, to them, ludicrous. I told Chantale and Marie-Claude how pervasive anxiety and uncertainty were among the non-Francophones I had encountered, and that people were talking openly and constantly about as many as a million people leaving Quebec, but to Chantale it sounded like just another attack. "We treat the Anglophones well," she said. "They don't do so badly."

On the night of the referendum, when Parizeau announced that ethnics were to blame for the loss and the crowd cheered, I had seen the color drain from Marie-Claude's cheeks. Caught between the monoculture of her childhood and cosmopolitan Montreal, she had always been worried about "the shadow of racism" in the separatist movement. "I would like everyone to be included in the project of a new country," she said now. "But I can understand their feeling of rejection. I know that it exists, but only because you tell me it does. I'm not so much in contact with these people. I don't have close friends that aren't Francophones. The thing that makes me sad is that I'm more conscious of the walls in my city. I don't know how to reach out. The walls were there before, but now they've been named."

I rode Montreal's absurdly quiet, rubber-wheeled Metro east—the guy beside me was reading a pamphlet on Esperanto grammar—to meet Pierre Vallières, the intellectual leader of the Front de Libération du Québec during the 1960s and the author of the best-selling *White Niggers of America*, a revolutionary tome in which Vallières likened the Québecois to slaves: "the workers of Quebec are aware of their conditions as niggers, exploited men, second class citizens. . . . Were they not imported, like the American blacks, to serve as cheap labor in the New World? The only difference between them is the color of their skin and the continent they came from." In the 1960s in Montreal, FLQ bombs were routinely exploding on the wealthy English west side of the city. Vallières was convicted of contributing to one bombing through "his writings, his words, his attitudes, etc."

In a Vietnamese restaurant in the Gay Village, Vallières, a frail Jesuitical man, said he had recanted the use of the term "nigger": "You have to understand the context. In the Sixties, it meant somebody who was downtrodden, somebody who was abused. That was the situation here. Now this is not the case. There is more poverty than there ever was before, but there are many, many Allophones who are poor as well."

I had heard Vallières on the radio talking about his frequent visits to Sarajevo over the last few years. When I asked him why he had gone, he said, "I felt it was my duty to see an experiment in self-management and self-determination and socialism fall into fratricidal wars and internecine killing." Vallières, who now says he was never a Québecois nationalist, doesn't see what happened in Sarajevo happening in Montreal. "Sarajevo is a small city, a unilingual city, and it's a city that is steeped in tradition. Montreal is younger, larger, and North American. In Sarajevo the war began outside the city, but if there is a conflict here, it would arise from inside, like the blacks in South-Central Los Angeles. I don't think it would be a real war with arms and bullets, but there might be some sparks."

André McLaughlin, Vallières's companion, who also spends a lot of time in Sarajevo, said, "I'm much more pessimistic about Montreal. After the referendum, a young man came to the house, very disappointed with the result, and he said he agreed with Parizeau's statement that the ethnics were to blame. He believes that Quebec is taking 40 percent of Canada's immigrants. That's not true, but try to convince that young man that what he thinks is based on emotion. When I tell my friends in Sarajevo about the referendum here, they say, 'Remember, that's how *we* started.' We have a lot of volunteers in Sarajevo who are willing to come here and teach us the art of survival."

In the parallel universes of French and English newspapers and television, politicians continued their poisonous post-referendum fighting—now, once again, pre-referendum fighting—always with a different interpretation. Jacques Parizeau resigned without apologizing for his remarks, and was given a statesman's send-off. Lucien Bouchard, the man of fate, gave up his position as leader of Her Majesty's Loyal Opposition in the federal parliament to take Parizeau's place as premier of the province and prepare for the next vote on independence. Bernard Landry remained the deputy premier. Prime Minister Chrétien, fulfilling promises he had made during the referendum campaign, introduced bills recognizing Quebec as a distinct society, giving the province a veto over constitutional change, and decentralizing power. Nothing Chrétien did seemed to matter. The popularity of sovereignty rose in the polls. The rest of Canada, as separatists hoped, was exhausted. Patience with the Quebec Problem was spent; the country had been desensitized to what seemed to be the certainty of its fragmentation. One of the enormous diaspora of ex-Montrealers now living in Toronto told me his eighty-year-old parents had left Montreal for Ontario. He laughed and said he now calls Quebec "the Old Country."

The only thing that no one I met, separatist or federalist, talked about was what would have happened if the vote had gone the other way. Nobody wanted to talk about the fact that a few days before the referendum a member of parliament of the Bloc Québécois, Bouchard's separatist party in the federal assembly, had sent a statement to army barracks in Quebec saying that "soldiers of Quebec origin" would be expected to transfer their loyalty to the new nation. No one mentioned the October Crisis of 1970, when Prime Minister Trudeau declared a state of emergency and sent tanks into the streets of Montreal and arrested hundreds to put down the picayune threat of the Front de Libération du Québec. No one wanted to think about the thick, sickening expectation of violence on the night of the referendum, when it seemed to me that it had, as the separatist campaign slogan promised, all become possible.

The surreal calm in Montreal after the referendum only hid the sense of dread among Anglophones and Allophones. In January, two months after I spoke to the English businessman, 1,200 Montrealers held a rally in support of the idea that the city should be partitioned from a sovereign Quebec and attached to what would be left of Canada, ignoring the fact that 2 million of the city's 3 million people are Francophone. The Cree, who have a land claim to most of the north of the province, repeated their long-standing demand to remain in Canada and not be "kidnapped" by separatists. Chrétien, once again resorting to scare tactics, replaced the economic threats he had made during the referendum campaign with a territorial threat. "If Canada is divisible, Quebec is divisible too," he said. "It's the same logic." Bouchard's comment was angry and cutting: "Canada is divisible because it is not a real country. There are two people, two nations, and two territories. And this one is ours."

Bouchard's words were disturbing to many Canadians precisely because they now rang so true. Perhaps Canada no longer *was* a country. I had come to Montreal in October thinking that the separatists would succeed and that Canada would die. The referendum failed, and the world media's attention moved elsewhere, but in the months since the vote it has seemed to me that Canada is dying anyway. The country was built on a paradox: what united Canada were its divisions. The conflict of the French and English, two dominant but co-existing cultures—what Canadian novelist Hugh MacLennan called "two solitudes"—created a tolerant, cosmopolitan nation. And Montreal was always its centerpiece, the only uniquely Canadian city. The hope that Montreal had offered was that there was a peaceful, compassionate way to live with difference, even a difference as profound as language. Now, in a few short weeks, the referendum had replaced the lived reality of compromise and tolerance with the abstractions of us and them.

A month after the referendum, in the Spanish restaurant on Boulevard St-Laurent, ghosts and twisters of snow drifted along the street outside the window. Sylvia, who had been raised by a Québecoise mother and an Anglophone father, but who identified herself as English, told me that she had seen graffiti spray-painted on walls all around Montreal: ANGLOS GO HOME. "Don't they realize this *is* my home?" she asked. And that, I thought, is how things will fall apart in Montreal. Not in the shouts and curses of an angry and divisive political campaign—that will come with the next referendum—but in the quiet desperation between fights, when Sylvia and all of us are left to wonder what, if anything, the word "home" is supposed to mean.

Germania Irredenta

Renouncing a provision of the 1945 Potsdam Declaration, Germans are looking more than wistfully at lands they lost in the war—and suing to get them back. Do some things never change?

Hans Koning

Hans Koning is at work on a novel, *Night and Day*, to be published next year.

I CLEARLY remember a newsreel of the state memorial ceremony for Reinhard Heydrich, which I saw in late 1942, when I was a very young sergeant in the British army. (Germany exported movie news to Sweden and Switzerland, and some got to England.) Heydrich, the German governor of Bohemia and Moravia (now the Czech Republic), had been killed by two Czech resistance fighters that spring. The service was in a dark hall in Berlin, lit by torches; a heathenish, Valhalla-like effect had been achieved. In his oration Hitler screamed that if the Czechs would not "co-exist peacefully" in the German Reich, they would at some future date be resettled in the Polar Circle. His audience shouted its approval. Earlier Hitler had picked the small town of Lidice, near the spot where the Czechs attacked Heydrich's car, as the focal point for immediate vengeance. Its adults were killed, its children shipped to camps and German orphanages and given German names.

Heydrich had not only been the ruler of Bohemia and Moravia; he had also been given the task of organizing the extermination of the Jews of Europe. The invitations to the Wannsee Conference of January 20, 1942, where the logistics of the gas chamber were worked out, had been sent out by him from Prague. "*Mit anschliessendem Frühstück*," his letters said—"With breakfast to follow."

Hitler's Polar Circle plans have, fifty-four years later, attracted unexpected new interest. Several Sudeten Germans have sued in Czech courts for the restitution of lands and property that were appropriated after the Sudetens were expelled from what is now the Czech Republic, at the end of the Second World War. The government of Chancellor Helmut Kohl, which wants an apology from the Czechs for those expulsions, announced last year through its Foreign Minister, Klaus Kinkel, that approval of the expulsions as part of the 1945 Potsdam Declaration by the Big Three (the United States, the United Kingdom, and the Soviet Union) did not make them legal. Kinkel sided with the Sudeten Germans, who assert that the declaration is in conflict with the United Nations Charter. (He uses the more circumspect phrase "in conflict with international law.")

A shiver must have gone through Germany's neighbors at this argument, which questions the very foundation of their states. Last February the ambassadors of the United States, the United Kingdom, and Russia published a statement in Prague reaffirming the Potsdam Declaration. But a feeling persisted that, just maybe, we were going back to square one.

As far as I could see, the U.S. media gave very little attention to this. It made me decide to take a trip, early this year, to southern Germany.

THE Second World War really started with those Sudeten Germans. Some two to three million of them lived in "the Sudetenland," as the Germans called a Czech region along the border. In 1938 Hitler declared that the Sudetenland was Germany's last irredenta—the last foreign territory that really belonged to Germany—and that to get it was his "last demand" in Europe. All through the summer he fought a war of nerves against the West, raving about the perfidious Czechs and their "stage actor President," Eduard Beneš, who were terrorizing Germans, beating German women and children who wore white stockings (the German "uniform") and murdering Germans in isolated villages. The circus of provocation was orchestrated for him by the leader of the Sudeten Germans, the Nazi Konrad Henlein. The United States was looking away at that time; England and France caved in and forced the Czechs to cede the Sudetenland. This was "Munich"—the shameful surrender led by the English Prime Minister, Neville Chamberlain, in the fall of 1938. Czechoslovakia lost its fortified border with Germany and its important armaments factories, and some six months later the rest of the country was taken by the Germans without a shot. Hitler came to Prague and slept in the government Hradčany Castle under the swastika flag. "I saw our enemies at Munich," he told his followers later. "They are little worms."

After 1945 maps continued to show the 1937 borders. East Germany was called "Middle Germany."

When one rethinks this story and the terror of the six-year German occupation that followed, in which some 350,000 Czechs lost their lives, one cannot be surprised that after the German surrender in 1945 there were numerous acts of local vengeance in which Sudeten Germans were killed. The bulk of those who remained were deported by the Czech government with a minimum of consideration—not to the Polar Circle, though, but back to their fatherland. These Germans and their descendants now want their lands and houses back. Meanwhile, the Czech survivors of the German concentration camps, some 17,000, still have not received any compensation from Bonn.

I learned on my visit that there is a specifically political angle to this: the Sudeten Germans have a pressure group within Germany, the Sudetendeutsche Landsmannschaft, with political clout that the millions of German deportees from Poland never had. Bavaria, where most of them live, is one of the sixteen *Länder* (states) in reunited Germany; it has a lot of autonomous power. A 1954 act of its government established the Sudeten Germans as one of the four population groups that make up Bavaria (with the Swabians, the Franconians, and the Old Bavarians) and guarantees them *Schirmherrschaft*—"high protection" or "guardianship." This gives the Sudetens a direct channel to the Bavarian government and through that to Bonn. Bonn's conservatives are particularly nervous right now about being outflanked on the right.

What is happening could be nothing more than a war of words. (Indeed, in a May speech Kinkel spoke of compensation for the Czech "victims of Nazi injustice.") It points, though, to a basic dilemma: either united Germany is an established country like any other, with all the egotism and arrogance of a major power, or it is still in a kind of quarantine. Europe's politicians and businesspeople have long accepted the first alternative, although I was often told that Kohl himself promotes a united Europe so fervently because he does not trust his country to be left on its own. He has called Germany's integration into Europe "a matter of life or death" for the twenty-first century.

One of the people who stressed this point of view to me was an editor of the *Stuttgarter Zeitung*, a serious and liberal south-German newspaper. The day we first met he wrote in his paper, "He who tries to demand certain rights based on the past prepares a European catastrophe." Those words were directed at the Sudeten Germans in Bavaria. Thoughtful as they sound, they gave me the feeling that even he still didn't "get it."

It's not a matter of the Sudetens' claiming their property on the basis of past records. It is a matter of the past's not being a source of *any* kind of German rights. If Germany had been a victor, even for a limited time, whole nations and many old and famous cities would have been wiped off the earth. The best that reunited Germany can ask for, it seems to me, is a clean slate. By no stretch of emotion or law should it expect a court to study the deportation of the Sudetens or any other such actions outside their contexts.

When my discussion with the editor turned to united Germany's border with Poland, he called it a *Wohlstandsgrenze*—a line between poor and well-off people. He was, perhaps unconsciously, downgrading a national border to an affair of economic zoning. After 1945, West German maps and atlases continued to show the 1937 borders. East Germany was usually called "Middle Germany." The Potsdam demarcations, the maps indicated, were but "temporary." Indeed they were—but no one in the West predicted that they would change again to Germany's advantage. Among the many who played along with this negation of postwar political reality was the American oil company Esso, as Exxon was then called; when one had to drive through a checkpoint, the East German guards confiscated Esso road maps and tore them up with great gusto. A conference of West German education ministers ruled that in schoolbooks "the loss of German land in the East is to be established as a loss to the entire civilized world."

When I traveled this spring from Paris to Frankfurt on an evening train, I saw to my horror that the railroad map in the corridor showed no border at all between Germany and Poland beyond a two-inch-long dotted line west of Szczecin. With the first daylight I discovered that there was indeed a border marked, so thin as to be almost invisible against the blue of the Oder River, which it followed. I am sure that German railroad officials would say this was done unthinkingly. The towns east of the border were shown with both their Polish and old German names.

I had a few years before traveled by train from Berlin to Warsaw in a compartment full of what are called here *Heimwehtouristen*—"homesickness tourists." At each stop they stood at the window and discussed what this or that town was "really" called. A German atlas from the time between the two world wars shows Strasbourg as a German town and omits the Polish corridor. One might say that German cartography is always one war behind.

NOTHING in this is so very surprising. I cannot think of a single historical example of a country's voluntarily giving up on its irredenta. That Germany is now as strong as it was in 1914, and Russia perhaps as weak as it was in 1914, does not make it any likelier that Germany will be the exception. The best chance for lasting peace would be if Germany under the Nazis was a historically unique situation.

A German historian, Fritz Fischer, in 1961 published a book about Germany's policies during the First World War, *Griff nach der Weltmacht*. The title translates as *Grab for World Power*, although "*Griff*" has a slightly less negative color than "grab." An abridged version was published by the New York publisher W. W. Norton under the calm title *Germany's Aims in the First World War*. In the book Fischer showed how the Kaiser's serious, polite, formalistic Germany was in its policies painfully close to Nazi Germany in the next war. Naturally, the book caused an outcry in West Germany, but its scholarship and the mass of documentation it presented left little room for factual criticism.

Fischer documented that Germany's war aim, almost until the bitter end, was the creation of a German Mitteleuropa that would include Belgium, Holland, Scandinavia, and, of course, Poland. In 1918 the Ukraine was added. (Analogous to it would be Mittelafrika, a German colony stretching across Africa from ocean to ocean.) Wartime German state documents said nonetheless that Germany was fighting for the "liberty of the continent of Europe and its peoples"; France, weakened "forever" by a German demand for 40 billion gold francs in reparations, would be forced to join the war against England.

A report to the Imperial Chancellery showed a map of the frontier strip isolating a rump Poland (perhaps to be ceded to Austria-Hungary), which was to be settled by Germans from the "Old Reich"—after being "cleared" by deporting part of its Polish population and all its Jews. A memorandum drawn up at the instruction of Chancellor Bethmann Hollweg declared, "The German people, the greatest colonising people of the world, . . . must be given wider frontiers within which it can live a full life." If the word *Lebensraum* isn't there yet, the concept certainly is.

I realize that it is not politically correct to generalize about an entire nation; still, centuries of a common history may put a stamp on a society which makes it hard for other societies to understand. I hope I am not venturing into an area of pseudoscience when I suggest that German aggressiveness was based not only on an overconfidence that the country presumably no longer feels about itself but also, paradoxically, on a lack of confidence it *does* feel. What is one to make otherwise of a report by Gustav Krupp, the arms manufacturer, written for the government in the fall of 1914? (The great industrialists of Germany played a large role in defining war policies.) Krupp wrote that German domination should continue in Belgium and extend to the north coast of France. He explained,

> Here we should be lying at the very marrow of England's world power, a position—perhaps the only one—which could bring us England's *lasting friendship* [italics mine]. For only if we are able to hurt England badly at any moment will she really leave us unmolested, perhaps even become our 'friend', in so far as England is capable of friendship at all.

The truth about nations is endlessly complicated, and political predictions based on generalization may go awry: the recent past provides plenty of examples. I find reason for some optimism in this. An experience I had toward the end of my visit may illustrate what I mean. One of my conversations about the German irredenta was with an academician whose real feelings about the matter didn't become quite clear to me. He seemed to feel that Germany's reunification had indeed created a "new legal context." He then started talking about himself.

> ***I was often told that Kohl promotes a united Europe because he does not trust his country to be left on its own.***

This man would have been born in Königsberg, in East Prussia, he told me, if his parents had not fled to the west from the approaching battles, in the winter of 1944–1945. He was born in West Germany just after the war ended.

Königsberg is now Kaliningrad, a town in Russia. As a naval base on the Baltic Sea, it was for many years closed to foreigners—but no longer. Two years ago the academician traveled there. He wandered through what he still considered to be his home town, accompanied by a Russian student guide who spoke German. Coming to the street where his parents had lived, he found that their house was still standing. He looked at it for a while and then hastened on. But his guide suggested that they go back and ring the bell and ask for a look inside. The man balked at first, but then his curiosity got the better of him and he agreed.

They were asked in. Three families now lived in the house. When the man explained the reason for his visit, the Russians made him sit down and brought out tea and cakes, and eventually (of course) vodka. They were clearly poor people, but they searched high and low for something to give him as a present. If he warned them in advance, they told him, the next time they would receive him in style.

The academician paused here, lost in thought. Then, to my astonishment, he ended, "And I now think that that was the best day in my entire life."

Size, Scope Of Hutu Crisis Hotly Debated

Refugees Caught In E. Zaire Chaos

Lynne Duke

Washington Post Foreign Service

NYABIBWE, Zaire, Nov. 23—High in the eastern Zaire mountains where the clouds hug the earth, gunfire crackled on the lush green slopes where a mass of Rwandan refugees was hidden. Believed to number between 150,000 and 400,000, they were driven here like cattle by the armed former Rwandan soldiers among them who have used the helpless as human shields for their pillaging of towns and villages.

Down below, this tiny hamlet of 8,000 people looked as if an apocalyptic prophecy had been realized. Several small wooden houses were burned and torn apart. The wreckage of 30 charred, twisted cars and tankers blocked the main dirt road, also littered with shrapnel as well as unexploded grenades and mortars. Men dug graves for those killed when the town was overrun Wednesday by the armed Rwandans, Who destroyed what they could not take, followed by Zairian rebels, who arrived to restore order.

With Nyabibwe still smoldering Friday, John Demescene Baragondoza and 70 other refugees, including about 20 small children, made their escape. They left the maelstrom of refugees behind them and began the long trek back to Bukavu, 65 miles to the south. Dusty but dignified in a double-breasted blazer, the former Rwandan postal worker stepped forward to issue a simple appeal to a group of journalists he encountered on the road: "Can you tell people that we need help? We need something to eat. We are very tired."

For the hapless Rwandan refugees remaining in eastern Zaire, weeks if not months of continued wandering and hardship appear to be in store. They are caught in the nexus of political, ethnic and military conflicts in Zaire, in Rwanda and in global capitals, were politicians continue to debate the refugees' numbers and whether they are significant enough to warrant help.

Traveling through the hinterlands of eastern Zaire, it becomes clear that many people—the numbers are uncertain—remain in desperate circumstances that will deepen without help and could sow the seeds for future instability in Central Africa's Great Lakes region.

These refugees are the remainder of what the United Nations says were 1.1 million Rwandan Hutu refugees who had been living in eastern Zaire camps since 1994 when they fled Rwanda after extremists among them perpetrated a genocide against Rwanda's minority Tutsis. Some 500,000 refugees have returned to Rwanda in recent days in a mammoth repatriation through the border station at Goma, Zaire. If 1.1 million were here to start with, then hundreds of thousands of refugees remain.

But the Goma exodus inspired a sense of diminished urgency among the world's political powers. A planned multinational peacekeeping force is on hold pending further deliberation. The United States believes that the bulk of the refugees have gone home and that about 200,000 remain. The United Nations contends that 700,000 refugees remain in Zaire—more than have been repatriated.

The rebel movement that controls eastern Zaire claims there are no more refugees in its territory—a claim clearly refuted by the Nyabibwe story—and that rebels will fight to stop a multinational force from bringing humanitarian assistance. Rwanda's Tutsi-dominated government, which has trained and supported the Zairian rebels, also is against the force.

"We are opposed to the multinational force because we believe that the innocent people who were not involved in the massacres in Rwanda have gone home," said Jonas Sebatunzi, spokesman for the rebel alliance. "The rest are assassins."

Instead of bringing humanitarian assistance, the Zairian Tutsi-led Alliance of Democratic Forces for the Liberation of Congo-Zaire, known generally as the Banyamulenge, wants an international force to come in to disarm the Hutu militias and former soldiers among the refugees and bring them to justice.

The refugee groups are largely under the control of Hutu soldiers of the former Armed Forces of Rwanda and the Interahamwe militia, both of which were under the old Hutu regime in Rwanda and are believed responsible for the 1994 genocide.

Human rights advocates accuse these former soldiers of using the Zairian refugee camps as launching pads for "ethnic cleansing" against Tutsis in eastern Zaire as well as for military attacks against Rwanda's Tutsi-dominated government. Tutsis in eastern Zaire are a minority group amid several other ethnicities, including Zairian Hutus.

The eastern Zairian instability gave rise to the Banyamulenge Tutsi movement. With Rwandan government training and support, the movement launched all-out war against Zairian government forces at the end of October and seized a swath of territory along Zaire's lakebound border. When the Zairian army fled in defeat, former Armed Forces soldiers and Interahamwe combatants among the refugees took up the slack and battled the rebels themselves. Low-level conflict between these two forces continues. Refugees report severe repression from former members of the Armed Forces and Interahamwe and that people who resist instructions are killed.

"There are many bodies in the mountains," said Baragondoza, who fled the Interahamwe, as he and his group rested on the road before gathering their belongings for the monthlong trek back to the border and, they hope, back home.

The fighting that broke out a month ago scattered refugees from a string of 40 U.N. camps. They surged toward the largest of the camps, called Mugunga, near Goma, Zaire, where Interahamwe forces held them under tight control until nine days ago, when the massive exodus began.

Since then, debate has raged about how many refugees remain and where they are. The Hutu refugees who last week were reported moving on Nyabibwe and points northwest are one of several groups still on the move. Another, smaller group is believed to be headed west from Bukavu, beyond rebel-held territory, toward the no man's land of the jungle. Already, the westward-moving refugees, believed to number 30,000, have encountered stiff resistance and fighting from villagers fearful of plundering by refugees. Residents of the region say some communities have destroyed small bridges to limit refugee access.

In the town of Walungu, about 30 miles west of Bukavu, a hospital director reported that Interahamwe fighters battled among themselves over provisions and medicine before pressing further west.

Humanitarian relief workers fear that a combination of battle, malnutrition and inaccessibility could seal the refugees' fate if they are not helped soon. But several factors are preventing aid workers, from finding or gaining access to the refugees.

The Zairian rebels holding eastern Zaire were, until recently, loath to allow aid workers into their area. And even when aid workers are able to circulate freely here, there are unknown numbers of refugees who have been pushed so far west that they may be beyond reach.

Still, the refugees keep marching. They are faceless masses to much of the world, which spots them on satellite photographs or hears of their numbers. With little to eat, they walk barefoot and weighed down with belongings, up and down the Lake Kivu region, in and out of the mountains, deep into the jungle.

Military-civilian schism widens, posing danger

As fewer and fewer citizens experience military service, society increasingly is dividing into two groups who disdain each other. That's bad for democracy.

Amy Waldman

Amy Waldman is an editor at The Washington Monthly.

The revelations of rape and sexual harassment at Aberdeen, Md., and other Army bases have drawn renewed—and deserved—attention to the military's difficulty in integrating women. But the stories about Aberdeen contain a detail illustrative of another side of the military: Soldiers found guilty of sexual liaisons with trainees may face charges of not just rape or sodomy but, if they are married, adultery as well.

Yes, adultery. As civilians from President Clinton to Jim Bakker make infidelity seem as common to modern marriage as the honeymoon, the armed services remain a bastion of traditional morality. In a society increasingly guided by "situational ethics" and moral relativism, the military evinces a steadfast commitment to right and wrong.

The difference is just one part of a broader schism between military and civilian views that could become dangerous. A military with little respect for amoral civilians, and civilian leadership that neither understands nor stands up to the military, is bad news for our democracy.

Forget the post-Vietnam military, when morale was low and desertion, illiteracy, drunkenness and drug abuse were rife. In the 1980s, the armed services began raising their standards; today they accept applicants of only the highest caliber. Recruits must have at least a General Educational Development degree, and most have high school diplomas.

Equally impressive is the quality of soldiers—and citizens—the military produces. Members of the armed services practice not only rigid self-discipline but also unflagging selflessness. As society at large increasingly exalts individual rights, the military continues to prioritize responsibilities—to your unit and, most of all, your country.

The armed services also have successfully addressed problems, most notably race, that still bedevil civilian society. Blacks in the military have attained leadership positions at a remarkable rate because the military practices the kind of affirmative action the rest of America should aspire to: Expand the pool of qualified applicants through recruitment or remedial education, then promote strictly on merit.

Yet few of us are learning the many lessons the military offers because the proportion of society with military experience has been shrinking dramatically. As a result, people in the military increasingly exude disdain for nonservers, whom they perceive as undisciplined, immoral and selfish. Civilians, in turn, traffic in blatant stereotypes of military people as stupid or fascistic.

These stereotypes have particular currency because the lack of military experience is most glaring among America's decision makers and opinion shapers. Bill Clinton is the most obvious—and troubling—example of a nonserver, but he has plenty of company. Close to 60% of men in the Senate are veterans, but only a third of the House (and only a quarter of the 104th and 105th Congresses' freshmen). Only 20% of Senate-confirmed Clinton appointees are veterans, and only 4% of White House staff. How many of our political leaders' children have served is unknown, but by all accounts the number is small.

So who is serving? Mostly the children of the poor and the working and middle classes. Of 220 Marines killed in the 1983 Beirut bombing, 78 were Catholic and 64 were Baptist, the denominations most common to the working class. There were two Episcopalians and two Presbyterians. Of the 19 Americans killed in June's terrorist bombing in Saudi Arabia, 10 were Roman Catholic and five were Baptist.

This class split is relatively new. Until Vietnam, military service was routine and honorable for elite and blue-collar youths alike. But as the Vietnam war machine geared up, leaders opened loopholes, notably educational deferments, exempting the well educated and well-off.

As the war's character became apparent, elites began to see military service as immoral (not to mention dangerous). By 1973, when we officially instituted an all-volunteer force, the morality of nonservice had been cemented. And with the draft's end, the children—or youthful versions—of Fortune 500 executives, professors, congressmen and journalists no longer had to evade service; they simply could ignore it.

The trend away from service among elites has perpetuated itself. The Reserve Officer Training Corps, for example, has long been a conduit for college students into military service. But in Vietnam's wake, student opposition prompted many colleges to phase out ROTC. In the 1970s and 1980s, ROTC made something of a comeback. But then the fight over gays in the military again drove ROTC programs from many campuses, this time with the support of professors who had been students during the first round of purgings.

That military service is becoming a rarity bodes ill for many reasons. Most dangerous is the growing abstractness of the military in the eyes of civilian leaders who decide to deploy it. Deciding to send troops to war or trouble spots is never easy, but it is easier if none of those deciding have children at risk.

Ignorance about the military, meanwhile, encourages a romanticized view of its ability to solve any problem, whether the influx of drugs here or hunger in Somalia. At the same time, guilt about not serving can make civilian policymakers loath to challenge the military industrial complex's demands. Combine that with military leaders' growing lack of respect for their civilian commanders—consider the open sniping at Clinton in the ranks—and the potential for an unhealthy concentration of power and hubris in the military becomes clear.

As with most problems, the civilian-military divide is easier to identify than remedy. Returning to the draft is politically and practically impossible: It would churn up far more recruits than a shrinking and technologically sophisticated military could train or use. But there are things we can do to encourage more military service. Expand, rather than curtail, ROTC programs, for example. Or institute a national-service lottery, with the option for civilian or military service. That, at least, would send the message that serving the country, whether by protecting its interests or caring for its elderly, is a task not for the few but for all of us.

Understanding Cultural Pluralism

The increase in racial violence and hatred on campuses across the country is manifested in acts ranging from hateful speech to physical violence. Strategies for dealing with this problem on a campus include increased awareness through mandatory ethnic studies, the empowerment of targets of violence, and fostering social and cultural interaction in festivals, folk-arts fairs, and literary and political forums. Systematic knowledge about ethnic groups has not been a central scholarly concern. In fact, mainstream literary, humanistic, and historical disciplines have only recently begun to displace sociological attention to the pathologies of urban ethnicity as the primary contact and source of information and interpretation of ethnic traditions. The historic role that voluntary groups have played in the reduction of bias and bigotry also needs to be revalued and revitalized. Voluntary associations can take part in a host of state and local initiatives to improve intergroup relations. Schools and parents can help children understand commonalities and differences among and within ethnic traditions and groups. The incorporation of everyday experiences of families and a formal pedagogy rooted in accurate and locally relevant resources are essential building blocks for understanding diversity.

The reemergence of the discussion of race, ethnicity, and intelligence that is included in the selections found in this unit reveals the embeddedness of interpretive categories that frame the discussion and analysis of race and ethnic relations. The enormity of the educational effort that is required as we attempt to move beyond the ethnocentrism and racism that bred hatred and destructive relationships between persons and communities is revealed in a variety of ways. Philosophic reflection on the epistemological issues associated with explaining human variety is rarely invited. However, it is precisely at this intersection of social philosophy and science that the crucial breakthroughs in understanding are likely to appear. The continual mismeasures of intelligence and misreadings of meaning indicate the long-term need for critical reformulation of the very idea of race.

At this time a variety of ways of measuring the development of race and ethnic relations are imposing the accuracy of their claims. Evidence cited by claimants to such authoritative knowledge and the attendant public criterion of credibility point to the expectation of a spirited debate. This unit challenges us to rethink the assumptions, contradictions, and aspirations of social development models.

Looking Ahead: Challenge Questions

What signs have you seen of an increase in racist, anti-Semitic, anti-immigrant, and antiminority group acts that recent studies apparently confirm?

What explains the fact that large population studies confirm that in the areas of ethnic, racial, and religious differences, Americans are more tolerant than ever?

Why do teenagers commit 80 percent of all bias-related acts?

Conflict in ethnic and race relations pose what problems for corporate and governmental institutions?

What media images of race and ethnicity are dominant?

What avenues are available for the authentic cultural resources of ethnic communities and traditions?

How can multiethnic expressions of traditions intersect with the breakdown of community and the isolationist tendencies related to individual and personal achievement?

How can the promotion of positive prototypes of ethnicity ever become as powerful as negative stereotypes?

How can dialogue among conflicting parties about dilemmas that are essential to technological and economic change enable us to share and shape the burden of social change?

Contrast local knowledge with national and local media as sources of information on race and ethnicity.

Why should advocates of multicultural development and diversity argue for the following: (1) Fair and equal protection under the law; (2) The compilation of full and accurate data on the ethnic composition of the American population; (3) Corporate and governmental leaders who are focused on issues that do not exacerbate relations among persons because of ethnicity and race.

What are the benefits if ethnic groups meet regularly with other ethnic groups and engage in friendly "what's your agenda" meetings?

Who, if anyone, benefits from the persistence of ethnic tension and conflict?

UNIT 9

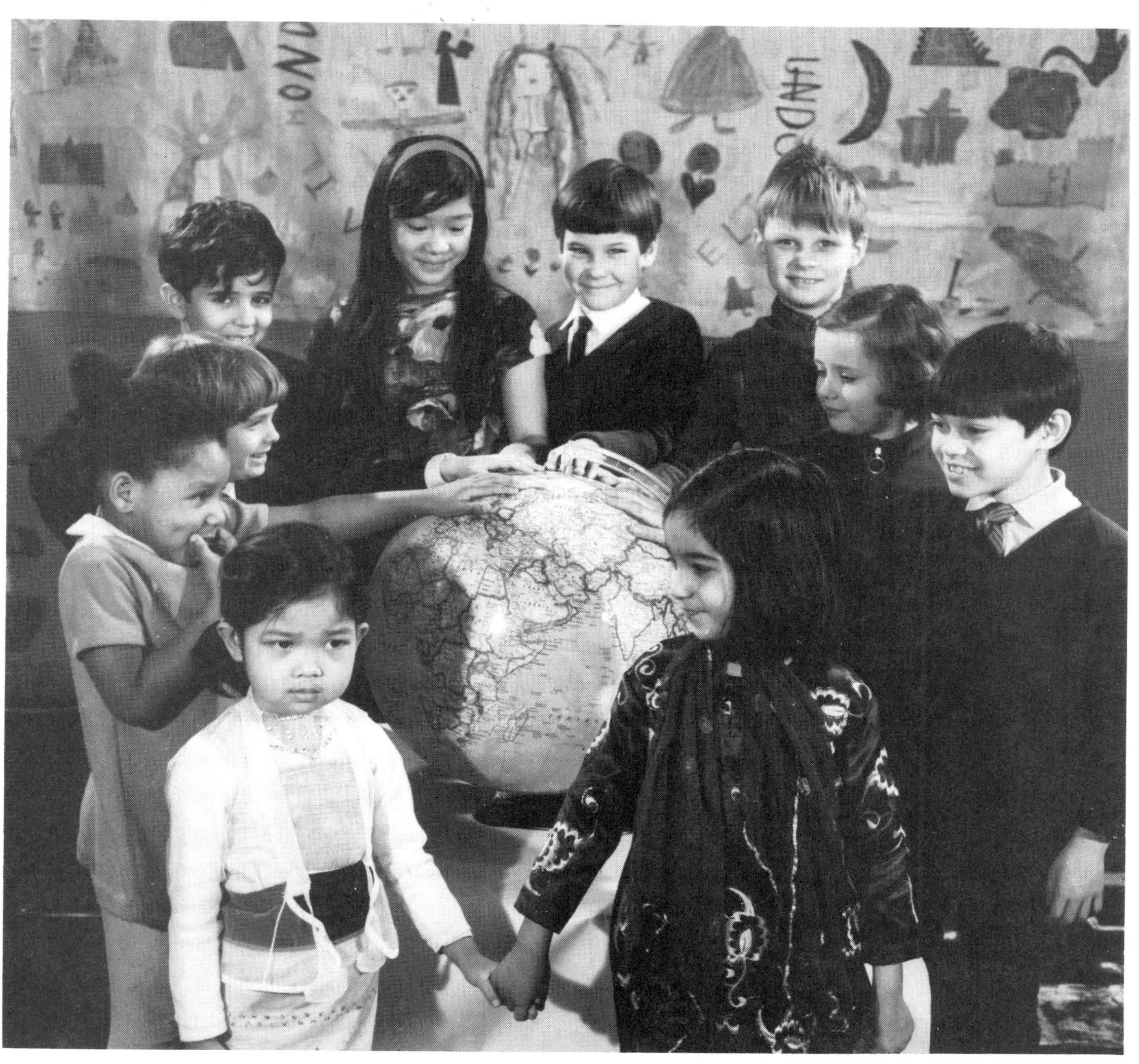

So You Want to Be Color-Blind

Alternative Principles for Affirmative Action

PETER SCHRAG

Peter Schrag is editorial page editor of the *Sacramento Bee*.

By now, there's not much doubt that when Americans are asked yes-or-no questions about the legitimacy of race preferences in public-sector hiring, contracting, and education, the answer is likely to be a flat no. Roughly 60 percent of Californian voters say that they support the proposed California Civil Rights Initiative (CCRI), which would prohibit all consideration of race or gender in public employment, education, and contracting; only 35 percent oppose it. Those findings are consistent with a decade of other survey data showing overwhelming opposition, among both men and women and among member of both political parties, to race and gender preferences. They suggest relatively few Americans will be troubled, and many will be delighted, when Newt Gingrich and other Republicans try to write prohibitions against contract set-asides and other minority preferences into the federal budget this summer. By next year, when CCRI is expected to be on the California ballot, the undoing of race preferences could become a political and social avalanche. The people who will be living under that avalanche are called liberals.

Republicans are relishing the difficulties that the rollback of preferences will cause Democrats forced to choose between their civil rights constituencies and what left of their blue-collar support. Which, of course, is why even such Republicans as Senate majority Leader Bob Dole and California Governor Peter Wilson, not long ago regarded as among the steadfast supporters of affirmative action, flipped on the issue—and why they'd just as soon keep it a question of either-or: color conscious or color-blind. It's hard to think of a better political wedge to use on the Democrats next year. It could kill Clinton in California, a state indispensable to his re-election. It could make today's racial tensions look benign next to what follows.

> Are we prepared to accept the larger effects of an absolute ban on racial preferences?

But this ought not to be that kind of question; the issue is too complex, too nuanced, too circumstantial, too slippery in definition, too divisive. To debate it in such terms is almost certain to embitter and distort whatever outcome the nation chooses—and to assure a Democratic disaster.

Between Black and White

Affirmative action has produced some clearly unreasonable results. In San Francisco, for example, substantial numbers of high-achieving Chinese students are denied entrance to Lowell High

School, a selective public institution, to make room for blacks and Hispanics (and even some whites) with lower scores and weaker records. At the University of California Medical School at Irvine, the blacks and Hispanics who are accepted have lower average medical school admission test scores than the Vietnamese applicants who are rejected. It would be hard to defend either of these policies against the charge that it is both unfair and academically debilitating.

But does the effort to eliminate such distortions also justify an absolute prohibition against efforts of the police chief of Los Angeles (or Detroit or Chicago) to seek out and promote qualified minority officers to diversify their departments? Why should a school system, seeking more effective models, not give some margin of preference to teacher candidates from underrepresented minority groups? If such private firms as the Bank of America or Nynex regard it as good business practice to seek out minorities to work in ethnically diverse markets and communities, why shouldn't the state Department of Motor Vehicles or the city zoning board do so for the same reasons?

There's no end of questions. Are we prepared to accept the larger effects of an absolute prohibition on racial preferences in all public-sector activities? Would we create an even larger playpen for lawyers and consultants to file reverse discrimination suits on the grounds that some practices were not truly color-blind? How, absent a court order, could any employer voluntarily mitigate the effects of past discrimination? Would it be better for the federal government (a) to encourage its contractors to take reasonable steps to diversify their workforces; (b) to adopt a fiercely neutral position; or (c) to prohibit its contractors from in any way noticing gender and ethnicity?

So far, however, instead of asking such questions, the parties in this debate—liberals and Democrats in thrall to their minority constituencies, Republicans exploiting the liberals' panic—are usually talking past the central issue: To what extent should merit be compromised for the sake of inclusion? the defenders of race-based affirmative action insist that no such preferences are ever given to unqualified people—that the choice is only made among the qualified—and that if that principle is violated, somebody or something, probably the courts, will crack down in righteous remedy. They are also quick to remind critics of race preferences—correctly, for the most part—that such practices were and still are used to benefit WASP legacies in the Ivy League and other selective colleges long before they were ever applied in favor of blacks and Hispanics. (What is not said is that the losers in both cases tend to be the same kinds of people: Jews and Asians.)

But what's the meaning of qualified? Some preferences clearly favor the less qualified. Under current law, contractors may win awards despite relatively high bids simply because they are black or Hispanic. In the ordinary sense, they are not as "qualified" as—and cost the taxpayers more than—lower (white) bidders passed over. But in trying to predict who will make a good cop or a good truck driver for the road crew, is there really any significant difference between the top three scores on the average civil service exam or perhaps even among the top ten? To what extent, indeed, are some affirmative action programs merely attempts to avert attacks on conventional hiring practices or university admission policies that are themselves based on shaky criteria and which, in any case, have never been fully disclosed, much less debated? The critics of affirmative action may have wildly exaggerated ideas of how much merit criteria are stretched in the cause of diversity. The defenders of race preferences may exaggerate how often relatives of union members get breaks in applying to apprenticeship programs, or how many alumni children get preferences in admission to Harvard or Princeton, but so far those institutions are not going out of their way to clarify what they do.

Shaky from the Start

The foundations were always shaky. From the earliest presidential orders of the 1960s—Kennedy's, Johnson's, Nixon's—calling on federal agencies and contractors to use "affirmative action" to eliminate discriminatory racial practices, to the introduction of goals and timetables in industry training and hiring, to the Reagan-era attempt, largely unsuccessful, to dismantle affirmative action, the country was always tentative and uncomfortable about formal racial distinctions, even when invoked for the most noble purposes. This, after all, was what the whole civil rights fight had been about, what the movement had tried to teach the country, and what for the most part—despite continuing subtle (and sometimes not-so-subtle) racism—it succeeded in doing.

What made race preferences tolerable—and what the Supreme Court in crucial cases accepted—was the assumption that they would be marginal and temporary. When candidates for a job were equally qualified, the obligation to remedy the effects of past discrimination justified preferences for people from races—later expanded to gender and handicap—that had been victims of that discrimination. In 1965, the year of the great triumphs of the civil rights movement, it made sense to argue, as Lyndon Johnson did, that "you do not take a person who has been hobbled by chains, liberate him, bring him up to the starting line" and then tell him "you are free to compete with all the others." But the consensus for preferences was always tentative. In *Bakke,* where the Court sanctioned the use of race as one "plus factor" among many extra-academic characteristics (musical or artistic or athletic talent, geographic background, unusual experiences, public service) that might be considered in university admissions—Justice Powell called it "the Harvard plan"—Justice Blackmun spoke of the need for a period of "transitional inequality." Within "a decade at most," he hoped, the need would disappear. "Then persons will be regarded as persons and discrimination of the type we address today will be an ugly feature of history that is instructive but that is behind us."

But that was 1978, and in the meantime almost precisely the opposite has happened. Race preferences, justified as a choice among equally qualified candidates, have been institutionalized and have grown to the point where the University of Texas Law School argues that if it did not use two sets of criteria in admissions there would be virtually no blacks or Hispanics at all, and where the average SAT scores for preferred minority groups at universities like Berkeley are now between 200 and 250 points lower than they are for whites and Asians. (It's between 150 and 200 points elsewhere in the University of California system.) Yet even that was not sufficient for the California legislature, then controlled by Democrats, which took note of the unsurprising fact that UC's minority graduation rates were significantly lower than those of whites and Asians and in 1991 quietly approved an "education equity act" to put fiscal and administrative pressure on the state's universities not just to admit students in the ethnic proportions in which they were graduating from the state's high schools, but to graduate them from college in the same proportions. Only Pete Wilson's veto kept the bill from becoming law. (It was that bill, incidentally, that prompted Glynn Custred and Thomas Wood, the two conservative academics who wrote CCRI, to begin work on the initiative.)

Elsewhere as well, inches have become yards. Outreach in contracting has turned to tax breaks and set asides for women and minority-owned businesses, even when the owners are themselves multimillionaires, and (increasingly) into a scandalous use of dummy ownerships by white- or male-controlled enterprises. Pressure on businesses from equal opportunity bureaucrats wielding the club of rigid disparate impact standards has pushed "goals and timetables" toward de facto quotas. (In one case, the Equal Employment Opportunity Commission sued a Chicago company that employed only blacks and Hispanics, charging that it did not have enough blacks.) The guarantee of voting rights has led to racially gerrymandered districts and Republican control of most Southern congressional delegations. In the process, what had been an informal understanding to pursue a high moral objective through a combination of stringent rules against discrimination and marginal race preferences has evolved into a system of quasi-entitlements and rigid legal impositions governed by a complex structure of quietly enacted law, appellate court decisions, civil service rules, university and graduate school admissions practices, set-asides, hiring goals, and EEOC formulas managed by armies of counselors, contract compliance auditors, diversity trainers, affirmative action officers, experts in disparate impact studies, and layer upon layer of lawyers—a huge panoply of law, regulation, and administrative practice affecting virtually every sector of the nation's life.

Rising Up Angry

It's hardly surprising that there's growing anger about this unsightly landscape of entitlements and demands. Working-class Americans and a great many others face tightening economic prospects. Talk radio and other new media now legitimize attitudes that were regarded as offensive, if not unspeakable, not so long ago.

Yet economic fears and the angry voices on the radio are hardly the whole explanation. We are now thirty years beyond the searing consciousness of what things were like before the Civil Rights Act and the Voting Rights Act, even among the majority of black people. There is much dispute about who has gained from race preferences, but there's little doubt that where the original argument for affirmative action rested in passionately assimilationist demands for equal justice, its consequences, especially on university campuses, have been increasingly manifest in segregated programs with their own criteria, shape-up courses for blacks and Latinos, "theme" housing, student-administered speech codes enforcing political correctness with the threat of suspension, even separate graduation exercises—plus the long train of racial tension that comes with them. The moral case that had started with "We Shall Overcome" and Martin Luther King seems to be ending with gangsta rap, Ice-T, melanism, Louis Farrakhan, and Khalid Muhammad. It is hard to defend affirmative action for an in-your-face separatism that rejects the western values that underlie and represent the only justification for the whole effort.

But if there are moral problems, there are practical ones as well. The proliferating list of protected groups—blacks, Latinos, women (in some circumstances), Asians (in others), the handicapped (plus veterans and legacies)—makes the future of group preferences increasingly dubious. It was almost inevitable that CCRI, which sparked our current affirmative action fight, would arise in the nation's most heterogeneous state. California's multicultural population makes it increasingly difficult to draw legitimate distinctions between who's to be favored and who is not, or even to make reasonable decisions, as the Census Bureau is now pointing out, about how individuals should be counted. And as intermarriage proliferates among all those groups, who's to say how their offspring should be counted? Should the son of an Argentinian immigrant, now a corporate executive in San Diego (or a Cuban in Miami), get preference as a Latino? How do you classify a student with a hyphenated name, half Hispanic and half Jewish? Why do we give preference to the child of the black doctor and none to the child of the Appalachian coal miner?

Historian Hugh Davis Graham of Vanderbilt University points out that the most overlooked law of the civil rights era, the Immigration Reform Act of 1965, which ended the system of national-origins quotas in U.S. immigration policy, had enormous consequences that we still don't fully comprehend. Although its sponsors claimed that it would produce little significant increase in immigration, it brought to the country more than 20 million legal immigrants during the thirty years after its enactment, approximately 75 percent of whom "qualified upon arrival for minority-group preferences over Americans whose citizenship reached back many generations." Surely that was not justified by any effort to remedy past injustices. Surely that was not part of any tacit bargain to which the country ever agreed.

Strains of Ambivalence

But does even that certify the wisdom of a decision that would, virtually overnight, impose the across-the-board prohibitions on race preferences that the opponents of affirmative action are now demanding? Or does it make more sense—political, social, moral—to return to the limited (*Bakke*) version of affirmative action, messy as it often was, to which the country seemed to give its consent a generation ago—and which it may still be willing to accept? To return to polls for a moment: If the question is changed from an either-or choice about explicit race preferences to more general matters about affirmative action, the answers change as well. In a *USA Today*/CNN poll this spring, 73 percent said they favor companies "making special efforts to find qualified minorities and women." Similar answers are given to questions about special training programs for minorities and women. The vast majority of respondents, white and black, don't believe that the country has been purged of racial discrimination. On a general question about affirmative action programs on the *USA Today* poll, 31 percent favored expansion, 37 percent favored a decrease, and 26 percent thought they should be kept about the same.

It may be impossible to fully articulate that ambivalence, much less write it into policy. But with the stakes as high as they are on this issue, it surely deserves the effort. Considerations in the appointment of scholars for a research university may not apply to the hiring of heavy-equipment operators or postal clerks. What applies to contracting with small businesses, regardless of the race and gender of their owners, may not apply to large corporations. And what may apply to some colleges may not apply to others. Many states have created two- or three-tiered higher education systems to serve both merit and inclusion—a highly selective university combined with readily accessible junior colleges and moderately selective four-year state colleges. Why should that principle be compromised by tempering admission standards for the selective institutions in order to further inclusion there as well?

Which brings the issue back to a more basic question: What is merit and to what extent are existing criteria merit-based? In the past year there has been a bitter fight in Chicago over the promotion of a handful of black cops who were ranked high on "merit" even though they scored lower on the civil service exam than some officers over whom they were promoted. In that case, either the word "merit" is fatuous or it raises serious questions about just what the exam measures. Admissions officers at colleges raise the same issue when they defend affirmative action by arguing that test scores aren't good predictors of performance in college. But if that's the case, why use the test at all?

Chances are that it's not the case. As the neoconservatives—some of whom defected from liberalism precisely over this issue—will tell you, the whole point of such tests was to foster merit against spoils systems at city hall and good-old-boy bias in the admission office at Yale. Ethnic spoils are no more acceptable now than the earlier varieties. In any case, nobody has yet shown what would be a better predictor of academic success for minorities.

And yet that hardly vitiates the general proposition: In many of the areas affected by public-sector racial preferences, there may be better ways of making choices than those we use now. If only court-ordered make-whole remedies to proven discrimination are permissible (which is what the opponents of race preferences advocate), how many more civil rights lawsuits would be filed that are now averted by voluntary action? Would any public employer, recognizing past discrimination, have to encourage a lawsuit before the victims could be made whole? Can race sometimes even be regarded—in practice, not in law—as part of the qualifications for certain jobs? If you seek out people not just for their technical knowledge, or their test-taking skills, but for their ability to deal with—and be trusted in—a community, why shouldn't ethnicity be a "plus factor" in the package?

The answers are hardly self-evident. None of these questions should suggest that it's proper for the police chief in Grosse Pointe to hire only white cops. This area doesn't lend itself well to across-the-board legal rules; it's better to build in flexibility and room to fudge. If there is a flat ban on any consideration of race in public policy, what happens to efforts to foster integration in elementary and secondary schools? John Bunzel, a former member of the U.S. Civil Rights Commission, now a fellow at the Hoover Institution and a sharp critic of the excesses of race preferences, has declined to support measures like CCRI which, he says, are too blunt; they simplify, and "I'm a complexifier." Shouldn't there be room at the margins, he asks, for ethnic diversity among all the other criteria? And that, of course is what the Supreme Court's *Bakke* decision, with all its flaws, sought to do.

Six Alternative Principles

It's not an easy task. Yet surely before the country is forced to a set of either-or choices, some alternative principles are worth considering:

1. *The more sophisticated the enterprise or skill for which candidates are chosen, the more important merit becomes and the weaker the claims for non-meritocratic criteria.* The kind of considerations we give in selecting people for blue-collar jobs should not be the same as the ones given to selecting graduate students in nuclear physics or brain surgery. The public junior college, by mandate, definition, and tradition, is more inclusive than the Institute for Advanced Study. Thomas Sowell makes a persuasive argument that the issue is not so much who should go to college but where. The frustration and tensions—not to mention the various distortions that have been created on many campuses to accommodate marginal students—result from the effort to bring people into academic situations for which they are not qualified. As a result, even those who are qualified are suspect and discredited.

2. *In public as well as private enterprises, diversity may well be a legitimate business consideration.* Where the choice is between candidates or contractors with similar bids or equal qualifications in skill, doesn't it make sense to consider first those who come from underrepresented groups and who will for that reason be more effective or make the enterprise more legitimate with clients and the community? In such choices, the lines of common sense, if they can be maintained, are better than the lines drawn by law.

3. *In college admission, economic disadvantage is a more legitimate extra factor for a borderline candidate than membership in a preferred racial group.* Why not shift the emphasis in affirmative action from minorities to children from families where no one has ever gone to college? Such policies may well result in smaller proportions of blacks or Hispanics at selective universities, at least in the short run, but it may have a far greater social impact. And unlike race preferences, economic disadvantage will not become a permanent entitlement. As such, it's far more consistent with the nation's historic principles. And to the extent that race preferences are forgotten, so will invidious assumptions about how minority students were accepted. What will become clear is the inadequate secondary school preparation, or worse, that causes the underrepresentation in the first place.

4. *All race preferences in public-sector activities—in contracting, hiring, and education—should be made fully public and subject to time limits and periodic public review by an objective, nonpartisan process.* We have already managed to do away with one of the most reprehensible practices: race-norming, the system of separately ranking candidates within their own ethnic groups on Labor Department job tests and hiring from the top of each list. The expectation ought to be that we will gradually do away with a great many more in coming years. An obvious way to

begin is to make affirmative action goals and the administrative definitions of disparate impact more flexible.

5. *Exclude all foreign-born residents, citizens, and aliens, and perhaps even the children of immigrants, from race preferences, excepting only children of American citizens who were living abroad.* There is no history of discrimination to justify such preferences. And they generate no end of resentment, as the passage of California's Proposition 187, the measure designed to deny social services to illegal aliens, has demonstrated.

6. *Vigorously enforce anti-discrimination law, not perhaps to the point of criminalizing discrimination as Shelby Steele proposes, but far more vigorously than we do now, and systematically review all public-sector merit systems to make certain that tests and other criteria are in fact appropriate to the tasks and positions for which they're used.*

This is hardly a complete list, much less an ideal one. But it recognizes that affirmative action—even race preference—has different meanings depending on the context, and that flexibility is critical. Affirmative action bears a heavy burden against the claims of real merit; where it favors rich over poor, strong over weak, it bears an insurmountable one. Yet rigid rules are likely to take us into a thicket of legal combat and social division more bitter than anything generated by the policies we have now. If the Democrats, rather than standing frozen in the headlights of the approaching disaster, were to try to articulate a third alternative, they might well reclaim some credibility on the issue.

The sense of a national moral imperative that once sustained affirmative action is rapidly eroding. It is only a matter of time before it's all gone. In those circumstances a soft landing—no phrase could be more appropriate in this context—would surely be better than a yes-or-no choice whose answer will almost certainly be no. But unless those who regard themselves as people of good will offer a third alternative, that's the answer we'll get.

Goin' Gangsta, Choosin' Cholita

Teens today "claim" a racial identity

Nell Bernstein

WEST MAGAZINE

Nell Bernstein is editor of YO! (Youth Outlook), *a Bay Area journal of teen life produced by Pacific News Service. Subscriptions: $12 young people/$75 supporter/yr. (6 issues) from Pacific News Service, 450 Mission St., Room 506, San Francisco, CA 94105.*

er lipstick is dark, the lip liner even darker, nearly black. In baggy pants, a blue plaid Pendleton, her bangs pulled back tight off her forehead, 15-year-old April is a perfect cholita, a Mexican gangsta girl.

But April Miller is Anglo. "And I don't like it!" she complains. "I'd rather be Mexican."

April's father wanders into the family room of their home in San Leandro, California, a suburb near Oakland. "Hey, cholita," he teases. "Go get a suntan. We'll put you in a barrio and see how much you like it."

A large, sandy-haired man with "April" tattooed on one arm and "Kelly"—the name of his older daughter—on the other, Miller spent 21 years working in a San Leandro glass factory that shut down and moved to Mexico a couple of years ago. He recently got a job in another factory, but he expects NAFTA to swallow that one, too.

"Sooner or later we'll all get nailed," he says. "Just another stab in the back of the American middle class."

Later, April gets her revenge: "Hey, Mr. White Man's Last Stand," she teases. "Wait till you see how well I manage my welfare check. You'll be asking me for money."

A once almost exclusively white, now increasingly Latin and black working-class suburb, San Leandro borders on predominantly black East Oakland. For decades, the boundary was strictly policed and practically impermeable. In 1970 April Miller's hometown was 97 percent white. By 1990 San Leandro was 65 percent white, 6 percent black, 15 percent Hispanic, and 13 percent Asian or Pacific Islander. With minorities moving into suburbs in growing numbers and cities becoming ever more diverse, the boundary between city and suburb is dissolving, and suburban teenagers are changing with the times.

In April's bedroom, her past and present selves lie in layers, the pink walls of girlhood almost obscured, Guns N' Roses and Pearl Jam posters overlaid by rappers Paris and Ice Cube. "I don't have a big enough attitude to be a black girl," says April, explaining her current choice of ethnic identification.

What matters is that she thinks the choice is hers. For April and her friends, identity is not a matter of where you come from, what you were born into, what color your skin is. It's what you wear, the music you listen to, the words you use—everything to which you pledge allegiance, no matter how fleetingly.

The hybridization of American teens has become talk show fodder, with "wiggers"—white kids who dress and talk "black"—appearing on TV in full gangsta regalia. In Indiana a group of white high school girls raised a national stir when they triggered an imitation race war at their virtually all white high school last fall simply by dressing "black."

In many parts of the country, it's television and radio, not neighbors, that introduce teens to the allure of ethnic difference. But in California, which demographers predict will be the first state with no racial majority by the year 2000, the influences are more immediate. The California public schools are the most diverse in the country: 42 percent white, 36 percent Hispanic, 9 percent black, 8 percent Asian.

Sometimes young people fight over their differences. Students at virtually any school in the Bay Area can recount the details of at least one "race riot" in which a conflict between individuals escalated into a battle between their clans. More often, though, teens would rather join than fight. Adolescence, after all, is the period when you're most inclined to mimic the power closest at hand, from stealing your older sister's clothes to copying the ruling clique at school.

White skaters and Mexican would-be gangbangers listen to gangsta rap and call each other "nigga" as a term of endearment; white girls sometimes affect Spanish accents; blond cheerleaders claim Cherokee ancestors.

"Claiming" is the central concept here. A Vietnamese teen in Hayward, another Oakland suburb, "claims" Oakland—and by implication blackness—because he lived there as a child. A law-abiding white kid "claims" a Mexican gang he says he hangs with. A brown-skinned

From *Utne Reader,* March/April 1995, pp. 87-90. Excerpted from *West* magazine, the Sunday supplement to the *San Jose Mercury News,* November 13, 1994.

girl with a Mexican father and a white mother "claims" her Mexican side, while her fair-skinned sister "claims" white. The word comes up over and over, as if identity were territory, the self a kind of turf.

At a restaurant in a minimall in Hayward, Nicole Huffstutler, 13, sits with her friends and describes herself as "Indian, German, French, Welsh, and, um...American": "If somebody says anything like 'Yeah, you're just a peckerwood,' I'll walk up and I'll say 'white pride!' 'Cause I'm proud of my race, and I wouldn't wanna be any other race."

"Claiming" white has become a matter of principle for Heather, too, who says she's "sick of the majority looking at us like we're less than them." (Hayward schools were 51 percent white in 1990, down from 77 percent in 1980, and whites are now the minority in many schools.)

Asked if she knows that nonwhites have not traditionally been referred to as "the majority" in America, Heather gets exasperated: "I hear that all the time, every day. They say, 'Well, you guys controlled us for many years, and it's time for us to control you.' Every day."

When Jennifer Vargas—a small, brown-skinned girl in purple jeans who quietly eats her salad while Heather talks—softly announces that she's "mostly Mexican," she gets in trouble with her friends.

"No, you're not!" scolds Heather.

"I'm mostly Indian and Mexican," Jennifer continues flatly. "I'm very little...I'm mostly..."

"Your mom's white!" Nicole reminds her sharply. "She has blond hair.

"That's what I mean," Nicole adds. "People think that white is a bad thing. They think that white is a bad race. So she's trying to claim more Mexican than white."

"I have very little white in me," Jennifer repeats. "I have mostly my dad's side, 'cause I look like him and stuff. And most of my friends think that me and my brother and sister aren't related, 'cause they look more like my mom."

"But you guys are all the same race, you just look different," Nicole insists. She stops eating and frowns. "OK, you're half and half each what your parents have. So you're equal as your brother and sister, you just look different. And you should be proud of what you are—every little piece and bit of what you are. Even if you were Afghan or whatever, you should be proud of it."

Will Mosley, Heather's 17-year-old brother, says he and his friends listen to rap groups like Compton's Most Wanted, NWA, and Above the Law because they "sing about life"—that is, what happens in Oakland, Los Angeles, anyplace but where Will is sitting today, an empty Round Table Pizza in a minimall.

"No matter what race you are," Will says, "if you live like we do, then that's the kind of music you like."

And how do they live?

"We don't live bad or anything," Will admits. "We live in a pretty good neighborhood, there's no violence or crime. I was just...we're just city people, I guess."

Will and his friend Adolfo Garcia, 16, say they've outgrown trying to be something they're not. "When I was 11 or 12," Will says, "I thought I was becoming a big gangsta and stuff. Because I liked that music, and thought it was the coolest, I wanted to become that. I wore big clothes, like you wear in jail. But then I kind of woke up. I looked at myself and thought, 'Who am I trying to be?'"

They may have outgrown blatant mimicry, but Will and his friends remain convinced that they can live in a suburban tract house with a well-kept lawn on a tree-lined street in "not a bad neighborhood" and still call themselves "city" people on the basis of musical tastes. "City" for these young people means crime, graffiti, drugs. The kids are law-abiding, but these activities connote what Will admiringly calls "action." With pride in his voice, Will predicts that "in a couple of years, Hayward will be like Oakland. It's starting to get more known, because of crime and things. I think it'll be bigger, more things happening, more crime, more graffiti, stealing cars."

"That's good," chimes in 15-year-old Matt Jenkins, whose new beeper—an item that once connoted gangsta chic but now means little more than an active social life—goes off periodically. "More fun."

The three young men imagine with disdain life in a gangsta-free zone. "Too bland, too boring," Adolfo says. "You have to have something going on. You can't just have everyday life."

"Mowing your lawn," Matt sneers.

"Like Beaver Cleaver's house," Adolfo adds. "It's too clean out here."

Not only white kids believe that identity is a matter of choice or taste, or that the power of "claiming" can transcend ethnicity. The Manor Park Locos—a group of mostly Mexican-Americans who hang out in San Leandro's Manor Park—say they descend from the Manor Lords, tough white guys who ruled the neighborhood a generation ago.

They "are like our...uncles and dads, the older generation," says Jesse Martinez, 14. "We're what they were when they were around, except we're Mexican."

"There's three generations," says Oso, Jesse's younger brother. "There's Manor Lords, Manor Park Locos, and Manor Park Pee Wees." The Pee Wees consist mainly of the Locos' younger brothers, eager kids who circle the older boys on bikes and brag about "punking people."

Unlike Will Mosley, the Locos find little glamour in city life. They survey the changing suburban landscape and see not "action" or "more fun" but frightening decline. Though most of them are not yet 18, the Locos are already nostalgic, longing for a Beaver Cleaver past that white kids who mimic them would scoff at.

Walking through nearly empty Manor Park, with its eucalyptus stands, its softball diamond and tennis courts, Jesse's friend Alex, the only Asian in the group, waves his arms in a gesture of futility. "A few years ago, every bench was filled," he says. "Now no one comes here. I guess it's because of everything that's going on. My parents paid a lot for this house, and I want it to be nice for them. I just hope this doesn't turn into Oakland."

Glancing across the park at April Miller's street, Jesse says he knows what the white cholitas are about. "It's not a racial thing," he explains. "It's just all the most popular people out here are Mexican. We're just the gangstas that everyone knows. I guess those girls wanna be known."

Not every young Californian embraces the new racial hybridism. Andrea Jones, 20, an African-American who grew up in the Bay Area suburbs of Union City and Hayward, is unimpressed by what she sees mainly as shallow mimicry. "It's full of posers out here," she says. "When *Boyz N the Hood* came out on video, it was sold out for weeks. The boys all wanna be black, the girls all wanna be Mexican. It's the glamour."

Driving down the quiet, shaded streets of her old neighborhood in Union City, Andrea spots two white preteen boys in Raiders jackets and hugely baggy pants strutting erratically down the empty sidewalk. "Look at them," she says. "Dislocated."

She knows why. "In a lot of these schools out here, it's hard being white," she says. "I don't think these kids were prepared for the backlash that is going on, all the pride now in people of color's ethnicity, and our boldness with it. They have nothing like that, no identity, nothing they can say they're proud of.

"So they latch onto their great-grandmother who's a Cherokee, or they take on the most stereotypical aspects of being black or Mexican. It's beautiful to appreciate different aspects of other people's culture—that's like the dream of what the 21st century should be. But to garnish yourself with pop culture stereotypes just to blend—that's really sad."

Roland Krevocheza, 18, graduated last year from Arroyo High School in San Leandro. He is Mexican on his mother's side, Eastern European on his father's. In the new hierarchies, it may be mixed kids like Roland who have the hardest time finding their place, even as their numbers grow. (One in five marriages in California is between people of different races.) They can always be called "wannabes," no matter what they claim.

"I'll state all my nationalities," Roland says. But he takes a greater interest in his father's side, his Ukrainian, Romanian, and Czech ancestors. "It's more unique," he explains. "Mexican culture is all around me. We eat Mexican food all the time, I hear stories from my grandmother. I see the low-riders and stuff. I'm already part of it. I'm not trying to be; I am."

His darker-skinned brother "says he's not proud to be white," Roland adds. "He calls me 'Mr. Nazi.'" In the room the two share, the American flags and the reproduction of the Bill of Rights are Roland's; the Public Enemy poster belongs to his brother.

Roland has good reason to mistrust gangsta attitudes. In his junior year in high school, he was one of several Arroyo students who were beaten up outside the school at lunchtime by a group of Samoans who came in cars from Oakland. Roland wound up with a split lip, a concussion, and a broken tailbone. Later he was told that the assault was "gang-related"—that the Samoans were beating up anyone wearing red.

"Rappers, I don't like them," Roland says. "I think they're a bad influence on kids. It makes kids think they're all tough and bad."

Those who, like Roland, dismiss the gangsta and cholo styles as affectations can point to the fact that several companies market overpriced knockoffs of "ghetto wear" targeted at teens.

But there's also something going on out here that transcends adolescent faddishness and pop culture exoticism. When white kids call their parents "racist" for nagging them about their baggy pants; when they learn Spanish to talk to their boyfriends; when Mexican-American boys feel themselves descended in spirit from white "uncles"; when children of mixed marriages insist that they are whatever race they say they are, all of them are more than just confused.

They're inching toward what Andrea Jones calls "the dream of what the 21st century should be." In the ever more diverse communities of Northern California, they're also facing the complicated reality of what their 21st century will be.

Meanwhile, in the living room of the Miller family's San Leandro home, the argument continues unabated. "You don't know what you are," April's father has told her more than once. But she just keeps on telling him he doesn't know what time it is.

In the eighteenth century a disastrous shift occurred in the way Westerners perceived races. The man responsible was Johann Friedrich Blumenbach, one of the least racist thinkers of his day.

the Geometer of Race

STEPHEN JAY GOULD

Stephen Jay Gould, a contributing editor of Discover, *is a professor of zoology at Harvard who also teaches geology, biology, and the history of science. His writing on evolution has won many prizes, including a National Book Award, a National Magazine Award, and the Phi Beta Kappa Science Award. For* Discover*'s November 1993 special section on ten great science museums, Gould wrote about the glass flowers at Harvard's Botanical Museum.*

INTERESTING STORIES often lie encoded in names that seem either capricious or misconstrued. Why, for example, are political radicals called "left" and their conservative counterparts "right"? In many European legislatures, the most distinguished members sat at the chairman's right, following a custom of courtesy as old as our prejudices for favoring the dominant hand of most people. (These biases run deep, extending well beyond can openers and scissors to language itself, where *dexterous* stems from the Latin for "right," and *sinister* from the word for "left.") Since these distinguished nobles and moguls tended to espouse conservative views, the right and left wings of the legislature came to define a geometry of political views.

Among such apparently capricious names in my own field of biology and evolution, none seems more curious, and none elicits more questions after lectures, than the official designation of light-skinned people in Europe, western Asia, and North Africa as Caucasian. Why should the most common racial group of the Western world be named for a mountain range that straddles Russia and Georgia? Johann Friedrich Blumenbach (1752–1840), the German anatomist and naturalist who established the most influential of all racial classifications, invented this name in 1795, in the third edition of his seminal work, *De Generis Humani Varietate Nativa* (On the Natural Variety of Mankind). Blumenbach's definition cites two reasons for his choice—the maximal beauty of people from this small region, and the probability that humans were first created in this area.

> *Caucasian variety.* I have taken the name of this variety from Mount Caucasus, both because its neighborhood, and especially its southern slope, produces the most beautiful race of men, I mean the Georgian; and because . . . in that region, if anywhere, it seems we ought with the greatest probability to place the autochthones [original forms] of mankind.

Blumenbach, one of the greatest and most honored scientists of the Enlightenment, spent his entire career as a professor at the University of Göttingen in Germany. He first presented *De Generis Humani Varietate Nativa* as a doctoral dissertation to the medical faculty of Göttingen in 1775, as the minutemen of Lexington and Concord began the American Revolution. He then republished the text for general distribution in 1776, as a fateful meeting in Philadelphia proclaimed our independence. The coincidence of three great documents in 1776—Jefferson's Declaration of Independence (on the politics of liberty), Adam Smith's *Wealth of Nations* (on the economics of individualism), and Blumenbach's treatise on racial classification (on the science of human diversity)—records the social ferment of these decades and sets the wider context that makes Blumenbach's taxonomy, and his subsequent decision to call the European race Caucasian, so important for our history and current concerns.

The solution to big puzzles often hinges upon tiny curiosities, easy to miss or to pass over. I suggest that the key to understanding Blumenbach's classification, the foundation of much that continues to influence and disturb us today, lies in the peculiar criterion he used to name the European race Caucasian—the supposed superior beauty of people from this region. Why, first of all, should a scientist attach such importance to an evidently subjective assessment; and why, secondly, should an aesthetic criterion become the basis of a scientific judgment about place of origin? To answer these questions, we must compare Blumenbach's original 1775 text with the later edition of 1795, when Caucasians received their name.

Blumenbach's final taxonomy of 1795 divided all humans into five groups, defined both by geography and appearance—in his order, the Caucasian variety, for the light-skinned people of Europe and adjacent parts of Asia and Africa; the Mongolian variety, for most other inhabitants of Asia, including China and Japan; the Ethiopian variety, for the dark-skinned people of Africa; the American variety, for most native populations of the New World; and the Malay variety, for the Polynesians and Melanesians of the Pacific and for the aborigines of Australia. But Blumenbach's original classification of 1775 recognized only the first four of these five, and united members of the Malay variety with the other people of Asia whom Blumenbach came to name Mongolian.

We now encounter the paradox of Blumenbach's reputation as the inventor of modern racial classification. The original four-race system, as I shall illustrate in a moment, did not arise from Blumenbach's observations but only represents, as Blumenbach readily admits, the classification promoted by his guru Carolus Linnaeus in the founding document of taxonomy, the *Systema Naturae* of 1758. Therefore, Blumenbach's only original contribution to racial classification lies in the later addition of a Malay variety for some Pacific people's first included in a broader Asian group.

This change seems so minor. Why, then, do we credit Blumenbach, rather than Linnaeus, as the founder of racial classification? (One might prefer to say "discredit," as the enterprise does not, for good reason, enjoy high repute these days.) But Blumenbach's apparently small change actually records a theoretical shift that could not have been broader, or more portentous, in scope. This change has been missed or misconstrued because later scientists have not grasped the vital historical and philosophical principle that theories are models subject to visual representation, usually in clearly definable geometric terms.

By moving from the Linnaean four-race system to his own five-race scheme, Blumenbach radically changed the geometry of human order from a geographically based model without explicit ranking to a hierarchy of worth, oddly based upon perceived beauty, and fanning out in two directions from a Caucasian ideal. The addition of a Malay category was crucial to this geometric reformulation—and therefore becomes the key to the conceptual transformation rather than a simple refinement of factual information within an old scheme. (For the insight that scientific revolutions embody such geometric shifts, I am grateful to my friend Rhonda Roland Shearer, who portrays these themes in a forthcoming book, *The Flatland Hypothesis.*)

BLUMENBACH IDOLIZED his teacher Linnaeus and acknowledged him as the source of his original fourfold racial classification: "I have followed Linnaeus in the number, but have defined my varieties by other boundaries" (1775 edition). Later, in adding his Malay variety, Blumenbach identified his change as a departure from his old mentor in the most respectful terms: "It became very clear that the Linnaean division of mankind could no longer be adhered to; for which reason I, in this little work, ceased like others to follow that illustrious man."

Linnaeus divided the species *Homo sapiens* into four basic varieties, defined primarily by geography and, interestingly, not in the ranked order favored by most Europeans in the racist tradition—*Americanus*, *Europaeus*, *Asiaticus*, and *Afer*, or African. (He also alluded to two other fanciful categories: *ferus* for "wild boys," occasionally discovered in the woods and possibly raised by animals—most turned out to be retarded or mentally ill youngsters abandoned by their parents—and *monstrosus* for hairy men with tails, and other travelers' confabulations.) In so doing, Linnaeus presented nothing original; he merely mapped humans onto the four geographic regions of conventional cartography.

Linnaeus then characterized each of these groups by noting color, humor, and posture, in that order. Again, none of these categories explicitly implies ranking by worth. Once again, Linnaeus was simply bowing to classical taxonomic theories in making these decisions. For example, his use of the four humors reflects the ancient and medieval theory that a person's temperament arises from a balance of four fluids (*humor* is Latin for "moisture")—blood, phlegm, choler (yellow bile), and melancholy (black bile). Depending on which of the four substances dominated, a person would be sanguine (the cheerful realm of blood), phlegmatic (sluggish), choleric (prone to anger), or melancholic (sad). Four geographic regions, four humors, four races.

For the American variety, Linnaeus wrote "*rufus, cholericus, rectus*" (red, choleric, upright); for the European, "*albus, sanguineus, torosus*" (white, sanguine, muscular); for the Asian, "*luridus, melancholicus, rigidus*" (pale yellow, melancholy, stiff); and for the African, "*niger, phlegmaticus, laxus*" (black, phlegmatic, relaxed).

I don't mean to deny that Linnaeus held conventional beliefs about the superiority of his own European variety over others. Being a sanguine, muscular European surely sounds better than being a melancholy, stiff Asian. Indeed, Linnaeus ended each group's description with a more overtly racist label, an attempt to epitomize behavior in just two words. Thus the American was *regitur consuetudine* (ruled by habit); the European, *regitur ritibus* (ruled by custom); the Asian, *regitur opinionibus* (ruled by belief); and the African, *regitur arbitrio* (ruled by caprice). Surely regulation by established and considered custom beats the unthinking rule of habit or belief, and all of these are superior to caprice—thus leading to the implied and conventional racist ranking of Europeans first, Asians and Americans in the middle, and Africans at the bottom.

Nonetheless, and despite these implications, the overt geometry of Linnaeus's model is not linear or hierarchical. When

Scientists assume that their own shifts in interpretation record only their better understanding of newly discovered facts. They tend to be unaware of their own mental impositions upon the world's messy and ambiguous factuality.

we visualize his scheme as an essential picture in our mind, we see a map of the world divided into four regions, with the people in each region characterized by a list of different traits. In short, Linnaeus's primary ordering principle is cartographic; if he had wished to push hierarchy as the essential picture of human variety, he would surely have listed Europeans first and Africans last, but he started with native Americans instead.

The shift from a geographic to a hierarchical ordering of human diversity must stand as one of the most fateful transitions in the history of Western science—for what, short of railroads and nuclear bombs, has had more practical impact, in this case almost entirely negative, upon our collective lives? Ironically, Blumenbach is the focus of this shift, for his five-race scheme became canonical and changed the geometry of human order from Linnaean cartography to linear ranking—in short, to a system based on putative worth.

I say ironic because Blumenbach was the least racist and most genial of all Enlightenment thinkers. How peculiar that the man most committed to human unity, and to inconsequential moral and intellectual differences among groups, should have changed the mental geometry of human order to a scheme that has served racism ever since. Yet on second thought, this situation is really not so odd—for most scientists have been quite unaware of the mental machinery, and particularly of the visual or geometric implications, lying behind all their theorizing.

An old tradition in science proclaims that changes in theory must be driven by observation. Since most scientists believe this simplistic formula, they assume that their own shifts in interpretation record only their better understanding of newly discovered facts. Scientists therefore tend to be unaware of their own mental impositions upon the world's messy and ambiguous factuality. Such mental impositions arise from a variety of sources, including psychological predisposition and social context. Blumenbach lived in an age when ideas of progress, and the cultural superiority of European ways, dominated political and social life. Implicit, loosely formulated, or even unconscious notions of racial ranking fit well with such a worldview—indeed, almost any other organizational scheme would have seemed anomalous. I doubt that Blumenbach was actively encouraging racism by redrawing the mental diagram of human groups. He was only, and largely passively, recording the social view of his time. But ideas have consequences, whatever the motives or intentions of their promoters.

Blumenbach certainly thought that his switch from the Linnaean four-race system to his own five-race scheme arose only from his improved understanding of nature's factuality. He said as much when he announced his change in the second (1781) edition of his treatise: "Formerly in the first edition of this work, I divided all mankind into four varieties; but after I had more actively investigated the different nations of Eastern Asia and America, and, so to speak, looked at them more closely, I was compelled to give up that division, and to place in its stead the following five varieties, as more consonant to nature." And in the preface to the third edition, of 1795, Blumenbach states that he gave up the Linnaean scheme in order to arrange "the varieties of man according to the truth of nature." When scientists adopt the myth that theories arise solely from observation, and do not grasp the personal and social influences acting on their thinking, they not only miss the causes of their changed opinions; they may even fail to comprehend the deep mental shift encoded by the new theory.

Blumenbach strongly upheld the unity of the human species against an alternative view, then growing in popularity (and surely more conducive to conventional forms of racism), that each major race had been separately created. He ended his third edition by writing: "No doubt can any longer remain but that we are with great probability right in referring all . . . varieties of man . . . to one and the same species."

AS HIS MAJOR ARGUMENT for unity, Blumenbach noted that all supposed racial characteristics grade continuously from one people to another and cannot define any separate and bounded group. "For although there seems to be so great a difference between widely separate nations, that you might easily take the inhabitants of the Cape of Good Hope, the Greenlanders, and the Circassians for so many different species of man, yet when the matter is thoroughly considered, you see that all do so run into one another, and that one variety of mankind does so sensibly pass into the other, that you cannot mark out the limits between them." He particularly refuted the common racist claim that black Africans bore unique features of their inferiority: "There is no single character so peculiar and so universal among the Ethiopians, but what it may be observed on the one hand everywhere in other varieties of men."

Blumenbach, writing 80 years before Darwin, believed that *Homo sapiens* had been created in a single region and had then spread over the globe. Our racial diversity, he then argued, arose as a result of this spread to other climates and topographies, and to our adoption of different modes of life in these various regions. Following the terminology of his time, Blumenbach referred to these changes as "degenerations"—not intending the modern sense of deterioration, but the literal meaning of departure from an initial form of humanity at the creation (*de* means "from," and *genus* refers to our original stock).

Most of these degenerations, Blumenbach argued, arose directly from differences in climate and habitat—ranging from such broad patterns as the correlation of dark skin with tropical environments, to more particular (and fanciful) attributions, including a speculation that the narrow eye slits of some Australian aborigines may have arisen in response to "constant clouds of gnats . . . contracting the natural face of the inhabitants." Other changes, he maintained, arose as a consequence of customs adopted in different regions. For example, nations that compressed the heads of babies by swaddling boards or papoose carriers ended up with relatively long skulls. Blumenbach held that "almost all the diversity of the form of the head in different nations is to be attributed to the mode of life and to art."

Blumenbach believed that such changes, promoted over many generations, could eventually become hereditary. "With

Blumenbach upheld the unity of the human species against an alternative view, then growing in popularity (and surely more conducive to conventional racism), that each race had been separately created.

the progress of time," Blumenbach wrote, "art may degenerate into a second nature." But he also argued that most racial variations, as superficial impositions of climate and custom, could be easily altered or reversed by moving to a new region or by adopting new behavior. White Europeans living for generations in the tropics could become dark-skinned, while Africans transported as slaves to high latitudes could eventually become white: "Color, whatever be its cause, be it bile, or the influence of the sun, the air, or the climate, is, at all events, an adventitious and easily changeable thing, and can never constitute a diversity of species," he wrote.

Convinced of the superficiality of racial variation, Blumenbach defended the mental and moral unity of all peoples. He held particularly strong opinions on the equal status of black Africans and white Europeans. He may have been patronizing in praising "the good disposition and faculties of these our black brethren," but better paternalism than malign contempt. He campaigned for the abolition of slavery and asserted the moral superiority of slaves to their captors, speaking of a "natural tenderness of heart, which has never been benumbed or extirpated on board the transport vessels or on the West India sugar plantations by the brutality of their white executioners."

Blumenbach established a special library in his house devoted exclusively to black authors, singling out for special praise the poetry of Phillis Wheatley, a Boston slave whose writings have only recently been rediscovered: "I possess English, Dutch, and Latin poems by several [black authors], amongst which however above all, those of Phillis Wheatley of Boston, who is justly famous for them, deserves mention here." Finally, Blumenbach noted that many Caucasian nations could not boast so fine a set of authors and scholars as black Africa has produced under the most depressing circumstances of prejudice and slavery: "It would not be difficult to mention entire well-known provinces of Europe, from out of which you would not easily expect to obtain off-hand such good authors, poets, philosophers, and correspondents of the Paris Academy."

Nonetheless, when Blumenbach presented his mental picture of human diversity in his fateful shift away from Linnaean geography, he singled out a particular group as closest to the created ideal and then characterized all other groups by relative degrees of departure from this archetypal standard. He ended up with a system that placed a single race at the pinnacle, and then envisioned two symmetrical lines of departure away from this ideal toward greater and greater degeneration.

WE MAY NOW RETURN to the riddle of the name Caucasian, and to the significance of Blumenbach's addition of a fifth race, the Malay variety. Blumenbach chose to regard his own European variety as closest to the created ideal and then searched for the subset of Europeans with greatest perfection—the highest of the high, so to speak. As we have seen, he identified the people around Mount Caucasus as the closest embodiments of the original ideal and proceeded to name the entire European race for its finest representatives.

But Blumenbach now faced a dilemma. He had already affirmed the mental and moral equality of all peoples. He therefore could not use these conventional criteria of racist ranking to establish degrees of relative departure from the Caucasian ideal. Instead, and however subjective (and even risible) we view the criterion today, Blumenbach chose physical beauty as his guide to ranking. He simply affirmed that Europeans were most beautiful, with Caucasians as the most comely of all. This explains why Blumenbach, in the first quote cited in this article, linked the maximal beauty of the Caucasians to the place of human origin. Blumenbach viewed all subsequent variation as departures from the originally created ideal—therefore, the most beautiful people must live closest to our primal home.

Blumenbach's descriptions are pervaded by his subjective sense of relative beauty, presented as though he were discussing an objective and quantifiable property, not subject to doubt or disagreement. He describes a Georgian female skull (found close to Mount Caucasus) as "really the most beautiful form of skull which . . . always of itself attracts every eye, however little observant." He then defends his European standard on aesthetic grounds: "In the first place, that stock displays . . . the most beautiful form of the skull, from which, as from a mean and primeval type, the others diverge by most easy gradations. . . . Besides, it is white in color, which we may fairly assume to have been the primitive color of mankind, since . . . it is very easy for that to degenerate into brown, but very much more difficult for dark to become white."

Blumenbach then presented all human variety on two lines of successive departure from this Caucasian ideal, ending in the two most degenerate (least attractive, not least morally unworthy or mentally obtuse) forms of humanity—Asians on one side, and Africans on the other. But Blumenbach also wanted to designate intermediary forms between ideal and most degenerate, especially since even gradation formed his primary argument for human unity. In his original four-race system, he could identify native Americans as intermediary between Europeans and Asians, but who would serve as the transitional form between Europeans and Africans?

The four-race system contained no appropriate group. But inventing a fifth racial category as an intermediary between Europeans and Africans would complete the new symmetrical geometry. Blumenbach therefore added the Malay race, not as a minor, factual refinement but as a device for reformulating an entire theory of human diversity. With this one stroke, he produced the geometric transformation from Linnaeus's unranked geographic model to the conventional hierarchy of implied worth that has fostered so much social grief ever since.

> I have allotted the first place to the Caucasian . . . which makes me esteem it the primeval one. This diverges in both directions into two, most remote and very different from each other; on the one side, namely, into the Ethiopian, and on the other into the Mongolian. The remaining two occupy the intermediate positions between that primeval one and these two extreme varieties; that is, the American between the Caucasian and Mongolian; the Malay between the same Caucasian and Ethiopian. [From Blumenbach's third edition.]

With one stroke, Blumenbach produced the geometric transformation from Linnaeus's unranked geographic model to the conventional hierarchy of implied worth that has fostered so much social grief ever since.

Scholars often think that academic ideas must remain at worst, harmless, and at best, mildly amusing or even instructive. But ideas do not reside in the ivory tower of our usual metaphor about academic irrelevance. We are, as Pascal said, a thinking reed, and ideas motivate human history. Where would Hitler have been without racism, Jefferson without liberty? Blumenbach lived as a cloistered professor all his life, but his ideas have reverberated in ways that he never could have anticipated, through our wars, our social upheavals, our sufferings, and our hopes.

I therefore end by returning once more to the extraordinary coincidences of 1776—as Jefferson wrote the Declaration of Independence while Blumenbach was publishing the first edition of his treatise in Latin. We should remember the words of the nineteenth-century British historian and moralist Lord Acton, on the power of ideas to propel history:

> It was from America that . . . ideas long locked in the breast of solitary thinkers, and hidden among Latin folios, burst forth like a conqueror upon the world they were destined to transform, under the title of the Rights of Man.

FOR FURTHER READING

Daughters of Africa. Margaret Busby, editor. Pantheon, 1992. A comprehensive anthology of prose and poetry written by women of African descent, from ancient Egyptian love songs to the work of contemporary Americans. The collection features the work of Phillis Wheatley, the first black to publish a book of poetry in the United States.

MINORITY RIGHTS: ON THE IMPORTANCE OF LOCAL KNOWLEDGE

I cannot stand forward, and give praise or blame to anything which relates to human actions, and human concerns, on a simple view of the object, as it stands stripped of every relation, in all the nakedness and solitude of metaphysical abstraction. Circumstances (which with some gentlemen pass for nothing) give in reality to every political principle its distinguishing colour and discriminating effect.
—Edmund Burke, *Reflections on the Revolution in France*

Daniel A. Bell

DANIEL A. BELL teaches political philosophy at the University of Hong Kong. He is the author of *Communitarianism and Its Critics* and the co-author of *Towards Illiberal Democracy in Pacific Asia.*

A small set of crucial human rights are valued, at least in theory, by all governments in the contemporary world. Rights against torture, murder, genocide, and slavery are simply not contested in the public rhetoric of the international arena. Of course, gross violations occur "off the record," but in such cases the task of the human rights activist is to expose the gap between public allegiance to rights and the sad reality of ongoing abuse. There is not much point deliberating about practices that everyone already condemns.

But political thinkers and activists can and do take different sides on many pressing minority rights conflicts. Whether the dispute is over the choice of language in schools and parliaments, the decentralization of govermental powers to regions controlled by minorities, or the protection of traditional homelands, there do not seem to be any readily available general proposals for noncontroversial solutions.

In my view, it is important to refrain from moral and political judgments about disputes of this sort until one has acquired detailed knowledge of local political circumstances and relevant cultural outlooks. Unlike most contemporary philosophers and political theorists, I want to found judgments not on principles derived from reasoning about universal human needs and interests but rather on the actual dispositions and pressing concerns of a society in this or that historically contingent condition. This "culturally sensitive" approach, needless to say, requires a great deal of time and energy spent learning a society's culture, history, politics, and language, but there may be no other path to sound and effective political judgments. In this essay I propose four arguments in favor of a "culturally sensitive" approach to minority rights.

Identifying the Group

Political thinkers tend to define cultural groups in terms of language, race, or religion. Vernon Van Dyke, for example, defines an ethnic community as "a group of persons, predominantly of common descent, who think of themselves as collectively possessing a separate identity based on race or on shared characteristics, usually language or religion." If the aim is to identify vulnerable minority groups deserving of special political rights, however, definitions in terms of shared language, race, or religion may have the effect of unjustifiably rewarding some groups and denying the legitimate aspirations of others.

It is instructive to look at some examples from China. According to the Chinese government, there are over fifty-five ethnic minorities in the country, amounting to more than 8 percent of the population. These officially recognized minorities are labeled as such by virtue of being "non-Han," meaning they do not use the Chinese script or bear all the physical characteristics of the Han Chinese. Leading experts on the subject such as June Teufel Dreyer (author of *China's Forty Millions*) and Colin Mackerras (author of *China's Minorities*) also operate with the government's definition of a minority group.

Contrary to popular belief, the Chinese government does recognize in principle that minority groups are entitled to special status in the Chinese political system. For example, the National People's Congress in 1984 passed "The Law on Regional Autonomy for Minority Nationalities" that allows for self-administration in Tibet and other "minority regions." Self-administration in practice, needless to say, does not amount to much. But some tangible benefits are in fact granted to officially recognized minority groups. Nicholas Tapp notes that "provisions for representation of minority nationalities in state organs, general exemption from the most stringent applications of the regulations on birth control, and the lower marks commonly required of members of minority nationalities who apply for admission to universities or colleges add up to a policy of positive discrimination."

The problem, however, is that under the current system benefits may accrue to individuals and groups not in need of special protection. Not surprisingly, the children of mixed marriages between Han and minority members usually choose minority rather than Han status. Whole counties and districts have applied for autonomous minority status on the basis of extremely slender evidence, such as the discovery of non-Han names in genealogies of several generations' depth.

At the same time, restricting the definition of minority groups to shared language or ethnicity can conceal vulnerable minority groups from political view—and so play into the hands of conservative majorities intent on denying legitimate aspirations for self-administration. As Emily Honig explains in her book *Creating Chinese Ethnicity: Subei People in Shanghai, 1850-1980*, the prejudice against Subei people is comparable to that experienced by African-Americans in the United States. Unlike African-Americans, however, the Subei are not physically distinct from the rest of the Shanghainese population, almost all of whom are Han Chinese. Rather, Subei are defined as such by virtue of being individuals whose families were originally poverty-stricken refugees from Jiangsu province. The political result is that Subei people do not benefit from the official Chinese policy of positive discrimination and special political representation for minority groups.

Consider as well the development of a distinctive Taiwanese identity defined primarily by a common experience with free market institutions and (more recently) a relatively democratic form of government rather than by shared language and ethnicity. Any prospect for a fair and workable reunification with the People's Republic of China cannot ignore the fact that many Taiwanese now think of themselves as sufficiently distinct to seek some form of self-administration. But this is a non-issue if one accepts the official Chinese view that the Taiwanese are not a distinct cultural grouping. And defining minority groups in terms of language or ethnicity leads one to endorse the official view.[1] Vulnerable minorities are more likely to be protected by policies sensitive to their actual history and self-understanding.

Trade-Offs

Much ink has been spilled debating whether or not civil and political rights need to be sacrificed in the interests of economic development. Proponents of "authoritarianism"—primarily government officials in East and Southeast Asia—argue that if factional opposition threatens to slow down economic development or to plunge the country into civil strife, then tough measures can and should be taken to ensure political stability. Liberal thinkers in the West then counter by reaffirming the value of civil and political liberties for human beings in general or by pointing out that social scientific evidence simply does not support the claim that there is a causal connection between authoritarianism and economic success.

There is, however, a narrower claim being presented by "authoritarian" governments that cannot be dismissed so readily: namely, that particular rights may need to be curbed in particular contexts, for particular economic or political purposes, as a short-term measure, in order to secure a more important right or to secure that same right in the long-term. Xin Chunying, a lawyer working at the Human Rights Center of the Chinese Academy of the Social Sciences, notes that East Asian governments emphasize "the particularity of human rights protection and the priority determined by the specific conditions of each country."[2] Justifications for the temporary suspension of a particular right are put forward by government officials, but often attract significant local support.

Consider for example the recent political history of Singapore. Kevin Tan, a professor of constitutional law at the National University of Singapore, notes that Singapore in the 1960s was plagued by a "communalism which pitted Singapore's majority Chinese population against the minority Malays." Communalism, and the attendant threat of racial riots, was dealt with by measures intended to construct an ethnically neutral national identity that might override particularist commitments to ethnic groups. This included such policies as a public housing program designed to break up ethnic enclaves and compulsory education in the unifying language of English.

These policies seem problematic: what do minority rights mean in practice if not the right to education in one's mother tongue and the right to live together as a community? Note, however, that the Singaporean government need not object to the principle of minority rights. If all it meant to say is that rights had to be curtailed in response to a pressing social problem (the need to curb racially motivated violence), then it seems besides the point to counter with the argument that rights are universal and cannot be restricted under any circumstances. Singaporean officials can concede that governments ought ideally to secure minority rights, adding that *in this case* these rights had to be sacrificed in order to secure more important rights to life and minimal subsistence.[3]

Nor would it be appropriate to respond with social scientific evidence based on generalizations. The specific argument that in the Singaporean context restricting minority rights was the most effective way of dealing with racial riots need not be (and may not be) a general argument for repression. It is simply not relevant to point out that other countries do not face similar problems or that social peace can sometimes be secured without similar restrictions.

When countering specific trade-off arguments for rights violations, one can question either the premise that the society under question is actually facing a social crisis requiring immediate political action or the idea that curbing minority rights is the best means of overcoming that crisis. But whatever the response, the social critic must be armed with detailed and historically informed knowledge of *that* society.

Of course, even if the critic were to concede (a) that the social crisis is real and (b) that curbing minority rights is the most effective way of overcoming it, such local justifications for the denial of minority rights are only of limited validity: they no longer apply once the crisis is overcome. But local knowledge is also necessary for the argument that the "state of emergency" can, and therefore should, be lifted.

Local Justifications

It is commonly believed that secular Western societies are uniquely tolerant and respectful of nonmainstream ways of life, including the cultural particularities of minority groups. From this it follows that policies designed to protect vulnerable minorities must draw on the social experiences and political ideals of Western societies, cast in universalist terms.

Against this view, however, it can be argued that *values* similar to Western conceptions of minority rights can also be found in some non-Western cultural traditions. For example, Nurcholish Madjid of the Indonesian Human Rights Commission notes that "Islam too recognizes . . . the right to use one's own language, the right to practice one's own culture, and the right to freedom of religion."[4] Moreover, if the purpose of rights is primarily to protect minority cultures from the political decisions of the majority, then clearly the *functional equivalents* of rights practices can sometimes be found in non-Western traditions. Chinese rule over Tibet in the mid-eighteenth century, for example, was primarily a matter of form, with the Tibetans in charge of their own affairs so long as they secured social peace and recognized a formal link with China. The Dalai Lama proposed a similar formula in 1988, but the Chinese government, seemingly oblivious to historical precedent, denounced the offer, calling it a "disguised form of independence."

Still, the struggle to promote minority rights is more likely to be won if it is fought in ways that build on, rather than challenge, local cultural traditions. Consider the case of the persecution of the Al-Arqam Islamic group in Malaysia. In accordance with a ruling from the "National Fatwa Council" and a decree by the Ministry of Home Affairs in August 1994, the Malaysian government launched a systematic campaign to suppress the Al-Arqam group. The Malaysian leader and founder of Al-Arqam, Ashaari Muhammad, was arrested and held without charge or trial; the group's written, audio, and visual presentations were banned; and Malaysian Muslims were prevented from joining Al-Arqam or participating in any of its activities.

In the eyes of Islamic legal scholar and human rights activist Abdullahi A. An-Na'im, however, the government of Malaysia "violated *Shari'a* law in the name of protecting Islam against 'deviationism.'" Deviationism, explains An-Na'im, is unknown to any orthodox formulation of *Shari'a*. The government of Malaysia could potentially have appealed to the notion of apostasy (although many Muslim scholars today oppose this view of *Shari'a*), but "by failing to apply even the notion of apostasy with its own legal safeguards under . . . Islamic law, the government of Malaysia has given itself licence to penalize and persecute Ashaari and his followers without conforming to the demands of the principle of legality and rule of law under *Shari'a* itself."

No doubt the government of Malaysia's behavior can also be criticized by appealing to non-religious political principles. An-Na'im notes, for example, that the "secular" human rights activist can criticize the government of Malaysia for denying a group of citizens their freedom of belief and for detaining them without charge or trial on the basis of a ruling from a council of "religious scholars," hence violating the principle that religion not be used for political ends. Perhaps the social critic could also invoke Article 27 of the United Nations International Covenant on Civil and Political Rights: "In those States in which ethnic, religious, or linguistic minorities exist, persons belonging to such minorities shall not be denied the right, in community with the other members of their group, to enjoy their culture, to profess and practice their own religion, or to use their own language." This right, the secular activist will argue, is due all human beings simply by virtue of their humanity, and does not depend on the interpretation of a particular religion or cultural tradition.

But how persuasive are these universal justifications in a country dominated by a Muslim majority where rights are generally thought to have theocentric foundations[5] and where Islamic legal codes already shape family and criminal law? In this context, arguments that appeal to widely shared religious values are far more likely to be effective than arguments founded on the principle that a human rights regime mandates a strict separation between religion and the state. And even if changes can be temporarily instituted on the basis of secular human rights principles, *long-term commitment* to minority rights is best secured by drawing on the expressed aspirations of those who adhere to a particular tradition.

In short, local cultural traditions may well provide sufficient resources to justify local commitment to values and practices similar to minority rights, and strategic considerations may speak in favor of using these resources to protect vulnerable groups.

Non-Liberal Cultural Traditions

But while some aspects of local culture may be invoked for this purpose, the problem is that other aspects can justify curtailing minority rights. For example, the many references in the Confucian tradition to "barbarians" may lend support to "civilizing missions" that have the effect of annihilating non-Han Chinese cultures. One response available to the proponent of a "culturally sensitive" approach is that even aspects of cultural traditions seemingly inconsistent with minority rights can sometimes be re-interpreted in ways that render them consistent. But these re-interpretations are unlikely to be widely accepted, and one might conclude that culturally sensitive approaches need to be buttressed by a U.S.-style right to free speech so that majority viewpoints can be challenged and eventually replaced by values more supportive of minority rights. As Professor An-Na'im puts it, "there must be the widest possible multiplicity of voices and perspectives on the meaning and implications of cultural norms and institutions."

I am inclined, however, to question the need for an internal cultural discourse that allows for "the *widest possible* multiplicity of voices and perspectives." What is needed is a mechanism for change within a tradition that allows minority viewpoints to become dominant or, at least, politically relevant. But this mechanism need not be an absolute right to free speech, and more generally it need not be the same in all times and places.

Consider the case of Dr. Sulak Sivaraksa, a leading pro-democracy activist in Thailand and a nominee for the Nobel Peace Prize. In 1991, the Thai ruler, General Suchinda, pressed charges against Dr. Sulak for *lèse majesté* and for defaming him (the general) in a speech given at Thammasat University. Fearing for his life, Sulak fled the country, but returned in 1992 after the Suchinda government had fallen to face the charges. In court, Sulak did not deny that he had attacked the "dictator" Suchinda, but he did deny the charge of *lèse majesté*, referring to the many services he had performed for the Royal Family. Sulak explains: "I did not . . . stake my ground on an absolute right to free speech. My defense against the charge of *lèse majesté* was my innocence of the charge; my defense was my loyalty to the King and Royal Family and, even where I discussed the use of the charge of *lèse majesté* in current Siamese political practice, it was to highlight abuse and to point to the ways in which abuse might undermine the monarchy, rather than to defend any theoretical right to commit this action. I am not affirming, nor would I affirm, a right to commit *lèse majesté*. This aspect of the case is particularly concerned with my being Siamese and belonging to the Siamese cultural tradition."[6]

In other words, Dr. Sulak aimed to persuade fellow citizens that the dominant political system should be replaced with an alternative, relatively democratic political structure, but he made it explicit that he did not want to challenge a mechanism for change that places a constraint on direct criticism of the Thai king. There is no reason to doubt Dr. Sulak's sincerity (perhaps he, like many Thais, would feel deeply offended, if not personally harmed, by an attack on the king). Is there anything wrong with a mechanism for changing a cultural tradition that has constraints like this one, endorsed by both defenders and critics of the prevailing views?

Liberal thinkers may worry about this line of argument. The claim that for strategic reasons the social critic should sometimes appeal to local traditions to justify values and practices that in the Western world are normally realized though a rights regime may be palatable, but few liberals will go along with the suggestion that cultural traditions can provide a genuinely moral foundation for illiberal norms and political practices. This latter argument may be employed as an excuse to justify or "tolerate" the subjugation of members of cultural groups who have been denied the opportunity to reflect on and criticize norms of deference and humility to powerful leaders.

Still, one can exaggerate this worry. For one thing, there may not be many other examples of illiberal constraints on challenges to prevailing cultural viewpoints endorsed by both political leaders and leading social critics (certainly one could not justify curtailing rights against murder, torture, slavery, and genocide on these grounds). Moreover, the argument for respecting the norms and practices endorsed by most adherents of particular cultural traditions (including leading social critics) can sometimes be employed to *expand* rather than *restrict* the set of rights typically enjoyed by members of liberal Western societies. For example, East Asian societies influenced by Confucianism strongly emphasize the value of filial piety or the idea that children have a profound duty to care for elderly parents, a duty to be forsaken only in the most exceptional circumstances. In political practice this means that parents have a right to be cared for by their children and that it is incumbent on East Asian governments to provide the social and economic conditions to facilitate the realization of this right. Political debate tends to center on the question of whether the right to filial piety is best realized by means of a law that makes it mandatory for children to provide financial support for elderly parents (as in Singapore or Japan), or whether the state should rely on more indirect methods such as tax breaks (as in Hong Kong) and housing benefits that simply make care for the elderly easier. But the argument that there is a pressing need to secure this right in East Asia is not a matter of political controversy.

Let me be more explicit about how these arguments may bear on the question of protecting vulnerable minorities from the decisions of majorities. On the one hand, respect for minority groups in liberal societies may translate into (illiberal) restrictions on criticism of aspects of cultural traditions held to be sacred by all (or nearly all) members of those groups. For example, Bhikhu Parekh suggests that laws against libel can be employed to protect minority cultures from various forms of defamation and hate speech. On the other hand, a richer and fuller respect for minorities may translate into expanding the set of social and economic rights typically granted in liberal societies. Perhaps the parents of East Asian immigrants can be given the right to immigrate as well, and adults of East Asian origin who care for their elderly parents can be given a special right to claim tax benefits. Nor should one rule out the possibility that liberal majorities learn from the cultural traditions of minority groups. In an age when Social Security payments may no longer be economically sustainable at their current level and when it is widely seen as morally acceptable in the West to commit relatively fit elderly parents to nursing homes, it may not be entirely implausible to promote the value of filial piety in liberal societies. But whether the issue is restricting rights, expanding rights, or learning from nonliberal cultures, the political proposals that we endorse should always be based on detailed knowledge of the cultural self-understandings of minority groups.

Notes

[1] It is worth noting, however, that in a different context even the Chinese government concedes that minority groups with legitimate aspirations for autonomy need not be defined in terms of language or ethnicity. In the case of Hong Kong the Chinese government officially endorses a "one country, two systems" political proposal for rule in the post-1997 period. What defines group particularity in this case is shared attachment to the rule of law and experience with a free economic system, not shared language or ethnicity.

[2] I quote from a paper presented at a workshop held in Hakone, Japan, June 1995, the first of three workshops on the theme "The Growth of East Asia and Its Impact on Human Rights." More generally, the second through fourth sections of this essay draw on papers presented in Hakone and at the second workshop held in Bangkok, Thailand, March 1996, as well as on ideas contained in my article "The East Asian Challenge to Human Rights: Reflections on an East West Dialogue," forthcoming in the *Human Rights Quarterly*, August 1996.

[3] It is worth noting that Article 4 of the United Nations International Covenant on Civil and Political Rights (1966) explicitly allows for short-term curbs on some rights (including the right to the protection of minority cultures, Article 27) if these are necessary to deal with particular social crises. Article 4 goes on to state that the derogation of rights against murder, torture, and slavery, among others, may not be made under this provision.

[4] It is not well known that the Iranian Parliament guarantees five seats for religious minorities. Jews, Zoroastrians, and Armenian and Assyrian Christians are allowed to elect deputies. A recent article in the *International Herald Tribune* noted that "Iran's 30,000 Jews turned out in force in general elections here to elect their representative to the Islamic republic's Parliament." (March 13, 1996)

[5] I do not mean to imply that Islamic countries are unique in this regard. Many religious Americans, for example, might think that the idea of human rights derives its ultimate justification from God's special concern for human beings.

[6] Dr. Sulak explains that he uses "the older terms *Siam* and *Siamese* rather than the government terms *Thailand* and *Thai* out of respect for the non-Thai minorities within the country. The word *Thailand* was initially imposed by the dictators in 1939."

ONE DROP OF BLOOD

Do ethnic categories protect us or divide us? The way that Washington chooses to define the population in the 2000 census could trigger the biggest debate over race in America since the nineteen-sixties.

LAWRENCE WRIGHT

WASHINGTON in the millennial years is a city of warring racial and ethnic groups fighting for recognition, protection, and entitlements. This war has been fought throughout the second half of the twentieth century largely by black Americans. How much this contest has widened, how bitter it has turned, how complex and baffling it is, and how far-reaching its consequences are became evident in a series of congressional hearings that began last year in the obscure House Subcommittee on Census, Statistics, and Postal Personnel, which is chaired by Representative Thomas C. Sawyer, Democrat of Ohio, and concluded in November, 1993.

Although the Sawyer hearings were scarcely reported in the news and were sparsely attended even by other members of the subcommittee, with the exception of Representative Thomas E. Petri, Republican of Wisconsin, they opened what may become the most searching examination of racial questions in this country since the sixties. Related federal agency hearings, and meetings that will be held in Washington and other cities around the country to prepare for the 2000 census, are considering not only modifications of existing racial categories but also the larger question of whether it is proper for the government to classify people according to arbitrary distinctions of skin color and ancestry. This discussion arises at a time when profound debates are occurring in minority communities about the rightfulness of group entitlements, some government officials are questioning the usefulness of race data, and scientists are debating whether race exists at all.

Tom Sawyer, forty-eight, a former English teacher and a former mayor of Akron, is now in his fourth term representing the Fourteenth District of Ohio. It would be fair to say that neither the House Committee on Post Office and Civil Service nor the subcommittee that Sawyer chairs is the kind of assignment that members of Congress would willingly shed blood for. Indeed, the attitude of most elected officials in Washington toward the census is polite loathing, because it is the census, as much as any other force in the country, that determines their political futures. Congressional districts rise and fall with the shifting demography of the country, yet census matters rarely seize the front pages of home-town newspapers, except briefly, once every ten years. Much of the subcommittee's business has to do with addressing the safety concerns of postal workers and overseeing federal statistical measurements. The subcommittee has an additional responsibility: it reviews the executive branch's policy about which racial and ethnic groups should be officially recognized by the United States government.

"We are unique in this country in the way we describe and define race and ascribe to it characteristics that other cultures view very differently," Sawyer, who is a friendly man with an open, boyish face and graying black hair, says. He points out that the country is in the midst of its most profound demographic shift since the eighteen-nineties—a time that opened "a period of the greatest immigration we have ever seen, whose numbers have not been matched until right now." A deluge of new Americans from every part of the world is overwhelming our traditional racial distinctions, Sawyer believes. "The categories themselves inevitably reflect the temporal bias of every age," he says. "That becomes a problem when the nation itself is undergoing deep and historic diversification."

Looming over the shoulder of Sawyer's subcommittee is the Office of Management and Budget, the federal agency that happens to be responsible for determining standard classifications of racial and ethnic data. Since 1977, those categories have been set by O.M.B. Statistical Directive 15, which controls the racial and ethnic standards on all federal forms and statistics. Directive 15 acknowledges four general racial groups in the United States: American Indian or Alaskan Native; Asian or Pacific Islander; Black; and White. Directive 15 also breaks down ethnicity into Hispanic Origin and Not of Hispanic Origin. These categories, or versions of them, are present on enrollment forms for schoolchildren; on application forms for jobs, scholarships, loans, and mortgages; and, of course, on United States census forms. The categories ask that every American fit himself or herself into one racial and one ethnic box. From this comes the information that is used to monitor and enforce civil-rights legislation, most notably the Voting Rights Act of 1965, but also a smorgasbord of set-asides and entitlements and affirmative-action programs. "The numbers drive the dollars," Sawyer observes, repeating a well-worn Washington adage.

The truth of that statement was abundantly evident in the hearings, in which a variety of racial and ethnic groups were bidding to increase their portions of the federal pot. The National Coalition for an Accurate Count of Asian Pacific Americans lobbied to add Cambodians and Lao to the nine different nationalities already listed on the census forms under the heading of Asian or Pacific Islander. The National Council of La Raza proposed that Hispanics be considered a race, not just an ethnic group. The Arab American Institute asked that persons from the Middle East, now counted as white, be given a separate, protected category of their own. Senator Daniel K. Akaka, a Native Hawaiian, urged that his people be moved from the Asian or Pacific Islander box to the American Indian or Alaskan Native box. "There is the misperception that Native Hawaiians, who number well over two hundred thousand, somehow 'immigrated' to the United States like other Asian or Pacific Island groups," the Senator testified. "This leads to the erroneous impression that Native Hawaiians, the original inhabitants of the Hawaiian Islands, no longer exist." In the Senator's opinion, being placed in the same category as other Native Americans would help rectify that situation. (He did not mention that certain American Indian tribes enjoy privileges concerning gambling concessions that Native Hawaiians currently don't enjoy.) The National Congress of American Indians would like the Hawaiians to stay where they are. In every case, issues of money, but also of identity, are at stake.

In this battle over racial turf, a disturbing new contender has appeared. "When I received my 1990 census form, I realized that there was no race category for my children," Susan Graham, who is a white woman married to a black man in Roswell, Georgia, testified. "I called the Census Bureau. After checking with supervisors, the bureau finally gave me their answer: the children should take the race of their mother. When I objected and asked why my children should be classified as their mother's race only, the Census Bureau representative said to me, in a very hushed voice, 'Because, in cases like these, we always know who the mother is and not always the father.' "

Graham went on to say, "I could not make a race choice from the basic categories when I enrolled my son in kindergarten in Georgia. The only choice I had, like most other parents of multiracial children, was to leave race blank. I later found that my child's teacher was instructed to choose for him based on her knowledge and observation of my child. Ironically, my child has been white on the United States census, black at school, and multiracial at home—all at the same time."

Graham and others were asking that a "Multiracial" box be added to the racial categories specified by Directive 15—a proposal that alarmed representatives of the other racial groups for a number of reasons, not the least of which was that multiracialism threatened to undermine the concept of racial classification altogether.

According to various estimates, at least seventy-five to more than ninety per cent of the people who now check the Black box could check Multiracial, because of their mixed genetic heritage. If a certain proportion of those people—say, ten per cent—should elect to identify themselves as Multiracial, legislative districts in many parts of the country might need to be redrawn. The entire civil-rights regulatory program concerning housing, employment, and education would have to be reassessed. School-desegregation plans would be thrown into the air. Of course, it is possible that only a small number of Americans will elect to choose the Multiracial option, if it is offered, with little social effect. Merely placing such an option on the census invites people to consider choosing it, however. When the census listed "Cajun" as one of several examples under the ancestry question, the number of Cajuns jumped nearly two thousand per cent. To remind people of the possibility is to encourage enormous change.

Those who are charged with enforcing civil-rights laws see the Multiracial box as a wrecking ball aimed at affirmative action, and they hold those in the mixed-race movement responsible. "There's no concern on any of these people's part about the effect on policy—it's just a subjective feeling that their identity needs to be stroked," one government analyst said. "What they don't understand is that it's going to cost their own groups"—by losing the advantages that accrue to minorities by way of affirmative-action programs, for instance. Graham contends that the object of her movement is not to create another protected category. In any case, she said, multiracial people know "to check the right box to get the goodies."

Of course, races have been mixing in America since Columbus arrived. Visitors to Colonial America found plantation slaves who were as light-skinned as their masters. Patrick Henry actually proposed, in 1784, that the State of Virginia encourage intermarriage between whites and Indians, through the use of tax incentives and cash stipends. The legacy of this intermingling is that Americans who are descendants of early settlers, of slaves, or of Indians often have ancestors of different races in their family tree.

Thomas Jefferson supervised the original census, in 1790. The population then was broken down into free white males, free white females, other persons (these included free blacks and "taxable Indians," which meant those living in or around white settlements), and slaves. How unsettled this country has always been about its racial categories is evident in the fact that nearly every census since has measured race differently. For most of the nineteenth century, the census reflected an American obsession with miscegenation. The color of slaves was to be specified as "B," for black, and "M," for mulatto. In the 1890 census, gradations of mulattoes were further broken down into quadroons and octoroons. After 1920, however, the Census Bureau gave up on such distinctions, estimating that three-quarters of all blacks in the United States were racially mixed already, and that pure blacks would soon disappear. Henceforth anyone with any black ancestry at all would be counted simply as black.

Actual interracial marriages, however, were historically rare. Multiracial children were often marginalized as illegitimate half-breeds who didn't fit comfortably into any racial community. This was particularly true of the offspring of black-white unions. "In my family, like many families with African-American ancestry, there is a history of multiracial offspring associated with rape and concubinage," G. Reginald Daniel, who teaches a course in multiracial identity at the University of California at Los Angeles, says. "I was reared in the segregationist South. Both sides of my family have been mixed for at least three generations. I struggled as a child over the question of why I had to exclude my East Indian and Irish and Native American and French ancestry, and could include only African."

Until recently, people like Daniel were identified simply as black because of a peculiarly American institution known informally as "the one-drop rule," which defines as black a person with as little as a single drop of "black blood." This notion derives from a long-discredited belief that each race had its own blood type, which was correlated with physical appearance and social behavior. The antebellum South promoted the rule as a way of enlarging the slave population with the children of slaveholders. By the nineteen-twenties, in Jim Crow America the one-drop rule was well established as the law of the land. It still is, according to a United States Supreme Court decision as late as 1986, which refused to review a lower court's ruling that a Louisiana woman whose great-great-great-great-grandmother had been the mistress of a French planter was black—even though that proportion of her ancestry amounted to no more than three thirty-seconds of her genetic heritage. "We are the only country in the world that applies the one-drop rule, and the only group that the one-drop rule applies to is people of African descent," Daniel observes.

People of mixed black-and-white ancestry were rejected by whites and found acceptance by blacks. Many of the most notable "black" leaders over the last century and a half were "white" to some extent, from Booker T. Washington and Frederick Douglass (both of whom had white fathers) to W. E. B. Du Bois, Malcolm X, and Martin Luther King, Jr. (who had an Irish grandmother and some American Indian ancestry as well). The fact that Lani Guinier, Louis Farrakhan, and Virginia's former governor Douglas Wilder are defined as black, and define themselves that way, though they have light skin or "European" features, demonstrates how enduring the one-drop rule has proved to be in America, not only among whites but among blacks as well. Daniel sees this as "a double-edged sword." While the one-drop rule encouraged racism, it also galvanized the black community.

"But the one-drop rule is racist," Daniel says. "There's no way you can get away from the fact that it was historically implemented to create as many slaves as possible. No one leaped over to the white community—that was simply the mentality of the nation, and people of African descent internalized it. What this current discourse is about is lifting the lid of racial oppression in our institutions and letting people identify with the totality of their heritage. We have created a nightmare for human dignity. Multiracialism has the potential for undermining the very basis of racism, which is its categories."

But multiracialism introduces nightmares of its own. If people are to be counted as something other than completely black, for instance, how will affirmative-action programs be implemented? Suppose a court orders a city to hire additional black police officers to make up for past discrimination. Will mixed-race officers count? Will they count wholly or partly? Far from solving the problem of fragmented identities, multiracialism could open the door to fractional races, such as we already have in the case of the American Indians. In order to be eligible for certain federal benefits, such as housing-improvement programs, a person must prove that he or she either is a member of a federally recognized Indian tribe or has fifty per cent "Indian blood." One can envision a situation in which nonwhiteness itself becomes the only valued quality, to be compensated in various ways depending on a person's pedigree.

Kwame Anthony Appiah, of Harvard's Philosophy and Afro-American Studies Departments, says, "What the Multiracial category aims for is not people of mixed ancestry, because a majority of Americans are actually products of mixed ancestry. This category goes after people who have parents who are socially recognized as belonging to different races. That's O.K.—that's an interesting social category. But then you have to ask what happens to their children. Do we want to have more boxes, depending upon whether they marry back into one group or the other? What are the children of these people supposed to say? I think about these things because—look, my mother is English; my father is Ghanaian. My sisters are married to a Nigerian and a Norwegian. I have nephews who range from blond-haired kids to very black kids. They are all first cousins. Now according to the American scheme of things, they're all black—even the guy with blond hair who skis in Oslo. That's what the one-drop rule says. The Multiracial scheme, which is meant to solve anomalies, simply creates more anomalies of its own, and that's because the fundamental concept—that you should be able to assign every American to one of three or four races reliably—is crazy."

These are sentiments that Representative Sawyer agrees with profoundly. He says of the one-drop rule, "It is so embedded in our perception and policy, but it doesn't allow for the blurring that is the reality of our population. Just look at— What are the numbers?" he said in his congressional office as he leafed through a briefing book. "Thirty-eight per cent of American Japanese females and eighteen per cent of American Japanese males marry outside their traditional ethnic and nationality group. Seventy per cent of American Indians marry outside. I grant you that the enormous growth potential of multiracial marriages starts from a relatively small base, but the truth is it starts from a fiction to begin with; that is, what we think of as black-and-white marriages are not marriages between people who come from anything like a clearly defined ethnic, racial, or genetic base."

The United States Supreme Court struck down the last vestige of anti-miscegenation laws in 1967, in Loving v. Virginia. At that time, interracial marriages were rare; only sixty-five thousand marriages between blacks and whites were recorded in the 1970 census. Marriages between Asians and non-Asian Americans tended to be between soldiers and war brides. Since then, mixed marriages occurring between many racial and ethnic groups have risen to the point where they have eroded the distinctions between such peoples. Among American Indians, people are more likely to marry outside their group than within it, as Representative Sawyer noted. The number of children living in families where one parent is white and the other is black, Asian, or American Indian, to use one measure, has tripled—from fewer than four hundred thousand in 1970 to one and a half million in 1990—and this doesn't count the children of single parents or children whose parents are divorced.

Blacks are conspicuously less likely to marry outside their group, and yet marriages between blacks and whites have tripled in the last thirty years. Matthijs Kalmijn, a Dutch sociologist, analyzed marriage certificates filed in this country's non-Southern states since the Loving decision and found that in the nineteen-eighties the rate at which black men were marrying white women had reached approximately ten per cent. (The rate for black women marrying white men is about half that figure.) In the 1990 census, six per cent of black householders nationwide had nonblack spouses—still a small percentage, but a significant one.

Multiracial people, because they are now both unable and unwilling to be ignored, and because many of them refuse to be confined to traditional racial categories, inevitably undermine the entire concept of race as an irreducible difference between peoples. The continual modulation of racial differences in America is increasing the jumble created by centuries of ethnic intermarriage. The resulting dilemma is a profound one. If we choose to measure the mixing by counting people as Multiracial, we pull the teeth of the civil-rights laws. Are we ready for that? Is it even possible to make changes in the way we count Americans, given the legislative mandates already built into law? "I don't know," Sawyer concedes. "At this point, my purpose is not so much to alter the laws that underlie these kinds of questions as to raise the question of whether or not the way in which we currently define who we are reflects the reality of the nation we are and who we are becoming. If it does not, then the policies underlying the terms of measurement are doomed to be flawed. What you measure is what you get."

SCIENCE has put forward many different racial models, the most enduring being the division of humanity into three broad groupings: the Mongoloid, the Negroid, and the Caucasoid. An influential paper by Masatoshi Nei and Arun K. Roychoudhury, entitled "Gene Differences between Caucasian, Negro, and Japanese Populations," which appeared in *Science*, in 1972, found that the genetic variation among individuals from these racial groups was only slightly greater than the variation within the groups.

In 1965, the anthropologist Stanley Garn proposed hundreds, even thousands, of racial groups, which he saw as gene clusters separated by geography or culture, some with only minor variations between them. The paleontologist Stephen Jay Gould, for one, has proposed doing away with all racial classifications and identifying people by clines—regional divisions that are used to account for the diversity of snails and of songbirds, among many other species. In this Gould follows the anthropologist Ashley Montagu, who waged a lifelong campaign to rid science of the term "race" altogether and never used it except in quotation marks. Montagu would have substituted the term "ethnic group," which he believed carried less odious baggage.

Race, in the common understanding, draws upon differences not only of skin color and physical attributes but also of language, nationality, and religion. At times, we have counted as "races" different national groups, such as Mexicans and Filipinos. Some Asian Indians were counted as members of a "Hindu" race in the censuses from 1920 to 1940; then they became white for three decades. Racial categories are often used as ethnic intensifiers, with the aim of justifying the exploitation of one group by another. One can trace the ominous example of Jews in prewar Germany, who were counted as "Israelites," a religious group, until the Nazis came to power and turned them into a race. Mixtures of first- and second-degree Jewishness were distinguished, much as quadroons and octoroons had been in the United States. In fact, the Nazi experience ultimately caused a widespread reëxamination of the idea of race. Canada dropped the race question from its census in 1951 and has so far resisted all attempts to reinstitute it. People who were working in the United States Bureau of the Census in the fifties and early sixties remember that there was speculation that the race question would soon be phased out in America as well. The American Civil Liberties Union tried to get the race question dropped from the census in 1960, and the State of New Jersey stopped entering race information on birth and death certificates in 1962 and 1963. In 1964, however, the architecture of civil-rights laws began to be erected, and many of the new laws—particularly the Voting Rights Act of 1965—required highly detailed information about minority participation which could be gathered only by the decennial census, the nation's supreme instrument for gathering demographic statistics. The expectation that the race question would wither away surrendered to the realization that race data were fundamental to monitoring and enforcing desegregation. The census soon acquired a political importance that it had never had in the past.

Unfortunately, the sloppiness and multiplicity of certain racial and ethnic categories rendered them practically meaningless for statistical purposes. In 1973, Caspar Weinberger, who was then Secretary of Health, Education and Welfare, asked the Federal Interagency Committee on Education (FICE) to develop some standards for classifying race and ethnicity. An ad-hoc committee sprang into being and proposed to create an intellectual grid that would sort all Americans into five racial and ethnic categories. The first category was American Indian or Alaskan Native. Some members of the committee wanted the category to be called Original Peoples of the Western Hemisphere, in order to include Indians of South American origin, but the distinction that this category was seeking was so-called "Federal Indians," who were eligible for government benefits; to include Indians of any other origin, even though they might be genetically quite similar, would confuse the collecting of data. To accommodate the various, highly diverse peoples who originated in the Far East, Southeast Asia, and the Pacific Islands, the committee proposed a category called Asian or Pacific Islander, thus sweeping into one massive basket Chinese, Samoans, Cambodians, Filipinos, and others—peoples who had little or nothing in common, and many of whom were, indeed, traditional enemies. The fact that American Indians and Alaskan Natives originated from the same Mongoloid stock as many of these peoples did not stop the committee from putting them in a separate racial category. Black was defined as "a person having origins in any of the black racial groups of Africa," and White, initially, as "a person having origins in any of the original peoples of Europe, North Africa, the Middle East, or the Indian subcontinent"—everybody else, in other words. Because the Black category contained anyone with any African heritage at all, the range of actual skin colors covered the entire spectrum, as did the White category, which included Arabs and Asian Indians and various other darker-skinned peoples.

The final classification, Hispanic, was the most problematic of all. In the 1960 census, people whose ancestry was Latin-American were counted as white. Then people of Spanish origin became a protected group, requiring the census to gather data in order to monitor their civil rights. But how to define them? People who spoke Spanish? Defining the population that way would have included millions of Americans who spoke the language but had no actual roots in Hispanic culture, and it excluded Brazilians and children of immigrants who were not taught Spanish in their homes. One approach was to count persons with Spanish surnames, but that created a number of difficulties: marriage made some non-Hispanic women into instant minorities, while stripping other women of their Hispanic status. The 1970 census inquired about people from "Central or South America," and more than a million people checked the box who were not Hispanic; they were from Kansas, Alabama, Mississippi—the central and southern United States, in other words.

The greatest dilemma was that there was no conceivable justification for calling Hispanics a race. There were black Hispanics from the Dominican Republic, Argentines who were almost entirely European whites, Mexicans who would have been counted as American Indians if they had been born north of the Rio Grande. The great preponderance of Hispanics are mestizos—a continuum of many different genetic backgrounds. Moreover, the fluid Latin-American concept of race differs from the rigid United States idea of biologically determined and highly distinct human divisions. In most Latin cultures, skin color is an individual variable—not a group marker—so that within the same family one sibling might be considered white and another black. By 1960, the United States census, which counts the population of Puerto Rico, gave up asking the race question on the island, because race did not carry the same distinction there that it did on the mainland. The ad-hoc committee decided to dodge riddles like these by calling Hispanics an ethnic group, not a race.

In 1977, O.M.B. Statistical Directive 15 adopted the FICE suggestions practically verbatim, with one principal exception: Asian Indians were moved to the Asian or Pacific Islander category. Thus, with little political discussion, the identities of Americans were fixed in five broad groupings. Those racial and ethnic categories that were dreamed up almost twenty years ago were not neutral in their effect. By attempting to provide a way for Americans to describe themselves, the categories actually began to shape those identities. The categories became political entities, with their own constituencies, lobbies, and vested interests. What was even more significant, they caused people to think of themselves in new ways—as members of "races" that were little more than statistical devices. In 1974, the year the ad-hoc committee set to work, few people referred to themselves as Hispanic; rather, people who fell into that grouping tended to identify themselves by nationality—Mexican or Dominican, for instance. Such small categories, however, are inconvenient for statistics and politics, and the creation of the meta-concept "Hispanic" has resulted in the formation of a peculiarly American group. "It is a mixture of ethnicity, culture, history, birth, and a presumption of language," Sawyer contends. Largely because of immigration, the Asian or Pacific Islander group is considered the fastest-growing racial group in the United States, but it is a "racial" category that in all likelihood exists nowhere else in the world. The third-fastest-growing category is Other—made up of the nearly ten million people, most of them Hispanics, who refused to check any of the prescribed racial boxes. American Indian groups are also growing at a rate that far exceeds the growth of the population as a whole: from about half a million people in 1960 to nearly two million in 1990—a two-hundred-and-fifty-nine-per-cent increase, which was demographically impossible. It seemed to be accounted for by improvements in the census-taking procedure and also by the fact that Native Americans had become fashionable, and people now wished to identify with them. To make matters even more confounding, only seventy-four per cent of those who identified themselves as American Indian by race reported having Indian ancestry.

Whatever the word "race" may mean elsewhere in the world, or to the world of science, it is clear that in America the categories are arbitrary, confused, and hopelessly intermingled. In many cases, Americans don't know who they are, racially speaking. A National Center for Health Statistics study found that 5.8 per cent of the people who called themselves Black were seen as White by a census interviewer. Nearly a third of the people identifying themselves as Asian were classified as White or Black by independent observers. That was also true of seventy per cent of people who identified themselves as American Indians. Robert A. Hahn, an epidemiologist at the Centers for Disease Control and Prevention, analyzed deaths of infants born from 1983 through 1985. In an astounding number of cases, the infant had a different race on its death certificate from the one on its birth certificate, and this finding led to staggering increases in the infant-mortality rate for minority populations—46.9 per cent greater for American Indians, 48.8 per cent greater for Japanese-Americans, 78.7 per cent greater for Filipinos—over what had been previously recorded. Such disparities cast doubt on the dependability of race as a criterion for any statistical survey. "It seems to me that we have to go back and reëvaluate the whole system," Hahn says. "We have to ask, 'What do these categories mean?' We are not talking about race in the way that geneticists might use the term, because we're not making any kind of biological assessment. It's closer to self-perceived membership in a population—which is essentially what ethnicity is." There are genetic variations in disease patterns, Hahn points out, and he goes on to say, "But these variations don't always correspond to so-called races. What's really important is, essentially, two things. One, people from different ancestral backgrounds have different behaviors—diets, ideas about what to do when you're sick—that lead them to different health statuses. Two, people are discriminated against because of other people's perception of who they are and how they should be treated. There's still a lot of discrimination in the health-care system."

Racial statistics do serve an important purpose in the monitoring and enforcement of civil-rights laws; indeed, that has become the main justification for such data. A routine example is the Home Mortgage Disclosure Act. Because of race questions on loan applications, the federal government has been able to document the continued practice of redlining by financial institutions. The Federal Reserve found that, for conventional mortgages, in 1992 the denial rate for blacks and Hispanics was roughly double the rate for whites. Hiring practices, jury selection, discriminatory housing patterns, apportionment of political power—in all these areas, and more, the government patrols society, armed with little more than statistical information to insure equal and fair treatment. "We need these categories essentially to get rid of them," Hahn says.

The unwanted corollary of slotting people by race is that such officially sanctioned classifications may actually worsen racial strife. By creating social-welfare programs based on race rather than on need, the government sets citizens against one another precisely because of perceived racial differences. "It is not 'race' but a *practice* of racial classification that bedevils the society," writes Yehudi Webster, a sociologist at California State University, Los Angeles, and the author of "The Racialization of America." The use of racial statistics, he and others have argued, creates a reality of racial divisions, which then require solutions, such as busing, affirmative action, and multicultural education, all of which are bound to fail, because they heighten the racial awareness that leads to contention. Webster believes that adding a Multiracial box would be "another leap into absurdity," because it reinforces the concept of race in the first place. "In a way, it's a continuation of the one-drop principle. Anybody can say, 'I've got one drop of *something*—I must be multiracial.' It may be a good thing. It may finally convince Americans of the absurdity of racial classification."

In 1990, Itabari Njeri, who writes about interethnic relations for the Los Angeles *Times*, organized a symposium for the National Association of Black Journalists. She recounts a presentation given by Charles Stewart, a Democratic Party activist: "If you consider yourself black for political reasons, raise your hand." The vast majority raised their hands. When Stewart then asked how many people present believed they were of pure African descent, without any mixture, no one raised his hand. Stewart commented later, "If you advocate a category that includes people who are multiracial to the detriment of their black identification, you will replicate what you saw—an empty room. We cannot afford to have an empty room."

Njeri maintains that the social and economic gap between light-skinned blacks and dark-skinned blacks is as great as the gap between all blacks and all whites in America. If people of more obviously mixed backgrounds were to migrate to a Multiracial box, she says, they would be politically abandoning their former allies and the people who needed their help the most. Instead of draining the established categories of their influence, Njeri and others believe, it would be better to eliminate racial categories altogether.

That possibility is actually being discussed in the corridors of government. "It's quite strange—the original idea of O.M.B. Directive 15 has nothing to do with current efforts to 'define' race,' says Sally Katzen, the director of the Office of Information and Regulatory Affairs at O.M.B., who has the onerous responsibility of making the final recommendation on revising the racial categories. "When O.M.B. got into the business of establishing categories, it was purely statistical, not programmatic—purely for the purpose of data gathering, not for defining or protecting different categories. It was certainly never meant to *define* a race." And yet for more than twenty years Directive 15 did exactly that, with relatively little outcry. "Recently, a question has been raised about the increasing number of multiracial children. I personally have received pictures of beautiful children who are part Asian and part black, or part American Indian and part Asian, with these letters saying, 'I don't want to check just one box. I don't want to deny part of my heritage.' It's very compelling."

This year, Katzen convened a new interagency committee to consider how races should be categorized, and even whether racial information should be sought at all. "To me it's *offensive*—because I think of the Holocaust—for someone to say what a Jew is," says Katzen. "I don't think a government agency should be defining racial and ethnic categories—that certainly was not what was ever intended by these standards."

Is it any accident that racial and ethnic categories should come under attack now, when being a member of a minority group brings certain advantages? The white colonizers of North America conquered the indigenous people, imported African slaves, brought in Asians as laborers and then excluded them with prejudicial immigration laws, and appropriated Mexican land and the people who were living on it. In short, the nonwhite population of America has historically been subjugated and treated as second-class citizens by the white majority. It is to redress the social and economic inequalities of our history that we have civil-rights laws and affirmative-action plans in the first place. Advocates of various racial and ethnic groups point out that many of the people now calling for a race-blind society are political conservatives, who may have an interest in undermining the advancement of nonwhites in our society. Suddenly, the conservatives have adopted the language of integration, it seems, and the left-leaning racial-identity advocates have adopted the language of separatism. It amounts to a polar reversal of political rhetoric.

Jon Michael Spencer, a professor in the African and Afro-American Studies Curriculum at the University of North Carolina at Chapel Hill, recently wrote an article in *The Black Scholar* lamenting what he calls "the postmodern conspiracy to explode racial identity." The article ignited a passionate debate in the magazine over the nature and the future of race. Spencer believes that race is a useful metaphor for cultural and historic difference, because it permits a level of social cohesion among oppressed classes. "To relinquish the notion of race—even though it's a cruel hoax—at this particular time is to relinquish our fortress against the powers and principalities that still try to undermine us," he says. He sees the Multiracial box as politically damaging to "those who need to galvanize peoples around the racial idea of black."

There are some black cultural nationalists who might welcome the Multiracial category. "In terms of the African-American population, it could be very, very useful, because there is a need to clarify who is in and who is not," Molefi Kete Asante, who is the chairperson of the Department of African-American Studies at Temple University, says. "In fact, I would think they should go further than that—identify those people who are in interracial marriages."

Spencer, however, thinks that it might be better to eliminate racial categories altogether than to create an additional category that empties the others of meaning. "If you had who knows how many thousands or tens of thousands or millions of people claiming to be multiracial, you would lessen the number who are black," Spencer says. "There's no end in sight. There's no limit to which one can go in claiming to be multiracial. For instance, I happen to be very brown in complexion, but when I go to the continent of Africa, blacks and whites there claim that I would be 'colored' rather than black, which means that somewhere in my distant past—probably during the era of slavery—I could have one or more white ancestors. So does that mean that I, too, could check Multiracial? Certainly light-skinned black people might perhaps see this as a way out of being included among a despised racial group. The result could be the creation of another class of people, who are betwixt and between black and white."

Whatever comes out of this discussion, the nation is likely to engage in the most profound debate of racial questions in decades. "We recognize the importance of racial categories in correcting clear injustices under the law," Representative Sawyer says. "The dilemma we face is trying to assure the fundamental guarantees of equality of opportunity while at the same time recognizing that the populations themselves are changing as we seek to categorize them. It reaches the point where it becomes an absurd counting game. Part of the difficulty is that we are dealing with the illusion of precision. We wind up with precise counts of everybody in the country, and they are precisely wrong. They don't reflect who we are as a people. To be effective, the concepts of individual and group identity need to reflect not only who we have been but who we are becoming. The more these categories distort our perception of reality, the less useful they are. We act as if we knew what we're talking about when we talk about race, and we don't."

The Place of Faith in Public Life: A Personal Perspective

John Brademas

On December 11, 1984, I delivered the annual Liss Lecture at the University of Notre Dame. Sponsored by the Department of Theology, the lecture came weeks after the 1984 presidential campaign that brought a potentially dangerous intrusion of religion into the national political arena.

In these observations, I discussed what I believe should be the relationship between religion and politics in the American democracy. I also reflected upon the importance of religion in my own life.

I AM DELIGHTED to be back on a campus and in a community that hold for me such deep personal meaning and so many warm memories.

As you know, I was born in Mishawaka, grew up in South Bend and so lived all my life in the shadow of Notre Dame.

For twenty-two years, I had the privilege of representing the people of the Third District in the Congress of the United States, and, without question, my most famed constituent was my longtime mentor, valued friend and now academic colleague, Father Theodore Hesburgh. He has, for an entire generation, served as president of Notre Dame, an extraordinary record in American higher education.

Beyond this stewardship, Father Hesburgh has been the conscience of our nation, bringing his religious vocation and a remarkable range of experience to bear on the most challenging issues of our times—civil rights, human rights, the struggle against poverty at home and abroad, and the control of nuclear arms.

I am proud now to serve on the Board of Trustees of the university he has done so much to build.

I am especially pleased to be here at the invitation of my dear friend, Bert Liss. The goal of the lecture series he created is to enhance communications across the boundaries of faith, a purpose with which I feel wholly at home. For my late father was Greek Orthodox, my mother is a member of the Disciples of Christ Church and I was brought up a Methodist. Before going to Congress, I taught at Saint Mary's College; and during my campaigns, I was enriched by the opportunity to represent people with a wide variety of religious traditions, including, beyond those I have mentioned, Amish, Mennonite, Brethren and, of course, Jewish.

Indeed, I recalled my own religious background in 1965 during a debate in the House of Representatives on aid to parochial schools. I recited the diversity of my family's religious ties and added that as one of the remaining bachelors then on Capitol Hill, all I needed to complete my experience was a Jewish wife.

Not long thereafter, I received a letter from New York City on Saks Fifth Avenue stationery, which began: "Dear Sir, I have read with interest your advertisement in the *Congressional Record.* I am 5′4″, green eyed, blonde, single and Jewish. Your attention will be appreciated!"

On a more serious note, I shall speak to you on the relationship of religious faith to the political order, first, because my own religious background had a definite effect on my career in public life; and, second, because of the explosion of attention to the question of religion and politics during this year's presidential campaign.

Religion and Politic

Of the latter point, I note some signs from contemporary American life:

- Debate has escalated in the last decade over such highly charged issues as abortion and school prayer.
- During 1980, we observed the emergence of the "Religious Right," spearheaded by the Reverend Jerry Falwell's Moral Majority, and the targeting for defeat of candidates for public office—I was one—on the basis of so-called "morality score cards" developed by this and related groups.
- We saw Falwell and his allies play an increasingly aggressive part in the presidential race—on behalf of Mr. Reagan—and in the congressional contests.
- Several Roman Catholic Bishops, led by Archbishop John J. O'Con-

From *Washington, D.C. to Washington Square* by John Brademas, 1986, pp. 238-252. Weidenfeld & Nicolson, New York.

nor of New York, publicly took to task Geraldine Ferraro, a Roman Catholic and first woman nominated for nationwide office by a majority party, for her position on abortion.

- The American Jewish community displayed rising apprehension both at the rhetoric of Jesse Jackson and his Muslim supporter Louis Farrakhan, on the one hand, and, on the other, the increasing influence of the Falwellians.
- Major candidates were pressed to clarify their understanding of the proper relationship between church and state.
- We heard some thoughtful statements on religion and political life, such as those made here at Notre Dame by Governor Mario Cuomo of New York and Congressman Henry Hyde of Illinois.
- Most recently, the National Conference of Catholic Bishops issued its Pastoral Letter on Catholic Social Teaching and the U.S. Economy; while one year earlier, the Bishops published another such letter on war and peace, with particular focus on the morality of nuclear war.
- Finally, theologians and other writers, like Harvey Cox, Richard Neuhaus and Michael Novak, have turned scholarly attention to the relationship of faith to political action in today's world.

International Religious Fervor

Beyond all these indications that religion and politics are becoming a potent combination at home, there is ample evidence that they are also a volatile mix abroad:

- In the unrelenting hostilities between Protestants and Catholics in Ireland;
- In the uneasy truce between church and state in Poland;
- In the repression of Jews and Christians in the Soviet Union;
- In debates over "liberation theology" within the Catholic Church of Latin America;
- In the ongoing strife in Lebanon among several religious and ethnic groups;
- In the assassination of Indira Gandhi by militant Sikhs; and
- In the unremitting hostility toward the West and the United States in particular of the followers of the Ayatollah Khomeini in Iran.

Given the range and complexity of the interplay between religion and politics, in our own country and others, I do not presume to address such weighty matters from the perspective of a scholar or theologian. Rather, I should like to offer some observations about the place of faith in public life based on my own experience, especially my service in Congress.

Today, of course, I speak from a different vantage point, as president of a large private, urban university. You may be interested to know that, although secular, New York University has more Roman Catholic and Jewish students than any other university in the United States.

Religious Heritage

Please allow me a few more comments about my own religious roots. Although as I have said, my father was Greek Orthodox and my mother a Disciple, my brothers and sister and I grew up in the First Methodist Church, 333 North Main Street, South Bend, Indiana; and that church was a vital part of our lives. Our ministers and Sunday School teachers were outstanding, and I also spent many Sunday evenings there as president of the Methodist Youth Fellowship.

Important as well were summer months in the small central Indiana farm town of Swayzee in Grant County, where we stayed with my mother's parents. In Swayzee, a kind of Thornton Wilder community of seven hundred, we attended the First Christian Church with my grandparents and also, occasionally, Taylor's Creek Baptist Church, a tiny rural church where my great-uncle, a successful farmer and part-time Primitive Baptist preacher, often filled the pulpit.

I loved going to these several churches, and so you will not be surprised to learn that years later, as a student for a brief time at Notre Dame before joining the navy, I befriended Father Roland Simonitsch, with whom I discussed the basic tenets of Roman Catholicism, or that in a sailor suit at the University of Mississippi, I attended the First Methodist Church in Oxford.

During four years in Cambridge—Massachusetts—my principal extracurricular life was at the Harvard-Epworth Methodist Church, where I was president of the Wesley Foundation and thought seriously about going into the Methodist ministry. I told my pastor that I was considering a career as either a Methodist minister or a politician, but that after attending an Annual Conference of the Methodist Church—which is when all the preachers get together—I knew it would be politics either way!

It must be obvious that religion played an important role in my own life and, accordingly, in the career I chose and followed for nearly a quarter of a century. That the Methodist church had a lengthy tradition of commitment to social justice made an impact on me.

Vivid, too, were recollections of my father's descriptions of street fights in South Bend between Ku Klux Klansmen and Notre Dame students and how his restaurant business was boycotted by the Klan because he was not a WASP.

And as a grade-schooler at James Madison School in South Bend, I remember the revulsion I felt on hearing Adolph Hitler's radio broadcasts, punctuated by the commentary of H. V. Kaltenborn, and having my first brush with censorship when the school principal refused to permit publication of my satirical attack on Hitler in the school's mimeographed newspaper. We were not yet at war with Germany, she explained, so that my little essay was not appropriate.

All these memories returned years later when as a Member of Congress I visited Auschwitz; when in Leningrad, I met surreptiously with Jewish dissidents and gave them mezuzahs and Hebrew-Russian dictionaries; and on an early snowy morning in Tashkent, Uzbekistan, attended services in an Orthodox synagogue.

I think as well of my audiences—two—with Cardinal Wyszynski in Warsaw; at the first, I found him brooding, pessimistic, depressed; at the second, not long after the election of Cardinal Wojtyla as the Holy Father, exultant, joyous, exuberant.

I recall, too, how years earlier, in 1957, when I was teaching at Saint Mary's College, I had an extraordinary day with the Benedictine monks at Montserrat near Barcelona and listened to their scathing criticism of those Bishops of the church of Spain who failed to attend to the poor and unemployed but instead made common cause with Franco.

During my later years in Congress, I also visited Cardinal Macharski of Krakow, who succeeded Wojtyla; Cardinal Lekai, Primate of the church of Hungary; in Bucharest and Moldavia, Patriarch Justin of the Rumanian Orthodox church, with whom I served on the Central Committee of the World Council of Churches; with Pimen, the Patriarch of Moscow; and earlier still, in Istanbul, with Athenagoras, Patriarch of the Eastern Orthodox church.

Yet I must tell you that I should not have been open to, indeed, eager for, such experiences had it not been for my roots here in South Bend and during my college years. Even as a student for a short time at Notre Dame, in 1945, I was moved by the encyclicals of Leo XIII and found the understanding in the Roman Catholic tradition of the social fabric of human existence richer in many ways than the often excessively atomistic, individualistic emphasis of much of mainstream Protestantism.

In like fashion, I was impressed as a young man by the thunderous passages of the Hebrew prophets, like Isaiah, whose denunciations of idolatry and corruption and whose call for justice I found in many respects consonant with the social teachings of Leo XIII and, years later, John XXIII, as well as with the writings of some of the Protestant reformers of the 1940s and 1950s.

Indeed, a principal influence on me was a course I took at Harvard nearly thirty-five years ago on the classics of the Christian tradition taught by the great historian of American Puritan thought, Perry Miller. We read Kierkegaard, Pascal, Augustine and Reinhold Niebuhr. Niebuhr was especially important to me, and I heard him preach at the Memorial Church in Harvard Yard, read most of his books and later had the privilege of meeting him a few times. Niebuhr's translation of the insights of Christian faith into the fundamentals of political democracy in his remarkable study *The Children of Light and the Children of Darkness* directly affected my decision to go into politics and helped shape my commitments as a legislator.

Now these were not the only encounters with religion that mattered to me, but I cite them because they illustrate the kind of experience that ultimately set me on the path of electoral politics.

Although I feel broadly heir to the Judeo-Christian tradition, my principal heritage is clearly Christian, and Protestant. Let me put my point as simply as I can by saying that I would find it difficult to imagine how I would even begin to understand the world and my place in it if I were not a Christian.

The Christian in Politics

Yet what do I mean when I say this? What does it mean to be a Christian? In my view, the central core of the Christian faith is *agape,* love, self-sacrificing, self-giving, other-regarding love, symbolized by, incarnated by, Christ on the cross.

What, in turn, is the relationship between the Christian faith, looked at in this way, and politics?

When I entered the political arena just thirty years ago, a problem for me was how to justify, from a specifically religious perspective, a political career. For a generation ago, I would remind you, certainly in Protestant circles, there were many, especially of conservative outlook, who argued that *agape* applied solely to private life and that the individual Christian and the Christian church must stand aside from the hurly-burly of politics.

Obviously, that was not my view, for I believed—and still do—that our religious faith must touch every dimension of human experience social, economic and political as well as personal.

I find it fascinating that the question that preoccupied me as a novice politician is still very much with us today. What is the link between the Christian law of love and the practice of politics?

The Role of Justice

If the question remains the same, as I think it does, the answer for me in 1984 is the same as it was in 1954—that the nexus between the law of love and the practice of politics is the concept of justice.

The idea of justice varies in human history, but I suggest that at the very least, justice means assuring every person his or her due, what he or she is entitled to as a human being.

Now justice is *not* the same as love. Love does not count or reckon, as Paul's First Letter to the Corinthians, chapter 13, reminds us. But justice does. Justice must be calculating. It is not love, therefore, but justice that must be the immediate objective of political action.

As Arthur Walmsley, an Episcopal church leader, has written:

> The balance of the rights and responsibilities of one group against those of another involves issues of justice. Justice seen in this light is not a crude approximation of love but the *means* by which the Christian co-operates with the will of God precisely in the midst of life.

Is love then irrelevant to political action? No! On the contrary, it is our love for our fellow human beings—commanded Christians by Christ—that generates in us a concern for justice among men and women.

The late Archbishop of Canterbury, William Temple, put the point this way:

> Associations cannot love one another; a trade union cannot love an employers' federation, nor can one national state love another. . . . Consequently, the relevance of Christianity in these spheres is quite different from what many Christians suppose it to be. Christian charity manifests itself in the temporal order as a supernatural discernment of and adhesion to, justice in relation to the equilibrium of power.

Given what I have said, you will better understand, if not agree with, my determination three decades ago to run for Congress and understand, too, what shaped my choices about where to put my energies as a legislator over the following years.

Religion and Politics

Although last month's election returns and this month's White House budget proposals point in just the opposite direction, the commitments of my years on Capitol Hill were to such purposes as the war on poverty; aid to disadvantaged schoolchildren; education of handicapped children; services for the elderly; scholarships, loans and work study for college students; and civil rights for blacks.

Having as an eighteen-year-old naval-officer candidate at the University of Mississippi stood in the little, William Faulkner-like town of Pontotoc and heard the late Senator Theodore G. Bilbo give vent to his virulent racism with attacks on "Clare Boothe Luce and those other communists [sic] up north who want to mongrelize the white race," I trust you will understand why, seventeen years later, I felt myself right where I thought I should be, standing on the steps of the Lincoln Memorial behind Martin Luther King, Jr.

I must add that through all my years in Congress, I took much comfort and derived more inspiration than I am sure my constituents ever knew from the knowledge that Father Hesburgh of Notre Dame shared those commitments.

I recall these several efforts not out of pride—although I am proud of them—but to remind us all that in a year when one political party and one strain of fundamentalism seem to have asserted a proprietary claim to God and so-called Christian values, many of the liberals I knew in Congress and I were raised in strong religious traditions that informed our choices and our vision of a just and open society.

Let me remind you that the major candidates for the 1984 Democratic presidential nomination included a Baptist preacher, the son of a Methodist minister and a graduate of the Yale Divinity School.

There is one other point I should like to make here, and that is that the Niebuhrian views with which I have expressed sympathy also prepared me for the combat style of American politics. For the Christian faith gives one an appreciation of the tentative nature of the human condition and so arms one for the uncertainties of political life. That perspective also equips one with the patience to work long and hard on one issue and the strength to endure defeat without being devastated.

It must be evident from what I have said that I have never understood the doctrine of separation of church and state to mean that religion has no role in politics. Nor can I agree with the assertion of my friend and former colleague Congressman Henry Hyde, in his speech here last September, that religious values have been driven from the public arena.

The question raised by recent events is not about *whether* but *how* religion and politics ought to mix.

Consider how this debate has shifted in the past twenty-five years. I remember how on April 8, 1960, I introduced on this campus a young Massachusetts Senator, then on his way to nomination and election as the first Roman Catholic President of the United States. I remember, too, the intensity, here in Indiana and elsewhere, of anti-Catholic sentiment during that campaign and how John Kennedy was repeatedly pressed not to assert his religious convictions but to deny that he spoke for his church or that his church spoke for him.

In his famous speech to the Greater Houston Ministerial Association before the election, Kennedy declared:

> I do not accept the right of any ecclesiastical official to tell me what I shall do in the sphere of my public responsibility as an elected official. . . .
>
> Whatever issue may come before me as President—on birth control, divorce, censorship, gambling, or any other subject—I will make my decision in accordance with what my conscience tells me to be in the national interest, and without regard to outside religious pressure or dictate.

In the 1984 presidential election, on the other hand, the situation was sharply reversed. Candidates and major public officials, most prominently Geraldine Ferraro, were challenged to explain why their decisions as public officeholders did not always conform to the tenets of their church and to their own religious convictions. Many of you heard the eloquent words of Governor Cuomo on just this question on this campus only three months ago.

Now if I have said yes to the question, "Does religious faith have a place in public life?," I must at the same time insist that there be limitations on the relationship. I should like, therefore, now to suggest some guidelines that can help us distinguish between appropriate and inappropriate mixtures of religion and politics.

Faith and Political Action

The first guideline concerns the level at which religious convictions are most properly applied in public debate. It seems to me obvious that our faith can—and should—be a source of guidance on basic values, yet I think it equally clear that we must be wary of those who insist—when it comes to public policy—that a principle of religious belief presents only one solution.

Here I am in agreement with Governor Cuomo that whereas we may be enjoined to accept the teachings of our faith,

> in the application of those teachings—the exact way we translate them into political action, the specific laws we propose, the exact legal sanctions we seek—there . . . is no one, clear, absolute route that the church says, as a matter of doctrine, we must follow.

In my view, strident insistence that there is only one way that a general principle of religion or morality can be written into the laws of the land comes dangerously close to using the instrument of government to impose doctrinally specific views on others who do not share them.

Certainly my respect for the rights of adherents to minority religions and of nonbelievers was among the reasons that, as a Member of Congress, I opposed legislation to permit organized prayer in public schools. Opposition to such prayer has been voiced, I note, by nearly every mainline Protestant church in this country as well as by most of the principal leaders of the Jewish community. Moreover, as the distinguished theologian John Bennett has noted: "Private prayer is voluntary and legal now!"

Let me make clear that I am not saying here that religious leaders or others should not speak out for or against specific policies or on single issues. Rather I am asserting that when they do so, they leave behind the authority and the moral force of their faith and become mundane—in the sense of earthly—political actors. Whatever they propose must be evaluated through the political process, according to the standards of feasibility and judgments about the public good that hold for all citizens of a democratic society.

But there is another point I must make here, one that Joseph Cardinal Bernardin made in his Gannon Lecture at Fordham University last year when he urged the church to adopt what he called "a consistent ethic of life" rather than focus on just one issue, whether nuclear war or abortion.

In similar vein, Professor Robert Bellah of the University of California at Berkeley has observed that Ronald Reagan is highly selective about the areas in which he finds a link between religion and public morality. In Bellah's words: "How can one hold that there is a relationship when it comes to matters of school prayer and abortion but not when it comes to matters of poverty, civil rights, and the prevention of nuclear war?"

In this respect, I remember well that the "right-to-life" advocates who used to visit me in Congress never said a word in support of legislation I was writing to help educate poor children and handicapped children, and to provide services to the elderly or the disabled. I found the silence of my constituents on these issues of human life eloquent—and distressing.

Candor constrains me here also to remark that many observers have noted how during the recent campaign, the Catholic Bishops, despite their representation of "a consistent ethic of life," targeted only one candidate on the national ticket for attack and on only one issue. These observers have reminded us that although there was a sharp divergence between the Bishops' Pastoral Letter on War and Peace and both the record of the Reagan Administration and the planks of the Republican Platform at Dallas, the Bishops voiced no similar criticism of Reagan and Bush.

In like fashion, such observers—who range from the *Washington Post* columnist Haynes Johnson to the Roman Catholic priest and professor at Saint John's University, Paul Surlis—note that the Bishops' Pastoral Letter on the U.S. Economy seems a near frontal attack on the Administration's domestic policies, yet this letter did not appear until after the election.

A Need for Tolerance

My second guideline for relating religion and politics follows from the first but is more a matter of tone than of scope or substance. It is that when we appeal to religious convictions in political life, we should do so in a spirit of tolerance and humility, and not with self-righteousness.

We must beware of those who claim for themselves a monopoly on morality and truth in any realm, but especially in politics. Groups like the Moral Majority and Christian Voice that call for the defeat of candidates on so-called moral grounds and that rank public officials on "Biblical scorecards" distort the political process. What kind of "morality" assigns a zero to Congressman Paul Simon and former Congressman Robert Drinan—the first a devoted Lutheran layman and the second a Jesuit priest—and a perfect, 100 percent record to another Congressman convicted in the Abscam scandal!

In similar fashion, I remind you that at a prayer breakfast in Dallas during the Republican convention, President Reagan asserted that those who opposed officially organized prayer in public schools were "intolerant of religion." Mr. Reagan went on to say that "morality's foundation is religion," as if nonbelievers were by definition immoral.

You will recall, too, the letter sent on behalf of the Reagan campaign by Senator Paul Laxalt of Nevada to forty-five thousand Christian ministers in which he attempted to make God a Republican county chairman—well, national chairman!—by warning the clergymen that "as leaders under God's authority we cannot afford to resign ourselves to idle neutrality." Jerry Falwell struck the same theme in Dallas when he proclaimed to the Republican delegates assembled that the party's standard-bearers were "God's instruments in rebuilding America."

Instead of such arrogance, I would urge on the part of those who invoke religion in the political process a degree of self-restraint, not to say humility. Religious leaders in particular should remind their followers that other solutions than the ones they propose are possible and appropriate and should be scrupulous in their respect of the right of others to disagree in the public arena. Otherwise, these leaders unfairly constrain debate with innuendos of faithlessness and even heresy.

The fact is each of us brings a particular heritage to bear when he or she enters the political fray, and each of us is obliged to listen intently and respectfully to the arguments of those with differing views. Each of us should be open to persuasion if the reasoning of others speaks more effectively for the public good.

For we must never forget the message that Abraham Lincoln delivered a war-torn nation on the occasion of his second inauguration as President: "Both [parties in the Civil War] read the same bible, and pray to the same God; and each invokes His aid against the other."

Surely it is fundamental in the Judeo-Christian heritage that all people and all nations are under the judgment of God.

Here I recall how Reinhold Niebuhr warned us that religious pluralism itself depends on a sense of our own imperfection. In his words:

> Religious diversity . . . requires a very high form of religious commitment. It demands that each religion, or each version of a single faith, seek to proclaim its highest insights while yet preserving a humble and contrite recognition of the fact that all actual expressions of religious faith are subject to historical contingency and relativity.
>
> Religious faith therefore ought to be a constant fount of humility.

The price of arrogance, pride, self-righteousness in the expression of religious convictions in political life is very steep. Even today we hear echoes of idolatry, religious chauvinism and political triumphalism in claims that America is a "Christian nation." Not so! America is a nation of Catholics, Jews, Protestants, Eastern Orthodox, Muslims, Buddhists, agnostics and nonbelievers. We must ever acknowledge, embrace and celebrate that religious and secular heterogeneity. For it is precisely in welcoming such diversity that we keep our society free.

Public Morality

The two guidelines I have discussed apply to the content and the tone of the relation between religion and the public order. My third guideline concerns the objective of that relationship, which in my view should be to fashion a working consensus on matters of public morality.

As Governor Cuomo made clear so eloquently in his speech here, concerns rooted in religious teachings influence both law and the policies of government most effectively and legitimately when they have gathered broad support. Of course, changes in law and policy also contribute to altering standards of public behavior. Ideally, however, the morality encoded in our laws represents a shared understanding of the common good. That morality ought not be the reflection of any one faith but of the varied traditions, secular and religious, of our Nation.

Obvious illustrations of how religious leaders can contribute to building consensus on issues that unqestionably have implications for public policy are the recent Pastoral Letters from the National Conference of Catholic Bishops.

Both the letters on nuclear war and peace and on poverty and the American economy expressed strong moral stands. Yet both letters also stressed principle over technique; allowed for, indeed, encouraged, debate over the implementation of the principles; and urged Catholics to work in *various* ways toward progress on the *same* objectives—reducing the threat of war and the circumstance of poverty. Both letters have, in fact, sparked considerable discussion and disagreement within the Roman Catholic church.

Let me here remind you that, as the great theologian John Courtney Murray once put it, "pluralism implies disagreement and dissension within a community [as well as] agreement and consensus." So that while we must marshal our convictions toward achieving consensus, we must also live peacefully with people we consider, by our particular standards of right and wrong, to be sinners.

These then are some of the guidelines I modestly suggest as we think about how to engage our religious faith on behalf of political purposes.

Those guidelines are, to repeat, first, that religious convictions should neither be too hastily nor too narrowly translated into public policy positions.

Second, in political debate, humility rather than self-righteousness should characterize our appeals to religious sources.

And, third, our objective should be, on matters of public morality, to reach consensus rather than to win legal victories that may incorporate our doctrines but divide us as a people.

Index

Credits/Acknowledgments

Cover design by Charles Vitelli

1. Race and Ethnicity in the American Legal Tradition
Facing overview—Dushkin/McGraw•Hill photo.

2. Immigration and the American Experience
Facing overview—Library of Congress photo. 69—Bettmann Archive illustration.

3. Indigenous Ethnic Groups
Facing overview—United Nations photo by Jerry Frank.

4. Hispanic/Latino Americans
Facing overview—Digital Stock photo.

5. African Americans
Facing overview—AP/Wide World photo.

6. Asian Americans
Facing overview—New York Convention and Visitors Bureau photo. 170-174—Pluralism Project photos.

7. The Ethnic Legacy
Facing overview—New York Convention and Visitors Bureau photo.

8. The Ethnic Factor: International Challenges for the 1990s
Facing overview—United Nations photo.

9. Understanding Cultural Pluralism
Facing overview—United Nations photo.

*PHOTOCOPY THIS PAGE!!!**

ANNUAL EDITIONS ARTICLE REVIEW FORM

■ NAME: ______________________ DATE: ______________

■ TITLE AND NUMBER OF ARTICLE: ______________________

■ BRIEFLY STATE THE MAIN IDEA OF THIS ARTICLE: ______________________

■ LIST THREE IMPORTANT FACTS THAT THE AUTHOR USES TO SUPPORT THE MAIN IDEA:

■ WHAT INFORMATION OR IDEAS DISCUSSED IN THIS ARTICLE ARE ALSO DISCUSSED IN YOUR TEXTBOOK OR OTHER READINGS THAT YOU HAVE DONE? LIST THE TEXTBOOK CHAPTERS AND PAGE NUMBERS:

■ LIST ANY EXAMPLES OF BIAS OR FAULTY REASONING THAT YOU FOUND IN THE ARTICLE:

■ LIST ANY NEW TERMS/CONCEPTS THAT WERE DISCUSSED IN THE ARTICLE, AND WRITE A SHORT DEFINITION:

*Your instructor may require you to use this ANNUAL EDITIONS Article Review Form in any number of ways: for articles that are assigned, for extra credit, as a tool to assist in developing assigned papers, or simply for your own reference. Even if it is not required, we encourage you to photocopy and use this page; you will find that reflecting on the articles will greatly enhance the information from your text.

MW00681047

VIPs

VIPs
very important pets

Compiled by

Priya Kapoor & Nandita Jaishankar

Lustre Press
Roli Books

Photo Credits

Corbis: 17, 24, 37, 44, 50, 56, 57 (top), 58-59, 68, 74-75, 102-103, 118-119, 126, 127, 132-133

***Dr. Johnson's Apple Orchard: The Story of America's First Pet Cemetery*:** 40, 64, 112, 113 (left), 113 (right), 115

Getty Images, Inc.: Front and back covers, 2, 3, 5, 6, 8-9, 10, 11, 13, 14, 15, 16, 18, 19, 20, 21, 22, 23, 25, 28, 29, 30, 31, 32, 33, 34-35, 39, 42-43, 44 (inset), 55, 47, 48, 49, 51, 52, 53, 54, 55, 57 (bottom), 61, 62-63, 66, 70, 71, 72, 73, 78, 80, 81, 82, 83, 84, 85, 86, 87, 89, 92-93, 95, 96, 97, 98, 100, 104, 105, 106, 107, 108, 111, 125, 128-129, 130, 131, 134-135, 136, 137, 138, 139, 140-141, 142, 143, 144

Jean-Louis Nou: 91

The Princely State of Junagadh: 90

The Liberace Foundation and Museum: 76, 77

The Lyndon Johnson Library and Museum: 26-27

The Rajiv Gandhi family collection: 116-117

The Royal Archives, H.M. Queen Elizabeth II, Windsor Castle: 120-121, 122, 123, 124

Facing Page: A couple preparing for the baptism ceremony of their pet dog, c. 1930.

Acknowledgements

We would like to thank Frances Dimond, The Royal Archives, H.M. Queen Elizabeth II, Windsor Castle, UK; Getty Images UK; Edward C. Martin Jr., Director of Hartsdale Pet Cemetery; Pauline Lachance, Archivist/Historian at the Liberace Foundation & Museum; Corbis; The Lyndon Johnson Library and Museum; Mrs. Priyanka Vadra; and Major General Dr. R.M. Kharb, for their kind assistance.

American comedian Harold Lloyd playing with a Great Dane on a beach, c. 1920.

Contents

Introd

What do Winston Churchill, Liberace, Marilyn Monroe and Martina Navratilova have in common? Their love for their pets! Through the ages animals have served as faithful and favourite companions to the rich, famous and powerful. You are about to meet some of these VIPs – Very Important Pets. These pets, hailing from different countries and across different eras are as diverse as their owners. Whether it is the Duke and Duchess of Windsor's beloved pugs or Mike Tyson's tiger, the stories in this book bring alive the loving bond pet owners share with their pets. For the famous, pets serve as devoted and constant friends with whom they can share a quiet moment away from the scrutiny of the public eye. According to movie actress and pet lover Alicia Silverstone, humans are greedy and selfish and spend a lot of time taking and not giving, whereas animals are not like that. Research indicates that pet ownership positively impacts the owner's life by reducing stress and depression.

In return these VIPs live a life of extravagance. And what a life it is! Like their owners, these pets are

The big and the small of it: comic actors Laurel and Hardy with dogs for a publicity shot.

accustomed to the best money can buy – crocodile collar encrusted with emeralds, treatments at special pet spas, engraved silver bowls and of course, invites to A-list parties. Many treat their pets as surrogate children; they are therefore treated like a child would be – complete with baptism ceremonies, day-care centres and even summer camps!

From John Steinbeck, who wrote an entire book about his travels with his dog Charley, to French writer Colette who wrote a novel based on her cat Saha, pets have inspired artists and intellectuals and even served as their muse. In battle, animals have served as a symbol of support and motivation for tired soldiers and leaders. From Alexander the Great to General Patton in both World War I and II, leaders have relied on their pets to be companions as well as protectors. There are numerous stories of brave animals who, because of the heroic actions

during wartime and otherwise, have become famous in their own right. To acknowledge such animals a special 'animals' Victoria Cross' – the Dickin Medal – was established. Other animals who rocketed to international fame include Laika, Belka, Strelka, and 10 other canines who the Russians sent to space as part of the space race.

American Presidents through the centuries too have been known to be ardent pet owners and never shy away from a photo opportunity with their beloved pets. In fact there is an entire museum devoted to White House pets. President Nixon's black and white Cocker Spaniel, Checkers, became a political issue during a presidential election as his owner was accused of accepting gifts during his campaign. The Spaniel was also the subject of the much remembered speech by Nixon that came to be known as the 'Checkers speech'. More recently Bill Clinton's dog Buddy proved to be a loyal companion during what must have been the most difficult time in the former president's life – the immediate aftermath of his grand jury testimony.

Royalty across the world have also lavished their love and attention on their pets. One extreme case is of the Maharaja of Junagadh in India, who organized a three-day extravagant wedding for his favourite dog. Great Britain's Queen Elizabeth II's love for dogs – Corgis in particular – is no secret. In fact, along with her late sister Princess Margaret, the Queen has created a whole new dog breed – Dorgis – which are a cross between Daschunds and Corgis.

Animals have also etched their names in celluloid history by playing lead roles in many box office successes. Take the case of canine heroine Lassie who, since first appearing on screen in 1941 has captured

Facing page: 14 year old Lady Diana Spencer who later became the wife of Prince Charles, being kissed by her pet pony.

Bottom: Henry Behrens, the smallest man in the world in 1956, dancing with his pet cat in the doorway of his Worthing home. Measuring only 30 inches high, Mr. Behrens made a living by travelling the world with Burton Lester's midget troupe.

the hearts of children and adults alike. She was even awarded a US Citation for the Program for Conservation at a reception hosted by First 'Lady Bird' Johnson at the White House. Rin Tin Tin, the German Shepherd is credited with saving Warner Brothers from financial ruin during the silent film era. At the peak of his career with Warner Brothers Rin Tin Tin received some 10,000 fan letters a week and was considered to be one of Hollywood's top stars. And did you know that the Winnie the Pooh, faithful companion to children for almost eight decades, was named after a real American black bear called Winnie who lived in the London Zoo? Winnie was first found during World War I when troops from Winnipeg (Canada) were being transported to Eastern Canada, and from there on to Europe.

These fascinating stories and many many more form this collection. Despite their famous owners, make no mistake – the VIPs here are very much the pets!

Adolf Hitler

To Die For: Hitler's Blondi

Blondi, a female Alsatian (German Shepherd) who belonged to Nazi dictator Adolf Hitler, had an unusual talent: Blondi could sing – and we are told, could even sing an octave higher on command! When the Soviet Army closed in on Hitler's bunker in Berlin in 1945, Hitler and some of his staff planned to commit suicide by consuming cyanide. The first pellet was tested on Blondi. Blondi was initially buried in a shell crater near Hitler's bunker.

On 30 April 1945, in keeping with Hitler's orders, Blondi, Hitler and his wife, Eva Braun were cremated with diesel fuel in the Reich Chancellery garden above his bunker. Later, the cremated remains were interred outside the emergency exit of Hitler's bunker. The charred remains were discovered by the Russians and shipped to Moscow to confirm their identity. In February 1946, the remains were again moved to a Soviet Smersh facility in Magdenburg. Allegedly, the remains were moved one last time in 1982 and finally immersed into a nearby Danube River tributary.

Top: Hitler with his wife, Eva Braun, photographed with their dogs at Berchtesgaden. The picture is from a photo album belonging to Eva Braun, discovered by the Americans at Frankfurt.

Left: Portrait of Corporal Adolf Hitler, right, with two other soldiers and a dog during his stay in a military hospital, WWI, Pasewalk, Pomerania.

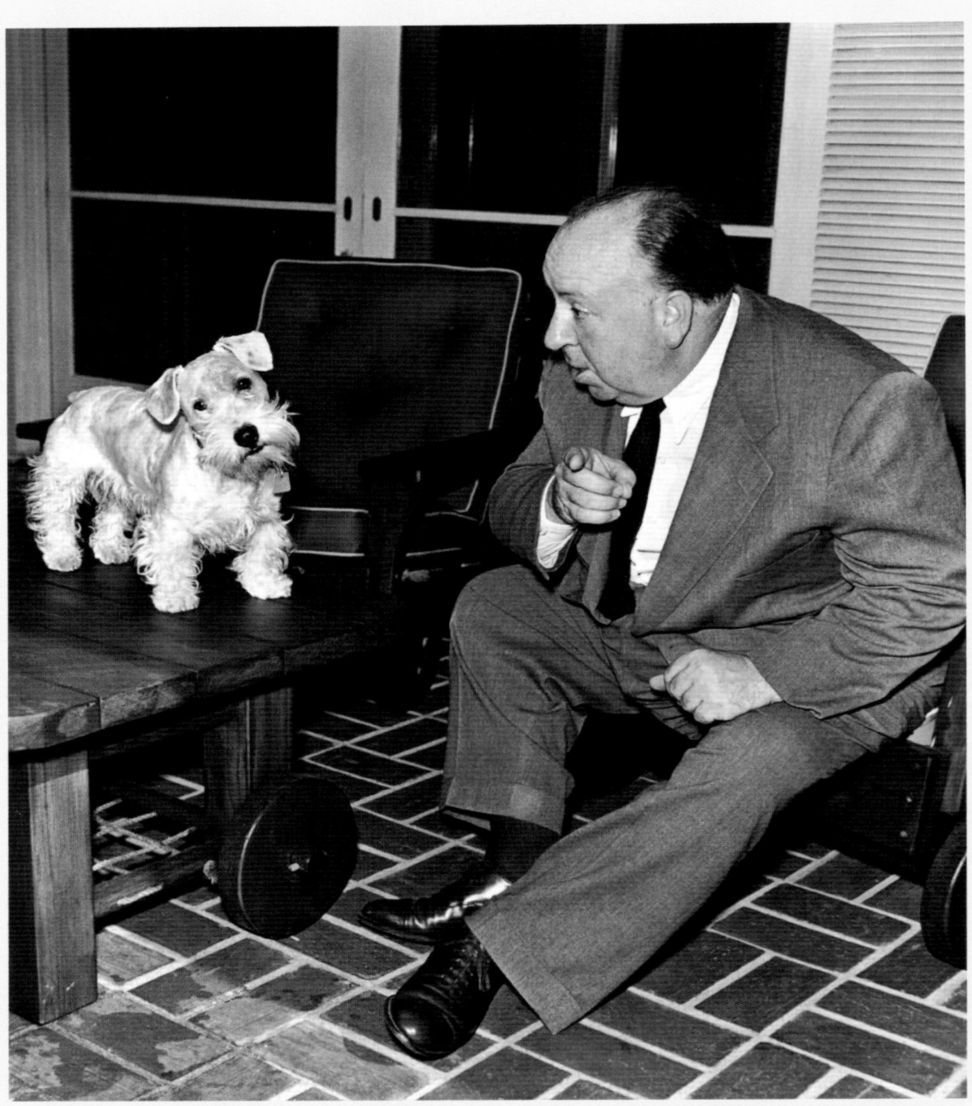

Alfred Hitchcock

Renowned film director Alfred Hitchcock, owned two white Sealyham Terriers who made guest appearances with him in his cameos in *Suspicion* (1941) and *The Birds* (1963).

Dr. Albert Schweitzer

Nobel Prize winner and renowned French medical missionary Dr. Albert Schweitzer was known to be a real animal lover. Sizi was one of Dr. Schweitzer's favourite cats, despite the fact she was domineering. Sizi would frequently fall asleep on the doctor's left arm. Rather than moving her (as he was left-handed), Dr. Schweitzer became ambidextrous so as not to disturb her while he wrote out prescriptions. He also had many exotic animal companions, including pelicans, antelopes, chimpanzees and gorillas. He raised his two antelopes, Leonie and Theodore (seen in the photograph) , from infancy and enjoyed taking evening strolls with the graceful creatures.

Audrey Hepburn

Audrey's Famous Love

The beautiful Audrey Hepburn's most beloved animal companion was her Yorkshire Terrier, Famous (also known as Mr. Famous or Famey). Famous appears in the Paris scene in *Funny Face*, in Audrey Hepburn's arm in the 'Anna Karenina' shot (facing page). She also loved taking Famous for cycle rides between film sets, in a basket made especially for him!

Famous was run over on Wiltshire Boulevard during the shooting of *The Children's Hour*, after which Hepburn's husband Mel Ferrer presented her with another Yorkshire Terrier, Sam. Later in life, Hepburn owned up to five Jack Russell Terriers named Missy, Tuppy, Penny, Piceri and Jackle.

All the Presidents' Pets

Presidential pets have often been the most popular residents of the White House. The presidential love affair with animals dates back to George Washington, who was devoted to his horse, Nelson. John Quincy Adams kept an alligator on the grounds, and Thomas Jefferson's family owned a pet bear!

During Lincoln's time, the White House was a menagerie of rabbits, turkeys, horses and goats. Theodore Roosevelt hosted more animals than any other President before or since. Roosevelt and his six children shared a deep affection for animals, and their collection included Guinea pigs, dogs, rabbits, lizards, bears, chickens, a badger, a blue macaw, a barn owl, a pony and a pig named Maude.

Some presidential pets were gifts from visiting dignitaries. Rutherford B. Hayes was gifted a Siamese cat from the American consul in Bangkok in 1878. The president named the cat Siam. His new pet is believed to have been the first Siamese cat ever to reach the United States. Rebecca, a raccoon, was presented to Calvin Coolidge, who built a special home for her and walked her by the leash on the White House grounds.

With the advent of popular media, the role White House pets have played in presidential lives as well as in history, has become more apparent. Fala, Franklin Roosevelt's Scottish Terrier, is remembered for being present when Winston Churchill and the President signed the Atlantic Charter in 1941 aboard the *USS Augusta*. Fala was the subject of the first presidential pet biography, a tradition that First Lady Barbara Bush continued with her book about the Bushs' Springer Spaniel, Millie, and by Hillary Clinton in her book about Socks, the Clintons' cat and Buddy, President Clinton's chocolate Labrador.

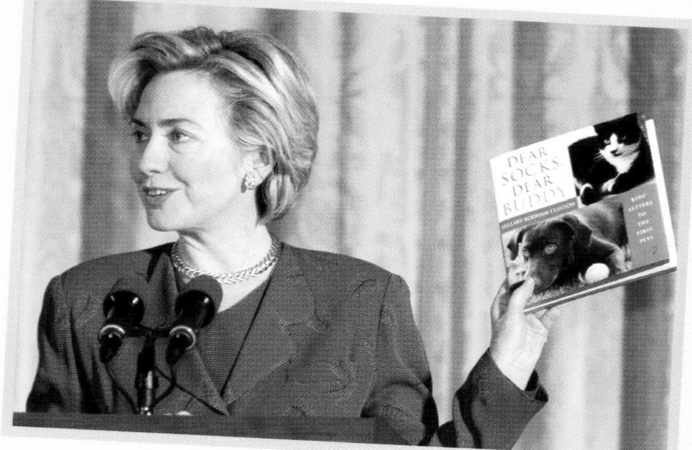

Top: Former First Lady Hillary Rodham Clinton during a White House ceremony to celebrate the launch of the children's book *Dear Socks, Dear Buddy.*

Facing page: Former President Lyndon Johnson's pet Beagles, Him and Her, sitting together on the White House lawn.

Pets have been used as political ploys. On the suggestion of an adviser, Herbert Hoover took in a German Shepherd named King Tut. This was said to enhance his image with the public. However, a pet could often harm a political career as well; when Lyndon Johnson was photographed holding his Beagle, Him, by the ears, the Republican leadership in Congress predicted it would damage Johnson's political career.

Presidential pets give us a glimpse into the more intimate, relaxed and caring side of these powerful figures. According to some reports, these pets have played a major role in alleviating stress and serving as listening posts for the commander in chief in challenging times, not to mention that many of them have been a part of history in the making!

Franklin D. Roosevelt

Fala, FDR's little black Scottish Terrier, was his constant companion, so much so that the Secret Service agents worried that the dog's presence drew too much attention to the President. FDR harboured no such fears – against advice, he brought Fala along to at least one of his three inaugurations, and was said to prefer his company to that of most people. In August 1941, Fala was at the Atlantic Charter Conference in Placentia Bay, Newfoundland with the President and British Prime Minister Winston Churchill. In September 1942 and April 1943, Fala went on inspection trips of defence plants and visited Monterey, Mexico and President Camacho of Mexico. In 1944, Fala was with the President on a sea trip to the Aleutian Islands. Rumours spread that Fala was accidentally left on one of the islands. During the 1944 presidential campaign, the Republicans accused FDR of spending millions

Top: Fala listening to President Roosevelt's speech on the radio on New Year Day, 1944.

Left: FDR pets Fala on a cruise ship to the Caribbean before heading for Warm Springs, GA.

of taxpayers' dollars in sending a destroyer back for Fala. The President answered the attack in his famous Fala speech while talking to the Teamsters Union, defending his loyal Scottish Terrier. When FDR died, the shaggy black dog rode his master's funeral train from Warm Springs to Washington D.C. Fala was heartbroken. Eleanor Roosevelt, FDR's widow tells the story of how Fala never really adjusted to his master's death. Once, in 1945, when General Eisenhower came to lay a wreath on FDR's grave, the gates of the regular driveway were opened and his automobile approached the house accompanied by the wailing of the sirens of a police escort. When Fala heard the sirens, his legs straightened out, his ears pricked up as if he expected to see his master coming down the drive as he had come so many times. When Fala died in 1952, he was buried at his master's feet. A statue of Fala accompanies FDR's Memorial in Washington D.C.

John F. Kennedy and Family

America's best-loved political family was also an animal-loving one. John Fitzgerald Kennedy and his family brought to the White House a collection of animals that continued to expand while he was in office. First Lady Jacqueline Kennedy designed a special play area for the children in the West Wing, complete with living quarters for their dogs, ducks, rabbits, guinea pigs, and ponies. The most famous of these was Caroline Kennedy's pony, Macaroni, given to her by then Vice-President Lyndon Johnson. Macaroni became a mini-celebrity in his own right receiving many letters from children all over the world. He would proudly pull the two Kennedy children in a sleigh around the South Lawn when the ground was covered with snow. In 1961 Soviet premier Nikita Khrushchev added to the Kennedys' menagerie by gifting them with a puppy named Pushinka. When asked about his earliest memories, John F. Kennedy Jr. recalled playing with his dog Pushinka on the slide as his first memory. In later years JFK Jr.'s love for animals

Jacqueline Bouvier, on her 10th birthday, seated with her dog Tammy at a dog show at East Hampton Fair, Long Island.

Christmas day, 1962. The Kennedy and Radziwill family at the White House with the Kennedy pets.

continued – the tabloids often caught him playing with his dog, Friday, a white Canaan, in Central Park.

When JFK Jr. died in 1999 Senator Edward Kennedy, in his eulogy, related a dog story about his nephew. 'He campaigned for me during my 1994 election and always caused a stir when he arrived in Massachusetts. Before one of his trips to Boston, John told the campaign he was bringing along a companion, but would need only one hotel room. Interested, but discreet, a senior campaign worker picked John up at the airport and prepared to handle any media barrage that might accompany John's arrival and his mystery companion. John landed with the companion alright – an enormous German Shepherd named Sam he had just rescued from the pound.'

May 1965: Jacqueline Kennedy standing with her daughter, Caroline (holding her pet Pug by the leash), her son JFK Jr., and her nephew, Anthony Radziwill, outside the Buckhingham Palace as they watch the Changing of the Guard ceremony. The family was in London for the inauguration of the Memorial to John F. Kennedy at Runnymede.

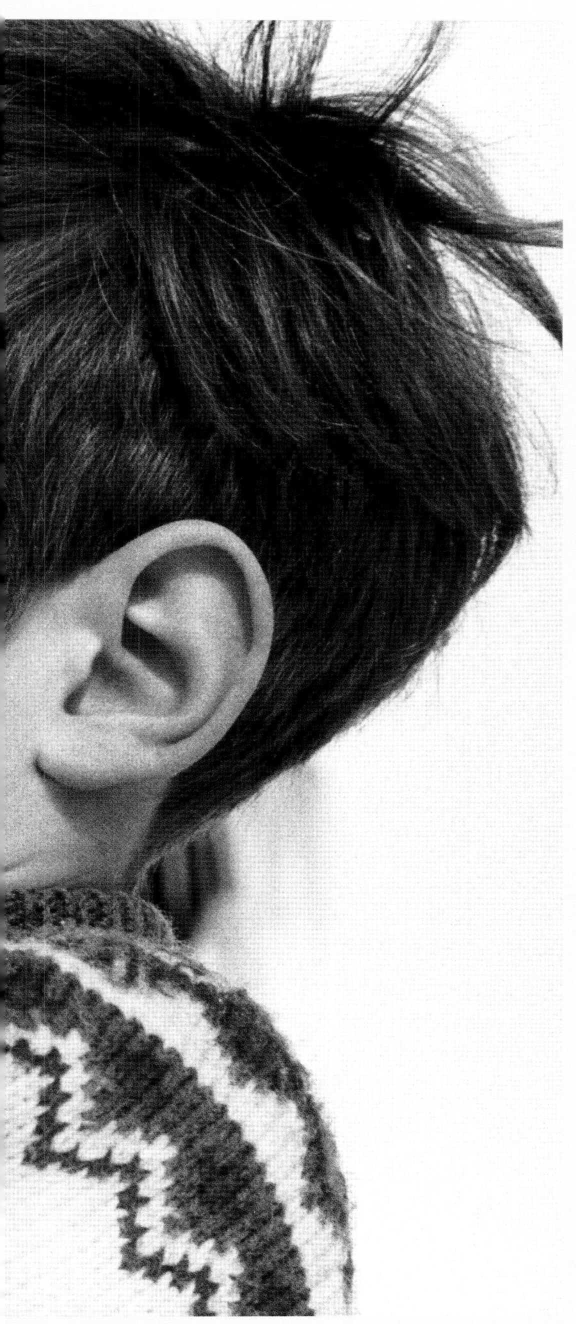

Top: JFK Jr. walks with his dog along the beach in Hyannisport, MA, the day after his grandmother, Rose Kennedy's death in 1995.

Left: JFK Jr. shares a moment with his puppy Pushinka, who was a gift from Russian President Nikita Krushchev to the Kennedys in 1961.

Lyndon B. Johnson

President Johnson had several dogs during his time at the White House. Him and Her, both Beagles, were often seen taking a stroll with the President and his wife, 'Lady Bird', on the lawns of the White House. J. Edgar Hoover, director of the Federal Bureau of Investigation, presented President Johnson with another Beagle, Edgar, after Him died. Blanco was a white Collie presented to the Johnsons by a little girl in Illinois. And finally, there was Yuki, the singing dog. Yuki was a mixed-breed dog found by President Johnson's daughter, Luci Nugent, at a gas station in Texas on Thanksgiving Day in 1966, on her way to the LBJ Ranch. Luci named the dog Yuki from *yukimas*, which means 'snow' in Japanese. At first, Yuki lived with Luci, but on a visit to the White House, Yuki won the President's heart and became his faithful companion. On the President's birthday, 27 August 1967, Luci told her father that he could keep Yuki. Yuki and President Johnson delighted visiting dignitaries by singing 'duets' together at the Oval Office. When President Johnson left office on 20 January 1969, Yuki returned to the LBJ Ranch with the President on Air Force One. After Johnson's death in January 1973, Yuki went to live with Luci Nugent and her family.

President Johnson singing with Yuki for British ambassador K.E. Bruce at the Oval Office on 6 February 1968.

Richard M. Nixon

One of the most famous presidential pets in U.S. history was a black and white spotted Cocker Spaniel named Checkers, who saved the career of Richard Nixon in 1952 when he was campaigning to be Vice-President of the United States. Accused of setting up a secret 'slush fund' with donations from political cronies, Nixon appeared on television and gave an emotional speech in which he referred to his 'little dog Checkers,' a gift from a supporter. He and his family loved this dog so much, he declared, that returning it was unthinkable. The public loved the Checkers reference, and Nixon secured the nomination. Nixon's beloved dog died in 1964 at the age of 18.

Left: President Ford studies budget matters at the Oval Office while petting his Golden Retriever, Liberty.

Top: President Ford takes a moment to play with Liberty at the Oval Office.

Facing page: President Nixon relaxing with Checkers after a long day.

Top: Nancy Reagan pets the Bushs' Golden Cocker Spaniel on their first visit to the Bush residence in Washington DC in 1981.

Bottom and right: The Reagans and their pet dogs and cats on holiday at their ranch in California.

Bill Clinton and Family

Buddy, a chocolate Labrador, became a part of the Clinton family in December 1997. Although the First Family received over 5,000 suggestions on what to name the dog, Bill Clinton finally named the dog Buddy, after his beloved great-uncle, Henry Oren 'Buddy' Grisham who had been a father figure to Clinton, and a dog trainer for 50 years. Buddy was frequently seen at the President's side at the White House and on his travels abroad where he was a great source of attraction.

Chelsea Clinton's cat Socks moved into the White House in 1993, and was the first cat to live in the White House after Jimmy Carter's daughter, Amy Carter's cat, Misty Malarky Ying Yang.

Socks and Buddy didn't get along at all. One of their fights was even caught on camera during a press conference at the White House! In 2000 Buddy moved to New York with Bill Clinton. Buddy died in 2002 when he was hit by a car.

Top: The Clintons and Buddy returning from a vacation in Martha's Vineyard in August 1998.

Left: Socks taking a ride on President Clinton's shoulders as he walks on the White House grounds.

George W. Bush and Family

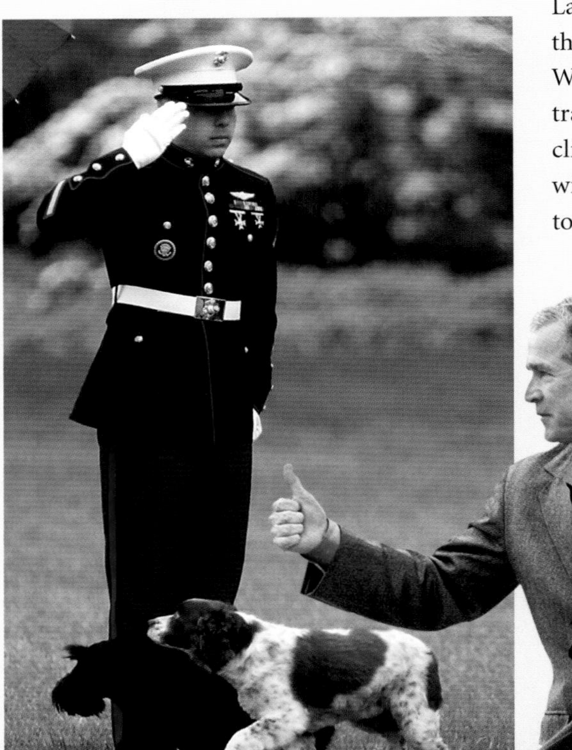

Spot, an English Springer Spaniel, was the daughter of Millie, a dog owned by the President George W. Bush's father and mother, former President George Bush and Barbara Bush. In fact, Spot was born in the White House in 1989, when the elder Bushes lived there. Spot was the only dog to have lived in the White House twice with two different presidents. The Bushes have another dog, Barney, a Scottish Terrier, who was a gift from New Jersey Governor Christie Whitman to Laura Bush. The two dogs animatedly greeted the President when he would return to the White House from trips, and often even travelled with the Bushes. Spot would dutifully climb onto a helicopter or Air Force One without being told, but Bush would always have to chase Barney down and hand him to an aide to be carried aboard. Mrs. Bush often said that with the Bushs' two daughters away at college talking about and playing with the dogs and the family cat, India, was a large part of the couple's entertainment. India 'Willie' Bush, a black cat, has been a beloved member of the Bush family for more than 10 years. The family named her after the former Texas Ranger baseball player, Ruben Sierra, who was called 'El Indio.' Spot was put to sleep in February 2004 after suffering a series of strokes. Her remains were taken to the President's ranch in Crawford, Texas.

Facing page:
Presidential dogs Spot and Barney walk past a saluting US Marine.

Right:
President Bush hands over Barney to First Lady Laura Bush before climbing aboard Air Force One.

Following page:
Former President George Bush relaxing on the White House lawn with three puppies nestled against him. Millie, an English Springer Spaniel gave birth to the puppies in March 1989. One of the puppies, named Spot, remained with the Bush family until her death in 2004.

Betty White

Heart of Gold

Kitta

Any book on celebrities and pets has to include Betty White. This *Golden Girl* is as passionate about animals as she is about acting. A member of the Television Hall of Fame and six-time Emmy Award winner for her roles on *The Mary Tyler Moore Show* and on *The Golden Girls*, this busy actress has been a part of television since 1949. Her love of animals, however, started long before that and was inculcated by her parents. There is an interesting story Betty often narrates about her father. During the Depression her father made radios to earn extra money. However, nobody had any money to buy radios. So he would trade them for dogs. Finding homes for dogs and cats is just one of the ways that Betty White helps animals. She is involved with numerous animal charities and is a board member of Actors and Others for Animals and has been appointed to the Los Angeles Zoo Commissioners.

The author of four books including one on animals, Betty has two dogs and a cat of her own. She is reported to have written a will that leaves her estate estimated at $5 million for the benefit of her pets. Kitta her Golden Retriever was socialized in Alaska to be a guide dog, but did not go in for formal training because his hips did not measure up to the required size. Her Shih Tzu, Panda, is a rescue. She spent the first six months of her life in a cage because she was impounded as evidence in the trial. A pet store sold this sick dog to a woman who took it back. The pet store said they would take care of it. But when she went back to check on it the next day, she found this same sick dog in the window for sale. So she blew the whistle and turned them in to the authorities. Panda closed a pet shop all by herself! Betty's Himalayan cat is named Bob Cat.

Betty White has often said that her animal work gives her the most joy. She says her favourite experience, however, was a show she created, wrote, produced, and hosted in 1970 and 1971, syndicated around the country, called *The Pet Set*. The show featured celebrities and their pets.

Lord Byron

Boatswain and Others

Lord Byron, the romantic English poet, shared his estate, Newstead Abbey, with a tame bear, a wolf, a hedgehog, tortoises, horses, monkeys and cats, to name a few. While a student at Cambridge, Byron was annoyed that the university rules banned keeping a dog. Instead, he decided to keep a tame bear; since there was no mention of bears in the statutes, the college authorities had no legal basis to complain!

But Byron's most beloved companion was his Newfoundland dog named Boatswain. The dog had a habit of following the post boy and on one such occasion was bitten by a rabid dog. As Boatswain foamed at the mouth, Byron gently wiped away the foam with his bare hands. After Boatswain's death, Byron erected a monument on the dog's grave at Newstead Abbey that read: 'One who possessed beauty without vanity, Strength without insolence, Courage without ferocity and all the virtues of man without his vices.'

Facing page: George Gordon Noel Byron, also known as Lord Byron, became an important figure in the Romantic movement of English poetry. He is seen here with one of his dogs, Lyon, in Greece, where he died whilst fighting in the Greek War of Independence c. 1715.

Christine Norman

Sandy

Crazy Love

In the 1920s Broadway actress, Christine Norman was considered one of the most beautiful women in the world. She seemed to have everything: beauty, talent, money and fame. Her suicide in 1930 was major news, but the bigger headlines came when her will was probated. As one newspaper announced: 'Miss Christine Norman's Will, Disposing of $150,000, Fails to Mention Mother.' Along with bequests to a number of friends, her will instructed a certain amount of money to be put aside for the upkeep of her Japanese Terrier, Sandy's grave at the Hartsdale Pet Cemetery. Ms. Norman's estranged husband, and her mother took the matter to court, confident that the 'insanity' of such a legacy would never be allowed to stand. Arthur Garfield Hayes, the well-known lawyer and civil libertarian successfully argued that Ms. Norman's will merely reflected a caring, loving woman of integrity. The court agreed and ruled the will valid. Her Terrier had won, and the actress' wishes were respected and carried out.

A rare photo of Christine Norman on stage, holding her dog Sandy in her arms.

Christine Norman's 'crazy' love for her dog, and her thoughtfulness in demonstrating and sustaining it in her will were much more important and far-reaching than the actress could have imagined. She probably never thought of her will as a document for the rights of pets and people, but that was the result. The legal precedent set in the lawsuit over Christine Norman's will has protected many others in a similar situation.

Doris Duke

Sole heir to her father, founder of American Tobacco Company, James Buchanan Duke's fortune at the age of 12, heiress Doris Duke came to be known as one of the world's most eccentric divas. At her home in Rough Point in Newport, Rhode Island, Doris is said to have let her pet camels, Baby and Princess, occupy the solarium during a hurricane. Even after her death, Duke continued to provoke controversy. Considered a shrewd money manager and investor, Duke's $30-million inheritance spiralled to a $750-million fortune due to her own money smarts. She was worth $1.5 billion when she died in 1993. In a will that provided for her camels, she settled a $100,000 trust fund on her beloved dog Minnie. Her widely publicized will briefly put her butler in charge as executor. The executor of the Duke estate went to court to can the canine trust, a move Minnie's new owner opposed. However, New York judge Eve Preminger's decision was in favour of Minnie.

Dusty Springfield

Dusty Springfield's love of cats is as much a legend as the great woman herself. The 60s pop star whose brooding, soulful voice won her international acclaim died in 1999 after a five-year battle with cancer. However, she made sure that her beloved cat Nicholas was going to be cared for even after she was gone. She arranged for the cat, a stray Californian Ragdoll she rescued, to be adopted by her friend Lee Everett-Alkin. Among the luxuries said to be enjoyed by Nicholas was a diet of imported American baby food. Dusty specified that Nicholas's bed was to be lined with her night-gown and that her recordings were to be played each night at his bedtime. Lee Everett-Alkin kept this promise and also moved the cat's 7-foot indoor tree house into her own home! Dusty had another cat, Malaysia, who died in 1990. When Malaysia was run over by a car, Dusty dedicated her 1990 album, *Reputation* to her, writing, 'May the great litter box in the sky have room for us all.' Nicholas too gets a mention on the sleeve notes of *A Very Fine Love*. Nicholas is reported to have died at the grand old age of 21.

Colette

The French author Colette **(right)** whose real name was Sidonie Gabrielle Claudine Goudeket, owned several Chartreux cats as pets. In 1933, she made one of them, Saha, the heroine of her book *La Chatte*, in which she devoted some beautiful descriptions to her cat. Saha was her muse and her inspiration to write beautiful verses. She referred to Saha as her 'blue pigeon', her 'pearl gray devil', and her 'little bear with fat cheeks and golden eyes'. The Chartreux is one of the oldest natural breeds of cats.

Charles Dickens

Victorian author Charles Dickens enjoyed the company of a cat called Williamina. Williamina insisted on dragging her kittens from their designated home in the kitchen and placing them in the master's study at his feet. One of these kittens was deaf and as nobody wanted it, Dickens kept it, and called it Master's Cat. In the evening, the cat, bored with watching Dickens read, learnt to distract the master's attention by extinguishing the candle with a swipe of its paw, making work impossible and play essential! Eleanor Poe Barlow, a Dickens scholar, wrote *The Master's Cat: The Story of Charles Dickens as Told by his Cat*. The book, written from a 'cat's eye' point of view is a biography of sorts.

Elizabeth Taylor

'Nibbles and Me'

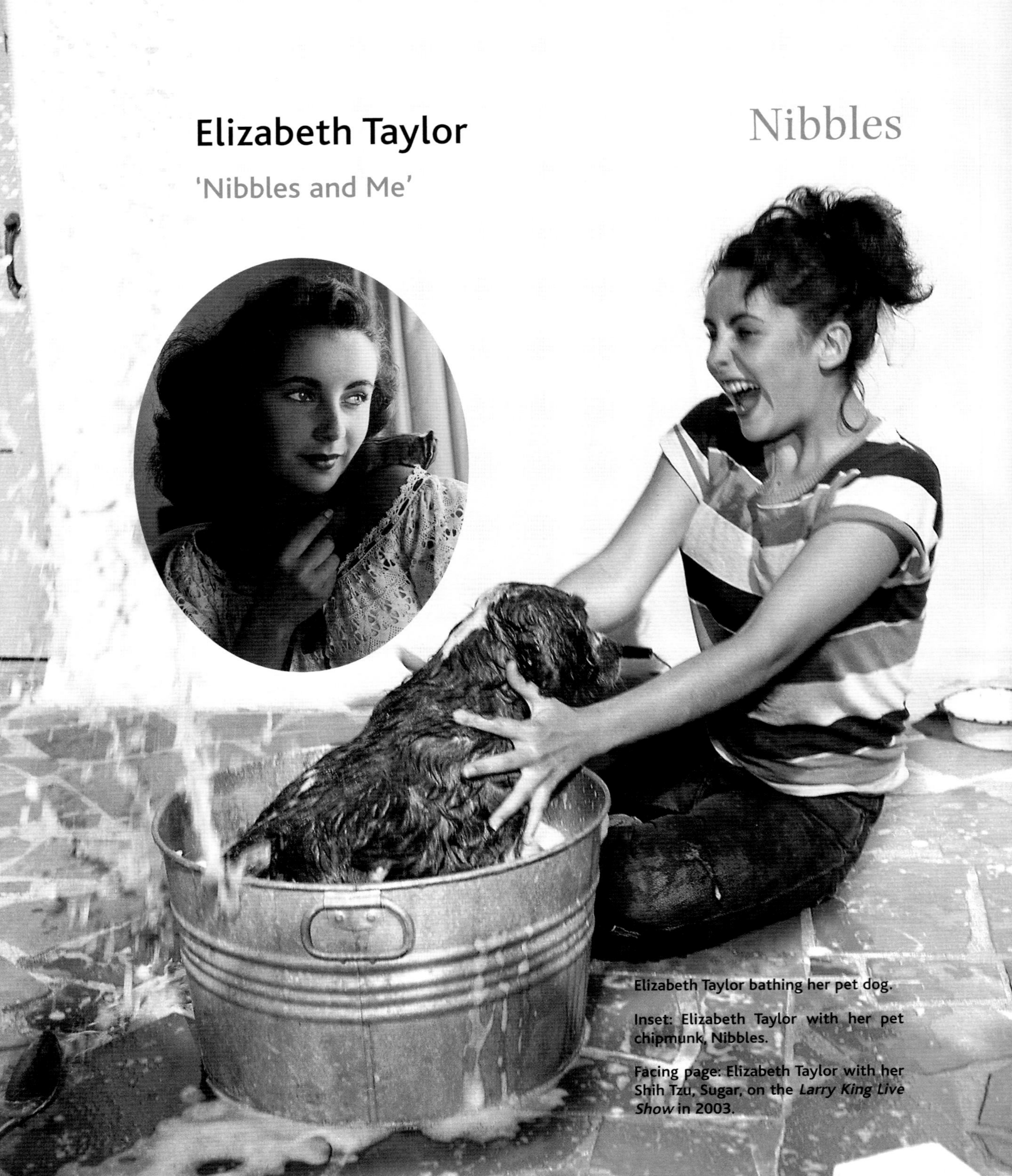

Elizabeth Taylor bathing her pet dog.

Inset: Elizabeth Taylor with her pet chipmunk, Nibbles.

Facing page: Elizabeth Taylor with her Shih Tzu, Sugar, on the *Larry King Live Show* in 2003.

In 1946, Elizabeth Taylor – then 14 and a major star at MGM – published a book about her pet chipmunk, Nibbles called *Nibbles and Me*. She and Nibbles (facing page, inset) were virtually inseparable during the shooting of *National Velvet* and other films; in fact the chipmunk almost got to appear in *The Courage of Lassie* – but he was so well behaved that he didn't look real, and his scene was cut! Elizabeth Taylor remembers the happiest birthday of her life, when she was given King Charles, the horse who was called The Pi in *National Velvet*, because only she could ride him. Taylor also has a great love for dogs. She currently owns Shih Tzus who are often seen with her at A-list events.

Elvis Presley

The King's Love of Dogs

The legendary Elvis Presley is known the world over for the impact he had on the world of music and fashion. One very important part of his life was his love for animals. Boy was the first dog Elvis acquired shortly after he began to achieve stardom. Baba, a Collie, went to Hollywood with Elvis and starred in the film *Paradise, Hawaiian Style* (1966). Getlo was a Chow who Elvis really adored. In 1975, before she was a year old, Getlo developed serious kidney problems and Elvis spent thousands of dollars in an effort to save her life. She eventually died very young. Elvis's Great Pyrenee, Muffin, seemed to have an incurably bad temper, which even obedience school couldn't improve. Even Elvis was bitten a few times! Elvis gave a tiny dog he called Sweetpea to his mother Gladys in 1956. After Gladys's death, Elvis continued to care for the dog. Teddy Bear of Zi-Pom-Pom was a pedigreed Poodle given to Elvis by a fan when he was in the army in Germany. Apparently the dog accompanied Elvis back to the United States when he returned. Elvis used to give dogs as gifts to people he loved. He gave his wife Priscilla a pair of Great Danes, Snoopy and Brutus, in the 60s. Brutus can be seen playing the role of Albert in the movie *Live a Little, Love a Little* (1968). The dog died not long after Elvis and Priscilla divorced. Snoopy later became Lisa Marie's (Elvis and Priscilla's daughter) dog. Elvis loved other animals besides dogs. Graceland, his home in Memphis, Tennessee, was also home for many other pets. Some were unusual, such as a chimpanzee named Scatter, a Mynah bird and even peacocks, but others were more common, like horses. Today there are still horses at Graceland, and the mansion has been open to the public since 1982.

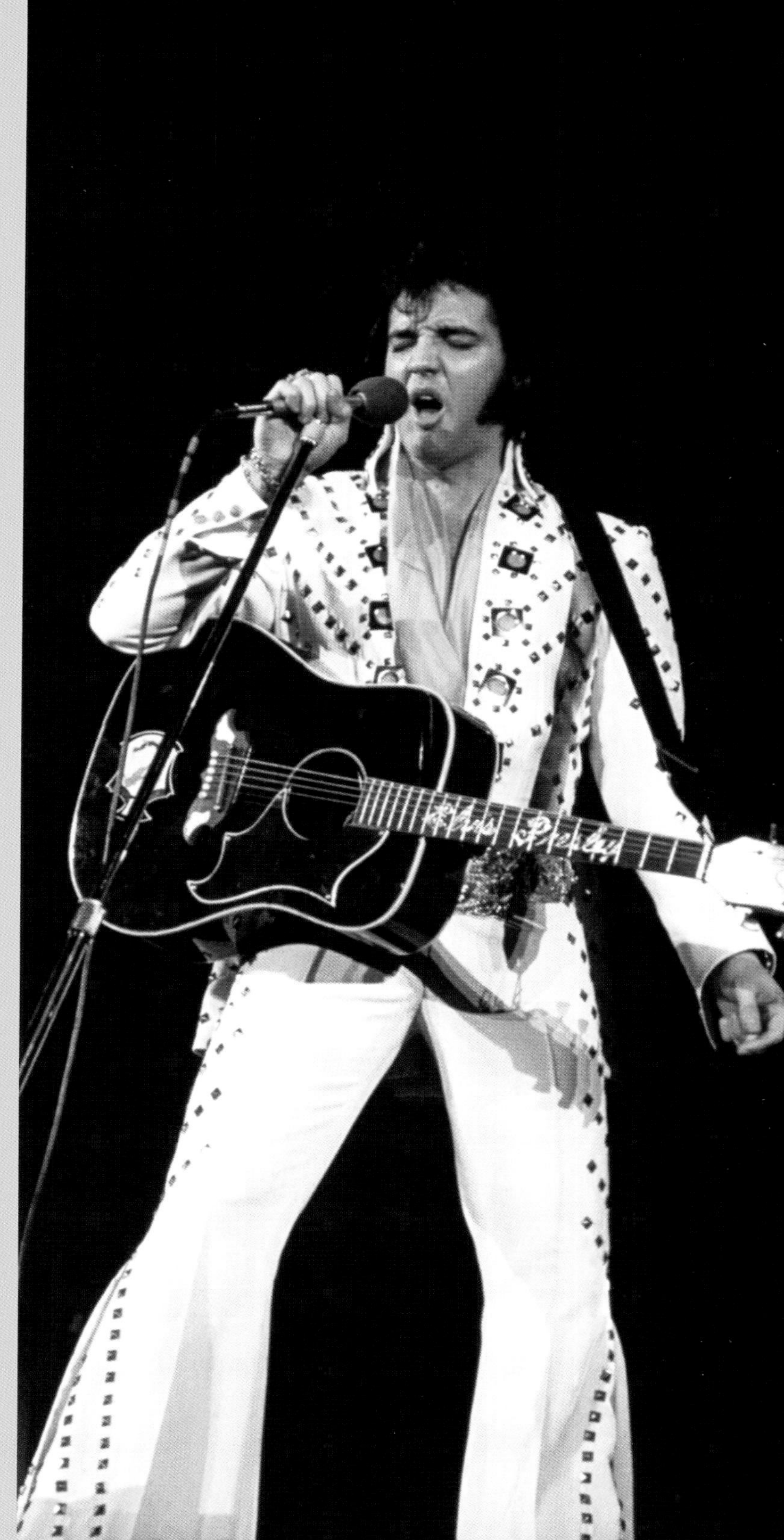

Ernest Hemingway

The Good Luck Cats

Ernest Hemingway, one of the most prolific and troubled writers of the last century was a great lover of the outdoors and had many pets during his lifetime. *Finca de Vigia,* the villa outside Havana where Hemingway lived from 1939-1960 includes the graves of four of Hemingway's dogs. Hemingway's fourth and last wife, Mary Welsh Hemingway, donated the estate to the Cuban government in 1961, just after the author committed suicide in his home in Ketchum, Idaho. Hemingway also had a villa in Key West, Florida, where he wrote some of his most famous works. The villa is now a museum. Its main attraction appears to be the inbred six-toed cats said to descend from Hemingway's pets. These cats who number up to 50 are cared for by the museum, as Hemingway stated in his will. Hemingway's first cat was a polydact, a cat with six toes. Hemingway was so taken with this unique character, which also was believed to bring good luck that he continued to acquire many polydacts. Hemingway held his cats in high regard because of their independent attitudes. The writer is said to have had 30 cats at one time with names ranging from Fats to Friendless Brother.

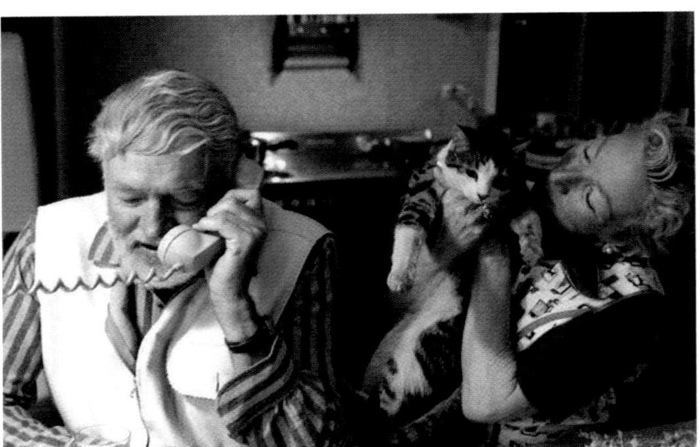

Ernest Hemingway with his wife and one of his numerous cats.

Facing page: Ernest Hemingway relaxing at home with his dog on the day he won the Nobel Prize for Literature for his novel *The Old Man And The Sea.*

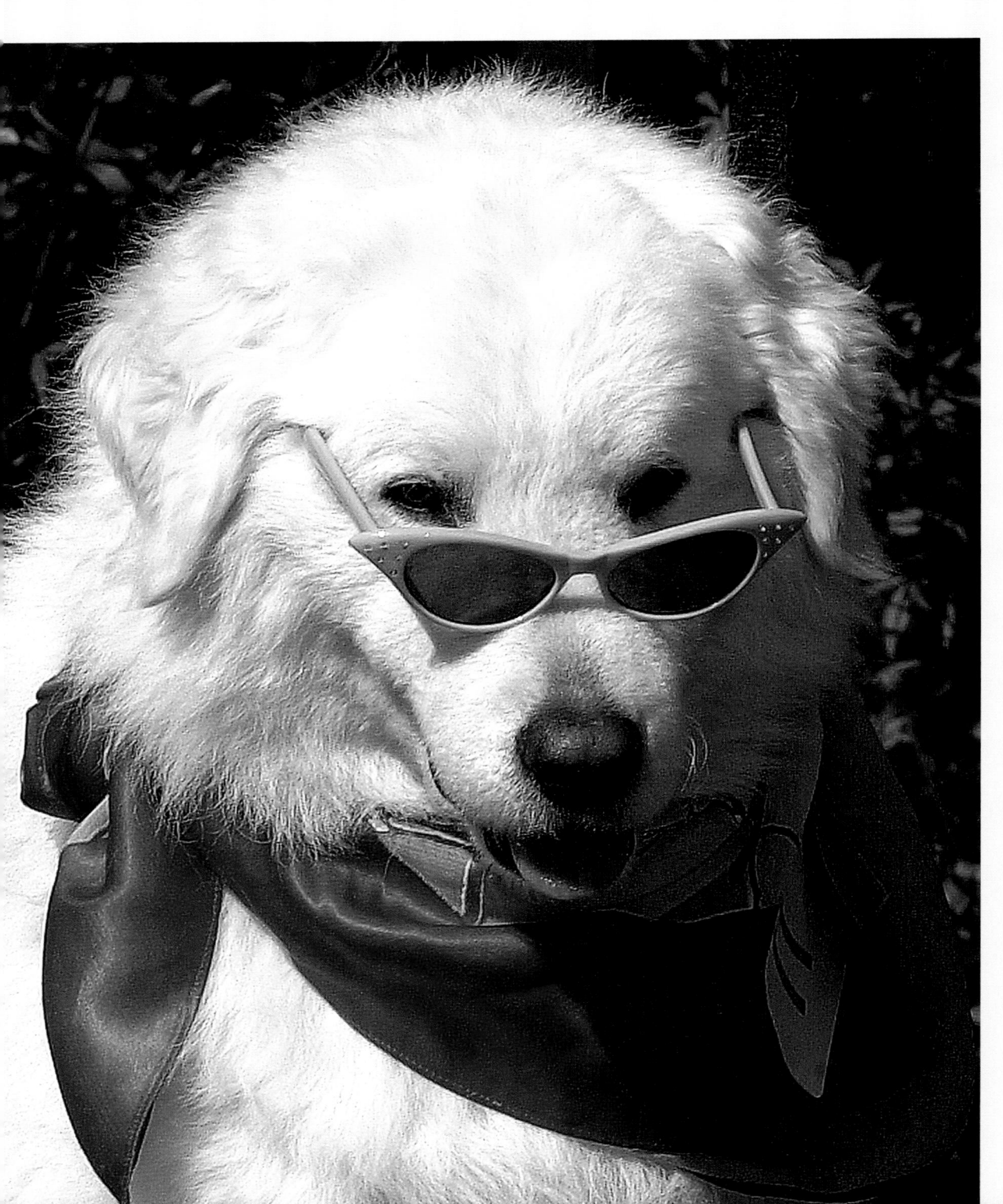

According to Joan Rivers, pets are extensions of their owners. Increasingly, pet owners want their pets to be well dressed, often in matching outfits and the latest trends. In Japan, there are magazines dedicated to 'dog couture,' and dog fashion is all the rage! This has sparked a line of pet fashions for special occasions, like Christmas and Halloween, as well as every day wear, and 'evening wear' for the glamorous pets accompanying their celebrity owners.

VIP Concierge

Animal Fair, a glossy lifestyle magazine for animal lovers, offers a service called VIP Concierge which puts canine lovers together with the top of pet merchandising ranging from designer doggie bags to canine cribs to veterinary products. They also arrange doggie birthday parties, and point out the latest in doggie fashion. Their white-gloved service directs owners to the best of dog groomers for canine coiffure and massages, customized dog-owner ensembles, as well as pet policy information for any form of travel. VIP Concierge was conceived when *Animal Fair*'s editors found themselves searching for custom-made products perfect for their pets.

Fashionable Dogs

Pets of the rich and famous have their own grooming salons, day-care centres and lines of accessories. Some pets even have their own wardrobes. Recently, no one has done more to promote this trend than Moonie (full name: Moondoggie) who played Bruiser, Reese Witherspoon's cherished companion and comic foil in the sequel to *Legally Blonde*. While Moonie doesn't have any dialogue in the movie, he manages to steal the film. How? With a lavish wardrobe ranging from an angora pom-pom sweater to an ermine-collared cloak! In the movie, Witherspoon's magnificently superficial Elle Woods, Harvard Law, Class of 2001,

Facing page: Marilyn Monroe's lookalike? A dog dressed like the Hollywood star.

Right: Supermodel Carmen Kass with her dog at the 2004 Sundance Film Festival.

Actress Susan Ward and her Boxer puppy Dixie **(left)**; Actress Ileana Douglas and her dog **(right)** at the launch party for the Fifi & Romeo Boutique in 2000. The Fifi & Romeo Boutique in Los Angeles sells luxury goods for dogs.

simultaneously organizes her wedding and sets out to find Bruiser's mother. Her quest takes her to the halls of Congress, where she lobbies for animal rights.

The studio called upon a specialist: doggie designer Yana Syrkin. Her Los Angeles dog boutique, Fifi & Romeo, is where Oprah Winfrey, Cameron Diaz, Diane Sawyer, the British royal family and many other celebrities purchase their pooches' threads. Moonie is accustomed to wearing togs. In winter, his trainer and owner Chipperton likes to drape him in sweaters to keep away the California chill. But getting him comfortable with *Legally Blonde 2*'s signature retro look – especially that pink Jackie O pillbox – took patience and an ample store of chicken tidbit treats. Moonie was rescued from the pound by Chipperton who envisioned him as a double for her most famous trainee, Gidget, the Taco Bell Chihuahua. But Moonie never got big enough for stand-in work. You can see the problem in *Legally Blonde 2*, in which Gidget plays Bruiser's mother.

Syrkin is an old hand at Chihuahua couture.

Her business grew out of her hobby of dressing up her own Mexican hairless, Yoda. At the time, Syrkin was a costume designer on *Ally McBeal.* Word spread through the Hollywood community and Syrkin was soon able to quit her day job to open Fifi & Romeo.

The Internet also sells a wide array of dog clothes and accessories – from fireman outfits, tennis togs, to kimonos and tuxedoes. Meatball, Adam Sandler's Bulldog, wore a tux to his master's wedding. High-end fashion houses including Kate Spade, Asprey & Garrard, Coach, Prada, Michael Simon, Gucci, Hermès and Louis Vuitton, all have a paw in the business. Not to miss out, MGM has licensed a pet accessory line inspired by *Legally Blonde 2*. So far, there's the Pink Collection (soft fleece beret with glittery star, reversible bandanas, a collar stamped 'Super Fun, Super Cute') and the Patriotic Collection (an Uncle Sam hat and harnesses in a star-and-bars pattern).

Gidget the Taco Bell Chihuahua

Gidget, the 'talking' Chihuahua shot to stardom in 1998 with the success of her Taco Bell ads, which featured her trademark slogan, '*Yo quiero Taco Bell.*' The adorable pooch was seemingly everywhere, with plush Chihuahua toys selling by the millions at Taco Bell stores. It was quite a rise for the former stray who was spotted by advertising directors, Chuck Bennett and Clay Williams, in Venice, California. They saw a Chihuahua 'cruising along down the boardwalk, looking large and in charge.' Gidget's bat-like ears, expressive eyes, and natural acting ability won her the spotlight. She made Chihuahuas all the rage, appearing in the Hollywood film, *Legally Blonde 2.* Celebrities like Madonna, Paris Hilton and Britney Spears now own this breed of dog.

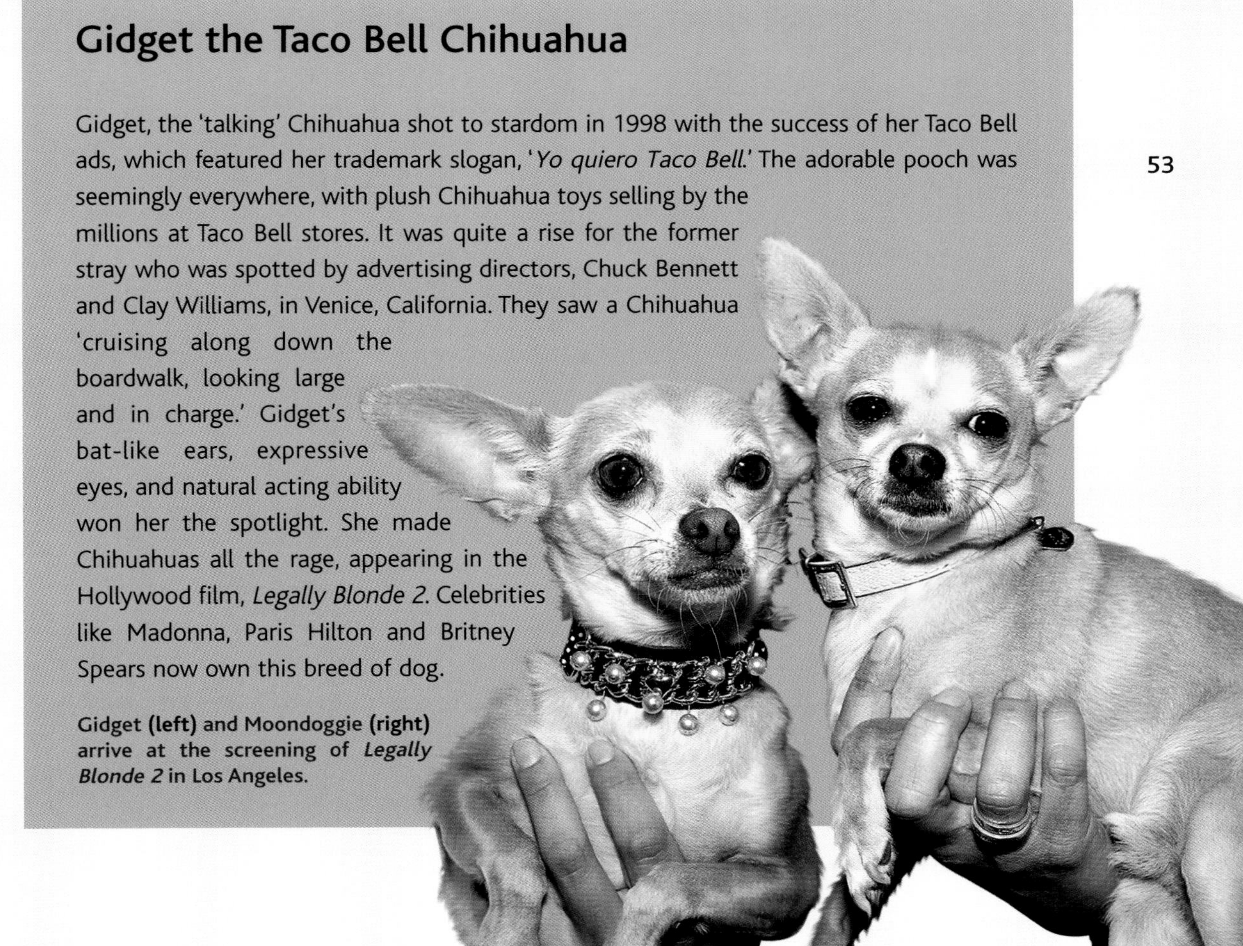

Gidget (left) and Moondoggie (right) arrive at the screening of *Legally Blonde 2* in Los Angeles.

Fitness centre and spa for pets in New York.

Yoga for Dogs

The latest trend in dog care is 'doga,' or yoga for dogs. This means, in between manicures and spa appointments chic pets will now also have to fit in regular yoga sessions with their owners. With books such as *Yoga for Pets* and *Doga: Yoga for Dogs* hitting the market, doga looks set to enter mainstream pet therapy. A fitness chain in New York holds monthly yoga classes for dogs called 'Ruff Yoga' at the Madison Square Gardens. Yoga poses are renamed to make them more appropriate for the canine clients – so child's pose becomes puppy's pose!

Top: Jane Fonda in a yoga pose with her cat.

Bottom: 'Ruff Yoga,' a monthly class for yoga enthusiasts and their canines in New York.

François Mitterand

Monsieur Baltique

In his will, former French President François Mitterand, asked that Baltique, his much loved black Labrador, should walk in his funeral procession. Baltique accompanied his master everywhere and was often seen walking with him near the family home in Lache. Baltique who was addressed in the polite French form *vous* by his masters, dined off Sèvres porcelain dishes, drank only mineral water, had two attendants and a car and chauffeur at his disposal. The dog joined the Mitterand family in 1986 and lived with them in the presidential quarters at the Palais de l'Elysée, where he would sniff up visiting dignitaries. On such occasions the President is said to have politely asked 'Monsieur Baltique' to please behave! Baltique shared the limelight at Mitterand's funeral along with world leaders such as Yasser Arafat, Prince Charles and Helmut Kohl. He was photographed at the funeral and the details of his behaviour gave rise to analyses of the way animals mourned – Baltique became listless, refused to eat, and visibly expressed his grief.

Frida Kahlo

Mother & Child

Caimito

When Mexican artist Frida Kahlo was left barren by an accident, her husband, Diego Riviera presented her with a pet spider monkey who Frida named Caimito. Caimito became the surrogate for a child Frida could not bear. Frida's inability to have children of her own was a central theme in her work. In many of her paintings and self-portraits, Frida would include her pet monkey as a surrogate child, looking like the infant Christ. In *Self Portrait with Monkeys*, an intense and rather strange painting, several monkeys' arms and tails wrap around her, but Frida's stoic gaze indicates her defiance in the face of the harshness of life.

General George Patton

'Willie the Conqueror'

Willie

General George Patton, a.k.a. Mad Dog, was mad about Bull Terriers. During World War II, General George S. Patton Jr. was often shown in photographs next to a small white dog. This dog was Willie, Patton's spunky Bull Terrier. Willie wasn't the first Bull Terrier that Patton owned. After World War I, Patton bought the first of several for his daughters Beatrice and Ruth Ellen, but Willie became the most famous. He wore bells around his neck – a sound that would often alert soldiers to the General's arrival – and supposedly Willie had his very own set of Army dog tags. Named after William the Conqueror, Willie was described as a bit gun-shy, but stayed at Patton's side during some of the worst battles of the war. He was devoted to General Patton and followed him everywhere. Willie had Patton's infamous stare and it was said that when people had to appear before Patton, they would also appear before Willie and would face the 'four meanest eyes ever witnessed.' Patton considered Willie his second in command and when the infamous General died, Willie was retired and sent to live out his days with Patton's wife and daughters.

Geri Halliwell

Harry

When Harry Met Geri

In her autobiography, *Just for the Record*, former Spice Girl Geri 'Ginger' Spice has outlined 36 essential requirements in a man, the last being 'Likes my dog.' This dog lover has been known to take her dogs to celebrity parties, signing events, recording studios and even London's Claridges Hotel where her Shih Tzu, Harry, accompanied her for high tea and gorged on cream cakes. One of Harry's first public appearances was at the South Bank Show Awards in London in 1999, where Geri took him up on stage to present an award. Harry has even made an appearance on the reality television show, *Popstars: The Rival* where Geri was a judge. Harry offered his own critique of the show by snoozing through most of it! Restaurants such as the former Notting Hill eatery Pharmacy, which had a strict no-dog policy, were known to make exceptions for Harry. At a photo shoot Geri was seen offering her cappuccino to the tiny pooch so he could lick all the froth, and lucky Harry was even allowed to eat food off her plate. Harry has his own room, but he prefers to sleep on Geri's bed, curled up against her stomach and is said to enjoy lukewarm tea! However it hasn't always been smooth sailing for Geri and Harry. When shopping at a designer store in West London, an embarrassed Geri had to apologize to the shop attendants when Harry decided to leave his mark on the shop's posh carpets. Harry and Geri have also featured on the cover of a lifestyle magazine in the UK. Other places where Harry has been spotted include the upmarket London restaurant Momo and Geri's gym, where she was told off for feeding Harry a muffin in the club restaurant. So protective is Geri of her pet pooch that she fired Harry's hair stylist when he revealed the name of his celebrity client to a British newspaper. Geri, who now spends an increasing amount of time in Los Angeles, has a new pet, a tiny Pomeranian, called Daddy, who friends say she got because she misses Harry who she left behind in the UK with her family.

Humphrey Bogart & Lauren Bacall

Named the Greatest Male Star of All Time by the American Film Institute, Humphrey Bogart (Bogie) and his fourth wife the actress, Lauren Bacall (Betty Joan Perske) purchased a home at 2707 Benedict Canyon Road in Beverly Hills, where they accumulated an array of animals. Their pets included 14 chickens, eight ducks and a large Boxer, seen here with his owners on their front lawn for a photo shoot.

DEDICATED
TO THE MEMORY OF
THE WAR DOG
ERECTED BY PUBLIC CONTRIBUTION
BY DOG LOVERS, TO MAN'S MOST
FAITHFUL FRIEND, FOR THE VALIANT
SERVICES RENDERED IN THE
WORLD WAR
1914 — 1918

To all faithful, loyal, brave and beloved animal friends – we salute you.

The Dickin Medal for Heroic Animals

In 1943, The PDSA'S (People's Dispensary For Sick Animals) founder Maria Dickin introduced the medal in order to honour animals that served with the Armed Forces and the Civil Defence units during World War II. The award is now given to an animal who displays conspicuous gallantry and devotion to duty associated with or under control of any branch of the Armed Forces or Civil Defence units. The medal will only be awarded on recommendation and is exclusive to the animal kingdom. The bronze medal bears the letters PDSA, with 'FOR GALLANTRY' written in the middle. Underneath is written, 'WE ALSO SERVE.' The PDSA Dickin Medal is recognized worldwide as 'the animals' Victoria Cross', the highest decoration for gallantry that can be bestowed on any animal member of the British and Commonwealth forces. To date it has been presented to 60 animals: 32 pigeons, 24 dogs, three horses and one cat.

The first dog to receive the Dickin Medal was Bob, a white mongrel. Attached to an infantry unit, he was sent on a mission along with the soldiers. Suddenly Bob froze and could not be moved. A sudden noise betrayed the enemy presence. Because of Bob the men were neither killed nor captured.

Facing page: A memorial to dogs who have been lost in battle at the Hartsdale Pet Cemetery, the oldest pet cemetery in America.

Most Recent Recipients

Buster: British Army dog Buster, a Springer Spaniel, became the most recent recipient of the PDSA Dickin Medal for gallantry in Iraq. In March 2003, in Safwan, Southern Iraq, Buster located a hidden cache of arms, explosives and bomb-making equipment in buildings thought to be the headquarters of extremists responsible for attacks on British Forces.

Following the find, all attacks ceased and shortly afterwards troops replaced their steel helmets with berets. Therefore Buster is considered responsible for having saved the lives of countless civilians and service personnel and for preventing untold misery for thousands of people.

Buster is the 60th animal to receive the PDSA Dickin Medal and does so in the Medal's 60th anniversary year.

The first recipient

Winkie: The first Dickin Medal recipient was a pigeon named Winkie. One of the most celebrated wartime animals, this blue

PDSA
For
Gallantry

checkered hen saved the lives of a bomber crew in World War II. With the advent of radio, radar and telephone communications, it was thought that carrier pigeons would become obsolete. But as war planes went down at sea and their radios were dunked in salt water, birds like Winkie still had a job to do. In 1942, a British Beaufort bomber was forced down in the North Sea. Winkie, thrown free of her on-board container and with wings clogged by oily water, flew toward the coast of Scotland some 129 miles away. Meanwhile, the bomber crew huddled in a dinghy shivering from the cold. Shortly before dawn, Winkie arrived in Scotland and a code tied to her leg helped lead a rescue team to the downed plane. A few days later, a banquet was held in Winkie's honour. She sat in her cage at the end of a long table and was toasted by admiring officers.

Facing page: Buster is awarded the Dickin Medal with his handler, Sergeant Danny Morgan. Buster helped save the lives of troops and civilians earlier this year when he located a hidden cache of arms, explosives and bomb-making equipment in southern Iraq.

A Home Away from Home

During Operation Desert Shield and Operation Desert Storm thousands of deployed soldiers were forced to sacrifice their pets. Many were forced to leave them in shelters. The lucky ones were adopted but most were euthanized. After 11 September 2001, Steve Albin and Dr. Linda Mercer decided to fix this problem by offering foster care for pets of those deployed in the American military abroad. Albin had been operating a website offering information about rescue groups and choosing the right pet, while Mercer, a Persian cat breeder for 11 years, had been overseeing another website that helped people adopt unwanted cats. The Military Pets Foster Project was started through Albin's website in December 2001. So far over a thousand dogs, various kinds of birds, horses, a pig and a boa constrictor have found homes thanks to this service. The aim of the project is to find homes close to where the deployed soldier lives. For many who agree to foster these pets, it's a way of showing their appreciation to those in the armed forces deployed overseas.

In many cases the owner opens a bank account in the pet's name. As of April 2002, the U.S. Government is actually paying for a portion of the pet expenses of deployed military, considering companion animals as members of the family, as opposed to mere property.

Other famous wartime animals

Bing: an Alsatian dropped in Normandy on D-Day, landed in a tree and was surrounded by shell fire all night until he could be rescued in the morning. Despite minor injuries, Bing took his place standing guard through continued heavy bombardment.

Chips: Perhaps the most famous war dog of World War II was Chips, who was donated to the U.S. Army by a civilian. Some 19,000 dogs

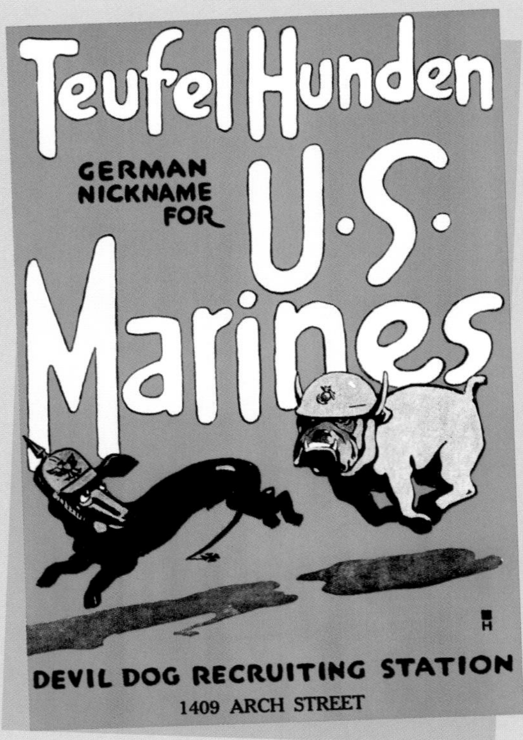

The U.S. Marine Corps earned an unofficial mascot during World War I that has remained an icon to this day. German soldiers reportedly referred to attacking Marines as *teufel-hunden*, or devil-dogs because of their aggressive fighting tactics. Upon hearing this, the Marines issued a recruiting poster depicting a snarling English Bulldog wearing a Marine Corps helmet, and a full-fledged mascot was born! The public took to the image quickly and in 1922 a registered English Bulldog named King Bulwark was officially enlisted in the Marine Corps as a private with a term for life and renamed 'Jiggs.'

By the time Jiggs died in 1927, he had risen to the rank of sergeant major. So he was interred with full military honours. Since then, numerous other Bulldogs have succeeded Jiggs as the official mascot of the U.S. Marine Corps, many of them named 'Chesty' after Lt. Gen. Lewis B. 'Chesty' Puller, the most decorated Marine in the history of the Corps.

Alexander the Great and Bucephalus

One of the best known legends about animals in battle is of Alexander the Great's faithful horse Bucephalus. The story goes that King Philip of Macedonia bought a horse for a large sum of money, but the horse proved to be vicious, stubborn and completely unmanageable. So the king ordered the horse to be destroyed. The king's twelve-year-old son Alexander asked to try the animal before he was put to death. Despite being warned not to do so by bystanders, Alexander stroked Bucephalus (ox-head, because of his wide skull) and nudged his head toward the sun when he noticed that the horse was afraid of his own shadow. Alexander then climbed on his back with no difficulty and from that day on Bucephalus allowed no one except the young prince to ride him. And Alexander never rode another horse, except Bucephalus, in any triumphant campaign.

In 326 BC, Alexander defeated the king of India at Hydaspes and Bucephalus, who was now 30 and wounded, carried Alexander out of harm's way before collapsing and dying beside his master. Bucephalus was buried with full military honours and the city of Bucephalus was built on his grave.

were procured in this way during the war, although only about half of them were deemed suitable for battle during a rigorous screening and training process. Chips was trained and in 1942 was one of the first dogs to be shipped overseas. He was assigned to the 3rd Infantry Division and served in North Africa, Italy, France and Germany. He even served as a sentry at the Roosevelt-Churchill summit in Casablanca in January 1943.

Although Chips was trained for sentry duty, on one occasion he reportedly broke away from his handler and attacked an enemy machine gun crew in a pillbox in Sicily. He seized one man and forced the entire group to surrender. Chips was also credited with the capture of numerous enemy soldiers simply by alerting Allied troops to their presence. According to the Army, the use of war dogs in this way lessened the danger of ambush and also served to boost the morale of soldiers on the ground.

Guide dog Roselle yawns as her owner Michael Hingson speaks at a luncheon where Roselle received an award for leading Hingson safely down 78 floors from the World Trade Center during the attack in 2001.

September 11 Dogs

On 11 September 2001, over 300 dogs were brought into the site now known as Ground Zero. The NYPD dogs were the there first. Apollo, part of the New York Police Department K9 Search and Rescue team was on the scene just fifteen minutes after the disaster, working hard to rescue people. Two guide dogs who saved their owners' lives just before the World Trade Center collapsed have been honoured for their bravery. Riva and Salty guided their blind owners through 78 floors of crowded and smoke-filled stairs.

On 5 March 2002 the Chairman of the PDSA presented Apollo, Riva and Salty with the Dickin Medal. Never before have three PDSA Dickin Medals been awarded for acts of conspicuous gallantry during a single event. This was also the first time the PDSA Dickin Medal has been awarded for actions outside the events of World War II and its aftermath.

Bottom left: An officer salutes near a painting of Sirius, a K9 dog killed during the terrorist attacks on the World Trade Center in 2001. Sirius was the only police dog to die in the attack.

Bottom right: Search and Rescue dog Apollo rests by the Langden Sarter award that he and his handler, NYPD K9 Officer, Peter Davis, received for their services during attack on the World Trade Center in 2001.

Gertrude Stein

Basket

Poodle Mania

Writer Gertrude Stein and her lifelong companion Alice Toklas owned at least three Poodles in their lifetime. The first was called Basket and when he died in 1937 he was replaced by Basket II who was later replaced by Basket III (seen here at their villa in Bilignin, France).

These Poodles were unusually well-connected as they met most greats and soon-to-be-greats at the Paris home of Stein and Toklas which was a centre for writers and painters such as Pablo Picasso, Henri Matisse, Ernest Hemingway, Clive Bell, André Gide and others.

The Poodles were very pampered. When her book, *The Autobiography of Alice B. Toklas*, became a bestseller, Gertrude Stein bought herself a new Ford car and 'the most expensive coat' made to order by Hermès for Basket, who was also gifted with two studded collars. Visitors to Stein's summer retreat in Bilignin were often forced to take Basket for a run!

Joan Rivers

Max

No Fashion 'Faux-paws' Allowed!

Nobody knows fashion dos and don'ts better than Joan Rivers. Joan, a talk show host/comedienne, cannot imagine life without her dogs, Max (a Pekinese, seen with Joan in the photograph), Spike (a Boston Terrier), Veronica and Lulu (Norwich Terriers). Joan regularly takes her furry friends on the set with her. She loves dressing her dogs in the latest fashion accessories and even allows them guest shots on her shows. Joan believes that the way the animal looks is an extension of its owner's personality: a well-groomed, presentable dog means that the owner is responsible and stays well groomed. However, if the dog is a mess, so is its owner! Her dogs have helped her sell a record-breaking 160 million dollars worth of baubles from the Joan Rivers Classic Jewellery Collection.

John Steinbeck

Charley

In Search of America

Three time Academy Award winner and Nobel Prize winner John Steinbeck kept dogs throughout his life. One of them, an Irish Setter called Toby, chewed up half of the only manuscript of *Of Mice And Men*. In a letter to his agent, the author was magnanimous towards the mutt: 'The poor little fellow may have been acting critically,' he explained.

In 1960, at the age of 58 John Steinbeck and his 10-year-old Poodle, Charley, set out on a 10 thousand mile journey across America in a camper. For three months these companions travelled the nation, meeting friends, strangers, relatives and immersing themselves in the fabric of the country. Steinbeck travelled in a van that he called Rocinante, after Don Quixote's horse. The result was *Travels With Charley: In Search of America.* Among other topics he reflects on in the book are burgers, trailer parks and truck drivers, and muses at length about dogs. The book went on to become a bestseller that initially sold more volumes than any of Steinbeck's other books and won the 1963 Paperback-of-the-Year Award and was later turned into a major television production.

'Intelligent and well-mannered, Charley is more than just a travelling companion; he is integral to the project. The dog helps break the ice with strangers: Charley is my ambassador,' wrote Steinbeck. Born Charles le Chien in Bercy, on the outskirts of Paris, Charley was a dog who chose diplomacy over aggression and was prone to vanity when groomed. Steinbeck wrote about his one-sided conversations, fretting over Charley's ailments, and the comfort of canine company.

Liberace

Dogs Forever

Wrinkles

Liberace was known for his outrageous sequined costumes and dazzling stage shows, but he was also a huge dog lover and surrounded himself with as many as 27 dogs of various breeds. Liberace referred to his dogs as his 'children' and no expense was spared to keep them in the lap of luxury. A recreation of his Palm Springs bedroom is on display at the Liberace Museum in Las Vegas. When asked why he had twin beds, Liberace would reply, 'One for me and one for the dogs.' The bedspreads on both beds were made of llama fur. Each time one of his dogs would pass away, Liberace would have them freeze-dried and stuffed in an appropriate pose to create a permanent keepsake. When Liberace died in 1987, a photo of his favourite dog Wrinkles was included in his casket.

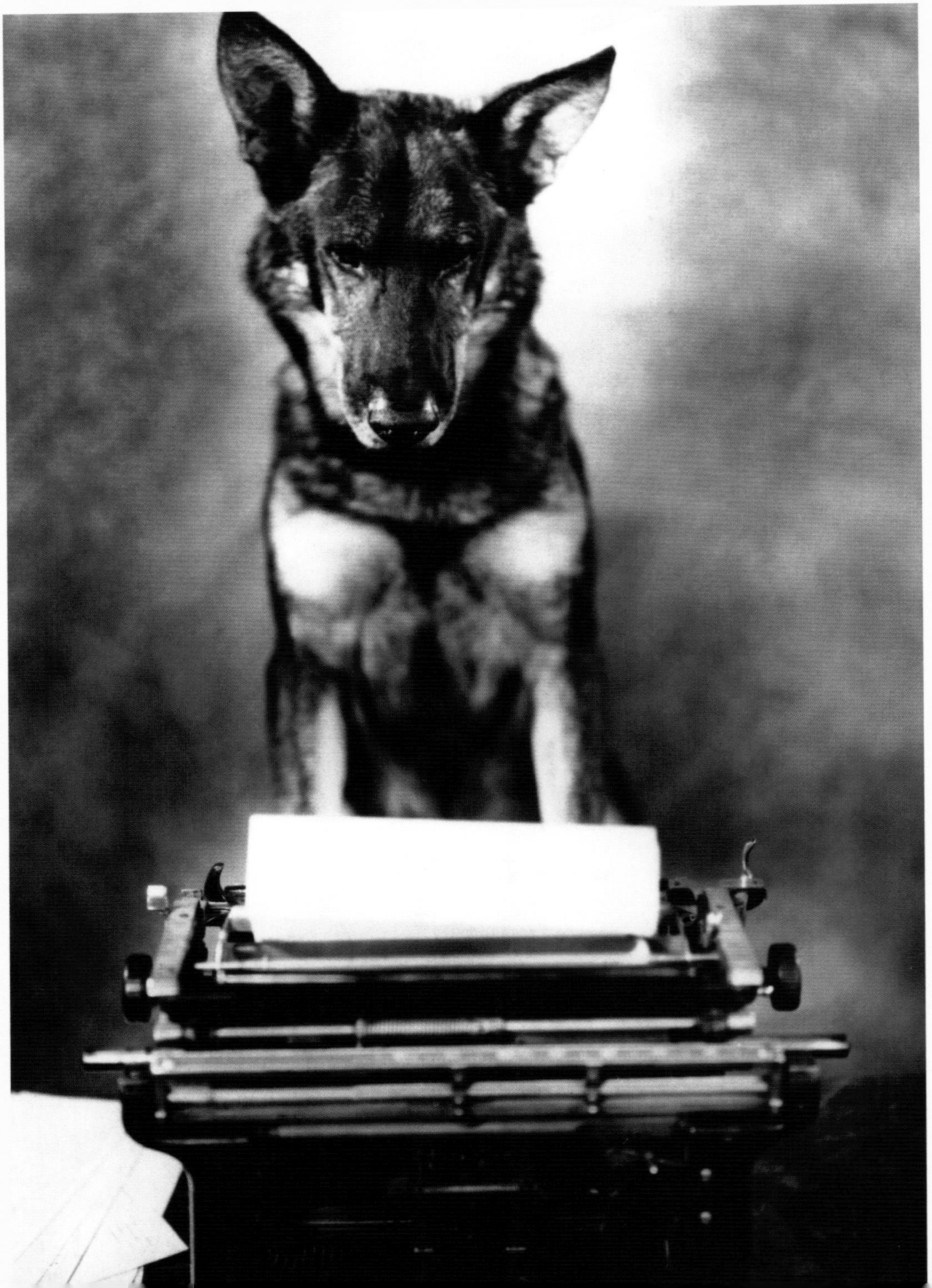

Legendary Animals

Some of the best known celebrities have been the four-legged variety. Who can forget the courage and loyalty of Lassie, the legacy of Rin Tin Tin, or Toto, Dorothy's faithful companion in *The Wizard of Oz?* Other animals have become equally famous in their own right – take Leo, the MGM lion who has been roaring for us for decades, or the curious photo of Nipper and His Master's Voice. Did you know that the beloved *Winnie the Pooh* series was based on an actual black bear? The stories of these famous animals have a timeless and heart-warming quality for every generation.

Beerbohm

Beerbohm was London's longest serving theatre cat. For 20 years he was the resident mouser at the Globe Theatre (now Geilgud). Occasionally he would wander on stage during a play, much to the delight of the audience, and dismay of the performers, who were always upstaged by his 'performance'. He died in March 1995, after retiring to Kent with the theatre's carpenter.

Boots

Boots' story is a Hollywood dream come true. From being the runt of the litter, Boots emerged as a big Hollywood dog star. Animal trainer Bert Rose noticed Boot's star qualities and his extraordinary ability to pay attention and understand commands. Boots understood more than eight hundred words, and had an uncanny ability to follow instructions. He made more than a dozen films (and was even awarded an Oscar for his performance in Paramount's *Emergency Squad*), but also travelled during World War II, both as an entertainer and as a star, making public appearances to raise money for the war effort. He gave a performance for President Franklin D. Roosevelt at Warm Springs, Georgia. Boots died in the early 1950s, and was buried in Hartsdale Pet Cemetery.

Facing page: Rin Tin Tin, the famous Warner Brothers animal film star, answering fan mail in 1938. Rin Tin Tin received thousands of letters every week.

Humphrey

Humphrey, a long-haired black and white cat, was described by many as one of the most popular and admired cats in Britain. As a resident of No. 10 Downing Street for eight years, his official role was mouser to the Cabinet Office. He first arrived as a stray when Mrs Thatcher was in power and remained throughout the term of John Major. In 1995 he disappeared for 3 months, to be later discovered at his new residency, the Royal Army Medical College. He was immediately returned to No. 10 Downing Street. In November 1997 Humphrey retired from No. 10 for health reasons. It is believed that Humphrey had been suffering from a kidney ailment for some years and had lost his appetite. Humphrey retired to a civil servant's home in south London.

Laika

The first living creature to go into space was a mongrel. Laika (Russian for 'barker') rocketed to international fame aboard Sputnik 2, the space satellite launched by the Soviets on 3 November 1957. In total the Soviets sent 13 dogs into orbit between 1957 and 1966, but it was Laika who became the most celebrated canine icon of the space race. Dubbed 'Muttnick' by the Americans, Laika became a heroine in her homeland; stamps bearing her picture were issued across the Soviet empire and a brand of cigarettes was named after her. More recently, a monument to honour Soviet cosmonauts was erected near Moscow and Laika is featured in it as well.

Despite Laika's ongoing celebrity status among books and websites on dogs, there was never any intention of bringing her back safely to earth – in fact, she was the only dog the Soviets sent into space with no hope of return.

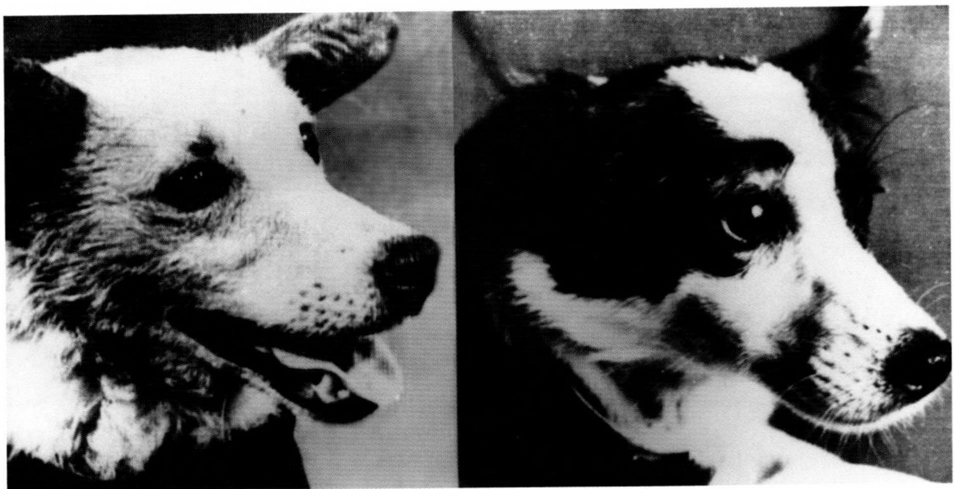

Belka and Strelka

Belka (left; 'squirrel' in Russian) and Strelka (right; 'little arrow' in Russian) were launched into space on board Sputnik 5 on 19 August 1960. They were accompanied on their flight by 40 mice, 2 rats and a number of plants. Belka and Strelka were safely recovered after spending a day in orbit. In 1961, at the height of the Cold War, Soviet premier Nikita Khrushchev gifted a dog named Pushinka ('fluffy' in Russian) to American president John F. Kennedy. Pushinka was Strelka's daughter.

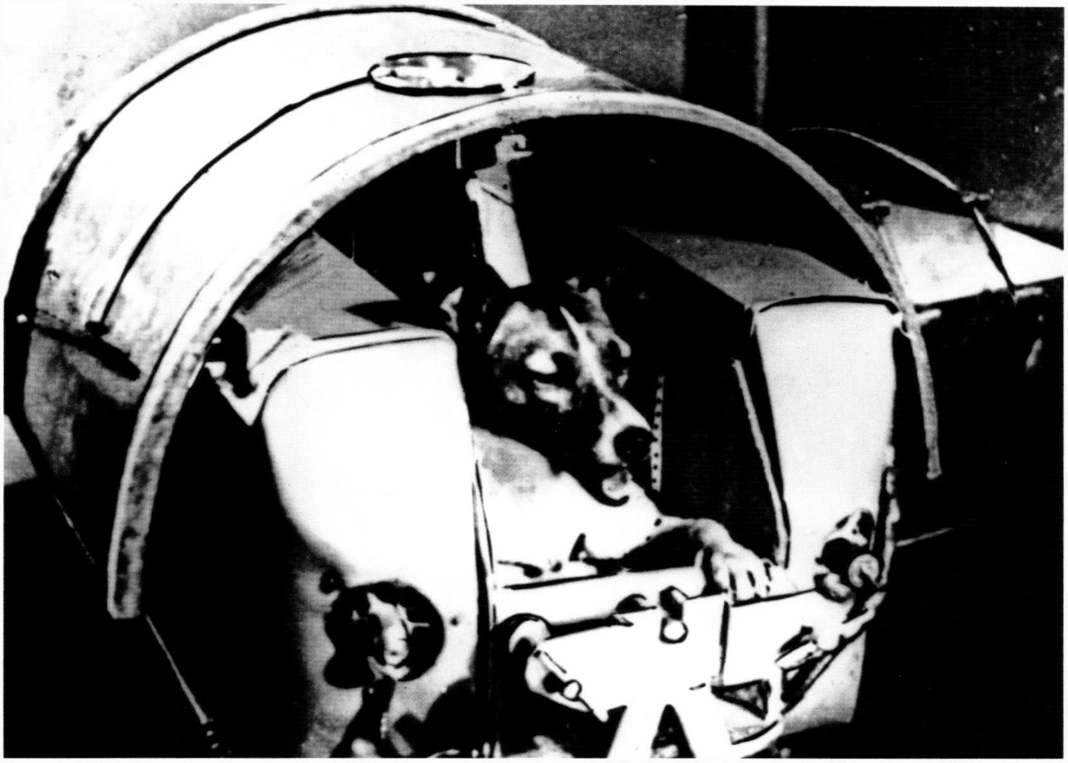

Laika the satellite dog in her specially designed contraption in Sputnik 2 before take-off.

The other four dogs did die in flight – Bars, Lisichka, Pchelka and Mushka – because recovery plans went awry. For decades, the Soviets maintained that Laika survived for seven days in orbit before dying painlessly. But in 2002 the truth was revealed: Laika died in a state of panic when the capsule overheated just hours after Sputnik 2 was launched.

Lassie

Lassie has single-handedly done more for the popularity of the Collie breed than any other dog. *Lassie Come Home,* written by Eric Knight, was first printed as a short story in 1938. In 1941 MGM, one of Hollywood's major studios, decided to make a movie out of

A packet of Russian *Laika* cigarettes.

the popular story. The movie titled *Lassie Come Home* premiered in 1943, starring the infamous Pal. A respected Hollywood dog trainer by the name of Rudd Weatherwax acquired Pal when his previous owners gave him up, and a legend was born! The beautifully shot film was the story of a loyal Collie who crossed hundreds of miles of rough terrain to return home to the boy she loved. The critics and public loved it. It made the 'Ten Best Movies' list at the end of the year. The movie featured two youthful stars, Roddy McDowell and Elizabeth Taylor. Lassie who came to represent traditional American values such as family and home, courage, loyalty and honesty, soon became an American institution, famous the world over. Lassie has reigned supreme since then as the undisputed canine heroine.

Facing page: Lady Bird Johnson, President Johnson's wife, meets Lassie at the White House in 1967.

Bottom: Leo the MGM lion in his travelling enclosure during a world publicity tour in 1928.

Leo the MGM Lion

MGM's trademark lion mascot, Leo, is seen at the beginning of every MGM feature film. Leo first roared on 31 July 1928 for the debut of the movie *White Shadows of the South Seas*. The roar was heard via a phonograph record since it was a silent film. The MGM lion logo was created in 1916 for the Goldwyn Pictures Corporation, and was based on the Columbia University fight song, *Roar, Lion, Roar*. Over the years, a number of lions, including Slats, Jackie and Tanner have portrayed Leo. Around the circle that framed Leo the Lion, the MGM motto *Ars Gratia Artis* (Art for Art's Sake) was displayed.

A cameraman and a sound technician record the roar of Leo the lion, in 1928, for MGM's famous movie logo. The footage was used on MGM's first talking picture *White Shadows in the South Seas.*

Marjan the Lion of Kabul

Marjan, the lion of Kabul, captured the hearts and minds of people all over the world when his life story was revealed in 2001. First acquired by Afghanistan's Kabul Zoo in 1978, Marjan survived five wars and one particularly brutal injury. In 1993, a soldier climbed into Marjan's pen to demonstrate his bravery to friends. When the soldier went to touch Chucha (Marjan's mate), Marjan leapt across the pen and mauled the man, who later died from his injuries. In retaliation, the soldier's brother threw a live grenade into Marjan's cage where it exploded. The blast badly mutilated Marjan's face, took out one of his eyes, damaged his jaw and left him deaf. But the lion survived. Taliban soldiers reportedly stoned Marjan in 1996 and considered eliminating all the neglected creatures of the zoo. After U.S. forces entered Kabul in November 2001, the plight of the Kabul Zoo's animals – and of Marjan in particular, who had become a symbol of survival against the odds – became widely known. Donations poured in from all parts of the globe to help the suffering animals. But for Marjan, despite a healthier diet and constant veterinary

Marjan was seen as a symbol of survival in war-torn Afghanistan.

Bottom: Habib Ullah, Marjan's caretaker, places paper flowers on Marjan's grave.

care, old age and mistreatment finally took their toll. He died in January 2002, at the age of 25.

Nipper and His Master's Voice

Over a century old, the 'His Master's Voice' trademark is still instantly recognized and is one of the Top 10 Famous Brands of the 20th Century. This is the story of Nipper, the dog looking into the gramophone.

Nipper was born in Bristol, England in 1884 and so named because of his tendency to nip the backs of visitors' legs. Though not a thoroughbred, Nipper had plenty of Bull Terrier in him. When his first master, Mark Barraud died destitute, his younger brother Francis, a painter, adopted Nipper and took him to Liverpool where he later painted the picture known as *His Master's Voice.*

In Liverpool Nipper discovered the phonograph and looked at it in amazement to make out where the sound came from. After Nipper died, Barraud committed this scence to canvas. He first registered the painting as *Dog looking at and listening to a Phonograph* and later renamed it *His Master's Voice.* A friend then suggested that he could make the picture more attractive by replacing the black horn with a brass one, so he called at the offices of The Gramophone Company hoping to borrow one. When Barraud showed the Manager, William Barry Owen, a photograph of his painting, Owen offered to buy it if Barraud replaced the phonograph with a gramophone. The deal was confirmed in 1899 and Barraud was paid £50 for the painting and further £50 for the full copyright.

This painting made its first public appearance on The Gramophone Company's advertising literature in 1900, but was registered as a trademark in 1910. Nipper the dog was buried in Kingston upon Thames, in an area that is now the rear car park of a bank. As one enters the bank, there is a plaque on the wall stating this.

Rin Tin Tin

In September 1918, a band of World War I airmen, including Corporal Lee Duncan, were scouting the countryside for a new headquarters. The men stumbled upon an abandoned German war dog station and in a shelled corner of the bunker discovered a mother German Shepherd and her five puppies. Corporal Duncan took two of the puppies home with him. Duncan named one of the dogs Rin Tin Tin and was determined the dog would make movie history. Rin Tin Tin appeared in a total of 24 films over his career

and was known for being a super stunt dog. His most successful movies include *Man From Hell's River* and *Where the North Begins*. He reportedly received 10,000 fan letters a week! Duncan says that the reason Rin Tin Tin could complete such amazing feats was because he and the dog had an understanding that was based on a strong loving bond. When Rin Tin Tin died at the age of 16, as a gesture of honour, Duncan had his body moved to a Paris pet cemetery, as France was Rin Tin Tin's country of birth. Rin Tin Tin's legacy lives on under a carefully monitored breeding programme and the majority of Rin Tin Tin puppies are trained to be service dogs.

Toto

Carl Spitz, a dog trainer and founder of the Hollywood Dog Training School, adopted a little Cairn Terrier in 1933 and named her Terry. Terry was very shy, but Spitz loved the little dog so much that he was determined to help her come out of her shell. After four years of confidence building, Terry was hired for her first movie. Terry appeared in six films, alongside such stars as Shirley Temple, Joan Crawford and Spencer Tracy, before getting her big break in *The Wizard of Oz*. After *Oz*, Terry's name was officially changed to Toto. Toto died of old age in 1943 and was buried in Spitz's backyard.

Winnie

Winnie was first found during World War I when troops from Winnipeg (Canada) were being transported to Eastern Canada, and from there, on to Europe. They stopped at White River, Ontario and a lieutenant named Harry Coleburn purchased a small female black bear cub for $20 from a hunter who had killed the cub's mother. Lt. Coleburn named that cub 'Winnipeg', after his own hometown. He called her 'Winnie' for short. Winnie became the mascot of the Brigade and went on to Britain with the unit. She was presented to the London Zoo in 1919. The bear became very popular with Christopher Robin, son of the author of the *Winnie the Pooh* books, A.A. Milne. Christopher Robin loved Winnie so much that he was even allowed to spend time inside the cage with Winnie when he was at the zoo! A.A. Milne started to write the books about Winnie and his son, and all of the characters in the 100-Acre-Woods. The other characters were Piglet, Eeyore, Tigger, Kanga, and Roo. These characters were based on stuffed animals that belonged to Christopher. Rabbit and Owl, like Winnie, were based on real-life animals near their home in Ashdown Forest, in Sussex, England. The 100-Acre-Woods is based upon this forest. The first story of *Winnie the Pooh* was published on 14 October 1926. Winnie the bear lived at the London zoo until 1934.

Judy Garland as Dorothy Gale, holding Toto the dog for the film *The Wizard of Oz* in 1939.

Maharaja of Junagadh

Roshnara

A Royal Treatment

Dog weddings were very much in vogue among rulers in North India during the 19th century. Maharaja Bhupinder Singh of Patiala and Maharaja Ranbir Singh of Jind celebrated the weddings of their dogs with great pomp and festivity. Perhaps the most ostentatious of these weddings was that of the Maharaja of Junagadh, Nawab Sir Mahabet Rasul Khan's dog, Roshnara, with the Nawab of Mangrol's dog, Bobby. A number of ruling dignitaries attended the marriage, in which the 'bride', Roshnara was perfumed, bejewelled and decked in brocade. She was carried in on a silver palanquin to the Durbar Hall. A military band and a guard of honour, and 250 dogs dressed in brocade received the 'groom', Bobby, who was bedecked in gold bracelets. Sir Irwin was invited to grace the occasion, but the Viceroy refused. Reportedly, the wedding festivities went on for three days.

The Maharaja of Junagadh owned 800 dogs, each with its own room, a telephone and a servant. When a dog died, mourning was declared, and Chopin's *Funeral March* was played. The Maharaja often had his liveried staff dress his dogs in formal evening suits, mount them on rickshaws and drive them on British summer capital Shimla's fashionable Mall. This infuriated the British women, who felt they were being mocked. The Maharaja was told to keep his dogs locked away. He grudgingly agreed, but got his ultimate revenge when there was a ball at the Viceregal Lodge. The Maharaja ordered his servants to round up every dog in Shimla. He set them loose in the grounds and was rewarded with the sound of horrified shrieks!

When the Maharaja migrated to Pakistan during the Partition of India in 1947, he left behind many weeping wives so that his pampered canines could fly with him on his plane.

The Maharaja of Junagadh seated with some of his famous hunting dogs.

Marilyn's One and Only Maf

Frank Sinatra gave Marilyn Monroe a Poodle after her divorce from writer Arthur Miller. Sinatra had purchased the dog from actress Natalie Wood's mother. Marilyn humorously named the poodle Maf after Sinatra's alleged Mafia connections. Interestingly, to spite Arthur Miller, Marilyn used to let Maf sleep on an expensive white beaver coat that Miller had presented her. With all of her emotional entanglements, difficulties with studios and deep feelings of loneliness, Maf remained the one true constant in Marilyn's life. When Marilyn returned to live in Hollywood, she had Maf flown back to be with her. After Marilyn's death in 1962, Maf was returned to Sinatra, as stated in her will. Sinatra's secretary, Gloria Lovell, eventually adopted Maf.

Martina Navratilova

Frodo

Love Match

Tennis ace Martina Navratilova was ranked No. 1 in the world seven different years. She won the Australian Open three times and the French Open twice. A lesser-known side of this tennis icon is that of a dog lover. In fact, Martina is so attached to her dogs that while she was in Australia a few years ago to play a match, she bought a Pug called Frodo because she was missing her dogs who she could not bring along because of the country's stringent pet travel laws. On the same trip, Martina was forced to make an 11-hour-drive to Melbourne from Sydney because Frodo was not allowed in the cabin and she was not happy to book him in as cargo. She said, 'We have rooms for computers, we have room for players, rooms for kids but you can't have room for dogs? If I couldn't take my dog to the tournament, I quite frankly wouldn't go there.'

To counter this problem, during the 2002 Family Circle Cup in Charleston, South Carolina, a tent was erected especially for pets of the players participating in the tournament. 'Martina's Puppy Park' housed 11 canines who were babysat by the local veterinary college students and were given food, water and toys to keep them busy. Among the pets present were Jennifer Capriati's Labrador Retriever, Happy; Lisa Raymond's Dachshund, Casy; Arantxa Sanchez-Vicaro's Chihuahua, Tina; and Serena Williams's Russell Terrier, Jackie. Martina brought along five of her own dogs. Recently, she adopted Duke, a blind special needs pet not many were willing to adopt. When Martina read about Duke's story in the newspaper she went to see him – it was a love match!

Françoise Durr

Born on Christmas Day in 1942 in Algiers, France's tennis champion, Françoise 'Frankie' Durr went on to hold 12 titles Grand Slam events (11 in doubles, 1 in singles). Durr will also be remembered for being the first woman to travel the circuit with her dog named Topspin who became a star by carrying Durr's racquet onto the court.

Mary Tyler Moore

A Passionate Cause

Mary Tyler Moore, the star of the hit American television programme *The Mary Tyler Moore Show* has had a passion for animals all her life. She says that she is most in touch with her spiritual side and laughs more when she is with her animals. A vegetarian for over 10 years, Mary does not wear any leather products and will not wear anything made of an animal. She wears fabric and synthetic shoes, belts and handbags. In recent years Mary has often been in the news for her role as an animal rights activist. In 1999 along with friend and Broadway star Bernadette Peters (facing page, right), Mary started *FIDO New York City*, an organization dedicated to helping find good homes for New York's homeless animals. The group sponsors several events, including the annual Broadway Barks, where stars of the Broadway stage bring attention to animals in need of a good home. Mary and her friends have also created a website, which helps homeless animals find homes. Mary has had many pets through the years including a Miniature Schnauzer, a Golden Retriever and a Petit Basset Griffon Vendeen – they all came from shelters. She also has two goats in the country and eleven horses, six of which are rescue animals. These include two police horses from the mounted police that at the age of 4 and 5 turned out to have physical problems that rendered them unsuitable for the kind of work they would have been required to do.

Mimsey the MTM Kitty Cat

A parody of the Leo the Lion mascot, this MTM (Mary Tyler Moore Productions) kitten concluded each episode with a sweet but timid 'meow.' Mimsey was rescued from a local animal shelter and became the kitten that would roar. After her foray into show business, the kitten lived the rest of its life in the San Fernando Valley home of an MTM staffer. Mimsey was born in 1968 and died in 1988. The Mimsey logo has appeared at the end of many MTM productions and with a number of variations.

Oprah Winfrey

Oprah Winfrey **(facing page)** is one of Hollywood's most famous dog lovers who refuses to travel without her dogs. Although Oprah has many dogs, her chocolate Cocker Spaniel Solomon and black Cocker Spaniel Sophie are the most well known of the pack.

Pamela Anderson

Actress Pamela Anderson is a celebrity who uses her star status to fight against cruelty towards animals. A vociferous spokesperson for PETA (People for the Ethical Treatment of Animals), Anderson, who is also a vegetarian, chooses leather-free clothing, including "pleather" cat suits and vinyl miniskirts, for her sleek look on the hit TV series *VIP*. In 2000, she began her crusade against the hidden cruelty of the leather industry, when she hosted PETA's first-ever video exposé of how animals are treated in the international leather trade, from dogs skinned in Korea, to cows in India. Pamela Anderson owns a Golden Retriever she calls Star. Star was rescued from a shelter. He was apparently the runt of the litter, and was still-born. He was given mouth-to-mouth resuscitation, and Pamela took the weak little puppy home to care for.

Renee Zellweger

Renee Zellweger loves spending time with her Golden Retriever-Collie mix, Dylan. Zellweger always keeps Dylan by her side, even when she's on the set. She knows every hotel that caters to pets. Dylan won Zellweger's heart when the actress was in her first year in college in Texas. Dylan even chose her own name – for a few weeks when she was still a puppy, her favourite sleeping spot was on a *Rolling Stone* magazine cover of Bob Dylan! Dylan shared the screen with her owner in *Nurse Betty*, where she played a guide dog.

The Osbournes

Ozzy's Zoo

Pipi

He may have bitten off a bat's head, but those familiar with *The Osbournes*, MTV's highest rated show ever, will know that Ozzy and his family are devoted animal lovers. MTV made Ozzy Osbourne's Pomeranian and Bulldog as famous as the rock star's children. With personalities to match their eccentric owners, the Osbournes' dogs have played a large part in the success of the show. One of the most entertaining episodes (*Bark at the Moon*) was the one dedicated to the Osbourne pets – the one where the dogs are running wild and Sharon has to call in a dog therapist to straighten things out as it is all getting a bit too much for the Prince of Darkness. There are three times as many animals in the Osbourne household as there are humans! Sharon Osbourne seems literally to collect dogs of every size, shape and colour. Sharon dotes on her animals and has had to pay the price of fame that the show has brought to the pets as well. Her dog was stolen for more than a month, but was later returned after an appeal was made on television. There was a $1,000 reward for Pipi, the missing Pomeranian's return, but the person who returned the dog refused to take any money. Sharon's Chihuahua, Lulu was killed when coyotes hopped a fence at their house in Beverly Hills. The coyotes attacked Pipi as well but Ozzy managed to rescue her. Pipi recovered fully after a successful surgery and now the Osbournes bring the dogs in at night. But it's Minnie the Pomeranian who as Sharon's Mini-Me has access to not only the entire house, but to jets, limos and salons. She has even shared the stage with Justin Timberlake at an awards function (as seen in the photo). Sharon refers to her as the top diva in the house and as her bodyguard. Ozzy has co-authored a book called *Bark at the Moon* about all the Osbourne pets including their breed, age, how they came to join the family, and even sexual orientation!

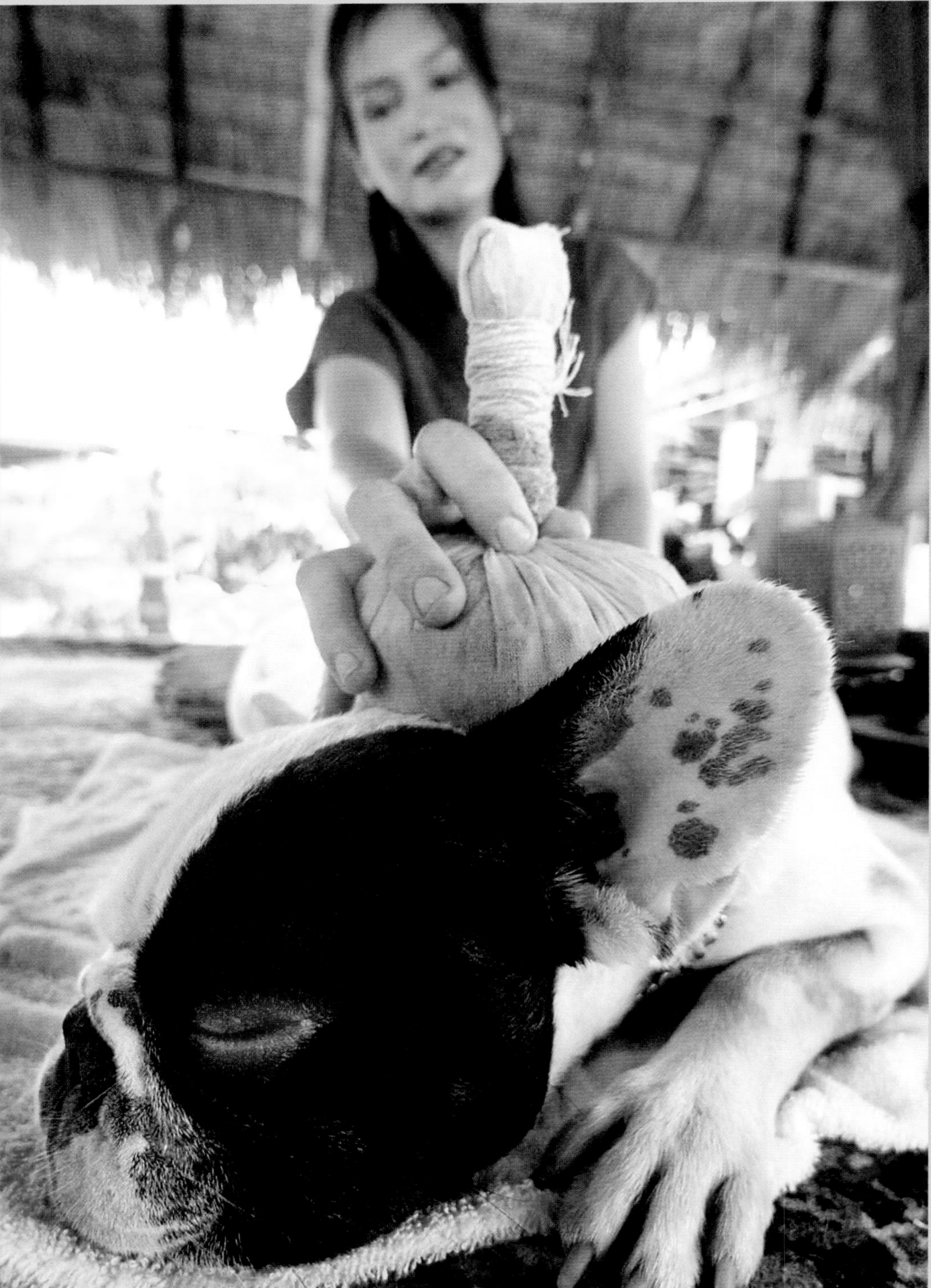

Pampered Pooches

Can't bear the thought of leaving your furry friends behind while travelling? Here is something to put you at ease. Hotels across North America and Europe now offer a cosy and comfortable 'home away from home' while you work or vacation. Services range from dog walking to oil massages, specially designed crockery to carefully chosen menus. Restaurants, too, are opening their doors for their very important customers, taking into account the likes and dislikes of their pampered clients. Indeed, a sure fire way to make your beloved pet feel like top pet for the day! Some celebrities who never travel without their pets – Oprah Winfrey, Martina Navratilova and Renee Zellwegger, to name just a few!

Pet Hotels

Pets Check In: Loews Hotel

Since the introduction of the Loews Loves Pets Program in 2000, many VIPs have made Loews their home away from home. Last year, Americans spent an estimated $29 billion on their pets. The Program includes a list of pet services ranging from pet 'room service', to dog-walking, pet-friendly restaurants, groomers, pet necessities and other attractions. Special menus are made up for finicky pets, designed to provide correct nutrition and help pets deal with travel stress. These services are developed and approved by a licensed veterinarian. Loews Hotels currently owns and operates 19 hotels in the US and Canada.

Hotel ZaZa

Dallas's first urban lifestyle hotel offers 24 hours of pampering for guests and their four-legged VIPs completed with an exclusive oil portrait of their pets. The luxurious ZaZa suite has been home to celebrities such as Britney Spears, Christina Aguilera, Ringo Starr and many others. This $5,000 package includes room-service, breakfast and dinner, special canine walking services twice daily, an in-room kennel and designer food and water bowls as gifts for guests. Special treats await the pets and their owners: pet toys, edible treats, a special 'pet lounging couch', a pet diary along with a picture frame, a ZaZa bandana and a bottle of house red or white wine to toast to great beginnings.

It's a dogs life! A Thai masseuse gives a dog a scented oil massage during the Dog Spa Treatment Program at The Dog Resort and Spa at a suburb of Bangkok, Thailand.

The Sutton Place: La Grande Residence

The Very Important Pet Program at La Grande Residence (Sutton Place Hotel) in Vancouver, Canada, caters to guests travelling with their faithful dog or cat. Services include the most delectable of gourmet delights, such as grilled Alberta beef T-bone steak, or seared fresh tuna fillet topped with caviar, and fresh Evian drinking water. There are also walking services and pet massages, offered for an additional fee. A special 'bedtime book' has been created for pets, and farewell gifts include charming porcelain food and water dishes.

Hotel Lancaster

Since its opening in 1996, Grace Leo-Andrieu, the owner of the posh Hotel Lancaster in Paris, France, noticed an increase in the number of inquiries from guests travelling with their dogs. So, for an additional charge there's doggie room-service available and special diet dishes can be arranged. Plus they get to sleep on designer Philippe Plein's state-of-the-art doggie bed, made of tobacco-coloured faux ostrich and stainless steel. If any dog loves the bed so much that it refuses to be parted from it, the owner can place an order for one.

Hotel de Crillon

In the heart of Paris, the grand five-star Hotel de Crillon has cashed in on the doggie trend by launching a special 'Dog de Crillon' programme. At the Crillon, visiting dogs are given an identification tag for their collar engraved with their name and the address of the hotel in case they lose their way, a toy, a bone containing fluorides, a bottle of mineral water and biscuits. Sitters and bilingual vets are available on request.

Four Seasons-George V and Meurice

Both these five-star hotels in Paris, also provide canine extras. The first has rubber mice and bones for pooches at play and a cover laid out on arrival embroidered with the animal's name. The second has a special groomer to take man's best friend for a walk in the Tuileries Gardens across the road.

The Dog's Bath Club in Lodon's fashionable Knightsbridge in 1959. Annual membership costs £5000.

Luxurious Kennels

If you can't take your pooch on your next holiday, offer him the next best thing: a stay in the Paris Suite at Kennelwood Village in St. Louis. Here, instead of a cage, he will lounge in a six-by-nine-foot room with his own TV and VCR. A valet feeds him, cleans the room, and takes him on supervised walks five times a day. And to make his holiday fun-filled he can participate in activities such as play school (tug-of-war, swimming, and tetherball with other dogs), 'yappy hour' (a daily treat of doggy ice cream and cookies), a nature walk, and spa treatments (hot-oil body massage and an anti-shedding rub).

For many years The Kennel Club-LAX, near Los Angeles Airport, held the record for luxury lodgings, with 14 eight-by-eight-foot, cheerfully decorated theme suites (choices include a farm, a lighthouse, and a fire station). However with demands for such luxurious kennels rising each year, places such as Kennelwood Village have sprung up across America.

Puppy Hut

Sheila Mullen **(left)** and Jackie Zajac, co-owners of Puppy Hut fast food restaurant for dogs in Toledo, Ohio, holding trays of dog food resembling human fast food such as French fries, chocolate chip cookies, pretzels, burgers, Kanine Cola and Cats-a-Cola.

Meanwhile for busy New Yorkers day care is another option. At The Doggy Gym in New York City, members, who can stay from 7 a.m. to 7 p.m., are separated into groups according to size and temperament and allowed to scamper over the indoor padded Astroturf running track for set periods of time. For an additional fee, dogs also visit Central Park in small groups. A vet is on the premises and grooming treatments are available. Many even leave their pets in day care for a day or two every week just so they can have the opportunity to play with other dogs.

French Eateries for Dogs

Walk into any brasserie, café or bistro in France and you are bound to get tangled up in Gucci dog leads. The French are known to do everything in great style, so it's only natural that man's best friend gets the best there is to offer. Take the luxury Trianon Palace Hotel in Versailles – it has a special canine menu, which includes poached queen's hambone with spring vegetables and low-fat yoghurt.

At Pierre Gagnaire's restaurant, off the Champs Elysées you may also see Jasper, Gagnaire's Labrador, peeping out from behind a screen, waiting to welcome guests and their dogs. Well-versed in the art of eating, he will fold himself elegantly under the table and graciously accept his dinner.

To celebrate the launch of his cookbook, *Masters and their Dogs*, Frederick E Grasser-Herme had a party at a restaurant at the top of Paris' Pompidou Centre. The launch party menu catered both to the masters as well as to the dogs.

At the Auberge d' L'Ill, Illhaeusern, the Michelin star hotel/restaurant near Strasbourg, all first-year apprentices have to learn to cook for dogs. Sundays at the Auberge are sacred, owners book not only for themselves, but also for their dogs.

Blue Dog Bakery

The demand for natural dog products is growing fast. Pets are considered a part of the family and pet owners want them to be as healthy as possible. This is what gave rise to the Blue Dog Bakery in Seattle, Washington, in 1998. Blue Dog Bakery President Margot Kenly is very particular about the bakery's products. The bakery takes pride in the delicious treats made from natural, high-quality and low-fat bakery ingredients. Concerned about chemical additives and animal by-products in other dog biscuits as well as the alarming increase in dog obesity, Kenly left the gourmet food industry in 1998 to start the Blue Dog Bakery. The Blue Dog Bakery is best known for its' Natural Cheese Flavoured Dog Treats and Low Fat Peanut Butter and Molasses Dog Biscuits.

There are no preservatives, artificial flavours, artificial colours or animal by-products in the biscuits – just healthy and nutritious ingredients. Blue Dog Bakery's crunchy biscuits are easily digested and help maintain strong teeth and fresh breath and provide a healthy alternative to treat your dogs good behaviour!

Paris Hilton

Tinkerbell

Arm Candy

Tiny dogs have become the latest fashion statement for many divas. Socialite Paris Hilton owns a Chihuahua, Tinkerbell, who she spoils by carrying around in a $1,500 designer tote bag. Tinkerbell accompanies Paris to A-list events wearing matching or similar outfits as her owner. These tiny dogs make for popular 'arm candy' with many celebrities. Other divas who own Chihuahuas are singer Madonna and supermodel Gisele Bundchen. Paris is also known to have owned some unusual pets. After winning $5,000 in Las Vegas, Paris Hilton sprung for a tiger, London, who she says is '75% wild'. The animal now lives on family property in Nevada. Recently, Paris was asked to disembark a plane after she tried to take a goat on board. She also had a monkey and a ferret when she turned up for the flight. When Paris was told that the flight was not a travelling circus, she had to take the pets home to Los Angeles in a six-hour limo drive.

buffalo
M

Hartsdale

The Hartsdale Pet Cemetery in New York was founded by Dr. Samuel Johnson. Dr. Johnson was a Professor of Veterinary Surgery at New York University, and he is most remembered for something he had never planned: the first pet cemetery in the United States. In 1896, a distressed client contacted Dr. Johnson. She had no place to give her dog a decent burial, and there was no way for this to be legally accomplished in New York city. Dr. Johnson offered her a place in his apple orchard in Hartsdale, in the little hamlet of Westchester. The idea was innocently given impetus when he mentioned this story to a journalist friend over lunch. To his surprise, the story appeared in print, and before long Dr. Johnson was flooded with calls from people who were looking for a burial place for their beloved pets. Dr. Johnson set aside a three-acre section of the apple orchard, and it began to look like a cemetery, dotted with gravestones. Today this location is known as the final resting point for nearly 70,000 pets, including dogs, cats, rabbits, birds and even a lion cub. Celebrities like Hungarian Princess Lwoff-Parlaghy, the legendary dancer Irene Castle, Broadway stage star Christine Norman, Pulitzer prize-winning author MacKinlay Kantor, singers Diana Ross and Mariah Carey have had their pets buried here. Many dogs of war and service dogs are buried at Hartsdale, as well as Hollywood canine stars like Boots.

A rare photograph of Dr. Johnson at the Hartsdale Pet Cemetery in 1899.

Pet Cemetery

Cimetière des Chiens

(et Autres Animaux Exotiques)

Famous American movie dog Rin Tin Tin is buried in a cemetery named the Cimetière des Chiens (et Autres Animaux Exotiques), in the suburb of Asnières, by the River Seine in France. The tombstone for the star of American films such as *Jaws of Steel* and *The Man from Hell's River* is made of fruity black onyx, with a gold-leafed 'star of the cinema' inscription.

Princess Lwoff-Parlaghy Goldfleck

The Princess and the Lion

Princess Vilma Lwoff-Parlaghy, a Hungarian born princess was a celebrity on both sides of the Atlantic. The princess was famous not only for her title and money, but was an accomplished portrait painter as well. She was an animal lover and any publicity about her always included something about her many pets and work in the field of animal welfare. She organized 'fashionable entertainments,' to raise money for animal protection societies, and she maintained a menagerie at a château she owned in the south of France.

Princess Lwoff-Parlaghy came to America with her favourite animals in 1899. In New York she stayed at the Plaza hotel for five years with a entourage that included a physician, a father confessor, several bodyguards and, of course, a great number of pets, which soon included a lion cub. Goldfleck first caught her eye on a visit to Ringling Brothers Circus. She fell in love with the cub and tried to buy it from the Ringlings, but they refused to sell him. Determined to obtain the cub, she called on one of her recent portrait subjects, Civil War hero General E. Sickles and begged him to use his influence on the Ringlings. Her scheme worked. General Sickles paid $250 for the cub and presented it to the princess who was overjoyed and sent for champagne for the christening of her new pet, officially named 'General Sickles,' but called 'Goldfleck'. Wrapped in an expensive wool blanket, Goldfleck was chauffeured in a limousine to the Plaza where the manager allowed the princess to keep him – under the care of a trainer – in a separate room in her apartment. Goldfleck was well behaved. Guests, who were at first appalled by his presence, were later not bothered by him. The princess took the lion with her wherever she could. When Goldfleck was four years old he fell ill and did not recover. The princess held a formal wake for him: Goldfleck lay in state surrounded by vases of flowers, his toys and his dishes. He was buried in Hartsdale Pet Cemetery in 1912. The inscription on the headstone reads: *Beneath This Stone Is Buried The Beautiful Young Lion Goldfleck, Whose Death Is Sincerely Mourned By His Mistress Princess Lwoff-Parlaghy, New York, 1912.*

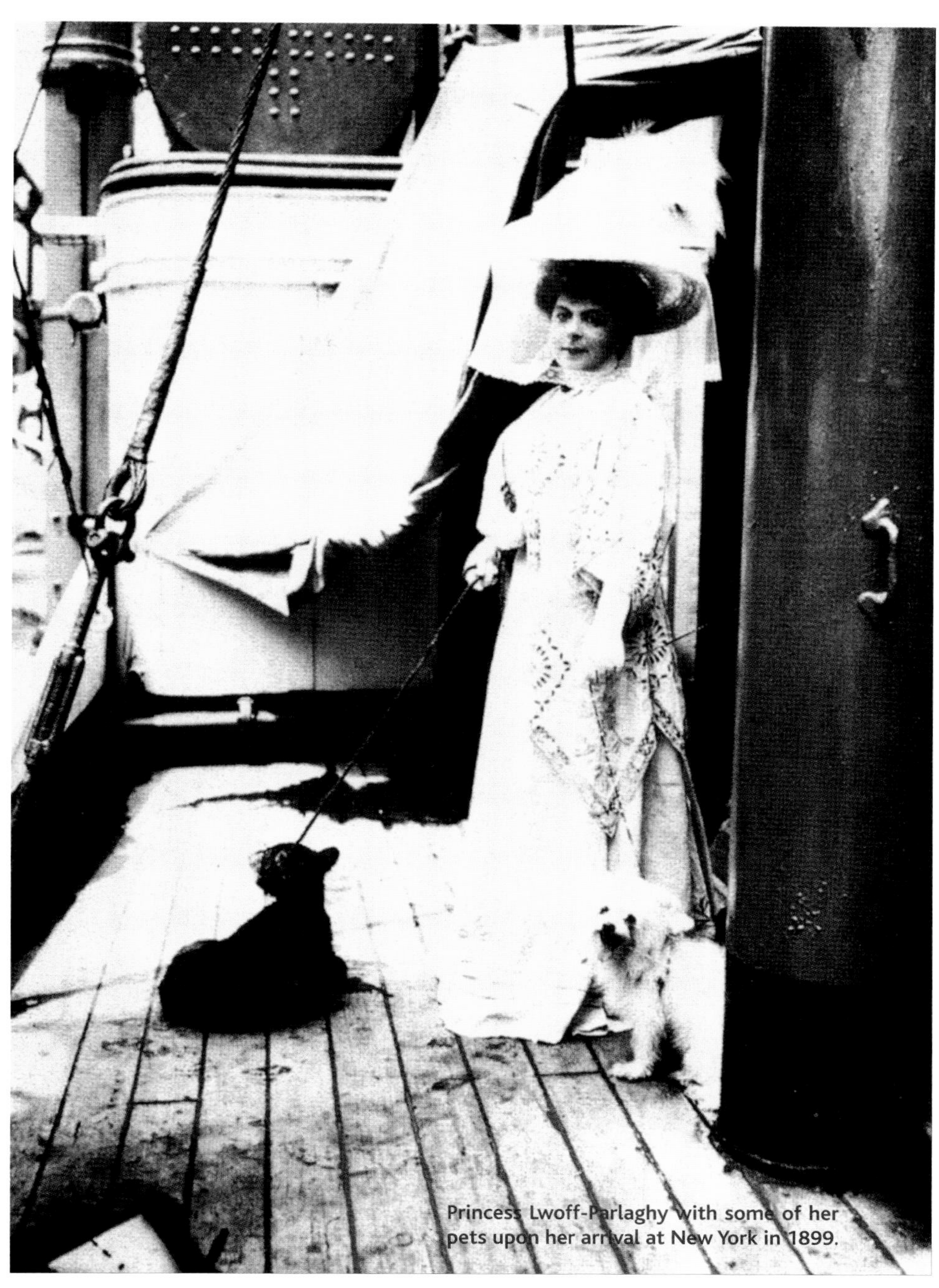
Princess Lwoff-Parlaghy with some of her pets upon her arrival at New York in 1899.

Rajiv Gandhi and Family

Golden Bond

Traditionally, the First Family of India, starting with Prime Minister Jawaharlal Nehru, has kept Golden Retrievers as their favourite pets. Madhu, Nehru's dog, provided excellent companionship to his young grandsons, Rajiv and Sanjay Gandhi during their formative years. Nehru's love of Golden Retrievers was passed down to his daughter, the late Prime Minister Indira Gandhi, who kept these dogs both as companions and guard dogs. Rajiv Gandhi's family continued keeping Golden Retrievers, eventually owning seven dogs when the family's matriarch dog, Toffee, whelped and gave birth to a litter of six puppies. The pups developed a bad case of haemorrhagic gastroenteritis, but through the care of Mrs. Sonia Gandhi and her daughter, Priyanka, all six puppies were saved. The near-death experience of the puppies created a strong bond with the family – none of the puppies were given away. They were named Sona, Patchy, Peppy, Reshma, Lassie and Snoopy. Toffee developed a very painful and severe case of arthritis when she turned 14, and the Gandhi family decided to put her to sleep. Toffee, who had been inseparable from Mrs. Gandhi, was given a very caring and emotional farewell from her, followed by prayers and offerings of holy water from the sacred river Ganges from Priyanka. Patchy, who had been a favourite of Rahul's (Rajiv Gandhi's son), outlived his siblings, living till the grand old age of 15. It took the family some time to have another pet. Priyanka recently took in Simba, another Golden Retriever puppy, while Rahul acquired a Terrier.

General Robert E. Lee

Travelling Far and Wide

Traveller

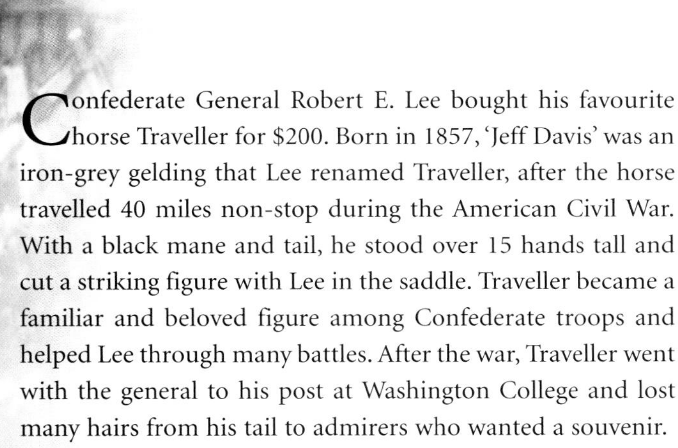

Confederate General Robert E. Lee bought his favourite horse Traveller for $200. Born in 1857, 'Jeff Davis' was an iron-grey gelding that Lee renamed Traveller, after the horse travelled 40 miles non-stop during the American Civil War. With a black mane and tail, he stood over 15 hands tall and cut a striking figure with Lee in the saddle. Traveller became a familiar and beloved figure among Confederate troops and helped Lee through many battles. After the war, Traveller went with the general to his post at Washington College and lost many hairs from his tail to admirers who wanted a souvenir.

When Lee died in 1870, Traveller followed his hearse in the funeral procession. One year later, at the young age of 13, Traveller developed tetanus after stepping on a rusty nail. To prevent suffering, he was shot since no treatment was available. Traveller's remains are interred in a plot outside the entrance of the Lee Chapel and Museum at Washington and Lee University in Lexington, Virginia.

Life imitates art: two of Queen Victoria's favourite dogs in royal repose.

Royals and their Pets

Royal history is full of fascinating stories of monarchs and their passion for animals. Kings and queens, raised in the atmosphere of regal palaces have often tolerated eccentric behaviour in their animals. Queen Victoria owned a total of 88 pets. George V, the founder of the House of Windsor, seemed to prefer animals to humans. He kept Sealyham terriers, Cairn Terriers, horses and a pink-grey parrot named Charlotte. Queen Elizabeth is said to have acquired a love of horses from her grandfather, King George V, while the love of Cairn Terriers was passed on from King George V to his eldest son, known to the family as David. The present Queen has always had Corgis in her life as well. She had one particularly ill-tempered Corgi, Dookie, who used to love taking nips at the legs of passers by. During King George VI and Queen Elizabeth's trip to Canada and the USA, the King and Queen would call their daughters, Princess Elizabeth and Margaret, who would end each call by putting Dookie to the phone and making him bark. Every year, the Queen would take endless dogs, ponies and horses with her to Scotland during summer. Here are some stories of the great romance of royals and their pets!

Top: Charlotte, King George V's parrot.

Right: Princess Victoria holding her pet cat with Tsarevitch Alexei of Russia in Reval, 1908.

Facing page: Queen Alexandra and Dowager Empress Fedorovna with their dogs in the Conservatory at Hvidore, Denmark, c. 1911.

Top: Francis Clark, Queen Victoria's Highland servant, with four of her dogs.

Right: King Edward VII and his dog, Caesar.

Bottom: Gazelles on board The Royal Yacht. They were given to Queen Alexandra in Algeria in 1905.

Napoleon Bonaparte & Josephine

Napoleon Bonaparte was a Dachshund lover, owning more than 20 such dogs in his lifetime. Napoleon loved his dogs so much that he refused to take them into battle for fear they may be harmed. Napoleon acquired a particularly small Dachshund and named it 'Napoleon' so that it could feel larger than its size. When Napoleon died, he left instructions that his surviving Dachshunds, when they passed on, be entombed with him.

General Napoleon Bonaparte's wife Josephine owned a Pug she called Fortune. The tiny black-faced dog had a nasty disposition and snapped at everyone except his mistress. On Napoleon and Josephine's wedding night, Fortune snarled when Napoleon entered the house and barked ferociously when he climbed into Josephine's bed, attacking Napoleon by nipping at his heels and sinking his teeth into his legs. Napoleon tried tossing the little monster out, but Josephine blocked the way, insisting that her sweet pet always slept beside her and getting married wasn't going to change that! Later on, Fortune carried secret messages under his collar to Napoleon when he was imprisoned at Les Carmes.

The Duke and Duchess of Windsor

Their romance is considered to be one the greatest of the past century. It shook the British Empire, rocked the Church of England, changed the succession and foretold the dissolution of the power of royalty. After their marriage, the Duke and Duchess of Windsor also came to be known for their great love of Pugs who became their surrogate children. During their marriage, the couple owned 12 Pugs. Living in exile in France, the Duke and Duchess of Windsor benefited from air fares and hotel suites paid for by nouveau riche hosts. This also allowed them to give their pets a royal lifestyle. The pampered Pugs accompanied them to all social activities, invited or not, much to the dismay of others in attendance who knew that the Windsor Pugs would be left to run wild and relieve themselves wherever they chose. They were fed out of silver bowls and had trained staff, including a chef and a servant to clean up after them and accompany them everywhere. They slept on monogrammed bed linen, wore silver collars with 14-Karat Cartier leashes and were sprayed with Christian Dior perfume everyday. Each evening, the Duchess would invite the Pugs onto her bed and hand-feed them special biscuits prepared daily by her chef.

Their house in the Bois de Boulogne is said to have housed an enormous collection of porcelain Pugs. When Sotheby's in New York auctioned off the Duke and Duchess of Windsor's collection of Pug figurines, Pug owners from all over the country descended on the auction house. Some of them carried their own Pugs in their arms, while a few wore slippers embroidered with pugs, perhaps to bring them good luck in the

Left: The Duke prepares to meet the press.

Facing page: The Duke and Duchess of Windsor at the International Canine Exhibition in Paris, in December 1956, with their two Pugs.

CARLINS

bidding. The two-bedroom Royal Suite at the Waldorf Astoria served as the New York City residence of the Duke and Duchess. The chairs in the seating area had needlepoint pillows of their beloved Pugs.

Queen Elizabeth II

The most famous Corgis in the world are accustomed to red carpet treatment everywhere. Queen Elizabeth II of Great Britain is extremely fond of pets which are famous for stealing the limelight at official photo shoots. This in the continuation of a long family tradition begun by her father, King George VI, who kept several Corgis. Corgis have since become a symbol of the present royal family. The Queen has owned more than 30 Corgis during her reign and now has three pedigree pooches, as well as three Dorgis, a cross breed originating from the then Princess Elizabeth's Corgi, Tiny with Princess Margaret's Dachshund, Pipkin. On her 18th birthday, Princess Elizabeth was gifted Susan, a Corgi, from her parents. She and her younger sister, the late Princess Margaret hand-fed the newcomer from a silver platter held by a footman and today the royal matriarch continues the custom, carefully mixing the ingredients and placing them in bowls in order of seniority. The royal pets are known to roam freely around Buckingham Palace and have made appearances at official functions.

The Queen's eye for horses has become quite renowned and she has passed her love of

Royals and their Pets

The Royal Princesses Elizabeth and Margaret at the windows of the Royal Welsh House in 1936 with two Corgis.

riding to her children as well as grandchildren. Prince Charles, her son, is a keen polo player and favours Labrador Retrievers, while Prince William rides horses and owns a black Labrador, Widgeon, who he received from his mother Princess Diana on his 14th birthday. Princess Anne has an interest in Greyhounds, Labrador Retrievers, Bloodhounds, Clumber Spaniels and Bull Terriers.

In December 2003 the British royal family met at the Queen's estate at Sandringham, Norfolk, for Christmas. Her daughter, Princess Anne, arrived with her English Bull Terrier Dotty, short for Dorothy. As the door was opened by a servant, one of the Queen's Corgis, Pharos, raced down to greet her. The Bull Terrier then attacked Pharos, injuring the

Mary Queen of Scots

The Queen of Scots had many small dogs, but her favourite was a King Charles Cavalier Spaniel. Imprisoned for treason, Mary's only company was her beloved Cavalier. On the day of her execution, Mary endured two strokes with an ax. Right after the beheading, Mary's separated body began to move. The little Cavalier had attended Mary's execution by hiding beneath her skirts. The dog refused to leave, lying between Mary's head and body and finally had to be carried away by Mary's ladies-in-waiting.

King George VI and Queen Elizabeth in 1936 with Princess Elizabeth and Princess Margaret on the grounds of Windsor Castle with their four dogs.

Members of the British Monarchy in 1979 walking their dogs. **(Left to right)** Prince Philip, the Duke of Edinburgh, Prince Edward, Queen Elizabeth II, Prince Charles, Princess Anne, Prince Andrew and Peter Philips holding his mother's hand.

Following pages: Queen Elizabeth II with the victorious Rugby Team England after they won the world championship in 2004. During the photo shoot at Buckingham Palace, one of the Queen's Corgis, always allowed to roam freely, inadvertently strolled into the frame.

Corgi's legs. He was treated by royal vets, but was eventually put down. The Queen was said to be 'absolutely devastated'. Buckingham Palace later issued a statement stating that it was not Dotty but another one of Princess Anne's Terriers, Florence who was the culprit. Princess Anne is the only royal to have a criminal record – in 2002 she was fined £500 for letting Dotty run out of control.

After the Queen Mother's death, the Queen took in her mother's dogs and now also owns Labradors and Spaniels.

Sigmund Freud

Freud's Dream Companions

Jofi

Sigmund Freud, founding father of psychoanalysis, was also the father to three dogs named Lun, Jofi and Wolf. Freud felt that dogs have a special sense that allows them to judge a person's character accurately. For this reason, his favourite Chow-Chow, Jofi, was allowed to attend all his therapy sessions. Freud admitted that he often depended upon Jofi for an assessment of the patient's mental state. The dog would lie down near a relaxed patient but across the room from those who seemed tense. Recent studies show that Freud was correct. Physiological measures show that petting a calm and friendly dog actually reduces stress, and that people who own dogs are likely to live longer and require less medical attention. Towards the end of his life, Freud suffered from jaw cancer, which made eating painful. Jofi was fed the choicest of scraps from his plate, often eating his entire meal! She was of great comfort to Freud during his period of illness. He wrote that she seemed to understand everything, and her sympathy for him was endless. Jofi's death in 1937 caused Freud intense grief.

Mahatma Gandhi

In India, the goat found a patron in Mahatma Gandhi. Gandhi had vowed not to drink cow or buffalo milk. But when his health deteriorated, doctors insisted he include milk in his vegetarian diet. So a goat always travelled with Gandhi to provide him with milk. When he visited England in 1931 to attend the second Round Table Conference, his pet goat accompanied him and stayed with him at the Claridge's Hotel. In London, Gandhi visited the Dairy Show at the Royal Agricultural Hall where the prize-winning goat was named 'Mahatma Gandhi.' In 1946, Gandhi was in a crucial meeting with members of the Cripps Mission when suddenly he left to tend to his injured pet goat. When he did not return for a while, Sir Stafford Cripps and his friends went looking for him. To their surprise and amusement, they found Gandhi applying mud over the goat's sprained ankle .

Mahatma Gandhi, Miraben (centre) and Pandit Madan Mohan Malaviya (right) with Gandhi's goat during his stay at the Claridge's Hotel, London in 1931.

George Clooney

Pot-bellied pig Max was a present from George Clooney's former girlfriend Kelly Preston. An accident in 2001 left the pig with cuts on his back and a squashed trotter. Clooney has been concerned about Max's health since then. Clooney is inseparable from the pig and he is said to allow the animal to sleep in his room. He even likes to snuggle up with Max after a long day on the set!

Mike Tyson

Mike Tyson claims he used to spar with his two tigers, Kenya and Storm, two female white Bengals, and Boris, a golden tabby male. They lived at his Texas home for seven years while Tyson tried to get a license to own them. When that never came through (and after Tyson filed for bankruptcy), the big cats were moved to a refuge in Colorado.

Hugh Hefner

With a zoo permit at his famous 5.5-acre Playboy mansion, apart from 'bunnies', Hugh Hefner keeps an assortment of peacocks and spider monkeys in the yard. It is heavily populated with wild rabbits, too.

Michael Jackson

Michael Jackson's Neverland Ranch is home to a giraffe, llama and an ostrich. But the exotic animal most associated with the singer is Bubbles, the chimpanzee, who used to appear in photo-ops wrapped around Jackson's arms. Now about 20 years old, Bubbles lives with a trainer in a nearby ranch. Jackson also bought two tigers, who live on a ranch in Texas.

Slash

Electric guitarist of rock group Guns n' Roses Slash loves reptiles. As a child he loved snakes, iguanas and all kinds of scaly, crawly things. In 1998 he made an appearance on *The Pet Shop*, a show on the Animal Planet cable channel. Slash owns an albino boa constrictor, as well as a variety of other snakes.

PUMA

Venus and Serena Williams

Dynamic Duo

Tennis aces Venus and Serena Williams both love dogs. To keep her company during long tournaments, tennis champion Serena Williams takes her Jack Russell Terrier, Jackie everywhere with her. Jackie travels in a small carry-on bag and is said to be very well behaved, be it in a plane or a hotel room. Serena also has a Pit Bull called Bambi who spends more time at home because he is known to be camera shy! When Serena was asked whether she had any problems with her dogs, she said that Bambi was particularly difficult to toilet train! Serena also admitted that she loves pampering her pooches and buying expensive gifts for them.

Older sister Venus has a Yorkshire Terrier, Pete, who is named after fellow tennis superstar, Pete Sampras. She also has another Yorkshire Terrier, Bobby, said to be her lucky mascot.

Venus Williams gets a good luck kiss from her dog Bobby before a match in 2001.

Facing page: Serena Williams reaches out to pet Jackie during a break at the Arthur Ashe Kid's Day Tennis Festival in 2002 in New York.

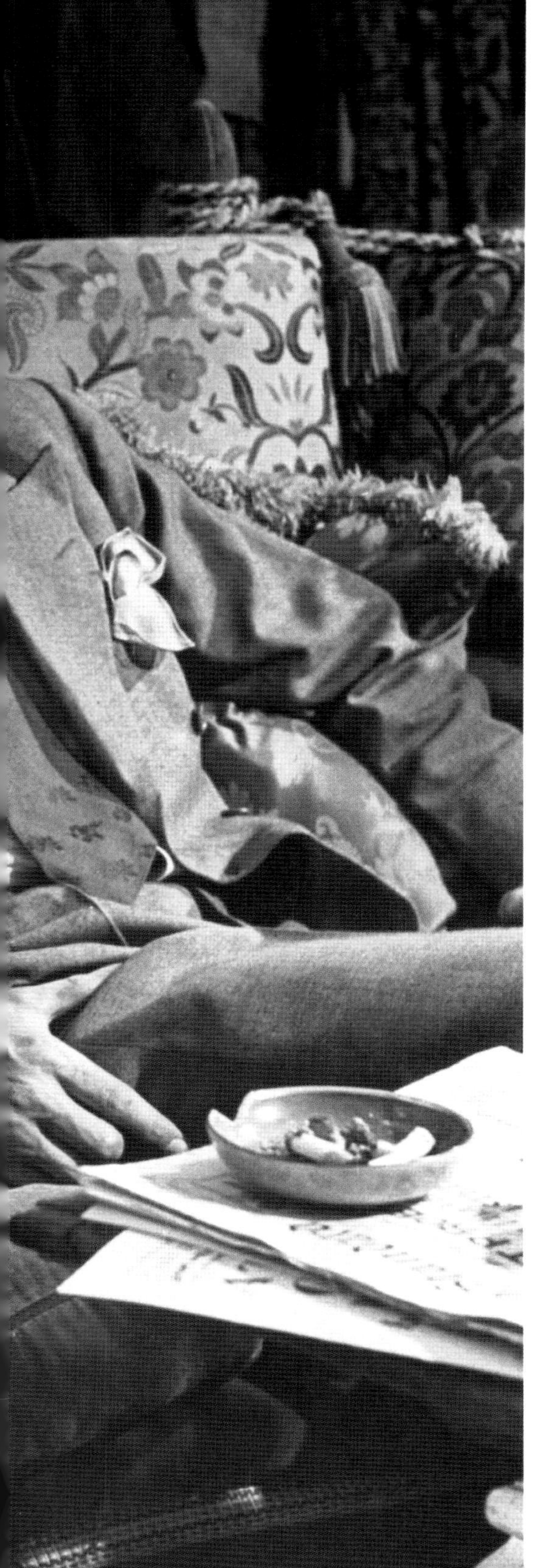

Vivien Leigh New

Crazy About Cats

Actress Vivien Leigh, best known for her portrayal of the headstrong Scarlett O'Hara in *Gone With Wind* had two great passions: acting and Siamese cats. During one period in her life, Vivien had 16 Siamese cats scattered around her houses and flats. Vivien's Siamese cat, New, always travelled with the actress. Vivien's husband, actor Lawrence Olivier (seen in the photo) brought back from France an elegant Parisian collar ornamented with small gilt bells for New. Unfortunately, New was run over by a car. Boy was the next Siamese cat Vivien owned. This pet was a gift from Olivier awaiting Vivien upon their return from their nine-month trip to Australia.

Poo Jones was one of Vivien's favourite cats. He was another Siamese cat who lived with the actress during the 1960s. Poo Jones was the last to see Vivien alive because the cat slept in her room, and was with her when Vivien died of tuberculosis in 1967.

Winston Churchill

Rufus I & II

Family of Animals

British wartime prime minister and Nobel winner Sir Winston Churchill may be best remembered for his stirring speeches and cigars, but he also had a great love for animals, especially of the exotic kind. Churchill's bizarre menagerie of pets included lambs, pigs, cattle, swans, a parrot and, at one point, a leopard! Churchill had two Poodles named Rufus I and Rufus II. Rufus I, who was presented to Churchill by his private secretary, Sir Colville, was brownish red and also responded to a nickname, Paprika. Rufus I was present at the historic signing of the Atlantic Charter, the document that outlined Allied war aims and set the foundation of the United Nations. Keeping him company was Fala, American President Roosevelt's Scottish Terrier. Rufus I was run over and killed while

Winston Churchill makes new friends during a vist to the house of Col. Frank Clarke in Miami Beach, accompanied by his wife and daughter in 1946. The parrots were especially brought to the house after Churchill expressed an interest in the creatures.

Left: Churchill at his private estate, Chartwell Manor, with his Poodle. **Right:** Churchill strokes a lion cub, held by Lady Churchill, on a visit to the London Zoo in 1943.

Churchill was attending the Conservative Party Conference at Brighton in October 1947. Rufus II, his replacement was a gift from Walter Graebner, Churchill's *Life* magazine editor for the war memoirs.

Churchill also kept a cat. Jock, a marmalade cat, was named after Churchill's private secretary Sir John 'Jock' Colville. Jock enjoyed living in the lap of luxury, sharing meals with Churchill and having his own reserved chair during wartime cabinet meetings. Before he died, Churchill asked that his home, Chartwell Manor, always keep an orange cat named Jock in memory his favourite cat.

Churchill bought Charlie, a blue and gold macaw in 1937. One of the first things she was taught was how to swear at the Nazis. The 104 year-old bird is believed to be Britain's oldest bird. For the past twelve years, Charlie has been living in Mr. Peter Oram's garden centre in Reigate, Surrey, attracting the public with her unmistakable Churchillian inflection!

ISBN: 81-7436-332-7

Published in India by
Roli Books in arrangement with
Roli & Janssen BV, The Netherlands
M-75 Greater Kailash II (Market)
New Delhi 110 048, India
Ph: ++91-11-29212782, 29210886
Fax: ++91-11-29217185
E-mail: roli@vsnl.com
Website: rolibooks.com

Text compiled by: Priya Kapoor, Nandita Jaishankar.
Design: Sneha Pamneja
Layout: Naresh Mandal, Kumar Raman

Printed and bound in Singapore

US President George W Bush carries Barney while Spot trails behind as they board Marine One. Spot, who died recently, dutifully climbed into planes. Barney has to be chased and carried into them, often by the President himself!